HIST 124: Canada and the World
Prof. Steven Maynard - 2018/2019

NELSON

NELSON

COPYRIGHT © 2019 by Nelson Education Ltd.

Printed and bound in Canada
1 2 3 4   21 20 19 18

For more information contact Nelson Education Ltd., 1120 Birchmount Road, Toronto, Ontario, M1K 5G4. Or you can visit our Internet site at nelson.com

This textbook is a Nelson custom publication. Because your instructor has chosen to produce a custom publication, you pay only for material that you will use in your course.

ISBN-13: 978-0-17-678481-2
ISBN-10: 0-17-678481-0

Consists of Selections from:

Visions: The Canadian History Module Project
P.E. Bryden, Colin Coates, Maureen Lux, Laura Macleod, Lynne Marks, Marcel Martel, Daniel Samson, Colin Coates, Jarett Henderson, Maureen Lux, Lynne Marks, Cindy Comacchio, Matthew Hayday
ISBN-10: 0-17-666069-0, ©

Cover Credit:

African Woman Sits With Her Basket, Credit: Library and Archives Canada e010771966 Working men, Credit: Library and Archives Canada C0476150 Shooting the rapids, Credit: Library and Archives Canada C-002774

Contents

Introduction   1

Chapter 1: Contact Zones from the 16th to 18th Century: How Did Aboriginal People Perceive European Newcomers?   3

Chapter 2: Fur Traders and Their Prey, 17th to 19th Centuries: Why Did Aboriginals Participate in the Fur Trade? 50

Chapter 3: Unfreedom in Early Canada: Race, Empire, and Slavery 97

Chapter 4: Schools, Prisons, and Asylums in Mid-19th Century British North America: What Did Institutional Reforms Have in Common? 139

Chapter 5: As Long as the Sun Shines and the Waters Flow: Treaties and Treaty-making in the 1870s 186

Chapter 6: The Early Canadian Women's Movement and the Struggle for the Vote, 1870s-1918 232

Chapter 7: Age Matters: Growing Up in the Interwar Years 279

Chapter 8: A National Crime: Residential Schools in Canada, 1880s to 1960s 322

Chapter 9: Medium and Message: Popular Culture, Mass Media, and National Identity, 1960s-2000s 367

Chapter 10: Queering Canada: Gay and Lesbian Political and Social Activism, 1969-1982 395

Index 442

INTRODUCTION

> The past is a foreign country; they do things differently there.
> —*The Go-Between*, L.P. Hartley (1953)

As editors and authors of the first set of modules in *Visions: The Canadian History Modules Project*, we tried to achieve a number of objectives. We wanted to provide introductory Canadian history students with a solid foundation for learning how to think like a historian in the context of their introductory Canadian history course. We also wanted instructors to be able to choose among a variety of teaching topics set within a common pedagogical framework that would support their students in their aim to become more sophisticated historical thinkers.

Each of the modules is designed to introduce a topic or key question that is commonly taught in introductory Canadian history classes. The short introductions set the basic context for the topic and draw attention to major historiographical themes and issues that have emerged as historians have studied it. They also attempt to show the interplay between the primary and secondary sources and illustrate how historians have used a wide variety of evidence to create their picture of the past. It is important for the students to note, however, that these introductions are merely starting points. Their job is to connect the material in the modules to the course lectures and core textbooks. A set of questions at the end of the introduction presents the framework for thinking critically about the material that follows. Each module contains a selection of primary sources from a broad range of materials, including government documents, diary entries and private letters, contemporary newspapers, and oral history interviews, as well as visual evidence in the form of maps, paintings, illustrations, and cartoons. Finally, a selection of secondary sources, the work of professional historians, foregrounds both the ways in which historians construct a narrative about the past and gives students insights into the differing ways in which evidence can be used.

The use of primary sources in conjunction with secondary sources is an essential component in the postsecondary study of history. To use an analogy, if the textbook for the course tells the overarching story of the history of Canada, the readings presented in these modules provide the rich detail that flesh out particular aspects of that story. They add the details that sensitize students to other viewpoints, other experiences, and other worldviews. If the past is indeed a foreign country, as Hartley said, then these modules are meant to give us an introduction to the tools to understand the assumptions, priorities, culture, and experience of people who lived 20 years ago or 200 years ago.

Learning to approach source material in a careful and nuanced way not only enhances students' ability to think critically, but also helps lower the barriers between the past and the present. It is important to apply these same critical approaches not only to the primary sources, but also to the secondary material. Historical actors are not the only ones influenced by the times in which they live. By showcasing different interpretations of evidence, we hope to help students realize that the past is not a set narrative, but rather that history is an argument created by historians based on how they choose and interpret the available evidence. Just as there are arguments today about issues such as climate change and how to interpret the scientific evidence for human impacts on climate, there are arguments among historians regarding a wide array of issues, from what Confederation meant to whether or not Canadians in the late nineteenth century experienced the secularization of their society.

We have carefully selected material that meets rigorous criteria of readability, significance, and variety. We include modules that cover a variety of approaches—social, political, environmental, religious, and so on—and a wide geographical range. One of the most difficult aspects of creating a reader is the need to exclude topics because of space limitations. In the case of *Visions*, however, the project has been conceived from the start as a living, growing database. We have therefore had the luxury of knowing that topics we were unable to cover in the first release will not be neglected but can be added as the project unfolds. To the instructors using this text we say, if you don't see what you need for your students, please join us!

Laura Macleod (Executive Editor, History)
P.E. Bryden (University of Victoria)
Colin Coates (Glendon College, York University)
Maureen Lux (Brock University)
Lynne Marks (University of Victoria)
Marcel Martel (York University)
Daniel Samson (Brock University)

CONTACT ZONES FROM THE SIXTEENTH TO EIGHTEENTH CENTURY

How Did Aboriginal People Perceive European Newcomers?

Colin Coates

Glendon College, York University

CONTACT ZONES FROM THE SIXTEENTH TO EIGHTEENTH CENTURY: HOW DID ABORIGINAL PEOPLE PERCEIVE EUROPEAN NEWCOMERS?

● **Introduction by Colin Coates**

▲ **Primary Sources**

Document 1: A Micmac Responds to the French
Chrestien LeClercq

Document 2: Of Laws
Baron de Lahontan

Document 3: How the Squamish Remember George Vancouver

Document 4: Engraving based on a drawing by Samuel de Champlain, 1613

Document 5: The Encounter Between Jacques Cartier and the Aboriginal Peoples at Stadaconé
Marc-Aurèle Suzor-Côté

■ **Secondary Sources**

Article 1: The Indians' Old World: Native Americans and the Coming of Europeans
Neil Salisbury

Article 2: Donnaconna Discovers Europe: Rereading Jacques Carter's *Voyages*
Ramsay Cook

Article 3: The *Other* in Early Canada
Cornelius J. Jaenen

● INTRODUCTION

Colin Coates

The encounter between Aboriginal peoples in North America and European newcomers changed the lives of people on both continents. While some aspects of this meeting were clearly very negative for Aboriginal peoples, they were not merely the passive victims of European expansion. European newcomers did not dominate Aboriginal peoples from the moment of first encounter. Rather, both groups influenced each other a great deal, and for many decades the Europeans relied on Aboriginal peoples for food and medicine. After all, the fate of the short-lived Viking settlement at L'Anse aux Meadows in northern Newfoundland around the year 1000 indicates that Europeans were not necessarily destined to flourish in the New World. By the sixteenth century, when Europeans returned to this part of the continent, they certainly enjoyed a degree of technological advantage in specific areas such as gunpowder and ships. Still, Aboriginal peoples were clearly better adapted to their terrain and climate.

Moreover, Aboriginal peoples had long experience adjusting to political and economic circumstances. The overview article by Neal Salisbury covers a variety of Aboriginal nations, showing the importance of considering the historical processes underway before the arrival of Europeans. This history of change helps us understand the nature of the contact experience. He also makes the point that the current national boundaries between Canada and the United States are irrelevant to our understanding of the early contact between Aboriginal peoples and Europeans.

One of the earliest records of the encounter of French and Aboriginal peoples is Jacques Cartier's (1491–1557) account of his voyage. But his account may not represent the first time the peoples met. When Cartier came upon Iroquoians at the Gaspé coast in 1535, they were eager to trade with him, an incident that suggests that they had established customs of trading with people who arrived on large sailing ships. Ramsay Cook's article on the extended encounter between the Iroquoians and Cartier and his men shows that not only did the French explorer "discover" North American Aboriginal society, but also the Iroquoians likewise discovered many aspects of European society. The Aboriginals, Cook argues, were not likely impressed. Likewise Cornelius Jaenen reminds us that, in this context, the French were "the other," and that it is important to try to understand Aboriginal attitudes toward the European newcomers. Aboriginal perspectives were not necessarily flattering. The material recorded by French missionary Chrestien Le Clercq (circa 1677) describes the negative Aboriginal attitudes toward many features of French society.

While Aboriginal peoples had many reasons to be wary of the newcomers, a few Europeans demonstrated some sympathy for and understanding of Aboriginal society. Indeed, Cartier and Samuel de Champlain (1567–1635) had visited other parts of the New World before coming to what is now Canada. Champlain in particular developed a broad and complex understanding of Aboriginal society. David Hackett Fisher's recent biography of Champlain argues that the French explorer developed a strikingly enlightened attitude toward Aboriginal society in New France.

In some circles, the exchanges between Aboriginal peoples and Europeans allowed for a new cultural critique to develop within European society. Europeans from the fifteenth to the eighteenth centuries undertook many voyages of exploration around the globe and saw many different societies and customs. One of the images that developed out of these encounters was the "noble savage." This personage exhibited great moral strength while living under more rudimentary conditions than most Europeans. One of the classic texts of this genre, Michel de Montaigne's famous essay, "Des Cannibales" (1580), provides a scathing comparison between contemporary French society and Aboriginal society in contemporary Brazil (at least as far as he understood it). Even though he failed to grasp many features of that Aboriginal society, de Montaigne showed how the Aboriginal peoples' moral code often surpassed that of their French contemporaries.

Another important contribution to the image of the "noble savage" is contained in the works of Baron Louis-Armand de Lom d'Ares Lahontan (1666–1715), a French military official who lived in New France in the late seventeenth century. He provided an influential account of the morality of Aboriginal life in his fictional dialogue between himself and the Iroquois leader Adario. Through this text, which contributed to changing the ways that Europeans understood Aboriginal society, Lahontan uses the literary device of portraying himself as gullible and unable to convince Adario of the virtues of French society. Adario, in contrast, provides a much more convincing account of the superiority of his way of life. Lahontan's work proved to be a significant influence on later Enlightenment thinkers in France. The Enlightenment concept of the "noble savage," while not necessarily doing justice to the complexities and subtleties of Aboriginal life in the New World, created a new image and changed European attitudes about the malleability of human nature.

The "first" encounters occurred over a long time period given the geographical expanse of the continent. The French and later the British slowly extended their reach toward the west, meeting different Aboriginal groups. Because the Rocky Mountains form such a formidable geographical barrier, relations with Aboriginal peoples on the West Coast of what is now Canada were not established until the late eighteenth century, almost 250 years after Cartier's arrival. The earliest newcomers were not always the same mix of British and French explorers. On the British Columbian coast, Russians and the Spanish arrived at the same time as the British. The excerpt from the oral history of the Squamish nation who live near present-day Vancouver deals with the arrival of the first British ship on their shore. It reminds us that "first contact" between Europeans and Aboriginal peoples occurred much later on the West Coast. In all parts of North America, as in other parts of the world, the nature of the contact experience between different peoples was complex, and it led to significant changes in the world views of both sides.

QUESTIONS

1. In the first document, what criticisms did the Mi'kmaq present about the nature of French society in the New World? Would such attitudes have influenced the likelihood of their embracing Christianity?

2. Was the encounter of Aboriginal peoples and Europeans described in "Of Laws" a positive or negative experience for the two sides? Considering that this dialogue was written in the late seventeenth century, was the nature of the cultural interaction different from that for the earlier periods discussed in this section?

3. To what extent are Adario's attitudes about the relationship between the individual and the state similar to attitudes commonly held by North Americans today? Are Adario's or Lahontan's views more "modern?"

4. Evaluate the importance of the technological advances that Europeans enjoyed over Aboriginal peoples. How does the image from Samuel de Champlain's map reflect this technological advantage?

5. Compare the attitudes toward Europeans among the Mi'kmaq in the early seventeenth century and the Squamish in the late eighteenth century? How important are the large differences in time and space?

FURTHER READINGS

Olive Dickason and David McNabb, *Canada's First Nations: A History of Founding Peoples from Earliest Times* (Toronto: Oxford University Press, 2008).

Olive Dickason, *The Myth of the Savage* (Edmonton: University of Alberta Press, 1984)

David Hackett Fisher, *Champlain's Dream* (New York: Simon & Schuster, 2009)

John S. Lutz, ed., *Myth and Memory: Stories of Indigenous–European Contact* (Vancouver: UBC Press, 2007).

Bruce Trigger, *The Children of Aataentsic: A History of the Huron People to 1660* (Montreal: McGill-Queen's University Press, 1976).

▲ Document 1: A Micmac Responds to the French

Chrestien LeClercq

Chrestien LeClercq was a Recollect missionary, who spent twelve years among the Mi'kmaq of the Gaspé peninsula (in present-day Quebec). Having learnt their language, he provides in this excerpt their response to some features of French society.

[...] the Indians esteem their camps as much as, and even more than, they do the most superb and commodious of our houses. To this they testified one day to some of our gentlemen of Isle Percée, who, having asked me to serve them as interpreter in a visit which they wished to make to these Indians in order to make the latter understand that it would be very much more advantageous for them to live and to build in our fashion, were extremely surprised when the leading Indian, who had listened with great patience to everything I had said to him on behalf of these gentlemen, answered me in these words: "I am greatly astonished that the French have so little cleverness, as they seem to exhibit in the matter of which thou hast just told me on their behalf, in the effort to persuade us to convert our poles, our barks, and our wigwams into those houses of stone and of wood which are tall and lofty, according to their account, as these trees. Very well! But why now," continued he, "do men of five to six feet in height need houses which are sixty to eighty? For, in fact, as thou knowest very well thyself, Patriarch—do we not find in our own all the conveniences and the advantages that you have with yours, such as reposing, drinking, sleeping, eating, and amusing ourselves with our friends when we wish? This is not all," said he, addressing himself to one of our captains, "my brother, hast thou as much ingenuity and cleverness as the Indians, who carry their houses and their wigwams with them so that they may lodge wheresoever they please, independently of any seignior whatsoever? Thou art not as bold nor as stout as we, because when thou goest on a voyage thou canst not carry upon thy shoulders thy buildings and thy edifices. Therefore it is necessary that thou preparest as many lodgings as thou makest changes of residence, or else thou lodgest in a hired house which does not belong to thee. As for us, we find ourselves secure from all these inconveniences, as we can always say, more truly than thou, that we are at home everywhere, because we set up our wigwams with ease wheresoever we go, and without asking permission of anybody. Thou reproachest us, very inappropriately, that our country is a little hell in contrast with France, which thou comparest to a terrestrial paradise, inasmuch as it yields thee, so thou sayest, every kind of provision in abundance. Thou sayest of us also that we are the most miserable and most unhappy of all men, living without religion, without manners, without honour, without social order, and, in a word, without any rules, like the beasts in our woods and our forests, lacking bread, wine, and a thousand other comforts which thou hast in superfluity in Europe. Well, my brother, if thou dost not yet know the real feelings which our Indians have towards thy country and towards all thy nation, it is proper that I inform thee at once. I beg thee now to believe that, all miserable as we seem in thine eyes, we consider ourselves nevertheless much happier than thou in this, that we are very content with the little that we have; and believe also

Source: Chrestien LeClercq, "A Micmac Responds to the French" circa 1677, in *New Relation of Gaspesia with the customs and religion of the Gaspesian Indians*, ed. by W.F. Ganong (Toronto: Champlain Society, 1910), pp. 103–06.

once for all, I pray, that thou deceivest thyself greatly if thou thinkest to persuade us that thy country is better than ours. For if France, as thou sayest, is a little terrestrial paradise, art thou sensible to leave it? And why abandon wives, children, relatives, and friends? Why risk thy life and thy property every year, and why venture thyself with such risk, in any season whatsoever, to the storms and tempests of the sea in order to come to a strange and barbarous country which thou considerest the poorest and least fortunate of the world? Besides, since we are wholly convinced of the contrary, we scarcely take the trouble to go to France, because we fear, with good reason, lest we find little satisfaction there, seeing, in our own experience, that those who are natives thereof leave it every year in order to enrich themselves on our shores. We believe, further, that you are also incomparably poorer than we, and that you are only simple journeymen, valets, servants, and slaves, all masters and grand captains though you may appear, seeing that you glory in our old rags and in our miserable suits of beaver which can no longer be of use to us, that you find among us, in the fishery for cod which you make in these parts, the wherewithal to comfort your misery and the poverty which oppresses you. As to us, we find all our riches and all our conveniences among ourselves, without trouble and without exposing our lives to the dangers in which you find yourselves constantly through your long voyages. And, whilst feeling compassion for you in the sweetness of our repose, we wonder at the anxieties and cares which you give yourselves night and day in order to load your ship [with cod]. We see also that all your people live, as a rule, only upon cod which you catch among us. It is everlastingly nothing but cod—cod in the morning, cod at midday, cod at evening, and always cod, until things come to such a pass that if you wish some good morsels, it is at our expense; and you are obliged to have recourse to the Indians, whom you despise so much, and to beg them to go a-hunting that you may be regaled. Now tell me this one little thing, if thou hast any sense: Which of these two is the wisest and happiest—he who labours without ceasing and only obtains, and that with great trouble, enough to live on, or he who rests in comfort and finds all that he needs in the pleasure of hunting and fishing? It is true," added he, "that we have not always had the use of bread and of wine which your France produces; but, in fact, before the arrival of the French in these parts, did not the Gaspesians live much longer than now? And if we have not any longer among us any of those old men of a hundred and thirty to forty years, it is only because we are gradually adopting your manner of living, for experience is making it very plain that those of us live longest who, despising your bread, your wine, and your brandy, are content with their natural food of beaver, of moose, of waterfowl, and fish, in accord with the custom of our ancestors and of all the Gaspesian nation. Learn now, my brother, once for all, because I must open to thee my heart: there is no Indian who does not consider himself infinitely more happy and more powerful than the French." He finished his speech by the following last words, saying that an Indian could find his living everywhere, and that he could call himself the seigneur and the sovereign of his country, because he could reside there just as freely as it pleased him, with every kind of rights of hunting and fishing, without any anxiety, more content a thousand times in the woods and in his wigwam than if he were in palaces and at the tables of the greatest princes of the earth.

No matter what can be said of this reasoning, I assert, for my part, that I should consider these Indians incomparably more fortunate than ourselves, and that the life of these barbarians would even be capable of inspiring envy, if they had the instructions, the understanding, and the same means for their salvation which God has given us that we may save ourselves by preference over so many poor pagans, and as a result of His pity ...

9

▲ Document 2: Of Laws

Baron de Lahontan

These selections show part of the fictitious dialogue between the Baron de Lahontan and the Huron chief Adario. Baron de Lahontan (1666–c. 1716) was a military officer stationed in North America in the late seventeenth century. Disaffected because of ill treatment by his superiors, he returned to Europe and wrote an account that helped create the image of the "noble savage" in European thought. While not entirely reflecting the reality of Aboriginal life or beliefs, the "noble savage" image suggested to European thinkers that humans who lived closer to a natural state enjoyed greater freedoms and lived more honourably than their European counterparts. Lahontan uses himself as a literary figure in this dialogue, and his words do not necessarily reflect his views; rather, they are used to reveal the wisdom of Adario's perspectives. The personage of Adario was patterned after the Huron chief Kondarionk (c. 1649–1701).

Note that these excerpts are from an early English-language translation of Lahontan's original French text. The spelling has been modified only slightly, and where necessary, in order to keep the flavour of the text.

Of Laws

Adario [...] let us therefore talk a little of what you call Laws; for you know that we have no such Word in our Language; tho' at the same time, I apprehend the force and importance of the Word, by virtue of the explication I had from you t'other day, together with the examples you mention'd, to make me conceive what you meant. Prithee tell me, are not Laws the same as just and reasonable Things? You say they are. Why then, to observe the Law, imports no more than to observe the measures of Reason and Justice: And at this rate you must take just and reasonable things in another sense than we do; or if you take 'em in the same sense. 'tis plain you never observe 'em.

Lahontan. These are fine Distinctions indeed, you please your self with idle Flams. Hast not thee the Sense to perceive, after twenty Years Conversation with the *French*, that what the *Hurons* call Reason is Reason among the *French*. 'Tis certain that all Men do not observe the Laws of Reason, for if they did there would be no occasion for Punishments, and those Judges thou hast seen at *Paris* and *Quebec* would be oblig'd to look out for another way of Living. But in regard that the good of the Society consists in doing Justice and following these Laws, there's a necessity of punishing the Wicked and rewarding the Good; for without that Precaution Murders, Robberies and Defamations would spread every where, and in a Word, we should be the most miserable People upon the Face of the Earth.

Adario. Nay, you are miserable enough already, and indeed I can't see how you can be more such. What sort of Men must the *Europeans* be? What Species of Creatures do they retain to? The *Europeans*, who must be forc'd to do Good, and have no other Prompter for the avoiding of Evil than the fear of Punishment. If I ask'd thee, what a Man is, thou wouldft answer me, *He's a Frenchman*, and yet I'll prove that your *Man* is rather a *Beaver*. For *Man* is not intitled to that Character upon the score of his walking upright upon two

Source: Lahontan, Baron Louis-Armand de Lom d'Ares, *New Voyages to North-America*, Vol. 2., Reuben Gold Thwaites, ed., (Chicago, IL: A.C. McClurg & Co., 1905), pp. 211 ff.

Legs, or of Reading and Writing, and shewing a Thousand other Instances of his Industry. I call that Creature a *Man*, that hath a natural inclination to do Good, and never entertains the thoughts of doing Evil. You see we have no Judges; and what's the reason of that? Why? We neither quarrel nor sue one another. And what's the reason that we have no Law Suits? Why? Because we are resolved neither to receive nor to know Silver. But why do we refuse admission to Silver among us? The reason is this: We are resolv'd to have no Laws, for since the World was a World our Ancestors liv'd happily without 'em. In fine, as I intimated before, the Word *Laws* does not signifie just and reasonable things as you use it, for the Rich make a Jest of 'em, and 'tis only the poor Wretches that pay any regard to 'em. But, pray, let's look into these *Laws*, or reasonable things, as you call 'em. For these Fifty Years, the Governors of *Canada* have still alledg'd that we are subject to the Laws of their great Captain. We content our selves in denying all manner of Dependance, excepting that upon the Great Spirit, as being born free and joint Brethren, who are all equally Masters: Whereas you are all Slaves to one Man. We do not put in any such Answer to you, as if the *French* depended upon us; and the reason of our silence upon that Head [topic] is, that we have no mind to Quarrel. But, pray tell me, what Authority or Right is the pretended Superiority of your great Captain grounded upon? Did we ever sell our selves to that great Captain? Were we ever in *France* to look after you? 'Tis you that came hither to find out us. Who gave you all the Countries that you now inhabit, by what Right do you possess 'em? They always belong'd to the *Algonkins* before. In earnest, my dear Brother, I'm sorry for thee from the bottom of my Soul. Take my advice, and turn *Huron;* for I see plainly a vast difference between thy Condition and mine. I am Master of my own Body, I have the absolute disposal of my self, I do what I please, I am the first and the last of my Nation, I fear no Man, and I depend only upon the Great Spirit: Whereas thy Body, as well as thy Soul, are doom'd to a dependance upon thy great Captain; thy Vice-Roy disposes of thee; thou hast not the liberty of doing what thou hast a mind to; thou'rt affraid of Robbers, false Witnesses, Assassins &c. and thou dependest upon an infinity of Persons whose Places have rais'd 'em above thee. Is it true, or not? Are these things either improbable or invisible? Ah! my dear Brother, thou seest plainly that I am in the right of it; and yet thou choosest rather to be a *French* Slave than a free *Huron*. What a fine Spark does a *Frenchman* make with his fine Laws, who taking himself to be mighty Wise is assuredly a great Fool; for as much as he continues in Slavery and a state of Dependence, while the very Brutes enjoy that adorable Liberty, and like us fear nothing but Foreign Enemies.

[....]

Adario. I'll tell thee one thing my dear Brother; I was a going one day from *Paris* to *Versailles*, and about half way, I met a Boor [peasant] that was going to be Whipt for having taken Partridges and Hares with Traps. Between *Rochel* [La Rochelle, in southwestern France, one of the main ports linking France and New France] and *Paris*, I saw another that was Condemn'd to the Gally's for having a little Bag of Salt about him. These poor Men were punish'd by your unjust Laws, for endeavouring to get Sustenance to their Families; at a time when a Million of Women were got with Child in the absence of their Husbands, when the Physicians Murder'd three fourths of the People, and the Gamesters reduc'd their Families to a Starving Condition, by losing all they had in the World; and all this with Impunity. If things go at this rate, where are your just and reasonable Laws; where are those Judges that have a Soul to be Sav'd as well as you and I? After this, you'll be ready to Brand the *Hurons* for Beasts. In earnest, we should have a fine time of it if we offer'd to punish one of our Brethren for killing a Hare or a Partridge; and a glorious sight 'twould be, to see our Wives inlarge the number of our Children, while we are ingag'd in Warlike Expeditions against our Enemies; to see Physicians Poison our Families, and Gamesters lose the Beaver Skins they've got in Hunting. In *France*, these things are look'd upon as trifles, which do not fall within the Verge of their fine Laws. Doubtless, they must needs be very blind, that are acquainted with us, and yet do not imitate our Example.

Laboutan. Very fine, my dear Friend; thou goest too fast; believe me, thy Knowledge is so confin'd, as I said before, that thy Mind can't reach beyond the appearances of things. Wouldst thou but give Ear to Reason, thou wouldst presently be sensible that we act upon good Principles, for the support of the Society. You must know, the Laws Condemn all without exception, that are guilty of the Actions you've mention'd. In the first place, they prohibit the Peasants to kill Hares or Partridges, especially in the Neighbourhood of *Paris;* by reason that an uncontroul'd liberty of Hunting, would quickly exhaust the whole Stock of those Animals. The Boors Farm the Grounds of their Landlords, who reserve to themselves the Priviledge of Hunting, as being Masters. Now, if they happen to kill Hares or Partridges, they not only rob their Masters of their Right, but fall under the Prohibition enacted by the Law: And the same is the Case of those who run Salt, by reason that the Right of Transporting it is solely lodg'd in the King. As to the Women and the Gamesters that you took notice of; you can't think sure that we'd shut 'em up in Prisons and Convents, and Condemn 'em to a perpetual Confinement. The Physicians 'twould be unjust to abuse, for of a hundred Patients they do not kill two; nay, on the contrary, they use their utmost efforts to Cure 'em. There's a necessity that Superannuated Persons, and those who are worn out, should put a Period to their Lives. And after all, tho' all of us have occasion to imploy Doctors, if 'twere prov'd that they had kill'd any Patient, either thro' Ignorance or Malice, the Law would not spare 'em no more than others.

Adario. Were these Laws observ'd, you would stand in need of a great many Prisons; but I see plainly that you do not speak all the truth, and that you're afraid of carrying the Thing farther, least my Reasons should put you to a stand. However, let's now cast our eyes upon those two Men who fled last year to *Quebec*, to avoid the being Burnt in *France*. If we look narrowly into their Crime, we'll find occasion to say, that *Europe* is pester'd with a great many foolish Laws.
[...]
Adario. The *French* in general take us for Beasts; the Jesuits Brand us for impious, foolish and ignorant Vagabonds. And to be even with you, we have the same thoughts of you; but with this difference, that *we* pity you without offering invectives. Pray hear me, my dear Brother, I speak calmly and without passion. The more I reflect up the lives of the *Europeans*, the less Wisdom and Happiness I find among 'em. These six years I have bent my thoughts upon the State of the *Europeans*: But I can't light on any thing in their Actions that is not beneath a Man; and truly I think 'tis impossible it should be otherwise, so long as you stick to the measures of *Meum* and *Tuum*. [That which belongs to me or you, i.e., private property] I affirm that what you call Silver is the Devil of Devils; the Tyrant of the *French*; the Source of all Evil; the Bane of Souls and the Slaughter-House of living Persons. To pretend to live in the Money Country, and at the same time to save one's Soul, is as great an inconsistency as for a Man to go to the bottom of a Lake to preserve his Life. This Money is the Father of Luxury, Lasciviousness, Intrigues, Tricks, Lying, Treachery, False-ness, and in a word, of all the mischief in the World. The Father sells his Children, Hus-bands expose their Wives to Sale, Wives betray their Husbands, Brethren kill one another, Friends are false, and all this proceeds from Money. Consider this, and then tell me if we are not in the right of it, in refusing to finger, or so much as to look upon that cursed Metal.

Lahontan. What! is it possible that you should always Reason so sorrily! Prithee, do but listen once in thy life time to what I am going to say. Dost not thou see, my dear Friend, that the Nations of *Europe* could not live without Gold and Silver, or some such precious thing. Without that Symbol, the Gentlemen, the Priests, the Merchants, and an infinity of other Persons who have not Strength enough to labour the Earth, would die for Hunger. Upon that lay, our Kings would be no Kings: Nay, what Soldiers should we then have? Who would then Work for Kings or any body else, who would run the hazard of the Sea, who would make Arms unless 'twere for himself? Believe me, this would run us to remediless Ruine, 'twould turn *Europe* into a Chaos, and create the most dismal Confusion that Imagination it self can reach.

Adario. You fobb me off very prettily, truly, when you bring in your Gentlemen, your Merchants and your Priests. If you were Strangers to *Meum* and *Tuum*, those distinctions of Men would be sunk; a levelling equality would then take place among you as it now do's among the *Hurons*. For the first thirty years indeed, after the banishing of Interest, you would see a strange Desolation; those who are only qualify'd to eat, drink, sleep and divert themselves, would languish and die; but their Posterity would be fit for our way of living. I have set forth again and again, the qualities that make a Man inwardly such as he ought to be; particularly, Wisdom, Reason, Equity, *&c.* which are courted by the *Hurons*. I have made it appear that the Notion of separate Interests knocks all these Qualities in the Head, and that a Man sway'd by Interest can't be a Man of Reason. As for the outward Qualifications of a Man; he ought to be expert in Marching, Hunting, Fishing, Waging War, Ranging the Forests, Building Hutts and Canoes, Firing of Guns, Shooting of Arrows, Working Canoes: He ought to be Indefatigable, and able to live on short Commons upon occasion. In a word, he ought to know how to go about all the Exercises of the *Hurons*. Now in my way, 'tis the Person thus qualify'd that I call a *Man*. Do but consider, how many Millions there are in *Europe*, who, if they were left thirty Leagues off in the Forrests, and provided with Fusees [guns] and Arrows, would be equally at a loss, either to Hunt and maintain themselves, or to find their way out: And yet you see we traverse a hundred Leagues of Forrests without losing our way, that we kill Fowl and other Beasts with our Arrows, that we catch Fish in all the places where they are to be had; that we Dog both Men and Wild Beasts by their Footsteps, whether in Woods or in open Fields, in Summer or in Winter; that we live upon Roots when we lye before the Gates of the *Iroquese*, that we run like Hares, that we know how to use both the Axe and the Knife, and to make a great many useful things. Now since we are capable of such things, what should hinder you to do the same, when Interest is laid aside? Are not your Bodies as large, strong and brawny as ours? Are not your Artisans imploy'd in harder and more difficult Work than ours? If you liv'd after our manner, all of you would be equally Masters; your Riches would be of the same Stamp with ours, and consist in the purchasing of Glory by military Actions, and the taking of Slaves; for the more you took of them the less occasion you would have to Work: In a word, you would live as happily as we do.

Lahontan. Do you place a happy Life, in being oblig'd to lye under a pittiful Hutt of Bark, to Sleep under four sorry Coverlets of Beaver Skins, to Eat nothing but what you Boil and Roast, to be Cloath'd with Skins, to go a Beaver Hunting in the harshest Season of the Year, to run a hundred Leagues on Foot in pursuit of the *Iroquese*, thro' Marshes and thick Woods, the Trees of which are cut down so as to render 'em inaccessible! Do you think your selves happy when you venture out in little Canoes, and run the risk of being drown'd every foot in your Voyages upon the Great Lakes; when you lye upon the ground with the Heavens for your Canopy, upon approaching to the Villages of your Enemies; when you run with full Speed, both days and nights without eating or drinking, as being pursued by your Enemies; when you are sure of being reduc'd to the last extremity, if the *Coureurs de Bois* [independent French fur traders] did not out of Friendship, Charity and

Commiseration, supply you with Fire-Arms, Powder, Lead, Thread for Nets, Axes, Knives, Needles, Awls, Fishing-Hooks, Ketties, and several other Commodities?

Adario. Very fine, come, don't let's go so fast; the day is long, and we may talk one after the other at our own leisure. It seems you take all these things to be great hardships; and indeed I own they would be such to the *French*, who like Beasts, love only to eat and to drink, and have been brought up to Softness and Effeminacy. Prithee, tell me what difference there is between lying in a good Hutt, and lying in a Palace; between Sleeping under a Cover of Beaver-Skins, and Sleeping under a Quilt between two Sheets; between Eating Boil'd and Roast Meat, and feeding upon dirty Pies, Ragou's, *& c.* dress'd by your greasy Scullions? Are we liable to more Disorders and Sicknesses than the *French*, who are accommodated with these Palaces, Beds and Cooks? But after all, how many are there in *France* that lye upon Straw in Garrets where the Rain comes in on all hands, and that are hard put to't to find Victuals and Drink? I have been in *France*, and speak from what I have seen with my Eyes. You rally without reason, upon our Clothes made of Skins, for they are warmer, and keep out the Rain better than your Cloth; besides, they are not so ridiculously made as your Garments, which have more Stuff in their Pockets and Skirts, than in the Body of the Garment. As for our Beaver-Hunting, you take it to be a terrible thing; while it affords us all manner of pleasure and diversion; and at the same time, procures us all sorts of Commodities in exchange for the Skins. Besides, our Slaves take all the Drudgery off our hands, (if so be that you will have it to be drudgery.) You know very well that Hunting is the most agreeable Diversion we have; but the Beaver-Hunting being so very pleasant, we prefer it to all the other sorts. You say, we have a troublesome and tedious way of waging War; and indeed I must own that a *French* Man would not be able to bear it, upon the account that you are not accustom'd to such long Voyages on Foot; but these Excursions do not fatigue us in the least, and 'twere to be wish'd for the good of *Canada*, that you were possess'd of the same Talent; for if you were, the *Iroquese* would not Cut your Throats in the midst of your own Habitations, as they do now every day. You insist likewise on the risk we run in our little Canoes, as an instance of our Misery; and with reference to that Point, 'tis true that sometimes we cannot dispense with the use of Canoes, because we are Strangers to the Art of Building larger Vessels; but after all, your great Vessels are liable to be cast away as well as Canoes. 'Tis likewise true, that we lye flat upon the open ground when we approach to the Villages of our Enemies; but 'tis equally true that the Soldiers in *France* are not so well accommodated as your Men are here, and that they are oftentimes forc'd to lye in Marshes and Ditches, where they are expos'd to the Rain and Wind. You object farther, that we betake our selves to a speedy Flight; and pray what can be more natural than to flye when the number of our Enemies is triple to ours. The Fatigue indeed of running night and day without Eating and Drinking, is terrible; but we had better undergo it than become Slaves. I am apt to believe that such extremities are matter of Horrour to the *Europeans*, but we look upon 'em as in a manner, nothing. You conclude, in pretending that the *French* prevent our Misery by taking pity of us. But pray consider how our Ancestors liv'd an hundred years ago: They liv'd as well without your Commodities as we do with 'em; for instead of your Fire-Locks, Powder and Shot, they made use of Bows and Arrows, as we do to this day: They made Nets of the Thread of the Barks of Trees, Axes of Stone; Knives, Needles and Awls of Stag or Elk-Bones; and supply'd the room of Kettles with Earthen Pots. Now, since our Ancestors liv'd without these Commodities for so many Ages; I am of the Opinion, we could dispense with 'em easier than the *French* could with our Beaver Skins; for which, by a mighty piece of Friendship, they give us in exchange Fusees, that burst and Lame many of our Warriors, Axes that break in the cutting of a Shrub, Knives that turn Blunt, and lose their Edge in the cutting of a

Citron; Thread which is half Rotten, and so very bad that our Nets are worn out as soon as they are made; and Kettles so thin and slight, that the very weight of Water makes the Bottoms fall out. This, my dear Brother, is the answer I had to give to your Reflexions upon the Misery of the *Hurons*.

Lahontan. 'Tis well; I find you would have me to believe that the *Hurons* are insensible of their Fatigue and Labour; and being bred up to Poverty and Hardships, have another notion of 'em than we have. This may do with those who have never stir'd out of their own Country, and consequently have no Idea of a better Life than their own; who having never visited our Cities and Towns, fancy that we live just as they do. But as for thee, who hast seen *France, Quebec* and *New-England*, methinks thy judgment and relish of things are too much of the Savage Strain; whilst thou prefers the Condition of the *Hurons* to that of the *Europeans*. Can there be a more agreeable and delightful Life in the World, than that of an infinity of rich Men, who want for nothing? They have fine Coaches, Stately Houses adorn'd with Rich Hangings and Magnificent Pictures, Sweet Gardens replenish'd with all sorts of Fruit, Parks Stock'd with all sorts of Animals, Horses and Hounds and good store of Money, which enables 'em to keep a Sumptuous Table, to frequent the Play-Houses, to Game freely, and to dispose handsomely of their Children. These happy Men are ador'd by their Dependants; and you have seen with your own eyes our Princes, Dukes, Marshals of *France*, Prelates, and a Mission of persons of all Stations, who want for nothing, and live like Kings, and who never call to mind that they have liv'd, till such time as Death alarms 'em.

Adario. If I had not been particularly inform'd of the State of *France*, and let into the knowledge of all the Circumstances of that People, by my Voyage to *Paris;* I might have been Blinded by the outward appearances of Felicity that you set forth: But I know that your Prince, your Duke, your Marshal, and your Prelate are far from being happy upon the Comparison with the *Hurons*, who know no other happiness than that of Liberty and Tranquility of Mind: For your great Lords hate one another in their Hearts; they forfeit their Sleep, and neglect even Eating and Drinking, in making their Court to the King, and undermining their Enemies; they offer such Violence to Nature in dissembling, disguising and bearing things, that the Torture of their Soul leaves all Expression far behind it. Is all this nothing in your way? Do you think it such a trifling matter to have fifty Serpents in your Bosom? Had not they better throw their Coaches, their Palaces and their Finery, into the River, than to spend their life time in a continued Series of Martyrdom? Were I in their place, I'd rather choose to be a *Huron* with a Naked Body and a Serene Mind. The Body is the Apartment in which the Soul is lodg'd; and what signifies it, for the Case call'd the Body, to be set off with Gold Trappings, or spread out in a Coach, or planted before a Sumptuous Table, while the Soul Galls and Tortures it? The great Lords, that you call Happy, lie expos'd to Disgrace from the King, to the detraction of a thousand sorts of Persons, to the loss of their Places, to the Contempt of their Fellow Courtiers; and in a word, their soft Life is thwarted by Ambition, Pride, Presumption and Envy. They are Slaves to their Passions, and to their King, who is the only *French* Man that can be call'd Happy, with respect to that adorable Liberty which he alone enjoys. There's a thousand of us in one Village, and you see that we love one another like Brethren; that whatever any one has is at his Neighbour's Service; that our Generals and Presidents of the Council have not more Power than any other *Huron;* that Detraction and Quarreling were never heard of among us; and in fine [in conclusion], that every one is his own Master, and do's what he pleases, without being accountable to another, or censur'd by his Neighbour. This, my dear Brother, is the difference between us and your Princes, Dukes, &c. And if those great Men are so Unhappy, by consequence, those of inferiour Stations must have a greater share of Trouble and perplexing Cares ....

▲ Document 3: How the Squamish Remember George Vancouver

The following is an account of the Squamish's first encounter with George Vancouver, as told by Squamish historian Louis Miranda (1892–1990), and presented at the Vancouver Conference on Exploration and Discovery by Chief Philip Joe in 1992. This represents an oral history passed down through the generations since 1792.

Vancouver's journal records that my ancestors who greeted him 'conducted themselves with the greatest decorum and civility.' He certainly liked the fish given and did not mind parting with a few iron tools in exchange. Vancouver took a look around the inlet and then headed into Howe Sound where an incident occurred that you may not be so familiar with, but which has been preserved in Squamish oral tradition.

As my elders tell the story, early one morning in the month called *Tim-kwis-KWAS* 'hot time,' an old man living near the mouth of the Squamish River had gone down to wash. As he raised his head, he saw an 'island' where no island had been before. The old man was alarmed and ran back to his house to wake his relatives. 'There is an island in the sound—a floating island,' he told them. The old man knew it was an island for it had skeletons of trees thrusting skyward. But it was like no island he had ever seen. Word was sent up the Squamish River for the people to come and see the mysterious floating island.

It was decided that the men would go out in their canoes to see the island. As they grew near, they saw that it wasn't a floating island at all, but a very large canoe, a strange canoe. Soon, men appeared and walked around the canoe. But what strange men they were! Every part of their body was covered except for their faces, which were white. My people scrutinized them. Finally, some of the elders came up with an explanation—these people are from the land of the dead. And they are wrapped in their burial blankets!

One of the dead people stepped forward. He had smoke coming from his mouth and it appeared that he was eating fire. The man motioned for my ancestors to go on board. They were hesitant, of course, but after much discussion, one brave young man decided that he would go, and others followed. Instantly, the dead man in the canoe extended his hand. 'Oh, he wants to play the "pulling fingers" game,' the Squamish men told one another. One man stepped forward, spit in his palm, rubbed his hands together, and thrust out his crooked finger. The fire-eating dead man shook his head no, no. 'A stronger opponent is wanted,' the Squamish decided. Another man stepped forward, spit on his hand and got ready to play the game. Again the white man shook his head, no. More Squamish men stepped forward, spit, and extended their finger, until only one man remained—a strong man from up the Squamish River. My people could see that the strangers were talking amongst themselves and we can only assume that they must have decided that this unusual behaviour was the Indian way of greeting. So the white man stepped forward to link fingers with the strong man of Squamish. The Squamish man pulled. He pulled hard. Oh, the smoke-blowing dead man hollered in pain as his finger was disconnected! Some of the Squamish had been sceptical of the strangers. Then they knew. 'Dead people don't feel pain, and this one is certainly having some!'

Fear of the strangers vanished. The Squamish looked around the strange, large canoe and when it came time to leave they climbed down into their own canoes. The white people lowered into the canoes some presents, including a barrel and a few boxes.

Source: Louis Miranda and Philip Joe, in Robin Fisher and Hugh J.M. Johnston, eds., *From Maps to Metaphors*, (Vancouver: UBC Press, 1993), pp. 3–5. Reprinted with permission of the Publisher from *From Maps to Metaphors: The Pacific World of George Vancouver* edited by Robin Fisher and Hugh Johnston. © University of British Columbia Press 1993. All rights reserved by the Publisher.

Back at the village the people huddled around as the men opened the treasure. When they pried the top from the barrel they were pleased to see that it contained good thick hair and face oil, much better than the deer tallow and salmon oil they had in storage. All hands dipped into the barrel and smeared it onto their faces and hair. But soon the oil began to thicken. Their hair got stiff! Their faces got thick! And they could hardly move their jaw! They ran for the water and washed it off. The gift of molasses was then emptied onto the ground.

My people had hoped that the second gift might be less trouble. Inside the box were shiny round pieces that attracted the attention of the women—who saw their value as ornaments—and the children—who thought they made fine toys. For the box of silver coins had no other value to the Squamish in 1792.

The story passed down by my ancestors tells how Vancouver provided gifts of pilot biscuits, whisky, and white flour—unfamiliar foods that they used with results that were initially comical, although history has recorded a less jovial aftermath.

Viewing the explorers' ships as 'floating islands' and the men, themselves, as 'dead people' was not a perspective unique to the Squamish. Our relatives—the Nanaimo Indians—were also visited one night by floating islands. In addition to the fire-eating habit of the strangers, they saw that their feet were wooden and made a great deal of noise when they walked! The Nanaimo people's barrel of molasses was used to mend their canoes, but it was soon found that molasses was as poor a canoe pitch as it was a hair oil.

Apparently Vancouver then sailed north, for his travels up the coast can be traced by the elders' stories of mysterious floating islands that appeared offshore, and then, just as quickly as they arrived, sailed beyond the next point.

Many of you have investigated the naming of the landscape by Vancouver and his Spanish counterparts. But perhaps you are not aware that the Squamish commemorated the historic 1792 meeting in Howe Sound by thereafter referring to the site by the Squamish name *Whul-whul-LAY-ton*, meaning "Whiteman place."

Indian stories and place names, like explorers' journals, are reminders of history that provide a glimpse into another era. As I hope my people's story has demonstrated, our mutual histories since 1792 have been inexorably entwined, although recalled from different perspectives.

This country, which so inspired the explorers and challenged the map makers, was the homeland of the Squamish and our neighbours the Musqueam and the Seleelwat. These beaches gave us shellfish, crabs, and eel grass. The forests and flatlands provided deer, large herds of elk, bear, and mountain goats. Food plants were harvested, and the trees supplied the wood for our houses, canoes, weapons, and ceremonial objects. The bark of red cedars was stripped to make our clothes. The inlet waters provided us with a wide variety of fish and sea mammals, and salmon returned regularly to the streams. And just as Captain Vancouver was said to have shared his molasses, biscuits, and flour, so our people shared our natural resources with those who followed in the wake of the floating islands.

▲ Document 4: Engraving based on a drawing by Samuel de Champlain, 1613

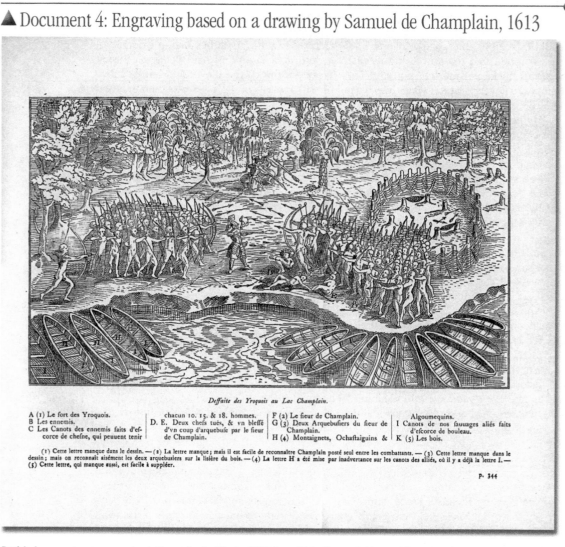

Deffaite des Yroquois au Lac Champlain.

A (1) Le fort des Yroquois.
B Les ennemis.
C Les Canots des ennemis faits d'ef-
corce de chefne, qui peuuent tenir

chacun 10. 15. & 18. hommes.
D. E. Deux chefs tués, & vn bleſſé
d'vn coup d'arquebuſe par le ſieur
de Champlain.

F (2) Le ſieur de Champlain.
G (3) Deux Arquebuſiers du ſieur de
Champlain.
H (4) Montaignets, Ochaſtaiguins &

Algoumequins.
I Canots de nos ſauuages aliés faits
d'eſcorce de bouleau.
K (5) Les bois.

(1) Cette lettre manque dans le deſſin. — (2) La lettre manque; mais il eſt facile de reconnaître Champlain poſté ſeul entre les combattants. — (3) Cette lettre manque dans le deſſin; mais on reconnaît aiſément les deux arquebuſiers ſur la liſière du bois. — (4) La lettre H a été miſe par inadvertance ſur les canots des aliés, où il y a déjà la lettre I. — (5) Cette lettre, qui manque auſſi, eſt facile à ſuppléer.

P. 344

● This is a contemporary depiction of a battle in 1609 in which Champlain used his arquebuse to fire on his Iroquois foes. What conclusions can we draw about Aboriginal–French relations based on this image?

Source: Deffaite des Yroquois au lac Champlain. In Champlain, Samuel de. Œuvres de Champlain / 2nd edition. Quebec : G.-É. Desbarats, 1870. Vol. 3, facing page 196. Archives of Ontario Library, 971.011 CHB http://www.archives.gov.on.ca/english/on-line-exhibits/franco-ontarian/pics/971_001_pg344_battle_520.jpg. LAC C-006780.

▲ Document 5: The Encounter Between Jacques Cartier and the Aboriginal Peoples at Stadaconé

● This image is a much later depiction of the encounter between Jacques Cartier and the Aboriginal peoples at Stadaconé (near present-day Quebec City). Quebec artist Marc-Aurèle Suzor-Côté painted this canvas in 1907. How does this image depict the encounter between the French and the Aboriginal peoples? Which group dominates the image? How well does this painting reflect the attitudes expressed in the readings for this section?

Source: http://www.mnba.qc.ca/Contenu.aspx?page=1529&langue=en. Suzor-Coté, Marc Aurèle de Foy, Jacques Cartier rencontre les Indiens à Stadaconé, 1535, Huile sur toile, 266x401 cm, Museé national des beaux-arts du Québec, Accession No. 34.12. Photographer Jean-Guy Kérouac.

Article 1: The Indians' Old World: Native Americans and the Coming of Europeans

Neil Salisbury

Scholars in history, anthropology, archaeology, and other disciplines have turned increasingly over the past two decades to the study of native peoples during the colonial period of North American history. The new work in Indian history has altered the way we think about the beginning of American history and about the era of European colonization. Historians now recognize that Europeans arrived, not in a virgin land, but in one that was teeming with several million people. Beyond filling in some of the vast blanks left by previous generations' overlooking of Indians, much of this scholarship makes clear that Indians are integral to the history of colonial North America.[1] In short, surveys of recent textbooks and of scholarly titles suggest that Native Americans are well on their way home to being "mainstreamed" by colonial historians.

Substantive as this reorientation is, it remains limited.[2] Beyond the problems inherent in representing Indian/non-Indian interactions during the colonial era lies the challenge of contextualizing the era itself. Despite opening chapters and lectures that survey the continent's native peoples and cultures, most historians continue to represent American history as having been set in motion by the arrival of European explorers and colonizers.[3] They have yet to recognize the existence of North American—as opposed to English or European—background for colonial history, much less to consider the implications of such a background for understanding the three centuries following Columbia's landfall. Yet a growing body of scholarship by archaeologists, linguists, and students of Native American expressive traditions recognizes 1492 not as a beginning but as a single moment in a long history utterly detached from that of Europe.[4] These findings call into question historians' synchronic maps and verbal descriptions of precontact Indians—their cultures, their communities, their ethnic and political designations and affiliations, and their relations with one another. Do these really describe enduring entities or do they represent epiphenomena of arbitrary moments in time? If the latter should prove to be the case, how will readings of Indian history in the colonial period be affected?

Far from being definitive, this article is intended as a stimulus to debate on these questions. It begins by drawing on recent work in archaeology, where most of the relevant scholarship has originated, to suggest one way of thinking about pre-Columbian North America in historical terms.[5] The essay then looks at developments in several areas of the continent during the centuries preceding the arrival of Europeans and in early phases of the colonial period. The purpose is to show how certain patterns and processes originating before the beginnings of contact continued to shape the continent's history thereafter and how an understanding of the colonial period requires an understanding of its American background as well as of its European context.[6]

In a formidable critique of European and Euro-American thinking about native North Americans, Robert F. Berkhofer, Jr., demonstrates that the idea of "Indians" as a single, discrete people was an invention of Columbus and his European contemporaries that has been perpetuated into our own time without foundation in historical, cultural, or ethnographic reality. On the contrary, Berkhofer asserts,

> The first residents of the Americas were by modern estimates divided into at least two thousand cultures and more societies, practiced a multiplicity of customs and lifestyles, held an enormous variety of values and beliefs, spoke numerous languages mutually unintelligible to the many speakers, and did not conceive of themselves as a single people—if they knew about each other at all.[7]

While there is literal truth in portions of Berkhofer's statement, his implication that Indians inhabited thousands of tiny, isolated communities in ignorance of one another flies in the face of a substantial body of archaeological and linguistic scholarship on North America and of a wealth of relevant anthropological literature on nonstate polities, nonmarket economies,

Source: Neil Salisbury, "The Indians' Old World: Native Americans and the Coming of Europeans" *The William and Mary Quarterly*, Third Series, Vol. 53, No. 3 (July 1996): 435–58. Reprinted with permission.

and noninstitutionalized religions. To be sure, indigenous North Americans exhibited a remarkable range of languages, economies, political systems, beliefs, and material cultures. But this range was less the result of their isolation from one another than of the widely varying natural and social environments with which Indians had interacted over millennia. What recent scholars of precolonial North America have found even more striking, given this diversity, is the extent to which native peoples' histories intersected one another.

At the heart of these intersections was exchange. By exchange is meant not only the trading of material goods but also exchanges across community lines of marriage partners, resources, labor, ideas, techniques, and religious practices. Longer-distance exchanges frequently crossed cultural and linguistic boundaries as well and ranged from casual encounters to widespread alliances and networks that were economic, political, and religious. For both individuals and communities, exchanges sealed social and political relationships. Rather than accumulate material wealth endlessly, those who acquired it gave it away, thereby earning prestige and placing obligations on others to reciprocate appropriately. And as we shall see, many goods were not given away to others in this world but were buried with individuals to accompany them to another.[8]

Archaeologists have found evidence of ongoing exchange relations among even the earliest known Paleo-Indian inhabitants of North America. Ten thousand years before Columbus, in the wake of the last Ice Age, bands of two or three dozen persons regularly traveled hundreds of miles to hunt and trade with one another at favored campsites such as Lindenmeier in northern Colorado, dating to ca. 8800 B.C. At the Lindenmeier site, differences in the flaking and shaping of stone points distinguished regular occupants in two parts of the camp, and the obsidian each used came from about 350 miles north and south of Lindenmeier, respectively.[9] Evidence from a wide range of settlement sites makes clear that, as the postglacial warming trend continued, so-called Archaic peoples in much of the continent developed wider ranges of food sources, more sedentary settlement patterns, and larger populations. They also expanded their exchanges with one another and conducted them over greater distances. Highly valued materials such as Great Lakes copper,

Rocky Mountain obsidian, and marine shells from the Gulf and Atlantic coasts have been found in substantial quantities at sites hundreds and even thousands of miles from their points of origin. In many cases, goods fashioned from these materials were buried with human beings, indicating both their religious significance and, by their uneven distribution, their role as markers of social or political rank.[10]

While the Archaic pattern of autonomous bands persisted in most of North America until the arrival of Europeans, the complexity of exchange relationships in some parts of the continent produced the earliest evidence of concentrated political power. This was especially so for peoples who, after the first century A.D., developed food economies that permitted them to inhabit permanent, year-round villages. In California, for example, competition among communities for coveted acorn groves generated sharply defined political territories and elevated the role of chiefs who oversaw trade, diplomacy, and warfare for clusters of villages. Similar competition for prime fishing and trading locations strengthened the authority of certain village chiefs on the Northwest Coast.[11] Exchange rather than competition for resources appears to have driven centralization in the Ohio and Illinois valleys. There the Hopewell peoples imported copper, mica, shell, and other raw materials over vast distances to their village centers, where specialists fashioned them into intricately crafted ornaments, tools, and other objects. They deposited massive quantities of these goods with the dead in large mounds and exported more to communities scattered throughout the Mississippi Valley. Hopewell burials differentiate between commoners and elites by the quantity and quality of grave goods accompanying each.[12] In the Southwest, meanwhile, a culture known as Hohokam emerged in the Gila River and Salt River valleys among some of the first societies based primarily on agriculture. Hohokam peoples lived in permanent villages and maintained elaborate irrigation systems that enabled them to harvest two crops per year.[13]

By the twelfth century, agricultural production had spread over much of the Eastern Woodlands as well as to more of the Southwest. In both regions, even more complex societies were emerging to dominate widespread exchange networks. In the Mississippi Valley and the Southeast, the sudden primacy of maize horticulture is marked archaeologically in a variety of ways—food remains, pollen profiles, studies of human bone (showing that maize accounted for 50 percent of people's diets), and in material culture by a proliferation of chert hoes, shell-tempered pottery for storing and cooking, and pits for storing surplus crops. These developments were accompanied by the rise of what archaeologists term "Mississippian" societies, consisting of fortified political and ceremonial centers and outlying villages. The centers were built around open plazas featuring platform burial mounds, temples, and elaborate residences for elite families. Evidence from burials makes clear the wide social gulf that separated commoners from elites. Whereas the former were buried in simple graves with a few personal possessions, the latter were interred in the temples or plazas along with many more, and more elaborate, goods such as copper ornaments, massive sheets of shell, and ceremonial weapons. Skeletal evidence indicates that elites ate more meat, were taller, performed less strenuous physical activity, and were less prone to illness and accident than commoners.[14] Although most archaeologists' conclusions are informed at least in part by models developed by political anthropologists, they also draw heavily from Spanish and French observations of some of the last Mississippian societies. These observations confirm that political leaders, or chiefs, from elite families mobilized labor, collected tribute, redistributed agricultural surpluses, coordinated trade, diplomacy, and military activity, and were worshipped as deities.[15]

The largest, most complex Mississippian center was Cahokia, located not far from the confluence of the Mississippi and Missouri rivers, near modern East St. Louis, Illinois, in the rich floodplain known as American Bottoms. By the twelfth century, Cahokia probably numbered 20,000 people and contained over 120 mounds within a five-square-mile area. One key to Cahokia's rise was its combination of rich soil and nearby wooded uplands, enabling inhabitants to produce surplus crops while providing an abundance and diversity of wild food sources along with ample supplies of wood for fuel and construction. A second key was its location, affording access to the great river systems of the North American interior.[16]

Cahokia had the most elaborate social structure yet seen in North America. Laborers used stone and wooden spades to dig soil from "borrow pits" (at least nineteen have been identified by archaeologists),

which they carried in wooden buckets to mounds and palisades often more than half a mile away. The volume and concentration of craft activity in shell, copper, clay, and other materials, both local and imported, suggests that specialized artisans provided the material foundation for Cahokia's exchange ties with other peoples. Although most Cahokians were buried in mass graves outside the palisades, their rulers were given special treatment. At a prominent location in Mound 72, the largest of Cahokia's platform mounds, a man had been buried atop a platform of shell beads. Accompanying him were several group burials: fifty young women, aged 18 to 23, four men, and three men and three women, all encased in uncommonly large amounts of exotic materials. As with the Natchez Indians observed by the French in Louisiana, Cahokians appear to have sacrificed individuals to accompany their leaders in the afterlife. Cahokia was surrounded by nine smaller mound centers and several dozen villages from which it obtained much of its food and through which it conducted its waterborne commerce with other Mississippian centers in the Midwest and Southeast.[17]

[...] Given the archaeological record, North American "prehistory" can hardly be characterized as a multiplicity of discrete microhistories. Fundamental to the social and economic patterns of even the earliest Paleo-Indian bands were exchanges that linked peoples across geographic, cultural, and linguistic boundaries. The effects of these links are apparent in the spread of raw materials and finished goods, of beliefs and ceremonies, and of techniques for food production and for manufacturing. By the twelfth century, some exchange networks had become highly formalized and centralized. Exchange constitutes an important key to conceptualizing American history before Columbus.

Although it departs from our familiar image of North American Indians, the historical pattern sketched so far is recognizable in the way it portrays societies "progressing" from small, egalitarian, autonomous communities to larger, more hierarchical, and centralized political aggregations with more complex economies. The image is likewise subverted when we examine the three centuries immediately preceding the arrival of Europeans. In both American Bottoms and the San Juan River basin [in present-day New Mexico], where twelfth-century populations were most concentrated, agriculture most productive, exchange most varied and voluminous, and political systems most complex and extensive, there were scarcely any inhabitants by the end of the fifteenth century. What happened and why?

Cahokia and other Mississippian societies in the Upper Midwest peaked during the late twelfth and early thirteenth centuries. Data from soil traces indicate that even then laborers were fortifying Cahokia's major earthworks against attack. At the same time, archaeologists surmise, Cahokia was headed toward an ecological crisis: expanded settlement, accompanied by especially hot dry summers, exhausted the soil, depleted the supply of timber for building and fuel, and reduced the habitat of the game that supplemented their diet. By the end of the fourteenth century, Cahokia's inhabitants had dispersed over the surrounding countryside into small farming villages.[18]

Cahokia's abandonment reverberated among other Mississippian societies in the Midwest. Fortified centers on the Mississippi River from the Arkansas River northward and on the Ohio River appear to have been strengthened by influxes of people from nearby villages but then abandoned, and signs from burials indicate a period of chronic, deadly warfare in the Upper Midwest. One archaeologist refers to the middle Mississippi Valley and environs during the fifteenth century as "the vacant quarter." A combination of ecological pressures and upheavals within the alliance that linked them appears to have doomed Cahokia and other midwestern Mississippian centers, leading the inhabitants to transform themselves into the village dwellers of the surrounding prairies and plains observed by French explorers three centuries later.[19]

The upheavals may even have extended beyond the range of direct Mississippian influence to affect Iroquois and Hurons and other Iroquoian speakers of the lower Great Lakes region. These people had been moving from dispersed, riverside settlements to fortified, bluff-top villages over the course of several centuries; the process appears to have intensified in the fourteenth century, when it also led to the formation of the Iroquois and Huron confederacies. The Hurons developed fruitful relations with hunter-gatherers to the north, with whom they exchanged agricultural produce for meat and skins, and Iroquois ties with outsiders appear to have diminished except for small-scale interactions with coastal peoples to the south and east. Across the Northeast, political life was characterized by violence and other manifestations

of intense competition. Whether the upheavals in exchange ties occasioned by the collapse of Cahokia were directly linked to the formation of the Iroquois and Huron confederacies, as Dena Dincauze and Robert Hasenstab have suggested for the Iroquois, or were simply part of a larger process generated by the advent of farming and consequent demographic and political changes, the repercussions were still evident when Europeans began to frequent the region during the sixteenth century.[20]

[...] Combinations of continuity and change, persistence and adaptability, arose from concrete historical experiences rather than a timeless tradition. The remainder of this article indicates some of the ways that both the deeply rooted imperatives of reciprocity and exchange and the recent legacies of competition and upheaval informed North American history as Europeans began to make their presence felt.

Discussion of the transition from pre- to post-contact times must begin with the sixteenth century, when Indians and Europeans met and interacted in a variety of settings. When not slighting the era altogether, historians have viewed it as one of discovery or exploration, citing the achievements of notable Europeans in either anticipating or failing to anticipate the successful colonial enterprises of the seventeenth century. Recently, however, a number of scholars have been integrating information from European accounts with the findings of archaeologists to produce a much fuller picture of this critical period in North American history.

[...] In the Northeast, [...] Iroquoian-speaking villagers on the Mississippian periphery and Archaic hunter-gatherers still further removed from developments in the interior met Europeans of several nationalities. At the outset of the century, Spanish and Portuguese explorers enslaved several dozen Micmacs and other Indians from the Nova Scotia-Gulf of St. Lawrence area. Three French expeditions to the St. Lawrence itself in the 1530s and the 1540s followed the Spanish pattern by alienating most Indians encountered and ending in futility. Even as these hostile contacts were taking place, fishermen, whalers, and other Europeans who visited the area regularly had begun trading with natives. As early as the 1520s, Abenakis on the coast of Maine and Micmacs were trading the furs of beavers and other animals for European goods of metal and glass. By the 1540s, specialized fur traders, mostly French, frequented the coast as far south as the Chesapeake; by the 1550s or soon thereafter, French traders rendezvoused regularly with Indians along the shores of upper New England, the Maritimes, and Quebec and at Tadoussac on the St. Lawrence.[21]

What induced Indians to go out of their way to trap beaver and trade the skins for glass beads, mirrors, copper kettles, and other goods? Throughout North America since Paleo-Indian times, exchange in the Northeast was the means by which people maintained and extended their social, cultural, and spiritual horizons as well as acquired items considered supernaturally powerful. Members of some coastal Indian groups later recalled how the first Europeans they saw, with their facial hair and strange clothes and traveling in their strange boats, seemed like supernatural figures. Although soon disabused of such notions, these Indians and many more inland placed special value on the glass beads and other trinkets offered by the newcomers. Recent scholarship on Indians' motives in this earliest stage of the trade indicates that they regarded such objects as the equivalents of the quartz, mica, shell, and other sacred substances that had formed the heart of long-distance exchange in North America for millennia and that they regarded as sources of physical and spiritual well-being, on earth and in the afterlife. Indians initially altered and wore many of the utilitarian goods they received, such as iron axe heads and copper pots, rather than use them for their intended purposes. Moreover, even though the new objects might pass through many hands, they more often than not ended up in graves, presumably for their possessors to use in the afterlife. Finally, the archaeological findings make clear that shell and native copper predominated over the new objects in sixteenth-century exchanges, indicating that European trade did not suddenly trigger a massive craving for the objects themselves. While northeastern Indians recognized Europeans as different from themselves, they interacted with them and their materials in ways that were consistent with their own customs and beliefs.[22]

By the late sixteenth century, the effects of European trade began to overlap with the effects of earlier upheavals in the northeastern interior. Sometime between Jacques Cartier's final departure in 1543 and Samuel de Champlain's arrival in 1603, the Iroquoian-speaking inhabitants of Hochelaga and Stadacona (modern Montreal and Quebec City) abandoned their communities. The communities were crushed militarily, and the survivors dispersed among both Iroquois and Hurons. Whether the perpetrators of these dispersals were Iroquois or Huron is a point of controversy, but either way the St. Lawrence communities appear to have been casualties of the rivalry, at least a century old, between the two confederations as each sought to position itself vis-à-vis the French. The effect, if not the cause, of the dispersals was the Iroquois practice of attacking antagonists who denied them direct access to trade goods; this is consistent with Iroquois actions during the preceding two centuries and the century that followed.[23]

The sudden availability of many more European goods, the absorption of many refugees from the St. Lawrence, and the heightening of tensions with the Iroquois help to explain the movement of most outlying Huron communities to what is now the Simcoe County area of Ontario during the 1580s. This geographic concentration strengthened their confederacy and gave it the form it had when allied with New France during the first half of the seventeenth century.[24] Having formerly existed at the outer margins of the arena of exchange centered in Cahokia, the Hurons and Iroquois now faced a new sources of goods and power to the east.[25]

The diverse native societies encountered by Europeans as they began to settle North America permanently during the seventeenth century were not static isolates lying outside the ebb and flow of human history. Rather, they were products of a complex set of historical forces, both local and wide-ranging, both deeply rooted and of recent origin. Although their lives and worldviews were shaped by long-standing traditions of reciprocity and spiritual power, the people in these communities were also accustomed—contrary to popular myths about inflexible Indians—to economic and political flux and to absorbing new peoples (both allies and antagonists), objects, and ideas, including those originating in Europe. Such combinations of tradition and innovation continued to shape Indians' relations with Europeans, even as the latter's visits became permanent.

The establishment of lasting European colonies, beginning with New Mexico in 1598, began a phase in the continent's history that eventually resulted in the displacement of Indians to the economic, political, and cultural margins of a new order. But during the interim natives and colonizers entered into numerous relationships in which they exchanged material goods and often supported one another diplomatically or militarily against common enemies. These relations combined native and European modes of exchange. While much of the scholarly literature emphasizes the subordination and dependence of Indians in these circumstances, Indians as much as Europeans dictated the form and content of their early exchanges and alliances. Much of the protocol and ritual surrounding such intercultural contacts was rooted in indigenous kinship obligations and gift exchanges, and Indian consumers exhibited decided preferences for European commodities that satisfied social, spiritual, and aesthetic values. Similarly, Indians' long-range motives and strategies in their alliances with Europeans were frequently rooted in older patterns of alliance and rivalry with regional neighbors.[26] Such continuities can be glimpsed through a brief consideration of the early colonial-era histories of the Five Nations Iroquois in the Northeast [...]

Post-Mississippian and sixteenth-century patterns of antagonism between the Iroquois and their neighbors to the north and west persisted, albeit under altered circumstances, during the seventeenth century when France established its colony on the St. Lawrence and allied itself with Hurons and other Indians. France aimed to extract maximum profits from the fur trade, and it immediately recognized the Iroquois as the major threat to that goal. In response, the Iroquois turned to the Dutch in New Netherland for guns and other trade goods while raiding New France's Indian allies for the thicker northern pelts that brought higher prices than those in their own country (which they exhausted by midcentury) and for captives to replace those from their own ranks who had died from epidemics or in wars. During the 1640s, the Iroquois replaced raids with full-scale military assaults (the so-called Beaver Wars) on Iroquoian-speaking communities in the lower Great Lakes, absorbing most of the survivors as refugees or captives. All the while, the Iroquois elaborated a vision of their confederation, which had brought harmony within their own ranks, as bringing peace to all people of the region. For the remainder of the century, the Five Nations fought a gruelling and costly series of wars against the French and their Indian allies in order to gain access to the pelts and French goods circulating in lands to the north and west.[27]

Meanwhile, the Iroquois were also adapting to the growing presence of English colonists along the Atlantic seaboard. After the English supplanted the Dutch in New York in 1664, Iroquois diplomats established relations with the proprietary governor, Sir Edmund Andros, in a treaty known as the Covenant Chain. The Covenant Chain was an elaboration of the Iroquois' earlier treaty arrangement with the Dutch, but whereas the Iroquois had termed the Dutch relationship a chain of iron, they referred to the one with the English as a chain of silver. The shift in metaphors was appropriate, for what had been strictly an economic connection was now a political one in which the Iroquois acquired power over other New York Indians. After 1677, the Covenant Chain was expanded to include several English colonies, most notably Massachusetts and Maryland, along with those colonies' subject Indians. The upshot of these arrangements was that the Iroquois cooperated with their colonial partners in subduing and removing subject Indians who impeded settler expansion. The Mohawks in particular played a vital role in the New England colonies' suppression of the Indian uprising known as King Philip's War and in moving the Susquehannocks away from the expanding frontier of settlement in the Chesapeake after Bacon's Rebellion.

For the Iroquois, such a policy helped expand their "Tree of Peace" among Indians while providing them with buffers against settler encroachment around their homelands. The major drawback in the arrangement proved to be the weakness of English military assistance against the French. This inadequacy, and the consequent suffering experience by the Iroquois during two decades of war after 1680, finally drove the Five Nations to make peace with the French and their Indian allies in the Grand Settlement of 1701. Together, the Grand Settlement and Covenant Chain provided the Iroquois with the peace and security, the access to trade goods, and the dominant role among northeastern Indians they had long sought.[28] That these arrangements in the long run served to reinforce rather than deter English encroachment on Iroquois lands and autonomy should not obscure their pre-European roots and their importance in shaping colonial history in the Northeast.

[...] As significant as is the divide separating pre- and post-Columbian North American history, it is not the stark gap suggested by the distinction between prehistory and history. For varying periods of time after their arrival in North America, Europeans adapted to the social and political environments they found, including the fluctuating ties of reciprocity and interdependence as well as rivalry, that characterized those environments. They had little choice but to enter in and participate if they wished to sustain their presence. Eventually, one route to success proved to be their ability to insert themselves as regional powers in new networks of exchange and alliance that arose to supplant those of the Mississippians, Anasazis, and others.

To assert such continuities does not minimize the radical transformations entailed in Europeans' colonization of the continent and its indigenous peoples. Arising in Cahokia's wake, new centers at Montreal, Fort Orange/Albany, Charleston, and elsewhere permanently altered the primary patterns of exchange in eastern North America. The riverine system that channelled exchange in the interior of the continent gave way to one in which growing quantities of goods arrived from, and were directed to, coastal peripheries and ultimately Europe.[29] [...] More generally, European colonizers brought a complex of demographic and ecological advantages, most notably epidemic disease and their own immunity to them, that utterly devastated Indian communities;[30] ideologies and beliefs in their cultural and spiritual superiority to native people and their entitlement to natives' lands;[31] and economic, political, and military systems organized for the engrossment of Indian lands and the subordination or suppression of Indian peoples.[32]

Europeans were anything but uniformly successful in realizing their goals, but the combination of demographic ecological advantages and imperial intentions, along with the Anglo-Iroquois Covenant Chain, enabled land-hungry colonists from New England to the Chesapeake to break entirely free of ties of dependence on Indians before the end of the seventeenth century. Their successes proved to be only the beginning of a new phase of Indian-European relations. By the mid-eighteenth century, the rapid expansion of land-based settlement in the English colonies had sundered older ties of exchange and alliance linking natives and colonizers nearly everywhere east of the Appalachians, driving many Indians west and reducing those who remained to a scattering of politically powerless enclaves in which Indian identities were nurtured in isolation.[33] Meanwhile, the colonizers threatened to extend this new mode of Indian relations across the Appalachians. An old world, rooted in indigenous exchange, was giving way to one in which Native Americans had no certain place.

Notes

1. See James Axtell, "A North American Perspective for Colonial History," *History Teacher*, 12 (1978–1979), 549–62. The beginning of this shift was signaled by Gary B. Nash, *Red, White, and Black* (Englewood Cliffs, N. J., 1973), and Francis Jennings, *The Invasion of America: Indians, Colonialism, and the Cant of Conquest* (Chapel Hill, 1975).

2. See James H. Merrell, "Some Thoughts on Colonial Historians and American Indians," *William and Mary Quarterly [WMQ]*, 3d Ser., 46 (1989), 108–10, and Daniel K. Richter, "Whose Indian History?" ibid., 50 (1993), 381–82.

3. See Frederick E. Hoxie, *The Indians Versus the Textbooks: Is There Any Way Out?* (Chicago, 1984); Hoxie, "The Problems of Indian History," *Social Science Journal*, 25 (1988), 389–99.

4. A volume that draws on all these approaches is Alvin M. Josephy, Jr., ed., *America in 1492: The World of the Indian Peoples Before the Arrival of Columbus* (New York, 1992). The best surveys of North American archaeology are Brian M. Fagan, *Ancient North America: The Archaeology of a Continent* (New York, 1991), and Stuart J. Fiedel, *Prehistory of the Americas*, 2d ed. (Cambridge, 1992). On languages see Harold E. Driver, *Indians of North America*, 2d ed. (Chicago, 1969), and Joseph H. Greenberg, *Language in the Americas* (Stanford, Calif., 1987), esp. chap. 2. Two especially interesting examples of work that utilizes oral traditions as historical sources to supplement "prehistoric" archaeology are Roger C. Echo-Hawk, "Kara Katit Pakutu: Exploring the Origins of Native America in Anthropology and Oral Traditions" (M.A. thesis, University of Colorado, 1994), and Donald Bahr et al., *the Short, Swift Time of Gods on Earth: The Hohokam Chronicles* (Berkeley, Calif., 1994).

5. On archaeology as a foundation for Indian history see Bruce G. Trigger, "Archaeology and the Image of the American Indian," *American Antiquity*, 45 (1980), 662–76, and "American Archaeology as

Native History: A Review Essay," *WMQ*, 3d Ser., 40 (1983), 413–52. Among works that incorporate archaeology into historical narratives, the most exemplary by anthropologists are Trigger, *The Children of Aataensic: A History of the Huron People to 1660* (Montreal, 1976), and Kathleen J. Bragdon, *Native People of Southern New England, 1500–1650* (Norman, Okla., 1996), and by historians, Daniel K. Richter, *The Ordeal of the Longhouse: The People of the Iroquois League in the Era of European Colonization* (Chapel Hill, 1992). The most thorough argument for the role of indigenous contexts in shaping post-Columbian American history is Francis Jennings, *The Founders of America: How the Indians Discovered the Land, Pioneered in It, and Created Great Classical Civilization; How They Were Plunged into a Dark Age by Invasion and Conquest; and How They Are Reviving* (New York, 1993). But Jennings argues for a pervasive "Mexican influence" in North America by the 15th century A.D. and makes several other inferences that are highly speculative at best. Lynda Norene Shaffer, *Native Americans before 1492: The Moundbuilding Centers of the Eastern Woodlands* (Armonk, N. Y., 1992), is a useful overview by a historian whose interest is world, rather than American, history.

6. The need for an understanding of its West African contexts is equally critical but outside the scope of this article and its author's expertise. For a beginning in this direction see John Thornton, *Africa and Africans in the Making of the Atlantic World, 1400–1680* (Cambridge, 1992), and the review of that volume by Ira Berlin in *WMQ*, 3d Ser., 51 (1994), 544–47.

7. Robert F. Berkhofer, Jr., *The White Man's Indian: Images of the American Indian from Columbus to the Present* (New York, 1978), 3.

8. The basic contribution to the vast literature on gift exchange economies are Marcel Mauss, *The Gift: Forms and Functions of Exchange in Archaic Societies*, trans. Ian Cunnison (London, 1954); Karl Polanyi, *The Great Transformation* (New York, 1944), chap. 4; Marshall Sahlins, *Stone Age Economics* (Chicago, 1972); and George Dalton, "The Impact of Colonization on Aboriginal Economics in Stateless Societies," in Dalton, ed., *Research in Economic Anthropology: An Annual Compilation of Research* (Greenwich, Conn., 1978), 1:131–84. On North America see William A. Turnbaugh, "Wide-Area Connections in Native North

America," *American Indian Culture and Research Journal*, 1:4 (1976), 22–28.

9. Edwin S. Wilmsen, *Lindenmeier: A Pleistocene Hunting Society* (New York, 1974); Turnbaugh, "Wide-Area Connections in Native North America," 23–24.

10. Fiedel, *Prehistory of the Americas*, chap, 4; Turnbaugh, "Wide-Area Connections in Native North America," 24–25; Jesse D. Jennings, "Epilogue," in Jennings, ed., *Ancient Native Americans* (San Francisco, 1978), 651; Barbara Bender, "Emergent Tribal Formations in the American Midcontinent," *American Antiquity*, 50 (1985), 52–62; Lynn Ceci, "Tracing Wampum's Origins: Shell Bead Evidence from Archaeological Sites in Western and Coastal New York," in Charles F. Hayes et al., eds., *Proceedings of the 1986 Shell Bead Conference: Selected Papers*, Rochester Museum and Science Center, Research Records No. 20 (Rochester, N. Y., 1989), 65–67.

11. Fiedel, *Prehistory of the Americas*, 133–43.

12. Joseph R. Caldwell, "Interaction Spheres in Prehistory," in Caldwell and Robert L. Hall, eds., *Hopewellian Studies*, Illinois State Museum, Scientific Papers, 12 (Springfield, 1964), 133–43; David S. Brose and N'omi Greber, eds., *Hopewell Archaeology: The Chillicothe Conference* (Kent, Ohio, 1979); Fiedel, *Prehistory of the Americas*, 240–51.

13. Linda S. Cordell, *Prehistory of the Southwest* (Orlando, Fla., 1984), 207–11; Fiedel, *Prehistory of the Americas*, 209–12.

14. Fiedel, *Prehistory of the Americas*, 251–60; Dan F. Morse and Phyllis S. Morse, *Archaeology of the Central Mississippi Valley* (New York, 1983), chaps. 10–11; Bruce D. Smith, "The Archaeology of the Southeastern United States: From Dalton to de Soto, 10,500–500 P.P.," *Advances in World Archaeology*, 5 (1986), 53–63; Vincas P. Steponaitis, "Prehistoric Archaeology in the Southeastern United States, 1970–1985," *Annual Review of Anthropology*, 15 (1986), 387–93.

15. The successful integration of archaeology, history, and theory as well as the range of approaches possible with these as foundations can be seen by surveying the relevant essays in Charles Hudson and Carmen Chaves Tesser, eds., *The Forgotten Centuries: Indians and Europeans in the American South, 1521–1704* (Athens, Ga., 1994). See also Chester B. De Pratter, "Late Prehistoric and Early Historic Chiefdoms in the Southeastern United States" (Ph. D. diss., University of Georgia, 1983);

Charles Hudson et al., "Coosa: A Chiefdom in the Sixteenth-Century Southeastern United States," *American Antiquity*, 50 (1985), 723–37; David G. Anderson, *The Savannah River Chiefdoms: Political Change in the Late Prehistoric Southeast* (Tuscaloosa, Ala., 1994). The most recent theoretical discussion is Randolph J. Widmer, "The Structure of Southeastern Chiefdoms," in Hudson and Tesser, eds., *Forgotten Centuries*, 125–55.

16. Melvin L. Fowler, "A Pre-Columbian Urban Center on the Mississippi," *Scientific American*, 233 (August 1975), 92–101; William R. Iseminger, "Cahokia: A Mississippian Metropolis," *Historic Illinois*, 2:6 (April 1980), 1–4.

17. Archaeologists disagree as to the complexity and power of Cahokia, but see Patricia J. O'Brien, "Urbanism, Cahokia, and Middle Mississippian," *Archaeology*, 25 (1972), 188–97; Fowler, "Pre-Columbian Urban Center on the Mississippi"; Iseminger, "Cahokia"; Fowler, *The Cahokia Atlas: A Historical Atlas of Cahokia Archaeology*, Studies in Illinois Archaeology, 6 (Springfield, 1989); George R. Milner, "The Late Prehistoric Cahokia Cultural System of the Mississippi River Valley: Foundations, Florescence, Fragmentation," *Journal of World Prehistory*, 4 (1990), 1–43; Thomas E. Emerson and R. Barry Lewis, eds., *Cahokia and the Hinterlands: Middle Mississippian Cultures of the Midwest* (Urbana, 1991). For European accounts of the Natchez and other Mississippians who sacrificed individuals when a paramount chief died see DePratter, "Late Prehistoric and Early Historic Chiefdoms," 64–77.

18. Fowler, "Pre-Columbian Urban Center," 8–11; Iseminger, "Cahokia"; Milner, "Late Prehistoric Cahokia Cultural System," 30–33.

19. Dena F. Dincauze and Robert J. Hasenstab, "Explaining the Iroquois: Tribalization on a prehistoric Periphery," in *Comparative Studies in the Development of Complex Societies*, 3 (Southampton, Eng., 1986), 5, 7–8; George R. Milner et al., "Warfare in Late Prehistoric West-Central Illinois," *American Antiquity*, 65 (1991), 581–603; Morse and Morse, *Archaeology*, chap. 12; Stephen Williams, "The Vacant Quarter and Other Late Events in the Lower Valley," in David H. Dye and Cheryl Anne Cox, eds., *Towns and Temples along the Mississippi* (Tuscaloosa, 1990), 170–80.

20. James A. Tuck, *Onondaga Iroquois Prehistory: A Study in Settlement Archaeology* (Syracuse, N. Y.,

1971), chaps. 2–4; James W. Bradley, *Evolution of the Onondaga Iroquois: Accommodating Change, 1500–1655* (Syracuse, N. Y., 1987), 14–34 passim; Trigger, *Children of Aataentsic*, 1:119–76 passim; Trigger, *Natives and Newcomers: Canada's "Heroic Age" Reconsidered* (Kingston, Ont., 1985), 38–110 passim; Dean R. Snow, *The Archaeology of New England* (New York, 1980), 307–19 passim; Dincauze and Hasenstab, "Explaining the Iroquois." One influential version of the oral account of the Iroquois Confederacy's founding confirms that it occurred against a backdrop of violence among the Five Nations Iroquois and their common enmity with the Hurons; see William N. Fenton. ed., *Parker on the Iroquois*, (Syracuse, N. Y., 1968), bk. 3, pp. 14–29.

21. Neal Salisbury, *Manitou and Providence: Indians, Europeans, and the Making of New England, 1500–1643* (New York, 1982), 51–56; Trigger, *Natives and Newcomers*, 118–44.

22. Christopher L. Miller and George R. Hammell, "A New Perspective on Indian-White Contact: Cultural Symbols and Colonial Trade," *Journal of American History [JAH]*, 73 (1986), 311–28; Trigger, *Natives and Newcomers*, 125–27; Bradley, *Evolution*, chap. 21 Calvin Martin, "The Four Lives of a Micmac Copper Pot," *Ethnohistory*, 22 (1975), 111–33; James Axtell, "At the Water's Edge: Trading in the Sixteenth Century," in Axtell, *After Columbus: Essays in the Ethnohistory of Colonial North America* (New York, 1988), 144–81; Trigger, "Early Native North American Responses to European Contact: Romantic versus Rationalistic Interpretations," *JAH*, 77 (1991), 1195–1215. Compare the barbed Delaware-Mahican tradition of early relations with the Dutch recorded by John Heckewelder in his *An Account of the History, Manners, and Customs of the Indian Nations, Who Once Inhabited Pennsylvania and the Neighbouring States* (Philadelphia, 1819), 71–75.

23. Trigger, *Natives and Newcomers*, 144–48.

24. Ibid., 157–61.

25. See Dincauze and Haasenstab, "Explaining the Iroquois."

26. See, for example, Kenneth E. Kidd, "The Cloth Trade and the Indians of the Northeast during the Seventeenth and Eighteenth Centuries," in Royal Ontario Museum, *Art and Archaeology Annual* (1961), 48–56; Wilcomb E. Washburn, "Symbol,

Utility, and Aesthetics in the Indian Fur Trade," *Minnesota History*, 40 (1966), 198–202; Donald J. Bladeslee, "The Calumet Ceremony and the Origin of Fur Trade Rituals," *Western Canadian Journal of Anthropology*, 7, No. 2 (1977), 78–88; Bruce M. White, "Give Us a Little Milk: The Social and Cultural Meanings of Gift Giving in the Lake Superior Fur Trade," *Minnesota History*, 48 (1982), 60–71, and "A Skilled Game of Exchange: Ojibway Fur Trade Protocol," ibid., 50 (1987), 229–40; Francis Jennings et al., eds., *The History and Culture of Iroquois Diplomacy: An Interdisciplinary Guide to the Treaties of the Six Nations and Their League* (Syracuse, N.Y. 1985), chaps. 1, 4–7; Richard White, *The Middle Ground: Indians, Empires, and Republics, 1650–1815* (Cambridge, 1991), chaps. 2–4 passim.

27. Richter, *Ordeal of the Longhouse*, 30–104.

28. Pennsylvania joined the Covenant Chain early in the 18th century; Francis Jennings, *The Ambiguous Iroquois Empire: The Covenant Chain Confederation of Indian Tribes with English Colonies from Its Beginnings to the Lancaster Treaty of 1744* (New York, 1984), chap. 8; Richter, *Ordeal of the Longhouse*, 105–213 passim.

29. Shaffer, *Native Americans before 1492*, esp. 10–11, 94–96.

30. Alfred W. Crosby, *Ecological Imperialism: The Biological Expansion of Europe, 900–1900* (Cambridge, 1986).

31. Roy Harvey Pearce, *The Savages of America: A Study of the Indian and the Idea of Civilization* (Baltimore, 1953); Richard Slotkin, *Regeneration through Violence: The Mythology of the American Frontier, 1600–1800* (Middletown, Conn., 1973); Berkhofer, *White Man's Indian*.

32. Jennings, *Invasion of America*, pt. 1.

33. For summaries of these developments see Salisbury, "The History of Native Americans from before the Arrival of the Europeans and Africans until the American Civil War," in Stanley L. Engerman and Robert E. Gallman, eds., *The Cambridge Economic History of the United States*, vol. 1: *The Colonial Era* (Cambridge, 1996), chap. 1, and "Native People and European Settlers in Eastern North America, 1600–1783," in *The Cambridge History of the Native Peoples of the Americas*, vol. 1: North America, ed. Trigger and Washburn (Cambridge, 1996).

■ Article 2: Donnacona Discovers Europe: Rereading Jacques Cartier's *Voyages*

Ramsay Cook

Jacques Cartier's *Voyages* is the most informative and reliable French description of the northern coast and the St Lawrence region of North America written in the sixteenth century. The report that the Florentine navigator Giovanni Verrazzano composed for the French king, Francis I, describing the 1524. voyage along the coast from the Carolinas to Cape Breton, captures both the changing topography and the different groups of people who lived on the Atlantic seaboard. But it lacks detail and depth. André Thevet,

Source: From Cook, R. *The Voyages of Jacques Cartier*, 1993, ix–x, xviii–xli. © 1993, University of Toronto Press. Reprinted with permission of the publisher.

cosmographer to Francis I, wrote two works about 'France antartique' during the second half of the century—though he may never have travelled to the St Lawrence area. His works, *Les Singularitez de la France antartique* (1556) and *La Cosmographie universelle* (1575), relied heavily on Cartier, with whom he was acquainted. He provides some fascinating details not found elsewhere—his description of the snowshoe for example—but his reliability is problematic. If Verrazzano approximated Montaigne's 'plain simple fellow' who did not 'construct false theories,' then Thevet exemplified the 'men of intelligence' who could not 'refrain from altering the facts a little' in order to substantiate their interpretation.[1]

Cartier's observations are frequently detailed and include an impressive range of information about the geography, natural history, and ethnography from Funk Island to the Amerindian settlement at Hochelaga at the foot of the mountain he named Mount Royal. The *Voyages*, for over 450 years, have provided almost the only documentation for the beginning of European contact with this region. They reveal a man with both the virtues of an honest observer and the assumptions and preoccupations of a shrewd Breton navigator. Since he interpreted what he saw, he 'never presents things just as they are' and, especially in his discussion of his relations with the people who lived along the St Lawrence, he 'could twist and disguise [facts] to conform to [his] point of view.' Like all historical documents, Cartier's *Voyages* can be both informative and misleading.[2] [...]

The critical test of Cartier's representation of what he saw in eastern North America is [...] his ethnology. For Cartier was, unwittingly Canada's first ethnologist, an activity practiced long before its invention as a science.[3] Cartier's *Voyages* can usefully be put to the test of a successful ethnographer set by Clifford Geertz: 'Ethnographers need to convince us ... not merely that they themselves have truly been there, but ... had we been there we should have seen what they saw, felt what they felt, concluded what they concluded.[4] Historians, from Marc Lescarbot in the seventeenth century to Samuel Eliot Morison and Marcel Trudel in the twentieth, have given Cartier almost uniformly high marks by that standard.[5] Cartier's descriptions of the native people he met carry conviction. But the question may fairly be posed: is it necessary to *conclude* what Cartier concluded, even if his description bears the mark of authenticity? That question can best be approached by focusing on the well-known story of Cartier's troubled relationship with Donnacona, 'the lord of Canada,' and his two sons Dom Agaya and Taignoagny, always remembering that all the evidence about that relationship is provided by Cartier, a judge on his own case.[6]

Can that same evidence be used to discover the voices and motives of Cartier's protagonists, to tease out a dialogue where too often only a single voice has been heard in the past? It is worth attempting, even if the results must be tentative, even conjectural, since it must be constructed from limited, often obscure, clues.[7] Moreover, it is important to realize that, in attempting to reconstruct the Cartier-Donnacona dialogue, the problem of language and communication is enormous. Naturally, on Cartier's first trip, the language barrier was total and native speech was almost always described as a 'harangue' or a 'sermon.'[8] Yet in his account of his contacts with the local inhabitants he confidently describes actions, motives, and relationships as though communication had been fairly straightforward. But was it? For example, he describes the relationship among Donnacona, Dom

Agaya, and Taignoagny as that of a 'father' and his 'sons.' How did Cartier know? The vocabulary compiled on the first voyage does not contain these words. On his second voyage he had, part of the time, the assistance of the two men he had carried off to France. How much French had they learned? How faithfully did they translate their own language that had developed in the North American context into an imperfectly understood European tongue? Many European concepts, as the missionaries would later discover, had no local equivalents.[9] The opposite was almost certainly true: the lack of European words for important Amerindian concepts. The more extensive vocabulary gathered during the second voyage still amounts to little more than a tourist's elementary phrase book: numbers, body parts, food, basic questions and commands. Writing of European accounts of contact with native people, Stephen Greenblatt remarks: 'The Europeans and the interpreters themselves translated such fragments as they understood or thought they understood into a coherent story, and they came to believe quite easily that the story was what they actually heard. There could be, and apparently were, murderous results.'[10] The *Voyages* certainly present a fairly coherent story of the Cartier-Donnaconna relationship. The more that relationship is examined, however, the more obvious it becomes that it was based on a dialogue of incomprehension, a dialogue in which Donnacona's actions were made to speak in European words. It ended, if not in murder, then certainly in tragedy.

IV

Cartier arrived in eastern North America already somewhat familiar with the character of its inhabitants.[11] That doubtless explains the matter-of-fact tone to his description of the scattered groups his expedition came across along the coast of Labrador. In 'the land God gave to Cain' he found a 'wild and savage folk' who painted themselves 'with certain tan colours'—Boethuk hunting seal. Before long he realized that these North American people were not all alike: they spoke different languages, practised contrasting lifestyles, and, he eventually realized, warred against one another. From first contact he feared them or at least doubted their trustworthiness, especially if he was outnumbered. He would retain that suspicion and fear even after numerous experiences of welcoming hospitality, though he would tell

King Francis I of 'their kindness and peacefulness'. When forty or fifty canoe-loads of Micmac in the Bay de Chaleur signalled a desire to trade with a French party in one longboat, Cartier 'did not care to trust to their signs.' When they persisted, he drove them off with gunfire. French security and potential dominance was established.

This meeting also suggests that Cartier and his party may not have been the first Europeans whom the local native people had met. They wanted to trade and showed no fear. In fact, by 1534, trade between Europeans—Bretons, Basques, English, and other people who lived and fished on the Atlantic seaboard—had a history of several decades, possibly beginning before Columbus.[12] Cartier provides the first detailed description of the ceremonials surrounding trade when the people he had previously driven off returned on 7 July, 'making signs to us that they had come to barter.' Cartier had brought well-chosen trade goods: 'knives, and other iron goods, and a red cap to give their chief.' The first exchange was brisk, the natives leaving stripped even of the furs that covered their bodies. Three days later, amid ceremonial gift exchanges, dancing and singing, business resumed. The young women hung back, suggesting earlier experiences with European sailors. Cartier watched these events with a careful eye, concluding that 'we perceived that they are a people who would be easy to convert'. This was not an immediate goal, but rather a thought for the future. It was an indication that from the outset the French were fishers of men as well as 'explorers,' and that Cartier saw no reason to accept these 'savages' on their own terms.

At Gaspé Harbour, later in July, Cartier made his first contact with members of the native community to which his future in Canada would be inextricably tied. These were people from Stadacona—Laurentian Iroquoians—making their annual fishing expedition to the east coast. Cartier's reports are the only record of these people who 'disappeared,' probably as a result of warfare and perhaps disease, by the end of the century.[13] His first impression of the Stadaconans is important because it illustrates Cartier's powers of observation again, and also provides a clear insight into his use of the term 'sauvaiges.' He wrote: 'This people may well be called savage; for they are the sorriest folk there can be in the world, and the whole lot of them had not anything above the value of five sous, their canoes and fishingnets excepted. They go

quite naked, except for a small skin, with which they cover their privy parts, and for a few old skins which they throw over their shoulders. They are not at all of the same race or language as the first we met. They have their heads shaved all around in circles, except for a tuft on the top of the head, which they leave long like a horse's tail. This they do up upon their heads and tie in a knot with leather thongs. They have no other dwelling but their canoes, which they turn upside down and sleep on the ground underneath. They eat their meat almost raw; only warming it a little on the coals; and the same with their fish [...] They never eat anything that has a taste of salt in it. They are wonderful thieves and steal everything they can carry off'.

For Cartier the word 'sauvaiges' was interchangeable with 'gens,' 'personnes,' 'peuple,' 'hommes du pays,' 'hommes,' 'femmes'—he never used 'Indiens.' This usage suggests that Cartier accepted the Amerindians as human, like himself—a matter much disputed in the aftermath of Columbus's initial encounter with the people in America.[14] That impression is supported by Cartier's belief that the inhabitants of the St Lawrence region could be converted to Christianity; had they not been 'men,' that potential would have been denied. But still they were 'savages,' which apparently meant poverty stricken, lacking in worldly possessions and civic institutions, bereft of religion and culture. (They certainly fulfilled Montaigne's definition: 'we all call barbarous anything that is contrary to our own habits'!)[15] Because of their 'savage,' 'wild' state, their lack of culture, Cartier believed that native people could easily be 'dompter': subdued, subjugated, tamed,[16] or as Biggar says, 'moulded.' Consequently, while native people were accepted as 'human,' they were only potential, not actual, equals of the Europeans. Only if the 'savage' characteristics that made them different were 'tamed' or 'moulded' could they become actual equals. Different *and* equal was inconceivable.[17] Finally, since these Laurentian people were 'savages' without culture, religion, or government, Cartier, like those European explorers who had preceded him, saw no reason to ask permission to explore and eventually settle their lands.

Nothing better emphasizes Cartier's assumptions about his rights—and Donnacona's reaction—than the drama that was acted out on 24 July 1534 at the entrance to Gaspé Harbour. There Cartier presided over the raising of a thirty-foot wooden cross to which was fixed a coat-of-arms bearing the fleurs-de-lys and a board on which was emblazoned the words: 'VIVE LE ROI DE FRANCE.' In the presence of Donnacona's people, the French 'knelt down with our hands joined, worshipping it before them; and made signs to them, looking up and pointing towards heaven, that by means of this we had our redemption, at which they showed many marks of admiration, at the same time turning and looking at the cross'.

Any 'marks of admiration' Cartier thought he detected were soon erased by a vigorous act of protest by native leaders. Cartier's account of this reaction demonstrates that what was viewed as an arbitrary European intrusion into eastern North America was not passively accepted. The protest was led by the person Cartier identified as 'the leader' and 'three of his sons and his brother.' Even the language barrier did not prevent Cartier from understanding—or thinking he understood—the meaning of the demonstration: 'pointing to the cross he [the leader] made us a long harangue, making the sign of the cross with two of his fingers; and then he pointed to the land all around about, as if he wished to say that all this region belonged to him, and that we ought not to have set up this cross without his permission'.

Neither the action of the French, in raising the cross, nor the reaction of the native people is totally unambiguous. Cross-raising, beginning with Columbus, had already become something of a tradition in the Americas. It contained both religious and political symbolism. Cartier had previously raised at least one cross—an undecorated one at St Servan's Harbour in June—and he would raise others later. Some of these crosses were raised unceremoniously and doubtless were intended to function as 'a landmark and guidepost into the harbour'. Though Cartier explained the Gaspé cross that way, its bold symbols of church and state, and the accompanying ceremony, surely represented something more. If it was not an explicit legal claim, recognizable in international law, to French possession of this territory, it was surely at least what Trudel calls 'une affirmation solennelle des droits de la France sur cette terre.'[18] This was not an anonymous directional sign; it distinctly affirmed the French presence. It is also worth emphasizing that in introducing the account of his second voyage, Cartier related his exploration both to the protection and promotion of Catholicism

against the threat of 'wicked Lutherans, apostates, and imitators of Mahomet' and to 'these lands of yours,' 'your possessions,' and 'those lands and territories of yours'. If, then, the crosses were merely traffic signals, they should at least be described as *French* traffic signals.

And what of the native people's protest? Cartier's interpretation of it as a rejection of the French right to act without permission can be seen, at the least, as a sign of a guilty conscience. Certainly he knew that no European sovereign would accept such an act on his or her territory. But did a North American 'leader,' especially one whose home territory was somewhere up the St Lawrence, have the same sense of sovereign or proprietary rights? Was the chief claiming the Gaspé harbour area as his people's fishing and hunting territory? It seems altogether likely. What is beyond doubt is that a protest did take place, a protest Cartier suspected was an expression of territorial jurisdiction. Moreover, Cartier acted quickly and deceptively to quell the protest.

When the chief—we later learn this was Donnacona[19]—completed his 'harangue,' a sailor offered him an axe in exchange for the black bear skin he was wearing. Responding to the offer of barter, Donnacona's party moved closer to the French ship only to have their canoe boarded and themselves taken prisoner, though Cartier did not use that term. On the second voyage he did, however, refer to them as 'captured' and 'seized'. Once on board they were cajoled—'made to eat and drink and be of good cheer' (was the drink alcoholic?)—into accepting the sign-post explanation. Cartier then announced that he intended to release only three of the prisoners—compensated with hatchets and knives. The other two, now decked out in shirts, ribbons, and red caps, would be taken 'away with us and afterwards would bring them back again to that harbour'. Since no destination was announced, it seems entirely unlikely that the two young men, or their father, understood this to mean an Atlantic crossing and a nine-month stay in France. Cartier made the final departure seem amicable, and perhaps it appeared that way to Donnacona's people who, if they understood what was taking place, probably recognized that resistance was hopeless. Cartier admitted that 'we did not understand the parting harangues,' and there is equally no reason to believe that Donnacona understood what Cartier had tried to tell him. At best the day ended in mutual misunderstanding—hardly the basis for an 'alliance.'[20]

In acting as he did—and the action seemed premeditated—Cartier followed an established European precedent. Europeans assumed a right to 'explore' new-found lands and to set up traffic crosses, indicating at least an intention to return and perhaps even staking a claim to possession. So, too, kidnapping native people began with Columbus, and Cartier may even have committed similar actions on earlier voyages to Brazil. Since at the time of the seizure of the natives Cartier had not determined whether to continue his explorations or to return to France before winter, his initial intention may have been simply to make use of the men as short-term guides. More plausible, however, is the view that Cartier planned to take the captives back to St Malo as concrete evidence of 'discovery' and to provide them with language training. With the aid of interpreters and go-betweens, the further penetration of North America, leading to the much sought after route to Asia—Cartier's primary goal—would be expedited. Or so Cartier doubtless hoped.

Exactly how Dom Agaya and Taignoagny, as the young men are identified in the account of the second voyage, spent their time between their arrival in St Malo on 5 September 1534 and their departure for home on 19 May 1535 is unrecorded. Nor is there any direct evidence revealing their reactions to their unexpected discovery of Europe. The harrowing experiences of an eighteenth-century Chinese visitor named John Hu, a man similarly untutored in French language and customs, offer some clues to the complexity of cultural contact: he was driven to such unpredictable behaviour that he was confined to the asylum at Charenton pondering the question, 'Why am I locked up?'[21] The two North Americans survived somewhat better, even though they must often have asked similar questions. They doubtless witnessed many strange and wonderful sights. Yet it seems unlikely that either the standard of living of ordinary Frenchmen—housing, food, or medical care—or the political and religious life of a country wracked with religious strife won their enthusiastic approval.[22] Perhaps they concluded, as Jean de Léry did after returning to France from Brazil, that 'one need not go beyond one's own country, nor as far as America, to see [...] monstrous and prodigious things.'[23]

By the time of their return home, they spoke some French, though the level of fluency cannot have been very high. They had learned to dress in the French manner. They may have calculated, and filed for future use, the comparative values of French trade goods, a knowledge that would earn them the epithet of 'rogues'. They had not been baptized, though they had observed that ceremony and other Catholic rites. To Cartier they may have seemed at least partly 'moulded' or 'tamed,' though he would continue to call them 'sauvaiges.' He apparently believed they were ready and willing to work for him. It was not yet in their interest to disabuse him of that notion. That could wait until they were safely back in Stadacona. Then their actions and attitudes would reveal that they had no wish to go on their foreign travels again.

V

During the winter of 1534–5, Dom Agaya and Taignoagny provided Cartier with much useful information about eastern North America. The French navigator certainly wanted to know whether a route to Asia could be found by continuing westward from the mouth of the St Lawrence. Perhaps they encouraged his hopes that a route existed. What he obviously did learn from them was that their home was far inland, up an enormous river at Stadacona, beyond a rich region known as the Saguenay. It was there that they wished to be returned, not to the Gaspé as their father had been promised. Consequently it was from knowledge gained from the two native men, and as a result of their directions, that Cartier was able to attain his principal geographical achievement: 'he was,' Marcel Trudel noted, 'the first to make a survey of the coasts of the St Lawrence [...] and, what is most to his credit, in 1535, he discovered the St Lawrence River.'[24] In fact, Cartier himself described what happened somewhat more accurately. On Friday, 13 August 1535, sailing from southwestern Anticosti, 'it was told us by the two savages whom we had captured on our first voyage, that this cape formed part of the land on the south which was an island; and that to the south of it lay the route from Honguedo where we had seized them [...] and that two days journey from this cape and island began the kingdom of the Saguenay, on the north shore as one made one's way towards this Canada'. Four days later, when Cartier was in some doubt about the route, 'the two savages assured us that this was the way to the mouth of the great river of Hochelaga [St Lawrence] and the route towards Canada [...] and that one could make one's way so far up the river that they had never heard of anyone reaching the head of it'. Cartier and his crew were the first known Europeans to be guided along the St Lawrence to Stadacona. They then insisted that the guide service be continued further up to Hochelaga. That demand resulted in a crisis in the hitherto satisfactory relationship with Dom Agaya, Taignoagny, and their father.

Not surprisingly, the return of the captives to their people in the Stadacona region was an occasion for great joy. At first the local inhabitants were cautious, even fearful, but once the returning men had identified themselves, the ceremonies and gift exchanges began. On 8 September, near the Ile d'Orléans, 'the lord of Canada' arrived alongside and began a 'harangue,' 'moving his body and his limbs in a marvellous manner as is their custom when showing joy and contentment.' Had Cartier interpreted the body language correctly? At this happy reunion, Cartier reported that the sons informed their father 'what they had seen in France, and the good treatment meted out to them there.' Donnacona expressed his gratitude with warm embraces for the French leader. Bread and wine were shared before the returning travellers departed with their father.

It was not until a week later, during which Dom Agaya and his brother had ample time to discuss their travels in more detail with their father, that Cartier met with them again. He was now impatient to move on, but he detected a marked, disturbing change in the mood of his former companions. Sailing towards Stadacona, Cartier met a large party of native people. 'All came over towards our ships,' he noted, 'except the two men we had brought with us [...] who were altogether changed in their attitude and goodwill, and refused to come on board our ships, although many times begged to do so. At this we began somewhat to distrust them.' Cartier's attitude was obviously changing, too. Nevertheless he believed they were willing to guide him to Hochelaga, a place of whose existence they had apparently informed him.

During the next five days, until Cartier pushed on up-river without his guides, the issue of the continuing service of Dom Agaya and Taignoagny resulted in an almost total break in relations between the Stadaconans and the St Malouins. The issue in dispute was simple. Cartier believed that his interpreters had promised to continue on with him to Hochelaga. Donnacona and his sons (Taignoagny more consistently, it would seem, than his brother) either did not want the French to continue westward at all or at least not without first making some binding commitment or alliance with the Stadaconans. If it is true, as some have concluded, that Donnacona hoped to prevent Cartier from making contact with other native groups so that Stadacona could control trade between the French and the hinterland, or that Donnacona hoped to enlist French military aid against the Hochelagans, there is nothing in Cartier's account to support these speculations.[25] Nor is it fair to accept Cartier's claim that on their return to Stadacona, Dom Agaya and Taignoagny began to 'intrigue' against him.[26] They had, after all, painfully concrete reasons for distrusting Cartier, and legitimate grounds for looking to their own interests in the face of French incursions into their territory. To judge these confusing events—which make it plain that the language barrier had not been effectively breeched—solely from Cartier's perspective implicitly denies the legitimacy of Donnacona's stance. Yet what Cartier viewed as 'treachery,' from Donnacona's point of view was a perfectly reasonable insistence that foreign visitors conduct themselves with due respect for the wishes and customs of their hosts. This is not to argue that the actions of the Stadaconans were so straightforward that Cartier was simply obtuse in failing to understand them. It does have to be remembered that the account of these events is Cartier's and therefore reflects his confusion and suspicion; it does not necessarily represent faithfully the intentions of the other actors whose behaviour may have had a logic of its own. A tentative analysis of a series of events that left Cartier impatient, suspicious, and frightened helps to reveal this logic.

On 16 September Taignoagny informed Cartier that Donnacona was 'annoyed' by the Frenchman's decision to visit Hochelaga and that he would not accompany him. Taignoagny then rejected Cartier's offer of a present—a bribe—in return for disobeying his father. The following day Donnacona appeared, and a ceremony—though Cartier may not have recognized it as such—took place in which the chief presented Cartier with a girl about twelve years old, said to be Donnacona's niece, and two younger boys, one of whom was said to be Taignoagny's brother, though these relationships seem confused. Cartier first understood these gifts as an attempt to convince him to forgo his Hochelaga trip—an apparent bribe. He refused that condition and was then told that the gifts were offered out of friendship and 'in sign of alliance'. Cartier attributed these conflicting stories to Taignoagny, 'as well by this as by other bad turns we had seen him do [...] was a worthless fellow, who was intent upon nothing but treason and malice'. He ignored or disbelieved, or failed to understand, the meaning of a 'sign of alliance.'

It is possible that in order to cement an alliance with the French, Donnacona was proposing a reciprocal gift, an exchange of persons? Cartier was familiar with gift-giving, for he had engaged in it since his first arrival in North America. But he probably did not understand its ceremonial implications in North American native societies, especially that such ceremonies could include the exchange of people.[27] This interpretation is perhaps borne out by the fact that after the Stadaconans failed in what, from Cartier's account, seemed to be a clumsy attempt to invoke the aid of their divinity to frighten the French away from the western trip, a new proposal was advanced. 'Taignoagny and Dom Agaya told the Captain that Donnacona was unwilling that either of them should accompany him to Hochelaga unless he [Cartier] should leave a hostage behind on shore with Donnacona'. It is, of course, possible that Donnacona suspected another kidnapping and wanted a hostage. Alternatively, this proposal may have been a misunderstood attempt to explain the reciprocal nature of the gift-exchange treaty ceremony.

Cartier summarily rejected this new proposal, for he had now completely lost confidence in his former interpreters. He would go without them, sweeping Donnacona's objections aside. But the questions remain: Did Cartier misinterpret Donnacona's objections and the proposal he made? Had Donnacona merely been asking Cartier to complete the reciprocal action that had begun when Cartier accepted the children who had been offered as a 'sign of alliance'? If an alliance had been offered and rejected, was it not quite natural for Donnacona's people to suspect that the French expedition to Hochelaga might have results that would be detrimental to the interests of Stadacona? 'In these primitive and archaic societies'— one might prefer the term stateless societies—Marcel

Mauss wrote in his *Essai sur le don*, 'there is no middle path. There is either complete trust or mistrust. One lays down one's arms, renounces magic and gives everything away, from casual hospitality to one's daughter or one's property. It was in such conditions that men, despite themselves, learnt to renounce what was theirs and made contracts to give and repay.'[28] Cartier had first refused to lay down arms ('to carry them … was the custom in France'; had then insisted that their magic, not his, should be renounced ('their god Cudouagny was a mere fool [...] Jesus would keep them safe'; and finally had refused the reciprocal gift that would have sealed an alliance, even when the lord of Canada's own niece and son were offered to him. Where complete trust might have been established, mistrust, on both sides, resulted.

Unable to understand the framework in which the Stadaconans acted, Cartier was reduced to denunciation, charging his lost allies with ill-will and treason. But the problem was a much deeper one. Cartier had taken Dom Agaya and Taignoagny to France to train them as interpreters so they could act as go-betweens, easing him along his way. On their return to the St Lawrence region armed with their new language skills, they were to act in his interests and aid him in achieving his objectives. In a sense, he expected them to act as Frenchmen. What he failed to comprehend, or accept, was that after a brief nine months of total immersion, Dom Agaya and Taignoagny remained pretty much as they had always been: St Lawrence Iroquoians. Once reunited with their own people, they reverted completely to their own identities and refused to collaborate unconditionally with their former captors.[29] When Cartier learned that what had appeared to be friendship in France had disappeared—a friendship he thought had been affirmed by the welcome he received on his first arrival at Stadacona—he could only explain it by character defects in the native people. They were unreliable, untrustworthy, treacherous rogues—a typical European conclusion.[30] Yet the behaviour that Cartier condemned as 'treason'—a word implying that loyalty was owed to the French— was, by Donnacona's logic, a rejection of that very idea, a rejection of French mastery. The first act of resistance had taken place at Gaspé Harbour. The struggle over Cartier's trip to Hochelaga was but another action in the same drama. Everything was now in place for the dénouement.

VI

Cartier's Hochelaga trip, as he recorded it, stands in marked contrast to the gathering atmosphere of mistrust and confused signals between the French and the Stadaconans. That contrast is seen in the first contact he made with native people up the river: 'they come towards our boats in as friendly and familiar manner as if we had been natives of the country'. Further along Cartier felt the same easy relationship, and at one point allowed a powerful man to carry him ashore 'as if he had been a six-year-old child'. There were gift exchanges; one local leader presented Cartier with 'two of his children,' though only the girl, who was eight or nine, was accepted. The culmination of this almost royal progress came at Hochelaga. As the French approached the village on 2 October they were greeted by 'more than a thousand persons, men, women and children, who gave us as good a welcome as ever father gave to his son [...] They brought us quantities of fish, and of their bread [...] throwing so much of it into our longboats that it seemed to rain bread'.

Cartier accepted this treatment as perfectly natural, perhaps even to be expected from people whom he may have assumed were familiar with Europeans. But what he interpreted as signs of familiarity were quite likely just the opposite, as he may gradually have realized. In fact, the character of the reception the French received at Hochelaga bore the marks of a first contact, one in which the native people mistook the French, marshalled in their armour and speaking a strange language, for something other than ordinary men. Women repeatedly brought their children to be touched, and the women showed none of the shyness evident in those earlier trading sessions when their men kept them at a distance. The next day, within the pallisaded village, a remarkable ceremony took place, one in which Cartier found himself in the role of shaman or healer—and accepted his unexpected casting. Cartier and his men were ushered to the centre of the town square and seated on elaborately woven mats. Soon they were joined by the village's leader, carried in on the shoulders of nine or ten strong men. When he took his seat on a deerskin near Cartier, it became obvious that he was severely paralysed and that he expected to be 'cured and healed' by his visitor. Cartier, taking his cue, 'set about rubbing his arms and legs with his hands. Thereupon this *Agouhanna*

took the band of cloth he was wearing as a crown and presented it to the Captain.' Then the sick, the lame, the blind, and the aged were brought forward for Cartier to 'lay his hands upon them, so that one would have thought Christ had come down to earth to heal them.' Cartier performed his appointed role in the only style he knew, 'making the sign of the cross over the poor sick people, praying God to give them knowledge of our holy faith'. So convincing was his interpretation that the local women tried to prevent the French from leaving by offering large quantities of food. Cartier rejected it for it was unsalted, though he was probably anxious to depart before being called for an encore.

Whether Cartier exaggerated these events of the early days of October 1535, and what exactly they meant to the St Lawrence Iroquoians, can only be guessed at. Certainly they were unlike any other ceremony recorded in the *Voyages*. It was obviously not an occasion for commerce, though some gifts were distributed by the French, for the Hochelagans showed none of the frenzied desire to exchange furs for European goods that was displayed at earlier meetings. Instead, the ritual performed in the village square bore the signs of some prophecy being fulfilled with the arrival of otherworldly healers.[31] Cartier's quick intelligence apparently allowed him to interpret the signals accurately. Perhaps it was the realization that his healing powers were at best untested that led to his hasty departure on the following day 'for fear of any misadventure'. Even the almost worshipful reception of the Hochelagans had not removed Cartier's distrust of the St Lawrence Iroquoians.

The French undoubtedly contrasted the respectful reception they had received at Hochelaga with what they interpreted as the cagey manoeuvring of Donnacona and his sons. Now they set out to return to Stadacona, convinced there was gold and silver to be found somewhere in the region and apparently under the impression that 'the Canadians and some eight or nine other peoples are subjects' of the Hochelagans. Perhaps this belief stiffened Cartier's determination to deal with Donnacona's people more firmly and, if necessary, harshly. The western trip had done nothing to dispel his suspicion that even the friendliest of gesture on the part of the leaders a Stadacona only masked treacherous intentions.

VII

Cartier's peremptory departure for Hochelaga on 19 September doubtless left the Stadaconans displeased, suspicious, and perhaps even hostile. When the French party returned a week later they found that the men they had left behind had built themselves a fort 'with artillery pointing every way'. Obviously relations had deteriorated further. Still Donnacona issued an almost immediate invitation to visit Stadacona—something Cartier had not done before going to Hochelaga, which may have been another cause for Donnacona's earlier unease. On visiting Stadacona, Cartier received a warm and formal welcome. He attached no particular significance to a display of scalps that Donnacona explained had been harvested during a war with the 'Toudamans,' though this may have been a request for French assistance.

During this period Cartier began closer observation of local customs, and concluded that the St Lawrence Iroquoians had 'no belief in God that amounts to anything.' He attempted to inform them about Christianity, but when Donnacona and his sons rounded up the whole village for baptism 'an excuse was made to them': there were no priests to conduct the ceremony and there was no consecrated oil. Whether this was the whole truth is unclear. Cartier had told Donnacona earlier that he had consulted his 'priests' before going to Hochelaga, at the time when an attempt had been made to prevent Cartier's departure by an appeal to the local god. Moreover, a mass was 'said and sung' some months later. If the priests had not died in the interim—and that is possible— then Cartier prevaricated on one of these occasions. It is significant that Cartier refused baptism for two reasons: 'we did not know their real intention and state of mind and had no one to explain to them our faith'. Yet the incident further convinced him that conversion would be easy.

Still, Cartier continued to distrust the Stadaconans, especially his two former guides after they urged their fellows to bargain for better prices. Both on his trip to Hochelaga and after returning, the French had been encouraged by some native people to beware of Dom Agaya and his brother. After a number of small incidents had heightened Cartier's apprehensions, and 'fearing that they should attempt some treasonable design,' he reinforced the fort and ordered a round-the-clock watch, thus provoking annoyance and puzzlement among Donnacona's

followers. Yet by the time winter had set in—and it was a terrible winter—relations had apparently been restored to 'as friendly a manner as before'.

December brought disaster in the shape of a scurvy epidemic, the best-known incident in Cartier's career. Disease was the scourge of sixteenth-century Europeans even more than for pre-contact North American people. In France disease was widespread, often epidemic, and cures were few. In March 1535, prior to Cartier's second trip, an 'epidemic and plague' broke out in St Malo and was perhaps carried up the St Lawrence. Europeans had, however, developed immunities, complete or partial, to a large number of communicable diseases, which meant they were no longer fatal. But European pathogens were largely unknown in America, making measles, small pox, tuberculosis, influenza, and other common diseases deadly. The cures—herbal and spiritual—that North Americans successfully applied to their own illnesses were impotent against the European biological invasion that silently accompanied Columbus.[32] Of course, Europeans could contact unexpected health problems in North America, too.

According to Cartier's account, the 'pestilence' that struck in December broke out first among the people of Stadacona and, despite efforts at quarantine, the French were soon infected. Since Cartier's graphic description of the disease makes it certain it was scurvy caused by a vitamin C deficiency, the suspicion of contagion was unfounded. Moreover, since the native people had an effective cure for scurvy, Cartier's assumption that both communities were suffering from the same illness may be questioned, especially when he reported 'more than fifty deaths' at Stadacona. Perhaps the native people had contracted a French imported virus. That the French brought diseases with them is documented by Cartier's observation that the scurvy remedy that was eventually used 'cured all of the diseases they had ever had. And some of the sailors who had been suffering for five or six years from the French pox [la grande vérole] were by the medicine cured completely'. What this disease really was—syphilis or small pox or something else— is impossible to say. But micro-organisms certainly entered the St Lawrence region with the French, likely began infecting the inhabitants by the early winter of 1535, and may even have played a part in the eventual disappearance of the St Lawrence Iroquoians.[33] Of course, native people suffered from vitamin C deficiencies, too; it is the reported fifty fatalities that suggests scepticism about Cartier's diagnosis.

What is incontestable is that while the scurvy raged through the French camp, afflicting all but three or four and killing twenty-five of the 110 members of the company, Cartier's fears and suspicions—his 'great dread' of the Stadaconans—grew. Utterly convinced that the native people bore the French ill will, Cartier resorted to a series of ruses to disguise the weakness of his stricken contingent from them—instead of asking for assistance. When, for example, a party led by Donnacona set off for the annual winter hunt and did not return exactly when expected, Cartier concluded that 'a large force to attack us' was being assembled. Nor were those suspicions and fears erased by the most obvious sign of Iroquoian good will imaginable in the circumstances. Dom Agaya, who had apparently himself suffered severely from a scurvy-like disease, not only prescribed the cure he had used but even ordered two women to gather the 'Annedda' (white cedar) branches for him.[34] It was not Cartier 'skillfully questioning'[35] Dom Agaya that is noteworthy in this episode, but rather the young Iroquois' quick, willing response to the plight of his one-time kidnappers. That Cartier was blind to this generosity is perhaps seen in his enthusiastic thanks to God, rather than to Dom Agaya, for the miraculous cure.

What even more obviously reveals Cartier's almost paranoid suspicion of the Stadaconans is the evidence that Dom Agaya's gift of the cure did nothing to undermine the 'dread' that Donnacona was plotting an attack on the French. When the headman returned from his trip, accompanied by a large number of hunters, and showed some signs that Cartier interpreted as secretiveness and caution, those fears were heightened. When Cartier learned that 'a leader of that region named Agona' was somehow a problem for Donnacona, he made no offer of support to the old man and his sons or to draw any connection between this problem and Donnacona's mysterious movements. Instead Cartier, 'on being informed of the large number of people at Stadacona, though un-aware of their purpose, yet determined to outwit them, and to seize their leader [Donnacona], Taignoagny, Dom Agaya, and the headmen. And moreover he had quite made up his mind to take Donnacona to France, that he might relate and tell to the king all he had seen in the west of the wonders of the world'. If Cartier believed

that by removing Donnacona's party he could place Agona in power and thus establish French control of the St Lawrence region through a puppet, there is nothing in his account that even hints at such 'a plan for a revolution.'[36]

Every effort was now focused on drawing Donnacona and his supporters into a trap. When the Stadaconans, perhaps suspecting foul play, proved reluctant prey, Cartier took this as a further sign of 'knavishness'. That the Stadaconans had the uneasy feeling that the French were planning a trip for them was revealed by Taignoagny's expression of relief when Cartier assured him that the king had 'forbidden him to carry off to France any man or woman, but only two or three boys to learn the language'. Taignoagny, the supposed scheming rogue, naïvely swallowed this blatant lie and promised to bring his father to the French fort the next day.

That day, 3 May, was Holy Cross Day, an appropriate occasion for a repetition of the events that had taken place at Gaspé Harbour two years earlier. First a cross raising, at a location where a traffic marker was hardly needed. Its Latin letters read: FRANCISCVSPRIMVS, DEI GRATIA, FRANCORVM REX, REGNAT.' Perhaps recalling the earlier ceremony, Donnacona was nervous and reluctant to enter the fort 'to eat and drink as usual'. Cartier became impatient with the cat-and-mouse game: he ordered his men to seize the chief, his two sons, and two others. A desperate attempt by Taignoagny to pull his father back came too late. Once the five 'had been captured and the rest had all disappeared, Donnacona and his companions were placed in safe custody'. They were prisoners.

Donnacona's followers, fully aware of the deadly fire power of the French canon, probably concluded that any attempt to free their leader would result in disaster. One apparent threat was made, but Cartier ordered Donnacona brought on deck to calm his people with the promise that within 'ten or twelve moons' he would return to his homeland. Ceremonies followed on this and subsequent days when Cartier was presented with large quantities of *esnoquy* or wampum, 'the most valuable articles they possess in this world; for they attach more value to it than to gold or silver'. These gestures were surely not made in homage to the French explorer who had deceived them but rather as a pathetic attempt to purchase a guaranteed return passage for their chief and his companions. Cartier generously repeated his promise, for what it was worth, and on 6 May 1536 his ships and their human cargo sailed away.

Cartier probably intended to return to Stadacona the next year, but King Francis was preoccupied by a war with Spain. The return journey was delayed for more than three years. None of the ten native people—the five captives plus five others who were 'gifts'—ever returned to Canada. All but one woman died before Cartier set out again, and she remained in France. She might have brought some embarrassing news had she returned. Before he died, Donnacona had been to court, apparently performing as Cartier had hoped. According to Thevet, he died 'a good Christian, speaking French.'[37] The fate of his companions is unrecorded except that, in all, three were baptized, whether voluntarily, or *in articulo mortis,* is unknown.[38] Probably the diseases that Dom Agaya and Taignoagny had escaped on their first trip now took their toll. Four years was a long time to be away from home. The 'slips of trees and the seeds of the rarest [plants] of Canada' that Cartier presented to Francis I were planted in the garden at Fontainebleau.[39] The 'lord of Canada' and his companions were presumably interred in humbler ground.

When the navigator of St Malo finally reappeared before Stadacona on 23 August 1541, he offered a self-serving account of the fate of the men, girls, and boys he had so callously transported to France. When he met with Agona who, he noted, 'was appointed king there by Donnacona,' Cartier told him that 'Donnacona was dead in France, and that his body rested in the earth, and that the rest stayed there as great Lords, and were married, and would not return back into their country.' The French leader was satisfied that the lie had been carried off convincingly, especially since Agona was now the unchallenged 'Lord and Governor of the Country'.

The third voyage, of which the record is so fragmentary, proved a complete fiasco. The settlement Cartier had been sent to help establish—leadership now rested with Sieur de Roberval—was short-lived. In the spring of 1542 the St Lawrence Iroquoians turned against him. Even Agona, whose loyalty the French so confidently believed had been bought by Donnacona's demise, apparently joined the opposition. Cartier, hoping a fistful of 'Canadian diamonds' would justify his desertion of Roberval, decided to flee.[40] Did he ever suspect that the St Lawrence Iroquoians had finally realized the true fate of Donnacona and the others?

Cartier's failure, for that is what it was, resulted from his ethnology, his attempt to understand the people who lived along the St Lawrence River. His description of them was careful and often perceptive. He leaves the impression of having truly 'been there.' But his judgment, and therefore his representation, of these people was mortally flawed. They existed only in European terms, never in their own, their *alterité* unrecognized because it was unaccepted. Though Cartier successfully mapped the St Lawrence, he misidentified the St Lawrence Iroquoians, who remained as mysterious as the *adhothuys* [belugas] and 'seahorses' [walruses] who played near the mouth of the Saguenay River. For Cartier, a flawed ethnology brought only failure; for Donnacona's people it proved fatal.

VIII

The *Voyages of Jacques Cartier* document the French discovery of the St Lawrence valley. They contain unique geographical, biological, and ethnological descriptions, but they also recount something else. Their pages record the St Lawrence Iroquoians' discovery of France, a country of overdressed and often underfed people, where men grew hair on their faces and did women's work in the fields. Women in France were said to be sexually voracious, babies consigned to wet nurses, and children subjected to harsh discipline. Most families lived huddled together while a few idle men enjoyed extensive estates, hunting and fishing for sport. Theirs was a religion of churches, priests, and preachers warring over dogma. From French ports sailed creaking ships filled with self-confident adventurers and sharp traders who carried arms, ignorant of local customs. These suspicious, scheming intruders brought unknown illnesses, frightened native women, told lies, and shamelessly kidnapped even those who helped them. The French, Donnacona's people might have concluded, 'are wonderful thieves and steal everything they can carry off.'

Notes

1. Laurence C. Wroth, *The Voyages of Giovanni de Verrazzano, 1524–28* (New Haven and London: Yale University Press 1970), Roger Schlesinger

and Arthur P. Stabler, eds., *André Thevet's North America: A Sixteenth-Century View* (Kingston and Montreal: McGill-Queen's University Press 1986). See also Frank Lestringant, *Le Huguenot et le Sauvage* (Paris: Aux Amateurs de Livres 1990).

2. The Montaigne quotations are from 'On Cannibals' in Michel Montaigne, *Essays* (London: Penguin Books 1958), 108.

3. Numa Broc, *La géographie de la Renaissance* 1420–1620 (Paris: Bibliothèque nationale 1980), where it is said of Renaissance explorers that 'par essence et par vocation, ils seront plus ethnologues que géographes' (80), Margaret Hogden, *Early Anthropology in the Sixteenth and Seventeenth Centuries* (Philadelphia: University of Pennsylvania Press 1964). Michèle Duchet in her *Anthropologie et histoire au siècle des lumières* (Paris: François Maspero 1971), argues that early travelers were not anthropologists in the modern sense because they failed to give up their civilized status 'to become participant-observers' (15). This is an elevated view of modern anthropologists, whose 'science' is effectively questioned in James Clifford, *The Predicament of Culture* (Cambridge, Mass.: Harvard University Press 1988), and by Clifford Geertz in *Work and Lives: The Anthropologist as Author* (Stanford: Stanford University Press 1988).

4. Geertz, *Work*, 16

5. Bruce Trigger's *The Children of Aataentsic: A History of the Huron People to 1660,* 2 vols. (Montreal and London: McGill-Queen's University Press 1976), I, 177–208, and Olive P. Dickason's *The Myth of the Savage* (Edmonton: University of Alberta Press 1984), 163–71, adopt a more sceptical approach to Cartier's evidence.

6. For a reconstruction of Amerindian views of European contact, based on sixteenth-century accounts and anthropological work, see Nathan Wachtel, *The Vision of the Vanquished: The Spanish Conquest of Peru through Indian Eyes 1530–1570* (New York: Barnes and Noble 1977). These rich sources are lacking for the sixteenth century in Canada. See Georges Sioui, *Pour une autohistoire amérindienne* (Québec: Les Presses de l'Université Laval 1989). For a brilliant discussion of the problems of documentation for nonliterate cultures see Inga Clendinnen, *Aztecs: An Interpretation* (Cambridge: Cambridge University Press 1991), 277–94. For an interpretation from an Amer-indian perspective see Bernard Assiniw, *Histoire des Indiens du Haut et du Bas Canada* (Montréal: Leméac 1974).

7. On the 'conjectural model' and the use of clues see Carlo Ginzburg,' Morelli, Freud and Sherlock Holmes: Clues and the Scientific Method.' *History Workshop* 9 (spring 1980): 5–36.

8. Cartier used several terms, including 'harangue' (26), 'sermon' (57), and 'prédication et preschement' (54), all suggesting a hortatory tone, a characteristic of formal Amerindian speech.

9. James Axtell, *The Invasion Within* (New York and Oxford: Oxford University Press 1985), 81–3

10. Stephen.J. Greenblatt, *Learning to Curse: Essays m Early Modern Culture* (New York and London: Routledge 1990), 27; see also Stephen Greenblatt, *Marvellous Possessions: The Wonder of the New World* (Chicago: University of Chicago Press 1991), 86–118. For valuable insights into the problem of communications see Lois M. Feister, 'Linguistic Communication between the Dutch and the Indians in New Netherlands, 1609–94,' *Ethno-history* 20, 1 (winter 1973): 25–38, David Murray, *Forked Tongues Speech: Writing and Representation in North American Indian Texts* (London: Pinter Publishers 1991), 1–48, and Robin Ridington, 'Cultures in Conflict: The Problem of Discourse,' in his *Little Bit Knowing Something* (Vancouver: Douglas and McIntyre 1990), 186–205. Charles Darwin's chapter on the Fuegians, in *The Voyages of the Beagle* (New York: Dutton 1977), is an interesting example of the way sixteenth-century attitudes to aboriginal peoples survived into the nineteenth century, though Darwin did recognize that 'wherever the European has trod, death seems to pursue the aboriginal' (418). Of particular interest is his comment on the problem of communication: 'Although all three could speak and understand, it was singularly difficult to obtain much information from them, concerning the habits of their countrymen: this was partly owing to their apparent difficulty in understanding the simplest alternative. Everyone accustomed to very young children knows how seldom one can get an answer even to so simple a question as whether a thing is black or white, the idea of black or white seems alternately to fill their minds. So it is with these Fuegians, and hence it was generally impossible to find out, by cross-questioning, whether one had rightly understood anything

which they had asserted' (198). Inga Glendinnen, '"Fierce and Unnatural Cruelty": Cortés and the Conquest of Mexico,' *Representations* 33 (winter 1991): 65–100

11. Michel Mollat, *Les explorateurs du XIIIe au XVIe siècles: Premiers regards sur des mondes nouveaux* (Paris: J.C. Lattès 1984), 184–5

12. David Beers Quinn, *England and the Discovery of America 1481–1620* (New York: Oxford University Press 1974), chap. 1, and James Axtell, 'At the Water's Edge: Trading in the Sixteenth Century,' in his *After Columbus* (New York: Oxford University Press 1988), 144–81; John Dickenson, 'Les précurseurs de Jacques Cartier,' in Fernand Braudel, *Le monde de Jacques Cartier* (Montreal: Libre-Expression 1984), 127–48

13. Bruce G. Trigger, ed., *Handbook of North American Indians, vol. 15: Northeast* (Washington: Smithsonian Institution 1978), 357–61

14. Anthony Pagden, *The Fall of Natural Man: The American Indian and the Origins of Comparative Anthropology* (Cambridge: Cambridge University Press 1986)

15. François-Marc Gagnon and Denise Petel, *Hommes effarables et bestes sauvaiges* (Montreal: Boréal, 1986), 91–115; Kupperman, *Settling*, 197–40; Montaigne, *Essays,* 108

16. *Cassell's Concise French-English French Dictionary* (New York: Macmillan 1968), 121

17. Tzvetan Todorov, *The Conquest of America* (New York: Harper and Row 1984), 42

18. Marcel Trudel, *Histoire de la Nouvelle-France: Les vaines tentatives* (Montréal: Fides 1963), 82; Brian Slattery, 'French Claims in North America, 1500–54,' *Canadian Historical Review* 59, 2 (June 1978): 139–69, argues convincingly that this act did not represent a legally recognizable claim, but in dismissing the symbolism he is, I think, too literal. Moreover, he underplays the importance of Cartier's remarks in the introduction to the Second *Voyage*. See also Olive P. Dickason, 'Concepts of Sovereignty at a Time of First Contacts,' in L.C. Green and Olive P. Dickason, *The Law of Nations and the New World* (Edmonton: University of Alberta Press 1989), 232, Cartier's action followed the precedent already set by Columbus on 12 October 1492, when he met his first group 'naked people.' In his brilliant *Columbus* (Oxford and New York: Oxford University Press 1991), Felipe Fernandez-Armesto writes: 'This was not just a description, but a classification. A late fifteenth century reader would have understood that Columbus was confronting "natural men," not citizens of a civil society possessed of legitimate political institutions of their own. The registering of this perception thus prepared the way for the next step, the ritual appropriation of sovereignty to the Castilian monarchs, with a royal banner streaming and a scribe to record the act of possession'. (82). For a fuller exposition of this argument see the same author's *Before Columbus: Exploration and Colonization from the Mediterranean to the Atlantic 1229–1492* (London: Macmillan 1987), 223–45.

19. Marcel Trudel, 'Donnacona,' *Dictionary of Canadian Biography* (DCB), I, (Toronto: University of Toronto Press 1966), 275–6. This biography, based on the only existing documentation, Cartier's *Voyages*, accepts unquestioningly Cartier's evaluation of Donnacona's actions.

20. Trudel, 'Cartier,' *DCB*, I, 167. There is no documentation for the claim that an 'alliance' was made. Nor is there any evidence that 'Cartier also stated that he wished to take two of Donnacona's sons to France for the winter.' Trigger, *Children,* 182

21. Jonathan Spence, *The Question of Hu* (New York: Knopf 1988), 126. Another suggestive source is Shusaku Endo's stories in *foreign studies* (Seven Oaks, England: Sceptre 1990).

22. Robert Mandrou, *Introduction to Modern France 1500-1640: An Essay in Historical Psychology* (London: Edward Arnold 1975), passim

23. Jean de Léry, *History of a Voyage to the Land of Brazil, Otherwise Called America* (Berkeley, Los Angeles, Oxford: University of California Press 1990), 133

24. Trudel, 'Cartier,' 171, though earlier Trudel gives some credit to the guides. See also Samuel Eliot Morison, *The European Discovery of America: The Northern Voyages A.D. 500–1600* (New York: Oxford University Press 1971), 395–423.

25. Trudel, 'Cartier,' 167; Trigger, *Children,* 187–8

26. Trudel, *Histoire*, 110; Cornelius Jaenen, *Friend and Foe: Aspects of French-Amerindian Cultural Contact in the Sixteenth and Seventeenth Centuries* (Toronto: McClelland and Stewart 1973), 13

27. See Marshall Sahlins, 'The Spirit of the Gift,' in his *Stone Age Economics* (Chicago: Aldine 1972), 149–84, and also a brilliant application of this idea in Peter Hulme, 'John Smith and Pocahontas,' in his

Colonial Encounters: Europe and the Native Caribbean 1492–1797 (London and New York: Methuen 1986), 147–52.

28. Marcel Mauss, *The Gift: Forms and Functions of Exchange* in *Archaic Societies* (London: Cohen and West 1954), 80; Trigger, *Children*, 187–90

29. Marie-Christine Gomez-Géraud, 'Taignoagny et Dom Agaya: Portrait de deux truchements,' in Alain Parent, *La renaissance et le nouveau monde* (Québec: Musée de Québec 1984), 52–4. This is perhaps the only article on Cartier that attempts to understand the viewpoint of Donnacona's sons.

30. Hulme, *Colonial, 163*; Karen O. Kupperman, 'English Perceptions of Treachery, 1583–1640: The Case of the American Savages,' *Historical Journal 20, 2* (1977): 263–87

31. George R. Hamell, 'Strawberries, Floating Islands, and Rabbit Captains: Mythical Realities and European Contact in the Northeast during the Sixteenth and Seventeenth Centuries,' *Journal of Canadian Studies* 21, 4 (winter 1986–7): 72–4; Christopher L. Miller and George R. Hamell, 'A New Perspective on Indian-White Contact: Cultural Symbóls of Colonial Trade,' *Journal of American History* 73, 2 (Sept. 1986): 311–28. Bruce Trigger, in 'Early Native North American Responses to European Contact: Romantic versus Rationalistic Interpretations,' *Journal of American History* 77, 4 (March 1991): 1195–1215, criticizes the 'cultural' interpretation of

early contact, though he admits that it may apply to first contacts. His position seems unnecessarily rigid.

32. H.P. Biggar, ed., *A Collection of Documents relating to Jacques Cartier and the Sieur de Roberval* (Ottawa: Public Archives of Canada 1930), 51; Alfred W. Crosby, Jr, *The Columbian Exchange: Biological and Cultural Consequences of 1492* (Westport, Conn: Greenwood Press 1972).

33. Bruce G. Trigger and James E. Pendergast, 'The Saint Laurence Iroquoians,' in Bruce G. Trigger, ed., *Handbook of North American Indians,* vol. 15: *Northwest* (Washington, DC: Smithsonian Institute 1978), 36. On syphilis see Crosby, *Columbian,* 122–64, and Claude Quétel, *History of Syphilis* (Baltimore: Johns Hopkins University Press 1990), chap. 1.

34. Jacques Rousseau, 'L'Annedda et l'arbre de vie,' *Revue d'histoire de l'Amérique français:* 7, 2 (Sept. 1954): 171–201

35. Trudel, 'Cartier,' 168

36. Ibid., Trudel, *Histoire*, 110–12

37. Schlesinger and Stabler, eds., *Thevet*, 9; Ch.-A. Julien, *Les voyages de découvertes et les premiers établissements XVe–XVIe siècles* (Paris: PUF 1948), 138–9

38. Trudel, 'Donnacona,' 276

39. Schlesinger and Stabler, eds., *Thevet*, 83

40. Trudel, *Histoire*, 142–68

■ Article 3: The *Other* in Early Canada

Cornelius J. Jaenen

[This article deals with] […] the image of the "other" at the time of New France, inspired to a certain extent by the magisterial works of Nathan Wachtel, *The Vision of the Vanquished: the Spanish conquest of Peru through Indian eyes, 1530–1570*, trans. by Ben and Siân Reynolds (New York: Barnes and Noble, 1977), Jean Meyer, *Les Européens et les autres* (Paris: Colin, 1975) and Tzvetan Todorov, *The Conquest of America: the question of the other*, trans. by Richard

Howard (New York: Harper & Row, 1984) among others. I believe that the issue of the complex relations between oneself and the "other", between identity and alterity exists in all time periods. Nonetheless, I distance myself from those who admire these great historians because I do not conceive of the "other" as being Amerindian, aboriginal, indigenous, seen either as a "cannibalistic and brutish beast" or as a "good man of nature" at the first stage of human history. These historians based their views on texts like the celebrated passage in the *Histoire naturelle* (1761) of Buffon, the naturalist, one of the most widely read works of 18th-century literature:

Source: Cornelius J. Jaenen, "L'autre" en Nouvelle France/ The 'Other' in Early Canada", Historical Papers (Vol. 24, 1989), pp. 1–12 with portions translated from the French. Reprinted with permission from the Canadian Historical Association.

The American [Indian], it is true, is little less in stature than other men, yet that is not sufficient to form an exception to the general remark—that all animated nature is comparatively diminutive in the new continent. In the [Indian] the organs of generation are small and feeble; he has no hair, no beard, no ardour for the female [...] possessed of less sensibility [sensitivity], yet he is more timid and dastardly; he has no vivacity, no activity of soul [...] he will remain for days together in a state of stupid inactivity.[1]

From this scientific tract, the transition is easy to the polemic work written by Corneille de Pauw, *Recherches philosophiques*, who declared that plants, animals, men and, I presume, even European institutions transplanted to America lost their vigour and strength. From this point, he concluded:

So far we have only considered the peoples of the Americas from their physical attributes, which being essentially tainted, have occasioned the loss of moral faculties: degeneration affects their senses and their organs: their soul has lost in proportion to their body. Nature, having taken everything away from one hemisphere of the globe to give it to another, placed in the Americas only children, who have not yet become men. When the Europeans arrived in the West Indies, in the fifteenth century, not a single American knew how to read or write; there is still today not a single American who knows how to reason.[2]

The polemic served to justify colonization since the Swiss jurist Emmerich de Vattel, the great authority in international law, could conclude that "the people of Europe, too closely pent up at home, finding land of which the [Indians] stood in no particular need, and of which they made no actual and constant use, were lawfully entitled to take possession of it, and settle it with colonies [...]" Still, [the eighteenth-century French philosopher] Diderot could not stop himself from asking if his compatriots would support the same argument in the circumstance whereby Amerindians "brought by chance to your coasts [...] would write in the sand of your shores or on the bark of your trees: 'This land belongs to us!'"[3]

This 18th-century Eurocentrism is hardly surprising to historians, as we are used to making the intellectual effort to place ourselves in the context of the past in which we are interested. But what worries me a little, is perhaps that we ourselves—am I wrong here?— maybe too often Eurocentric as well. Is it not true that we always are content with the idea that the "other" in the Americas is always the Amerindian, in the Congo, the Congolese, or in India, the Tamil? The first inhabitants of this vast continent were clearly the Amerindians. Am I wrong, consequently, in formulating the thesis that the "other" on this continent, was and still is the European, whether Viking, Breton or Basque!

As for New France, it seems to me that the French—the *newcomers* of [historical anthropologist] Bruce Trigger and the *virtuous settlers* of [nationalist historian] Lionel Groulx—are the true "others". These "others" appear in a number of guises, from the fisher from St Malo who ravished aboriginal women, the *coureur de bois* rapidly assimilated to indigenous values, to the *Black Robes*, the great Christian shamans, capable of solving droughts and dangerous floods or of avoiding the negative consequences of smallpox. What I want to sketch is the great variety of images, or stereotypes of the "other"—the invader who came from beyond the Atlantic in search of gold, precious stones, a maritime passage, land to cut timber or to grow crops, that is with motives largely incomprehensible to the first inhabitants of this world that would be baptized "the New World."

The European, in this case the French, was perceived by Amerindians, at least by Algonquian and Iroquoian peoples, according to different aspects of his culture and beliefs, as both strangers and strange. In the first place, his physical appearance provided little reassurance. Of course, they appeared to be creatures that resembled the Amerindians, but this meant little in itself, because the moose and the beaver also shared the spirit of life, possessed an intelligence adapted to their environment, and were worthy of respect as "persons", that is in European terms as "persons other than humans." Brother Sagard, Recollect missionary to the Huron, related, "And in this connection I must relate that a savage one day seeing a Frenchman with a beard turned to his companions and said as if in wonder and amazement, 'O, what an ugly man! Is it possible that any woman would look favourably on such a man [...]'"[4]

Was there a link between the physical appearance of this European "other" and his intelligence? The Nipissings were clear on this point, according to Sagard:

It happened that after the interpreter of the Epicerinys had spent two years among them they, thinking they were paying him a compliment, said to him: Well, now that you are beginning to speak our language well, if you had no beard you would have almost as much intelligence as such and such a people, naming one that they considered much less intelligent than themselves, and the French still less intelligent than that people. Thus these good folk judge us to be very unintelligent by comparison with themselves, and at every moment and on the slightest occasion they say to you *Téondion* or *Tescaondion*, that is to say 'You have no sense'; *Atache*, 'ill balanced.'[5]

The missionary Louis Hennepin informs us that certain Amerindians of the *pays d'en haut* [the Upper Country], "added, that we had all Tails like Beasts, that the European Women have but one Pap in the middle of the Breast, and bear five or six Children at a time [...]"[6] This representation of the "other" is worthy of the image of the man of the woods, the *wildeman*, and the world of monsters left to us by the folklore of the Middle Ages.

In fact, in comparison to Amerindians, the French appeared puny, weak and skinny. They had "legs of wool" when it was necessary to traverse the great Canadian forests and "brains of rabbits" as far as the *petite guerre* ["guerilla" warfare tactics] was concerned. This "other" was generally weak in spirit, vain, boasting, boisterous, quarrelsome and, worst of all, without courage and lacking honesty. This was the stereotype of the colonizing Frenchman. Even Amerindian children believed themselves superiors in intelligence to the missionaries, "so good a conceit have they of themselves and so little esteem for others," according to a Recollect father.[7] [The Algonquin chief] Iroquet's band refused to take a young interpreter that Champlain wished to impose on them,[8] and whom they found too weak and inexperienced, "fearing that harm might come to the youth, who was not accustomed to their manner of life, which is in all respects hard, and that if any accident befell him the French would be their enemies."[9]

Can the intelligence—or rather the Frenchman's lack of intelligence—be seen in his material culture? Our historiography has always depicted the primitive "savage" confronting superior European technologies and science. But we should perhaps ask ourselves if the Amerindian found the firearms, the wagons, European clothing, and so on, superior to his own possessions. It is true that in the early 16th century, Gonneville provided important evidence of the first contacts between French and Amerindians and the reactions of the latter: "They were completely amazed by [the] size of the ship, the artillery, the mirrors, and other things that they saw on the ship, and especially by writing that was sent from the ship to the crewmen who were in the villages. These men did what had been asked of them, although the Indians could not explain to themselves how the paper could talk."[10]

However, some twenty years later, Verrazzano remarked that they were not impressed by all the Europeans' products. He tells us:

They did not esteem the silk, gold or other cloths, and did not wish to receive them. The same was true of metals like iron and steel. Again and again they declared that they had no admiration for the arms which we showed them. They did not want any from us and were only interested in their mechanisms. They even did not wish to receive mirrors: after they looked at themselves in the mirrors, they returned them to us, laughing.[11]

We know that fifty years later, Breton and Norman fishers exchanged knives, combs, needles and bronze pots for beaver and moose hides, a trade that is often qualified as being of unequal value. But I believe that we would do well to ask ourselves how Amerindians perceived these exchanges. If it really involved an unequal exchange, in what ways did they perceive the inequality? Who was fooled? Here is an example which illustrates well the problem: "you [Frenchmen] are also incomparably poorer than we, and [...] you are only simple journeymen, valets, servants, and slaves, all masters and grand captains though you may appear, seeing that you glory in our old rags and in our miserable suits of beaver which can no longer be of use to us."[12]

In answer to Recollect missionaries who wished to make the Amerindians into French people by making them believe that from all points of view the lifestyle of Europeans was superior to their own, a chief of Ile Percée replied that he was astonished that the French had "so little cleverness." Why, for instance, construct houses "which are tall and lofty [...] as these trees [for] men of five to six feet in height, [why do they] need houses which are sixty to eighty?" He continued, "my brother, hast thou as much ingenuity and cleverness as the Indians, who carry their houses and their wigwams with them so that they may lodge wheresoever they please, independently of any seignior whatsoever? [...] [W]e can always say, more truly than thou, that we are at home everywhere [...]"[13] "The other" in this case did not enjoy the liberty which characterized the life of Amerindians. The Frenchman was always, it seems, enslaved to a master, a superior, whether it was an authoritarian head of family, a priest, a seigneur, an officer, a magistrate, a governor, or a king.

How did Amerindians perceive the society that "the other" transplanted to American territory? First of all, it was hierarchical, therefore fundamentally based upon inequalities in all areas, favouring a small class of privileged people, in contrast to the Amerindian society generally lauded for their equality and their fraternity. It was possible to find "the other" authoritarian, intolerant and close-minded. French society focused on profits, often to the point of lacking charity and compassion for one's neighbour. I return to our Gaspesian chief who expressed so clearly his people's sentiments.

Well, my brother, if thou dost not yet know the real feelings which our Indians have towards thy country and towards all thy nation, it is proper that I inform thee at once. I beg thee now to believe that, all miserable as we seem in thine eyes, we consider ourselves nevertheless much happier than thou in this, that we are very content with the little that we have; and believe also once for all, I pray, that thou deceivest thyself greatly if thou thinkest to persuade us that thy country is better than ours. For if France, as thou sayest, is a little terrestrial paradise, art thou sensible to leave it?[14]

If the French were so attached to their inferior lifestyle, it was their choice, but it was not necessary to impose it in America. "*Aoti Chabaya,* [they say] That is the [Indian] way of doing things. You can

have your way and we will have ours; every one values his own wares."[15]

The "other's" diet was also disliked: the salted dishes, the bread that tasted of wood ash and the wine which resembled bitter absinthe.

We see also that all your people live, as a rule, only upon cod which you catch among us. It is everlastingly nothing but cod—cod in the morning, cod at midday, cod at evening, and always cod, until things come to such a pass that if you wish some good morsels, it is at our expense; and you are obliged to have recourse to the Indians, whom you despise so much, and to beg them to go a-hunting that you may be regaled. Now tell me this one little thing, if thou hast any sense: Which of these two is the wisest and happiest?[16]

In sum, almost all aspects of life and culture of the European "other" had little attraction for the Amerindians because, among them, individual autonomy and responsibility were the dominant values. The individual recognized no master and was never the subject of coercion. In a culture which held in high regard liberty, they also valued generosity and collective commitment. The conclusion of all these comparisons, according to Chief Gachradodow, in 1744, was a condemnation of European colonization.

The World at the first was made on the other Side of the Great Water different from what it is on this Side, as may be known from the different Colours of our Skin, and of our Flesh, and that which you call Justice may not be so amongst us; you have your Laws and Customs, and so have we. The Great King might send you over to conquer the *Indians*, but it looks to us that God did not approve of it; if he had, he would not have placed the Sea where it is, as the Limits between us and you.[17]

In few realms is the Amerindian vision of the European intruder and of the worth of his own culture better demonstrated than in the responses to evangelization, to the efforts of French missionaries to francize and christianize the Natives in a context which confused the kingdom of God with the kingdom of France. In responding to missionary intrusion the Native peoples were also responding to a variety of economic, social, and political values and assumptions. The Jesuits, for example, have been praised by some historians for their principle of accommodation to foreign cultures, their cultural relativism. Nevertheless, in the Canadian missions they still worked towards altering to some extent the structures of what they perceived to be a primitive society, to introduce new domestic values, agricultural techniques, a more serviceable political system, formal schooling, and so forth. Amerindian reactions, therefore, were not simply to a new theology or belief system but also to a radically different social organization in which this theology and belief system were embedded. Missionaries, as I have said elsewhere, were aggressive purveyors of a new and supposedly superior way of life, whose purpose was to remake individuals and whole societies in the image of their ideal. The Amerindians dealt with this challenge in a variety of ways and in so doing reveal to us their vision, their perception of this "other being" so intent on converting and transforming them, as well as their view of the culture and beliefs he represented.

It has often been stated that the Amerindians, in general, were attracted by the liturgy and sacraments and were convinced by the preaching of the missionaries. Those who became what some evangelizers called "people of prayer" saw virtues in Catholicism, to be sure, but it is from their point of view that any assessment must be made. Wampum was used in the public confessions that preceded festivals, funeral rites were ended by the interment of the dead "near whom they took good care to bury a sufficient quantity of provisions," in battle a crusader-like cry was raised to the Master of Life, and Christian prayers on crucial occasions could be accompanied by offerings of tobacco and salutations to the sun. Amerindians were able to assimilate the other's religion to their own spiritual concepts. God and devil might emerge from such a fusion with the same appelation, Jesus as the Sun, and the Holy Spirit as Thunder. Some Innu hunters were delighted Jesus had appeared in a dream to promise a successful hunt. They could not understand why their missionary was upset when they recounted how Jesus expected tobacco in return for His intercession. Was He not the Supreme Shaman? Could they not enlist His aid as did their

French brothers in their daily problems? Father Biard had acknowledged that "they accept baptism as a sort of sacred pledge of friendship and alliance with the French." Was the desire of some to convert any less sincere because it seemed to afford access to greater spiritual power, to useful trade and military relations, to possible protection from disease and famine, and to revitalization of one's own spiritual heritage?[18]

Of such Native converts Luc-François Nau was able to write: "I know a great number who serve God as faithfully as is observed in the best regulated religious communities."[19] On the other hand, Corneille de Pauw seriously doubted that, from an objective and detached point of view, this interpretation of conversion was accurate. He quoted from an inquiry into Native beliefs made after the British conquest, therefore a presumably anti-Catholic report: "Several were questioned on the articles of faith which were absolutely unknown to them, although these dogmas had been preached in their country for two centuries. Others had a very uniform notion of the story of Christ. They answered that he was a shaman, French by origin; that the English had hanged him in London; that his mother was French; and that Pontious Pilatous had been a lieutenant in the service of Great Britain."[20] De Pauw attributed this travesty of sacred history more to Native assimilation of the other's religion than to missionary intrigues.

All Amerindian cultures shared an ability to entertain and give assent to a variety of views, even if they were contrary to their better judgement, in what has been called institutionalized hospitality.[21] Sister Duplessis de Ste. Hélène reported that "the greatest number listen to the mysteries which are preached as to a fairy tale" and these left few impressions. The abbé Gaulin believed that they were "sufficiently enlightened to formulate an infinity of difficulties concerning all our mysteries." Did not the soldiers and *coureurs de bois* tell them that "it is the work of a black robe to preach, but one must not be concerned by what he says." So the Baron de Lahontan observed that they listened "to all the Jesuits preached without ever contradicting them, contenting themselves with scoffing between sermons." He explained their viewpoint as he understood it:

When they preach the incarnation of Jesus Christ to them, they reply that is admirable;

when they ask them do they wish to become Christians, they answer that it is laudable, that is to say they will think about it. And if we Europeans exhort them to come in crowds to church to hear the word of God, they say it is reasonable, that is to say they will come; but in the end it is only to obtain a pipeful of tobacco that they approach the holy place; or else to mock our Fathers, as I have said already, for they have such fortunate memories that I am acquainted with more than ten of them who know Holy Writ by heart.[22]

This value placed on deference and detachment was interpreted by the missionaries as dissimulation, which they traced back to their supposedly faulty permissive child-rearing practices: "Dissimulation, which is natural to those Savages, and a certain spirit of acquiesence, in which the children of that country are brought up, make them assent to all that is told them; and prevent them from ever showing any opposition to the sentiments of others, even though they may know what is said to them is not true."[23] Louis Hennepin, true to his own independence of mind, saw this tolerant indifference as part of their conscious antipathy to aggression. He wrote:

Notwithstanding that seeming Approbation, they believe what they please and no more; and therefore 'tis impossible to know when they are really persuaded of those things you have mentioned to them, which I take to be one of the greatest Obstructions to their Conversion; For their Civility hindering them from making any Observation or contradict what is said unto them, they seem to approve of it, though perhaps they laugh at it in private, or else never bestow a Moment to reflect upon it, such being their indifference for a future Life.[24]

The Sorbonne theologians eventually advised the colonial bishop to warn against baptizing those who made their profession of faith "only because they do not wish to contradict the Missionary."[25]

Another response was the assertion of a dichotomous universe, with a present and a hereafter designed for themselves, and separate ones for the "others." The western tribes told Jean-Pierre Aulneau that they "were not made for that religion." Just as there were two paths on earth so there were separate places for the souls of the departed. The Catholic concept of the hereafter was challenged: "This [...] 'tis like all the rest of your fine lies, all the souls, among our people at least, go to the same place; two of our souls came back once and told us all I have said."[26] On another occasion another missionary was interrupted with the same argument: "It's well for those of your Country: but we do not go to heaven after Death. We go only to the Country of Souls, whither our People go to hunt fat Beasts, where they live in greater Tranquility [....]"[27] An Innu shaman said, "Thy God has not come to our country and that is why we do not believe in him; make me see him and I will believe in him." When Paul Le Jeune countered such a statement with the assertion that Jesus Christ had not gone to Europe either, it only brought the noncommittal, "I have nothing to say against all this, for I have not been taught anything to the contrary."[28]

It was commonly believed that the missionaries possessed peculiar spiritual powers. When employed for ends that served their bands and tribes, they were perceived as powerful intercessors. When their intrusion was accompanied by epidemics, famine, or disastrous defeat at the hands of enemies, however, a cause-effect relationship was postulated. So, smallpox and Iroquois assaults on the Huron confederacy brought charges of witchcraft to bear against the missionaries. As a correspondent noted, "They were on the dock as criminals in a council of natives. The fires were lit closer to each other than usual, and they seemed to be so only because of them, for they were esteemed guilty of witchcraft, and of having poisoned the air which caused the pestilence throughout the country."[29] The same charges were not made against the traders, however. A young fisherman reported a visitation dream in which it was revealed to him by Iouskeha, "the true Jesus," that it was "the strangers who alone are the cause of it; they now travel two by two through the country, with the design of spreading the disease everywhere."[30]

I underscore the fact that there was great tolerance for the religion of the "other," but witchcraft was one of the few crimes in their society punishable by death. One of the first missionaries to come to Canada had opined that "no one must come here in the hope of suffering martyrdom [...] for we are not in a country where the natives put Christians to death on account of their religion."[31] He added that, quite to the contrary, they "leave every one to his own belief." The martyrs, in most cases, were victims of intertribal war.

I believe that the views of Amerindian women deserve attention. They believed that their persons and their social roles were the objects of a two-fold attack on the part of the missionaries—first as women, and secondly as natives. Among the nomadic bands the proscription of polygamy, if adhered to, would have greatly increased a woman's workload. Among the sedentary agricultural tribes the women, especially the "grandmothers" as the Jesuits called the matrons, refused to give up their children to be educated at Quebec. The men as hunters, traders, and warriors might be more amenable to conversion as a means of consolidating their relationship with the French, but the women saw few immediate advantages. What right had the missionary to undermine a woman's authority in the clan, or to assign a man to women's agricultural work? More than one matron drove the converted son-in-law from the longhouse. The men who were appointed "prayer captains" by the missionaries on one reserve exclaimed: "It is you women who [...] are the cause of all our misfortunes. It is you who keep the demons among us. You do not urge to be baptized; you are lazy about going to prayers; when you pass before the cross you never salute it; you wish to be independent. Now know that you will have to obey your husbands and our prayer captains. [. . .]"[32]

This introduction of so-called Christian discipline was deeply resented by many women. At Sillery a runaway wife was returned chained by one foot to her husband. Another woman was beaten by her "young Christian" husband; they were reprimanded but, the *Relations* specify, "especially the woman, who was more guilty than her husband." When a priest suggested that the disobedient had a fire "kindled in the other world" to torment them, women replied "in a deriding way," that, if so, then "the Mountains of the other World must consist of the Ashes of souls." One boldly asserted on another occasion: "I do not recognize any sins."[33]

We can understand why a missionary in the upper country complained that there were "no persons more attached to silly customs, or more obstinate in their error, than the old women, who will not even lend an ear to our instructions."[34] Were they not protecting their culture and traditional belief system? This sometimes required some unusual action. It was a woman who alerted the Huron council to the Jesuit peril: "Do you not see that when they move their lips, what they call prayers, those are so many spells that come forth from their mouths? It is the same when they read in their books. [...] If they are not promptly put to death, they will complete their ruin of the country, so there will remain neither small nor great."[35]

Finally, it might be objected that the missionaries in New France were not without success. Indeed, as I have said, there were conversions at various levels of understanding and for various motives. There were even a few who renounced their identity and heritage to join the "others," saying "I am French." Chief Garakontié of the Onondaga, for example, was derided by traditionalists because "he was no longer a man, that he had become French, that the Black Gowns had turned his head." Even so, the vision of the "other" may not have been what Europeans expected. The Innu are reported to have said their own mass in the absence of missionaries. The Micmacs, we are told, "have often been seen dabbling with, and affecting to perform the office and functions of missionary, even to hearing confessions. [...]" Even more disturbing was the knowledge that Micmac women had taken on a spiritual role in the "new religion" which was not denied them in their traditional religion. "These in usurping the quality and name of *religieuses* [nuns] say certain prayers in their own fashion, and affect a manner of living more reserved than that of the commonalty of Natives, who allow themselves to be dazzled by the glamour of a false and ridiculous devotion." Not only did women dare to take on a role the clergy disapproved of but they were also generally honoured for doing so: "They look upon these women as extraordinary persons, whom they believe to hold converse, to speak familiarly, and to hold communication with the sun, which they have all adored as their divinity." One woman in particular was honoured among the Abenakis. She was 114 years old, and said her prayers on unstrung beads of a rosary which she gave out as relics saying they had fallen from heaven into her hands.[36]

The vision of the "other" in the religious domain was conditioned by the fact that French and Amerindian cultures confronted each other as entities and that, by that fact, the conversion of individuals demanded much more than a superficial revision of personal convictions. Nonetheless, converts and non-converts seem to have been in agreement on one point: the "other" had a lifestyle and beliefs that were appropriate for him, but these should only be adopted after serious reflection. It is true that I have especially used missionaries' writings to show the vision that Amerindians could have of the "other" come from France, but I remind you of a sentence from Montesquieu: "It is necessary for them to tell the truth when they have no interest in hiding it in order to be believed when they wished to lie."

Notes

1. *Buffon's Natural History containing a Theory of the Earth, [....] from the French*, vol. VII (London, T. Gillet, 1807), p. 39.
2. Corneille de Pauw, *Recherches philosophiques sur les Américains*, London, 1770, t. II, p. 153 (translated by editor).
3. Emmerich de Vattel, *The Law of Nations or the Principles of Natural Law*, quoted in Walter B. Scaife, "The Development of International Law as to Newly Discovered Territory", *Papers of the American Historical Association*, 4, 3 (July 1890), p. 275. Diderot, quoted in Yves Bénot, *Diderot: De L'athéisme à l'anticolonialisme*, (Paris; Maspero, 1970), p. 197 (translated by editor).
4. George M. Wrong, ed., *Sagard's Long Journey to the Country of the Hurons* (Toronto: Champlain Society, 1939), p. 137.
5. Ibid., p. 138.
6. Louis Hennepin, *A New Discovery of a Vast Country in America* (Chicago, 1903), vol. 2, p. 84.
7. Wrong, ed., *Sagard's Long Journey*, p. 138.
8. Marc Lescarbot, *The History of New France*, trans. by W. L. Grant (Toronto: Champlain Society, 1914), vol. III, p. 21–22.
9. Ibid., p. 22.
10. "Le Voyage de Paulmier de Gonneville à Brésil (1503–5)" in Ch. A. Julien, *Jacques Cartier: Voyages au Canada. Avec les relations des voyages en Amérique de Gonneville, Verrazano et Roberval*, (Paris, 1981), p. 53 (translated by editor).
11. "Le voyage de Giovanni Da Verrazono à la Francesca (1534) ", ibid., pp. 89–90 (translated by editor).
12. William F. Ganong, ed., Chrestien Le Clercq, *New Relations of Gaspesia with the Customs and Religion of the Gaspesian Indians* (Toronto: Champlain Society, 1910), p. 105.
13. Ibid., pp. 103–04.
14. Ibid., p. 104.
15. R. G. Thwaites, *The Jesuit Relations and Allied Documents*, (New York, 1959), vol. 3, p. 121.
16. Ganong, ed., Le Clercq, *New Relation of Gaspesia*, p. 105.
17. *The Treaty held with the Indians of the Six Nations*, (Williamsburg, 1744), p. 42.
18. W.I. Kip, ed., *The Early Jesuit Missions in North America* (New York, 1846), 166–67; Library and Archives Canada, MG 17, A 7-1, Vol 4, No. 1, "Relation d'une expédition contre les Renards," p. 2658; Thwaites, *Jesuit Relations*, 4:201; 5:223; 8:27–37; 9:213; 11:259. See also James Axtell, *After Columbus* (New York, 1988), Chap. 7.
19. *Rapport de l'Archiviste de la Province de Québec pour 1926–27* (Québec, 1927), 313.
20. De Pauw, *Recherches philosophiques*, 161–62.
21. Calvin Martin, *Keepers of the Game* (Berkeley, 1975), 153.
22. NA, MG 3, Series T, Carton 77, pp. 27, 104; *ibid.*, Series K. Carton 1232, No. 4, p. 112; Baron de Lahontan, *Mémoires de l'Amérique septentrionale* (Baltimore, 1931), 107.
23. Thwaites, *Jesuit Relations*, 52:203.
24. Louis Hennepin, *A New Discovery of a Vast Country in America* (London, 1698), 2:70.
25. Mgr. H. Têtu and Abbé C.-O. Casgrain, eds., *Mandements, lettres pastorales et circulaires des évêques de Québec* (Québec, 1887), 1:447.
26. François du Creux, *The History of Canada or New France* (Toronto, 1951), 1:119.
27. Hennepin, *A New Discovery*, 577.
28. Thwaites, *Jesuit Relations*, 7:101; 11:157.
29. Dom Guy Oury, *Marie de l'Incarnation, Ursuline (1599–1672). Correspondance* (Solesmes, 1971), Lettre XXX, 67–68.
30. Thwaites, *Jesuit Relations*, 20:27–29.
31. Joseph LeCaron, *Au Roy sur la Nouvelle-France* (Paris, 1626), n.p.
32. Thwaites, *Jesuit Relations*, 28:105–07.
33. *Ibid.*, 18:155 and 23:111.
34. *Ibid.*, 54:143.
35. Oury, *Marie de l'Incarnation*, Lettre L, 117–18.
36. LeClercq, *New Relation*, 229–30.

FUR TRADERS AND THEIR PREY, SEVENTEENTH TO NINETEENTH CENTURIES

Why Did Aboriginals Participate in the Fur Trade?

Colin Coates
Glendon College, York University

FUR TRADERS AND THEIR PREY, SEVENTEENTH TO NINETEENTH CENTURIES: WHY DID ABORIGINALS PARTICIPATE IN THE FUR TRADE?

● **Introduction by Colin Coates**

▲ **Primary Sources**

Document 1: Account of the Beaver Hunt from *Relations des Jésuites*
Father Paul Le Jeune, 1634

Document 2: Indian Trade at York Factory, 1769–1771 from *Andrew Graham's Observations on Hudson's Bay*
Glyndwr Williams, ed.

Document 3: Detail from "A Map of the Inhabited Part of Canada from the French Surveys"

Document 4: Translation of Letter in Montagnais, circa 1785
René Pituabanu

Document 5: Original Letter in Montagnais, circa 1785
René Pituabanu

Document 6: David Thompson's Narrative of His Explorations in North America, 1784–1812
Joseph Burr Tyrell, ed.

■ **Secondary Sources**

Article 1: The Trade Assortment: The Meanings of Merchandise in the Ojibwa Fur Trade
Bruce M. White

Article 2: 'Beaver'
Shepard Krech III

● INTRODUCTION

Colin Coates

It may appear obvious why the fur trade became a thriving enterprise in the territory that would later become Canada and indeed why it played such a large role in the economies of both Europeans and Aboriginal peoples. Having hunted many fur-bearing animals to extinction in Europe, Europeans had to turn to new regions to acquire desirable pelts. Aboriginal peoples in North America had access to furs of excellent quality. They could be induced to trade them for items they lacked: metal items, cloth, guns and decorative items, like beads. According to a simplistic view of the operation of the fur trade, supply and demand, the characteristic twins of standard economic theory, should explain why Europeans and Aboriginal peoples became involved in this commerce.

The supply of beavers depended not only on the efforts of Aboriginal hunters, but also on the ecology of the animal itself. The beaver was quickly hunted to extinction or near-extinction in many regions. If the supply of pelts could vary, Aboriginals' desires to trade were not as predictable as French, British and Dutch merchants would have liked. Even the motivations and tactics of European traders could reflect non-economic impulses.

Thus, many historians argue that the fur trade was much more than an economic relationship. Certainly Aboriginal peoples and Europeans traded their items for goods that had a greater use value from their perspective. Neither thought they were getting a bad bargain. But there were many different contexts to the fur trade. Trade was important to diplomatic and military alliances between Europeans and diverse Aboriginal nations. As the French discovered on occasion, even if there were a glut of beaver furs, it remained necessary to maintain the trading relationship for reasons related to colonial security and expansion. The French often had to participate in an unprofitable commerce in order to pursue imperial goals. As fur-bearing animals were hunted to extinction in specific regions, the trade extended farther to the north, west and south, drawing French, Dutch and British traders and their Aboriginal partners into longer chains of economic and diplomatic relations.

Moreover, European fur traders often commented on how they had to adapt to Aboriginal practices in order to pursue the fur trade. Gifts were important in convincing Aboriginal peoples to maintain relations with specific forts and individual traders. The fur trade also encouraged the development of personal and emotional connections between Aboriginal peoples and Europeans. The fur traders were far from home and family, and many established deep ties with Aboriginal women and the children who resulted from their relationships. Intermarriages of French and Hudson's Bay Company traders with Aboriginal women cemented economic and political ties between the different groups, and smoothed the operations of the trade.

To achieve a full understanding of the North American fur trade it is necessary to consider Aboriginal motivations. Certainly some of the trade goods that Europeans brought with them had technological advantages over Aboriginal practices. Metal spear heads are lighter, sharper and more durable than stone spear heads, for instance. And a gun may prove more effective—though by no means was this always the case—than a bow and arrow. Bruce White's article discusses the trade items that proved of interest to the Ojibwa (Anishinaabe). He also examines the extent to which individuals wished to acquire wealth, pointing out that generosity could be a more effective means of establishing prestige than merely accumulating goods. Furthermore, Aboriginal peoples had developed over millennia an effective technology for surviving and thriving in North America, and while many features of European technology may have been practical, they were by no means necessary for survival. Europeans may have believed that Aboriginal peoples quickly became dependent on the trade; however, the indigenous traders did not always behave in that fashion. One key issue is, of course, the use of addictive substances as trade items, specifically alcohol, and one Scottish fur trader, Andrew Graham, from the Hudson's Bay Company discusses this exchange in "Indian Trade at York Factory, 1769–1771" below.

Although there were many differences among the variety of Aboriginal nations in the Americas, many Aboriginal peoples espoused a spirituality that revered the natural world in which they lived: the animals, trees, and rocks. Jesuit Father Paul Le Jeune's account of Aboriginal hunting practices provides some evidence of Aboriginal beliefs in reciprocity with nature. Given this clearly sincere respect for other species, then why did Aboriginal peoples hunt the beaver to extinction in specific areas, thus creating a dynamic of trade that would push the search for good-quality furs farther and farther into the interior of the continent? Ethnohistorian Shepard Krech III assesses the evidence for human–animal relations in the beaver trade in the article reproduced here. In trying to understand the motivations of Aboriginal peoples in the early centuries of contact between them and Europeans, historians usually have to rely on sources produced by non-Aboriginal peoples. The intelligent and sensitive fur trader and explorer David Thompson recounted an explanation for the decline in the numbers of beaver in his meeting with two elders in 1797 in what is now western Manitoba. A very rare example of a surviving document produced by an Aboriginal person in the eighteenth century is a letter from circa 1785 written in Montagnais (Innu) and provided below.

There are clearly many sides to the question of how to assess the motivations of Aboriginal peoples in their involvement in the fur trade. Aboriginal peoples may have made their choices from a variety of economic, spiritual, emotional, or political perspectives. Historians often grapple with the complex issue of motivation. It is one matter to rely on the expressed (and often written) views of individuals. But individuals may also have motivations that they do not feel the necessity to record or that maybe they do not even realize. As the excerpt from David Thompson's account shows, Aboriginal elders clearly acknowledged the deleterious effects of the beaver hunt. Yet despite this awareness, the fur trade continued.

QUESTIONS

1. What technologies and skills were required for hunting beaver? In what ways did Aboriginal peoples demonstrate their respect for the beaver?
2. What did Andrew Graham's experience in the Hudson Bay forts tell him about why Aboriginal peoples traded furs?
3. The accounts in Documents 1 and 6 describe different Aboriginal nations and discuss encounters that occurred about 150 years apart. How similar are the descriptions of Aboriginal attitudes toward the beaver among the Innu (Montagnais) and the Ojibwe (Anishinaabe)?
4. What does the letter from René Pituabanu tell us about the relationship between these Montagnais and the traders in Quebec?
5. What does the form of the Document 5 letter tell us about the Montagnais ability to communicate in writing?
6. How did the elders explain the decline in the beaver population in their region?

FURTHER READINGS

Denys Delâge, *Bitter Harvest: Amerindians and Europeans in Northeastern North America, 1600–64,* trans. by Jane Brierley (Vancouver: UBC Press, 1993).

W. J. Eccles, "The Fur Trade and Eighteenth-Century Imperialism," *William & Mary Quarterly* Third Series, Vol. 40, Issue 3 (July 1983): 341–362.

Carolyn Podruchny, *Making the Voyageur World: Travelers and Traders in the North American Fur Trade* (Toronto: University of Toronto Press, 2006).

Arthur J. Ray, *Indians in the Fur Trade: Their Role as Hunters, Trappers and Middlemen in the Lands Southwest of Hudson Bay, 1660–1870* (Toronto: University of Toronto Press, 1974).

Sylvia Van Kirk, *Many Tender Ties: Women in Fur-trade Society* (Winnipeg: Watson & Dwyer, 1999).

Richard White, *The Middle Ground: Indians, Empires, and Republics in the Great Lakes Region, 1650–1815* (Cambridge, U.K.: Cambridge University Press, 1991).

▲ Document 1: Account of the Beaver Hunt from *Relations des Jésuites*

Father Le Jeune was a Jesuit missionary among the Aboriginal peoples of the St Lawrence Valley in the seventeenth century, and in these excerpts from the Jesuit Relations, he describes Innu (Montagnais) hunting practices and spiritual beliefs.

Father Paul Le Jeune

The [Indians] do not throw to the dogs the bones of female Beavers and Porcupines,—at least, certain specified bones; in short, they are very careful that the dogs do not eat any bones of birds and of other animals which are taken in the net, otherwise they will take no more except with incomparable difficulties. Yet they make a thousand exceptions to this rule, for it does not matter if the vertebræ or rump of these animals be given to the dogs, but the rest must be thrown into the fire. Yet, as to the Beaver which has been taken in a trap, it is best to throw its bones into a river. It is remarkable how they gather and collect these bones, and preserve them with so much care, that you would say their game would be lost if they violated their superstitions. As I was laughing at them, and telling them that Beavers do not know what is done with their bones, they answered me, "Thou dost not know how to take Beavers, and thou wishest to talk about it." Before the Beaver was entirely dead, they told me, its soul comes to make the round of the Cabin of him who has killed it, and looks very carefully to see what is done with its bones; if they are given to the dogs, the other Beavers would be apprised of it and therefore they would make themselves hard to capture. But they are very glad to have their bones thrown into the fire, or into a river; especially the trap which has caught them is very glad of this. I told them that the Hiroquois [Iroquois], according to the reports of the one who was with us, threw the bones of the Beaver to the dogs, and yet they took them very often; and that our Frenchmen captured more game than they did (without comparison), and yet our dogs ate these bones. "Thou hast no sense," they replied, "dost thou not see that you and the Hiroquois cultivate the soil and gather its fruits, and not we, and that therefore it is not the same thing?" I began to laugh when I heard this irrelevant answer. The trouble is, I only stutter, I take one word for another, I pronounce badly; and so everything usually passes off in laughter. What great difficulty there is in talking with people without being able to understand them. Furthermore, in their eat-all feasts they must be very careful that the dogs do not taste even the least of it; but of this in another chapter.

"On Their Hunting and Fishing"

The Castor or Beaver is taken in several ways. The [Indians] say that it is the animal well-beloved by the French, English and Basques,—in a word, by the Europeans. I heard my host say one day, jokingly, *Missi picoutau amiscou,* "The Beaver does everything perfectly well, it makes kettles, hatchets, swords, knives, bread; and, in short, it makes everything." He was making sport of us Europeans, who have such a fondness for the skin of this animal and who fight to see who will give the most to these Barbarians, to get it; they carry this to such an extent that my host said to me one day, showing me a very beautiful knife, "The English have no sense; they give us twenty knives like this for one Beaver skin."

Source: Father Paul Le Jeune. *Relations des Jésuites*, 1634, Vol. 6, pp. 210–11 and Chapter IX, "On Their Hunting and Fishing," 297–301.

In the Spring, the Beaver is taken in a trap baited with the wood it eats. The [Indians] understand perfectly how to handle these traps, which are made to open, when a heavy piece of wood falls upon the animal and kills it. Sometimes when the dogs encounter the Beaver outside its House, they pursue and take it easily; I have never seen this chase, but have been told of it; and the [Indians] highly value a dog which scents and runs down this animal.

During the Winter they capture them in nets and under the ice, in this way: They make a slit in the ice near the Beaver's House, and put into the hole a net, and some wood which serves as bait. This poor animal, searching for something to eat, gets caught in a net made of good, strong, double cord; and, emerging from the water to the opening made in the ice, they kill it with a big club.

The other way of taking them under the ice is more noble. Not all the [Indians] use this method, only the most skillful; they break with blows from the hatchet the Cabin or house of the Beaver, which is indeed wonderfully made. In my opinion no musket ball can pierce it. During the Winter it is built upon the shore of some little river or pond, is two stories high, and round. The materials of which it is composed are wood and mud, so well joined and bound together that I have seen our [Indians] in Midwinter sweat in trying to make an opening into it with their hatchets. The lower story is in or upon the edge of the water, the upper is above the river. When the cold has frozen the rivers and ponds, the Beaver secludes himself in the upper story, where he has provided himself with wood to eat during the Winter. He sometimes, however, descends from this story to the lower one, and thence he glides out under the ice, through the holes which are in this lower story and which open under the ice. He goes out to drink and to search for the wood that he eats, which grows upon the banks of the pond and in the pond itself. This wood at the bottom is fastened in the ice and the Beaver goes below to cut it and carry it to his house. Now the [Indians] having broken this house, these poor animals, which are sometimes in great numbers under one roof, disappear under the ice, some on one side, some on the other, seeking hollow and thin places between the water and ice, where they can breathe. Their enemies, knowing this, go walking over the pond or frozen river, carrying a long club in their hands, armed on one side with an iron blade made like a Carpenter's chisel, and on the other with a Whale's bone, I believe. They sound the ice with this bone, striking upon it and examining it to see if it is hollow; and if there is any indication of this, then they cut the ice with their iron blade, looking to see if the water is stirred up by the movement or breathing of the Beaver. If the water moves, they have a curved stick which they thrust into the hole that they have just made; if they feel the Beaver, they kill it with their big club, which they call *ca ouikachit*; and, drawing it out of the water, go and make a feast of it at once, unless they have great hopes of taking others. I asked them why the Beaver waited there until it was killed. "Where will it go?" they said to me; "its house is broken to pieces and the other places where it could breathe between the water and ice are broken; it remains there in the water, seeking air, and meanwhile it is killed." Sometimes it goes out through its House, or some hole; but the dogs which are there, scenting and waiting for it, have soon caught it.

When there is a river near by, or an arm of water connecting with the pond where they are, they slip into that; but the [Indians] dam up these rivers when they discover them, breaking the ice and planting a number of stakes near each other, so that the Beaver may not escape in that direction. I have seen large lakes which saved the lives of the Beavers; for our people, not being able to break all the places where they could breathe, therefore could not trap their prey. Sometimes there are two families of Beavers in the same House, that is, two males and two females, with their little ones.

The female bears as many as seven, but usually four, five, or six. They have four teeth, two below, and two above, which are wonderfully drawn out; the other two are small, but these are large and sharp. They are used to cut the wood for their food, and the wood with which they build their house; they sharpen these teeth when they are dull, by rubbing and pressing them against each other, making a little noise which I have myself heard.

The Beaver has very soft fur, the hats made of it being an evidence of this. It has very short feet which are well adapted to swimming, for the nails are united by skin, in the same way as those of river-birds or seals; its tail is entirely flat, quite long and oval-shaped. I measured one of a large Beaver; it was a palm and eight fingers or thereabout in length, and almost one palm of the hand in width. It was quite thick, and was covered, not with hair, but with a black skin looking like scales; however, these are not real scales. The Beaver here is regarded as an amphibious animal, and therefore it is eaten in all seasons. My idea is that the grease when melted is more like oil than grease; the flesh is very good, but it seems to me a little stale in the Spring, and not so in Winter. But if the pelt of the Beaver excels the pelt of the sheep, the flesh of the sheep is superior, in my opinion, to that of the Beaver,—not only because it tastes better, but also because the Sheep is larger than the Beaver.

▲ Document 2: Indian Trade at York Factory, 1769–1771

Andrew Graham served in a number of Hudson Bay Company forts between 1749 and 1775, eventually rising to the position of chief factor, the leading company official, at Prince of Wales's Fort (present-day Churchill, Manitoba). He recorded his observations of the natural history and trading practices for the company.

I have heard great talking off and on concerning Hudson's Bay being laid open to all adventurers. The climate will not allow it; every necessary must be brought from England excepting fish, flesh and fowl, and that could not be got without the assistance of the natives who would enhance the price according to the demands. Each Factory [fort] at present are obliged to employ forty able hunters to bring in provisions, notwithstanding the supplies yearly sent out. There are not natives sufficient inhabiting between the Forts and the muscuty [prairie] country, where the Archithinue [Blackfoot] and Aseenepoets [Assiniboine or Stonys] inhabits, to raise the fur trade above 20,000 skins more than is now sent home yearly from the Bay. And if the trading standard was enlarged in favour of the natives, would ruin it all; for I am certain if the natives were to get any more for their furs, they would catch fewer, which I shall make plainly appear viz. one canoe brings down yearly to the Fort one hundred made beaver in different kinds of furs, and trades with me seventy of the said beaver for real necessaries. The other thirty beaver shall so puzzle him to trade, that he often asks me what he shall buy, and when I make an answer, Trade some more powder, shot, tobacco and hatchets etc., his answer is, I have traded sufficient to serve me and my family until I see you again next summer; so he will drink one half, and trade the other with me for baubles.

I am certain that inland settlements would be more for the natives' interest than for the Company's advantage, as their being supplied so nigh would encourage their wretched indolence, prevent them from visiting the lower Forts and as before observed they would catch no more furs than seventy or one hundred beaver, which fully supplies their annual wants [...] The long knowledge I have of the affairs in Hudson's Bay makes me affirm, that however advantageous it may be to two or three poor pedlars from Canada to drive a wretched and vagabond life after a few furs, I do not think it is, and am certain it would not be, worth the notice of a Honourable Company of Gentlemen [e.g. the Hudson's Bay Company] to follow such pitiful game [...]

[...] All gentlemen that are acquainted with the natives in Hudsons Bay know that it is not altogether by giving large presents to the leaders that will gain a trade, but by an affable, kind, easy behaviour to the whole body of natives; for as all natives are master over their own families they give no ear to the leader if they have any disgust to the fort. In short no leader has power to enforce what he would have put in execution. The trade will fluctuate a little let a person be never so careful, but when it gives way to a yearly decline it then plainly appears they don't love the usage [...]

To prevent the natives from hurting themselves with brandy and strong waters, we at none of the settlements exchanges [sic] that commodity for any furs but the following viz. martens, cats, foxes coloured, wolves, and bears. This has been the case from the time the Company had the Charter and wisely done. If the natives were to receive brandy for whatever kind of furs etc. they bring down, they would trade little or nothing else, which

Source: Glyndwr Williams, ed., *Andrew Graham's Observations on Hudson's Bay 1676–1791* (London: Hudson's Bay Record Society, 1969), Vol. XXVII, pp. 263–265, 281.

would end in their ruin, and the Company's affairs. Please to observe keeping up spirituous liquors to the above value makes the natives trap valuable furs. In Europe the higher value that is set upon any commodity the greater the price he is given, so should spirituous liquors be highly valued in Hudson's Bay, and not be made a drug as it is now at York Fort.

▲ Document 3: Detail from "A Map of the Inhabited Part of Canada from the French Surveys"

A Map of the
INHABITED PART
OF
CANADA
from the French Surveys; with
the FRONTIERS of
NEW YORK and NEW ENGLAND
from the Large Survey
By CLAUDE JOSEPH SAUTHIER.
Engraved by Wᵐ FADEN, 1777.

LONDON, Published as the Act directs Feb 25. 1777 by Wᵐ FADEN, Corner of St Martin's Lane, Charing-Cross.

● Detail from "A Map of the Inhabited Part of Canada from the French Surveys; with the Frontiers of New York and New England from the Large Survey by Claude Joseph Sauthier" (1777). The detail (called by cartographers a "cartouche") provides a stylized view of the trading process between Aboriginals and Europeans. How does the style of this image illustrate European perceptions about Aboriginal peoples involved in the fur trade? Does this image fit the material presented in the primary source accounts?

▲ Document 4: Translation of Letter in Montagnais from René Pituabanu, circa 1785

Some historians claim a very high level of literacy among the Innu (Montagnais) in the late eighteenth century, higher even than among the European population of the St Lawrence Valley. This letter was possibly addressed to Peter Stuart, who was involved in the fur trade in this region. The author of the letter was René Pituabanu, and it dates from around 1785, when Pituabanu was about 70 years of age. The post at Ishuamiskutsh or the Îlets-Jérémie was located north of Tadoussac on the north shore of the St Lawrence River.

I tell thee brother.

Tho' the Young men, my sons, are industrious in hunting, there are hardly any beaver to be found. It there were, they would kill them because the people of Ishuamiskutsh [the Îlets-Jérémie] want to do what they can.

Send us red checked cloth… The people of Îlets-Jérémie shall go into the interior this autumn, before it is possible to go hunting seals. They will go first in the forests to hunt, then when the time is ready they will go on the water for seals. Doubtless they will not want to go for seals if they find nothing for themselves in the interior. I demand a large boat. It is too difficult to carry casks in our birchbark canoes. This winter I'll stay at Îlets-Jérémie if I am still alive. Even if there are always people who stay here, I warn you that not everyone at Îlets-Jérémie will stay here in my opinion. This is all that I tell you.

I write from Îlets-Jérémie.

I salute thee,

I, Rné

Source: Translation of Letter in Montagnais, circa 1785, René Pituabanu. The translation is based on the eighteenth-century translation into English and a more recent French version, both published in José Mailhot, "Deux lettres montagnaises du XVIIIe siècle" *Recherches amérindiennes* XVII, 1 (1992):

tſhi uitamatin ni kanitſhs

At ma ui manitugaſuuats ni kuſhiſats he natauiutuau
utſhinitſhiſhiuatſh tapuenama muetſh teuatſh.

amiſkuats tſhi ma tatakuaue. Amiſkuats pua ma ni patatſhe
uatſh at ma ui manitukaſhuuatſh iſkuamiſkuuiriniuatſh,
ka miruaſits iſkueuakup ka mikuats gate ka katſhiteuats
natauentakaniu nama kata hapuuatſh uneuahunanitſh
iſkuamiſkuuiriniuatſh pitta ma ka takuſpiuatſh tekua
tſhitſh etku eka miruatſh he Akumuſtauaniuitſh
pitta nutſhimitſh katanatauihuuatſh mag iſhpiſh
miruatſh he akumuſtauaniuits egu tſhe akumuſt auatsits, atit
lli akumuſtauatuau eka tſhekuariu miſkamaſutuau nutſhimitſh
ni nataueriten tſharipaus ueſa ariman uaſkueutitſh
uauiatagana he puſhitakanitſh (piputſh iſkuamiſkutſh
ni ka iapin iriniuian at ma eiapitſh apinaniupin
iſkuamiſkutſh tſhi uitamatin nama uir kaſſinau
iſkuamiſkutſh iriniuatſh ka taiapuuats nititeriten
egu iſpiſh tſhi uitamaten

iſkuamiſkutſh ni maſſinagan

tſhi tatamiſkatin

nir Rne

N. B the above was wrote when he was about 70 years old &
about 26ᵗʰ Year of his reign

▲ Document 6: David Thompson's Narrative of His Explorations in North America, 1784-1812

David Thompson was one of the most important European explorers in eighteenth- and nineteenth-century British North America. He spent much of his life in what is now western Canada, from 1784 to 1815, in the employ first of the Hudson Bay Company and then its Montreal-based rival, the North West Company. Towards the end of his long life, in the late 1840s, he recorded his travels and encounters across North America. This excerpt recounts his experiences travelling from Aspen House to Snake Creek in 1797, to the west of Lake Manitoba.

[...] When we had proceeded over more than half way of the [beaver] Dam, which was full mile in length, we came to an aged Indian, his arms folded across his breast, with a pensive countenance, looking at the Beavers swiming [sic] in the water, and carrying their winter's provision to their houses, his form tall and erect, his hair almost white, which was almost the only effect that age appeared to have on him, though we concluded he must be about eighty years of age, and in this opinion we were afterwards confirmed by the ease and readiness with which he spoke of time long past. I enquired of him, how many beaver houses there were in the Pond before us, he said, "there are now fifty two, we have taken several of their houses; they are difficult to take, and those we have taken were by means of the noise of the water on their houses from a strong wind which enabled us to stake them in, otherwise they would have retired to their burrows, which are very many." He invited us to pass the night at his tent which was close by, the Sun was low, and we accepted the offer.

In the Tent was an old man, almost his equal in age with women and children; we preferred the open air, and made a good fire, to which both of the old men came, and after smoking a while conversation came on. As I had always conversed with the Natives as one Indian with another, and been attentive to learn their traditions on the animals[,] on Mankind, and on other matter in ancient times, and the present occasion appeared favourable for this purpose. Setting aside questions and answers which would be tiresome; they said, by ancient tradition of which they did not know the origen [sic] the Beavers had been an ancient people, and then lived on the dry land; they were always Beavers, not Men, they were wise and powerful, and neither Man, nor any animal made war on them.

They were well clothed as at present, and as they did not eat meat, they made no use of fire, and did not want it. How long they lived this way we cannot tell, but we must suppose they did not live well, for the Great Spirit became angry with them, and ordered Weesaukejauk to drive them all into the water and there let them live, still to be wise, but without power; to be food and clothing for man, and the prey of other animals, against all which his defence shall be his dams, his house and his burrows. You see how strong he makes his dams, those that we make for fishing wiers [weirs] are often destroyed by the water, but his always stands. His House is not made of sand, or loose stones, but of strong earth, with wood and sometimes small stones; and he makes burrows to escape from his enemies, and he always has his winter stock of provisions secured in good time. When he cuts down a tree, you see how he watches it, and takes care that it shall not fall

Source: Joseph Burr Tyrrell, ed., *David Thompson's Narrative of His Explorations in North America, 1784–1812* (Toronto: Champlain Society, 1916), pp. 202–06.

on him. "But if so wise, for what purpose does the Beaver cut down large trees of which he makes no use whatever." "We do not know, perhaps an itching of his teeth and gums."

The old Indian paused, became silent, and then in a low tone [they] talked with each other; after which he continued his discourse. I have told you that we believe in years long passed away, the Great Spirit was angry with the Beaver, and ordered Weesaukejauk (the Flatterer) to drive them all from the dry land into the water; and they became and continue very numerous; but the Great Spirit has been, and now is, very angry with them and they are now all to be destroyed. About two winters ago, Weesaukejauk showed to our brethren, the Nepissings and Algonquins the secret of their destruction; that all of them were infatuated with the love of the Castor[e]um [the secretion of the beaver's glands] of their own species; and more fond of it than we are of fire water: We are now killing the Beaver without any labor, we are now rich, but shall soon be poor, for when the Beaver are destroyed we have nothing to depend on to purchase what we want for our families, strangers now over run our country with their iron traps, and we, and they will soon be poor.

The Indian is not a materialist, nor does he believe in Instinct, a word of civilized Man, which accounts for great part of the actions of Mankind, and of all those of animated nature; the Indian believes that every animal has a soul which directs all it's [sic] motions, and govern all it's [sic] actions; even a tree, he conceives must somehow be animated, though it cannot stir from it's [sic] place.

[...] The Nepissings, the Algonquins and Iroquois Indians having exhausted their own countries, now spread themselves over these countries, and as they destroyed the Beaver, moved forwards to the northward and westward; the Natives, the Nahathaways, did not in the least molest them; the Chippaways and other tribes made use of Traps of Steel; and of the Castorum. For several years all these Indians were rich, the Women and Children, as well as the Men, were covered with silver brooches, Ear Rings, Wampum, Beads, and other trinkets. Their mantles were of fine scarlet cloth, and all was finery and dress. The Canoes of the Furr [sic] Traders were loaded with packs of Beaver, the abundance of the article lowered the London prices. Every intelligent Man saw the poverty that would follow the destruction of the Beaver, but there were no Chiefs to controul [sic] it; all was perfect liberty and equality. Four years afterwards (1797) [i.e., in 1801] almost the whole of these extensive countries were denuded of Beaver, the Natives became poor, and with difficulty procured the first necessaries of life, and in this state they remain, and probably for ever. A worn out field may be manured, and again made fertile; but the Beaver, once destroyed cannot be replaced; they were the gold coin of the country, with which the necessaries of life were purchased.

Article 1: The Trade Assortment: The Meanings of Merchandise in the Ojibwa Fur Trade

By Bruce M. White

In July 1791, after a winter of trading among a group of Ojibwa, or Anishinaabeg, from Leech Lake (in present-day north-central Minnesota near the Crow Wing River), Jean-Baptiste Perrault returned to Michilimackinac to pay off his supplier, a Mr Todd, who had provided him with goods the previous fall. After paying his debts, Perrault had a credit of £31, Halifax currency, on his account. He did not receive any of this in cash but used his credit to resupply with Todd for the next year. Obtaining seven bolts ("pieces") of woollen cloth, or "drap," and what he called the "assortment" of goods, which were wrapped into the cloth bales and packed in cases, barrels, and other packages, Perrault set off for the western end of Lake Superior. On the fifth day he arrived at the mouth of the Rivière au Poisson qui rit, the present-day Laughing Whitefish River in Michigan, where he encountered a trader of his acquaintance named Dufaut.[1]

Dufaut was on his way to Michilimackinac from his wintering place at Lac du Flambeau to the south. As they floated in the lake in their two canoes—manned by canoemen who are never mentioned—the two men began to converse. Dufaut wished to know how furs were selling at Mackinac [Michilimackinac]. The prices were low, said Perrault, offering him a shot of alcohol, presumably rum. After drinking it, Dufaut said, "Well the season is pretty far along, it will soon be too late for me to go back to Lac du Flambeau."[2]

Perrault replied, "Well how about trading with me? How many packs do you have?" Dufaut said he had one pack of otter, five packs of beaver, two packs of martin, three packs of bear, and one pack of fisher, wolverine, and muskrat, adding, "The rest is deerskins." He then asked Perrault, "And you, what is in your canoeload?" Perrault said that he had the following: "7 assorted bales, 12 barrels of drink, 2 do. powder, 5 sacks of shot and ball, 1 case of axes and chisels, 6 trade guns, 1 bale of tin kettles, 2 sacks of flour, 4 sacks of wheat, 1 barrel of grease & one ditto of sugar."

Dufaut considered for a moment: "Let's land, it's done." Before they landed, Perrault made sure that Dufaut understood that he (Perrault) would need to keep enough provisions in his canoe to get him back to Mackinac. Dufaut agreed. They went ashore at the mouth of the river. Perrault had his tent put up. Dufaut told him: "It's not necessary for you to open your packages. Just show me your manifests. That will be enough." Dufaut was satisfied. In the same way Perrault received Dufaut's fur bales *sous cordes*, all wrapped up, without opening them. The men both spent the night there and went their separate ways the next morning.[3] Perrault arrived at Mackinac fourteen days later. Finding Mr Todd, who was quite surprised to see him, Perrault was able to sell his furs at a better price than he had gotten earlier. He made a profit of £132 on the transaction. He obtained more merchandise and set out again for his wintering post.[4]

This anecdote from Perrault's memoirs describes a fairly minor incident in the long life of a trader. Yet it is an account that brings together many threads in the history of the fur trade.[5] A striking aspect of this encounter is the easy understanding between the two traders, especially with respect to the merchandise Perrault carried in his canoe. When the two men discussed this merchandise, they spoke in a common language of trade. Dufaut knew well what was in Perrault's canoe. He did not need to look at the goods or check their quality because he knew the bales contained goods that all the traders in this region brought to their trading posts. With little variation these were the goods that he himself would have gotten had he gone to Mackinac. They were a set of goods that had proven, in both the French and British fur trades, to satisfy the Ojibwa with whom the two men traded. But more than that, the trade assortment had a special meaning in the trade process itself.

An aboriginal group's preference for specific kinds of goods was related to its culture, the history of its dealings with European traders, and the

Source: Bruce M. White, "The Trade Assortment: The Meanings of Merchandise in the Ojibwa Fur Trade " in Sylvie Dépatie, et al., *Vingt ans après Habitants et Marchands,* (McGill-Queen's University Press), pp. 115–37. Reprinted with permission from McGill-Queen's University Press.

economics of the trade. The goods that made up the trade assortment satisfied native demand in a variety of ways. They could be used to keep people warm, to kill animals, or to cook food. They could increase the prestige and power of the person who owned them or who gave them away in religious and political ceremonies.

The Ojibwa of Lake Superior first obtained French merchandise sometime in the early to mid-seventeenth century. There are many unanswered questions about the nature of the Ojibwa's interest in European technology and the effect of the technology on Ojibwa culture. It is not clear, as some have argued, that the Ojibwa became dependent on European technology in the sense that they could not survive without it.[6] Nonetheless, by the eighteenth century many Ojibwa people had developed a strong liking for a range of French, and later British, tools, utensils, cloth, clothing, guns and ammunition, silver ornaments, and beads. Further, Ojibwa interest in these kinds of trade merchandise persisted well beyond the era of the fur trade. Many of the same goods they had sought from traders were later supplied by US government officials during annuity payments. There were, however, variations in the Ojibwa demand for merchandise. Men and women often desired a different set of goods, in accordance, in part, with Ojibwa subsistence patterns. Men used guns and ammunition for hunting. Women made use of awls for sewing and for their birch-bark work, scrapers for working hides, and metal utensils for preparing food. Men and women may have chosen different sizes of the "point" blankets offered by the trader and different silver ornaments or other articles of adornment. Finally, some of the demand was based on needs that were not immediately material. In addition to being worn or used as bedding, blankets were also used as shrouds for the bodies of people who had died, as gifts at the Feast of the Dead or at Midewiwin religious ceremonies, and as offerings to be dropped in the water as a way of calming spirits on dangerous canoe voyages on Lake Superior.[7]

While much has been written about the aboriginal people's interest in European merchandise, few scholars have offered detailed descriptions of the nature and quantities of trade goods supplied at Great Lakes trading posts during the French and British fur trades. One of the first to attempt this kind

of exhaustive research was Louise Dechêne, in her path-breaking study *Habitants et Marchands de Montréal au XVIIe Siècle*. Using notarial documents as well as the records of Montreal merchant Alexis Lemoine Monière, she enumerated the merchandise imported into North America by French businessmen of the seventeenth and eighteenth centuries and shipped from Montreal in birch-bark canoes to supply the growing demand from native consumers. Rather than describing these goods piecemeal, Dechêne categorized them according to a variety of types, including cloth, clothing, blankets, beads and other "trinkets," utensils, tools, wine and brandy, and ammunition, and recorded the value of the merchants' investments in these categories. Dechêne's work revealed the rich assortment of goods sought by aboriginal people and demonstrated something that may have startled many: cloth, clothing, and blankets accounted for over 60 per cent of the merchant's investment in goods for trade with aboriginal people.[8]

Others have now followed Louise Dechêne's lead. In my own 1987 essay, "Montreal Canoes and Their Cargoes," I studied the goods shipped from Montreal to a Sault Ste Marie trader in the 1780s.[9] The archaeologist Dean Anderson also delved into the Monière accounts to provide an archaeological perspective on the flow of merchandise into native societies. Anderson compared the goods found in eighteenth-century Great Lakes archaeological sites with the goods listed in the Monière accounts of shipments to the same region. By keeping track of the posts to which the goods were sent and categorizing the merchandise according to a series of functions (such as clothing, hunting, adornment, and grooming), Anderson provided some insights into the way such items were used in native societies. His study corroborated many of Louise Dechêne's conclusions about the nature of the merchandise shipped by Montreal merchants.[10]

Anderson pointed out that the account books he had relied on in his study were not necessarily a record of the merchandise acquired by aboriginal people. Some of the goods might have been intended for sale to traders and mixed-blood residents of the region. However, Anderson argued that by and large these account books, while not "an exact record of the goods Indians obtained," did record "goods intended for trade," an inventory that was based on the traders' understanding of the aboriginal people's interest in European goods. The accounts, he went on, were therefore records of "the flow of European goods into Indian societies," shaped "predominately by Indian demand." Extrapolating from his study, Anderson stated that there was broad consistency in the types and quantities of goods shipped to a variety of native communities in the Great Lakes region.[11]

Such a conclusion is not surprising given the fact that Great Lakes native groups shared similar languages, cultures, and woodland subsistence patterns, which would have influenced the choice of goods shipped there. On the other hand, information on the trade patterns in other regions suggests that these may have differed in important ways from the patterns of the Great Lakes peoples. According to the traders themselves, knowing of these differences was crucial to the trader's success. An individual who was familiar with one or more groups of Indians in one region was not necessarily equipped to deal properly with those of another region. As Pierre-Antoine Tabeau, a trader of the Upper Missouri around 1800, put it, "Those who are not versed in the Savage trade cannot imagine how important is the selection of articles and how far an individual, unfit or evilly intentioned, can be harmful to the process of commerce and to good order."[12] Certain Indian groups had a preference for certain kinds of merchandise over others. The Sioux and Arikira liked many of the things that the Osage and the Kansas favoured, but they also liked blue glass beads, brass wire, and iron for arrows and spears. The Arikira would not trade for any item that was over the value of a buffalo robe. They were fond of vermilion but would not trade for it; they expected it as a gift accompanying other items.[13] Tabeau wrote, "Ammunition, knives, spears, blue beads, tomahawks, and framed mirrors are the only articles for which they are willing to exchange their robes."[14]

Tabeau's remarks suggest an important aspect of the trade assortment, one that is not mentioned at all in the records of goods shipped from Montreal, but that is also a product of native demand: the patterns according to which these goods were traded. The mere fact that a blanket and a knife were both sought by aboriginal people did not mean that they could be traded in precisely the same way. The trade assortment was not merely a set of goods; it was also a set of practices, a game with specific rules, a language according to which each object could be made

to represent a variety of meanings. European merchandise was never traded as a unit; different goods were traded in different ways. For these reasons, the characteristic trade assortment of a particular region or community can only be fully understood in terms of the process through which the goods were traded.

THE TRADE PROCESS

The earliest exchanges between the peoples of the western Great Lakes and the French newcomers were probably sporadic, occurring when traders or merchants met with Indians who had packs of furs ready to trade for merchandise. Transactions like this took place when fleets of canoes manned by people usually called "Ottawa" (though this would have included ancestors of the present-day Ojibwa) came down the Ottawa River to Montreal in spring or summer. On these visits there were speeches, ceremonies, and the smoking of pipes, followed by the direct exchange of furs for goods.[15] Early on, however, a system became established in which traders ventured west and wintered in or near native villages. In this context, trade was not confined to gifts and one-for-one exchanges once a year. Credit was added to the range of possible transactions, and the trade involved more than furs and merchandise, since traders were dependent on the native community for the food and supplies needed to survive the winter.[16]

It is difficult to gauge the exact structure of the early trade among the Ojibwa, since few narrative or business sources survive from the seventeenth century.[17] However, by the mid-eighteenth century, trade. in native communities had become a formalized system, including gifts, credit, and direct exchanges. Though much of the information about this system of trade comes from records of the so-called British trade, there is strong evidence that the methods used were inherited from the French, or rather were continued by French traders—such as Perrault and Dufaut—who remained in the region and passed their expertise on to the new British traders.[18]

A trading year in a native community near Lake Superior began in the fall when the trader from Sault Ste Marie or Michilimackinac arrived with a new supply of goods. Once settled in his trading house, he met with members of the community and exchanged ceremonial gifts. He then gave out goods on credit, and his aboriginal customers set off on their fall and winter hunts, in small family groups. During the subsequent winter, the trader or his men might go *en drouine* (a term with obscure origins),[19] visiting native families to collect the furs they had secured. Aboriginal people might revisit the trading post, bringing in furs. In both cases, further gifts and further credit might be given. At the end of the trading year, before the departure of the trader, goods were exchanged and there might be concluding gifts and ceremonies.[20]

Trade participants brought to each of these various trade transactions a set of expectations specific to each encounter. Both the aboriginal people and the traders had an understanding of what they might expect when they met to trade. The work of economic anthropologist Marshall Sahlins helps to explain how this worked. In his study of "the sociology of primitive exchange," Sahlins delineated a "spectrum of reciprocities." At one extreme was what he and others have called "generalized reciprocity," exchanges that were "putatively altruistic." Sharing or generosity, for example, would prompt the pure gift; in such transactions the gift was not reciprocated with an immediate return gift, but rather with a long-term obligation. "Receiving goods lays on a diffuse obligation when necessary to the donor and/ or possible for the recipient. The requital thus may be very soon, but then again it may be never."[21] In the middle of the spectrum lay "Balanced reciprocity," or direct exchange—"The reciprocation is the customary equivalent of the thing received and is without delay." Sahlins suggested that the term could be loosely applied to transactions "which stipulate returns of commensurate worth or utility within a finite and narrow period." At the other extreme was "negative reciprocity," the attempt to get something for nothing. The most extreme example would be theft through violence, but Sahlins suggested that there were other forms of negative reciprocity in which "various degrees of cunning, guile, stealth" were used to "maximize utility at the other's expense." Sahlins's analysis suggests that the occurrence of these various forms of reciprocity was dependent on social distance; that is, generalized reciprocity was most likely to occur among the closest kin, whereas negative reciprocity was the most "impersonal sort of exchange" and from the present-day "point of view the 'most economic.'"[22]

Anthropologists have often applied ideas such as these to the analysis of material and social exchange within societies or between peoples with similar social systems. It is more challenging, however, to analyse exchanges between societies that appear to be radically different.[23] How do the variety of exchanges in the fur trade fit Sahlins's model? What accommodations were made between aboriginal people and fur traders to shape the process?

Many aspects of fur trade exchange make sense in the context of Sahlins's theories. At one extreme was what is usually called gift giving, the presentation of items by both traders and aboriginal people that helped to reduce the social distance between strangers, making long-term relationships possible. In the middle were a variety of balanced exchanges in which the parties to the trade exchanged items one-for-one. At the other extreme was what was usually called "pillaging," the plunder of objects by trader or aboriginal.[24]

Neatly categorizing any transaction is not always easy. It may appear, for example, that a trader's gift fits the category of generalized reciprocity, a freely given object designed to reduce social distance. A closer examination might reveal that the gift was solicited or coerced through various means and was actually the opposite, a form of near-pillage in which guile has taken the place of violence. North West Company trader François Victoire Malhiot stated that on his way to Lac du Flambeau on 25 July 1805 he had met an Ojibwa man named Le Genou. The man was very unhappy with the trader Simon Chaurette of the competing XY Company, and he also complained of the lack of food and ammunition at the post. It seemed to Malhiot that Le Genou was planning to do some harm to Chaurette, "at least to pillage him." Malhiot came to this conclusion because Le Genou, speaking of Chaurette, had said, "Oh Dog, you will be pitiful." Said Malhiot, "These last words contain a lot of things."[25]

For traders like Malhiot, pity was a familiar concept. It was something that their customers often referred to in the speeches they made when they sought to establish a relationship with government officials or traders or when they hoped to receive gifts from individuals of power.[26] Clearly Le Genou had been frustrated in his attempts to secure for himself a satisfactory relationship with Chaurette. He may have felt that Chaurette was not showing the proper generosity. Traders who were not generous or who violated the proper way of dealing with aboriginal people were quite commonly threatened with pillage, the sanction of losing all their goods. If pillage occurred, the trader would then be "pitiful," the condition he had ignored in others. More often the trader would respond to the threat by being more generous. Generosity in traders, then, was not always freely exhibited; rather it could be motivated by fear, the product of threats and guile.[27]

Similarly, credit was shaped by a variety of sometimes ambiguous motivations and understandings. Much of the exchange of goods for furs took place in credit transactions. While fur-trade credit has often been described as debt slavery—a means of binding aboriginal people to traders year after year—the logic of credit is much more complex than that.[28] The meaning of credit was hinted at in a description given by Alexander Henry the Elder of his first trading year among the Lake Superior Ojibwa. In 1765 Henry, one of the pioneer British traders in the region, set out for the south shore of Lake Superior. He had never traded in the region before but drew on the knowledge of several French businessmen, including Étienne-Charles Campion, who had advised him in 1761, and Jean-Baptiste Cadot, the trader at Sault Ste Marie who had helped to save his life after the siege of Fort Michilimackinac in 1763 and who became his business partner in 1765.[29] Historian Harold Innis described Henry and Cadot's partnership as "symbolic of the necessary combination between English capital and French experience" that helped to shape the fur trade in the British period.[30]

Henry purchased four canoeloads of goods at Fort Michilimakinac on twelve-month credit. After passing Point Iroquois west of Sault Ste Marie, Henry "fell in with Indians, of whom," he wrote, "I purchased provisions. One party agreed to accompany me, to hunt for me, on condition of being supplied with necessaries on credit."[31] Farther on, at Ontonagon, Henry met more Indians, "whom I furnished with merchandise on credit." He recorded the basis on which he gave credit, in the process delineating the kinds of goods he supplied in such transactions: "The prices were for a stroud blanket, ten beaverskins; for a white blanket, eight; a pound of powder, two; a pound of shot, or of ball, one; a gun, twenty; an axe, of one pound weight, two; a knife, one."[32]

At Chequamegon, or La Pointe, his wintering place, Henry found fifty lodges of aboriginal people "who were almost naked, their trade having been interrupted, first by the English invasion of Canada, and next by Pontiac's War." Henry also noted: "Adding the Indians of [Chequamegon] to those which I had brought with me, I had now a hundred families, to all of whom I was required to advance goods on credit. At a council, which I was invited to attend, the men declared, that unless their demands were complied with, their wives and children would perish; for that there were neither ammunition nor clothing left among them. Under these circumstances, I saw myself obliged to distribute goods, to the amount of three thousand beaver-skins."[33] Despite the recent interruption in trade, these Ojibwa remembered how to deal with traders and what to say to get what they wanted. Statements about their great need were often part of the speeches given by aboriginal people at the beginning of a trading year.[34] And these people were neither naked nor destitute, though the clothing Henry found them wearing qualified as nakedness by European standards; they wore clothing made of deerskin, "European manufactures having been for some time out of their reach."

The kinds of goods that Henry gave on credit, as well as the circumstances that led to his giving credit, reveal some of the logic behind the credit relationship: credit was necessary to supply and clothe the people for the coming winter so that they could supply the trader with furs. The alternative to credit could have been that they would use their time and resources in clothing and feeding themselves, not in hunting or trapping furs for the trader. In Henry's case, his willingness to give credit was amply rewarded. As a return on his investment, he received 150 packs of beaver and 25 packs of otter and marten.[35]

Transactions such as this were generally balanced, insofar as aboriginal people were able and willing to produce the furs and traders to supply goods. Yet credit is not a balanced transaction in terms of time: When goods are given out on credit, reciprocation does not take place immediately. In this sense, though technically a form of balanced reciprocity, the credit relationship at first mimics generalized reciprocity, with the difference being that repayment is obligatory, in the credit relationship and a length of time is set after which the person receiving credit has to repay the debt.

One of the reasons that traders gave goods on credit was to influence the trapping behaviour of aboriginal clients. Aboriginal people repaid their debts because that is what they had agreed to do and because reciprocity was ingrained in their culture. But they did not always repay them entirely. Opinions have differed about the extent to which debts remained unpaid, on the average, at the end of the trading year. Johann Georg Kohl, an ethnographer who visited the Ojibwa of the south shore of Lake Superior in 1855, stated that Canadian traders "often give the Indians credit for large supplies, and rarely find any difficulty in getting their accounts settled."[36] Others have disagreed.[37] Sometimes a less-than-full repayment was influenced by an inability to gather enough furs. Anthropologist Mary Whelan has a more complex explanation. In her study of the Dakota fur trade, she stated that "in situations where social and economic behavior are organized around reciprocity, 'debt' is actually required to keep the system functioning. Full repayment is not intended and no notion of 'getting out of debt' is involved. The point is to stay in debt so that social ties are maintained and you are assured of having an ally when future need arises."[38]

From the beginnings of the fur trade, a recurring theme was the desire of aboriginal people to establish a consistent and reliable source of supply of European technology and goods.[39] Given this interest in a continuing supply, a certain amount of debt might have been deemed useful in influencing traders to return to the community. The degree to which repayment of debt took place probably varied according to local circumstances. What also varied was the degree to which complete repayment was of real concern to the traders, since it is probable that traders factored in differing amounts of unpaid credit in their rates of exchange.[40]

If aboriginal people sometimes were unable or unwilling to repay the credit they received from traders, this did not mean that they were confused about the difference between gift and credit. There was an important relationship between the two transactions. Neither could exist without the other. Gifts made credit relationships possible because they helped create good feeling and trust. Even though credit was not always repaid, suggesting the hypothesis that credit was actually assumed to be a gift, in fact gift and credit were not interchangeable.

In his book *The Middle Ground*, historian Richard White suggested that while credit was central to the fur trade, the aboriginal people in the Great Lakes region "never fully acknowledged advances as debts."[41] Instead, he said, they treated such advances as they would other generalized exchanges, whereby the original gift would be "reciprocated at a time when the giver needed aid and the recipient was able to give it." But with respect to the Ojibwa people, since they tried to repay their debts yearly, this theory would only make sense if one assumed that the perceived need White referred to occurred regularly on a seasonal basis—that is, if the Ojibwa believed that traders "needed aid" in the form of various furs, in the winter and spring each year. Otherwise, White's theory appears to assert that aboriginal people had only one form of exchange, generalized reciprocity, and that they were incapable of distinguishing other forms of exchange with other rules and other expectations. Such an argument is in keeping with the frequent tendency to collapse all forms of material interaction in non-Western societies into the category of the "gift." As anthropologist Nicholas Thomas made clear in his description of similar trade situations in the Pacific, "we cannot understand these systems as unitary gift economies or, for that matter, as economies dominated by any particular transaction form." Whether or not aboriginal economies in North America were ever limited to what might be called the gift, that does not appear to have been the case by the eighteenth century. By that time reciprocal exchanges in the trade were consistent with White's later statement that the fur trade was a "precarious amalgam of exchanges that ranged from gifts to credit transactions, to direct commodity exchanges, to extortion, to theft," though one can argue with the term "precarious."[42]

The aboriginal ability to negotiate alliances, described so thoroughly by White in his account of aboriginal-French diplomacy in the seventeenth and eighteenth centuries, was also present in the fur trade, though the patterns of trade have yet to be so clearly explained.[43] Both aboriginal people and traders had a sense of the complexity of the trade transactions, whether or not they agreed on precisely what transactions were being undertaken at any particular time or on what the reciprocal obligations were. The various kinds of transactions could be distinguished from one another by the way in which both parties spoke as they negotiated them. The fur trade was never a silent trade.[44] Both traders and customers gave speeches in which they explained what they expected of their relationship as a whole and of any transaction in particular. Thus, the verbal context of any transaction was important in interpreting its meaning. The temporal and seasonal context was also important. Certain transactions were more likely to happen following certain other kinds of transactions or to take place at a particular season of the year.[45] Finally, the objects themselves (that is, their cultural definitions in trade and in native life or what Nicholas Thomas called the "cultural differentiation of artifacts") helped to differentiate the transactions.[46]

OBJECTS OF TRADE

In the Ojibwa fur trade, certain kinds of objects came to have a certain significance, and thus certain kinds of goods were more likely to have a place in certain transactions. This particularity, in and of itself, helped make clear to both trader and aboriginal customer what was expected during particular transactions. Cloth goods and alcohol, for example, were two kinds of merchandise defined and treated in strikingly different ways. Alcohol, whether brandy, high wines, or rum, had obvious cultural significance in the fur trade as well as in aboriginal-European diplomacy.[47] Among traders in the Lake Superior region in the eighteenth and early nineteenth centuries, alcohol, in the form of rum or brandy, was chiefly given to aboriginal people in two kinds of transactions: as gifts and in exchange for food. The trading ceremonies at the beginning and end of the year and on the repayment of debts usually featured gifts of alcohol. The food on which the trader depended, such as wild rice, game, and maple sugar, was in large part obtained with liquor, XY trader George Nelson wrote of his experiences while trading on the Chippewa River in 1803–4: "We don't pay provisions here with anything else than with rum sometimes tobacco, but seldom tho[ugh], & ammunition. The Indians are so accustomed to it that they are quite surprised when any other payment is given them."[48] By contrast, cloth, clothing, and blankets were mainly exchanged either in the context of the credit/debt transactions—as in the circumstances in 1765 described by Alexander Henry—or directly, for furs or possibly for supplies such as canoes.

The contrast between these two kinds of merchandise and between the transactions through which they were characteristically exchanged may suggest evidence for what anthropologists have called "spheres of exchange," that is, categories of exchange involving different goods and services with differing cultural values. Generally, there were rules and social sanctions against exchanging goods appropriate to different spheres.[49] Marshall Sahlins stated that many societies make "distinctive categorizations of food versus other goods, i.e. 'wealth.'" He suggested that in such societies "food for goods transactions" would "rend the solidary bonds."[50] A problem with applying a spheres-of-exchange theory to the Ojibwa fur trade lies in the difficulty in determining the basis—cultural, social, and economic—for the existence of such spheres, the kinds of goods that might fit in the various categories, and the relative rigidity or permeability of these categories. It is also not altogether clear how binding such distinctions might be in intercultural exchanges.

It was often noted that, among the Ojibwa, the reluctance to share food and the insistence on selling it or demanding goods in return for it were considered to be violations of cultural rules.[51] Beyond that, however, no comprehensive effort has been made to describe Ojibwa ideas concerning what anthropologist A. Irving Hallowell called the concept of property, that is, "the pattern of rights, duties, privileges, powers, etc., which control the behavior of individuals or groups in relation to one another and to the custody, possession, use, enjoyment, disposal, etc. of various classes of objects." As Hallowell stated, any such study would involve "an exceedingly complex network of structural relations and a wide range of variables."[52]

One helpful source, however, does offer suggestions concerning Ojibwa beliefs about the rights and duties of people towards material goods. Johann Georg Kohl, who recorded a variety of such beliefs, stated that among the Ojibwa the willingness to share "reaches such a pitch that it is one of the chief obstacles to their conversion." He noted that "next to the liar, no one is so despised by the Indians as the narrow-hearted egotist and greedy miser … As long as a man has anything, according to the moral law of the Indians, he must share it with those who want; and no one can attain any degree of respect among them who does not do so most liberally." Most of the examples that Kohl gave had to do with the willingness of the Ojibwa to share their last bit of food if others were in need.[53]

The obligation to share food, according to Kohl, did not mean that all food resources were open to exploitation by everyone. Kohl described certain aspects of food gathering and of exploitation of the natural surroundings for which other rules applied. He said that the places in which resources were harvested, such as a sugar bush, a cranberry patch, and even beaver dams, all had owners—that is, people who controlled their use. In the case of beaver dams, Kohl said that ownership could be "handed down from father to son." In the case of the other resources, he noted that they were "family property." He said that "no Indian family would think of making sugar at a place where it had no right."[54] While society encouraged the sharing of food, it still placed the ownership of some resources with individuals or family groups.

A further implication in the idea that resources were owned by those individuals who made use of them is that ownership was shaped by a gendered division of labour. When he wished to have a bark house built so that he would have lodging during his visit, Kohl negotiated with women to erect the structure and buy the rolls of bark to cover it, because they were responsible for this activity in Ojibwa society. In this sense, bark houses were the property of women in general. Specific houses or rolls of bark were the property of specific women. There is some suggestion that similar factors applied to the meat obtained by a hunter but prepared by women. In describing the importance of sharing meat, Kohl stated that before the hunter ate anything himself, "his feeling of honour insists that he must first of all consult with his wife how the deer is to be divided among his neighbours and friends."[55]

Kohl, along with many others, reported that when a person asked for food from people who had it, they felt obligated to give it. This was not the case with other kinds of goods. For example, it is likely that among the Ojibwa, as among other aboriginal groups, furs were treated differently from the meat of the animals from which the furs were taken. Instead of being shared, they would be the property of the hunter or trapper who took them, or of his family.[56] To obtain furs and other kinds of property, negotiations were necessary to determine the proper return. Another special class comprised religious objects,

which required high returns and special negotiations when exchanged. Kohl stated that "all their information about religious matters, every exchange of magic remedies, every copy and explanation of a picture-writing, must be paid for, and they ask enormous prices. They will often give a horse, a handsome fowling-piece, or a packet of beaver skins, for a piece of bark that has figures scratched on it. For how little is a packet of skins in comparison with a magic song, to which all the beavers in the world listen, and must go into traps on hearing it."[57]

Generosity with food was expected of all people, and those who were generous were considered to be fulfilling their obligations towards other members of the society. Generosity with other objects, however, brought greater returns: it could help give a person power and influence in the society. Kohl noted that the most powerful men in the community were the worst dressed: "They give to the tribe not only what they obtain by the chase, but also all the presents even to their tribute-money. Frequently, when a chief receives very handsome goods, either in exchange for his peltry, or as recognition of his high position, he will throw them all in a heap, call his followers, and divide all among them," including sometimes the shirt off his back. Ultimately, said Kohl, such giving away of goods was an investment: "A man who lays up such capital in the hearts of his followers is thence much richer than if he had all the wares under lock and key. In case of need, all his followers blindly obey his orders."[58] The implication of these statements is that the Ojibwa made a distinction between food and other objects in terms of the rights and duties of their owners, and in terms of the value of these objects in exchanges.

In his discussion of the separation of food and "wealth" in many societies, Sahlins argued that there had to be an important qualification: "These food and nonfood spheres are sociologically based and bounded." At a certain social distance, the spheres dissolved. Exchanges that were not possible inside a society might be possible in dealings with people from outside the society. In the case of the fur trade, however, a system of interaction was established between the Ojibwa and Europeans in which social and cultural distances were overcome. This was made possible because Europeans accommodated themselves to native beliefs and culture. Aboriginal beliefs about food and other objects were applied to the material goods of the fur trade. Thus, logically, alcohol and tobacco were incorporated into the food sphere of exchange and treated as objects to be shared or traded for other objects of food. Many other trade goods were treated, in Sahlins's terms, as wealth—that is, as objects for which there was no obligation to share. Most of the time they were traded directly.

However, there were exceptions to the rules suggested here. Both cloth goods and alcohol were sometimes exchanged in ways that did not fit this pattern. For example, special coats were given to chiefs at trading ceremonies at which the trader sought to reward Ojibwa leaders for their loyalty. And, as stated before, chiefs often passed these articles on to their followers. Blankets and other cloth articles might also be given to "cover the body" of a person who had died. Long speeches were delivered to explain what these articles of clothing were meant to represent.[59]

There were also occasions when the usual food/alcohol transactions could not occur because one or the other was not available. For example, according to XY trader George Nelson, food was scarce at his trading post on the Chippewa River in March 1804. Nelson's men had to be fed in other ways. Nelson wrote that one of the men had "gone with his family to his father in law's lodge as we have nothing here to eat. I give him a little ammunition & a few silverworks to trade provisions—for we have now nothing else to trade. We subsiste [sic] upon indian Charity."[60] Without the alcohol they needed to trade for food, Nelson's men were forced either to use other trade goods or to rely on their relatives in the native community. Similarly, there were occasions when, for a variety of reasons, alcohol was traded directly for furs or other items.

How did such uses fit into the distinctive spheres of exchange discussed here? Gifts of clothing to chiefs were intended to serve a very specific purpose—to increase the traders' influence in a community by showing honour to the leaders of that community. For the purposes of the transaction, clothing was redefined from an item designed to keep its wearer warm to an intangible symbol of respect, something with an intangible reciprocal, loyalty. Symbols like this could not be bought, but had to be given freely. On the other hand, when alcohol was traded for furs or other objects, it ceased to be a symbol of the close social relationship that both aboriginal people

and traders were seeking to establish. It became a mere commodity, with no implication of a close relationship. Such exchanges of alcohol occurred not in credit transactions, but in one-for-one exchanges when aboriginal people who were not indebted to a trader purchased a quantity of alcohol with what would presumably be a surplus of furs. Evidence suggests that such purchases occurred more frequently at places like Sault Ste Marie, to which aboriginal people travelled from distant places in the summer, having the opportunity for only short-term dealings with the trader. On such occasions, gifts might be given to initiate or cement a transaction, but there was no question of credit.[61]

The nature of these exceptional transactions involving cloth goods and alcohol suggests something of the logic of the normal spheres of exchange. Alcohol, food, and tobacco were usually exchanged in ways that decreased social distance between traders and aboriginal people. As Louise Dechêne noted, liquor served more as a "token of goodwill than as a commodity."[62] Objects in this category could be given away or traded one for the other. Such transactions created a trader-aboriginal society in which trust was possible. Similarly, the giving away of clothing was intended to foster loyalty. By contrast, most cloth, clothing, and blankets were given on credit or traded directly. These transactions made up the bulk of transactions in which traders obtained furs. This was only fitting, since cloth, clothing, and blankets replaced furs in aboriginal society.

SUMMARY AND CONCLUSIONS

For traders who operated in the western Great Lakes region in general and among the Ojibwa in particular, the choice of goods was crucial. Every trader needed to bring an assortment of goods designed to fulfil native demand. Aboriginal people used merchandise to meet a variety of material, social, and religious needs. Beyond fulfilling these needs, the assortment of goods brought by fur traders had another role to play in the patterns of trade. The trade assortment consisted of a specific set of goods, each of which was used in various ways in trade encounters, as gifts, in credit transactions, and in one-for-one exchange. Some goods, such as alcohol, tobacco, and food, were usually given as gifts and in exchange for food. Other goods, such as clothing, cloth, and blankets, were usually exchanged in credit transactions and in direct trade. The particular uses of the different goods in this way reflected native beliefs, the way in which aboriginal people categorized and valued food and other material objects.

Whether or not other trade goods fit into the trade categories or spheres of exchange identified here remains to be demonstrated. To explore this question, it is necessary to make detailed use of trade narratives that describe the attitudes and behaviour of trade participants. It is also important to make use, when possible, of fur trade account books that record in detail the many kinds of transactions that took place during a trading year. With such data it may be possible to measure the proportion of goods traded, given away, and given on credit for furs, food, and supplies, and to determine when during the trading year these different exchanges occurred. Such an analysis would increase our understanding of the patterns that existed in the way merchandise reached aboriginal people.

Another point that needs further exploration is the degree to which the patterns described here were influenced by financial considerations on the part of traders. Traders may have resisted receiving food in exchange for such expensive items as cloth, clothing, or blankets, except in cases where they hired people to hunt for them.[63] Aboriginal people who could pay off the bulk of their debts by bringing in food would not have had an incentive to hunt for furs, which were after all the ultimate purpose of the fur trade from the European point of view. Traders would probably have been quite happy to trade liquor for furs, since concentrated liquor was denser and more easily transported and handled than cloth, clothing, and blankets. But aboriginal people who obtained only liquor would not have had the clothing or tools necessary to survive and hunt and trap furs during the winter. Thus, some of the patterns of the fur trade made sense both from the point of view of native spheres of exchange and business economics.

The way in which some trade goods were expended in the fur trade, however, was probably viewed as an unfortunate necessity by the traders. Louise Dechêne made this clear when she stated that traders "had to provide a whole range of articles, some not very profitable."[64] Trade merchandise used in gift giving or used to pay for supplies was, from the trader's point of view, overhead. The traders had to pay for it one way or another. The profits made by

fur traders, then, cannot be determined, as is sometimes attempted, simply from an analysis of credit or one-for-one exchanges of furs for merchandise. Any detailed study of the operations of the fur trade business must take into account the many meanings of merchandise, both in fulfilling aboriginal demand and in making possible the smooth operation of trade.

Notes

1. The original manuscript of Jean-Baptiste Perrault's narrative is in the Henry R. Schoolcraft Papers, Library of Congress, Washington, DC. The narrative was first published in English in *Michigan Pioneer and Historical Collections* (Lansing, Mich.: Michigan Pioneer and Historical Society, 1909, 1910), 37:508–609. The first French edition, from which the author has translated all quotations used here, was titled *Jean-Baptiste Perrault marchand voyageur parti de Montréal le 28e de mai 1783* (Montreal: Boréal Express, 1978). Perrault uses the French term "assortiment," to describe the merchandise (82). See also pages 80, 89, and 98 of his narrative for other uses of the term.

2. Perrault, *Jean-Baptiste Perrault*, 82.

3. Ibid., 83.

4. Ibid.

5. One important aspect of the encounter is the nationality of the traders. For many people who write about the fur trade, Perrault, Dufaut, and the men who worked for them would probably be described as British traders. They were agents of British-controlled companies, in the midst of what is normally called the "British period" of colonial history. Yet for the Ojibwa of Lake Superior, the British fur trade was simply a continuation of the trade that had begun in the mid-seventeenth century—a trade through which they obtained valued European goods. Well into the nineteenth century, these Ojibwa called the European traders with whom they dealt "les français" or in their own language "wemitigoozhi." The French term, for example, was used in relation to the North West Company traders under the command of François Victoire Malhiot. See Malhiot, Journal, 13 (3 September 1804), original in McGill University Libraries, Rare Books and Special Collections. On the Ojibwa word, see John Nichols and Earl Nyholm, *An Ojibwe Word Resource Book* (St Paul: Minnesota Archaeological

Society, 1979), 151. Except for a scattering of Scots, Irish, and English, mostly at the higher-level positions, the bulk of those active in the Lake Superior fur trade were of French ancestry, people whose ancestors had worked in the fur trade since its beginnings. For an attempt to explore the extent of the continuing French influence in the British trade in the early 1800s, see Bruce M. White," 'Give Us a Little Milk': Economics and Ceremony in the Ojibway Fur Trade" (MA thesis, McGill University, 1985), 94–7.

6. On questions about dependency, see Richard White, *The Middle Ground: Indians, Empires, and Republics in the Great Lakes Region, 1650–1815* (Cambridge: Cambridge University Press, 1991), 482–3.

7. For a description of the goods supplied during Ojibwa annuity payments, see Frances Densmore, *Chippewa Customs* (St Paul: Minnesota Historical Society, [1929] 1979), 138–9. For a summary of the range of goods sought by the Ojibwa and their multiple uses, see Bruce M. White, "Encounters with Spirits: Ojibwa and Dakota Theories about the French and Their Merchandise," *Ethnohistory* 41 (summer 1994): 376.

8. Louise Dechêne, *Habitants et marchands de Montréal au XVIIᵉ siècle* (Paris: Librairie Plon, 1974), 151, 507. The English translation of Dechêne's book was published as *Habitants and Merchants in Seventeenth-Century Montreal* (Montreal and Kingston: McGill-Queen's University Press, 1992).

9. Bruce M. White, "Montreal Canoes and Their Cargoes," in Bruce Trigger et al., eds, *'Le castor fait tout': Selected Papers of the Fifth North American Fur Trade Conference, 1985* (Montreal: Lake St Louis Historical Society, 1987), 164–92.

10. Anderson's work also revealed that cloth goods accounted for more than 60 per cent of the trader's investment, something that was, of course, not evident from the fragments of mainly non-perishable goods found in archaeological sites. See Anderson, "Documentary and Archaeological Perspectives on European Trade Goods in the Western Great Lakes Region" (Ph D dissertation, Michigan State University, 1992), 104, 113–23, 148; and idem, "The Flow of European Trade Goods into the Western Great Lakes Region, 1715–1760," in Jennifer S.H. Brown, W.J. Eccles, and Donald P. Heldman, eds, *The Fur Trade Revisited: Selected Papers of the Sixth North American Fur Trade Conference, Mackinac Island, Michigan,* 1991 (East Lansing and Mackinac Island: Michigan State University Press/Mackinac State Historic Parks), 101, 109.

11. See Anderson, "Documentary and Archaeological Perspectives," 66–68; and idem, "Flow of European Trade Goods," 113.

12. Pierre-Antoine Tabeau, *Tabeau's Narrative of Loisel's Expedition to the Upper Missouri,* ed. Annie Heloise Abel (Norman: University of Oklahoma Press, 1939), 170.

13. For examples of other such preferences, see Shepard Krech, "The Early Fur Trade in the Northwestern Subarctic: The Kutchin and the Trade in Beads," in Trigger et al., *'Le castor fait tout'*, 236–77.

14. Tabeau, *Tabeau's Narrative*, 171.

15. R. White, *The Middle Ground*, 105. For accounts of Ottawa expeditions to Montreal, see Nicolas Perrot's account in Emma Helen Blair, ed., *Indian Tribes of the Upper Mississippi Valley and Region of the Great Lakes* (Cleveland, Ohio: Arthur H. Clark Company, 1911), 1:175, 210–20. For a description of the speeches and ceremonies, see Louis-Armand, Baron de Lahontan, *New Voyages to North-America*, ed. Reuben G. (Chicago: A.C McClurg, 1905), 1:92–5. On French gift-giving practices, see Cornelius J. Jaenen, "The Role of Presents in French-Amerindian Trade," in Duncan Cameron, ed., *Explorations in Canadian Economic History: Essays in Honour of Irene M. Spry* (Ottawa: University of Ottawa Press, 1985), 231–50.

16. See Harold A. Innis, *The Fur Trade in Canada: An Introduction to Canadian Economic History* (Toronto: University of Toronto Press, [1930] 1956), 57–62, for a discussion of the transition from trade at Montreal to trade in the interior of the Great Lakes region. Most early discussions of the role of credit in the fur trade concern the Hudson's Bay Company, though there is evidence that the French granted credit at an early date in inland trade. See Toby Morantz, "'Gift-Offerings to Their Own Importance and Superiority': Fur Trade Relations, 1700–1940," in William Cowan, ed., *Papers of the Nineteenth Algonquian Conference* (Ottawa: Carleton University, 1988), 137, 140; and Daniel Francis and Toby Morantz, *Partners in Furs: A History of the Fur Trade in Eastern James Bay, 1600–1870* (Kingston and Montreal: McGill-Queen's University Press, 1983), 52.

17. Dechêne, *Habitants et Marchands*, 168.

18. Continuity in gift giving and ceremonies is discussed in B.M. White, "Encounters with Spirits," 381.

19. A variant of the term was *en dérouine*. See John Francis McDermott, *A Glossary of Mississippi Valley French, 1673–1850*, Washington University Studies, n. s., Language and Literature, no. 12 (St Louis: Washington University, 1941), 66; and André Bergeron, *Dictionnaire de la langue québécoise* (Montreal: VLB Editeur, 1980), 179–80.

20. For a more detailed description of the process, see Bruce M. White, "A Skilled Game of Exchange: Ojibway Fur Trade Protocol," *Minnesota History* 50 (summer 1987): 229–40.

21. Marshall Sahlins, *Stone Age Economics* (New York: Aldine Publishing Co., 1972), 193, 194.

22. Ibid., 194, 195.

23. One anthropologist who has sought to study the economic exchange between societies is Nicholas Thomas. See his *Entangled Objects: Exchange, Material Culture and Colonialism in the Pacific* (Cambridge, Mass.: Harvard University Press, 1991), particularly 84–8.

24. Bruce M. White, "The Fear of Pillaging: Economic Folktales in the Western Great Lakes," in Brown, *Fur Trade Revisited*, 199–216.

25. Malhiot, Journal, 3.

26. B.M. White, "Give Us a Little Milk," 22–23, 38–39.

27. Sometimes a threat of pillage was made as a way of improving rates of exchange or coercing gifts, occasionally at the encouragement of rival traders. See B.M. White, "Fear of Pillaging," 207.

28. See Morantz, "Gift Offerings," 140.

29. The partnership helps demonstrate the way in which the methods perfected in the French period were carried over in new circumstances. Alexander Henry, *Travels and Adventures in Canada and the Indian Territories* (New York: Garland Publishing, [1809] 1976), 11, 192–6. On Étienne-Charles Campion, see *Dictionary of Canadian Biography* (Toronto: University of Toronto Press, 1979), 4:132–3. On the career of Jean Baptiste Cadot, see David Armour's biographical sketch in *Dictionary of Canadian Biography*, 4:128–30; Theresa M. Schenck, "The Cadottes: Five Generations of Fur Traders on Lake Superior," in Brown, *Fur Trade Revisited*, 189–94; and B.M. White, "Montreal Canoes," 164.

30. Innis, *Fur Trade in Canada*, 167–8.

31. Henry, *Travels and Adventures*, 194.

32. The rates of exchange described by Henry in 1765 were much higher than those described for later periods. This was probably due to the scarcity of goods after many years of war. Ibid., 195–6.

33. Ibid.

34. On speeches of this kind, see B.M. White, "Give Us a Little Milk," 40.

35. Henry, *Travels and Adventures*, 204.

36. Johann Georg Kohl, *Kitchi-Gami: Life among the Lake Superior Ojibway* (St Paul: Minnesota Historical Society Press, [1860] 1985), 78.

37. See R. White, *The Middle Ground*, 114.

38. Mary K. Whelan, "Dakota Indian Economics and the Nineteenth-Century Fur Trade," *Ethnohistory* 40 (spring 1993): 246–76.

39. B.M. White, "Encounters with Spirits," 389.

40. According to Royce Kurtz, in the trade among the Fox and Mesquakie in the 1820s, "a return in skins of 50 percent on credit was necessary to break even." See Kurtz, "Looking at the Ledgers: Sauk and Mesquakie Trade Debts, 1820–1840," in Brown, *Fur Trade Revisited*, 148. According to Innis (*Fur Trade in Canada*, 374), in the Hudson's Bay Company fur trade in the late nineteenth century, a return of 75 per cent was regarded as "a very favorable recovery."

41. R. White, *The Middle Ground*, 114.

42. Ibid., 480; and Thomas, *Entangled Objects*, 50.

43. R. White, *The Middle Ground*, 84, 93, for example, and throughout the book.

44. The idea of a "silent trade"—an exchange of goods between people from different societies who carried out the process without speaking to each other—is a kind of economic myth. See Philip D. Curtin, *Cross-Cultural Trade in World History* (Cambridge: Cambridge University Press: 1984), 12–13.

45. On fur trade speeches and seasonal aspects of the trade, see B.M. White, "A Skilled Game of Exchange," 231–4.

46. Thomas, *Entangled Objects*, 206. Thomas wrote, "If inadequate and over-generalized notions of 'gift economies' are displaced by more locally particular models of prestations, alienability, and debts, and if this discussion is integrated with the interpretation of the cultural differentiation of artifacts, some sense can be made of the process of colonial contact in different areas."

47. See B.M. White, "Give Us a Little Milk," 32–5.

48. George Nelson, Journal, 1803–04, 35 (15 September 1803), Metropolitan Toronto Central library. See

also B.M. White, "A Skilled Game of Exchange," 235.

49. Sex and money may represent two such spheres of exchange in modern European-American society. Sex is something that is supposed to be given away, on the basis of love, friendship, or marriage, not to be exchanged for money. Characteristically, economic anthropologists define as entrepreneurs those who are able to cross the boundaries between such spheres and reap potential profits from doing so. See Frederick Barth, *The Role of the Entrepreneur in Social Change in Northern Norway* (Bergen: Norwegian Universities Press, 1963), 10; and Paul Bohannan and George Dalton, eds, *Markets in Africa* ([Evanston]: Northwestern University Press, 1962), 3.

50. Sahlins, *Stone Age Economics*, 218.

51. Ibid., 269–70, gives several examples of this attitude towards food, taken from the narrative of John Tanner, a white man who lived for many years among Ottawa and Ojibwa on the Red River. See John Tanner, *A Narrative of the Captivity and Adventures of John Tanner* (New York: Garland Publishing, [1830] 1975).

52. Ibid., 218. For a discussion of "property" as a set of rights and duties, see A. Irving Hallowell, "The Nature and Function of Property as a Social Institution," in his *Culture and Experience* (New York: Schocken Books, 1967), 236–49.

53. Kohl, *Kitchi-Gami*, 66, 70.

54. Ibid., 421. A variety of sources have suggested that Ojibwa ownership was communal while at the same time noting that people had "rights" in various kinds of property. As Hallowell suggested, however, having a right to do something is seen as one kind of ownership even among Europeans. See Hallowell, *Culture and Experience*, 236–49. Inez M. Hilger noted that "maple groves were not claimed by any particular family, but it was well understood that no one tapped trees that were customarily tapped each season by the same family." See Hilger, *Chippewa Child Life* (St Paul: Minnesota Historical Society, 1991), 146–7. See also Peter Grant, "The Sauteux Indians: About 1804," in Louis R. Masson, ed., *Les bourgeois de la Compagnie du Nord-Ouest* (Quebec: Côté et Cie., 1889–90), 2:326; and Joseph N. Nicollet, *The Journals of Joseph N. Nicollet: A Scientist on the Mississippi Headwaters with Notes of Indian Life, 1836–37* (St Paul: Minnesota Historical Society, 1970), 253. Ownership of particular resources for a season or a longer period of time did not necessarily imply the existence of so-called hunting territories, the meaning and pre-European existence of which has been widely debated. See Eleanor Leacock, *The Montagnais 'Hunting Territory' and the Fur Trade*, American Anthropological Association, Memoir no. 78 (Menasha, Wise: American Anthropologist, [1954]); and John M. Cooper, "Is the Algonquian Family Hunting Ground System Pre-Columbian?" *American Anthropologist* 41 (1939): 66–90.

55. Kohl, *Kitchi-Gami*, 70.

56. Samuel W. Pond discussed this distinction among the Dakota. See Pond, *The Dakota or Sioux in Minnesota as They Were in 1834* (St Paul: Minnesota Historical Society, [1908] 1986), 49. Peter Grant stated that, among the Ojibwa, even provisions could be differentiated based on whether or not they were "reserved for the traders or for some other particular purpose." See Grant, "Sauteux Indians," 326.

57. Kohl, *Kitchi-Gami*, 161, stated that "it is often possible to receive as a present from an Indian a richly decorated pipe without any return; you can eat your fill in his lodge, and, in some cases he will refuse to take anything for it ... but if you try to get from him a piece of written bark and the requisite explanation of the hieroglyphics, you must pay its weight in silver. Brother keeps such secrets hidden from brother, son from father, and will only surrender them for payment." Kohl suggested that these beliefs were dictated, in part, by a sense of obligation to the spirit from whom the knowledge was gained, quoting one person as saying, "The Great Spirit would be angry were we to squander his gifts."

58. Ibid., 66–67.

59. On chiefs' coats, see B.M. White, "A Skilled Game of Exchange," 14. On gifts for "covering the body," see North West Company partner John Sayer's 1804–5 journal, erroneously labelled as that of Thomas Connor, in Charles M. Gates, ed., *Five Fur Traders of the Northwest* (St Paul: Minnesota Historical Society, [1933] 1965), 266, 269; and Perrault, *Jean-Baptiste Perrault*, 68–69, 70–72, 75.

60. On Sayer's wife making sugar, see Curot, Journal, 39 (8 March 1804). See also John Sayer's journal (1 March 1805), in Gates, *Five Fur Traders*, 270; and Nelson, *Journal*, 25.

61. Preliminary calculations by the author based on an account book of Jean-Baptiste Barthe, a trader at Sault Ste Marie in the 1770s, show exchanges of alcohol for furs amounting to over 23 per cent of

the value of all exchanges of trade goods for furs. Cloth, clothing, and blankets amounted to over 55 per cent. See Barthe account book, 1775–79, Burton Historical Collection, Detroit Public Library.

62. Dechêne wrote that "the trader who wanted to secure a faithful clientele and convince the Indians to hunt on his behalf, in order to secure steady returns, did not turn brandy into a major item for sale." Dechêne, *Habitants and Merchants*, 82, 88.

63. See B.M. White, "A Skilled Game of Exchange," 232.

64. Dechêne, *Habitants and Merchants*, 82, 88.

■ Article 2: "Beaver"

By Shepard Krech III

[…] The beaver, *Castor canadensis*, was amazingly abundant in North America. The naturalist Ernest Thompson Seton speculated that in 1600 as many as fifty million swam in waters across the continent. Today, their traces can be read in the countless banks, creeks, runs, brooks, rivers, ponds, meadows, mountains, valleys, and towns bearing their name. Anthropomorphized and occasionally domesticated, beavers have attracted intense scrutiny over the centuries. Many authors have commented on the architecture and engineering of their dams and lodges, and on their character and mentality, enshrining them in a cloak of cleanliness, monogamous family values, and—as "eager beavers"—industriousness. Indeed, beavers are monogamous, local, and sedentary—the basic winter social group lives in a lodge and consists of a mated pair and their young from two years—and like all rodents must chew, else their continuously growing incisors would curve fatally into their skulls.

If beavers did not construct dams, lodges, canals, dens, and escape tunnels, they would not have a suitable, secure living habitat near their food sources. Herbivores, they prefer aquatic plants and the leafy parts and bark of trees like aspen and poplar. They can fell six-inch-diameter trees in an hour; larger ones are sometimes collaborative projects. When they exhaust the food resources bordering their pond, they often excavate fifty-foot-long canals to nearby tree-lined ponds. Their lodges are free-standing or located in dams; some have multiple chambers and hunters have killed more than thirty-five beavers in such apartment complexes.

Source: Shepard Krech III, "Beaver" in *The Ecological Indian: Myth and History* (New York: W.W. Norton, 1999), pp. 173–195, 288–297. Copyright © 1999 by Shepard Krech III. Used by permission of W.W. Norton & Company, Inc.

Beavers construct wood, stone, and mud dams over several nights, and given enough beaver power, a colony, which consists of the beavers associated with one dam, can erect impressively large dams—from twelve to eighteen feet high and from four hundred to eight hundred feet long. One dam reportedly was four thousand feet long. These are products of larger beaver colonies. Not surprisingly, beavers alter their habitat profoundly through all their activity, forming pond ecosystems when dams are built, and meadow ecosystems when dams are destroyed due to fast streamflow, flood, or abandonment.[1]

European explorers and fishermen became involved in a trade for beaver pelts the instant they put to shore in North America. The exchange started in the Northeast in the late fifteenth and early sixteenth centuries, grew to tens of thousands of beaver pelts annually by the early seventeenth century, and eventually became almost continental. Since the items exchanged for them cost little to manufacture and transport and the pelts brought handsome profits at home, it is easy to understand why Europeans pushed the trade. But Indians relished it also, eager to exchange common pelts, worth a trifling amount to them, for novel foods like bread, peas, beans, and prunes and for rare and useful manufactured goods like copper kettles, axes and knives, and cloth. In seventeenth-century New France, a Montagnais leader, knife in hand, jested to a Jesuit missionary, "'The English have no sense; they give us twenty knives like this for one Beaver skin.'" Some Indians might have been wary of the Europeans, some neutral, and others aggressive from knowing that these foreigners were dangerous—but few were reluctant to trade. In this atmosphere, can it be coincidental that complaints of a dearth of beavers poured in as early as the late seventeenth century?[2]

Europe, where otter, beaver, marten, and other furs were in popular demand, provided the predominant market for North American pelts. For centuries the beaver pelt was paramount in that market. It appeared as the emblem of the famed Hudson's Bay Company (HBC), which obtained a Royal Charter over a vast territory in North America in 1670, and became the standard of exchange as the Made Beaver, which was an average-size male pelt in prime condition. Merchants found beavers attractive not for their lustrous pelt, however, but for the underhairs held together by interlocking barbs when pressed together, a quality making them without parallel in felt hat production. The significance of the underhairs was reflected in the HBC's motto, *pro pelle cutem*, meaning "the skin for the fur or wool." For years traders literally traded furs known as coat beaver (*castor gras*) from Indians' backs. Worn for months as clothing, hair inside, coat beaver was primed for felting: friction from the wearer's body loosened the coarse guard hair roots and thinned the pelts, while sweat—a natural fulling agent in felting—and oils penetrated downy and absorbent underhairs.

The French defined the fashion for felt hats or *castors* until the mid–sixteenth century, when the English and others adopted it. Felt hats became an essential part of the male wardrobe throughout Europe for three hundred years. Once European beaver populations were decimated, hatters cast their eyes toward America. As imperial and colonial powers jockeyed for power and economic control, hunters killed millions of beavers. Hats went through many styles, and as fashion changed, so did the trade. A preference for smaller brims in the late seventeenth century, together with an influx of low-grade dry (*sec*) and summer pelts damaged the trade. In the 1840s, consumers accepted silk as a substitute for beaver felt in their hats, and the market for beavers shifted to fur coats and fancy furs, where they vied with martens and minks. From that time on, beaver trapping was never again as intense, yet merchants shipped millions of beaver pelts to London in the second half of the nineteenth century.[3]

As it moved inland, the beaver trade repeatedly obliterated beaver populations. A number of scholars proposed that hunters devastated fur bearers and other resources in most places where the fur trade was carried on more or less permanently. Ultimately, this may have been the case but it did not happen in the same way everywhere. As Toby Morantz, an anthropologist, and others suggested, the trade was complicated by local circumstances; by migration, warfare, disease, middlemen, trespassers, and poachers; as well as by culturally determined and historically contingent attitudes toward animals, exchange, and accumulation.[4]

Thus there were many beaver trades, not one; and the narrative of the trade must account for both local variations and regional or continental patterns. Each region had its own history. In New England, for example (where beavers were not overly numerous to start with), the acquisitiveness was strong on both sides—for beaver pelts and for manufactured goods— and hunters all but exterminated beavers (and other animals) by the end of the seventeenth century.[5]

Beavers were scarce in the greater Northeast by this date. The Huron and Iroquois pressured these animals intensely; Gabriel Sagard, a Récollet missionary, was prophetic when he wrote after a visit to the country of the Huron in the 1620s that "I cannot think but that the end is in sight." By the mid-1630s beavers were almost gone in southern Ontario, and the Huron spent even more time as traders.[6] Over the next four decades, the five tribes that formed the Iroquois Confederacy killed most beavers nearby, "absolutely exhaust[ing]" their lands, and in trapping parties of hundreds of men, trespassed aggressively and successfully on the territories of their neighbors. As in the South, politics and warfare often affected both animals and the trade. In general, when hostilities raged, hunters left beavers alone and when peace reigned, they made war on beavers.[7]

Farther west the beaver trade took on a different narrative, as competing interests made some Indians desultory trappers, and religious reasons (perhaps stemming from the importance of medicines relating to beaver in prosecuting buffalo hunts) precluded trapping for others. This left the field open to the few foreigners daring enough to trespass and poach, and into the breach stepped trappers of European extraction, so-called "mountain men" who killed formidable quantities in the Rocky Mountains and elsewhere in the West, as well as Iroquois, hired by fur trade companies or on their own and the most renowned Indians for roaming far afield for beavers.[8] They and many others used steel traps baited with castoreum, the powerful attractant from the glands of the beaver. Algonquian Indians had used castoreum since at least the seventeenth century, and merchants distributed steel traps widely after the mid-eighteenth century; in the nineteenth century, as mass production put millions of traps into circulation, both were commonplace. Lethal in combination, they hastened the decimation of beavers: Nineteenth-century trapping records of mountain men show tallies of 250 beavers in a season, and even 150 in a day.[9]

By the late nineteenth century, the beaver harvest was 10 percent of its level one century before, and beavers were scarce or locally extinct in North America. They disappeared from New Jersey by 1820 and New Hampshire by 1865. By 1890, they were rare or absent in Pennsylvania, Wisconsin, Minnesota, most of New York, many parts of Quebec and Ontario, and elsewhere.

Concerned legislators passed laws designed to halt the destruction of beavers as they had with deer. Men and women active in the conservation movement that formed in the last three decades of the nineteenth century were appalled by the eradication of buffaloes, passenger pigeons, and other wildlife including beavers. New conservationists spoke of a "mad rush at the counter for fur and pseudo-fur" and the fashion for fur as a "craze." In the twentieth century, conservation sentiments and regulations had taken stronger hold and for beavers, the tide turned. Many understood with Roderick MacFarlane, long employed by the HBC, that "if let alone, or not much disturbed by hunting, the beaver will rapidly increase in numbers." In the first two decades of the twentieth century, restocking programs were instituted widely in the United States and Canada. Together with stringent laws restricting trapping, the programs succeeded—to the extent that within just a few years in the Adirondacks, where beavers had been extinct, New York's Conservation Commission called them "interesting but destructive," responsible for flooding highways and railroads. This success brought renewed trapping during fur booms in the 1920s and 1940s. Soon most states again allowed beaver trapping and the annual harvest in North America climbed to hundreds of thousands of pelts.[10]

Like white-tailed deer, beavers survived to recover much of their former range. Deer regained their place as a result of restricted seasons, lowered hunting pressures, and greatly expanded edge habitats between grain fields and new forests. Beavers recovered as a consequence of trapping restrictions, restocking, changes in fashion, and conservation.

In the 1990s, antifur lobbies and changing fashions have cast trapping as a pariah profession, leaving beaver populations unchecked. Anthropomorphized, beavers are loved in the abstract—until like deer their unbridled populations explode into suburban cultural landscapes as pests, attracting headlines like "Busy Beavers Gnaw on Suburban Nerves" and "Besieged by Beavers in Rural New York." As the millennium approaches, these "annoying overachievers" once again busily and eagerly are altering every conceivable habitat in North America.[11]

In Canada, the fur trade figures significantly in national identity and national history, and *Castor canadensis* has often been proposed for the nation's coat of arms. The trade was paramount in the eastern half of Canada. This is a vast region, containing hundreds of thousands of square miles of prime beaver habitat in lakes, ponds, and rivers in boreal and deciduous forests. Complex culturally, this region has been home for centuries to tens of thousands of people speaking Iroquoian and Northern Algonquian languages. Our interest here is in the latter, whom linguists classify as speakers of Ojibwa (in the south and west) and Cree and Montagnais (in the north). Through time these Northern Algonquians have used different names for themselves. Their group or band names came originally from natural features or territories. Then outsiders gave them names associated with trading posts, regions, or labels applied by their neighbors. With naming so clearly linked to identity and power, some today prefer the names with origins in traditional self-designations—for example, Innu ("human being"), not Montagnais (applied by seventeenth-century French to the people living in the mountains north of the St. Lawrence River); or Anishinaabe ("Indian, human being, ordinary man") rather than Ojibwa/Chippewa ("puckered up"—from the toe of a moccasin), which white people generalized widely beyond one specific group using the label for themselves.

The Montagnais and Cree speakers include the Montagnais/Innu, Naskapi, Attikamek, and various Cree groups; their lands extend from the Labrador Sea and Gulf of St. Lawrence to central Alberta over two thousand miles west. To their south, Ojibwa speakers have a history of expansion, often at the expense of the Cree. Pushed by their neighbors the Iroquois, who threatened or initiated trade-related wars, and pulled by lands ripe for exploitation and middleman trade, Ojibwa speakers spread north and south of Lake Superior in the late seventeenth century from north of Lake Huron and Superior's east end, and Michigan's Upper Peninsula. By 1800 Ojibwa speakers occupied lands across Ontario and Manitoba and in northern Michigan, Wisconsin, and Minnesota; in these places they were known as the Algonquin, Nipissing, Ottawa, Saulteaux, Ojibwa, and Chippewa.[12]

Before Europeans appeared, Northern Algonquians found beavers a vital source of food and clothing, and also used their prominent orange-enameled incisors as cutting, gouging, and sharpening tools, and their scapulas (stripped of their flesh) as instruments of divination. After the arrival of Europeans, beavers continued to be valuable in the domestic economy but they also obviously became commodities in the European marketplace, which altered through time their use in domestic contexts. Not surprisingly, against animals so important, Northern Algonquians have marshaled an impressive and changing battery of weapons including traps, deadfalls, snares, nets, clubs, spears, bows and arrows, axes, ice chisels, and guns.

They also have controlled the hunting of beavers (and other animals) in defined areas known as family hunting territories. The territory is a bounded piece of land, and the "family" in question is a group of people united by kinship, marriage, and other ties of social solidarity and led by someone in whom authority and management rights are vested. Both territory and authority descend from one generation to the next—often, but not always, from a man to his son. The family is especially likely to use the territory (and to exercise control over or manage renewable and nonrenewable, and sedentary and mobile, resources) from late fall through spring.

There is considerable variation in an institution so widespread—variation in the size, ecology, and resources of a territory, in the size and composition of the family, in the definition of trespass and sanctioning of intruders, in the nature of "ownership" or management, in which resources are reserved to the family and which are not, and in what happens to the territory from one generation to the next. Despite differences, many Northern Algonquians distinguish the use of mobile animals important for subsistence from sedentary animals significant as commodities. Anyone can kill the former (caribou, for example) without consequence, especially when needy; but the latter (beavers, for example) are usually reserved for the territory's managing partners—unless a person is starving, in which case he can kill a beaver for its lifesaving flesh as long as he delivers the pelt to the rightful owners. Clearly, without territories, management—including efficient hunting or conservation—of sedentary animals is difficult, and with territories, management is possible; the animal most often managed is the beaver.

One question is whether territories resulted from the fur trade or were aboriginal. They do seem to have become increasingly prominent through time. Debate has raged for eighty years. Almost always cast as a choice between alternatives, the prevailing argument was initially that the territories were ancient. Then scholars identified the fur trade as the cause. This disagreement entered general debates in sociological and historical theory, because Marxist theorists denied that precapitalist hunting and gathering people could have private property, and if these Northern Algonquians did, through their family hunting territories, then where did that leave the general theory?

Today, that row seems esoteric, and most will agree that an institution so widespread and varying surely had multiple beginnings under specific historical and ecological circumstances.[13]

Although the decline of beavers in eastern and central Canada was widespread, we cannot assume that it is explained in the same way everywhere. Not all Northern Algonquians were equally enthusiastic participants in the trade, especially when it conflicted with traditional subsistence activities. Here, a series of single snapshots or frames of specific people, times, and places, each depending entirely on the existence of adequate historical evidence, will provide a range of opportunities to understand the history, culture, and behavior in specific locales as we seek answers to the question, Did Indians possess conservation ideals and family hunting territories prior to the onset of the trade only to abandon them in the face of a seductive array of novel goods, or did they develop both as a result of outside influences?

The first snapshot is of the Montagnais in the 1630s. These people had probably been drawn into the transatlantic trade in the preceding century when European mariners put to shore to dry and process fish, but the near absence of documentation leaves the period hazy. In the seventeenth century, record-keeping Jesuit proselytizers arrived in New France and set down the first comments about the exchange and its impact on beavers. Like Europeans, these Montagnais seem to have relished the trade, one "jokingly" telling Father Paul Le Jeune, head of the Jesuit mission in Quebec, one day that "the Beaver does everything perfectly well, it makes kettles, hatchets, swords, knives, bread; in short, it makes everything."[14]

There was more than banter in these remarks. Montagnais and many other native people were indeed fond of items like copper kettles, clothing, metal tools, guns, and many other goods that rapidly took the place of bark containers, stone tools, and a host of traditional artifacts. They eagerly exchanged beavers for these objects, which may have had a rapid impact on beaver populations, for there is evidence for an immediate decline. By 1635, for instance, beavers were very scarce near Three Rivers and elsewhere along the St. Lawrence, evidently because of overtrapping.[15] The year before, Le Jeune spent the winter with a Montagnais band. He alluded vaguely to this group's "boundaries" and spoke of Indians who came "to hunt upon our very grounds, taking away our game and our lives at the same time" during a time of extreme hardship. This band (and others later in the century), it seems, lived in lands that band members considered theirs to exploit and perhaps manage. But when Le Jeune remarked that one goal of his mission was to settle Montagnais near Three Rivers so that they would hunt in specific territories—or cultivate the soil—he gave the impression that the families possessed no such territories.[16]

Le Jeune's remarks relating to conservation were emphatically negative. When the Montagnais he knew found a beaver lodge, they "kill all, great and small, male and female." Le Jeune prophesied that they "will finally exterminate the species in this Region, as has happened among the Hurons, who have not a single Beaver." The nearby Mi'kmaq, similarly intent on trade, also possessed a "disposition," according to Nicolas Denys, a trader and governor of Acadia in the years following 1635, to "take all" beavers, in a lodge,

and "not to spare the little ones any more than the big ones." Involved in an exchange with Europeans for several generations, they treated all animals the same, killing "all of each kind" they captured; before Europeans arrived, Denys speculated, they took meat they needed and left skins on the ground.[17]

To prevent these Montagnais from following the example of the Huron, Le Jeune proposed "locating" specific families so that each would take "its own territory for hunting, without following in the tracks of its neighbors." He also thought of "counseling" them "not to kill any but the males and of those only such as are large." This way, Le Jeune thought, "they will have Beaver meat and skins in the greatest abundance." This not only represents one of the earliest recorded European designs to promote conservation and family-managed hunting territories in North America but implies that both were novel ideas.[18]

The second frame is of the seventeenth- and eighteenth-century Cree who lived on the East Main—a large area east and southeast of James Bay. The Cree in this region were initially associated with specific bands identified with inland or coastal regions, rivers, or individual leaders. They later drew a group identity from trading posts and their regional geographical location on the East Main or east of James Bay.

While the East Main Cree took part in the fur trade in the seventeenth century, little is known of the central issues of conservation and control over beaver populations prior to the eighteenth. The evidence is simply too thin. It does seem, however, that in the southern parts of the region in south-central Quebec, the Cree used beavers extensively for food and clothing and pursued them with bows, arrows, deadfalls, and nets, and by breaking into lodges or burrows located with the help of dogs, and that native people in the northern parts of this region considered caribou more important than beaver for food and clothing. The Cree who traded at Rupert House in the southernmost part of James Bay evidently possessed hunting territories in the 1670s: Each spring they were said to decide how to adjust the boundaries of hunting grounds and allocate them to "families" in the coming year. Even though this is a secondhand account written forty years after the fact, it does open the possibility that men negotiated hunting territories anew each year, with the entire band in mind.[19]

As for what form that management took, we are in the dark except for an enigmatic note from the 1650s to 1660s, in which Pierre Esprit Radisson remarked that some Crees who came south to the Great Lakes to trade were unlike other Indians in not killing young beavers. We know neither who these Crees were nor whether they left young beavers so that they might mature and reproduce the colony or acquire larger, more valuable prime winter pelts.[20]

From Eastmain, a HBC post on the southeast coast of James Bay, where beaver was by far the most valuable fur exchanged in the eighteenth century, comes evidence of lands hunted out. Probably as a result of French competition and Iroquois and other poachers, the number of pelts traded at this post declined sharply in the 1730s (and again in the 1760s). By 1730, lands in the southern parts of this region were "Drained of animals" and "ruined." One Jesuit wrote that beaver populations might rebound only if lands were abandoned, but that "would be asking The Impossible from the savages. They would travel ten leagues to kill a beaver a year old, summer or winter, if they could find it." In the following decades, trespass and poaching by outside Indians and the East Main Cree themselves continued to be an issue. In 1745, one East Main Cree reported restrictions on killing fur bearers "in one anothers Leiberty." Another Cree on whose lands he was hunting told him that he could kill and keep rabbits or caribou but not martens—thus distinguishing animals consumed from those destined for exchange (which is a sign of commodification) and signaling the existence of hunting territories (evidently also possessed by the Cree who traded at Fort Albany to the west), for which evidence becomes more marked in the second half of the eighteenth century.[21] Were hunting territories born in events like these? Did trespassers from outside the band or tribe initially cause resentment when they stripped the lands of resources newly transformed into commodities; and embittered, did people subsequently clamor for hunting territories over which they could exercise control when members of their own band emulated the outsiders?

For the next snapshot we move west to York Factory, the HBC post on the southwest side of Hudson Bay, in the period 1738–75.[22] Competition for the Cree trade was keen throughout the eighteenth century. Before 1763, the value of beaver, expressed as a percent of the total return, declined steadily and at times sharply at York Factory. The decline was due in part to gift giving and French competition but also to faunal cycles, disease, and a static demand for trade goods.

These Crees had a fairly inelastic need for goods. For each hunter each year the demand amounted to a gun (if the hunter's gun was broken beyond repair) plus powder and shot, a powder horn, two hatchets, an ice chisel, four knives, a fishing net, a file, six awls, one brass kettle, four yards of cloth, and over seven pounds of tobacco. To purchase these goods, a hunter required seventy beaver pelts or the equivalent in other furs. Andrew Graham, resident at York Factory for two decades in the second half of the eighteenth century, commented that a standard of trade adjusted "in favour of the natives, would ruin it all; for I am certain if the natives were to get any more for their furs, they would catch fewer." Graham thought this was because "one canoe brings down yearly to the Fort one hundred made beaver in different kinds of furs, and trades with me seventy of the said beaver for real necessaries. The other thirty beaver shall so puzzle him to trade, that he often asks me what he shall buy, and when I make an answer, Trade some more powder, shot, tobacco and hatchets etc., his answer is, I have traded sufficient to serve me and my family until I see you next summer; so he will drink one half, and trade the other with me for baubles."

The trade in brandy, as well as in other goods requiring measures that the traders might leave "short," resulted in tidy profits for the traders. But even when traders signaled a greater demand for furs in the prices (in goods) they were willing to pay, Indians did not respond by increasing the supply. Instead they brought the same number or sometimes less (producing what is known as a backward-sloping supply curve, contradicting the idea that "economic man" invariably responds "rationally" to heightened demand with a greater supply). Working against an increased supply were the limited capacity of canoes and human bodies, a mobile life, a greater interest in being generous by giving away than in accumulation for its own sake, and lavish gift giving on the part of European traders to offset temptation to trade with their competitors.[23]

According to Graham and his predecessor James Isham, the York Factory Cree hunted beavers during all seasons, and Isham thought it "a Little strange" that the animals did not "Diminish greatly considering the many thousands that is Killd. of a Year." Like the East Main Cree, the York Factory Cree distinguished the domestic from the commodity value of beavers. In Isham's words, "When Severall Indians is together, they have sett Rules to the Right of the Beaver skin, which is;—if one finds a beaver house, all the Rest goes with and assists him to Kill them, he that found the house having all the skins, and the flesh Equaly Divided, otherwise some wou'd gett all and other's none."

On measures designed to conserve beavers, neither trader is very helpful despite their combined five decades of residence. Isham remarked equivocally that "in some houses an Indian will Kill 15 or 20 beaver, and in other's not above 2 or 3"—surely inconclusive on whether beavers were deliberately left alive in a lodge. On the one hunt he witnessed, Graham reported that the Cree killed all the beavers they found in a lodge, which amounted to two. Following a single winter in residence at York Factory, T. F. Drage said in contrast that when the Cree "take a house" of beavers, "they generally leave two to breed." His comment is intriguing and perhaps linked to Radisson's report a century earlier on the Cree leaving young beavers to mature, perhaps to control multiple "harvests" of beavers from the same lodge. Yet in 1700, the soldier and author Bacqueville de la Potherie remarked that Indians who traded at Fort Nelson/York Factory marked beaver lodges, claiming the pelts within for themselves, but then went about their business destroying beaver lodges and dams and netting or killing beavers with spears and arrows seemingly without regard for the morrow.

In contrast to sedentary beavers, the hunting of which could be controlled in theory, caribou migrated rapidly through territories and across major rivers. Their numbers, as well as the carnage and waste hunting them, astounded the traders at York Factory. Isham remarked that the Cree "frequently" killed "scores" of caribou, taking "only the tongues or heads" and letting "the body or carcass go a Drift with the tide." Over a three-week period, they "Kill'd upwards of 1,000 Deer [caribou] by the Quantity of tongues I have Rec'd from them." Drage linked the assault on pregnant cows in spring for their tongues to a recent decline in numbers of caribou and

remarked that HBC traders "reproved" some Crees who "uselessly destroy'd" these caribou.

The great destruction and waste struck Graham also. He used almost identical language as Isham had in talking about the hunt for migrating caribou in May and September: The Cree killed "several score" at once and took only "the tongues, heads, hearts and feet, according as they choose; letting the carcasses go adrift in the river." Graham branded the coastal-dwelling Cree as indolent gourmands, yet argued that behavior "unaccountable to Englishmen" made sense to people who were mobile and carried their belongings. They killed the animals for their own use, and for tongues, fat, and other choice products to exchange for brandy and other trade goods. They then set the carcasses adrift. They killed more than they needed, and more than they used. Graham thought that they believed they could not kill too many. "They kill animals out of wantonness," he said, "alleging the more they destroy the more plentiful they grow."[24]

Graham's observations were largely for the years 1753–74. The period between roughly 1750 and 1830 was a watershed era for the development of conservation and family hunting territories. Before, their traces were fleeting, local, or absent. After, the evidence for both was widespread. There were two important reasons for the change: the great decline in the numbers of beavers and other mammals, and the active promotion of conservation and territories by the HBC.

During this eighty-year era, the assault on beavers was continuous and the decline in beaver populations ubiquitous. Competition for furs was stiff throughout the eighteenth century. The French and English vied with each other on Hudson Bay and inland, with especially keen competition in the two decades before mid-century. In 1763, the English emerged victorious but in the Northern Algonquian trade, free market conditions ruled widely. Trading companies, with the HBC and North West Company as the main antagonists from the 1780s onward, and the XY and other short-lived companies in supporting roles, intensified the struggle for pelts. They waged bitter contests for fur in the final decades of the eighteenth century, and after the end of the first decade of the nineteenth, traders voiced sharp complaints about the "great scarcity of Beaver" everywhere east of the Rocky Mountains. Beavers were decimated in most productive boreal forest, deciduous forest, parkland, and river-bottom tall grass prairie habitats. Few remained in southwestern Ontario, southern and central Manitoba, or central Saskatchewan; these and other regions were "nearly exhausted in Fur bearing Animals," and to find beavers Indians had to go farther afield every year. There is no doubt that persistent and aggressive trapping, fueled by competition and an influx of new trappers who were mainly Indian but also of European descent, were principally responsible for the decline. Abetting them were drought, lodge-destroying fires, mismanagement, and—twice—disease, which one time left beavers "red and bloody about the heart" and caused great mortality.

In the last decade of this period, traders urged that conservation measures and a territorial system be developed in order to curb the carnage of beavers. The pivotal moment occurred in 1821 with the merger of the HBC and North West Company, which marked the end, for the time being, of fierce competition in lands that drained into Hudson Bay. With George Simpson at the helm of the newly amalgamated firm, the victorious HBC faced lands over which it asserted monopoly control but which with rare exception were depleted of furs. Beginning with Simpson, few doubted that action was needed if beaver were ever again to be traded. Determined to reverse the course, he called upon traders to conserve the severely depleted populations. His twin priorities were to "nurse the country," that is, not to hunt it and allow beavers and other depleted fur-bearing animals to "recruit" or recover; and to encourage native people to develop hunting territories in which they could conserve beavers. "Nursing" included halting the trade in pelts from young and summer-killed beavers, whose pelts were small or inferior in quality; dissuading the use of steel traps, "the scourge of the Country"; and installing a quota system in districts where animals were especially depleted. The policy was reiterated in formal resolutions at HBC council meetings in the 1820s to 1830s. Hunting territories were also seen as part of the solution. By "alloting certain tracts of the country to the different bands," Simpson thought it possible to control hunting and allow animal populations to recover.

The results were admittedly uneven. Simpson did report later that the attempt "to confine the natives throughout the country now by families to separate and distinct hunting grounds" seemed "to take among them by degrees." But, skeptical of the reach of his authority, he also confessed that "it is a difficult matter to change the habits of Indians" even when they "may see the ultimate benefit" of action. Two problems linked to subsistence intervened: Some Indians depended on beaver flesh and others had to search widely for food of any kind. Given this, Simpson realized that it was not entirely practical to expect all people to confine themselves to certain localities or to refrain from killing summer or small beavers. Success in curtailing the summer hunt was sometimes impermanent. "By entreaties and threats," Simpson reported that he succeeded in curbing some destructive summer hunts of roaming Indians but that in the winter they returned to kill beavers in lodges they discovered the previous summer. Even if one could persuade hunters to leave beavers to breed or mature, an adverse season would undo that success. But the results were not entirely bleak. In some instances, where muskrats were an acceptable substitute for trade and subsistence, beavers recovered, and when trading posts closed, all fur-bearer populations rebounded.

Despite its monopoly, the HBC did not conduct the trade in identical fashion everywhere, nor was its control absolute. Traders varied in their willingness to enforce policies. They could not prevent Indians from dealing with competing American and Métis traders on the border with the United States, nor could they control the inroads of "free traders" not in their employ, who filtered north as the nineteenth century wore on. Neither native people nor traders seemed able to develop a renewable harvest of beavers, and the decline in these animals continued until the 1840s, when the HBC introduced more stringent measures against trapping, as well as premium prices for other furs. In combination, they relieved pressure on the beaver populations, which rebounded. Then almost immediately silk hats replaced felt hats, and the most intense action shifted away from beavers to other furs. Thus, market forces in combination with HBC policies and perhaps other factors led to the eventual recovery of beaver populations.[25]

The next three snapshots in quick succession are of the Cree near Lake Winnipegosis from the 1790s through the 1820s, the Cree on the East Main in the period 1820–50, and the Northern Ojibwa in northern Ontario from the 1790s through the 1840s.

Like some other regions, Lake Winnipegosis was the scene, of fierce and escalating competition involving the HBC and North West and XY companies in the late eighteenth and early nineteenth centuries. David Thompson, the HBC surveyor who was among the Western Woods Cree in the 1790s, spoke generally about the destructive consequences of the era of intense rivalry, and especially of the lethal combination of castoreum (the product of a set of paired glands near the beaver's anus), whose seductive properties had been known to some Algonquian-speaking Indians since the seventeenth century, and steel traps, which became available in the eighteenth. By the late eighteenth century, trappers combined both in the beaver hunt, and here, as elsewhere, beavers disappeared rapidly.

According to Thompson, one old Cree linked the decline to his tribesmen's desire for manufactured goods, to the lack of control over hunting, and to the attitude of a Cree creator. That old man said that for some reason, the "Great Spirit"—probably Kihcimanitōw the benevolent creator—twice became "angry" with beavers. The first time was long ago when beavers lived on land as ancient people and were wise and powerful until Kihcimanitōw ordered Wīsahkēāhk, a trickster-transformer being, to "drive them all into the water and there let them live, still to be wise, but without power; to be food and clothing for man, and the prey of other animals...." The second time, Kihcimanitōw determined that beavers "are now all to be destroyed" and Wīsahkēcāhk subsequently showed the Algonquin and Nipissing the "secret of the destruction"—castoreum—of which beavers were "more fond ... than we are of fire water." The old man concluded, "We are now killing the Beaver without any labor, we are now rich, but [shall] soon be poor, for when the Beaver are destroyed we have nothing to depend on to purchase what we want for our families, strangers now run over our country with their iron traps, and we, and they will soon be poor." Thompson remarked, "For several years all these Indians were rich, the Women and Children, as well as the Men, were covered with silver brooches, Ear Rings, Wampum, Beads and other trinkets. Their mantles were of fine scarlet cloth, and all was finery and dress." But predicated on an endless supply of beaver, this consumption could not last. "Every intelligent man saw the poverty that would follow the destruction of the Beaver, but there were no Chiefs to controul it; all ways perfect liberty and equality. Four years afterwards (1797) almost the whole of these extensive countries were denuded of Beaver, the Natives became poor, and with difficulty procured the first necessaries of life...."[26]

These Crees obligingly hunted beavers. If they possessed territories, they resisted complaining about or taking action against trespass. Others surely trespassed and poached during this period. Outsiders like Mohawk trappers and "Freemen," who were former employees of Canadian fur companies, poured into Cree territory. They and the Cree reaped the benefits of steel and castoreum. One trader complained that Iroquois had "dispersed all over where ever a beaver was known to be which will finish the Destruction of the Country as they leave nothing wherever they come."

After 1821, HBC traders pushed conservation policies at Cumberland House northwest of Lake Winnipegosis. While some Crees did evidently lay off the summer muskrat hunt so that these animals might raise their young, most Crees continued to bring in summer beaver pelts, against HBC policy. When one trader said five years later that he was willing to cut the price for beaver by 50 percent in order to "allow" them "to increase," the Cree responded "very coolly" by stating that "Beaver meat was too good to let Pass when there was any chance of killing it." With great ambiguity, this trader remarked that "Sacrificing" beavers "is the preservation of the Lives of the Indians." Did he mean merely that the flesh was a food on which the Cree depended? Or that the pelts were sacrificed? Or that in sacrifice they somehow assured a continuing supply?[27]

Some distance away from Cumberland House, the Cree who lived on the east side of James Bay and traded at Rupert House had a different history of development of territories and conservation. As Toby Morantz showed, the development of hunting territories among the James Bay Cree could not have originated with George Simpson's policies. These Crees had restricted hunting in one another's areas as far back as the mid—eighteenth century. They possessed loosely organized territories one decade before the amalgamation of the HBC and North West Company, and the Rupert House Cree were said to be "tenacious of their Property in their Lands and are not pleased when other Indians encroach on them" only two years after the HBC monopoly began. For this reason, perhaps, when traders asked them the next year to spare "Cub Beaver," they responded that it was "perfectly accordant with their own Ideas on the subject and their Desires of not impoverishing their Lands."

But because beaver continued to be important for subsistence, it had been necessary to ask. To help the Cree resist the temptation, the traders lowered the tariff on fishing tackle and ammunition—but not uniformly. In the southern parts of the region where competition lingered, the HBC did not discourage the use of steel traps or killing young and summer beavers, but developed a scorched-earth policy to encourage the trade to them, not to their competitors, even if it meant killing all animals.

The potential for conservation in family hunting territories was clear. In "alternate years" in the early 1840s, the Rupert House Cree hunted "different sections of their lands, leaving such to recruit two or even three years"—a rotational practice that would have conserved beavers. If they had not done so, one trader speculated, "Long ago their lands (particularly the Coast Indians whose beaver grounds are so limited) would have been exhausted." The HBC nevertheless felt the need to curtail further the beaver pelt trade in that decade. The Rupert House Cree complained that Indians from other posts trespassed on lands they had deliberately left idle and, to the east, the Mistassini Cree had identical complaints about poachers who killed beavers during the summer and other seasons. That decade the HBC also established beaver preserves on two islands in James Bay to go along with the rules against hunting young or summer animals. When restrictions were lifted, the total value of beavers traded at Rupert House almost doubled within a decade, a visible sign of newly robust populations.[28]

The story of the Northern Ojibwa who moved into northwestern Ontario in the eighteenth century is familiar: Indians unhesitatingly exchanged mundane beaver pelts for rare and useful European technology, competition fueled exchange, and beavers became scarce. At the start, beavers were up to the pressure, by one report "so plentiful" between Lakes Superior and Winnipeg that Indians "place little value on it and only collect the large skins which they send to the English." At first, many Northern Ojibwas threw smaller pelts away and folded the quest for furs into their primary hunt for moose and caribou. But later in the century, the fierce competition between the HBC and North West Company left a lasting impact on beavers, and after the turn of the nineteenth century, the trade deteriorated rapidly. Over the next two decades, traders on both sides reported "impoverished," "barren and poor," or "exhausted" country; scarce, few, or absent beavers; and plummeting profits. At Osnaburgh House, an HBC post, the number of large pelts dropped by 50 percent in one year and by 90 percent in a decade. Caribou also declined greatly and moose disappeared entirely, and starving Indians increasingly turned to fish for subsistence, and rabbits for food and clothing.[29]

Prior to the nineteenth century there was no sign of conservation or territoriality among the Northern Ojibwa of Osnaburgh House-Lac Seul, as Charles Bishop, an anthropologist, showed. In the 1790s, beavers were still so plentiful that Indians continued to throw small pelts away. Then, moose, caribou, and beaver (in the wake of competition) declined in numbers. In these conditions, an indigenous system to control the hunt for beaver was born. Previously, lands were allotted to specific individuals by consensus or group leaders. Now, Ojibwa hunters, more focused on sedentary resources than ever before, started to mark beaver lodges as their own. HBC traders might have influenced this effort to claim lodges and territories because it coincided with developing HBC policy to get the Osnaburgh House-Lac Seul Ojibwa and other Indians to conserve beavers and exert firmer control over where they hunted. In the 1820s traders alerted the Northern Ojibwa to beaver-hunting restrictions, refused cub or summer-killed beaver pelts at some posts, and attempted to outlaw the lethal steel traps.

Lodge marking notwithstanding, trespass loomed as a major impediment to conservation in the 1820s. One trader complained, "One tribe pays no attention to the mark of another." Indians commonly trapped territories considered by other bands as their own; they killed beavers "when they see them." Territoriality was not firmly institutionalized everywhere; "it is very hard if not impossible to prevent the Natives from killing every little animal they see as well as the larger," one trader remarked, "so long as the ground is common among them." The Northern Ojibwa roamed and poached and with familiar results, "[flew] upon everything they can catch even beavers of a span long," and "destroyed all the Furred animals."

The Northern Ojibwa sometimes stepped up their own kill as a management strategy as well as to combat poachers. In the late 1830s one Ojibwa "almost ruined his lands," evidently by overtrapping, but then moved to a different area "to let his Beaver recover." Some eight years later, he was using the same strategy but this time when he returned to a river he had deliberately not hunted for three years in order to let beavers recover, he discovered that "Strange Indians" armed with steel traps had trapped it out. He was determined not to let poachers gain advantage over him again—but the only option he had was to trap out the lands himself.

The Northern Ojibwa adopted territories and conservation haltingly. For two decades, HBC traders pushed the conservation policy but did not enforce it in the same way everywhere. Ignoring traders, some Indians continued to eat beavers and bring summer and cub beaver pelts to posts. If these pelts were refused, they simply traded them to other Indians who in turn took them to less discriminating traders whose regions held more beavers. Trespassers were uninterested in conservation, and Indians who pre-emptively stripped their own lands ahead of poachers apparently could not afford to be interested themselves. In the 1830s, the evidence for family hunting territories becomes clearer and finally abundant, and by mid-century, complaints against trespass declined, perhaps signaling a general acceptance of territorial boundaries and rights. In the ensuing decades, family hunting territories with sanctions against trespass were common among the Osnaburgh House Ojibwa.[30]

From having been rare in the teens, beavers recovered in the 1830s, and for the rest of the century, their populations fluctuated from scarcity (1840s) to abundance (1870s to 1880s) to scarcity again (1890s), a pattern produced mainly by alternating conservation and overtrapping and by the mid-1840s substitution of silk in the manufacturing of hats. In the final decade of the century, Indians once again "exterminated" beavers; "annually driven further back by the encroachment of hunters from other places," they evidently "no longer spare a few animals for breeding, even on their own lands, as has hitherto been their custom." The trader who reported this was right: Beavers were again being hunted out. But if by "hitherto" he meant at some primordial

pre-European time, he produced no evidence (and we have none); the origins of that custom, an artifact of historical circumstances that began some seventy years before, were already obscure.[31]

Thus far we have six frames of Northern Algonquians from the seventeenth through nineteenth centuries. In the first three—the Montagnais in the 1630s, the East Main Cree in the period from 1650 to 1745, and the York Factory Cree from 1738 to 1775—the concept of conservation seems to have been largely absent; most Indians—but not all—had no interest whatsoever in it. These Indians killed as many beavers as they needed to satisfy their desire for trade goods and domestic consumption. And while some staked claims to beaver lodges or hunting territories, others evidently did not honor those rights. Perhaps family hunting territories emerged where people wished to repel trespassers and manage their own beaver lodges to produce renewable commodities; perhaps outsiders like Le Jeune had some sway over conservation attitudes; perhaps Northern Algonquians felt toward beavers, as the York Factory Cree did toward caribou, that "the more they destroy the more plentiful they grow."

The last three frames—the Cree near Lake Winnipegosis in the 1790s to 1820s, the Cree on the East Main in the 1820s to 1840s, and the Northern Ojibwa in northern Ontario in the 1790s to 1840s—took place during a period of intense fur-trade company competition followed by monopoly; of dedicated trapping and consumerism; of steady destructive pressure on the beaver populations; and of stated interest on the part of traders in the conservation of beavers and territorial behavior. The Cumberland House Cree, needing beavers for food, paid no attention to the calls for conservation. The Rupert House Cree, in contrast, appear to have had a tradition of both conservation and hunting territories. And while some Northern Ojibwas developed both conservation and territorial systems at the same time as, and seemingly in response to, new HBC regulations, others lived by trespassing and poaching.

Conservation and territoriality in this vast region clearly were affected by local variations in ecological, demographic, social, cultural, and historical circumstances.[32] As among Ojibwa speakers[33] and other Algonquian speakers[34] farther south, population pressure, fur-trade company competition, game depletions, and fur traders concerned that destroyed commodities would erode their profits hastened the moment that conservation and territoriality became concrete for the nineteenth-century Northern Ojibwa, and perhaps for the eighteenth-century East Main Cree and others.

Notes

1. Lewis Henry Morgan, *The American Beaver: A Classic of Natural History and Ecology* (New York: Dover Publications, 1986 [orig.1868]); John Richardson. "Castor fiber, Americanus. The American Beaver," in *Fauna Boreali-Americana; or the Zoology of the Northern Parts of British America. Part First Containing The Quadrupeds* (New York: Arno Press, 1974 [orig. 1829–1837]), 105–13; John James Audubon and John Bachman, "American Beaver," in *The Quadrupeds of North America*, Volume 1 (New York: Arno Press, 1974 [orig. 1846]), 347–59; J. A. Allen, *Monographs of North American Rodentia. No. VI. Castoridae*, by Elliott Coues and Joel Asaph Allen, Department of the Interior, U.S. Geological Survey of the Territories, Report 11, No. 6 (1877), 427–54; Horace T. Martin, *Castorologia or the History and Traditions of the Canadian Beaver* (Montreal: William Drysdale and Company, 1892); Ernest Thompson Seton, "Canadian Beaver," in *Life-histories of Northern Animals: An Account of the Mammals of Manitoba*, Volume 1 (New York: Charles Scribner's Sons, 1909), 447–79; Edward Royal Warren, *The Beaver: Its Work and Its Ways* (Baltimore: The Williams & Wilkins Company, 1927), 20–21 and passim; Leonard Lee Rue III, *The World of the Beaver* (Philadelphia: J. B. Lippincott Co., 1964); A. W. F. Banfield, "Beavers," in *The Mammals of Canada* (Toronto: University of Toronto Press, 1974), 157–62; Edward P. Hill, "Beaver," in *Wild Mammals of North America: Biology, Management, and Economics*, ed. Joseph A. Chapman and George A. Feldhamer (Baltimore: Johns Hopkins University Press, 1982), 256–81; Milan Novak, "Beaver," in *Wild Furbearer Management and Conservation in North America*, ed. Milan Novak et al. (Ontario: Ministry of Natural Resources, 1987), 282–312.

2. Reuben Gold Thwaites, ed., *The Jesuit Relations and Allied Documents: Travels and Explorations of the Jesuit Missionaries in New France 1610–1791* (Cleveland: Burrows Brothers, 1897), Volume 6, 297, 299 ("the English …"); Jean Elizabeth Murray, *The Fur Trade in New France and New Netherland prior to 1645*, Ph.D. dissertation (University of Chicago, 1936), 1–23 and passim; Eleanor Leacock, "The Montagnais 'Hunting Territory' and the' Fur Trade," *Memoirs of the American Anthropological Association* No. 78 (Menasha, WI, 1954), 1–59, pp. 10–12 (Champlain); Dean R. Snow, "Abenaki Fur Trade in the Sixteenth Century," *Western Canadian Journal of Anthropology* 6, No. 1 (1976): 3–11; Herbert C. Kraft, "Sixteenth and Seventeenth Century Indian/White Trade Relations in the Middle Atlantic and Northeast Regions," *Archaeology of Northeastern North America* 17 (1989): 1–29; Arthur J. Ray and Donald Freeman, *'Give Us Good Measure': An Economic Analysis of Relations between the Indians and the Hudson's Bay Company before 1763* (Toronto: University of Toronto Press, 1978), 19ff.

3. Martin, *Castorologia*, passim; Warren, *The Beaver*, 19; Rue, *The World of the Beaver*, 135; Novak, "Beaver"; Harold A. Innis, *The Fur Trade in Canada: An Introduction to Canadian Economic History*, revised edition (Toronto: University of Toronto Press, 1970), 386–96 and passim; Murray G. Lawson, *Fur: A Study in English Mercantilism, 1700–1775* (Toronto: University of Toronto Press, 1943); Murray G. Lawson, "The Beaver Hat and the North American Fur Trade," in *People and Pelts*, Selected Papers of the Second North American Fur Trade Conference, ed. Malvina Bolus (Winnipeg: Peguis Publishers, 1972), 27–37.

4. For example, Harold Hickerson, "Fur Trade Colonialism and the North American Indians," *Journal of Ethnic Studies* 1 (1973): 15–44, p. 24. Toby Morantz was an early proponent of the idea that there was not one but many trades. See Toby Morantz, "The Fur Trade and the Cree of James Bay," in *Old Trails and New Directions: Papers of the Third North American Fur Trade Conference*, ed. Carol M. Judd and Arthur J. Ray (Toronto: University of Toronto Press, 1980), 39–58; Shepard Krech III, ed., *The Subarctic Fur Trade: Native Social and Economic Adaptations* (Vancouver: University of British Columbia Press, 1984); Jacqueline Peterson and John Afinson, "The Indian and the Fur Trade: A Review of Recent Literature," *Manitoba History* 10 (1988): 10–18; Ray and Freeman, *'Give Us Good Measure'* 20.

5. William I. Roberts III, *The Fur Trade of New England in the Seventeenth Century*, Ph.D. dissertation (University of Pennsylvania, 1958); Peter A.

Thomas, "The Fur Trade, Indian Land and the Need to Define Adequate 'Environmental' Parameters," *Ethnohistory* 28 (Fall 1981): 359–79; Neal Salisbury, *Manitou and Providence: Indians, Europeans, and the Making of New England, 1500–1643* (New York: Oxford University Press, 1982).

6. Bruce G. Trigger, "Ontario Native People and the Epidemics of 1634–1640," in *Indians, Animals, and the Fur Trade: A Critique of "Keepers of the Game,"* ed. Shepard Krech III (Athens: University of Georgia Press, 1981), 19–38; Bruce G. Trigger, "The Road to Affluence: A Reassessment of Early Huron Responses to European Contact," in *Out of the Background: Readings on Canadian Native History*, ed. Robin Fisher and Kenneth Coates (Toronto: Copp Clark Pitman Ltd., 1988), 88–101; Conrad Heidenreich, *Huronia: A History and Geography of the Huron. Indians 1600–1650* (Toronto: Historical Sites Branch, Ontario Ministry of Natural Resources, McClelland and Stewart Ltd., 1971), 207–8; Conrad E. Heidenreich and Arthur J. Ray, *The Early Fur Trades: A Study in Cultural Interaction*, ed. John Wolforth and R. Cole Harris (Toronto; McClelland and Stewart Ltd., 1976), 27–28 (Sagard), 63–65; Murray; *The Fur Trade in New France and New Netherland*, 103–12, 184–85; Paul Chrisler Phillips, *The Fur Trade*, Volume 1 (Norman: University of Oklahoma Press, 1961);

7. Long before 1670, the Iroquois were said to have "absolutely exhausted" the south side of Lake Ontario, and as a consequence roamed north and west to fight the Illinois and Miami who had poached on Iroquois lands. In light of the Iroquois' role in the eradication of beavers in their own lands, their report to Baron de Lahontan that "contrary to the custom of all the Savages" the Illinois and Miami "have carried off whole Stocks, both Male and Female" seems self-serving. Allen W. Trelease, "The Iroquois and the Western Fur Trade: A Problem in Interpretation," *Mississippi Valley Historical Review* 49 (June 1992): 32–51, p. 43; Thwaites, *The Jesuit Relations*, Volume 40, 211–15; Innis, *The Fur Trade in Canada*, 21, 36–37, 51 ("absolutely exhausted"), 54–55; Bruce Alden Cox, "Indian Middlemen and the Early Fur Trade: Reconsidering the Position of the Hudson's Bay Company's "Trading Indians,'" in *Rendezvous, Selected Papers of the Fourth North American Fur Trade Conference, 1981,* ed. Thomas C. Buckley (St. Paul: North American Fur Trade Conference, 1984), 93–99; George T. Hunt, *The Wars of the Iroquois: A Study in Intertribal Trade Relations* (Madison: University of Wisconsin Press, 1968); Thomas Elliot Norton, *The Fur Trade in-Colonial New York 1686–1776* (Madison: University of Wisconsin Press, 1974).

8. Peter Fidler, a Hudson's Bay Company surveyor and trader, said that the Piegan were "so full of superstition" in the 1790s that they would not bring dead beavers inside their tipis, or touch or eat them. Perhaps the aversion was linked to the significance of beavers, at least among the closely related Blackfeet, in sacred ceremonies, medicine bundles, and ritual conducive to success hunting buffaloes. Peter Fidler, "Journal of a Journey over Land from Buckingham House to the Rocky Mountains in 1792 & 3." Accession No. 79.269/89. Provincial Archives of Alberta, Edmonton, Alberta, 11. For the Plains and Upper Midwest, see Annie Heloise Abel, ed., *Tabeau's Narrative of Loisel's Expedition to the Upper Missouri* (Norman University of Oklahoma Press, 1939), 83–88; Oscar Lewis, *The Effects of White Contact upon Blackfoot Culture with Special Reference to the Role of the Fur Trade*, Monographs of the American Ethnological Society, Volume 6 (Seattle: University of Washington Press, 1942); Joseph Jablow, *The Cheyenne in Plains Indian Trade Relations 1795–1840*, Monographs of the American Ethnological Society, Volume 19 (Seattle: University of Washington Press, 1950); John E. Sunder, *The Fur Trade on the Upper Missouri, 1840–1865* (Norman: University of Oklahoma Press, 1965); James L. Clayton, "The Growth and Economic Significance of the American Fur Trade, 1790–1890," in *Aspects of the Fur Trade*, Selected Papers of the 1965 North American Fur Trade Conference (St. Paul: Minnesota Historical Society, 1967), 62–72; Josiah Gregg, *Commerce of the Prairies*, ed. Max L. Moorhead (Norman: University of Oklahoma Press, 1974); Jeanne Kay, "Wisconsin Indian Hunting Patterns, 1634–1836," *Annals of the Association of American Geographers* 69, No. 3 (1979): 402–18; Robert A. Trennert, Jr., *Indian Traders on the Middle Border: The House of Ewing, 1827–54* (Lincoln: University of Nebraska Press, 1981); Jeanne Kay, "Native Americans in the Fur Trade and Wildlife Depletion," *Environmental Review* 9 (1985): 118–30; Fred R Gowans, *Rocky Mountain Rendezvous: A History of the Fur Trade*

Rendezvous, 1825–1840 (Layton, UT: Gibhs M. Smith, Inc., 1985); Hiram Martin Chittenden, *The American Fur Trade of the Far West*, Volumes 1–2 (Lincoln: University of Nebraska Press, 1986); David J. Wishart, *Fur Trade of the American West 1807–1840"* (Lincoln; University of Nebraska Press, 1992); R. Grace Morgan, *Beaver Ecology/Beaver Mythology*, Ph.D. thesis (Department of Anthropology, University of Alberta, 1991), 1–13, 45–47, 102–4, 172–90, and passim; Robert Glass Cleland, *This Reckless Breed of Men: The Trappers and Fur Traders of the Southwest* (Lincoln: University of Nebraska Press, 1992); Mary K. Whelan, "Dakota Indian Economics and the Nineteenth-Century Fur Trade," *Ethnohistory* 40 (Spring1993): 246–76.

9. In the 1820s, Sewell Newhouse began making traps at Oneida Community, which five decades later produced 300,000 annually. On castoreum and the steel trap: Richard Glover, ed., *David Thompson's Narrative 1784–1812* (Toronto: The Champlain Society, 1962), 204–5; Innis, *The Fur Trade in Canada*, 263–64; A. W Schorger, "A Brief History of the Steel Trap and Its Use in North America," *Wisconsin Academy of Sciences, Arts and Letters* (1951): 171–99; Carl P. Russell, *Firearms, Traps, & Tools of the Mountain Men* (New York: Alfred A. Knopf, 1967), 97–163; Robin F. Wells, "Castoreum and Steel Traps in Eastern North America," *American Anthropologist* 74 (June 1972): 479–83; Christian F. Feest, "More on Castoreum and Traps in Eastern North America," *American Anthropologist* 77 (September 1975): 603; Richardson, "Castor fiber, Americanus. The American Beaver," 108; Martin, *Castorologia*, 147 (Iroquois); Warren, *The Beaver*, 19; Rue, *The World of the Beaver*, 135 (mountain men).

10. James A. Tober, *Who Owns the Wildlife? The Political Economy of Conservation in Nineteenth-Century America* (Westport, CT: Greenwood Press, 1981); John F. Reiger, *American Sportsmen and the Origins of Conservation*, revised edition (Norman: University of Oklahoma Press, 1986); R. MacFarlane, "Notes on Mammals Collected and Observed in the Northern Mackenzie River District, Northwest Territories of Canada, with Remarks on Explorers and Explorations of the Far North," *Proceedings U. S. National Museum* 28, No. 1405 (1905): 673–764, p. 743; William T. Hornaday, "The Fur Trade and the Wild Animals," *Zoological Society Bulletin* 24, No. 2 (1921): 29–52, p. 29 ("craze," "mad rush");

Martin, *Castorologia*, 50–59, 143–45; Seton, "Canadian. Beaver"; Ernest A. Sterling, "The Return of the Beaver to the Adirondacks," *American Forests* 19, No. 5 (1913): 292–99; G. B. Heath, "The Beaver Coming Back," *Fins, Feathers and Fur* 6 (19/16): 3–5; Robert B. Peck, "The Renaissance of the Beaver," *Forest and Stream* 91 (April 1921): 152–54, 182–87, p. 184 ("interesting but destructive"); Vernon Bailey, "Beaver Habits, Beaver Control, and Possibilities in Beaver Farming," *U.S. Department of Agriculture*, Bulletin No. 1078 (Washington, DC, 1922): 1–29; Lee E. Yeager, "Trouble in the High Country—Beaver Mismanagement," *Colorado. Conservation* 3, No. 4 (1954): 11–15; Lee E. Yeager, "Let's Argue … about Beaver!" *Hunting & Fishing* 31, No. 10 (1954): 22–25, 66–67; Rue, *The World of the Beaver*, 138–43; Julius F. Wolff, Jr., "Hot Fur," in *Rendezvous*, 215–30; Novak, "Beaver"; Martyn E. Obbard et al., "Furbearer. Harvests in North America," in *Wild Furbearer Management and Conservation in North America*, 1007–34; Milan Novak et al., *Furbearer Harvests in North America, 1600–1984*, supplement to ibid.

11. John R. Luoma, "Back to Stay," *Audubon* 98 (January–February 1996): 53–58; Elizabeth Bumiller, "Besieged by Beavers in Rural New York," *New York Times* September 3, 1996, B1; Todd Shields, "Busy Beavers Gnaw on Suburban Nerves," *Washington Post*, December 14, 1996, A1; Robert Whitcomb, "We Humans Subdivide Nature at Our Own Whim," *Providence Sunday Journal,* July 27, 1997.

12. Linguistic classification and ethnonymy are complex in this region. Following expansion, various Ojibwa-speaking people—ethnonyms from *Handbook of North American Indians*—lived in Ontario (the Algonquin, Nipissing, Northern Ojibwa, Southeastern Ojibwa, Southwestern Chippewa, Ottawa, and Saulteaux), Manitoba (the Saulteaux), Michigan (the Ottawa), Wisconsin (the Southwestern Chippewa and Ottawa), and Minnesota (the Southwestern Chippewa). (The exact linguistic relationship of Ottawa and Algonquin to "Ojibwa" is under discussion.) For the Montagnais, Naskapi, East Cree, Attikamek, Eastern and Western Swampy Cree, Woods Cree, Ottawa, Saulteaux, Severn Ojibwa, Central Southern Ojibwa, and Eastern Ojibwa languages in the Algonquian (or more broadly, Algic) language family, see lves Goddard, "Introduction," in *Handbook of North American*

Indians, Volume 17, Languages (Washington, DC: Smithsonian Institution, 1996), 1–16; Ives Goddard, "Native Languages and Language Families of North America," in *ibid*, endmap; Michael K. Foster, "Language and the Culture History of North America," in *ibid*, 64–110, pp. 97–100. On ethnonymy, see Bruce Trigger, ed., *Handbook of North 'American Indians, Volume 15, Northeast* (Washington, DC: Smithsonian Institution,1978); Ives Goddard, "Synonymy," in "Southeastern Ojibwa" by Edward S. Rogers, in *ibid.*, 760–71, pp. 768–71 ("puckered up"); June Helm, ed., *Handbook of North American Indians, Volume 6, Subarctic* (Washington, DC: Smithsonian Institution, 1981); Daniel Francis and Toby Morantz, *Partners in Furs: A History of the Fur Trade in Eastern James Bay 1600–1870* (Kingston: McGill-Queen's University Press, 1983), 11–13; Charles A. Bishop, *The Northern Ojibwa and the Fur Trade: An Historical and Ecological Study* (Toronto: Holt, Rinehart and Winston of Canada, Ltd., 1974), 305–39; Charles A. Bishop, "Ojibwa, Cree, and the Hudson's Bay Company in Northern Ontario: Culture and Conflict in the Eighteenth Century," in *Western Canada: Past and. Present*, ed Anthony W. Rasporich (University of Calgary, 1975), 150–62; Shepard Krech III, "The Subarctic Culture Area," in *Native North Americans: An Ethnohistorical Approach*, second edition, ed. Molly Mignon and Daniel Boxberger (Dubuque, IA: Kendall Hunt, 1997), 85–112.

13. The debate over family hunting territories extends over eight decades. See Adrian Tanner, "The Significance of Hunting Territories Today," in *Cultural Ecology Readings on the Canadian Indians and Eskimos*, ed. Bruce Cox (Toronto: McClelland and Stewart Ltd., 1973), 101–14; Charles A. Bishop and Toby Morantz, eds., "A Qui Appartient Le Castor? Les Régimes Fonciers Algonquins Du Nord Remis En Cause/Who Owns the Beaver? Northern Algonquian Land Tenure Reconsidered," *Anthropologica* 28, Nos. 1–2 (1986): 1–220; Colin Scott, "Property, Power, and Aboriginal Rights among Quebec Cree Hunters," in *Hunters and Gatherers 2: Property, Power, and Ideology*, ed. Tim Ingold, David Riches, and James Woodburn (New York: Berg, 1988), 35–51.

14. Le Jeune remarked that this man "was making sport of us Europeans, who have such a fondness for the skin of this animal and who fight to see who will give the most to these Barbarians, to get it; they carry this to such an extent my host said to me one day, showing me a beautiful knife, 'The English have no sense; they give us twenty knives like this for one Beaver skin.'" Thwaites, *The Jesuit Relations*, Volume 6, 297, 299. On these Montagnais, see also John M. Cooper, *The Northern Algonquian Supreme Being*, Catholic University of America Anthropological Series No.2 (Washington, DC: Catholic University of America, 1934), 60–61. Later that century, Father Chrétien Le Clercq, a Récollet missionary to the Mi'kmaq in northern New Brunswick (across the St. Lawrence from the Montagnais) echoed Le Jeune when he reported being "unable to keep from laughing on overhearing an Indian" say "in banter" as follows, "In truth, my brother, the Beaver does everything to perfection. He makes for us kettles, axes, swords, knives, and gives us drink and food without the trouble of cultivating the ground" (see Innis, *The Fur Trade in Canada*, 27–28; Leacock, "The Montagnais 'Hunting Territory,'" 11–12; compare John M. Cooper, "Is the Algonquian Family Hunting Ground System Pre-Columbian?," *American Anthropologist* 41 [1939]: 66–90).

15. Thwaites, *The Jesuit Relations*, Volume 8, 57; Innis, *The Fur Trade in Canada*, 28.

16. Thwaites, *The Jesuit Relations*, Volume 8, 57, Volume 7, 171, Volume 31, 209, Volume 32, 269, 271, Volume 59, 29. On Le Jeune, see, for example, Leacock, "The Montagnais 'Hunting Territory,'" 14–15; Cooper, "Is the Algonquian Family Hunting Ground System Pre-Columbian?," 76; Frank G. Speck and Loren C. Eiseley, "Significance of Hunting Territory Systems of the Algonkian in Social Theory," *American Anthropologist* 41 (1939): 269–80, pp. 271, 274–75. Toby Morantz (personal communication, June 7, 1998) rightly cautions about generalizing beyond Le Jeune given the equivocal nature of evidence at his time.

17. There is no indication that Indians deliberately left beavers alive (Thwaites, *The Jesuit Relations*, Volume 8, 57, 59, Volume 6, 299–303; see also Leacock, "The Montagnais 'Hunting Territory,'" 3; Thomas L. Altherr, "'Flesh Is the Paradise of a Man of Flesh': Cultural Conflict over Indian Hunting Beliefs and Rituals in New France as Recorded in *The Jesuit Relations*," *Canadian Historical Review* 64 [1983]: 267–76, p. 276; Heidenreich and Ray, *The*

Early Fur Trades, 65). On Denys and his remark that the Mi'kmaq saved "few" beavers (which does not necessarily contradict other things that he said), see Calvin Martin, "The European Impact on the Culture of a Northeastern Algonquian Tribe: An Ecological Interpretation," *William and Mary Quarterly* 31 (1974): 3–26, pp. 4, 11, 16. Following Denys, Martin stated that the Mi'kmaq formerly took only what they needed for subsistence, and that the taking was governed by "spiritual consideration." But is there evidence for this or for Martin's thesis that "overkill of wildlife would have been resented by the animal kingdom as an act comparable to genocide" in any sources prior to the 20th century? For a recent account of Mi'kmaq history, see Harald E. L. Prins, *The Mi'kmaq: Resistance, Accommodation, and Cultural Survival* (Fort Worth: Harcourt Brace, 1996).

18. Thwaites, *The Jesuit Relations* Volume 8, 57, 59.

19. The Rupert House account is reported by J. Oldmixon in 1741 from a journal of Thomas Gorst dated 1670–75. See Diamond Jenness, *The Ojibwa Indians of Parry Island, Their Social and Religious Life*, Canada Department of Mines, National Museum of Canada, Bulletin No. 78, Anthropological Series No. 17, (Ottawa: National Museum of Canada, 1935), 5; Toby Morantz, "Old Texts, Old Questions: Another Look at the Issue of Continuity and the Early Fur-Trade Period," *Canadian Historical Review* 73 (1992): 166–93, p. 184; Cooper, "Is the Algonquian Family Hunting Ground System Pre-Columbian?," 77–78; Leacock, "The Montagnais 'Hunting Territory,'" 16; Bishop, "Ojibwa, Cree, and the Hudson's Bay Company in Northern Ontario," 153–54.

20. Additional problems stem from Radisson's still-debated claims to have reached James Bay and other places. Arthur T. Adams, ed., *The Explorations of Pierre Esprit Radisson*, (Minneapolis: Ross and Haines, 1961), 88, 95, 147; Charles A. Bishop, "The Western James Bay Cree: Aboriginal and Early Historic Adaptations," *Prairie Forum* 8 (1983): 147–55; Robert A. Brightman, "Conservation and Resource Depletion: The Case of the Boreal Forest Algonquians," in *The Question of the Commons: The Culture and Ecology of Communal Resources* (Tucson: University of Arizona Press, 1987), 121–41, p. 123; Murray, *The Fur Trade in New France and New Netherland*, 8; Francis and Morantz, *Partners in Furs*, 22; Germaine Warkentin, personal communication (e-mail), June 2, 1998. The evidence for conservation or hunting territories elsewhere in this era is thin. Le Clercq (also see note 16) mentioned that the Mi'kmaq elders and a chief determined (in 1675–87) how territories should be assigned to hunters the following season (Frank G. Speck, "Family Hunting Territories of the Lake St. John Montagnais and Neighboring Bands," *Anthropos* 22 [1927]: 387–403, p. 392; Cooper, "Is the Algonquian Family Hunting Ground System Pre-Columbian?," 78–79). In 1689, Baron de Lahontan remarked that each fall the Algonquian Fox agreed to the allotment of hunting grounds, each with fur-bearing resources, and not to trespass, but Cooper ("Is the Algonquian Family Hunting Ground System Pre-Columbian?," 75) and others wonder whether Lahontan is dependable.

21. Thwaites, *The Jesuit Relations*, Volume 68, 109, Volume 69, 113 ("asking The Impossible"); Edward S. Rogers, "The Hunting Group-Hunting Territory Complex among the Misstassini Indians," National Museum of. Canada, Bulletin No. 195, Anthropological Series No. 63. (Ottawa; National Museum of Canada, 1963); Toby Morantz, "The Probability of Family Hunting Territories in Eighteenth Century James Bay: Old Evidence Newly Presented," in *Papers of the Ninth Algonquian Conference*, ed. William Cowan (Ottawa: Carleton University, 1978), 224–36, p. 233; Francis and Morantz, *Partners in Furs*, 33–64, 96 ("in one anothers Leiberty"); Charles A. Bishop, "Demography, Ecology and Trade among the Northern Ojibwa and Swampy Cree," *Western Canadian Journal of Anthropology* 3 (1972): 58–71 (Fort Albany). Toby Morantz (personal communication, June 7, 1998) emphasizes that evidence for hunting territories increased in the 18th century.

22. Discussion is confined to the Cree who traded at York Factory—generalization beyond would be hazardous—at a period selected because three York Factory residents left reports: James Isham, present except for several years from the late 1730s to 1761; T. F. Drage, who spent one winter with Isham in the late 1740s; and Andrew Graham, at York Factory from 1753 to 1774. Their accounts are not independent and require careful reading. E. E. Rich, ed., *James Isham's Observations on Hudsons Bay*, 1743 (London: The Champlain Society

for the Hudson's Bay Record Society, 1949); T. F. Drage, "An Ethnographic Account of the Northern Cree, 1748," *Manitoba Archeological Quarterly* 6, No. 1 (1982): 1–40; Glyndwr Williams, ed., *Andrew Graham's Observations on Hudson's Bay 1767–91* (London: The Hudson's Bay Record Society, 1969).

23. Williams, *Andrew Graham's Observations*, 263, 275–77; E. E. Rich, "Trade Habits and Economic Motivation among the Indians of North America," *Canadian Journal of Economics and Political Science* 26 (1960): 35–53; Heidenreich and Ray, *The Early Fur Trades*, 75–87; Arthur J. Ray, "Competition and Conservation in the Early Subarctic Fur Trade," *Ethnohistory* 25 (1978): 347–57; Ray and Freeman, *'Give Us Good Measure,'* 125–74, 223–28, and passim. Ray and Freeman reveal beaver trade fluctuations at HBC posts on Hudson Bay in 1700–1760, the era of French-English competition. At Fort Albany and Eastmain, the value of beaver pelts (expressed as a percent of the total return) declined from roughly 80 percent to 50 percent, then recovered to 70 to 80 percent. Elsewhere the change in value was in one direction down. At Moose Factory the value shot down from 80 to 50 percent and at York Factory, from 70 to 94 to under 50 percent, and notable declines in value occurred at Eastmain in the 1730s to 1740s, Fort Albany in the 1750s, and Moose Factory and York Factory in the 1760s.

24. Graham drew on Isham for his depiction of caribou hunting. Rich, *James Isham's Observations*, 81, 116, 143; 147; Williams, *Andrew Graham's Observations*, xiv, 10–11, 15–16, 154, 280–81; Drage, "Ethnographic Account," 18–21; J. B. Tyrrell, ed., "Letters of la Potherie," in *Documents Relating to the Early History of Hudson Bay* (Toronto: The Champlain Society, 1931), 143–370, pp. 233–36, 341–42; Brightman, "Conservation and Resource Depletion: The Case of the Boreal Forest Algonquians," 123; Bishop, "The Western James Bay Cree," 147–55. According to Bishop ("Ojibwa, Cree, and the Hudson's Bay Company in Northern Ontario," 159), the Fort Albany Cree "were taught conservation measures" but it is unclear when or by whom. It is difficult to know what to make of the report that the Illinois Indians angered Canadian Indians because they "killed or carried off both male and female beavers," which "the tribes who trade beaver skins for supplies with the Europeans" considered

"criminal and cowardly" (Seymour Feiler, ed., *Jean-Bernard Bossu's Travels in the Interior of North America 1751–1762* [Norman: University of Oklahoma Press, 1962], 77).

25. For the 1750–1830 era and Simpson's policy, see Innis, *The Fur Trade in Canada*, 261–80, 326–35, p. 261 ("great scarcity of Beaver"); E. E. Rich, *The Fur Trade and the Northwest to 1857* (Toronto: McClelland and Stewart Ltd., 1967); Frederick Merk, ed., *Fur Trade and Empire: George Simpson's Journal*, revised edition (Cambridge: Belknap Press of Harvard University Press, 1968); Arthur J. Ray, *Indians in the Fur Trade: Their Role as Trappers, Hunters, and Middlemen in the Lands Southwest of Hudson Bay, 1660–1870* (Toronto: University of Toronto Press, 1974), 117–24, 195–204; Arthur J. Ray, "Some Conservation Schemes of the Hudson's Bay Company, 1821–50: An Examination of the Problems of Resource Management in the Fur Trade," *Journal of Historical Geography* 1 (1975): 49–68, pp. 51, 54, 57, 64, 67; Ray, "Competition and Conservation in the Early Subarctic Fur Trade"; Bishop, *The Northern Ojibwa and the Fur Trade*, 124–28, 184, 210–11 (quotes from Simpson), 245–49, 284, Calvin Martin, *Keepers of the Game: Indian Animal Relationships and the Fur Trade* (Berkeley: University of California Press, 1978), 136–43 ("red and bloody"—the description was John Tanner's and may have referred to tularemia); Ann M. Carlos, *The North American Fur Trade, 1804–1821: A Study in the Life-cycle of a Duopoly* (New York: Garland Publishing, Inc., 1986), 140–41, 155–64, 177.

26. As Glover remarks, the date on this particular account (1797) may well be incorrect (Glover, *David Thompson's Narrative*, 154–57); see also Martin, *Castorologia*, 144–46. For Kihcimanitōw and Wīsahkēcāhk, see Jennifer S. H. Brown and Robert Brightman, *"The Orders of the Dreamed": George Nelson on Cree and Northern Ojibwa Religion and Myth, 1823* (St. Paul: Minnesota Historical Society Press, 1988), 107–8; 119–38. According to a story reported by Alexander Henry, beavers once possessed speech but Nanabozho/Great Hare/the Great Spirit took it away from them "lest they should grow superior in understanding to mankind." In different versions, animals conspired against men but by stripping from them the power of speech, the Great Hare ensured that men would continue to exist. Alexander Henry, *Travels and Adventures*

in Canada and the Indian Territories (Rutland, VT: Charles E. Turtle, 1969), 126, 205-6. For castoreum and steel, see note 11.

27. Paul S. Thistle, *Indian-European Trade Relations in the Lower Saskatchewan River Region to 1840* (Winnipeg: University of Manitoba Press, 1986), 63–64, 72–73, 77, 88 ("dispersed all over ..."; "Sacrificing ...").

28. Julius Lips, "Naskapi Law," *Transactions of the American Philosophical Society* NS Volume 37, Part 4 (Philadelphia: American Philosophical Society, 1947), 379–492, pp. 433–34, 458; Morantz, "The Probability of Family Hunting Territories," 226, 234; Francis and Morantz, *Partners in Furs*, 97, 125–32; compare Rolf Knight, "A Re-examination of Hunting, Trapping, and Territoriality among the Northeastern Algonkian Indians," in *Man, Culture, and Animals: The Role of Animals in Human Ecological Adjustments*, ed. Anthony Leeds and Andrew P. Vayda (Washington, DC: American Association for the Advancement of Science, 1965), 27–42, p. 32.

29. With minor exceptions, quotations are from Charles A. Bishop, "The Emergence of Hunting Territories among the Northern Ojibwa," *Ethnology* 9 (January 1970): 1–15; Bishop, *The Northern Ojibwa and the Fur Trade*, 11–12, 108–10, 245–49, 277; Bishop, "Ojibwa, Cree, and the Hudson's Bay Company in Northern Ontario," 160. See also Innis, *The Fur Trade in Canada*, 91 ("so plentiful" etc.—La Verendrye); Ray and Freeman, *'Give Us Good Measure,'* 35f.

30. Bishop, "The Emergence of Hunting Territories," 4–5, 11; Bishop, *The Northern Ojibwa and the Fur Trade*, 11–12, 110–11, 124–28, 184, 206–20, 245–49, 284, 289–96; Edward S. Rogers, "Cultural Adaptations: The Northern Ojibwa of the Boreal Forest 1670–1980," in *Boreal Forest Adaptations: The Northern Algonkians*, ed. A. Theodore Steegman (New York: Plenum Press, 1983), 85–141; Harold Hickerson, "Land Tenure of the Rainy Lake Chippewa at the Beginning of the 19th Century," *Smithsonian Contributions to Anthropology 2* (Washington, DC: Smithsonian Institution, 1967), 37–65, pp. 58–59. In 1826, Mattagamis who lived 240 miles southwest of James Bay had family "allotments" in part hunted and in part rested in a given year (Bishop, *The Northern Ojibwa and the Fur Trade*, 212).

31. Bishop, *The Northern Ojibwa and the Fur Trade*, 94–95, 124–28, 184, 196–97. Perhaps "encroachment"

was broadly common; in 1885 some Mistassini Crees and Lac St. Jean Montagnais evidently sought to conserve beavers but others poached if they could get away with it (Lips, "Naskapi Law," 402–3).

32. On variation within the region, see A. Irving Hallowell, "The Size of Algonkian Hunting Territories: A Function of Ecological Adjustment," *American Anthropologist* 51 (1949): 35–45; Hickerson, "Land Tenure of the Rainy Lake Chippewa," 42; Edward S. Rogers, "Subsistence Areas of the Cree-Ojibwa of the Eastern Subarctic: A Preliminary Study," *Contributions to Ethnology V*; National Museum of Canada, Bulletin No. 204, Anthropological Series No. 70 (Ottawa: National Museum of Canada, 1967), 59–90. Toby Morantz (personal communication, June 7, 1998) suggests that at Abitibi in 1823, the Cree left beavers to breed if the numbers were sufficient; that Indians who were "poor" trapped out-their own lands and then poached on their neighbors' lands; and that conservation, poaching, etc. might always have depended on how easy or difficult it was to obtain food and basic supplies.

33. There are possible links elsewhere between population pressure, competition, game depletions, and territoriality and conservation: In the 1690s the Ottawa evidently tried to leave some beavers alive in lodges; in 1700 the Algonquin apparently marked beaver lodges yet allowed others to have access to meat; in the 1760s the Algonquin possessed territories descending within families and punished trespass severely and Southeastern Ojibwa families had exclusive rights to territories; and in 1800 the Southwestern Ojibwa hunted beavers in roving bands or areas alloted informally to them by a leader for the season (Alexander Henry, *Travels and Adventures in Canada and the Indian Territories* [Rutland, VT: Charles E. Turtle, 1969], 23; Cooper, "Is the Algonquian Family Hunting Ground System Pre-Columbian?," 73; Leacock, "The Montagnais 'Hunting Territory,'" 15–16; Harold Hickerson,. "The Southwestern Chippewa: An Ethnohistorical' Study," *Memoirs, of the American Anthropological Association*, No. 92 [Menasha, WI, 1962], 14, 40–45; W. Vernon Kinietz, *The Indians of the Western Great Lakes 1615–1760* [Ann Arbor: University of Michigan Press, 1965 (orig. 1940)], 237; Brightman, "Conservation and Resource Depletion: The Case of the Boreal Forest Algonquians," 123 [for Baron de Lahontan].

34. The "Abenaki" (perhaps including the Penobscot, Passamaquoddy, Maliseet, and others) reportedly possessed and defended family hunting territories against trespass in 1710 (Cooper, "Is the Algonquian Family Hunting Ground System Pre-Columbian?," 73–74 [A. Raudot]); the Penobscot reported in the 1760s that "their hunting ground and streams were all parcelled out to certain families, time out of mind" but that "it was their rule to hunt every third year and kill two-thirds of the beaver, leaving the other third part to breed, and that their Beavers were as much their stock for a living as Englishman's cattle was his living; that since the late war English hunters kill all the Beaver they find on said streams, which had not only empoverished many Indian families, but destroyed the breed of Beavers, etc." Disentangling their complaint against the English from the rest of this statement is difficult (Dean R Snow, "Wabanaki Family Hunting Territories," *American Anthropologist* 70 [1968]: 1143–51, p. 1149 [Joseph Chadwick]).

UNFREEDOM IN EARLY CANADA

Race, Empire, and Slavery

Jarett Henderson
Mount Royal University

UNFREEDOM IN EARLY CANADA: RACE, EMPIRE, AND SLAVERY

- **Introduction by Jarett Henderson**

▲ **Primary Sources**

Document 1: Aboriginal Slave Halter

Document 2: French Iron Shackles

Document 3: "The Cruelty of the Savage Iroquois"

Document 4: Father Hennepin's Writing on Indigenous Slavery

Document 5: The *Code Noir* (1685)

Document 6: Like Negroes of the Islands

Document 7: Purchasing People

Document 8: Freedom Before Abolition

■ **Secondary Sources**

Article 1: I Make Him My Dog/My Slave
  Brett Rushforth

Article 2: Slavery in New France
  Robin Winks

Article 3: Slaves in Île Royale, 1713–1758
  Kenneth Donovan

● INTRODUCTION

Jarett Henderson

In 1858, just months before his death, Jacques Viger, a former Patriot and Mayor of Montreal, was again practising his habit of collecting matters of history.[1] This time, and in connection with the Historical Society of Montreal, Viger was cataloguing whatever documents he could that archived the long history of unfreedom in Canada. *De L'esclavage en Canada / The Slave in Canada,* published just months after Viger's death, contained the documents of colonial and imperial administrators, both French and British: government ordinances, court transcripts, and notorial records.[2] These are the sources that archive the purchase, regulation, and manumission of *Panis* (Aboriginal) and Black slaves in early Canada. For Viger's contemporaries, his work was noteworthy because it contradicted the nationalist argument made by François-Xavier Garneau in his *Histoire du Canada.* Canada, Garneau wrote in 1860, "happily escaped the terrible curse of Negro slavery."[3] Rather *L'esclavage en Canada* illustrates that both Black and Indigenous people lived lives of unfreedom in, and along, the empire of the St. Lawrence. This module introduces you to the varied and often ignored history of slavery in northeastern North America. In what follows you will interrogate the social and political complexities of race, slavery, and empire on the Indigenous lands that were becoming early Canada.

Generations before white French colonizers arrived in the "New World," Indigenous people across the continent, through a diverse system of knowing, ordered their societies by ascribing various meanings to different human bodies. On the northwestern coast of North America, for example, Leland Donald has explored the nuanced social and economic histories of Indigenous slavery.[4] Closer to the St. Lawrence, and throughout the region that French colonizers termed the *Pays d'en Haut,* Brett Rushforth explores the complicated ways that the Huron, Ottawa, Iroquois, Sioux, Illinois, and Fox nations understood human bondage. Through a methodology that draws from archeology, history, ritual, and linguistics, Rushforth traces how central Algonquian and Siouan peoples spoke about slavery. His chapter reproduced here draws upon the French dictionaries created and used by Jesuit missionaries to learn Indigenous languages. These sources reveal that Indigenous people often used metaphors of domestication and mastery and compared their captives to dogs and other domesticated animals. Anishinaabe-speakers, for example, called their slaves *awakaan,* which meant captive, dog, or animals kept as pets. Rushforth has found that Indigenous slavery—often a diplomatic act of exchanging "a little flesh"—was central to the maintenance of Indigenous and Indigenous–French alliances in the fledgling outposts that constituted New France.[5]

As New France sputtered into existence, Indigenous understandings of human unfreedom encountered French imperial understandings of enslavement. The images of an Indigenous slave halter and French iron shackles reproduced here vividly expose the similarities and differences between unfreedom in these cultures. As Robin Winks illustrates, over the seventeenth and eighteenth centuries, missionaries, merchants, and government officials increasingly worked to ensure that French imperial understandings of slavery took hold in a colony marked by settler–Aboriginal violence, an exhaustingly slow rate of population growth, and a frigid reputation.[6] Missionaries struggled to remedy this situation by instructing the *sauvage* in the teachings of Christianity. In 1698, Father Hennepin published, for European audiences, accounts of his travels through the *Pays d'en Haut,* his mission work, and his capture; these were tales that would have simultaneously intrigued and worried his contemporaries. *A New Discovery of a Vast Country in North America* recounted how Hennepin and his two French servants were captured by Sioux warriors on 20 April 1680. Hennepin's vivid account appears to have been insufficient at capturing the exigency of Indigenous slavery, for he also included a horrific image that fused all that he knew, and likely had heard about Indigenous slavery, into an image that depicted "The Cruelty of the Savage Iroquois."[7]

As missionaries like Hennepin worked and travelled among Indigenous nations, white French colonizers from fur traders to merchants through to government and church officials increasingly purchased both Black and Indigenous peoples, fusing Indigenous and French imperial understandings of slavery.[8] In 1685, the French Empire established, for the first time, the legal and social distinctions between masters and slaves through the *Code Noir*. Though historians continue to debate the extent to which the *Code* applied to the unfree peoples of northeastern North America, it nonetheless marked a significant shift in how ideas of race and freedom were mobilized in the French Empire to order its peoples.[9] Regardless of the *Code's* application in New France, it nonetheless regulated nearly every aspect of the master–slave relationship and would come to have important repercussions for *Panis* and Black slaves, free Indigenes and Blacks, and white colonizers in early Canada. So much so that 50 years later it had become necessary for French imperial administrators to sanction an ordnance for the local colonial context of New France. In April 1709, Jacques Radout rendered an ordinance on the subject of "the Negroes and the Indians called Panis." Radout's ordinance, reproduced here, established that Indigenous slaves in New France were to be treated and regulated "like Negros in the Islands."[10] It is yet a further indication of the wider imperial context that shaped the institution of slavery as it struggled to take hold in early Canada.

As was true of the Indigenous peoples who practised forms of human unfreedom prior to, and after, contact, no two sites of France's Empire in northern North American yielded the same experience of slavery. Exciting projects such as the *Great Unsolved Mysteries in Canadian History—Torture and the Truth: Angelique and the Burning of Montreal* and Afu Cooper's *The Hanging of Angelique* have brought to light the history of Angelique, a Black domestic slave whose act of resistance led to not only the burning of significant portions of eighteenth-century Montreal, but also a trial that culminated with the burning of her body.[11] Kenneth Donovan explores the interactions that slaves had with the families for whom they worked in Louisbourg, on Île Royale. As a central node in the French Empire's expansive trade network that included both sugar and slaves, this case study illustrates the differing conditions of domestic enslavement that *Panis* and Black slaves experienced in this cosmopolitan imperial outpost.[12]

Though slaves were often vulnerable, sometimes abused, and purchased for a variety of social and sexual purposes, the mixing of Indigenous and French systems of enslavement did offer pathways to freedom. Long before the abolitionist campaigns of the late-eighteenth century, female slaves who lived in the *Pays d'en Haut* and married French settlers were often freed by their new husbands. Other slaves could be manumitted by verbal agreement or by purchasing their own freedom. Running away, of course, was also an option and a tactic slaves frequently employed.[13] As the rising number of manumitted slaves increased in the first decades of the eighteenth century, it became necessary for French colonial administrators to establish a uniform system to distinguish free from slave. On 1 September 1736, Giles Hocquart issued the ordinance, reproduced here, which made it necessary that for a slave to be freed, by either gift or purchase, a notary must record his or her manumission and register it with the royal registry office. This decision indicates, Winks argues, that slavery had grown to such an extent that it required both records and regulation.[14] When the Indigenous territories that constituted New France were transferred to the British in 1763, the Articles of Capitulation that Viger chose to archive in 1858 indicate that both white French and British imperial administrators were careful to make concessions for slave owners.[15] The institution of slavery would continue in Quebec, Britain's newest imperial territory to the century's end, as the notorial records documenting the purchase and subsequent manumission of "a certain Negro boy or lad called Rubin" indicate.[16] Early Canada remained a place where contrasting and competing ideas of human unfreedom, both Indigenous and European operated, creating a colonial order that revolved around the complex intersection of empire, race, and slavery.

QUESTIONS

1. How did Indigenous societies in the Great Lakes region speak of unfreedom/captivity? What role did Indigenous captives have in Indigenous societies?
2. How do the two tools of enslavement pictured here differ? How are they similar? Can you speculate as to the effect of the confluence of French and Indigenous slavery in early Canada?
3. How does Hennepin represent Indigenous enslavement and captivity? Why do you think he depicted this history in such a fashion? In what ways is Hennepin helpful for understanding the history of unfreedom in early Canada? Can you identify any problems with his depictions of Indigenous enslavement and captivity?
4. What did the *Code Noir* regulate? Do you think this had any effect on how colonists in early Canada understood the connection between race and freedom? Why or why not?
5. Why do you think imperial administrators felt they needed to regulate slavery in New France in 1709? How can we gauge the success of their efforts? What types of information do the records of notaries teach us about unfreedom in early Canada? How can we use these documents to make historical inferences about the institution of slavery in eighteenth-century northeastern North America?
6. What types of work did slaves perform in early Canada? How convinced were you by Donovan's argument? Would you characterize slavery in New France as a "benign" form of slavery as some historians have? Why or why not?

FURTHER READINGS

Cooper, Afua. "Acts of Resistance: Black Men and Women Engage Slavery in Upper Canada, 1793–1803." *Ontario History* 99, no. 1 (Spring 2007): 5–17.

Donovan, Kenneth. "Slaves in Île Royale," *French Colonial History* 5 (2004): 25–42.

Harris, Jennifer. "Black Life in a Nineteenth Century New Brunswick Town," *Journal of Canadian Studies* 46, no. 1 (Winter 2012): 138–66.

Lee, Maureen Elgersman. *Unyielding Spirits: Black Women and Slavery in Early Canada and Jamaica*. New York: Garland Publishing, 1999.

Rushforth, Brett. *Bonds of Alliance: Indigenous and Atlantic Slaveries in New France*. Chapel Hill, NC, University of North Carolina Press, 2012.

Sapoznik, Karlee. "Where the Historiography Falls Short: La Vérendrye through the Lens of Gender, Race and Slavery in Early French Canada, 1731–1749." *Manitoba History*, no. 62 (Winter 2009): 22–32.

Vidal, Cécile, and Emily Clark. "Famille et Esclavage à la nouvelle-orléans sous le régime français, 1699–1769." *Annales De Demographie Historique*, no. 2 (Novembre 2011): 99–126.

Whitfield, Harvey Amani. "The Struggle Over Slavery in the Maritime Colonies," *Acadiensis* XLI, no. 2 (Summer/Autumn 2012): 17–44.

Winks, Robin W. *The Blacks in Canada: A History*. Second Edition. Montreal-Kingston: McGill-Queen's Press, 1997.

NOTES

1. Bettina Bradbury, *Wife to Widow: Lives, Laws, and Politics in Nineteenth-Century Montreal,* (Vancouver: UBC Press, 2011).

2. Jacques Viger, Louis Hippolyte Lafontaine, Eds., *De l'esclavage en Canada,* (Montréal: Société historique de Montréal, 1859).

3. François–Xavier Garneau, *History of Canada: From the Time of Its Discovery to Till the Union Year*, Trans, Andrew Bell, (Montreal: John Lovel, 1860), 95.

4. Leland Donald, *Aboriginal Slavery on the Northwest Coast of North America,* (Berkeley, CA: University of California Press, 1997).

5. Brett Rushforth, *Bonds of Alliance: Indigenous and Atlantic Slaveries in New France,* (Chapel Hill, NC: University of North Carolina Press, 2012).

6. Allan Greer, *The People of New France,* (Toronto: UTP, 1997).

7. Father Louis Hennepin, *A New Discovery of a Vast Country in America,* Edited by Reuben Gold Thwaites, (Chicago: A. C. McClurg and Company, 1903).

8. Karlee Sapoznik, "Where the Historiography Falls Short: La Vérendrye through the Lens of Gender, Race and Slavery in Early French Canada, 1731–1749," *Manitoba History* 62 (Winter 2009) and Marcel Trudel avec Micheline D'Allaire, *Deux siècles d'esclavage au Québec,* (Montreal: Éditions Hurtubise, 2004). See also the recent exhibitition on Slavery in New France at the Grand Bibliothèque in Montreal, Canada. Unfortunatley, as of yet, no publication has resulted from this exhibit.

9. *Le code noir, ou Recueil des règlements rendus jusqu'à présent: Concernant le gouvernement, l'administration de la justice, la police, la discipline & le commerce des Nègres dans les colonies françaises,* (Paris: Chez L.F. Prault, imprimeur du Roi, quai des Augustins, à l'Immortalité, 1788).

10. "Ordinance Rendered on the Subject of the Negroes and the Indians Called Panis," Bibliothèque et Archives nationales du Québec, Centre de Québec, Ordonnance des Intendants, E1, S1, P509, Raudot, Jacques, Ordinance Relative to Slavery in Canada, April, 13, 1709.

11. *Great Unsolved Mysteries in Canadian History: Torture and the Truth,* www.canadian mysteries.ca and Afua Cooper, *The Hanging of Angelique,* (Toronto: Harper Collins, 2006).

12. Kenneth Donovan, "Slaves in Île Royale, 1713–1758," *French Colonial History,* Volume 5 (2004): 25–42.

13. Maureen G. Elgersmanm, "Slavery in Early Canada," in *Unyielding Spirits: Black Women and Slavery in Early Canada and Jamaica,* (New York, Garland Pub: 1999).

14. Robin Winks, *Blacks in Canada: A History,* Second Edition (Montreal-Kingston: McGill-Queen's University Press, 2000).

15. Viger, *De l'esclavage en Canada,* (1859).

16. *Rapport de L'Archiviste de la Province de Québec pour 1921–22,* (Quebec: Louis-Amable Proulx, Imprimeur de Sa Majesté Le Roi, 1922).

▲ DOCUMENT 1: ABORIGINAL SLAVE HALTER

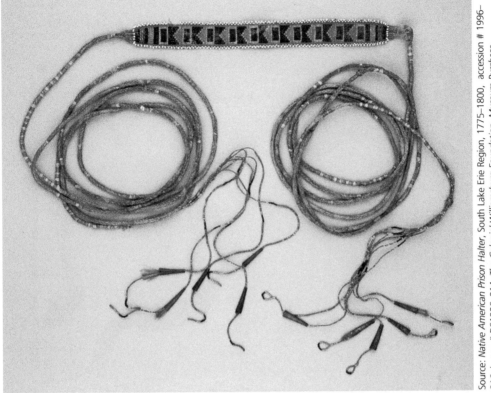

Source: *Native American Prison Halter, South Lake Erie Region, 1775–1800*, accession # 1996–816, image # DS1996–914. The Colonial Williamsburg Foundation. Museum Purchase.

● Because of their delicate nature, few indigenous halters like this one have survived. Yet they were common across north america in the seventeenth and eighteenth centuries. Jesuits identified these tools of enslavement as bridles or harnesses, while algonquians around the great lakes called them "sacant8tagane."

▲ DOCUMENT 2: FRENCH IRON SHACKLES

Source: © Chicago History Museum/The Bridgeman Art Library

● To be in irons was to be a slave. Though very different from the Aboriginal Slave Halter in Document 1, both of these tools were symbols of unfreedom. What was their physical purpose? What social or cultural messages did they imply?

▲ DOCUMENT 3: "THE CRUELTY OF THE SAVAGE IROQUOIS"

Source: From "The Cruelty of the Savage Iroquois," in Father Louis Hennepin, *A New Discovery of A Vast Country in America*, Edited by Reuben Gold Thwaites, Chicago: A. C. McClurg and Company, 1903.

● This image, from Father Hennepin's *A New Discovery of a Vast Country*, was designed to depict the "cruelty" of the "savage" Iroquois. After reading Hennepin's account that follows in Document 4, what do you realize about this image? How can we use this image to understand how captives/slaves were viewed by Iroquoian society?

▲ DOCUMENT 4: FATHER HENNEPIN'S WRITING ON INDIGENOUS SLAVERY

On 11 April 1680, Louis Hennepin, a Recollect missionary and his two French servants were captured by a war party of Sioux Indians. Hennepin, who was eventually adopted by Chief Aquipaguetin, was held captive for eight months among the Sioux. Although not an account of his transition to life in captivity, the excerpt below chronicles Hennepin's interpretation of the cultural, social, and political aspects of enslavement in Iroquoian society.

There are no Savages in all the Northern America but what are very cruel to their Enemies. We are astonished at the Cruelties which the Neroes, the Dioclessans, and the Maximins inflicted upon the Christians, and have their Names in Detestation and Horror; but the Inhumanity of the Iroquois towards the Nations they make Slaves goes beyond theirs.

When the Iroquois have killed a Man, they tear off the Skin of his Skull, and carry it home with them as a certain Mark of their Victory. When they take a Slave, they tie him, and make him run after them; if he is unable to follow them, they stick their Hatchet into his Head, and there leave him, after they have torn off Skin and Hair together. They don't spare sucking Infants: If the Slave can march after them, they tie him every Night to a piece of Wood made in the form of a St. Andrew's Cross, and leave him exposed to be stung by the Mosquitoes and other Flies, in Summer-time, and use him as cruelly as may be.

Sometimes they fix four Pegs into the Ground, to which they Fasten their Slaves by the Feet and Hands, and so leave them all Night long upon the Ground in the sharpest Weather. I omit a hundred other Sufferings, which these miserable Wretches undergo in the daytime. When they are near their Villages, they set up loud Cries, whereby their Nation knows that their Warriors are returned with Slaves. Then the Men and Women put on their best Apparel, and go to the entrance of the Village to receive them; there they make a lane for the Slaves to pass through them. But 'tis a lamentable Reception for these poor People: The Rabble fall upon them like Dogs or Wolves upon their Prey, and begin to torment them, whilst the Warriors march on in File, mightily puffed up with their own Exploits.

Some kick the Slaves, some cudgel them, some cut them with Knives, some tear off their Ears, cut off their Noses or Lips, insomuch that most of them die in this pompous Entry. Those that resist against these rude Treatments are reserved for exemplary Punishment. Sometimes they save some, but very rarely. When the Warriors are entered into their Cabins, the Ancients assemble themselves to hear the relation of what passed in the War.

If the Father of a Savage Woman has been killed, they give her a Slave for him, and 'tis free for that Woman either to put him to Death, or save him alive. When they burn them, this is their manner; They bind the Slave to a Post by the Hands and Feet, then they heat red-hot Musket-barrels, Hatchets, and other Iron Instruments, and apply them red-hot from head to foot, all over their Body; they tear off their Nails, and pluck out their Teeth; they cut Collops of flesh out of their Backs, and often flay their Skin off from their Skull: After all this they throw hot Ashes upon their Wounds, cut out their Tongues, and treat them as cruelly as they can devise. If they don't die under all these Torments, they make them run and follow them, laying them on with Sticks. It is reported, that once a Slave ran so well,

Source: "The Cruelty of the Savage Iroquois," in Father Louis Hennepin, *A New Discovery of a Vast Country in America*, Edited by Reuben Gold Thwaites, Chicago: A. C. McClurg and Company, 1903. Republished by Toronto: Coles Publishing Company, 1974, 507–12. Link: http://archive.org/stream/anewdiscoveryav00paltgoog#page/n176/mode/2up

that he saved himself in the Woods, and could not be caught again. It is probable he died there for want of Succour. But what is more surprising is that the Slaves sing in the midst of their Torments, which frets their Executioners exceedingly.

An Iroquois told us, that there was one Slave whom they tormented cruelly; but he told them, You have no Ingenuity, you don't know how to torment your Prisoners, you are mere Blockheads; if I had you in my Circumstances, I'd use you after another manner: but whilst he ran on so boldly, a Savage Woman gets a little Iron Spit heated red-hot, and runs it into his Yard: this made him roar; but he told the Woman, You are cunning, you understand something, this is the Course you should take with us.

When the Slave, which they burn, is dead, they eat him; and before his Death they make their Children drink some of his Blood, to render them cruel and inhumane. Those that they give their Lives to, live with them, and serve them like Slaves: But in length of time they recover their Liberty, and are looked upon as if they were of their own Nation.

The Savages of the Louisiana that dwell along the River Mississippi, and are situated seven or eight hundred Leagues beyond the Iroquois, as the Issati and Nadouessans, among who I was a Slave, are no less brave than the Iroquois; they make all the Nations round them tremble, tho' they have nothing but Bows, Arrows, and Maces. They run swifter than the Iroquois and make excellent Soldiers; but they are not so cruel: they don't eat the Flesh of their Enemies; they are content to burn them only. Once having taken a Huron, who eat human Flesh as the Iroquois, they cut off pieces of Flesh from his own Body, and said to him; You that love Man's Flesh, eat of your own, to let your Nation know, who now live among the Iroquois, that we detest and abominate your Barbarities; for these People are like hungry Dogs that devour any sort of Meat.

The Iroquois are the only Savages of North America that eat human Flesh; and yet they don't do but in cases extraordinary, when they are resolved to exterminate a whole Nation. They don't eat human Flesh to satisfy their Appetites; 'tis to signify to the Iroquois Nation, that they ought to fight without ever submitting to their Enemies; that they ought rather to eat them than leave any of them alive: They eat it to animate their Warriors; for they always march out of their five Cantons the day after, to fight with their Enemies; for the Rendezvous for next day is always given notice of by these Feasts of human Flesh.

... I don't describe these five Cantons of the Iroquois here, I only treat of their Barbarity and Cruelty, and add, that they have subdued a very large Country since within these fifty Years; that they have extended their Territories, and multiplied their Nation by the Destruction of other People, the Remainder of whom they have made Slaves, to increase the number of their Troops.

NEL

▲ DOCUMENT 5: THE *CODE NOIR* (1685)

The Code Noir *was first issued in 1685. It legalized slavery in the French Atlantic Empire, while detailing the duties and conditions of slaves as well as the responsibilities that masters had to their property.*

II. All slaves in our said province will be baptized and instructed in the Catholic, Apostolic, and Roman religion. We order those inhabitants who purchase newly arrived Negroes to inform the Governor and Intendant of the said islands within a week at the latest or face a discretionary fine …

III. We forbid any public exercise of any religion other than the Catholic, Apostolic, and Roman; we wish that any offenders be punished as rebels and disobedient to our orders. We prohibit all congregations for this end, declare them illicit and seditious, and subject to the same penalty, which will be levied, even against masters who allow or tolerate them among their slaves.

IV. No overseers will be given charge of Negroes who do not profess the Catholic, Apostolic, and Roman religion …

VI. We charge all our subjects, whatever their status and condition, to observe Sundays and holidays that are kept by our subjects of the Catholic, Apostolic, and Roman religion. We forbid them to work or to make their slaves work on these days from the hour of midnight until the other midnight, either in agriculture, the manufacture of sugar or all other works, on pain of fine and discretionary punishment of the masters and confiscation of the sugar, and of the said slaves who will be caught by our officers in their work.

VII. Equally we forbid the holding of Negro markets and all other markets the said days on similar pains, including confiscation of the merchandise that will be found then at the market and discretionary fine against the merchants.

IX. The free men who will have one or several children from their concubinage with their slaves, together with the masters who permitted this, will each be condemned to a fine of two thousand pounds of sugar; and if they are the masters of the slave by whom they have had the said children, we wish that beyond the fine, they be deprived of the slave and the children, and that she and they be confiscated for the profit of the [royal] hospital, without ever being manumitted. …

XI. We forbid priests to officiate the marriages of slaves unless they can show the consent of their masters. We also forbid masters to use any means to constrain their slaves to marry [them] against their will.

XII. The children who will be born of marriage between slaves will be slaves and will belong to the master of the women slaves, and not to those of their husband, if the husband and the wife have different masters.

XIII. We wish that if a slave husband has married a free woman, the children, both male and girls, will follow the condition of their mother and be free like her, in spite of the servitude of their father; and that if the father is free and the mother enslaved, the children will be slaves the same.

XV. We forbid slaves to carry any weapon, or large sticks, on penalty of the whip and of confiscation of the weapon to the profit of those who seizes them; with the exception of those sent to hunt by their master or who carry their ticket or known mark.

Source: *Le code noir, ou Recueil des règlements rendus jusqu'à présent: Concernant le gouvernement, l'administration de la justice, la police, la discipline & le commerce des Nègres dans les colonies françaises,* (Paris: Chez L.F. Prault, imprimeur du Roi, quai des Augustins, à l'Immortalité, 1788): 28–58. Link: http://archive.org/details/lecodenoirourecu00fran

XVI. We also forbid slaves belonging to different masters to gather together in the day or night on pretexts such as a wedding or otherwise, whether on their master's property or elsewhere, and still less in the main roads or faraway places, on pain of corporal punishment, which will not be less than the whip and the fleur-de-lis and which in cases of frequent violations and other aggravating circumstances can be punished with death …

XIX. We forbid slaves to expose for sale, at the market or to carry to private houses for sale any kind of commodity, even fruits, vegetables, firewood, herbs for their food and animals of their manufacture without express permission of their masters by a ticket or by known marks, on pain of confiscation of the things thus sold, without restitution of the price by their masters, and of a fine of six livres tournois to their profit for the buyers.

XXII. Each week masters will have to furnish to their slaves ten years old and older for their nourishment two and a half jars in the measure of the land, of cassava flour, or three cassavas weighing at least two-and-a-half pounds each or equivalent things, with two pounds of salted beef or three pounds of fish or other things in proportion, and to children after they are weaned to the age of 10 years half of the above supplies.

XXVI. Those slaves who are not fed, clothed and supported by the masters according to these orders will notify our attorney and give him their statements, based on which and even as a matter of course, if the information comes to him from elsewhere, the masters will be prosecuted by him and without cost, which we want to be observed for the cries and barbarous and inhumane treatments of masters towards their slaves.

XXX. Slaves will not be invested with offices or commissions having any public function, nor act as agents for any other than their masters in acting or administering any trade or judgment in loss or witnesses, either in civil or criminal matters; and in cases where they will be heard as witnesses, their dispositions will only serve as memorandum to aid the judges in the investigation, without being the source of any presumption, conjecture or proof.

XXXIII. A slave who strikes his master or the wife of his master, his mistress, or their children to bring blood, or in the face will be punished with death.

LV. Masters twenty years old will be able to manumit their slaves by all [legal] deeds or by cause of death, without being required to provide the reason for this manumission, neither will they need the permission of parents, provided that they are minors twenty-five years of age.

LVIII. We command manumitted slaves to retain a particular respect for their former masters, their widows and their children; such that the insult that they will have done be punished more severely that if it had been done to another person: we declare them however free and absolved of any other burdens, services and rights that their former masters would like to claim, as much on their persons as on their possessions and estates as patrons.

LIX. We grant to manumitted slaves the same rights, privileges and liberties enjoyed by persons born free; desiring that they merit this acquired liberty and that it produce in them, both for their persons and for their property, the same effects that the good fortune of natural liberty causes in our other subjects.

▲ DOCUMENT 6: LIKE NEGROES OF THE ISLANDS

This 1709 ordinance archives the confluence of local concern and imperial policy in the rules guiding the practice of slavery in the French settlements of northern North America. In making comparisons to French imperial slavery in the Caribbean, this ordinance, issued in Quebec City, established the legal precedent that made Panis slaves akin to Negro slaves on the French islands: full chattel slavery had come to New France.

April 13, 1709

Ordinance rendered on the subject of the Negroes and the Indians called Panis

It is well known how this colony would benefit were its inhabitants able to securely purchase the Indians called Panis, whose country is far distant from this one, and who can only be obtained from Indians who capture them in their territory and sell them to the English of Carolina, and who have at times sold them to the people of this country, who at times find themselves cheated out of the considerable sums that they must pay for them because of the notions of liberty inspired in them by those who did not purchase them, which means that they almost always abandon their masters under the pretext that there are no slaves in France, which is not necessarily true for the colonies attached to it, since in the islands of this continent all the Negroes bought by the inhabitants are always regarded as such, and as all colonies must be considered on the same footing, and as the people of the Panis nation are needed by the inhabitants of this county for agriculture and other enterprises that might be undertaken, like Negroes in the Islands, and as these bonds are very important to this colony, it is necessarily to ensure ownership to those who have purchased or will purchase them.

We, according to His Majesty's good pleasure, ordain that all the Panis and Negroes who have been purchased, or who shall be purchased hereafter, shall be fully owned as property by those who have purchased them and be known as their slaves; we forbid the said Panis and Negroes from abandoning their masters and order a 50 livres fine against anyone who corrupts them. We order that the present ordinance be read and published in the customary locations in the towns of Quebec, TroisRivières, and Montreal, and that it be registered by the notaries of these jurisdictions, under the diligence of our sub-delegates, done and given at our resident at Quebec the 13 of April 1709,

[Signed] Raudot

Read and published at the church in lower town after seven o'clock and at the door of the parish church of Quebec after high mass the 21st of April 1709 by me, court bailiff in the jurisdiction of Quebec and resident of Rue. St. Pierre, [Signed] Congnet

---

Source: "Ordinance Rendered on the Subject of the Negroes and the Indians Called Panis," Bibliothèque et Archives nationales du Québec, Centre de Québec, Ordonnance des Intendants, E1, S1, P509, Raudot, Jacques, Ordinance Relative to Slavery in Canada, April, 13, 1709. http://pistard.banq.qc.ca/unite_chercheurs/description_fonds?p_anqsid=20120716124331702&p_centre=03Q&p_classe=E&p_fonds=1&p_numunide=806897

▲ DOCUMENT 7: PURCHASING PEOPLE

Historians of early Canada owe much to the work, and registers, of public nota-ries. What do we learn about slave owners from these documents? What details are we provided about the lives of slaves in the colony?

I. THE SALE OF FIVE NEGROES BY CHARLES RHÉAUMÉ, TO LOUIS CUREUX DE SAINT-GERMAIN (25 SEPTEMBER 1743).

Before the undersigned Royal Notary, at the Provostship of Quebec, therein Residing, and the witnesses named below, was present Mr. Charles Rhéaumé merchant usually Residing on The Seigneury of the Isle of Jesus near the City of Montreal and presently in this city, who has sold, with a guarantee against all problems and hindrances whatsoever, to Mr. Loüis Cureuxdit St Germain, bourgeois of this city, who accepts the acquisition for him-self and his assignees, five Negro slaves, two men and three women and girls, whom the said purchaser has seen currently at the house of the widow Madame Cachelievre. The said vendor promises to deliver them shortly to the said purchaser for the sum of three thou-sand livres, which the said purchaser, promises to pay to the said seller, upon the delivery of the said slaves.

Thus it was &c, obliging, &c. done and passed in Quebec, at the Office of the said notary, on the morning of the twenty-fifth of September seventeen hundred forty-three, in the presence of Mr Loüis Lambert and Mr. Nicolas Bellevüe, witnesses residing at Québec, who along with the said Mr. Rhéaumé and the notary did sign, the said Mr. St Germain having declared to not know how to write or sign as requested, following a reading done of it.

[SIGNED] L. LAMBERT
[SIGNED] BELLEVÜE
[SIGNED] C RHÉAUMÉ
[SIGNED] PINGUET

Source: *Rapport de L'Archiviste de la Province de Québec pour 1921–22,* (Quebec: Louis-Amable Proulx, Imprimeur de Sa Majesté Le Roi, 1922): 113. http://archive.org/details/rapportdelarchiv02arch

II. SALE OF A PANIS NAMED FANCHON, AGED ABOUT TEN OR ELEVEN YEARS, NON-BAPTIZED, BY JACQUES-FRANCOIS DAGUILLE, A MERCHANT OF MONTREAL, TO MATHIEU-THÉODOZE DE VITRÉ, SHIP CAPTAIN (4 NOVEMBER 1751)

In attendance were, Mr. Jacques-François Daguille, Merchant of Montreal, currently in this city to voluntarily sell to Mr. Mathieu-Théodoze de Vitré, a ship captain, the terms presented deemed acceptable, a Panis named Fanchon, who is not yet baptized, aged about ten or eleven. Mr. [Daguille] willingly made the sale, subject to the price and sum of four hundred pounds, which was paid by Mr. de Vitré, who happily accepted the sum. Whereby, the above mentioned seller, Mr. Daguille, agrees that Mr. de Vitré is able to enjoy the above named Panis as he sees fit, etc., done and passed at Quebec, in the study of Master Panet, one of the undersigned notaries, in the year one thousand seven hundred fifty one, before noon on 4 November, and signed.

DAGUILLE
DENYS VITRE
BAROLET
PANET

Source: *Rapport de L'Archiviste de la Province de Québec pour 1921–22*, (Quebec: Louis-Amable Proulx, Imprimeur de Sa Majesté Le Roi, 1922): 118. Link: http://archive.org/details/rapportdelarchiv02arch

III. SALE OF A NEGRO NAMED RUBIN, BY DENNIS DALY, TAVERN KEEP OF QUEBEC, TO JOHN YOUNG, MERCHANT, ALSO OF QUEBEC (15 AUGUST 1795)

Before the Public Notaries for the City of Québec and Province of Lower Canada here unto subscribing Personally came and appeared Mr. Dennis Daly of the city of Quebec, tavern keeper, and John Young, of the said city of Quebec, Esquire, merchant, when the said Dennis Daly of his own free will and accord acknowledged and declared that for, and in consideration of the sum of seventy pounds Halifax currency to him the said Dennis Daly satisfied and paid by the said John Young Esquire the Receipt whereof is by the said Dennis Daly hereby acknowledged was bargained and sold and by these presents doth bargain and sell unto the said John Young Esquire a certain Negro boy or lad called Rubin. To have and to hold the Negro lad named Rubin unto the said John Young Esquire his heirs, executors, administrators and assigns from henceforth and forever, which said Negro lad was purchased and acquired by him the said Dennis Daly from John Cobham, of the city of Quebec, as appears by deed of sale bearing date the sixth day of September in the year of Our Lord one thousand seven hundred and eighty six delivered up to the said John Young Esquire at the execution hereof.

The said Dennis Daly hereby covenanting, promising and agreeing for himself, his executors, curators or administrators, to guarantee, warrant and defend this present sale against all claims and demands whatsoever of him, the said Dennis Daly, or all and every person or persons whatsoever. Thus done and passed at Québec in the office of Charles Stewart this fifteenth day of August in the year of Our Lord one thousand seven hundred and ninety five the said Dennis Daly having hereunto set his hand and the said John Young as testifying his acceptance to this minute deposited in the office of the said Charles Stewart the same having been first read over.

DENNIS DALY
JOHN YOUNG
A. DUMAS
CHAS. STEWART

Source: *Rapport de L'Archiviste de la Province de Québec pour 1921–22*, (Quebec: Louis-Amable Proulx, Imprimeur de Sa Majesté Le Roi, 1922): 122. Link: http://archive.org/details/rapportdelarchiv02arch

▲ DOCUMENT 8: FREEDOM BEFORE ABOLITION

In the years before the abolition of slavery, a slave depended on the humanity of their master if they were to become free. In 1736, it became necessary to establish a legal framework for manumission (the process of becoming legally free) as numerous slaves had sought freedom by running away from their masters. Laws were created to curtail this; the Code Noir *addressed this "problem" directly. Running away, however, was not the only path to freedom. As this notary record from 1797 indicates, some owners willfully emancipated their slaves. Can you speculate as to why Rubin's master decided to free him only two years after he had purchased Rubin?*

I. ORDINANCE BY GILLES HOCQUART RELATIVE TO THE LIBERATION OF SLAVES [1 SEPTEMBER 1736]

1 September 1736
Ordinance Concerning the Liberation of Slaves
Gilles Hocquart

Upon having been informed that a number of Individuals in This Colony have liberated their Slaves with no more formality than verbally granting them their freedom, And it being necessary to determine the Status of Slaves that may be liberated hereafter, We after having conferred with M. le Marquis de Beauharnois, Governor and lieutenant general for the king in this Colony, Ordain that in the future all individuals in this Country, regardless of their status, who wish to liberate their Slaves will be required to do so according to an act signed by Notaries for which minutes will be kept, And which will be Recorded at the registry of the closest Jurisdiction Royale; we Declare that all other liberations not concluded according to the above form will be Null and Void, and the present ordinance will be read and published in the customary manner, and recorded in the Registries of the Royal Jurisdictions of Québec, Montréal, and TroisRivières. Mandated, etc, done at Quebec on the first of September 1736.

[Signed] Hocquart

Source: Archives nationales du Québec, Centre de Québec, Registre des Commissions et Ordonnances rendues par monsieur Hocquart Intendant de justice, police et finances en la Nouvelle france, E1, S1, P2855, Hocquart, Gilles, Ordinance relative to the liberation of slaves, September 1, 1736, fol. 99.

II. THE EMANCIPATION OF A NEGRO LAD NAMED RUBIN, AGE EIGHTEENTH YEARS, BY JOHN YOUNG, MERCHANT OF QUEBEC (8 JUNE 1797)

Before the public notaries, personally appeared, John Young, Esquire of the city of Québec, merchant, who freely and voluntarily declared that whereas by deed of sale passed before Charles Stewart Esquire and his fellow notaries bearing date at Quebec the fifteenth day of August which was in the year of Our Lord one thousand seven hundred and ninety five, he, the said John Young, for the sum of seventy pounds currency, being the consideration expressed in the said deed, did purchase and acquire from Mr. Dennis Daly, of the said city of Québec, tavern-keeper, a certain Negro lad, named Rubin, about the age of eighteen and, whereas he, the said John Young, being desirous of emancipating the said Negro lad Rubin, and as an encouragement to honesty and assiduity in the said lad, Rubin, declared in the presence of Charles Stewart, one of the subscribing notaries, that if he, the said Rubin, should faithfully serve him, his executors or assigns for and during the term of seven years from the date hereof at the end and expiration of that time he would give him his free and full liberty and in the meantime he would give maintain and cloth him in a decent manner suited to one in his station.

The above declaration however is made upon this express condition that if he, the said Rubin, shall at any time during the said term of seven years to be computed from the date of these presents get drunk absent himself without leave or neglect the business of the said John Young Esq. his master he shall forfeit his title to his liberty anything herein contained to the contrary notwithstanding. But on the other hand if he shall will and truly perform his duty and in all things demean and behave himself as a good and faithful servant he may at the end of the said term of seven years demand of the said John Young his free liberty to which he shall be entitled by virtue of these presents. And further on condition of his good behaviour he shall be allowed monthly as pocket money the sum of two shillings and six pence per month.

Thus done and passed at Quebec aforesaid the eight day of June one thousand seven hundred and ninety seven this minute having been first duly read to and subscribed by the said John Young and explained to the said Rubin who engaged to fulfill the condition of this agreement and accepted with gratitude the generous offer made him by John Young Esq. his master in the presence of the said subscribing notaries these presents remaining of record in the office of the above named Charles Stewart.

JOHN YOUNG
RUBIN X [his mark] YOUNG
A. DUMAS
CHS. STEWART

Source: *Rapport de L'Archiviste de la Province de Québec pour 1921–22,* (Quebec: Louis-Amable Proulx, Imprimeur de Sa Majesté Le Roi, 1922): 123. Link: http://archive.org/details/rapportdelarchiv02arch

ARTICLE 1: I MAKE HIM MY DOG /MY SLAVE

Brett Rushforth

On April 12, 1680, a Belgian monk-turned-missionary named Louis Hennepin tinkered with a canoe on the banks of the Mississippi River. As two French servants boiled a wild turkey for his lunch, Hennepin surveyed the strange and beautiful country before him. His party had traveled the Mississippi for eleven days without incident, but, as he awaited his meal, Hennepin "suddenly perceived ... fifty bark canoes, conducted by 120 Indians, entirely nude, who descended this river with great speed." Hennepin called out to them, twisting his tongue around rudimentary Algonquian to assure the Indians of his good intentions. "Mistigouche," he cried, using the Algonquians' name for his people to identify himself and his servants as their friends. As Siouan speakers, the approaching war party did not understand his words. But, unfortunately for Hennepin, they got the message: these bearded foreigners were allies of the Algonquian-speaking peoples of the Mississippi Valley, the very peoples the Sioux had to attack.[1]

Hennepin and his party quickly realized the danger and scrambled to evade an impending assault. Ditching the turkey in the brush, the servants ran to the canoe, joining Hennepin in a hasty retreat. Within seconds, Sioux canoes surrounded them. Raising ceremonial war cries, the attackers boarded Hennepin's canoe and took him captive. "We offered no resistance," Hennepin later recalled, "because we were only three against so great a number." Now using signs because he "did not know a word of their language," Hennepin tried to urge the Sioux on to their original target, but to no avail. Next he offered bribes, first tobacco from Martinique, then two wild turkeys they had saved for dinner. This pleased his captors, and their demeanor seemed to soften, but by nightfall Hennepin and the Frenchmen still feared for their lives. The servants resolved to die fighting like men, but Hennepin was more resigned to his fate, whispering a vow that he would "allow them to kill me without resistance in order to imitate the Savior, who gave himself voluntarily into the hands of his executioners."[2]

Rather than dying a martyr, Hennepin lived the next eight months as a captive among the Sioux. For nineteen days he and his companions were forced to row their overburdened canoe against the Mississippi's strong current. Reaching the northern edges of navigable waters, the Sioux destroyed Hennepin's canoe to prevent his escape and then marched the prisoners over half-frozen marshlands toward their villages. The prisoners faced daily threats to their lives, enduring "hunger, thirst, and a thousand outrages ... marching day and night without pause." When Hennepin's hunger and fatigue caused him to lag, his captors set fire to the meadows only behind him, forcing him to push ahead. In short, according to Hennepin, "The insults that these barbarians committed against us during our journey are beyond all imagining."[3]

When they reached the Sioux villages, the prisoners faced another wave of humiliating assaults. They were stripped naked, their bodies were painted, and they were forced to sing and dance as they drummed a rattling gourd. The warriors stood the prisoners in front of tall stakes, set in the ground and surrounded by straw and wood, erected to burn incoming captives. Then they began to negotiate Hennepin's fate. A few urged good treatment to curry favor with the French, but their voices were overwhelmed by those arguing for his execution. They began to torture him but were cut short when an influential war chief named Aquipaguetin stepped forward and claimed the priest as a replacement for his son, who had fallen at the hands of Hennepin's allies. In Aquipaguetin's charge Hennepin entered the chief's village, injured and demoralized but glad to be alive.[4]

As he made the transition to life in captivity, Hennepin found it difficult to make sense of his position in Sioux society or even to find the right word to define it. His captors themselves said that "they considered [him] a slave that their warriors had captured in their enemies' territory." Yet, because of his ceremonial adoption as Aquipaguetin's son, he expected a level of independence and respect he never achieved. He was beaten. He faced repeated

Source: Brett Rushforth, *Bonds of Alliance: Indigenous and Atlantic Slaveries in New France*, (Chapel Hill: University of North Carolina Press, 2012): 35–51; 70–71. Published for the Omohundro Institute of Early American History and Culture. Copyright © 2012 by the University of North Carolina Press. Used by permission of the publisher. www.uncpress.unc.edu

death threats. He performed forced labor, farming with Aquipaguetin's wives and children on a nearby island. And he was under almost constant surveillance: "The more I hid myself, the more I had Indians after me ... for they never stopped watching me." But it was hunger that troubled him the most. To keep him weak and dependent, Hennepin's newly adopted kin fed him only five or six meals a week, giving him just enough wild oats and fish eggs to keep him alive. "I would have been very content had they given me something to eat, as they did their children," he remembered. "But they hid [their food] from me ... conserving what little fish they had to feed their children." Despite the metaphorical kinship conferred by his adoption, he and his captors understood the difference between real and fictive sons. "They thus preferred the lives of their children to mine," a distinction that even Hennepin admitted was only reasonable. If the priest could not fully grasp his experience as a Mississippi Valley captive, he was eager for it to end: "It must be said that it is a sweet and pleasant thing to come out of slavery."[5]

The Indians who would engage in a century-long slave trade with French colonists brought their own complex and evolving practice of slavery to the colonial encounter. The act of enslavement dominated and defined Natives' thinking about slavery far more than the long-term status of those they enslaved. Indigenous slaves lived under a wide range of conditions, some dehumanizing and others nearly familial, and a particular slaves's place in the community could change over time. But all of them had to pass through the ritualized system of enslavement designed to strip them of former identities and forcibly integrate them into the capturing village. In war dances and diplomatic ceremonies, through the binding and marking of bodies, and with a sophisticated language of dominion and ridicule, the Native peoples of the Pays d'en Haut articulated an elaborate idiom of slavery as a form of human domestication that reduced enemy captives to the status of dogs and other domesticated animals. Simultaneously expressing and seeking power, enslavement involved a series of scripted acts of physical and psychological dominion designed, in the words of several Algonquian and Siouan languages, to tame and domesticate captured enemies. In so doing, captors harnessed the enemy's power to serve the needs of their own people.

Although slaves were defined by their place in Native war culture, they also labored in agriculture and performed other useful tasks. For men, this work often violated gender norms, as they were compelled to perform traditionally female tasks like hoeing in the fields or carrying baggage on hunting expeditions. Female slaves often became subordinate wives, adding their reproductive and domestic labor to the households that incorporated them. Full of possibilities for social integration, enslaved women's work also carried many dangers, including the potential for sexual violence that seems to have been a hazard unique to their slave status. Some of enslaved individuals' most important labor was performed in the area of diplomacy. As both agents and objects of intercultural relations, indigenous slaves mediated between the violent impulses that led to their enslavement and the alliance building that their bodies facilitated as symbols of generosity. As a regionally and temporally specific system of human bondage, Algonquian and Siouan slavery differed in important ways not only from European chattel slavery but also from other forms of Indian captivity in North America.

NIT'AOUAKARA—I MAKE HIM MY DOG / MY SLAVE

"This reception is very cruel; some tear out the prisoners' nails, others cut off their fingers or ears; still others load them with blows from clubs."

–Sébastien Rale, Jesuit, 1723

Indians of the Pays d'en Haut expressed their relationship to slaves through metaphors of domestication and mastery, comparing captives to dogs and other domesticated animals. More than a simple insult, the metaphorical domestication of enemy captives represented an elaborate cultural idiom that shaped the practice and defined the meaning of indigenous slavery. To shame and intimidate their enemies, Algonquians and Siouans treated their prisoners with great disrespect through symbolic acts of humiliation designed to strip them of their former identities and incorporate them as subordinate domestics. Beginning with demeaning abuse on the journey home, continuing through acts of torture as captives were received into the village, and culminating in ceremonial killing or forced incorporation, Indians designed their rituals of enslavement to demonstrate their mastery over weaker enemies and to secure the allegiance and passivity of those they would keep alive as slaves.

Anishinaabe-speakers called their slaves *awakaan*, which meant "captive," "dog," or "animals kept as pets." The earliest French lexicon of central Algonquian languages, recorded between 1672 and 1674 by Jesuit Father Louis Nicolas, included *aouakan*, meaning "slave or prisoner of war," as one of eight essential nouns for missionaries to know to effectively teach western Indians. After living among the Anishinaabes of Michilimackinac and Sault Sainte Marie, Lahontan composed his own dictionary of essential Anishinaabe terms, listing *Ouackan* for "slave."[6]

The most-advanced French linguist of Anishinaabemowin in the seventeenth century was Louis André, a Jesuit trained in Latin linguistics and later a linguistics professor at Quebec's Jesuit college. Living in several Native villages and working closely with Ottawa informants, he conducted a fourteen-year study of their language and produced an eight-hundred-page manuscript dictionary and phrase book designed to teach other missionaries the language. André recorded dozens of Anishinaabe terms and phrases relating to slavery, most of which expressed the metaphor of slaves as domestic animals. André wrote that the verb to enslave (*nit'aouakara*), for example, literally meant to make someone a dog. Often rendered in the first person possessive, it described enslavement as an act of animal domestication: to say "I make him my slave" was to say "I make him my dog." One of the most intriguing variations of this verb was translated by another Jesuit among the Ottawas as "I make him my plaything, my slave." Rendered in the diminutive form, it could be translated more literally as "I make him my little dog/puppy."[7]

The act of domestication—turning enemies into dogs—began even before the warriors left their village for the raid. Raids originated in communal, and quite often contested, discussions of issues ranging from the need for retaliation to preemptive raids designed to weaken a threatening enemy. Among the Illinois, elder male relatives of anyone killed by an outsider could call a council and demand revenge. "If my strength and my courage equalled yours, I believe that I would go to avenge a relative as brave and as good as he was," one Illinois elder said in a late-seventeenth-century war council. "But being as feeble as I am, I cannot do better than address myself to you," the young warriors. He persuaded them to fight by appealing to their sense of collective revenge and individual masculine honor.[8]

Louis Hennepin witnessed similar negotiations among the eastern Sioux, seeing for himself the beginning of a process that had led to his own enslavement. The warrior or family initiating the raid sent invitations around the village, and sometimes to neighboring villages, to join in a war feast. Accepting this invitation meant accepting the call to war. Those who wished to join the war party gathered at the home of the one who invited them, singing their warrior songs as they arrived. In these songs, Sioux men recounted their deeds of bravery and recalled the captives they had taken, vowing similar success on this raid: "I am going to War, I will revenge the Death of such a Kinsman, I will slay, I will burn, I will bring away Slaves, I will eat Men." A feast and dance followed, called by the Sioux *šunkahlowanpi*—literally "ceremonial song of the dog"—described by later Sioux informants as "a parade with singing made by those who are on the point of going to war."[9]

Eating men and taking slaves expressed the central theme of the *šunkahlowanpi* and other war feasts in the Pays d'en Haut. As Pierre-François-Xavier de Charlevoix explained, warriors "say also in direct Words, that they are going to *eat a Nation;* to signify that they will make a cruel War against it; and it seldom happens otherwise." The metaphorical equation of eating men and taking slaves found its physical expression in the ritual consumption of dog meat, which was the centerpiece of the warriors' feast that preceded the raid. "This feast is one of dog's flesh," explained Nicolas Perrot of the rite among the Anishinaabes, "which [among them] is ranked as the principal and most esteemed of all viands. ... Feasts of this sort are usually made only on the occasion of a war, or of other enterprises in which they engage when on expeditions against their enemies." The practice was so entrenched in the Pays d'en Haut that one colonial official concluded, "The feast of dogs is the true war feast among all the savages." Dog feasts sometimes continued into the journey toward an enemy's territory, and evidence suggests that war parties sometimes killed and ate enemy dogs as sign of power over them.[10]

When captured, slave raiders could find their own logic turned disastrously against them. An Ottawa war chief named Sinagos, who had a reputation as a brutal slaver, conducted a raid in Sioux territory in the early 1670s "putting the men to flight and carrying away the women and children whom they found there." Those who escaped the raid gathered reinforcements who pursued and captured Sinagos and the surviving captives. Recognizing his prominence, the Sioux decided to make an example of him rather than kill or enslave him. "They made him go to a repast," wrote Nicolas Perrot, "and cutting pieces of flesh from his thighs and all other parts of his body, broiled these and gave them to him to eat—informing Sinagos that, as he had eaten so much human flesh and shown himself so greedy for it, he might now satiate himself upon it by eating his own."[11]

Because Indians imagined enslavement as the violent consumption of flesh, they compared freeing captives to vomiting: a violent release of the flesh they had eaten. When a Fox war chief entertained a French delegation in the 1680s, he offered his French guest some venison. When the Frenchman refused on the grounds that he was unhappy with Fox slave raids against French-allied Indians, the Fox man called for four captives, whom he released to his French guest. "Here is how reasonable the Fox can be ... he vomits up the meat that he had intended to eat ... even as it is between his teeth he spits it out, he asks you to return it to where he captured it." Jacques Gravier recorded an expression for releasing captives among the Illinois: "nisicarintamaꙗa acꙗ8ssemahi. je done la vie a cinq prisoniers," I give life to five prisoners. The Algonquian verb means "to vomit."[12]

Carrying mental images drawn from this rich verbal and ceremonial milieu, warriors began their journey to enemy territory seeking slaves to domesticate. In the indigenous war culture of the Pays d'en Haut, taking captives took precedence over killing enemies and especially over territorial conquest, which was extremely rare. "When a Savage returns to his own country laden with many scalps, he is received with great honor," wrote Sébastien Rale, "but he is at the height of his glory when he takes prisoners and brings them home alive." Such feats of bravery, Rale explained, allowed a warrior to be considered "truly a man." "They are so eager for this glory that we see them undertake journeys of four hundred leagues through the midst of forests in order to capture a slave."[13]

Once warriors carried captives a safe distance away from a raided village, they bound them tightly by the hands and neck with a halter. Keeping the captives' legs free except when they slept, the captors "immediately tie their hands and compel them to run on before at full speed, fearing that they may be pursued ... by the companions of those whom they are taking away." Louis Hennepin explained the danger of slowing the captors down. "When they have taken a slave, they garrote him and make him run," he wrote shortly after his own release from slavery among the Sioux. "If he cannot keep up they strike him on the head ... and scalp him. "This was a second wave of sorting strong captives from those who might become an immediate liability or a long-term drain on local resources. The old and infirm were rarely taken from the village, and the necessity of running, bound, for long stretches with little food ensured another level of fitness for surviving slaves"[14]

Led along by a leash, captives faced physical and verbal abuse during their long march to the captors' village. An Illinois warrior might refer to a slave he had captured as *ninessacanta*, "my slave, the one whom I bring," a phrase drawn from the root word "to beat, batter, bludgeon" and occasionally, "to beat to death." Louis Hennepin found his repeated beatings more terrifying than debilitating, enhancing his captors' arbirary power by making him fear constantly for his life. Indeed, the march northward to the Sioux villages was so disorienting for Hennepin that he lost all sense of place and distance, sketching on his return to Europe a map of the Upper Mississippi Valley that stretched it hundreds of miles north of its headwaters. Copied by several subsequent cartographers, Hennepins's bewilderment registered in European cartography long after his release from captivity.[15]

As the returning warriors neared their village, the war chief signaled their arrival with a series of high-pitched cries, one for each captive in the party. In some accounts, individual warriors also cried out once for each of the captives they had taken, "As soon as he arrives, all the people of the village meet together, and range themselves on both sides of the way where the prisoners must pass," wrote Sébastien Rale. "This reception is very cruel: some tear out the prisoners' nails, others cut off their fingers or ears: still others load them with blows from clubs." Among the most degrading of the gauntlet's many torments was the participation of women and children, whose taunts fell with special poignancy on captured male warriors. Like the ceremonies that initiated the slave raid, the logic of subordination required that captives' incorporation into village society be a public affair involving all segments of Native society.[16]

Those disfigured by the gauntlet bore permanent marks of their status as a captive enemy, especially when such wounds occurred in conspicuous locations like the face or hands. Maiming the hands also served another purpose: preventing escape or rebellion. Describing a similar strategy used by the Iroquois, one Jesuit observed. "They began by cutting off a thumb of each [captive], to make them unable to unbind themselves." According to one account, Algonquians adopted this practice to avenge those captured by their Iroquois enemies. The resulting scarring and disfiguration were considered "the marks of their captivity," which remained with living captives long after the trauma of initiation had passed.[17]

Strategic slave marking registered in the Algonquian languages of the Pays d'en Haut. The Anishinaabes used a phrase that Louis André translated as "I cut a young slave to mark him. "The Illinois had a whole family of expressions dealing with personal marking of slave bodies, all drived from the root word *isc8*, meaning "mark of imperfection/defect." These included *isc8chita*, "someone who has a cropped ear"; *isc8chipag8ta*, "bitten on the ear, ear removed with the teeth"; *nitisc8ic8rep8a*. "I crop his nose with my teeth." Other Indians of the Pays d'en Haut marked men in an especially painful way, using "red-hot javelins, with which they pierced the most sensitive parts of his body." Even these physical markers of slavery narrated the act of enslavement as domestication, emphasizing the very personal power exercised over these enemies by capturing warriors. Like enslavement itself, biting the tip from a captive's nose or ear was at once an alienating and terribly intimate act of dominion.[18]

Cropping the nose of the wild thunderer tamed him and transferred his significant power to the dominating village. Consistent with the intent of enslavement generally, this rite expressed the prowess of the captor while appropriating the power of the captive. Perhaps this is why enemy warriors percieved as especially threatening were made to "suffer according to their Merits." Those who cried out during torture were considered less potent and thus less worthy of an honorable death. "When a victim does not die like a brave man," according to Charlevoix, "he receives his death's wound from a woman or from children; he is unworthy, say they, to die by the hands of men."

Even in death male captives faced the prospect of emasculation from their enemies.[19]

After being beaten and marked, slaves were undressed and forced to sing (in some cases the singing began before entering the village). This was the final metaphorical act of stripping slaves' former identities from them, preparing them for death or the forced integration that would follow. At least one Algonquian language made explicit the connection between the humiliation of stripping and slavery: Illinois-speakers used the phrase *nilci8i-nakiha arena*, which meant both "I lift up his loin cloth" and "I treat him like a slave."[20]

Once the initial tortures subsided, another round of sorting divided captives marked for death from those who would stay alive as slaves. Among the Illinois, male heads of household "assemble and decide what they will do with the prisoner who has been given to them, and whether they wish to give him his life." Hennepin came to understand that his fate had been decided in the same way among the Sioux. "When the warriors have entered their lodges, all the elders assemble to hear the account of all that has happened in the war, then they dispose of the slaves. If the father of an Indian woman was killed by their enemies, they give [her] a slave in his place, and the woman is free to give him life or have him killed." "The Anishinaabes did much the same, granting life to some and subjecting others to a slow and painful death. Although the particular reasons for sparing individual captives varied from family to family and village to village, captives could be kept alive to augment population growth, to replace a dead relative or to facilitate alliances through trade. Once the captive had been granted life, he or she was washed, clothed, and given a new name, often that of the deceased he or she was intended to replace. One Illinois word describing the decision to grant life to a captive derives from the word meaning "to cure or heal."[21]

Captives marked to die were forced to sing what the French described as "chansons de mort," or death songs, according to Pierre Deliette, " to afford entertainment to their executioners." François de Montigny witnessed the spectacle when a Winnebago war party passed by an Illinois village "in triumph" with two Missouri slaves, "who were forced to sing their death songs, which is a custom among all the Indians." Called *kikit8inaki8a*, meaning "slave songs," by the Illinois, captives were forced to sing at the entrance of each household that had lost a family member to the captive's people, allowing grieving kin a chance at violent (or at least verbal) catharsis. Condemned slaves were handed a special staff and forced to march from cabin to cabin as they sang. At ten to twelve feet long, the staff was wrapped in feathers to signify the captors otherworldly power over the slave. It must have also become a physical burden to captives who had to carry it around the village for hours. The staff was eventually planted in the ground to become torture stake, where condemned slaves spent their final hours enduring a slow, smoldering death.[22]

Captors spared women and children more often than men. In addition to targeting the male warriors for revenge killings, this strategy maximized the demographic benefits of slavery, as increasing the number of adult males in a village would do little to change its reproductive capacity. During times of high mortality due to disease or warfare, female captives often represented the best hope for rapidly restoring lost population. Especially in the frequently polygynous societies of the Pays d'en Haut, female captives integrated smoothly into present social structures as second or third wives of prominent men. Children were especially prized because of the relative case with which they assimilated into the capturing society, learning new languages and customs much more quickly than older captives. This selection process left a surplus of male captives, who were often traded outside the village. Welcomed communally, slaves were controlled individually. The warrior who captured each slave exercised mastery over the person as a private possession, and any family wishing to kill or adopt a slave would have to negotiate terms with the original master. This process could lead to conflict among the captors as the ultimate future of each slave became a matter of group deliberation.[23]

Of the many possible fates facing a captive who survived the rituals of domestication, the most familiar to modern readers is a captive's adoption into a household to take the place of the dead. If it was not the most common outcome, it was certainly the status that French observers recognized most readily. "When there is any dead man to be resuscitated, that is to say, if any one of their warriors has been killed, and they think it a duty to replace him in his cabin," wrote Sébastien Rale, "they give to this cabin one of their prisoners, who takes the place of the deceased; and

this is what they call 'resuscitating the dead'." In times of peace this role was played by other members of the same village, who took the place of prominent villagers who had died, thereby assuming their full identity and status. Nicolas Perrot insisted that among the ottawas a dead person of high status was sometimes replaced by another resident of the village, "and they regard themselves as united to this family, as much as if they were actually kindred." But because the adoptee "must be of the same rank" as the dead, captives were rarely chosen to replace influential men and women.[24]

What captive adoption meant in Native societies is elusive at best. French law and culture granted an adopted father an essentially proprietary authority over the adopted child, and this shaped what French observers meant to convey with the notion of captive "adoption," never intended by French authors to indicate the creation of true kinship. Even captives themselves, like Louis Hennepin, found their relationship with adopted relatives hard to comprehend, not familial in any sense that they recognized yet still expressed as kinship. When it came to difficult choices, as it did with Sioux food supplies, Hennepin acknowledged that his adopted kin favored their actual relatives over the fictive kinship created by his ceremonial adoption. Transcending the limits of European observations and filling in their silences, indigenous languages provide a glimpse of how Indians themselves understood the category of kinship created by captive adoption. Their own metaphors suggest meanings much more complex than colonists understood.[25]

Kinship terminology was conspicuously absent from Algonquian idioms describing adopted captives. Rather than using the common verb *nintoohsimaa*, "I have him as a father," for example, Illinois captives identified their master by the household where they stayed. Only two recorded kinship terms applied to adopted captives or slaves. The first was an expression used by families who wanted to kill a slave from a returning war party. They would say to the warrior who captured the slave, *nita8embima*, a unique word from meaning "that is my relative," which was said only "by the executioner to whoever brings a slave" to the village. Rather than indicating actual kinship, the term condemned the captive to death in memory of the dead relative. The Jesuit Thierry Beschefer recorded the presence of a second kinship term in 1683, specifically used to demean adoptees. Using a different form of the word *son*, captors signified "a submission of which They make use to command us, as They do the Slaves whom they have adopted." According to a French trader, among the Anishinaabes adopted captives "never lie in their Masters Huts," another mark of distinction from the household's actual kin similar to the exclusion experienced by Hennepin among the Sioux. The master was, in the words of Pierre Chaumonot, a "feigned parent," or fictive kin.[26]

Adopted slaves, then, were bound to a household of fictive kin, occupying the physical and metaphorical place of a child but constantly aware that they were not actual relatives. Slaves' history and the terminology used to describe them equated them more with the family's domestic animals than with their children. And because they had no actual kin but were attached to a household at the master's pleasure, they were bound to the family at a single point rather than through the multiple lines created by kinship. Like dogs, their linguistic equivalents, adopted slaves were thus part of the household but never really part of the family.

The presence of fictive kinship bonds created by slaves' ritual adoption followed a pattern of linking family and slavery in a wide range of historical slave systems. The expression of mastery in familial terms—what sociologists of slavery call "quasi-filial" kinship—pervaded slaveries from ancient Rome to the antebellum southern United States, Indeed, the English word *family* derives from the Latin *famulus*, meaning household slave. Across vast cultural differences, masters have imagined themselves fathers, but they have always understood the difference between their slaves and their biological family. This was especially evident in the particular language of kinship used by those adopting slaves in the Pays d'en Haut, where they made careful distinctions between real and fictive sons, between actual kin and those forced to take their place in the household.[27]

The French did not find in the Pays d'en Haut a benign system of captivity that they would transform into slavery. The Siouan and Algonquian peoples there had an elaborate and often brutal war culture centered on a form of slavery, built on different assumptions and employed for different reasons than the plantation slavery developing in the contemporary Atlantic. Focused on the act of enslavement rather than the production of commodities, indigenous slavery was at its heart a system of symbolic dominion, appropriating the power and productivity of enemies

and facilitating the creation of friendships built on shared animosity toward the captive's people. The intensely personal violence experienced during the first few months could be brutal and often deadly, but those who survived and weathered the storm of insults that followed found themselves in a system with many well-worn pathways out of slavery. These paths were often difficult to take, they were not available to everyone, and the prevalence of diplomatic slave trading served as a constant reminder of slaves' marginal and precarious position. And it goes without saying that, given the choice, no one would have sought enslavement, no matter what the outcome. But, if only in the next generation, slaves could at least hope to rise to full acceptance by the society that enslaved them, becoming identified with a people they once considered less than fully human.

Slavery in the Pays d'en Haut simultaneously disrupted and facilitated the broader political economy of trade and intermarriage that linked peoples and places throughout the region and beyond. Among allies, the sharing of enslaved enemies cemented alliances and created the bonds of fictive kinship that linked the region's peoples to one another across ethnic and linguistic lines. Among enemies, enslavement provided outlets for violent expressions of enmity that stopped short of total destruction and provided mechanisms of repopulation and enhanced productivity. As in all historical contexts, enslaved individuals in the Pays d'en Haut were agents as well as objects, responding to the trauma and alienation of slavery with creative adaptation to their new surroundings. French colonizers would bring their own evolving notions of slavery to the colonial encounter, which began a century-long conversation that would transform the vocabularies and structures of slavery in both the Pays d'en Haut and the French Atlantic world.

NOTES

1. "J'apperçus tout d'un coup ... cinquante Canots d'ecorce conduits par six vingt Sauvages tous nuds, qui décendoient d'une fort grande vitesse sur ce Fleuve." Louis Hennepin, *Nouvelle découverte d'un très grand pays situé dans l'Amérique, entre le Nouveau Mexique et la mer glaciale* (Utrecht, 1697), 314–315. Catherine Broué discusses problems with Hennepin's credibility, concluding that the 1697 edition is largely reliable and highly valuable. Broué, "En filigrane des récits du Pére Louis

Hennepin: 'trous noirs' de l'exploration louisianaise, 1679–1681," *Revue d'histoire de l'Amérique française*, LIII (1999–2000), 339–366. For the negative view, see Jean Delanglez, *Hennepin's Description of Louisiana: A Critical Essay* (Chicago, 1941). Perhaps the foremost authority on seventeenth- and eighteenth-century Sioux history and culture, Raymond J. DeMallie concludes that Hennepin's writings, if evaluated carefully, "present valuable ethnographic detail" about the eastern Sioux. DeMallie, "The Sioux at the Time of European Contact: An Ethnohistorical Problem," in Sergei A. Kan and Pauline Turner Strong, eds., *New Perspectives on Native North America: Cultures, Histories, and Representations* (Lincoln, Nebr., 2006), 243.

Throughout this study I use the term "Sioux" rather than the recently fashionable "Dakota" because the latter term excludes those Sioux who are Lakota or Nakota and because "Sioux" is a much more widely recognized term among Anglophone readers. French sources from the seventeenth and eighteenth centuries do not allow a clear distinction between various Sioux bands, so the broader term also better reflects the historical record. Several modern tribal organizations in the United States use "Sioux" in their official names, but none uses "Dakota" except to designate their location. See Raymond J. DeMallie, "Sioux until 1850," in *Handbook*, XIII, *Plains*, part 2, 718; and, for a different perspective, Gary Clayton Anderson, *Kinsmen of Another Kind: Dalzota-White Relations in the Upper Mississippi Valley, 1650–1862* (Lincoln, Nebr., 1984).

2. "Nous ne faisons aucune resistance, parce que nous n'étions que trois contre un si grand nombre," 316: "Je ne savois pas un mot de leur langue," 320; "J'avois resolu de me laisser tuer sans resistance afin d'imiter le Sauveur, qui s'étoit remis volontairement entre les mains de ses bourreaux," 319: Hennepin. *Nouvelle découverte*.

3. "Le faim, la soif, et mille outrages ... marché jour et nuit sans delai," 342: "Les Insultes, que ces Barbares nous firent pendant nôtre route, sont au dessus de toute imagination," 322: Hennepin, *Nouvelle découverte*.

4. Ibid., 355.

5. "Elles me consideroient comme un Esclave, que leurs Guerriers avoient fait dans le pays de leurs Ennemis," 362; "plus je m'enchois, plus j'avois de Sanvages à ma suite ... car ils ne me quittoient point de veuë." 320–321; "J' aurois esté fort content, s'ils m'eussent

donné à manger, comme à leurs enfans. Mais ils se cachoient de moy ... conservoient le peu de poisson, qu'elles avoient, pour en nourrir leurs enfans. ... Elles préféroient donc la vie de leurs enfans à la mienne. En quoy il est certain, qu'elles avoient raison," 362; "Il Paul avoüer. qu'il est bien doux et bien agreeable de sortir de l'Esclavage," 463: Hennepin, *Nouvelle découverte* For mistreatment and labor, see Louis Hennepin, *Description de la Louisiane, nouvellement découverte au Sud'Ouest de la Nouvelle France* (Paris. 1683), 246; Hennepin, *A New Discovery of a Vast Country in America, Extending above Four Thousand Miles, between New France and New Mexico* (London, 1698) (Wing H1451), I. log. William Henry Foster similarly argues that the power of Native women to control slaves "came not from physicality but from the hearth." Foster. *The Captor's Narrative: Catholic Women and Their Puritan Men on the Early American Frontier* (Ithaca, N.Y., 2003), 9.

6. John D. Nichols and Earl Nyholm, *A Concise Dictionary of Minnesota Ojibwe* (Minneapolis, Minn., 1995), 14; Frederic Baraga, *A Dictionary of the Otchipwe Language, Explained in English* (Cincinnati, Ohio, 1853), 49–50, 453; C. Douglas Ellis, *Âtalôhkâna nêsta tipâcimôwina: Cree Legends and Narratives from the West Coast of James Bay* (Winnipeg, 1995), 55, 85, 159, 449. Although there are many variant spellings of *awakaan*, I use Nichols and Nyholm's version as the most recent standardization of the orthography. For Nicolas, see Diane Daviault, ed., *L'algonquin au XVIIe siêele: une édition critique, analysée et commentée de la grammaire algonquine du Père Louis Nicolas* (Sainte-Foy, Que., 1994), 5, 34, 106–107; [Louis-Armand de Lom d'Arce], Baron de Lahontan, *Voyages du Bon de Lahontan dans l'Amérique Seplentrionale* (Amsterdam, 1705), II, 321. Jonathan Carver echoed Lahontan's spelling in his own word list more than sixty years later; "Esclave, Ouackan." See Carver, *Voyage dans les parties intérievres de l'Amérique Septentrionale pendant les années 1766, 1767, et 1768* (Yverdon. Switzerland, 1784), 312.

Linguists tend to distinguish between words historically recorded forms and their standardized spellings by placing those words quoted from historical sources in quotation marks and placing standardized non-English words in italics. I break from that convention, here—by generally italicizing all Algonquian words—for two reasons. First, because the MiamiIllinois language lost most of its native speakers quite early, it has relatively few standardized words, and none of the Algonquian languages has standardized forms for much of the seventeenth-century vocabularies I discuss here. Second, the large number of Algonquian words in the text would make the use of quotation marks cumbersome, interfering with the narrative rather than clarifying its meaning. Algonquian words quoted from historical sources are spelled as they were recorded in the original manuscript or printed text.

7. "Je le fais esclave": André, "Preceptes, phrases, et mots de la langue algonquine outaouaise," s.v. "esclave," "J'en fais mon joiiet, mon esclave": Pierre Du Jaunay, "Dictionarium gallico-outaouakum, "MS, 1748, copy in Smithsonian Institution Anthropology Library, s. v. "esclave." Du Jaunay also confirms Andre's translation of *nit'aouakara:* "nit'a8akan. mon [ésclave] nit'a8akara. Je le fais esclave."

8. Pierre Deliette, "Memoir of De Gannes [Deliette] concerning the Illinois Country," in Theodore Calvin Pease and Raymond C. Werner, ed. and trans., *The French Foundations, 1680–1693*, Collections of the Illinois State Historical Library, XXIII (Springfield, Ill., 1934), 377 (hereafter cited as Deliette, "Memoir").

9. Hennepin, *New Discovery*, II. 72: Eugene Buechel and Paul Manhart, *Lakota Dictionary: Lakota-English/English-Lakota* (Lincoln, Nebr., 2002), 191, 291.

10. Charlevoix, *Letters to the Dutchess of Lesdiguieres,* 131 ("*eat a nation*"); Perrot, *Memoir*, in Blair, ed. and trans., *Indian Tribes*, 53–54 ("most esteemed"); Antoine Denis Roudot, "Memoir concerning the Different Indian Nations of North America," in W. Vernon Kinietz ed., *The Indians of the Western Great Lakes, 1615–1760* (Ann Arbor, Mich., 1940), 403 ("true war feast"); Henri Joutel, *The La Salle Expedition to Texas: The Journal of Henri Joutel, 1684–1687*, ed. William C. Foster, trans. Johanna S. Warren (Austin, Tex., 1998), 119.

11. Perrot, *Memoir,* in Blair ed, and trans., *Indian Tribes,* 189, 190.

12. "Le Chef prenant la parole dit, voici en quoi I Outagamis peut etre raisonnable ... il vomit la viande qu'il a eû dessein de manger ... et l'ayant entre ses dents il la crache, il te prie de la remettre eû il l'a prise." Bacqueville de La Potherie. *Histoire de l'Amérique Septentrionale.* II 214; Gravier and Largillier, "Dictionnaire illinois–français." 527 ("to vomit").

13. Raudot, "Memoir," in Kinietz,ed.. *Indians of the Western Great Lakes*, 355–356. For the Rale quote. see *Jesuit Relation*. LXVII. 171–173.

14. "Quand ils ont pris un esclave. ils le garotttent [sic] et le font courir; s'il ne peut les suivre. ils luy donnent un coup de hache à la teste et le laissent après lay avoir enlevè la peruque ou cheveleure": Hennepin. *Déscription de la Louisiane*, 63. *Jesuit Relations.* LXVL, 275 ("tie their hands").

15. Gravier and Largillier, "Dictionnaire illinois-français." 28, 340. The first map influenced by Hennepin's information was a 1681 Paris map titled *Carle de la Nouvelle France*, which could have been drawn only from Hennepin because of its placement of the "Issati," or Sioux villages. Derek Hayes, *American Discovered: A Historical Atlas of North American Exploration* (Vancouver, 2004), map 92. Hennepin's own map, first published in his 1689 *Description de la Louisiane,* was reprinted several times into the early eighteenth century, including in his *Nouvelle decouverte* (1697 and subsequent editions).

16. *Jesuit Relations,* LXVII, 173. Rale speculated that the Illinois adopted these cruelties only after their similar treatment as captives of the Iroquois: "It was the Iroquois who invented this frightful manner of death, and it is only by the law of retaliation that the Illinois, in their turn, treat these Iroquois prisoners with an equal cruelty," See *Jesuit Relations*, LXVII, 173–175. This statement should be assessed cautiously, however, as the French frequently minimized the violence of their allies and exaggerated that of the Iroquois. See, for example, a report from 1660 that describes French-allied Indians' tearing out fingernails, cutting off fingers, and burning hands and feet at Quebec, dismissed by another Jesuit as "merely the game and diversion of children" (*Jesuit Relations*, XLVI, 85-101, esp. 93). "Tout le Village assiste à cette derniere Ceremonie" (Bacqueville de La Potherie. *Histoire de l'Amérique Septentrionale.* II, 26). For a description of the gauntlet among eastern Algonquians, see James Axtell, "The White Indians of Colonial America," *WMQ*. 3d Ser., XXXII (1975), 70—71. For the Iroquois, see Daniel K. Richter, "War and Culture: The Iroquois Experience," *WMQ*. 3d Ser., XL (1983), 557.

17. *Jesuit Relations*, L. 39 ("cutting off a thumb"). XLV, 257 ("marks"). For the best descriprion of Iroquoian disfiguration, see Roland Viau, *Enfants du néant et mangeurs d'âmes: guerre, culture, et société en Iroquoisie ancienne* (Montreal, 1997), 172–186; William A. Starna and Ralph Watkins, "Northern Iroquoian Slavery," *Ethnohistory*, XXXVIII (1991), 43–45. For additional eaxmples from the Pays d'en Haut, see *Jesuit Relations*, XLVIII, 85–101, LXVIII,

171–175. For hand mutilation, see also Gravier and Largillier, "Dictionnaire illinois-francais," 176.

18. "Je coupe un jeu[n] esclave pour marquer": Andre, "Preceptes, phrases, et mots de la langue algonquine outaouaise," s.v. "marquer." "Qui a l'oreille coupèe": "mordu a l'oreolle, oreille emportee avec les dents": "je luy coupe le nès avec le dents": Gravier and Largillier. Dictionnaire illinois-francais," 111. 176, *Jesuit Relations*, XLVIII, 99 ("red-hot javelins").

19. For the long-nosed god and thunderers, see James R. Duncan, "Of Masks and Myths." *Midcontinental Journal of Archacology*, XXV (2000), 1–26. Hennepin. *New Discovery*. L. 186 ("according to their Merits"). P. de Charlevoix, *Journal of a Voyage to North-America* (London, 1761), II. 107.

20. "Je luy oste son brayet, la traite en esclave": Gravier and Largillier, "Dictionnaire illinois-français." 209.

21. Deliette, "Memoir," 384 ("assemble and decide"). "Quand les guerriers sont entrés dans leurs cabannes, tous les anciens s'assemblent pour entendre la relation de tout ce qui s'est passé en guerre, ensuitte ils disposent des Esclaves. Si le pere d' une femme Sauvage a esté tué par leurs ennemis, ils luy donnent un Esclave à la place, et il est libre à cette femme de luy donner la vie ou de le faire mourir." Hennepin, *Description de la Louisiane*, 65–66, For post-torture healing and naming, see Bacqueville de La Potherie, "History of the Savage Peoples Who Are Allies of New France," in Blair, ed. and trans., *Indian Tribes*, II, 36–43; Daniel K. Richter, *Ordeal of the Longhouse: The Peoples of the Iroquois League in the Era of European Colonization* (Chapel Hill, N.C., 1992), 59–74; Viau, *Enfants du néunt*, 137–160. For "nimpelakiihaa," see Antoine-Robert Le Boullenger. "Dictionnaire français-illinois." MS, ca, 1720s, John Carter Brown Library, Brown University, Providence R.I.; Daryl Baldwin personal communication.

22. Deliette, "Memoir," 383 ("chansons de mort"); *Jesuit Relations*.XLV.183 ("entertainment") "En triomphe… ces pauvres prisonniers qu' on obligeoit de chanter leur chanson de mort, qui est une maniere qu' ont tous les sauvages": the Illinois demanded the slaves release because they were Missouris, "comme ayant toujours este amis" (as they had always been friends"): frangois de Montigny, "Lettre de M. de Montigny sur les missions du Mississippi." Aug. 25, 1699, 1–2, ASQ.SME (text nt clear), For the torture staff, see Deliette, "Memoir"383–384: Gravier and largillier "Dictionnaire Illinois-franeais, 373."

23. Richter, *Ordeal of the Longhouse,* esp. 67–68; Gordon M. Sayre, *Les Sauvages Américains: Representations of Native Americans in French and English Colonial Literature* (Chapel Hill, N.C., 1997), 248–304. For Illinois social structure, see Susan Sleeper-Smith, *Indian Women and French Men: Rethinking Cultural Encounter in the Western Great Lakes* (Amherst, Mass., 2001), esp 1–37, where she indicates the importance of women to integrating outsides into Illinois kin structures. For a similar captive selection process among the Indians of the Southwest, see James F. Brooks. *Captives and Cousias: Slavery, Kinship and Community in the Southwest Borderlands* (Chapel Hill, N.C., 2002), esp. 1–40.

24. *Jesuit Relations,* LXVII, 173 ("resuseitating"): Perrot, *Memoir* in Blair. ed. and trans., *Indian Tribes*. 1, 84 ("same rank") 85 ("actually kindred").

25. Kristin Elizabeth Gager, *Blood Ties and Fictive Ties: Adoption and Family Life in Early Modern France* (Princeton, N.J., 1996); Hennepin, *Nouvelle découecrle*, 362. Compare this to Perrot's report that Anishinaabe wives could turn to their extended kin when they needed protection or redress. Perrot, *Memoir,* in Blair, ed. and trans., *Indian Tribes*, 1, 64–65.

26. "Cest mon parent, dit le boureau a qui conque amene un esclave": Gravier and Largillier, "Dictionnaire illinois–français," 36. For Illinois kinship terms, see David J. Costa, "The Kinship Terminology of the Miami-Illinois Language," *Anthropological Linguistics*, XLI (1999), 28–53: *Jesuit Relations,* LXII, 213 ("to command us"). Pierre Deliette confirmed Beschefer's sense that calling adoptees "son" was a mark of disrespect. See Deliette, "Memoir," 363. For "never lie in their Masters Huts," see Lahontan, *New Voyages,* II, 37. For "feigned parent," see *Jesuit Relations*. XVIII, 29.

27. Orlando Patterson, *Slavery and Social Death: A Comparative Study* (Cambridge, 1982), 62–65; *Oxford English Dictionary*. s.v. "family." In 1376, the French political philosopher Jean Bodin wrote. "For the very name of a Familie came of *Famulus* and *Famulativ,* for that it had in it a great number of Slaves: and so of the greatest part of them that are in subjection in the Familie, men call all the whole household a Familie: or else for that there was no greater means to gather wealth than by slaves and servants, which the Latines call *Famuli,* the auntients not without cause have called this multitude of Slaves and servants a Familie." Bodin. The Six Bookes of Commonweule. ed. Kenneth Douglas McRae (Cambridge. Mass., 1962), 32.

◼ARTICLE 2: SLAVERY IN NEW FRANCE

Robin Winks

Slavery was given its legal foundation in New France between 1689 and 1709, and had the timing been different, the institution might well have taken a firmer hold than it did. Prior to 1663 New France had been a seigneury of the Compagnie des Cent-Associés, administered by the company with an eye to quick profits from the fur trade and fitfully aided by the Society of Jesus as a mission colony. Colonization had been subordinated, and economic rather than social ends had shaped the conventional wisdom of the time. The fur trade required no skilled labor; it required no gang labor either. A full-blown slave system had not been needed, and although the Indians enslaved many of their captives, on occasion selling a *pani* to work as a field hand or as a domestic servant for the French, there had been no economic base upon which slavery could profitably be built and little demand for either slave or *engagé* ("indentured") labor.

When New France was transferred from company to royal control in 1663, this conventional wisdom was broken temporarily and Louis XIV set about building a new colony. Upon the wilderness he imposed an effective form of administration, with a governor who was responsible for external affairs and the military and an intendant who was to maintain law and order, to provide a secure financial basis for the colony and to take charge of internal development. The following year the Coutume de Paris was introduced by a newly created Conseil Souverain, thus bringing local laws into conformity with those of the metropole. Jean-Baptiste Colbert, the Minister of the Marine, encouraged intermarriage between French and Indians so that a new people of one blood might emerge, with their loyalties and their future pinned to the revitalized colony. And for five years Jean Talon, "The Great Intendant," labored to diversify the economy of New France.

Under Talon and his immediate successors the colony was a projection into the New World of a growing, centralized society near the height of its power. Religious orthodoxy was mandatory after the revocation of the Edict of Nantes in 1685. A local militia began training in Montreal. Talon brought in purebred livestock, tested seed grain, encouraged the development of industry, investigated the fisheries, tapped the filling reservoir of skilled workers, and endeavored to begin trade with the French West Indies. More seigniories were granted, and in order to increase population the state brought in *filles de roi*, gave dowries to the needy and grants to those who went forth and multiplied, and forced bachelors into marriage. Careful censuses were taken to measure the colony's growth in manpower, to gauge the proper use of the skilled immigrants, and to forecast possibilities for new industries and new channels of trade.

During this period of imaginative and expansive thinking, slavery appeared to be one means of increasing manpower. In 1677 Jean-Baptiste de Lagny, Sieur des Bringandières, obtained royal permission to exploit the mines of New France. He soon found that there was too much to do and too few to do it: the fisheries, the mines, and agriculture all offered potential wealth too great for only nine thousand colonists to tap. Consequently, sometime in 1688 apparently, he communicated his conviction to the governor, Jacques-René de Brisay, Marquis de Denonville, who in turn and together with the intendant, Jean Bochart de Champigny, that year appealed to France for Negro slaves. "Workers and servants are so rare and extraordinarily expensive," they wrote, "... as to ruin all those who attempt to be enterprising. We believe that the best means to remedy this is to have Negro slaves here. The Attorney General of the Council, who is in Paris, assures us that if His Majesty agrees to this proposition, some of the principal inhabitants will have some [slaves] bought for them in the Islands as vessels arrive from Guinée, and he will do so as well."[1]

Denonville was an aggressive governor who already had shown little regard for other races and who was determined to build the economy of New France, at least in some measure, along the lines laid down by Talon. Two years earlier he had sought diligently for two Negro slaves who had escaped from New York, and in 1687 he had seized forty Iroquois whom he had invited to a peace conference and had shipped them to France as slaves. Now he was in the midst of a war precipitated by his duplicity. By the end of the year

Source: Robin Winks, "Slavery in New France, 1628–1760" in *Blacks in Canada: A History*, Second Edition, (Montreal-Kingston: McGill-Queen's University Press, 2007): 3–9.

he was to be defeated and, in 1689, recalled by Louis XIV. In 1685 the *Code Noir* had been promulgated for the West Indies, and Denonville reasoned that the *Code*, as well as the slaves, might be brought from the islands to help solve New France's chronic shortage of unskilled labor. In this wish he was helped by the Attorney General, Charles-François-Marie Ruette d'Auteuil, who early in 1689 sent a memorandum to the King in which he argued that slavery would be profitable for New France, since even the expense of clothing the slaves might be turned to advantage; the Negroes could, as the Algonquins did, wear dry beaver skins which, through use, would become *castor gras* of doubled value.[2]

Whether moved by a vision of more productive mines or of prime pelts from black backs, Louis XIV assented on May 1, 1689.[3] In doing so, he rather carelessly limited his remarks to the importation of Negro slaves to help with agriculture, and he cautioned that since these expensive purchases would be coming from a radically different climate, the entire project might well fail should the sudden contrast in environment prove too much for the Negroes. Almost immediately thereafter, the outbreak of King William's War, and Denonville's recall, virtually nullified the royal assent. The King gave a second authorization in 1701,[4] four years after the Treaty of Ryswick. Queen Anne's War, or the War of the Spanish Succession, broke out during the following year, however, once again making sea routes dangerous and transport scarce. Thereafter, the colony was left to its own devices for obtaining slaves, and when, in 1704, Paris declared that colonies existed solely to serve the mother country and should not compete for industry, commerce, or population, New France reverted to an economy based in part upon the declining fur trade, effectively ending any likely need for a large number of slaves.

Nonetheless, slavery continued to grow slowly, for domestic servants and field hands were wanted by the wealthier families, and local authorities tried to give to it a more secure legal base when they could. The word *esclave* itself had not been used in the civil registers of New France before 1694,[5] but thereafter it became increasingly common. Clearly, confusion as to the formal status of the slave and how to give him his freedom lay back of the final step by which slavery acquired its tenuous footing in New France. On April 13, 1709, the intendant, Jacques Raudot, disturbed by the presence of a number of Indians who,

despite the widespread assumption that they were slaves by law, were claiming to be free men, read a lengthy *ordonnance*[6] in which he declared that "all the *panis* and Negroes who have been purchased and who will be purchased, shall be the property of those who have purchased them* and will be their *slaves.*" Anyone who induced a slave to run away from his master was to be fined fifty livres.[7]

But if Raudot were to provide an official statement in support of slavery, official action also was necessary to ensure that those *panis* and Negroes whom their masters genuinely wished to set free might enjoy that freedom. Between 1706 and 1736 the number of slaves who had been given their freedom—or claimed they had—increased rapidly, leading to confusion (especially among the unchristianized who shared the same or similar names) about who was slave and who was free. Accordingly, in the latter year the intendant, Gilles Hocquart, issued a new *ordonnance* that provided for a uniform means of manumission. Verbal agreements were no longer sufficient: to free a slave by gift or by purchase, the owner or purchaser was to obtain a notary's certificate, and all such transactions were to be registered immediately with a royal registry office. Previous manumissions were valid, but none could depart from this procedure after the first of September. Clearly, slavery had grown sufficiently to require records as well as regulation; equally clearly, there was a body of opinion that wished to extend freedom to the slaves, since we may presume that Hocquart's *ordonnance* was in response to a petition, although the initiative may have come not from owners but from freed Negroes and *panis*.[8]

The status of slaves in New France also was regulated by the *Code Noir*, which though never proclaimed in the colony[9] appears to have been used as customary law. There were, in fact, two codes: the first, of 1685, was limited specifically to the West Indies; a revised code of 1724 applied to the new colony of Louisiana as well. The second code did not depart from the first in any significant way except to forbid intermarriage. The original *Code* was drafted to protect the white man from forms of slave violence: theft, revolt, and escape. Since slaves were not numerous in New France, little attention was given to specific regulations covering such eventualities until a specific case arose, which then was dealt with on its merits and within the spirit of the code. Because gang labor was virtually impossible, and since most Negro slaves in particular were domestic servants, less attention needed to be given to safeguards—either for owner or for slave—with respect to clothing, housing, and working conditions. The memory of Colbert and Talon appears to have lingered, for no steps were taken to prevent intermarriage in New France, and if a white man took a Negro slave wife, she was freed by the act of marriage, Further, by the Coutume de Paris, Negro slaves were chattels (*meubles*), and as personal property they were not attached to the land as serfs but solely to their owners.

Hocquart issued his ordinance partially because, as he said, slaves were deserting their masters almost daily under the mistaken belief that there could be no slavery in France or in her dominions. There had been slaves in France, in fact, from early in the seventeenth century. Slavery, it was true, never had been expressly recognized in France: in 1571, when a cargo of Negroes was landed at Bordeaux for sale, the *parlement* ordered their release because slavery did not exist there; and in 1691 the Minister of the Marine declared that Negroes who were brought into the country would be free upon arrival. But his order did not touch upon the legality of slavery in the colonies. In any case, regulations of this sort were seldom enforced, and slaves did serve government officials, ship captains, soldiers, and planters throughout the century. That de facto slavery existed is proven by the suits for freedom undertaken in the eighteenth century.[10]

King and colony were by no means in agreement about slavery, adding to the confusion created by having one set of regulations in France, another—the *Code Noir*—in the Antilles, and a third for New France. A concert of opinion between governor and intendant in 1688 and 1701 had elicited formal approvals of slavery from the King, but by 1716 such a bond of opinion was broken. In October the intendant, Michel Bégon, repeated Champigny's plea: as there were only twenty thousand inhabitants in New France, he wrote, labor was expensive and scarce. If the colony were encouraged to enter into the slave trade, local industry, agriculture, and commerce would improve much as they had in the English colonies to the south. Boston supported a thriving economy partially on slaves, and in New York the land was cultivated by Negroes so that white energies could be directed to trade. In New France, the intendant suggested, Negroes could till the soil,

fish for cod, saw timber, build ships, and exploit the iron mines "out of which the King and the colony could derive the greatest advantages" if there were but workers to develop them.

Apparently Bégon anticipated the major objection at its source, for the governor, Philippe de Rigaud, Marquis de Vaudreuil, later wrote in the margin of Bégon's *mémoire* that the climate was too cold and the expense of clothing slaves too great. In prior refutation Bégon pointed out that the climate of Boston and New York was not markedly different and that those Negroes already in New France were in good health. Further, the expense need not be lasting, for the free trade in beaver skins, fresh letters of exchange, and the normal royal funds spent on the colony would provide sufficient revenue. Since in 1716 the slave-trading monopolies enjoyed by the Compagnie de Guinée and the Compagnie du Sénégal were broken by opening the trade to the Guinea Coast to all, Bégon may also have hoped to create in New France a small center for building slave ships. In this he would have been frustrated, however, for the King required that vessels engaged in the Guinea trade should be fitted out exclusively at Bordeaux, Nantes, Rochelle, or Rouen.[11]

Although persistent, without Vaudreuil's support Bégon could accomplish very little. In 1720, one month after the Compagnie des Indes was given a new monopoly over the Guinea trade, Bégon asked the King to send Negroes to work in the hemp market, and he forwarded a memorial in which the inhabitants of New France undertook to buy one hundred and one Negroes from the company at six hundred livres each. In June 1721, the Navy Board informed Bégon that it would have the company carry a cargo of Africans to Quebec, but no action appears to have been taken after the Board learned that the Negroes of Sénégal, who might be sent, were worth one thousand livres each in the West Indies.[12]

Other evidence that the intendants, and on occasion the governors, wished to push slavery while the King was reluctant to do so may be found in the circumstances of Hocquart's *ordonnance* in 1736. The intendant apparently had wished to be more sweeping than his statement reveals, for the King told both him and the governor, Charles, Marquis de Beauharnois, that he did not approve of their proposal to decide on the status of *panis* and other slaves by an explicit law, and it was he who ordered that the colony's judges should be content to follow the custom that considered *panis* to be slaves until those masters who wished to do so granted them freedom by notarial deed.[13] Any move to advance the assumption that all Negroes were slaves—as was occurring for Negroes in the English colonies at this time—and thus to formalize their condition along purely racial lines, was thereby blocked.

NOTES

1. On Lagny, see Benjamin Sulte, "L'eselavage en Canada," *La revue Canadienne,* n.s., *8* (1911), 318, who gives more prominence to Lagny's letter than do other authors. Extracts from the letters of Denonville and Champigny, dated August 10, October 31, and November 6, 1688, are printed in [Jacques Viger and Louis Hippolyte Lafontaine, eds.], "De l'esclavage en Canada," in La Société Historique de Montréal, *Mémoires et documents relatifs à l'histoire du Canada I* (1859), 1–2, The translation is my own. Francis Parkman, while engaged in research for *The Old Regime in Canada* (1874) and *A Half-Century of Conflict* (1892), had extracts copied from these and other pertinent documents; the copies are in the Parkman Papers in the MHS. Viger kept his notes in books that he called *Ma Saberdache,* from which he quotes: When Viger died in 1858, Lafontaine carried the work forward. Lafontaine's copies of the documents are in the PAC., Lafontaine Papers, *14*, file 64, fols. 5552–65; the originals are in the Laval University library.

2. Viger and Lafontaine, "L'esclavage," pp. 2–3; Trudel, pp. 20–21; Parkman Papers, *25*, 294, on d'Auteuil; A. Judd Northrup, "Slavery in New York: A Historical Sketch," *83d Annual Report 1900*, New York State Library, Appendix 6: *State Library Bulletin History No. 4* (Albany), pp. 258–59, 275.

3. Several brief summaries of slavery erroneously state that it was authorized in New France by the rescript of 1688, a mistake apparently perpetuated from Hubert Neilson, "Slavery in Old Canada Before and After the Conquest," *Transactions of the Literary and Historical Society of Quebec,* ser. 2, no. 26 (1906), p. 21. It was Louis's reply of 1689 that legalized slavery.

4. Archives de la Province de Québec, Quebec, Ordres du Roi, ser. B, 22: King to Louis Hector de Callière, governor of New France, and to Champigny, May 31, 1701. On October 5, the governor

and intendant reported that they permitted colonists to hold Negro slaves (Parkman Papers, 6, 238).

5. Trudel, p. 315.

6. Presumably Raudot acted upon a petition or remonstrance from slave-owners, for an *ordonnance* normally arose from a petition addressed to the King or to his representative.

7. Printed in Viger and Lafontaine, pp. 4–5.

8. *Arréts et Règlements du Conseil Supérieur de Québec, et Ordonnances et Jugements des intendants du Canada* (Quebec, 1955), p. 371.

9. There is some disagreement on this point. William Renwick Riddell, in "Le Code Noir," *JNH, 10* (1925), 321, n. 1, feels there is "no sufficient ground" for doubting that the code was applied to New France, but the only evidence he gives is dubious. While Neilson ("Slavery in Old Canada," p. 26) asserts that, since the code of 1685 was incorporated in the Coutume de Paris, which received royal sanction as being applicable to all colonies in the New World, it did apply, he appears to confuse the code itself with the Coutume's regulation concerning *meubles.* Trudel (pp. 27, 163, 213, 316) points out that he could find no evidence that the code was promulgated formally.

10. On slavery and attitudes toward slavery in France, see Gaston Martin, *Histoire de l'esclavage dans les colonies françaises* (Paris, 1948); Paul Trayer, *Etude historique sur la condition légale des esclaves dans les colonies françaises* (Paris, 1887); Charles de la Ronciére, *Nègres et négriers,* 9th ed. (Paris, 1933); and Shelby T. Mc. Cloy, *The Negro in France* (Lexington, Ky., 1961), especially pp. 5–6, 12–14, 22–51, Hilda M. Neatby, *The Administration of Justice under the Quebec Act* (Minneapolis, 1937), pp. 9–11, discusses the validity of the Coulume de Paris in New France.

11. *Collection de manuscrits contenant lettres, mémoires et autres documents historiques relatifs à la Nouvelle-France …* (Quebec, 1884), *3*, 21.

12. See Ordres du Roi, *44*, fols. 3, 528 1/2; *47*, fol. 1242. These are summarized by Edouard Richard in *Report concerning Canadian Archives for the Year 1904* (Ottawa, 1905), App. K. 21, 28, 54. See also Joseph-Noël Fauteux, *Essai sur l'industrie au Canada sous le régime française,* (Quebec, 1927), *1*, 476–77.

13. Ordres du Roi. *63*, fol. 642 1/2, as printed by Richard in *Canadian Archives Report 1904,* p. 211.

ARTICLE 3: SLAVES IN ÎLE ROYALE, 1713–1758

Kenneth Donovan

Charles, an 18-year-old black slave, produced much of the food consumed in his owner's household in 1733. Charles was the property of Pierre Benoist, an ensign in the garrison at Louisbourg, who lived with his family in block two of the town. By 1733, Pierre and his wife, Anne Levron, residents of the town since 1722, had two daughters, 15-year-old Anne and eight-year-old Marie Anne. Maintaining the Benoist household was a full-time job for Charles. The courtyard of the property had a garden measuring 34 by 45 feet, and three animal sheds housing two goats, a sow, 30 hens and roosters, eight ducks, and six turkeys. In addition, Benoist had a half share of an ox and a heifer. Besides their backyard garden, the Benoists had another 900-square-foot garden in nearby block 22 of the town. When not planting, weeding, harvesting the vegetables, or feeding the livestock, Charles was kept busy cutting kindling and keeping the stoves and fireplaces supplied with wood. By December 1733 the Benoists had ten cords of wood in their backyard. A prized member of the household, Charles was valued at 512 *livres* in 1733.[1]

At least 266 individuals like Charles were enslaved in Île Royale from 1713 to 1758, with 232 or 87.2 percent of them in Louisbourg. Recent scholarship on the slave trade has emphasized how slaves in communities such as Île Royale were part of "Atlantic history," and as such, slaves circulated like ambulant property throughout the Atlantic basin, connecting communities around the Atlantic word.[2] Yet, in spite of the thematic unity, the new scholarship has also highlighted the heterogeneous nature of the slave experience. "No one slavery, no unitary slave trade, no single black experience existed," wrote Philip D. Morgan.[3] The lives of slaves who came to Île Royale reinforced Morgan's contention of "no single black experience," since their work and situation were shaped by the unique history and culture of the island.

Most of the 266 slaves in Île Royale, with different backgrounds but a common experience as slaves,

spoke French and had similar occupations.[4] This paper asserts that Île Royale slaves, although designated as property, were by no means passive. The majority of slaves in Île Royale—246 or 92.4 percent—were domestics, performing work to support the functioning of households; they became servants, nursemaids, gardeners, and did most of the daily chores. Only 19 slaves—one fisherman, two cabin boys, 15 sailors, and one executioner—worked outside the household.[5] This paper shows that the increase of slaves in Île Royale followed the growth of the general population, especially the number of families and children. Slaves removed the burden of heavy domestic work and thus, in effect, supported French women in bearing more children than they otherwise would have done: during the years 1722 to 1758 there were 2,200 children born in Louisbourg.[6] Female slaves helped to rear these children. Much of the literature on slaves to date has shown little concern for the humanity or individual behavior of slaves and the relations between the enslaved and their masters.[7] This paper discusses how individuals, both slave and free, interacted with each other within a French and New France context. By focusing on the lives of 23 slaves (14 women 9 men), the paper provides evidence of the importance of slave work to the success and comfort of households and family life in Île Royale.[8]

With the end of the War of the Spanish Succession in 1713, the French were forced to leave Newfoundland and move to Île Royale. By 1714 there were more than three hundred refugees at Louisbourg, including Georges, a black slave who had been purchased by Pastour de Costbelle, the governor of the colony, prior to leaving Newfoundland.[9] George appears to have been the first enslaved African in Île Royale. The nature of the African slave trade ensured that slaves such as George had been separated from their families, their communities, and their heritage: slavery, as Orlando Patterson has observed, entailed "social death," the loss of all recognition of previous marks of identity.[10] The slaves of Île Royale, like most slaves, were not literate, and they were not named or counted as persons in most of the numerous censuses that were conducted on the island. The slaves had no names except those given by their masters, and even then 25 of the 266 slaves in this study had to be recorded as "anonymous."[11] Nor did Île Royale slaves leaves narratives or other significant traces of their identity. Nevertheless, it is possible to

Source: Kenneth Donovan, "Slaves in Île Royale," *French Colonial History*, Volume 5 (2004): 25–42. Adapted with permission by the French Colonial History Society.

study their lives by examining a variety of sources such as records of birth, marriage, and death; lists of returning settlers (1749); contracts of sale; court proceedings; ship departures and arrivals; military enlistment rolls; official correspondence; diaries; and newspapers. Relying on a cumulative methodology, the lives of the 266 slaves have been reconstructed from a mass of disparate primary materials.

The first slave in Île Royale came with Governor Pastour de Costbelle, but it was another eleven years before slaves in significant numbers began to appear on the island. In 1724 there were four slaves in Louisbourg out of a total civilian population of 894. By 1726 there were only three slaves in the colony; but over the next eight years, there was a dramatic increase in the slave population. There were 28 slaves in Louisbourg by 1734 (2.4 percent of the town's population); in 1737 there were 50 slaves (3.3 percent of the population). During the same period (1734–1737) the number of children had grown from 394 to 664, an increase of 40.6 percent. Over the same period, Louisbourg families purchased 22 slaves, an increase of 44 percent in three years. And the trend continued. Over a period of 33 years (1724–1757), there was a steady advance in the number of slaves as the population of Louisbourg and Île Royale increased. By 1752 there were 63 slaves in the town, and five years later, in 1757, that number had more than doubled to 125 slaves, representing 3.1 percent of Louisbourg's estimated civilian population of 4,000. With slaves representing a maximum of slightly more than three percent of Louisbourg's people, they composed a small fraction of the society. Thus, Île Royale was a society *with* slaves, not a "slave society" dominated by the ramifications of slaveholding. Although the remaining records can provide only a glimpse of the world of the slaves in eighteenth-century Louisbourg, they demonstrate that in spite of their relatively small numbers, black and *panis* slaves were in demand throughout the colony's history, and that they contributed significantly to its sustainability.

There was a constant shortage of labor in Île Royale, but there was apparently little inclination to purchase slaves to do most of the labor that produced saleable commodities. As the capital and commercial center of the colony, Louisbourg had an economy that depended on the fishery, the military, and trade.[12] By 1718 Île Royale was producing and exporting 150,000 *quintals* (7.5 million kilos)

of dried codfish per year. (One *quintal* equals approximately 50 kilograms). Île Royale cod production in the first half of the eighteenth century accounted for one-third of all the cod caught by the French in North American waters; but free and indentured men, not slaves, operated the fishery. Only one slave is known to have participated in the Île Royale fishery: George, "the Black," a slave of fishing proprietor Marie Anne Peré, who was paid as a member of fishing crews.[13]

Louisbourg started out as a simple base for the cod fishery, but as the town prospered and also took a major role in the re-export of Caribbean sugar products, Louisbourg developed into one of the most important ports in New France. By 1734 the town was basically completed. Fishing properties—most with landing stages, drying platforms, and a few buildings—surrounded the harbor. At the same time, Louisbourg became the main French military stronghold in the Atlantic region. As a fortress, Louisbourg resembled a European fortified town: it was enclosed by walls, and had batteries and outer works. By the 1730s more than 150 ships were sailing into Louisbourg, making it one busiest seaports in North America. Besides its economic and commercial importance, Louisbourg was the capital and administrative center of Île Royale.

Louisbourg's stratified society was dominated by senior colonial officials, military officers, and successful merchants: categories that were not mutually exclusive. Down the social scale, petty marchants, innkeepers, and artisans served garrison, port, and fishery. By the 1740s Louisbourg's full-time population ranged from 2,500 to 3,000. Each summer, Breton, Norman, and Basque migrant fisherman swelled the population. In Louisbourg's newly formed society, people tended to change occupations more readily than in France, but because almost all manufactures were imported, their occupational choice was narrow. As in small French towns of the day, people of different status lived side by side.[14] Slaves were part of the local society, and yet they were cosmopolitan as well. They were multilingual and came from the West Indies, Africa, India, France, Canada, and the British-American colonies.[15]

Slaveholding in Île Royale was part of a broader phenomenon that began in the sixteenth century when the first slaves were brought from Africa to America; but slaveholding was not significant in terms of numbers. The French enslaved the first blacks in Canada as early as 1608. By 1759, the end of French regime, there were 3,604 slaves in Canada—1,132 of whom were black.[16] The majority of the slaves in New France—69 percent—were not African but *panis,* a term derived from the Caddoan tribes of the Great Plains. The *panis* included slaves from more than 20 aboriginal societies such as the Fox, Sioux, Iowa, Kansa, Chickasaw, Blackfoot, and Comanche. The French name *panis* had become a generic term for "aboriginal slaves" by 1750.[17] During the period from 1713 to 1758, Île Royale, which had a smaller population than the communities along the St. Lawrence, included some 266 slaves: 144 males, 97 females, and 25 whose gender could not be determined. Unlike Canada, where the majority of the slaves were *panis*, most of the slaves in Île Royale—90.9 percent (242 out of 266)—were blacks, reflecting the colony's close trade links with the French West Indies. There were, however, at least 24 *panis* enslaved in Île Royale.

Official French policy toward slavery was established in 1685 with the adoption of the Black Code (*Code Noir*) for the West Indies, which was reissued, with minor revisions, in 1724. In principle, the 60 articles of the Black Code offered some protection to slaves, for it "insisted on the basic humanity of the slave: each was to be instructed, baptized, and ministered unto as a Christian, families were to be recognized, and freed slaves were to receive the rights of common citizens—in theory the African could aspire to become a Frenchman."[18] Slave owners were forbidden to have children by concubinage with their slaves, and those who broke the law were subject to a fine of two thousand pounds of sugar. Various articles of the code also obliged masters to provide minimum weekly quantities of food to all slaves ten years old or over, and forbade them from substituting *guildive* (sugar-cane brandy) for edibles. Slave owners were also required to provide each slave with two suits of clothing or four ells of cloth per year. Finally, masters had to take care of slaves in their old age. Even in slave societies of the West Indies, however, a wide gap yawned between the theory expressed in the code and the practice of slave owners; the Black Code was never even registered in Île Royale and Canada, although it was observed to the extent that slaves were to be baptized, and adults were not to work on Sundays and holy days of obligation.[19]

The overwhelming majority of slaves in Île Royale engaged in some sort of domestic service, and there was a rough division of labor by gender. The men, such as Charles, worked outdoors. They tended gardens, fed animals, cleaned stables, carried water, cut firewood, mowed hay, picked berries, gathered seaweed, shoveled snow, and ran errands. Thus, for those who could afford it, purchasing a slave not only brought higher status but also significantly improved living conditions. Slaves were highly valued because they could do most of the daily chores, especially the heavy and demanding work. Since they had considerable work experience, mature slaves such as François *dit* Jasmin could take on even more responsibility. Born in the French West Indies in 1688, François was a slave of Elie and Simone Thesson *dit* La Floury. Though the Floury family had an extensive fishing and mercantile operation, with two schooners and six shallops, and hired upwards of 80 fishermen each spring, they also owned farm animals, meadowland along the road to the Mira River, and farm and fishing property in Little Bras d'Or and at Scatary Island. François doubtless helped with the farm chores; besides feeding and caring for three cows and two horses, he had to cut hay, churn butter, and attend to numerous other duties associated with a fishing and mercantile property.[20]

Whereas François looked after the outdoor chores, an unnamed New England slave woman assisted Simone Floury with the household, which included nine girls and two boys. Enslaved women performed a wide range of household duties, from looking after children to cleaning clothes, scrubbing floors, preparing meals, and washing dishes. A similar role was intended for Rosalie, a 14-year-old female purchased by Andre Carrerot and his wife Marie for 550 *livres* in June 1736. At the time of purchase, the Carrerots had five children ranging in age from two to ten years, and Marie Carrerot was expecting her sixth child. Rosalie became a live-in nanny and servant in the Carrerot home. Rosalie was considered to be an adult. Besides looking after the children, she had numerous household chores, since the Carrerots lived in a large two-story, half-timbered house on rue Toulouse in block 2 of the town. If Rosalie did not have the necessary household skills, that posed little difficulty, since the law permitted the Carrerots to train Rosalie in the manner that suited their lifestyle. The sale agreement noted that Jean

Gouin transferred to "Carrerot any right of ownership of the said Negress, to be disposed of as he sees fit, in accordance with the usual practice in like cases."[21] The Carrerots eventually had 11 children, and Rosalie worked hard to help raise the children and maintain the household.

Slaves like Rosalie were much sought after in communities such as Louisbourg and Halifax, and slaves were traded between the ports after Halifax was founded in 1749, even though it was a British colony. By 1750 there were 14 enslaved black people in Halifax.[22] The types of slaves being sold there were clearly comparable to those employed in Île Royale. In September 1751 when the schooner *Success* arrived in Halifax, having made its second voyage from Antigua that summer, it brought "9 negro men, the property of Captain Bloss."[23] The following year, Joshua Mauger, a Halifax merchant who had commercial dealings in Louisbourg, offered six additional slaves for sale, including one female and five males. Promoting the domestic skills of the female slave, Mauger described her as "a very likely Negro Wench, of about thirty five years of Age." She was "Creole born," he noted, adding that she had been "brought up in a Gentleman's Family, and [was] capable of doing all sorts of Work belonging thereto, as Needlework of all sorts, and in the best manner; also Washing, Ironing, Cookery, and every other Thing that can be expected from such a slave."[24]

Slave women in Île Royale practiced similar skills and specific occupations in Louisbourg households. Maria, for instance, was a chambermaid in the home of Jean Laborde, the treasurer of the colony during the 1750s. She was one of six slaves in this large household, which included another woman who worked as a servant, Adelaise; Cezar and Thomas, also domestic servants; while Polidor was the personal servant of Sebastien, Laborde's son. Touissant was the cook for the household, in which six slaves looked after five people: Laborde, his wife, a son, a daughter, and a nephew.[25] Since Laborde was one of the leading colonial officials and therefore was obliged to entertain in the town's highest social circles, many of the slaves in the Laborde household were called upon to perform their tasks in a relatively public way. By the late 1750s Laborde, whose property and holdings were valued at quarter of a million *livres*, could easily afford six slaves and host lavish dinner parties and social events.[26] As testimony to his vast wealth, Laborde purchased an additional slave for 805 *livres* at a Louisbourg auction in November 1756. The unnamed slave was one of 13 crewmembers aboard the Newport schooner *New Brunswick* that had been captured off Île Royale after returning from the Newfoundland Grand Banks with a cargo of whale oil.[27] Laborde thus had seven slaves, including one from New England.

Numerous other skilled slaves lived in Île Royale. Among them were Dauphine (the cook) and Anne Honiche Nanon, a servant in the home of Nicolas Larcher.[28] An African native, Anne, who was born in 1734, helped to run Larcher's household affairs. Although a bachelor, Larcher, like Andre Carrerot, was also a member of the Superior Council and a wealthy merchant who lived in a large house outside Louisbourg's walls.[29]

Dauphine, Touissant, and Anne Honiche might have known another cook, Marie Marguerite Rose, a slave also skilled in food preparation. A native of Guinea in West Africa, Marie Marguerite helped to prepare the meals in the home of Louisbourg officer Jean Loppinot and his wife Magdelaine. Purchased in 1736, Marie Marguerite worked as a slave in the Loppinot household for 19 years and helped to raise their 12 children (plus her own) until she was freed in 1755. Upon obtaining her freedom, Marie Marguerite married Jean Baptiste Laurent, a Mi'kmaq, and opened a tavern in Louisbourg. Although illiterate, Marguerite had a cookbook entitled *Le Cuisinier Royal* among her goods when she died two years later. Documents suggest that she did not learn to read and write after her marriage, so she may have kept the cookbook as a prized gift from her mistress. Marie also had an extensive wardrobe of used clothing, some of which she may have received used from her former owner.

The inventory of Marie Marguerite Rose's estate, drawn up in 1757, revealed that she had an even broader range of household skills. A capable tavern-keeper, Marie was also a seamstress who could knit, dye and iron clothes, as well as make her own soap. Since Marie died suddenly in August 1757, the inventory recorded some of her projects in progress at the time of her death, including "a pair of woollen stockings, half made, along with two balls of wool of the same colour." In addition, she had "a ball of white wool and another of brown" and "three small balls of cotton." Apparently, Marie was also making her husband a shirt, since there was a new man's shirt "having only one sleeve, the other being attached with a pin." Marie may have valued blue-hued clothing,[30] as she had "a little blue starch" in her chest for dyeing clothes. Marie also collected remnants of numerous fabrics that she intended to reuse in order to make different types of clothing, along with five balls of her own home-made soap to wash the clothes, and a laundry iron to ensure that they were neatly pressed. Nor did Marie confine herself to the interior of her home. A skilled gardener with her own shovel, she had vegetables in her garden that brought 40 *livres*, 15 *sols* when her effects were sold, making them the most valuable item in her entire estate. She also had "a barrel in which there were some raspberries," together with six pounds of sugar that was doubtless to be used for making preserves.[31]

In one instance, there is more evidence about what a personal servant might be expected to do. Catharine Congo, a slave of Louisbourg merchant Bernard Detcheverry and his wife Jeanne, was one of 14 people seated at Captain Gerard Jaulery's table on the ship *Le Comte de Maurepas* when it departed Bayonne for Louisbourg on 30 May 1749 with 83 passengers, 69 of whom received ordinary rations. Catharine Congo and her owners were entitled to extra rations and special treatment at the captain's table for a passage fee of 62 *livres*, 10 *sols* per person.[32] Self-interest on the part of the Detcheverrys probably played a role in Catharine's seating arrangement, since it was only at the captain's table that she could cater to her owner's wishes.

Of the slaves like Catharine Congo and Marie Marguerite Rose whose birthplace are known, 13 were natives of French West Africa, 25 were from the French West Indies, nine were from Canda, nine from British North America, and 33 people were born in Île Royale.[33] The majority of the remaining 186 slaves in Île Royale were doubtless from the French West Indies also; it is likely that only a small percentage were born in Africa. Much the same patterns held for black slaves in British North America during the eighteenth century. Unlike Île Royale or New France, the data for the origins of New England slaves is more conclusive. Most slaves in the British northern colonies such as Pennsylvania, New Jersey, New York, Connecticut, Rhode Island, Massachusetts, and New Hampshire were born in the British West Indies or were purchased in the southern colonies of North America. The merchants of these British colonies, like their counterparts in Île Royale, did not participate in the international slave trade, but took orders or requests for slaves from merchants or others who often had connections with the Caribbean islands.[34] Northern merchants also sold one or two slaves with a West Indies or North American cargo, solely on a speculative basis. Thus, well-known Boston merchant Peter Faneuil, who traded with Louisbourg throughout the 1730s and 1740s, occasionally sent black slaves as part of cargoes of foodstuffs—including the ship, which was to be sold as well. In July 1737 Faneuil insructed Thomas Kilby, his agent at Canso, Nova Scotia, to sell a sloop at Louisbourg, as well as its cargo of bread, flour, pork, and beef. Included among the shipment were "Two young negro men which if you can get a good price for pray dispose of them." If the price was not suitable, the slaves were to be returned to Boston.[35] On another occasion, 27 April 1753, Captain James Spellen of New York sold Jean, an 11–year-old slave, in Louisbourg. Spellen was a regular trader between New York, Louisbourg, and Halifax.[36]

Only ten slaves, however, came to Île Royale via the British North American colonies. The majority of slaves, such as Marie Flore, arrived in Île Royale from the French West Indies. A native of Martinique, Marie Flore was a one-year-old child when she debarked at Louisbourg in 1741 with her owner, ship captain Pierre Boullot. Boullot had made 13 voyages from Martinique to Louisbourg from 1737 to 1751. Settling in Louisbourg in 1753, Boullot married Jeanne Richard, a Louisbourg native, two years previously, and during the 1750s they had six children.[37] Marie Flore, like Rosalie in the Carrerot household, became a nanny and servant in the Boullot family, and eventually gave birth to a son, Denis. Marie Flore, who was 12 years old in 1753, was likely Boullot's daughter. Describing her in 1762, Boullot noted that "he kept a creole from Martinique at his home for approximately 20 years.[38] The Boullots also had an unnamed slave who was merely described as a "carib," and another *"negresse"* as well.[39]

With the constant demand of feeding, changing diapers, washing, and caring for six young children, Marie Flore, the *"negresse,"* and the "carib" assumed responsibility for the household and the outdoor chores of the Boullot family. Similarly, two slaves who were contemporaries of Marie Flore—Louise, an 18-year-old slave, and her fellow worker, Cezar—undertook the same tasks in the home of Louis La Groix. Like Boullot, La Groix married a Louisbourg native, Magdelaine Morin, in 1753 and settled in Louisbourg. A native of Quebec, La Groix was a ship captain and merchant who had been trading from Quebec to Louisbourg to the French West Indies since the 1730s. La Groix purchased Louise and Cezar just prior to his marriage. Within three years of their wedding, the La Groixs had three children. Unfortunately, Louise died on 24 May 1755, when her mistress was five months pregnant with her second child. Another slave, Marie Anne—who would in turn have her own child, Jeanne Joseph, in 1758—soon replaced Louise.

The birth of Jeanne Joseph, as well as the death of Louise, was recorded in Louisbourg's parish records. In most Roman Catholic colonies, the church's response to slavery was driven not so much by a humanitarian concern about the plight of slaves in colonial society as by a religious conviction that slaves had souls to save and therefore represented potential converts. Accordingly, the church maintained that the moral and spiritual nature of the slave was more significant than the slave's temporary servile status.[40] One hundred and twenty-three black and aboriginal slaves appear in the Île Royale parish records: 80 baptisms, five weddings, 18 burials, 11 witnesses, and nine mothers of babies.

Even though many of the 80 baptized slaves were adults who hailed from the French West Indies, where according to the stipulations of the Black Code, slaves "were to be baptized" and "masters were to instruct their slaves in the Catholic religion, on pain of a discretionary fine," they had not been baptized before their arrival in Louisburg.[41] As elsewhere in New France, slaves were baptized more readily in Île Royale because there were no powerful interests—primarily slave owners and plantation managers—who opposed religious instruction of the slaves.[42] But in some cases, such baptisms occurred only on their deathbeds, after years of service in their masters' households. Some slaves were never baptized in Louisbourg. Anne Honiche Nanon was only baptized in 1759 after she and her owner had returned to France.[43] Moreover, the baptismal ceremony might have been a demeaning experience for slaves. Young children of the owners often served as godparents at most baptisms, as they also did for newborn French infants. This practice may have served to create a formal bond between child and nurse, but we know nothing of what the slave thought of it.

No matter what their particular situation, slaves in Île Royale were forced to adapt to a life they did not choose and could not control. And yet the evidence reveals that these slaves were individuals, with particular life and work skills, who established identities for themselves individually and a significant presence in Île Royale as a group. Male slaves such as Charles, François *dit* Jasmin, Cezar, Thomas, and Polidor were crucial workers in the daily exploitation of the local properties of Louisbourg because they cut wood, carried water, cut hay, milked the cows, fed the chickens, and weeded the gardens. A shortage of workers in Île Royale ensured that slaves' labor was highly valued, especially among growing families, and thus the number of slaves increased as the general population expanded. Over 92 percent of Île Royale slaves were domestics. Slaves such as Touissant, Dauphine, and Anne Honiche Nonon were skilled cooks who prepared meals for prominent members of the Superior Council. Maria was a chambermaid and Adelaise a servant; another servant, Catharine Congo, received special treatment while traveling with her master's family from Europe. Female slaves such as Rosalie, Marie Marguerite Rose, Catharine Françoise, Marie Flore, Louise and Marie Anne were especially highly prized because they helped to rear children as well as to maintain their masters' households. Clearly the work they did supported the demographic expansion of Louisbourg, thereby contributing to the success of the settlement in a fundamental way.

Slaves in Louisbourg did not remain socially dead. They formed relationships with the families for whom they worked and the children they likely nursed. They also formed relationships with each other. Few in numbers, the slaves in Île Royale would have known each other, and may even have collaborated on work in this small society where a few slaves together did not constitute a threat. Dauphine, Touissant, and Anne Honiche, for example, were cooks for three prominent members of the Superior Council, and they may have shared recipes and collaborated on preparing special meals for official gatherings. There is evidence that slaves also gathered on their own account, on occasions such as slave weddings and baptisms; at least five slaves were allowed to marry. Most important, the enslaved people of this society became parents, since nine enslaved women are listed in the records as mothers. The humanity of these enslaved people becomes apparent because they were individuals with their own story to tell; they were part of an evolving African-French colonial culture. Although Île Royale was a small colony, the world of the slaves was even smaller since they were not permitted to work in the large-scale exploitation of the fishery for commodity production, or on the construction of the fortifications. Instead, they provided support for the domestic and personal aspects of life, and thus they were integrated tightly into the life of the town.

NOTES

This paper was first presented at the 27th Annual Meeting of the French Colonial Historical Society, East Lansing and Detroit, Michigan, 2001. I want to thank the anonymous reviewers for their comments, and Robert DuPlessis, the former editor, and Patricia Galloway, the current editor, for their insightful criticisms of this article.

1. Inventory after death of Anne Levron at the request of Pierre Benoist, her husband, 19 December 1733, Centre des Archives d'Outre-mer, Aix-en-Provence, France [hereafter CAOM], G 2, vol. 182, fols. 986–1009. See also Brenda Dunn, "The Private Properties of Block 2," unpublished manuscript, Fortress of Louisbourg Library, National Historic Site of Canada 1978 [revised], 78–85.

2. In a recent work, Robert Harms uses the voyage of the French ship *Diligent* in 1731–32 to link the communities or "worlds" of the French slave trade in the eighteenth century. Harms's "worlds" include France, West Africa, and Martinique, as well as some offshore islands. See Robert W. Harms, *The Diligent: A Voyage through the Worlds of the Slave Trade* (New York: Basic Books, 2002).

3. Philip D. Morgan, "African and American Atlantic Worlds," preface to a special issue on African and American Atlantic Worlds, *William and Mary Quarterly* 56, no. 2 (April 1999), 241–42. In the same issue, see Robin Law and Kristin Mann, "West Africa in the Atlantic Community: The Case of the Slave Coast," 307–34. On studying "Atlantic history," see Bernard Bailyn, "The Idea of Atlantic History," *Itinerario* 20, no. 1 (1996): 38–44. On the African contribution to Atlantic history, see John Thorton,

Africa and Africans in the Making of the Atlantic World, 1400–1680 (Cambridge: Cambridge University Press, 1992).

4. The colony of Île Royale included the islands of Île Royale (Cape Breton) and Île St. Jean (Prince Edward Island). The French used the names Île Royale and "Cap Breton" interchangeably. I have compiled a nominal list of 216 slaves found in the Île Royale documentation. See Kenneth Donovan, "A Nominal List of Slaves and Their Owners in Île Royale, 1713–1760," *Nova Scotia Historical Review* 16, no. 1 (June 1996): 151–62. The list includes the name, age, and origin of the slaves, if available, together with the date of their arrival in the colony. The names and occupations of the owners are also part of the data. Since 1996, I have identified an additional 197 slaves for the years 1713–1810 for a total of 413 people. See Kenneth Donovan, "Slavery in Cape Breton, 1713–1810," unpublished manuscript, Fortress of Louisbourg, National Historic Site of Canada. The list comprises 266 slaves during the French regime, 1713–1758.

5. Donovan, "Slavery in Cape Breton, 1713–1810," lists the occupations of all 266 slaves in Île Royale.

6. A. J. B. Johnston, *Religion in Life at Louisbourg, 1713–1758* (Kingston: McGill-Queen's University Press, 1984), 113.

7. Philip D. Morgan, *Slave Counterpoint: Black Culture in the Eighteenth-Century Chesapeake and Lowcountry* (Chapel Hill: University of North Carolina Press, 1998), xxii.

8. On family life, see Kenneth Donovan, "Communities and Families: Family Life and Living Conditions in Eighteenth-Century Louisbourg," in Eric Krause, Carol Corbin, and William O'Shea, eds., *Aspects of Louisbourg: Essays on the History of an Eighteenth-Century French Community in North America* (Sydney, Nova Scotia: University College of Cape Breton Press, Louisbourg Institute, 1995), 117–49; A. J. B. Johnston, *Control and Order in French Colonial Louisbourg, 1713–1758* (East Lansing: Michigan State University Press, 2001), 223–42.

9. Purchase of the slave Georges, account of Governor Costebelle with George De Lasson and Michel Daccarette, 1711–1713, CAOM, G 2, vol. 178, fols. 18–23.

10. See Orlando Patterson, *Slavery and Social Death: A Comparative Study* (Cambridge, Mass.: Harvard University Press, 1982).

11. Donovan, "Slavery in Cape Breton, 1713–1810."

12. Louisbourg's permanent civilian population was 633 in 1720; 813 in 1724; 1,463 in 1737; and 2,690 in 1752. These figures do not include totals for the garrison, fishermen, or other transients who were in the colony on a seasonal basis. By the late 1750s Île Royale's population, including soldiers, approached 10,000 people. See A. J. B. Johnston, "The Population of Eighteenth-Century Louisbourg," *Nova Scotia Historical Review* 11, no. 2 (December 1991), 75–86.

13. CAOM, 1735, G 2, vol. 194, dossier 80. George was a slave of Marie Peré, a widow of fishing proprietor Antoine Peré. Included among the debts owed to Madame peré was a list of her fishermen who owed for supplies. Georges, "the Black," owed 70 *livres*.

14. Kenneth Donovan, "Île Royale, Eighteenth Century," in R. Cole Harris, ed., *Historical Atlas of Canada: From the Beginning to 1800*, vol. 1 (Toronto: University of Toronto Press, 1987), plate 24; Kenneth Donovan, "Tattered Clothes and Powdered Wigs: Case Studies of the Poor and Well-to-Do in Eighteenth-Century Louisbourg," in Kenneth Donovan, ed., *Cape Breton at 200: Historical Essays in Honour of the Island's Bicentennial* (Sydney, Nova Scotia: University College of Cape Breton Press, 1985), 2–3.

15. Kenneth Donovan, "Slaves and their Owners in Île Royale, 1713–1760," *Acadiensis* 25, no.1 (1995), 3–32.

16. Robin W. Winks, *The Blacks in Canada: A History* (Montreal: McGill-Queen's University Press, 1971), 9; Marcel Trudel, *Dictionnaire des esclaves et de leurs propriétaires au Canada francais* (Quèbec: presses de l'Université Laval, 1990), xiii-xxviii. See also Marcel Trudel, *L'Esclavage au Canada français: Histoire et conditions de l'esclavage* (Quèbec: Presses de l'Université Laval, 1960), 20–21.

17. Brett Rushforth, "Savage Bonds: Indian Slavery and Alliance in New France." Ph.D. diss., University of California-Davis, 2003; Cornelius J. Jaenen, *Friend and Foe: Aspects of French-Amerindian Cultural Contact in the Sixteenth and Seventeenth Centurics* (New York: Columbia University Press, 1976), 138; Dale Miquelon, *New France, 1701–1744: A Supplement to Europe* (Toronto: McClelland and Stewart, 1987), 238–39; Trudel, L'Esclavage au Canada, 60–64; J. R. Miller, *Skyscrapers Hide the Heavens: A History of Indian-White Relations in Canada* (Toronto: University of Toronto Press, 1989), 45; James Cleland Hamilton. "The Panis: An Historical Outline of Canadian Indian Slavery in the Eighteenth Century." *Proceedings of the Canadian Institute* (February 1897), 19–27.

18. D.W. Meinig, *The Shaping of America*, (New Haven: Yale University Press, 1986), 171. For a contemporary description of the Black Code, see Le Romain, "Negroes," in *Encyclopedia, Selections: Diderot, d'Alembert, and a Society of Men of Letters*, translated with an introduction by Nelly S. Hoyt and Thomas Cassirer (Indianapolis: Bobbs-Merrill, 1965), 258–73. The Black Code has been printed in Mederic Louis Elie Moreau de Saint-Mèry, ed., *Loix et constitutions des colonies francoises* (Paris, 1784–1790). A complete version is available in *Le Code Noir, au Recueil des Reglemens* (Basse-Terre, Gaudeloupe, 1980), 446.

19. Cornelius J. Jaenen, *The Role of the Church in New France* (Toronto: University of Toronto Press, 1976), 152.

20. Inventory of the estate of Elie Thesson *dit* La Floury, 22 March 1741, CAOM, G 2, vol. 197, dossier 143. By 22 March 1741, there were 448 pounds of butter in the La Floury storehouse, together with three sickles. For background on the La Floury family and business operations, see Kenneth Donovan, "Property of Elie Thesson dit La Floury," unpublished paper, Fortress of Louisbourg Library, Louisbourg National Historic Site of Canada, 1992.

21. Sale of the slave Rosalie, 19 June 1736, CAOM, G 3, 2039–1, pièce 168.

22. James W. St. G. Walker, *The Black Loyalists: The Search for a Promised Land in Nova Scotia and Sierra Leone, 1783–1870* (New York, 1976), 41.

23. The Naval Office Shipping Lists for Nova Scotia, 1730–1820, in the Public Record Office, London, 1981, p. 132. The *Success*, a thirty-ton schooner under Captain Mathew Milbourn, had a three-man crew. Registered in Antigua on 18 April 1750, the *Success* was owned by Charles Hay and Company. Microfilm copy consulted from Memorial University, St. John's, Newfoundland.

24. *Halifax Gazette* (Halifax). 30 May 1752. For some of Mauger's trading activities at Louisbourg, see the sale of the cargo of the schooner *Speedwell*, with Joshua Mauger as the supplier of the cargo, Louisbourg, 8 May to 14 August 1751 , AC, C11B, vol. 30, fols. 123–34.

25. Louisbourg residents debarking at La Rochelle, 28 April 1759, AC, C11B, vol. 38, fol. 268.

26. T. A. Crowley, "Government and Interests: French Colonial Administration at Louisbourg 1713–1758," Ph.D. diss., Duke University, 1975, 298; J. F. Bosher, "Jean Laborde," *Dictionary of Canadian Biography* 4:421.

27. Sale of a slave from the schooner *New Brunswick*, Louisbourg. 12 November 1756, no. 19, B, 6112, A.C.M. The complete court case includes documents numbered from 14 to 34.

28. Louisbourg residents debarking at La Rochelle, 28 April 1759, AC, C11B, vol. 38, fol. 267.

29. Declaration by Nicolas Larcher that Anne Honiche Nanon was his slave in Louisbourg, 5 April 1762, Admiralty of France, 4th register, AC, F 1B4, fol. 16. For details on Larcher, see Christopher Moore, "Nicolas Larcher," *Dictionary of Canadian Biography* 4:438–39; Nicolas Larcher, AC, E256, Dossiers Personnels, Archives de la Marine.

30. Robert Louis Stein, *The French Slave Trade in the Eighteenth Century: An Old Regime Business* (Madison: University of Wisconsin Press, 1979), 71–72.

31. Inventory and sale of the estate of Marie Marguerite Rose, CAOM, G2, vol. 212, dossier 552, 27 August 1757.

32. List of people at the Captain's table on the ship *Le Comte de Maurepas*, Bayonne, 30 May 1749, AC, F5 B. No folio number given.

33. See Donovan, "Slavery in Cape Breton, 1713–1810."

34. Ira Berlin, *Many Thousands Gone: The First Two Centuries of Slavery in North America* (Cambridge, Mass.: Harvard University Press, 1998), 47.

35. Peter Faneuil to Thomas Kilby, Boston, 20 June 1737, Faneuil Letter Book, Baker Library, Harvard University, Boston.

36. Captain James Spellen of New York sold the slave Jean in Louisbourg on 27 April 1753, and was also trading in Halifax during 1753. Sale of the slave Jean, 27 April 1753, CAOM, G 3, 2047–2, no. 74. For Spellen in Halifax, see the *Halifax Gazette* (Halifax), 10 November 1753.

37. The six children included Anne Louise, Charles Pierre, Marguerite Louise, Jean Pierre, Bertrand Joseph, and Josephine Louise. For the children of Pierre Boullot and Jeanne Magdelaine Richard, see the family reconstitution file at Fortress Louisbourg National Historic Site, and Louisbourg residents debarking at La Rochelle, 28 April 1759, AC, C11B, vol. 38, fol. 271.

38. Declaration of Pierre Boullot, 23 June 1762, Archives Departmentales, St. Servan, Brittany, Ile and Valine, 9B8, fol. 99.

39. Louisbourg residents debarking at La Rochelle, 28 April 1759, AC, CIIB, vol. 38, fol. 271. For details regarding Boullot's voyages from Martinique to Louisbourg, see AC, C7, 41, Dossiers Personnels, Archives de la Marine. For the death of Marie Flore's son Denis on 25 September 1760 in France, see Registre Paroissial St Jean des Champs, Normandy; for a declaration by Pierre Boullot that he had the slave Marie Flore for 20 years, see registers of the admiralty of St Malo, 23 June 1762, cited in research note, Madame Michèle Godret to A. J. B. Johnston, Paris, 4 March 1997. This letter and note is on file at the Fortress of Louisbourg archives.

40. Jaenen, *The Role of the Church*, 151–53; Winks, *The Blacks in Canada*, 12. See also Marcel Trudel, "L'Attitude de l'église Catholique vis-à-vis l'esclavage au Canada français," *Canadian Historical Association Report* (1961); "The Attitude of the Roman Catholic Church toward the Negro during Slavery," in W. D. Weatherford, *American Churches and the Negro* (Boston, 1957); Mary Veronica Miceli, "The Influence of the Roman Catholic Church on Slavery in Colonial Louisiana under French Domination, 1718–1763," Ph.D. diss., Tulane University, 1979. More recent scholarship has challenged the role of all Christian churches, citing an "African spiritual holocaust" in which the psychological balm of Christianity helped to control slaves. See Jon F. Sensbach, "Charting a Course in Early African-American History," *William and Mary Quarterly* 50, no. 2 (April 1993): 401; Norrece T. Jones, *Born a Child of Freedom, Yet a Slave: Mechanisms of Slave Control and Strategies of Resistance in Antebellum South Carolina* (Middletown, Conn.: Wesleyan University Press, 1990); Peter Kolchin, *Unfree Labor: American Slavery and Russian Serfdom* (Cambridge, Mass.: Belknap Press of Harvard University Press, 1987); and Jon Butler, *Awash in a Sea of Faith: Christianizing the American People* (Cambridge, Mass.: Harvard University Press, 1990).

41. Le Romain, "Negroes," 270. See also E. V. Goveia, *The West Indian Slave Laws of the Eighteenth Century* (Barbados, 1970), 39.

42. Many plantation managers opposed religious instruction of the slaves in the West Indies. The French Catholic Church in the sugar islands

during the eighteenth century was also a pale imitation of the church in France. See Robert Forster, "Slavery in Virginia and Saint-Domingue in the Late Eighteenth Century," in Philip Boucher, ed., *Proceedings of the Thirteenth and Fourteenth Meetings of the French Colonial Historical Society* (Lanham, Md.: University Press of America, 1990), 9; Eugene D. Genovese, *Roll, Jordan, Roll: The World the Slaves Made* (New York: Pantheon Books, 1974), 174; C. L. R. James, *The Black Jacobins: Toussaint L'Ouverture and the San Domingo Revolution* (London: Secker and Warburg, 1938); Alfred Metraux, *Voodoo in Haiti, trans.* H. Charteris (New York: Schocken Books, 1972); A. Gisler, *L'Esclavage aux Antilles françaises (XVIIe–XIXe siècle): Contribution au problème de l'esclavage* (Paris: Karthala, 1981).

43. For the baptism of Anne Honiche Nanon, see the declaration by Nicolas Larcher that he had his slave baptized at St Méry in 1759, in extracts from the registers, 1760 to 1777, AC, F1B4, fol. 16.

SCHOOLS, PRISONS, AND ASYLUMS IN MID-NINETEENTH CENTURY BRITISH NORTH AMERICA

What Did Institutional Reforms Have in Common?

Colin Coates
Glendon College, York University

SCHOOLS, PRISONS, AND ASYLUMS IN MID–NINETEENTH CENTURY BRITISH NORTH AMERICA: WHAT DID INSTITUTIONAL REFORMS HAVE IN COMMON?

● **Introduction by Colin Coates**

▲ **Primary Sources**

Document 1: Report of the Commissioners on the Subject of Prisons, Pentitentiaries, etc., etc. etc.
Charles Duncombe

Document 2: Excerpt from Part I of the Report on a System of Public Elementary Education for Upper Canada
Rev. Egerton Ryerson

Document 3: "Schooldays, Schooldays ... Cocagne Academy in the 1840s"
Gordon McCall Theal

Document 4: *A Meeting of the School Trustees*, 1885 (National Gallery of Canada)
Robert Harris

Document 5: Visit to the Toronto Asylum
Susanna Moodie

Document 6: Untitled Painting of the Provincial Asylum
William James Thomson

■ **Secondary Sources**

Article 1: The Development of the Lunatic Asylum in the Maritime Provinces
Daniel Francis

Article 2: "Open to the Public": Touring Ontario Asylums in the Nineteenth Century
Janet Miron

Article 3: Awakening a Demand for Schooling: Educational Inspection's Impact on Rural Nova Scotia, 1855–74
Robert Lanning

● INTRODUCTION

Colin Coates

Schools, penitentiaries, and insane asylums are different types of state-run institutions that together reflected and created new relationships between individuals and the state. In the areas that became parts of Canada in 1867, these institutions all took shape during the middle decades of the century. Colonial governments followed the lead of other jurisdictions, such as Massachusetts and of course Great Britain. Elites placed great stock in the new institutions. The imposing buildings were signs of "progress," fine displays of the appropriate use of government revenue to effect societal change. Government officials and politicians pointed proudly to the substantial investments made in these institutions, a gauge of the promise of the country.

In recent years, historians have seen the middle decades of the nineteenth century as a key period of "state formation." Of course, Confederation itself was a clear sign of the state-formation process. But the previous decades had seen major growth in the responsibilities and capacities of the colonial state, as well as increases in the number of institutions required to oversee these new roles. Asylums, prisons, schools, and hospitals were the most obvious of these new institutions. Yet we should also note the dramatically expanded role played by the state in developing infrastructure, most notably the construction of railways and canals. Taken together, these were massively expensive undertakings, requiring the state not only to raise new revenues through taxation and tariffs, but also to assemble bureaucracies to oversee their operation and to collect and administer the taxes to build them. By mid-century, colonial governments that had once prided themselves on their inexpensive operations were running major budgets and assuming significant debts.

In the 1840s and 1850s, politicians and bureaucrats were faced with huge waves of immigration, and they felt the need to address the arrival of thousands of relatively poor people in British North America. The school system offered the opportunity to form the young minds of children, the penitentiary promised a punishment regime to reform the individual criminal, and the asylum represented a means to restore the sanity of the misguided. In each case, the institutions aimed at reforming the individual. Surveillance and self-regulation were the means to effect these changes, a significant shift from the earlier reliance on physical punishment. As was the case in the countries of western Europe and the United States, British North American proponents of institutional reform in the nineteenth century believed that the publicly funded schools, prisons, and asylums constituted a break with past techniques and methods. The document written by Gordon McCall Theall, who left British North America for a distinguished career in South Africa, reflects on an older form of schooling in the 1840s and reveals the physical punishment and rote learning that he expected had disappeared from schools in subsequent decades. Reformers recommended moving away from physical punishment and restraint as a way of dealing with undesirable behaviour to focusing instead on the attitudes of the individual. They thus intended to provide a more just treatment encouraging the individual to become a productive member of society. However, Charles Duncombe's report on penitentiaries in the United States submitted to the legislature of Upper Canada in 1836 contains some recommendations on reforms of punishment techniques that may not appear so benign today.

Furthermore, there was often a discrepancy between the stated goals of such institutions and the ways in which they were managed and experienced. Many of the institutions cost a great deal of money, not only to build but also to staff. The relatively limited taxation base of the British North American colonies meant that the institutions often lacked the funds that would have been necessary to meet the goals of their founders. The article by Daniel Francis conveys this point in looking at the insane asylums in New Brunswick and Nova Scotia.

The institutions represented an important shift in the relationship between individuals and the state. Through inspectors, the government-funded schools demanded certain types of behaviour from youth and their families, insisting, for instance, that the young attend school rather than help out with farm work. In his article, Robert Lanning discusses the role of school inspectors in Nova Scotia from the 1850s to the 1870s. Many members of the public remained distrustful of taxation, and some protested the use of public funds for such projects. Therefore, while the magnificent asylum buildings might prove venues for public tours in nineteenth-century Canada West/Ontario, as Janet Miron's article points out, and as Susanna Moodie's chapter illustrates, the public was often less enthusiastic about having to expend government funds. Others feared the intrusion of these institutions into their lives. The expansion of the schooling system in Canada East/Quebec in the 1840s, for instance, led in some districts near the town of Trois-Rivières to what some at the time called the "Candlesnuffers' War." Local elites and farmers greeted school inspectors and tax collectors with a great deal of hostility, recognizing how their activities infringed upon the rural autonomy previously enjoyed. The proponents of the new schools claimed that those who defended local concerns were trying to snuff out the candle of learning. Robert Harris's famous painting of the meeting between the local school trustees and the new female schoolteacher in a small rural schoolhouse on Prince Edward Island conveys some of the complexity of the relations between the state-appointed educator and local citizens.

State intervention in individual lives had different implications in Quebec than it did in other jurisdictions. In Quebec, the majority of the population was French speaking and Catholic, while English-speaking Protestants dominated much of the political life. This period saw the beginning of a long-lasting issue in Canadian public life, the question of whether schooling should respect denominational boundaries. In Quebec, many institutions did not develop from state funds, but rather were offered by the Catholic Church and, indeed, until recently, education remained divided along denominational lines.

The story of institutional development in the middle decades of the nineteenth century is rather mixed. Reform-minded leaders attempted to influence behaviour through creating new large-scale institutions and channelling taxes to such projects. Although they saw a clear break with the past, in some cases their proposals were less innovative, at least in retrospect, than they may have appeared at the time. Meanwhile, they faced important limitations on what they could achieve: individuals resisted elements of the reforms and a limited tax base restricted what could be done. Even today, citizens and politicians continue to debate self-consciously "humanitarian" perspectives on societal problems and the significant expenditures that are involved in such processes.

QUESTIONS

1. According to Charles Duncombe, what is the purpose of the penitentiary or prison? Is punishment or reform the main purpose? What methods would ensure that the prisoner became more docile?
2. What assumptions underlie the school system as conveyed in Rev. Egerton Ryerson's report? What was the goal of mass education, according to Rev. Ryerson?
3. Compare the reasons for and methods of controlling the populations of Upper Canada (Ontario) as outlined in the proposals by Charles Duncombe and Rev. Egerton Ryerson. Which groups of people did the proposed reforms aim to control?

4. In what ways do the goals of Rev. Egerton Ryerson's school system differ from the type of school experience that Gordon McCall Theal had had in Nova Scotia in the 1840s?
5. Compare the exterior view of the Ontario provincial asylum as depicted in Susanna Moodie's account and William James Thomson's painting and the interior observations as recounted by Moodie. Did the exterior and interior perspectives match?

FURTHER READINGS

Axelrod, Paul, *The Promise of Schooling: Education in Canada, 1800–1914* (Toronto: University of Toronto Press, 1997).

Curtis, Bruce, *Building the Educational State: Canada West, 1836–1871* (London: The Althouse Press, 1988).

Nelson, Wendie, "'Rage against the Dying of the Light': Interpreting the Guerre des Éteignoirs" *Canadian Historical Review* 81, 4 (December 2000): 551–581.

Oliver, Peter N., *'Terror to Evil-doers': Prisons and Punishments in Nineteenth-Century Ontario* (Toronto: University of Toronto Press, 1998).

Shortt, S.E.D., *Victorian Lunacy: Richard M. Bucke and the Practice of Late Nineteenth-Century Psychiatry* (Cambridge: Cambridge University Press, 1986).

▲ Document 1: Report of the Commissioners on the Subject of Prisons, Penitentiaries, etc., etc. etc.

Charles Duncombe

Charles Duncombe was a doctor and political figure in Upper Canada. In 1837, he would become involved in the Rebellion against the government. The year previously he presented a report to the colonial legislative on his investigation into penal practices in various parts of the United States.

The great object of the institution of civil government, is to advance the prosperity, and to increase the happiness of its subjects. The agents of the government, become, in this point of view, the fathers of the people; and it may surely be ranked among the duties incident to this paternal care, not only that those who are guilty of crime should receive the chastisement due to their offences; but that no pains should be spared to remove the causes of offence, and to diminish, as far as possible, the sources of temptation and corruption. This obligation applies with peculiar force to the case of juvenile offenders; a class whose increasing numbers, and deplorable situation loudly calls for more effective interposition, and the benevolent interference of the legislature.

Every person that frequents the streets of this city [Toronto] must be forcibly struck with the ragged and uncleanly appearance, the vile language, and the idle and miserable habits of numbers of children, most of whom are of an age suitable for schools, or for some useful employment. The parents of these children, are, in all probability, too poor, or too degenerate to provide them with clothing fit for them to be seen in at school; and know not where to place them in order that they may find employment, or be better cared for. Accustomed, in many instances, to witness at home nothing in the way of example, but what is degrading; early taught to observe intemperance, and to hear obscene and profane language without disgust; obliged to beg, and even encouraged to acts of dishonesty to satisfy the wants induced by the indolence of their parents—what can be expected, but that such children will in due time, become responsible to the laws for crimes, which have thus, in a manner, been forced upon them?—Can it be consistent with real justice that delinquents of this character should be consigned to the infamy and severity of punishments, which must inevitably tend to perfect the work of degradation, to sink them still deeper in corruption, to deprive them of their remaining sensibility to the shame of exposure, and establish them in all the hardihood of daring and desperate villainy? Is it possible that a christian community can lend its sanction to such a process, without any effort to rescue and to save?

If the agents of our municipal government stand towards the community in the moral light of guardians of virtue; if they may be justly regarded as the political fathers of the unprotected, does not every feeling of justice urge upon them the principle, of considering these juvenile culprits as falling under their special guardianship, and claiming from them the right which every child may demand of its parent, of being well instructed in the nature of its duties, before it is punished for the breach of their observance? Ought not every one who has a just sense of the reciprocal obligations of parents and children to lend his aid to the administrators of the law, in rescuing those pitiable victims of neglect and wretch-

Source: *Journal of the House of Assembly of Upper Canada* (1836), Appendix 71, pp. 4–5.

edness, from the melancholy fate which almost inevitably results from an apprenticeship in our common prisons?

It is well worth the attention of the legislature to devise some means by which criminals may be speedily brought to trial after arrest; and while imprisoned for crimes in the common gaols of the different districts of the province that they should be classed so that the unfortunate debtor and the highly culpable criminal, should have no communication with each other—Nor would I, if it were possible to do otherwise, allow criminals to have any communication among themselves during their confinement previously to or after trial: and when sentence of condemnation to hard labor had been passed upon them, I would advise that the punishment should be carried into effect in the manner least likely to debase the human mind, and the most calculated to produce the *reformation* of the convict. I would still treat him as an accountable being, both to God and to society. His treatment should be just and consistent and as lenient as his situation would admit of. He should be taught to feel, that upon himself still, to a certain extent, depended his future prospects in life wherever the term of sentence admitted of a rational prospect of a return to society; and even where that was not the case, he should be brought to acknowledge that much of his present comfort or misery must as a matter of course, depend upon himself,—and where he had no hope of enjoyment from society beyond the walls of the prison, he should be directed to look for happiness from within his own bosom *here*, and the hope of future blessedness hereafter. He would then become a better man as a convict—enjoy more comfort in confinement, and be likelier, in consequence, to be liberated.

The flogging in penitentiaries is highly reprehensible. Fear should not be the only incentive to action—convicts should feel a respect for themselves; for the good opinion of the keepers; and even of their fellows.

In the penitentiary at Frankfort in Kentucky, I witnessed a new mode of punishment, that of *suspended animation*—which appeared to me to be better adapted to penitentiary punishment than any thing I had before seen; for while it instantly subdued the most turbulent and obstinate spirits, it neither debased the mind, nor left it in that sour, unhappy and degraded state; the usual concomitant of corporal punishment.

This suspended animation was inflicted in the easiest and quietest manner possible; without much loss of time, or danger to the health, or injury of the convict,—and from the short experience of this institution upon man, and from comparisons long since made upon the brute creation, it is admitted to be one of the most potent subduers of the malevolent animal passions ever had recourse to. It is thus produced:—

The convict is placed in an easy chair resembling the tranquilizing chair, used in Lunatic asylums.—The convict, sitting, apparently, at perfect ease, has his feet, legs, body, and arms, safely secured, a box (or spout) with a box at one end of it is brought up behind his chair. The spout stands upon three legs, and just high enough from the floor to place the body of the convict on a horizontal line with it, when his easy chair resting upon a broad bottom, shall be inclined backwards so as to admit his head into one end of it. The side and partition next the top of his head are a little higher than the top of his nose as he lies on his back with his head in the box. In that position the collar is put down about his neck and secured. The partition at the top of his head does not rest on the bottom of the box by one inch; so that the water poured in will run out and be conducted into a large pot or tub placed under the lower end of the spout to receive the water. The keeper then takes a bucket of water and fills the box until it covers the convict's face and mouth entirely, and thereby suspends animation as long as may seem necessary to subdue his passions, and on allowing him to breathe he has invariably become a reformed man; with his turbulent passions quite subdued. He pursues his work in the penitentiary without

145

any of that morose and unhappy feeling which so often succeeds the flogging, and other usual corporal punishment that only restrains the convict by fear from the repetition of the offence. Fear debases, never ennobles the mind, and therefore should be had recourse to as seldom as possible, as a mode of punishment in any system of improvement. In our civil or political institutions teach children from their infancy *to govern themselves*: early accustom them to the exercise of the *moral* and *intellectual* faculties, thereby giving those organs of the mind an ascendency over the malevolent animal passions and propensities. Let all our literary civil and political institutions be so conducted, that the organs of benevolence, veneration, conscientiousness and hope may predominate. Thus shall we most effectually and permanently promote the peace, prosperity, welfare and good government of this province.

All which is respectfully submitted

Charles Duncombe, Acting Commissioner for obtaining certain information etc. etc.

▲ Document 2: Excerpt, "Part I of the Report on a System of Public Elementary Education for Upper Canada"

Rev. Egerton Ryerson

Egerton Ryerson was the key figure in developing the educational system of Upper Canada. He patterned the school system after that available in Ireland, but in this report he compared educational practices in many European jurisdictions and in the United States.

Part I Of The Report On A System Of Public Elementary Instruction For Upper Canada.

[...] What [is] meant by Education

By Education, I mean not the mere acquisition of certain arts, or of certain branches of knowledge, but that instruction and discipline which qualify and dispose the subjects of it for their appropriate duties and employments of life, as Christians, as persons of business and also as members of the civil community in which they live.

Basis and Extent of the System

The basis of an Educational structure adapted to this end should be as broad as the population of the country; and its loftiest elevation should equal the highest demands of the learned professions, adapting its gradition [sic] of schools to the wants of the several classes of the community, and to their respective employments or profession, the one rising above the other—the one conducting the other; yet each complete in itself for the degree of education it imparts; a character of uniformity as to fundamental principles pervading the whole; the whole based upon the principles of Christianity, and uniting the combined influence and support of the Government and the people.

The branches of knowledge which it is essential that all should understand, should be provided for all, and taught to all; should be brought within the reach of the most needy, and forced upon the attention of the most careless. The knowledge required for the scientific pursuit of mechanics, agriculture and commerce, must needs be provided to an extent corresponding with the demand, and the exigencies of the country; while to a more limited extent are needed facilities for acquiring the higher education of the learned professions.

Comparative Neglect of Elementary Education

Now, to a professional education, and to the education of the more wealthy classes, no objection has been made, nor even indifference manifested. On the contrary, for these classes of society, less needing the assistance of the Government and having less claims upon its benevolent consideration than the laboring and producing classes of the population, have liberal provision been made, and able Professors employed, whilst Schools

Source: J. George Hodgins, ed., *Documentary history of education in Upper Canada, from the passing of the Constitutional Act of 1791, to the close of Rev. Dr. Ryerson's administration of the Education Department in 1876,* Vol. 6 (Toronto: Warwick Bro's & Rutter, 1899): 142–146.

of Industry have been altogether overlooked, and primary Instruction has scarcely been reduced to a system; and the education of the bulk of the population has been left to the annual liberality of Parliament. Nay, even objections have been made to the education of the laboring classes of the people; and it may be advisable to show, at the outset, that the establishment of a thorough system of primary and industrial education, commensurate with the population of the country, as contemplated by the Government, and as is here proposed, is justified by considerations of economy as well as of patriotism and humanity.

First, such a system of general education amongst the people is the most effectual preventative of pauperism, and its natural companions, misery and crime.

General Education a Preventive of Pauperism

To a young and growing country, and the retreat of so many poor from other countries, this consideration is of the greatest importance. The gangrene of pauperism in either cities or states is almost incurable. It may be said in some sort to be hereditary as well as infectious,—both to perpetuate and propagate itself,—to weaken the body politic at its very heart,—and to multiply wretchedness and vice.

What Statistics of Pauperism Prove

Now, the Statistical Reports of pauperism and crime in different countries, furnish indubitable proof that ignorance is the fruitful source of idleness, intemperance and improvidence, and these the fosterparent of pauperism and crime. The history of every country in Europe may be appealed to in proof and illustration of the fact,—apart from the operation of extraneous local and temporary circumstances,—that pauperism and crime prevail in proportion to the absence of education amongst the labouring classes, and that in proportion to the existence and prevalence of education amongst those classes, is the absence of pauperism and its legitimate offspring. [...]

System of Education should be universal

1. The first feature then of our Provincial system of Public Instruction, should be *universality*; and that in respect to the poorest classes of society. It is the poor indeed that need the assistance of the Government, and they are proper subjects of their special solicitude and care; the rich can take care of themselves. The elementary education of the whole people must therefore be an essential element in the Legislative and Administrative policy of an enlightened and beneficent Government.

Should be practical

2. Nor is it less important to the efficiency of such a system, that it should be *practical*, than that it should be universal. The mere acquisition or even the general diffusion of knowledge without the requisite qualitites to apply that knowledge in the best manner, does not merit the name of education. Much knowledge may be imparted and acquired without any addition whatever to the capacity for the business of life. There are not wanting numerous examples of persons having excelled, even in the higher departments of knowledge, who are utterly incompetent to the most simple, as well as the most important, affairs of every day life. [...]

▲ Document 3: Schooldays, Schooldays ... Cocagne Academy in the 1840s

Gordon McCall Theal

These reminiscences were published in 1894 after Theal, having emigrated to South Africa, returned to Canada for a visit. He describes his childhood experiences at his local school. This excerpt provides an example of the punishment regime that humanitarians were attempting to reform.

[...] Let us look first at the Cocaigne Academy, a good specimen of a Canadian public school—regarded as of the first class—in the olden time. The building, erected by public subscription, stood close to the shore, at one end of the long wooden bridge that spanned the river at its mouth, so as to be in a central position. All the classes were taught in one large room, which was warmed in winter by an immense stove in the centre, round which the desks were ranged. The principal was the reverend Alfred Horatio Weeks, a clergyman of the church of England, and the assistant, or usher as he was termed, was Mr. David Miller, a layman. The government did not contribute anything to the support of the institution, which was maintained entirely by school fees and by subscriptions guaranteed in case the fees fell short. The hours of attendance were from 9 to 4, with an hour for lunch, except on Saturdays, when the school closed at 1. The holidays were about half as long as those at present given. The discipline was cruelly severe. The reverend principal was conscientious, and as he really believed that to spare the rod was to spoil the child, he tried to do his duty regardless of his muscles.

I asked my old classmate if he remembered the punishment inflicted on a particular occasion upon several boys for what would now be regarded as a very trifling fault. I have need to, he replied, and baring one of his wrists he showed me a large mark which he has borne ever since as the result of it.

Yet the reverend principal was not naturally a cruel man. He was a very strict disciplinarian, but he could say kind words and act generously enough outside the schoolhouse. He made me a present of a pair of skates once, so, in spite of the drubbings I received, I have a warm place in my memory for him. He was still living, though at a very advanced age, a widower, and childless, when I was in Canada, but I had not time to visit the part of the province where he was then residing, and shortly after my return to London I received intelligence of his death.

The school being a place of terror, it was a natural result that no one went to it of his own free will. If a boy did not know his lessons, he would argue he might as well play truant for the day, as the punishment for the one offence would be no worse than for the other. And there was frequently a strong temptation to play truant, even when a boy could repeat his home task, but knew he would likely be belaboured for something else. In the spring time a habitant was making maple sugar only half-a-dozen miles up the river, and it would be so nice to help carry the little bark dishes of sap from the trees to the boiler, and get a block when it was taken from the mould. Or later the wild strawberries—the delicious wild strawberries of Canada—were ripening in some warm locality, and each boy

Source: Gordon McCall Theal, "Schooldays, Schooldays ... Cocagne Academy in the 1840s" *Acadiensis: Journal of the History of the Atlantic Region*, Vol. 5, 2 (1976): 134–147 (Excerpted). Reprinted with permission.

thought he would like to be the first to eat them. And then as the season advanced there were the wild raspberries and the blueberries in the newly burnt clearings on the border of the forest, and later still the hazel nuts on the Island, all powerful magnets for schoolboys dreading the reverend principal's cane. Or a report would pass round that the fishing was particularly good in a certain stream, or that a big wolf had been trapped by somebody, or a schooner was to be launched, or in winter the river and the harbour would be one great sheet of ice inviting races on skates; with these on one side and the rod on the other, the pupils of the Cocaigne Academy often turned away from the path that led to knowledge.

One day—it was the 3rd of November 1847—four boys were standing on the bridge watching great clouds of wahwahs [wild geese] and wild ducks of other kinds that were on the wing from the north towards warmer latitudes, knowing by instinct that winter was approaching. The oldest of the four had a gun, but somehow the flocks all took a course that led away from the bridge, and he had no chance of testing his skill. A light canoe was fastened to one of the piers, so, tired of waiting, three of the boys jumped in, and with two of them paddling and the other holding the gun in readiness, shot out into the harbour to a spot that the birds were passing over. The chance came, but the gun recoiled, and with even so slight a shock the canoe turned over. The water was so cold that to swim very far was impossible. One of the boys who clung to the canoe was saved, the corpse of the one who had the gun was found that night just where the accident took place, and the body of the other was recovered nearer the shore. The effect of this sudden death of two of the brightest boys in the school was felt long afterwards.

One day there was a violent storm. The north-west wind in its fury swept over the Strait, and piled the water in Cocaigne harbour higher than had ever been known before. The moon was full, and under ordinary circumstances the tide line would have been within a few feet of the schoolhouse, but now the water surrounded the lonely building, great waves came rolling in before the gusts to dash against the outer wall of wood, and soon the place was a wreck, to the intense delight of every boy that saw it. But our mutual congratulations were soon over. A gentleman who lived close to the other end of the bridge, and who had a number of sons, offered a wing of his house, and in a few days the school was opened again.

I have yet to describe the method of teaching, and to enumerate the subjects taught. The usher took spelling, reading, geography, arithmetic, what was called philosophy, and once a week French. Only once a week was there a lesson in one of the principal languages of the country, and then it was bare reading without any explanation whatever. The geography lessons were home tasks, and were nothing more than the repetition by each boy of a certain quantity of matter in a book. It was really a test of memory, and nothing else. The philosophy meant answering by rote a series of questions from a long catechism, and for practical value may be classed with the geography. The arithmetic was better, and as this was Mr. Miller's strong point, we really got some explanation of rules and were helped forward in our work.

The principal took the Latin and Greek languages, history, and penmanship. His own handwriting was remarkably good, almost like copperplate, and he laid down the sensible rule that the test of writing was the ability of any one whatever to read it without hesitation or difficulty. He used to set a copy for us to follow, and then warm with his cane the hands of those whose performance was not to his satisfaction. The history taught was that of Greece, Rome, and England, but we learnt little more than lists of events and names of rulers. Of the life of the Greek people, of the effects of Roman institutions upon modern nations, and of everything in fact that would be really useful for us to know, we remained ignorant. The great movements of our own times, the stirring events of modern Europe and America, even past occurrences in Canada, were utterly ignored. We could repeat the legend of Romulus, and could remember the name of Miltiades, but we never heard in school of Frederick the Great or of George Washington, except indirectly as their actions affected England. A knowledge of the Latin and Greek languages was, in the opinion of the principal, the first and highest object of a schoolboy's life, and consequently a very large portion of time was taken up with those studies. I went to the Cocaigne Academy from an infant school, where English grammar was beyond the capacity of the pupils, and the day I entered it I had a copy of the Eton Latin grammar put into my hands, with a long home task marked off in it. Thereafter two hours every day I stood before the principal declining Latin nouns and adjectives and conjugating verbs, without ever a word of explanation or comparison with the structure of English speech, with no help or guidance whatever but the rod when a mistake was made. So it went on, through the Delectus, and the Commentaries of Caesar and the Lives of Cornelius Nepos and the Aeneid of Virgil, all dull rote, with no life and no real teaching in it at all, so that I believe unless a boy had an extraordinary natural inclination for Latin lore, his training at this school would forever have repelled him from it. Mathematics were not taught at all, and if I had not at a later date had the advantage of a course of lessons in this branch of knowledge from an Irishman named O'Donnell—an eccentric but very estimable man—of algebra and geometry I should have remained absolutely ignorant.

The institution which I have been describing was a fair specimen of a public school in Canada half a century ago. The system of instruction was then generally held to be good, and the severe discipline was regarded as scriptural and correct. No parent dreamed of complaining about it. There was but one exception that I know of the Grammar School of St. John, of which Dr. James Paterson was the principal, under whose guidance many boys were trained who have made their mark in Canada. It was my good fortune to attend this school for some time after leaving the Cocaigne Academy, and to Dr. Paterson more than to any other teacher I owe what little knowledge I had when I entered upon the duties of active life … His idea of a school was that it should be a place of preparation for a boy to educate himself, the teacher could only lay a foundation, the pupil must build upon it; but he took care to lay the foundation strong and well, and he pointed out the way in which the edifice should be raised. He devoted more time to Latin than to all other subjects put together—it was the custom of the day.—but the Aeneid in his hands was a thing of life and beauty to his pupils. A single lesson from him on the use of globes was worth more than all the geography ever taught at Cocaigne. He pointed out too the good for admiration, and cast scorn upon the mean and bad, till every boy felt an enthusiasm to do what was right. He worked by attraction, not by fear, and I never knew of a case of truancy from his school. But, as I said before, the Grammar School of St. John was exceptional in its system, and I think just on that account many people looked somewhat askance upon it; the other institution, which I described first, represents the ideas of education at that time.

▲ Document 4: Robert Harris, *A Meeting of the School Trustees,* 1885 (National Gallery of Canada)

● Robert Harris (1849–1919) was a well-known Canadian painter, most famous perhaps for his depiction of the Fathers of Confederation. This painting illustrates the disagreement between a young female teacher in Prince Edward Island and the school trustees, ostensibly over the introduction of new teaching methods. What message does this painting attempt to convey? What are the gender dynamics of the painting? How does the artist use light to underline the point he is making?

Source: Harris, Robert, *A Meeting of the School Trustees,* 1885. National Gallery of Canada, Ottawa. Photo © National Gallery of Canada.

▲ Document 5: Visit to the Toronto Asylum

Susanna Moodie

As Janet Miron's article suggests, tourists often visited asylums in nineteenth-century Ontario. Susanna Moodie, one of the most celebrated authors of British North America, describes her visit to the Toronto Queen Street asylum in her 1853 book, Life in the Clearings versus the Bush. *What access did Moodie and her family have to the inmates? Why did she visit the asylum? What did she learn in doing so?*

Our next visit was to the Lunatic Asylum. The building is of white brick,—a material not very common in Canada, but used largely in Toronto, where stone has to be brought from a considerable distance, there being no quarries in the neighbourhood. Brick has not the substantial, august appearance that stone gives to a large building, and it is more liable to injury from the severe frosts of winter in this climate. The asylum is a spacious edifice, surrounded by extensive grounds for the cultivation of fruits and vegetables. These are principally worked by the male patients, who are in a state of convalescence, while it affords them ample room for air and exercise.

A large gang of these unfortunates were taking their daily promenade, when our [horse-drawn] cab stopped at the entrance gate. They gazed upon us with an eager air of childish curiosity, as we alighted from our conveyance, and entered the building.

We were received very politely by one of the gentlemen belonging to the establishment, who proceeded to show us over the place.

Ascending a broad flight of steps, as clean as it was possible for human hands to make them, we came to a long wide gallery, separated at either end by large folding-doors, the upper part of which were of glass; those to the right opening into the ward set apart for male patients, who were so far harmless that they were allowed the free use of their limbs, and could be spoken to without any danger to the visitors. The female lunatics inhabited the ward to the left, and to these we first directed our attention.

The long hall into which their work-rooms and sleeping apartments opened was lofty, well lighted, well aired, and exquisitely clean; so were the persons of the women, who were walking to and fro, laughing and chatting very sociably together. Others were sewing and quilting in rooms set apart for that purpose. There was no appearance of wretchedness or misery in this ward; nothing that associated with it the terrible idea of madness I had been wont to entertain—for these poor creatures looked healthy and cheerful, nay, almost happy, as if they had given the world and all its cares the go-by. There was one thin, eccentric looking woman in middle life, who came forward to receive us with an air of great dignity; she gave us her hand in a most condescending manner, and smiled most graciously when the gentleman who was with us inquired after her *majesty's* health. She fancies herself Victoria, and in order to humour her conceit, she is allowed to wear a cap of many colours, with tinsel ornaments. This person, who is from the lowest class, certainly enjoys her imaginary dignity in a much greater degree than any crowned monarch, and is perhaps far prouder of her fool's cap than our gracious sovereign is of her imperial diadem.

The madwomen round her appeared to consider her assumption of royalty as a very good joke, for the homage they rendered her was quizzical in the extreme.

Source: Susanna Moodie, *Life in the Clearings versus the Bush* (London: Richard Bentley, 1853), pp. 299–308.

There are times when these people seem to have a vague consciousness of their situation; when gleams of sense break in upon them, and whisper the awful truth to their minds. Such moments must form the drops of bitterness in the poisoned cup of life, which a mysterious Providence has presented to their lips. While I was looking sadly from face to face, as these benighted creatures flitted round me, a tall stout woman exclaimed in a loud voice—

"That's Mrs. M——, of Belleville! God bless her! Many a good quarter dollar I've got from her;" and, running up to me, she flung her arms about my neck, and kissed me most vehemently.

I did not at first recognise her; and, though I submitted with a good grace to the mad hug she gave me, I am afraid that I trembled not a little in her grasp. She was the wife of a cooper, who lived opposite to us during the first two years we resided in Belleville; and I used to buy from her all the milk I needed for the children.

She was always a strange eccentric creature when sane—if, indeed, she ever had enjoyed the right use of her senses; and, in spite of the joy she manifested at the unexpected sight of me, I remember her once threatening to break my head with an old hoop, when I endeavoured to save her little girl from a frightful flagellation from the same instrument [...]

She is at present an incurable but harmless maniac; and, in spite of the instance of cruelty [...] towards her little girl, now, during the dark period of her mind's eclipse, gleams of maternal love struggled like glimpses of sunshine through a stormy cloud, and she inquired of me earnestly, pathetically, nay, even tenderly, for her children. Alas, poor maniac! How could I tell her that the girl she had chastised so undeservedly had died in early womanhood, and her son, a fine young man of twenty, had committed suicide, and flung himself off the bridge into the Moira river only a few months before. Her insanity saved her from the knowledge of events, which might have distracted a firmer brain. She seemed hardly satisfied with my evasive answers, and looked doubtingly and cunningly at me, as if some demon had whispered to her the awful truth.

It was singular that this woman should recognise me after so many years [...]

Another stout, fair-haired matron, with good features and a very pleasant face, insisted on shaking hands with us all round. Judging from her round, sonsy [cheerful], rosy face, you never could have imagined her to have been mad. When we spoke in admiration of the extreme neatness and cleanness of the large sleeping apartment, she said very quietly—

"Ah, you would not wonder at that could you see all the water-witches at night cleaning it." Then she turned to me, and whispered very confidentially in my ear, "Are you mad? You see these people; they are all mad—as mad as March hares. Don't come here if you can help it. It's all very well at first, and it looks very clean and comfortable; but when the doors are once shut, you can't get out—no, not if you ask it upon your knees." She then retreated, nodding significantly.

Leaving this ward, we visited the one which contained the male lunatics.

They appeared far more gloomy and reserved than the women we had left.

One young man, who used to travel the country with jewellery, and who had often been at our house, recognised us in a moment; but he did not come forward like Mrs.—— to greet us, but ran into a corner, and, turning to the wall, covered his face with his hands until we had passed on. Here was at least a consciousness of his unfortunate situation, that was very painful to witness. A gentlemanly man in the prime of life, who had once practised the law in Toronto, and was a person of some consequence, still retained the dress and manners belonging to his class. He had gone to the same school with my son-in-law, and he greeted him in the most hearty and affectionate manner, throwing his arm about his shoulder, and talking of his affairs in the most confidential manner. His mental aberration was only displayed in a few harmless remarks, such as telling us that this large house was his, that it had been built with his money, and that it was very hard he was kept a prisoner in his own dwelling; that he was worth millions; and that people were trying to cheat him of all his money, but that if once he could get out, he would punish them all. He then directed my son-in-law to bring up some law books that he named, on the morrow, and he would give him a dozen suits against the parties from whom he had received so many injuries [...]

There were two boys among these men who, in spite of their lunacy, had an eye to business, and begged pathetically for coppers, though of what use they could be to them in that place I cannot imagine. I saw no girls under twelve years of age. There were several boys who appeared scarcely in their teens.

Mounting another flight of snowy stairs, we came to the wards above those we had just inspected. These were occupied by patients that were not in a state to allow visitors a nearer inspection than observing them through the glass doors. By standing upon a short flight of broad steps that led down to their ward, we were able to do this with perfect security. The hands of all these women were secured in mufflers; some were dancing, others running to and fro at full speed, clapping their hands, and laughing and shouting with the most boisterous merriment. How dreadful is the laugh of madness! how sorrowful the expressions of their diabolical mirth! tears and lamentations would have been less shocking, for it would have seemed more natural. [...].

▲ Document 6: William James Thomson, Untitled Painting of the Provincial Asylum, Toronto, 1890

● This image demonstrates the size and grandeur of the Provincial Asylum in Toronto. How does the landscaping indicate the public nature of this building? What is the purpose of a painting such as this?

Source: William James Thomson, untitled painting of the Provincial Asylum (opened 1850), Toronto. Ink and watercolour on paper, 1890. Collection of the Centre for Addiction and Mental Health (CAMH), Toronto. Courtesy CAMH Archives. An ink and sketch version originally appeared as an illustration in the *Toronto Globe*, 5 April 1890.

■ Article 1: The Development of the Lunatic Asylum in the Maritime Provinces

Daniel Francis

Late in the year 1835 some two dozen reputed lunatics who had been imprisoned in the county gaol in Saint John were removed first to the city's almshouse and then, early the next year, to the basement of a small, wooden building on Leinster Street. This building, constructed originally as a cholera hospital but as of February 1836 housing fourteen lunatics in its depths and as many sick paupers upstairs, was Canada's first mental institution. It would be another twelve years before New Brunswick had a permanent treatment center and another twenty-three years before its sister province of Nova Scotia had one.[1] Yet this little hospital, inadequate as it was, represented an important change in the treatment of the insane in the Maritimes. At last it was being recognized that the most important thing about the mentally ill was that they were mentally ill, not poor or violent or criminal, and that they required a specific kind of supervision in a specific kind of institution. It had not always been so.

The first law regarding the insane in the two colonies was a 1759 statute establishing a workhouse in Halifax. No special accommodation was provided for insane paupers in the building who were lumped indiscriminately with "all disorderly and idle persons, and such who shall be found begging, or practising any unlawful games, or pretending to fortune telling, common drunkards, persons of lewd behaviour, vagabonds, runaways, stubborn servants and children, and persons who notoriously misspend their time to the neglect and prejudice of their own and their family's support". Special consideration was given only to the retarded and lunatics who were physically incapable of labouring. Others were to be put to work alongside their fellow inmates and with them to be whipped "moderately" upon entering the workhouse and strenuously if they proved "stubborn

or idle".[2] In 1774 a second statute, entitled "An Act for Punishing Rogues, Vagabonds, and other Idle and Disorderly Persons", provided that persons "furiously mad and dangerous to be permitted to go abroad" should be "safely locked up in some secure place".[3] In New Brunswick an 1824 statute directed dangerous lunatics to be "kept safely locked up in some secure place" and if necessary chained, a practice which was already being followed.[4] Lunatics who fell afoul of the law were thus placed in conditions which could only aggravate their illness and then expected to behave normally or suffer for it.

Yet the insane certainly were not actively persecuted. If they caused no problems and could look after themselves, they were left to wander at will. Those who were either wealthy themselves or had wealthy relations were usually packed off to a private madhouse in the United States or Britain. Far from seeking out inmates for the prisons and poorhouses, the authorities hoped a mentally ill person's family would assume the responsibility of caring for him at home. But since many of the insane were quite understandably paupers, those who could not support themselves or rely on their families were placed in almshouses or workhouses. From their beginnings the two colonies adopted the British poor law system which was based on the administrative principle that each town or parish had to support its own poor by a compulsory assessment of the inhabitants.[5] While able-bodied unemployed were either gaoled for being "idle and disorderly persons" or set to work by an Overseer of the Poor, some kind of accommodation was found for the infirm poor, often in private homes or in buildings rented for the purpose. A major drawback to this system of relief was that many communities did not have the resources to care for their poor and as a result the practice of auctioning off paupers developed.[6] Overseers of the Poor were authorized to pay local residents to take paupers into their homes and support them for a year. The price was arrived at by a process of down-bidding at a public auction. The person willing to take the pauper for the least amount of money won his or her services. Originally the practice was regulated but gradually controls were relaxed and the system became one of brutal abuse. Paupers became a kind of slave labour in the backwoods of the provinces and people began to use the auctions as a means of making an income and as a source

Source: Daniel Francis, "The Development of the Lunatic Asylum in the Maritime Provinces," *Acadiensis: Journal of the History of the Atlantic Region,* Vol. 6, 2 (1977): 23–38. Reprinted with permission.

of subsidized labour. Clearly, many of the victims of the auction block, at least before asylums were built, would have been paupers suffering from mild forms of mental illness.

In Nova Scotia the mentally ill first were provided for in the Halifax Poor's Asylum in 1812. It was originally intended that they be confined apart from the healthy paupers but as the institution became overcrowded this distinction was not enforced. In 1832 a legislative committee touring the poorhouse reported that "every room from the cellar to the garret is filled to excess" and told of one room with eighteen beds which nightly held forty-seven persons.[7] The committee urged the erection of a hospital but did not consider a separate lunatic asylum necessary. It was not really until Hugh Bell became mayor of Halifax in 1844 that an energetic movement for the establishment of an asylum began. Bell had arrived in the colony from Ireland in 1782 at the age of two years and had been in turn a journalist, a Methodist preacher, a successful brewer and a politician. He was sixty-four when, apparently influenced by a term as commissioner of the Poor's Asylum, he undertook to persuade the government to build an asylum.[8] His first move was to pledge his own salary as mayor to a special asylum fund. Next, he organized public meetings to gather similar private pledges, hoping to force the government's hand. Bell's campaign was supported by a number of wealthy Haligonians and endorsed by at least two Halifax newspapers, the *Novascotian* and the *Times,* but the scheme did not seem to capture the imagination of the populace. As the *Times* reluctantly reported. Bell's activities "do not appear to be well seconded".[9] In 1845, prompted by an abortive suggestion from New Brunswick that it, Nova Scotia and Prince Edward Island build a joint asylum, a commission was established with Bell as the chairman to investigate the possibility of establishing an asylum in Nova Scotia. The Bell Commission enthusiastically endorsed the project the next year but no action was taken and in 1848 another legislative committee argued that "it would be improper at this time to recommend any appropriation of the public monies which would require so great an expenditure".[10] Early in 1850 Dorothea Dix, the American psychiatric reformer, delivered an impassioned plea to the legislature on behalf of the mentally ill but she failed to prompt any action and not until 1852 did "an Act for Founding a Lunatic Asylum" pass the Assembly and not until January 1859 were the first patients admitted.[11]

A number of factors may have contributed to this delay. During the 1840s, when Hugh Bell was trying to get government backing for an asylum, the assembly was preoccupied with the noisy struggle for political power between James Johnston's faction and the "Liberals" led by Joseph Howe. Another explanation, the one advanced at the time, was that other demands were being made on the provincial treasury.[12] For the first half of the century the hospital annexed to the Halifax Poor's Asylum was the only public hospital in the city. During the typhus epidemic in 1847 this facility was woefully overcrowded and the local medical community began to petition the government for a new hospital. In 1849 a legislative committee conducted an investigation into the matter which resulted in funds being allotted. Since at the same time the assembly was financing the construction of a new prison, the legislators apparently felt justified in putting off the asylum recommended by the 1846 commission. Furthermore, in the early 1850s railway fever absorbed the attention and the revenues of the province. "Provincial finances were completely compromised by railway legislation and there was a powerful aversion to new taxation for any other purpose".[13]

Agitation for the reform of treatment of the mentally ill began earlier in New Brunswick than in its neighbouring colony, perhaps because in the former the social dislocation associated with higher rates of immigration made the plight of the insane more evident and more urgent. The movement was led by a medical man, Dr. George Peters. Peters had been born in Saint John in 1811 but had been exposed to more advanced ideas about insanity during his years as a medical student in Edinburgh.[14] In the 1830s he was the visiting medical officer at the Saint John almshouse and county gaol and it was the degraded condition in which he found the insane incarcerated in these institutions which prompted him to petition the assembly for the provision of an asylum. In the gaol Peters was horrified to find that warders were making no attempt to separate the mentally ill from other criminals and he discovered many lunatics under heavy restraint, "some of them perfectly naked and in a state of filth"[15] At the Almshouse Peters found similarly inadequate conditions. This institution had been built in 1819 to house sixty persons.[16]

In 1836 it held one hundred and forty paupers, forty of whom required medical treatment and were kept in a makeshift two-room infirmary big enough to handle eight people comfortably.[17] Sick patients overflowed these two rooms into the section of the almshouse reserved for the mentally ill. It was this situation which provoked Peters into seeking permission from the government to move the insane from the almshouse to the basement of the cholera hospital. Unfortunately, the situation did not improve. Lunatics were able to mingle freely with the sick paupers who were being treated in the upper stories of the hospital and the building was too crowded to allow Peters to practice any kind of treatment. The temporary asylum was really just an extension of the almshouse; as Peters himself described it, it was "essentially a pauper institution".[18]

At the same time as the temporary asylum was opening in 1836, the justices of the peace in Saint John County, alarmed at the growing number of mentally disturbed inmates in the gaols, petitioned the assembly to establish a more permanent asylum.[19] A legislative committee was appointed with instructions to gather information from the United States and Europe about the treatment of the insane and to plan a permanent facility. Although this committee reported in December of that year, it was a decade before the assembly was convinced of the inadequacy of the temporary building and appropriated funds that allowed construction of the new asylum to begin.[20] It is not difficult to account for this reluctance to commit provincial funds to the asylum project. While it is true that between 1838 and 1841 the newly acquired control over the revenues from the crown lands swelled the provincial coffers, the decentralized manner in which these funds were dispensed meant that provincial projects did not always receive financial support. As MacNutt has pointed out, the individual assemblyman had control over how and where government money was spent in his constituency.[21] Control of the purse strings was crucial to him because by deploying the money skillfully he could ensure electoral support. He might be reluctant, therefore, to surrender any portion of his patronage money to projects of a more general purpose. Yet the parochialism of legislators should not be exaggerated. The late 1830s and early 1840s were years of heavy immigration and economic crisis in the colony and the assembly was faced

with a variety of immediate needs. In response, it undertook in the years between 1834 and 1847 four major welfare measures aside from the asylum.[22] In 1834 a cholera hospital was opened in Saint John; in 1836 funds were authorized for the construction of a county gaol in the city and a house of correction; in 1838 a new alms-house-workhouse-infirmary complex was approved; and in 1847 the Emigrant Orphan Asylum opened its doors in Saint John. Proponents of a mental asylum had to vie with all these different interests for a share of the public funds and were actually at a disadvantage since gaols and poorhouses could if necessary double as mental institutions.

The Maritime mental institutions which eventually were established in the 1840s and 1850s were designed to accommodate a specific treatment technique known as moral treatment. A few simple drugs, both tranquillizers and purgatives, were administered to control behaviour; assorted bathing techniques were advised for manic or depressed patients; and blood-letting had not entirely been discredited. But moral treatment, or the humane method, was the principal therapeutic technique. It was to the nineteenth century what psychoanalysis became to our own. Moral treatment had its origins in the last decade of the eighteenth century in Europe where it developed out of the practical experiences of Philippe Pinel in France and William Tuke in England. Pinel (1745–1826) attained legendary stature in the history of psychiatry by being the first to strike the chains from the insane and free them from confinement in dungeons, first at the Hopital de Bicêtre in Paris in 1793 and two years later at the Saltpetrière, a hospital for women. His major work, *A Treatise on Insanity*, was published in an English translation in 1806 and his theories were known in the Maritimes as he was referred to approvingly in the New Brunswick report of 1836. Tuke (1732–1822), an English tea merchant and Quaker, pioneered moral treatment in the York Retreat for the Insane which he founded in 1792. His grandson, Samuel Tuke, wrote *Description of the Retreat* in 1813, which was published in the United States the following year and became a standard text for reformers throughout the English-speaking world. Really not treatment in a medical sense at all, the moral method employed compassion and lenience within a strictly controlled environment in an attempt to coax the mind back to sanity. The intention was first of all to relieve the patient's fears and then to distract the mind from its morbid preoccupations. In this manner the patient was encouraged to exercise self-control and to reassert the primacy of will over passion. At mid-century this technique was extended by John Conolly, a British asylum doctor, to include the complete abolition of all mechanical and physical restraints.

The principles of moral treatment were carried into the Maritimes by reform-minded laymen such as Hugh Bell and more importantly by doctors who had been educated in Europe or the United States. At the beginning of the century most Maritime medical men were trained as apprentices but by the 1830s a number were being educated at universities in Great Britain and this was certainly true of the doctors who became medical superintendents at the new asylums and the main exponents of moral treatment in the two colonies.[23] George Peters, the original superintendent of the New Brunswick institution, and his successor John Waddell, superintendent for twenty-seven years, both received their degrees from Scottish universities affiliated with mental hospitals where modern treatment techniques were employed. James DeWolf, the first superintendent of Mount Hope, likewise was a graduate of Edinburgh University. Later in the century aspiring doctors began to attend American medical schools; for example, James Steeves, Waddell's successor, studied in Pennsylvania and New York.[24] Even when these early alienists were not formally trained in the United States, their annual reports indicate that they kept a close watch on developments there and frequently toured the more famous American institutions where moral treatment was practiced. While the broad principles of moral treatment were endorsed by all the asylum superintendents, there were differences in the way these principles were applied. This was especially true of the elimination of physical restraints. In New Brunswick Waddell early on rejected the "indiscriminate and frequent use" of mechanical restraints but argued that sometimes they had to be applied for the good of the patient and this moderate position was adopted by his successors.[25] In Nova Scotia, on the other hand, there were quite radical differences of opinion at different points in time. Dr. DeWolf invoked Conolly and endorsed "the total disuse of mechanical restraint" whereas his successor, Dr. A. P. Reid, defended physical restraints as a form of discipline.[26] Despite these differences of emphasis, however, medical personnel at the Maritime asylums shared a perception of themselves as practitioners of moral treatment.

Moral treatment enjoyed such unequivocal allegiance because it was believed to be effective. The decades of the 1840s and 1850s were a period of unbridled optimism regarding the curability of mental illness. "It is the decided opinion of most persons who have investigated the subject," the New Brunswick commissioners reported in 1836, "that insanity is on the increase. But at the same time it is consolatory to observe, that the disease is not now considered of so formidable a nature as it used to be. because it is found easily to yield to judicious treatment timely applied."[27] In the United States optimism reached a high point in the period 1830–1850 and it is not surprising that the same is true of the Maritime colonies since they looked across the border for proof that their asylums would be successful.[28] The Bell Commission, for example, reported recovery rates of 82½ per cent and 86½ per cent respectively at the Worcester Asylum in Massachusetts and Boston's McLean Asylum and concluded confidently that "Wherever an Asylum is established, there the numbers of Insane in proportion to the population begin to diminish".[29] An important qualification invariably made was that a lunatic was curable primarily in the very early stages of his illness, usually in the first three months. If madness could be detected at the outset and the afflicted person removed from his home to an asylum before temporary symptoms became permanent illness, then cure was virtually assured. If not, if family or friends hesitated before bringing the mentally ill to the asylum, then doctors promised nothing. In fact, they hinted at the worst. When John Waddell stated categorically that "No insane man recovers at home" he was speaking for all his colleagues.[30] Insanity demanded moral treatment and moral treatment demanded the asylum.

A clear idea of the aim of moral treatment is best obtained by examining how it was intended to be implemented in the new, Maritime asylums. Practitioners began with the building itself. The ideal location was on a height of land commanding a scenic view, right at the edge of civilization. Such a site offered the insane the scenery which was expected to soothe their frenzies and divert their attention. Advocates of moral treatment had great faith in the remedial influence nature exerted over the deranged mind: "[…] the sounds caused by rushing water is the music of nature, and is always in harmony with, and soothing in its effects on, the nervous organism".[31] Diversion was also a rationale for building the asylum on the edge of a city, remote enough so that the insane were insulated from the excitement of urban life but close enough so that they had "constant proofs that they are in a world of hope, and among beings who are engaged in the every day business of life."[32] These asylums were not built on secluded sites far from the centers of population. On the contrary, as examples of the charitable character of the populace, they were trophies to be displayed.

The physical appearance of the institution was an important aspect of moral treatment. As in all things, the emphasis was on symmetry and good taste, what came to be called "moral architecture".

> As it is found that the external appearance, as well as the internal economy of the Hospital for the Insane, exert an important moral influence … it is a principle now generally recognized and acted on, that good taste and a regard for comfort, should characterize all the arrangements both external and internal, as calculated to induce self-respect and a disposition to self-control.[33]

As important as the countenance of the asylum was the arrangement of its buildings. Within the Maritime asylums certain classes of patients were to be isolated from each other. For example, patients were segregated by sex and special accommodation was provided for "frantics" whose violent behaviour might disturb the other inmates. Another criterion for separating patients was social class. In part the rationale for this practice was economic. Asylum administrators hoped to attract wealthy patients whose fees would contribute to the upkeep of the institutions. It was thought necessary to offer this class of patient comfortable surroundings and assurances that it would not be subjected to the unsettling manners and morals of lower class lunatics.[34] This reasoning also betrays a therapeutic rationale. Patients had to be insulated from all that was offensive to them and which might cause them to retreat into their derangement. Segregation by class was one of the practices asylum personnel anticipated would make Maritime institutions superior to their American counterparts

in which conditions were distressingly democratic.[35] As it turned out, however, overcrowding and lack of funds kept asylums in Nova Scotia and New Brunswick from achieving a rigorous separation of social classes. It was a recurring complaint throughout the century that the indiscriminate mixing of classes was diverting wealthier patients to foreign institutions, thereby losing local asylums desperately needed funds.[36]

As for the organization of time within the asylum, moral treatment combined three elements—work, play and worship. The most important of this trinity was work, physical labour within the asylum itself or in the gardens surrounding the institutions. Useful employment was intended to have a variety of effects, not the least of which was to defray the expenses of maintaining the institution. More importantly, labour had therapeutic value, if for no other reason than it exhausted the patients, improving their sleeping habits and their physical health. Like the scenery, physical work, by forcing the patient to concentrate on something other than himself, diverted his attention from his sickness, theoretically weakening the irrational forces in their struggle with the will. Since many of the insane seemed to suffer from excess energy which made their behaviour frenzied and unpredictable, regular labour was intended to divert and give vent to some of this energy in a more useful and healthy way. But perhaps the most important influence labour was expected to have on the insane was its moral influence. If a patient was to rejoin society as a productive member, then he or she had to be taught independence, industry and self-respect. Useful employment was as much a way of instilling moral values as it was of healing broken minds.[37] But work could not occupy all the time nor all the patients in an asylum. It was anticipated that upper class inmates, who apparently did not require the moral lessons of useful employment, would be exempt from physical labour. For them, and for the lower classes in their spare time, instructive recreation had to be provided. As well, regular religious observances were scheduled, though for reasons more behavioural than spiritual. Religion was useful as another distraction and the services, because of their communal nature, were considered excellent opportunities for practicing decorum and restraint.[38]

The final element of moral treatment, and one which circumscribed all the others, was isolation.

While it was considered healthy that the mentally ill be aware of, and to some degree witness to, the daily life of society beyond the asylum walls, it was also considered crucial that the individual patient be removed from the immediate social surroundings which had been witness to his fall from reason.

> The first and most important step is to remove the patient from his own home and from all the objects which he has been accustomed to see. His false notions and harassing impressions are associated in his mind with the objects exposed to his senses during the approach of his disease. His relations have become to him stale and uninteresting, and afterwards cause of angry irritation. [...] The most favourable situation is a retirement, where the patient will be surrounded by objects which have a composing influence.[39]

The mind, once shattered, needed a quiet place, a kind of laboratory, in which it could be carefully reconstructed. Throughout the century medical men repeatedly warned the public that the insane could not be treated at home, that they had to be surrendered up to the asylum if they were not to become forever incurable.

When all these elements were combined, the result was a self-enclosed, rightly organized institution, the aim of which was the reformation of its inmates' behaviour into socially conventional patterns. Perhaps the most revealing statement about moral treatment can be found in the Nova Scotia report of 1846—"without system there cannot be success".[40] The asylum was a system. Everything from its location to the table manners of its inmates was interrelated to transform behaviour. In charge of this process was the medical superintendent, "the very light and life of the Institution", who was expected not to practice medicine but to attract the confidence, the obedience and the emulation of his charges.[41] The system ignored causes because the understanding of them was rudimentary.[42] Instead, doctors concentrated on symptoms—the hallucination, the frenzy, the melancholy—and tried to eliminate them by reinforcing the patient's self-control. This was the moral system and it flowered in a brand new institution, the asylum.

At the same time as the new Maritime asylums were opening their doors, a noticeable change occurred in the attitude of the law to the incarceration of the insane. Prior to this time statutes had illustrated a reluctance on the part of the lawmakers to take responsibility for the care of the mentally ill. However, as the asylum began to be emphasized as the only proper place for treatment, legislators became much more aggressive in their attitude toward the insane. In New Brunswick the original bylaws governing the new asylum restricted inmates to "lunatics proper" and refused admission to all but exceptional cases of idiocy and delerium tremens.[43] This changed in 1852 when "An Act to Amend the Law Relating to Lunatics and Insane Persons" provided that "any person furiously mad or so far disordered in his reason as to be dangerous when at large" was to be taken forcibly to the asylum and incarcerated there on the orders of two Justices of the Peace.[44] No doctor need be consulted and the superintendent of the asylum could not refuse a patient. Seven years later the law was changed to ensure that no one was admitted to the provincial asylum without first being certified by a doctor but the asylum's superintendent still had no right to refuse admittance to anyone so certified, be they senile, retarded or epileptic.[45] The legal emphasis was on making it as easy as possible to get the mentally ill into the asylum. In Nova Scotia the situation was similar. Prompted by four murders committed within a year, all by men who were subsequently found to be insane, the legislature passed a law which allowed two Justices of the Peace to hold in custody any person who "seemed" to be insane and "seemed" to have "a purpose of committing some crime".[46] If found to be mentally disturbed by a doctor, the individual was held either in gaol or in the poorhouse, or in the asylum when it opened four years later. The Nova Scotia asylum superintendents had more discretionary power than their New Brunswick counterparts. From the beginning the Nova Scotia asylum at Mount Hope was governed by a law which allowed recent and acute cases of insanity to be given preference over more chronic cases.[47] This meant that when the institution became crowded, which it very soon did, mental defectives and cases of long-term illness were refused admittance. While at no time were persons ever legally committed to the Nova Scotia asylum without certification by a physician, there was a perceptible shift in the legal attitude. An 1858 statute, "An Act For the Management of the Hospital for the Insane", provided for the incarceration of any person who could be proven to be "by reason of insanity, unsafe to be at large or suffering any unnecessary duress or hardship".[48] By 1872 the law made no reference to public or personal safety. It merely stated that "any lunatic being at large may be apprehended".[49]

Unhappily, the medico-legal campaign to institutionalize the mentally ill had an effect quite opposite to that intended by reformers and medical men. To be effective, moral treatment required a small number of patients, all of whom were in the acute stage of their illness, and a large staff to work with them. What happened, however, was that the asylums were immediately and continuously overcrowded, especially with what were considered chronic incurable cases, and had neither the staff nor the facilities to be anything more than places of confinement. The heady optimism of mid-century evaporated into exasperation, and sometimes plain brutality, as asylums proved unable to fulfill their role as successful treatment centers.

The New Brunswick asylum opened in December 1848 and in his report for the following year the medical superintendent, John Waddell, was already asking that the institution be enlarged.[50] When completed, it was intended to handle 180 patients in a complex of three buildings, but these were not finally built until 1864, at which time the daily average of patients at the asylum was 194.[51] Demands for expansion continued but it was not really until 1885, when a farm annex capable of handling 150 of the more long-term cases was built, that a satisfactory patient population was achieved.[52] New Brunswick now had facilities for 320 acute cases and almost half that many chronics and complaints about overcrowding were seldom heard. In Nova Scotia the Mount Hope Asylum was also constantly overcrowded from its opening in 1859 until the commencement in 1886 of the county asylum system. The county institutions were meant to accommodate "harmless insane, idiotic persons, and epileptic persons who are insane but who have not manifested symptoms of violent insanity".[53] By 1897 there were fifteen of them throughout Nova Scotia.[54] Crowded conditions at the asylums made the successful treatment of patients almost impossible and cure rates never approximated the heady forecasts of eighty and ninety per cent. By 1882 Dr. A. P. Reid was admitting that at Mount Hope only about ten per cent of the four hundred patients had much hope of regaining their mental health.[55] In 1891 the superintendent of the New Brunswick institution admitted that "Out of four hundred and forty-two patients, only sixteen were expected to be restored to mental health".[56] That is barely more than three per cent. The asylum had become a place of confinement for hundreds of mentally ill people who were given next to no hope of recovery.

Not only were the asylums hopelessly overcrowded, they were also poorly staffed. At first, the superintendent was the only medically qualified staff member. Later in the century he was given an assistant. It was the intention of both asylums that these doctors make daily visits to all the patients but evidence given at a number of enquiries suggests that these duties were frequently neglected. Daily care of asylum inmates devolved upon a small number of attendants who had no training and often, because of overwork, or simple meanness, no sympathy. Since turnover in these jobs was rapid and steady, the insane seldom even had the benefit of experienced care. Given these conditions, it is not surprising to find that there were a number of publicized incidents of attendants abusing patients. In New Brunswick, just a year after the asylum opened, two attendants were dismissed for what was delicately called "gross misconduct".[57] A short while after Mount Hope opened in Nova Scotia the institution's steward, Amos Black, was dismissed by a committee of investigation, apparently for having sexual relations with a number of the patients. In any event Black and DeWolf, the superintendent, were frequently at odds, the committee terming the situation at the asylum a "civil war" between the two men with the patients neglected as a result.[58] Five years after the Black incident, the bruised, lice-ridden corpse of Richard Hurley became the center of a controversy about the standard of care at the asylum. During the twenty-four-year-old Hurley's six-month stay at Mount Hope no members of his family were permitted to visit him until the day the father was summoned to take the consumptive body of his son home to die. A committee investigating the incident concluded that parts of the asylum were indeed overcrowded and filthy, although it declared that there was "no evidence to fix any blame on either Dr. DeWolf or any of the attendants".[59]

While unqualified attendants were undoubtedly the cause of some abuse, the biggest problem in the asylums was lack of space. In 1877 Dr. James Steeves, superintendent of the New Brunswick hospital from 1876 to 1896, travelled to Fredericton to try and convince the legislature to finance an addition to the building. There were 284 patients in an institution built to accommodate only two hundred, Steeves told the Saint John *Daily Telegraph,* and one hundred of these did not have the separate rooms they required for proper treatment. "The evils involved in this simple fact are such as could not well be described in our columns," wrote the interviewer, "for the details would be offensive and even shocking".[60] In Nova Scotia the "offensive" details of overcrowding were described publicly, as a result of an investigation into conditions at the asylum in May, 1877.[61] It was established that because of crowding, patients were being neglected, wards were filthy and no treatment was being carried out. Kate Cameron, an attendant at Mount Hope for four years, told the committee that she had once seen a female patient stripped, bound and left unattended in a room with no bed and no heat, simply because she had torn her clothes. It was December and the woman froze to death but no inquest was held into the incident.[62] Michael Meagher, another attendant, told the following story:

> A patient named Graham was in the dark room (solitary confinement) while I was at the Hospital. It was in the Winter time. The glass was broken, and the rain came in and wet the floor. Graham was lying on the floor on a mattress. The room was in a very dirty condition. There was straw on the floor, and human excrements. I saw the snow not melted on the floor. We put the food in over the door sometimes. The doctor would occasionally enquire how he was. [...] He never went to see him. A man put in the dark room was entirely neglected. Graham was subject to fits: he might have died without assistance during the night: he was left entirely to his own resources after locking him up. Graham was a powerful, muscular man. It was the practise of the attendants to give as little food as possible to patients in that state to reduce their strength: just enough food to sustain them. The doctors never enquired into the quantity of food given them. Graham was in the dark room from one to three weeks. The room was bitterly cold; it was hardly fit for a dog: it was not fit for a human being.[63]

These abuses at Mount Hope may have been aggravated by Superintendent DeWolf, an arrogant man with whom most of his employees found it difficult to work. But the fact that both the New Brunswick and Prince Edward Island asylums were also, in different degrees, found to be inadequate institutions, suggests that Mount Hope was not the exception but the rule.[64]

The evidence indicates that the Maritime asylum failed to live up to its founders' expectations. Instead of a place of treatment it had become a place of confinement Good intentions were one thing, but lack of adequate space and facilities meant inevitably that the emphasis at the asylums was on custody, not treatment. Organization became paramount as the logistics of caring for hundreds of mentally ill inmates became complicated and costly. Behaviour was subordinated to a rigidly controlled pattern of daily institutional life. The county asylums built in Nova Scotia after 1885 epitomized this trend. The regulations for one of these institutions warned that "any inmate guilty of drunkenness, disobedience, obscenity, disorderly conduct, profane or indecorous language, theft, waste or who shall absent himself or herself from the premises without the permission of the Superintendent or who shall injure or deface any part of the house or furniture therein, or who shall commit waste or destruction of any kind in regard to property connected with the Asylum shall be subject to merited punishment".[65] "Merited punishment" included solitary confinement on a diet of bread and water for up to twenty-four hours. All activity at these institutions—getting up in the morning, eating meals, taking exercise, going to bed at night—was done en masse and regulated by the sounding of bells. Given the intolerable conditions of the asylum, the humane aspect of moral treatment had been sacrificed to the requirements of the system. The Maritime asylum had become more a jail than a hospital.

Notes

1. Prince Edward Island is not considered in this article because not until very late in the period

under discussion was a hospital for the mentally ill constructed on the Island. An asylum was opened near Charlottetown in 1847 but it doubled as a house of industry and in construction resembled a workhouse more than a hospital. This building, chronically overcrowded and underfinanced and poorly lit and ventilated, remained the only facility for the mentally ill until 1879 when the first proper hospital built for the purpose was opened. See R. N. Stalwick, "A History of Asylum Administration in Canada Before Confederation" (unpublished Ph.D. thesis. University of London, 1967), pp. 89 *passim*; Henry Hard, ed., *The Institutional Care of the Insane in the United States and Canada* (Baltimore 1917), vol. 4, pp. 203 *passim*. When the term Maritime is used in the article, therefore, it is meant to refer to New Brunswick and Nova Scotia only.

2. *Statutes of Nova Scotia,* 32 Geo 11, c.1.

3. *Ibid.,* 10 Geo III. c.5.

4. *Consolidated Statutes of New Brunswick,* 5 Geo IV. c.9.

5. For the following discussion of poor relief I am indebted to Brereton Greenhous,. "Paupers and Poorhouses: The Development of Poor Relief in Early New Brunswick", *Social History,* I (April. 1968), pp. 103–26, and James Whalen, "New Brunswick Poor Law Policy in the Nineteenth Century" (M.A. thesis. University of New Brunswick. 1968), part of which was published in *Acadiensis,* II (I).

6. See Greenhous, *op.cit.,* and Grace Aiton, "The Selling of Paupers by Public Auction in Sussex Parish". *Collections of the New Brunswick Historical Society,* 16 (1961). pp. 93–110.

7. Nova Scotia. Legislative Assembly, *Journals,* 1832. App. 49 [hereafter references to Assembly journals in the Maritimes will be to *JLA*].

8. Henry Hurd. *op. cit.,* p. 549.

9. *Novascotian.* 25 November 1844 and *Times.* 5 November, 22 December 1844.

10. Nova Scotia, *JLA.* 1846. App. 32; *JLA.* 1848. App. 54.

11. Nova Scotia. *JLA,* 1850. App. 72.

12. *Novascotian,* 23 March 1846.

13. W. S. MacNutt *The Atlantic Provinces* (Toronto, 1965), p. 261.

14. Hurd, *op.cit.,* p. 584.

15. George Peters to Executive Council, 28 November 1836, New Brunswick, Records of the Executive Council, Health and Sickness, vol. 2, Provincial Archives of New Brunswick [hereafter PANB].

16. Whalen. *op.cit.,* p. 55.

17. *New Brunswick Courier* (Saint John), 24 December 1836.

18. George Peters to Executive Council, 3 May 1845, New Brunswick, Executive Council Pupers, vol. 118, p. 1442, PANB.

19. Hurd, *op.cit.,* p. 37.

20. Report of the Commissioners, December 1836, New Brunswick, *JLA.* 1836–7. App. 3.

21. W. S. MacNutt. *New Brunswick* (Toronto, 1963), pp. 258–9.

22. Whalen, *op.cit.*

23. See K. A. Mackenzie, "Nineteenth Century Physicians in Nova Scotia". *Collections of the Nova Scotia Historical Society.* 31 (1957). pp. 119–20 and J. W. Lawrence, "The Medical Men of St. John in its First Half Century". *Collections of the New Brunswick Historical Society.* 1 (1897), pp. 273–305.

24. Hurd. *op.cit.,* pp. 561, 584, 591, 595.

25. Report from the Medical Superintendent of the Provincial Lunatic Asylum, New Brunswick. *JLA,* 1851. App.

26. Report of the Medical Superintendent of the Nova Scotia Hospital for the Insane, Nova Scotia, *JLA.* 1872. App. 20: 1881. App. 3A.

27. New Brunswick, *JLA.* 1836–7. App. 3.

28. See Norman Dain. *Concepts of Insanity in the United States, 1789–1865* (New Brunswick, N.J., 1964), p. 114.

29. Nova Scotia, *JLA,* 1846. App. 32.

30. Report of the Medical Superintendent, New Brunswick, *JLA,* 1849. App.

31. Report of the Medical Superintendent, New Brunswick, *JLA,* 1875. App. 6.

32. Report of the Commissioners, New Brunswick, *JLA,* 1836–7. App. 3.

33. Nova Scotia, *JLA,* 1846. App. 32.

34. Report of the Commissioners, New Brunswick, *JLA,* 1836–7. App. 3.

35. Report of the Medical Superintendent, New Brunswick, *JLA.* 1849. App.

36. See, for example, New Brunswick, *JLA,* 1850, 1851. App. and Nova Scotia, *JLA,* 1860. App.; 1874. App. 6.

37. See Report of the Commissioners, New Brunswick. *JLA,* 1836–7. App. 3 and Nova Scotia, *JLA,* 1846. App. 32.

38. Report of the Commissioners, New Brunswick. *JLA,* 1836–7. App. 3.

39. *Ibid.*

40. Nova Scotia. *JLA,* 1846. App. 32.

41. *Ibid.*

42. For a detailed discussion of contemporary theories of insanity and its causes see my thesis, "That Prison on the Hill; The Historical Origins of the Lunatic Asylum in the Maritime Provinces" (unpublished M.A. thesis, Carleton University. 1975).

43. Correspondence, Reports and Returns, New Brunswick, Records of the Executive Council, vol. 118, Lunatic Asylum, 1843–57, pp. 1540–6, PANB.

44. Report of the Medical Superintendent, New Brunswick. *JLA*. 1854. App.

45. *Consolidated Statutes of New Brunswick, 1903,* vol. 1, c. 101.

46. *Nova Scotian,* 1 January 1855; *Statutes of Nova Scotia,* 1855, c. 34. ser. 1–6.

47. Nova Scotia, *JLA,* 1859. App. 10.

48. *Statutes of Nova Scotia,* 1858. c. 38.

49. *Ibid.,* 1872. c. 3.

50. Report from the Medical Superintendent, New Brunswick, *JLA,* 1850. App.

51. *Ibid.,* 1865. App. 14.

52. *Ibid.,* 1886. App.

53. *Statutes of Nova Scotia,* 1886, c 44.

54. Report of the Medical Superintendent. Nova Scotia, *JLA,* 1899. App. 3A.

55. *Ibid.,* 1883. App. 3A.

56. Report from the Medical Superintendent, New Brunswick. *JLA,* 1891. App.

57. *Morning News* (Saint John), 7 December 1849.

58. Nova Scotia, *JLA,* 1861. App. 6; *Novascotian,* 28 May 1860.

59. Report of Committee on Humane Institutions, Nova Scotia, *JLA*. 1867. App. 38.

60. *Daily Telegraph.* 28 August 1877.

61. Report of Commission to investigate the condition and general management of the Provincial Hospital for the Insane, Nova *Scotia, JLA,* 1878. App. 10.

62. Nova Scotia. *Supplementary Evidence as to the Management of the Hospital for the Insane* (Halifax. 1872).

63. *Ibid.*

64. In 1874 a Grand Jury visited the Prince Edward Island asylum and reported that they "find it difficult to ask your Lordships to believe that an institution, so conducted, would be allowed to exist in a civilized community. In a cell below the ground, about six feet by seven feet, they found a young woman, entirely naked, beneath some broken, dirty straw. The stench was unbearable. There were pools of urine on the floor, evidently the accumulation of many days, as there were gallons of it". The superintendent of the institution was apparently "an ordinary labourer" and the Jury concluded that "the whole Asylum is one state of filth". (Grand Jury Presentment on the state of the Asylum. P.E.I., *JLA,* 1875. App. G).

65. *Bylaws,* Cumberland County Hospital for the Insane, 1895, Public Archives of Nova Scotia.

■ Article 2: "Open to the Public": Touring Ontario Asylums in the Nineteenth Century

Janet Miron

In the 1880s E. Katharine Bates embarked on a transatlantic tour of North America, visiting such cities as Montreal, New York, Boston, Philadelphia, and Washington. While in Toronto for a few days, she included in her sightseeing itinerary the law courts of Osgoode Hall, the University of Toronto, Rosedale Park, and the insane asylum on Queen Street.[1] A few years earlier, Thomas Dick, a young farmer living outside the city, came to Toronto for a visit on the occasion of the national exhibition and chose to spend his time seeing not only the Central Prison but the asylum grounds as well.[2] The visits by Bates and Dick to Toronto's asylum were part of an extremely popular pastime in Ontario in the nineteenth century, whereby large numbers of people poured into the asylums hoping to inspect both the buildings and the people confined within them.[3]

Historians have tended to dismiss visitors such as Bates and Dick as cruel voyeurs who were drawn to mental institutions in search of cheap thrills and excitement, and as irritating intruders who greatly vexed institutional officials.[4] However, when the aims of these visitors, their experiences on their tours, and

Source: James E. Moran and David Wright, eds., *Mental Health and Canadian Society: Historical Perspectives* (Montreal: McGill-Queen's University Press, 2006), pp. 19–20, 21, 22–26, 30–32, 34–42. Reprinted with permission.

the attitudes of asylum employees towards them are critically analyzed, institutional tourism becomes a complex phenomenon that represented more than a mere "shameful" or "degrading spectacle."[5] Indeed, the practice embodies invaluable information for the historian and helps to illuminate both the relationship between asylums and their broader community and popular attitudes towards the insane. In particular, the discourse surrounding visitors demonstrates that many asylum superintendents and government inspectors believed the public had the potential to influence both the success of the asylum and the treatment of mental illness. Moreover, it suggests that an array of motives lay behind people's decisions to visit a hospital for the mentally ill. While not all alienists shared the views of visitors and not all visitors were propelled by the same considerations, the debates that arose and the records left behind by officials and visitors provide important insights into the role these institutions served in the nineteenth century, the influence the public had upon their functionings, and the relationships that were forged with the communities beyond the asylum's walls. [...]

It is the thousands of casual observers with which this chapter primarily is concerned. When we explore asylums through the eyes of such individuals, it becomes clear that nineteenth-century Canadians and tourists from abroad were not mere passive receptacles of the ideologies espoused by those in the medical profession but, instead, were active participants in the effort to understand and study what was deemed to be aberrant behaviour. [...]

Proponents Of Visiting

Most superintendents and government inspectors did not believe that asylums could be easily isolated from greater society; nor did many of them actually desire complete segregation. Instead, a number of administrators strove to foster close ties with the communities beyond their walls, arguing that such relationships were beneficial for a variety of reasons. Moreover, many recognized that the public was crucial to these institutions in a number of ways and that perceptions of and attitudes towards asylums were as dependent on "official" discourse as they were on the laity's experiences while passing through them. As state-run institutions relied on government funding, public approval was essential for asylums, and inevitably, this dependence led asylum officials to embark on campaigns to bolster popular support through the practice of visiting.

Many officials perceived visiting as an important part of the process of social legitimization and believed that the practice was the best means by which public confidence could be gained. These officials were aware of the public's growing fascination with asylums, evinced by the fact that the reports of superintendents, government inspectors, and commissioners were regularly reprinted in the popular press and that the recommendations, criticisms, and impressions of "professional" visitors or prominent reformers commonly appeared in newspapers as well. However, officials were also cognizant of the prejudice towards asylums that pervaded society and undermined the view of their institutions as curative. Indeed, much of the printed information available to the general populace painted a grim picture of institutions for the mentally ill. In the nineteenth century, "shocking" tales of conditions inside asylums appeared regularly in newspapers, sparking concern over the treatment of the institutionalized and fostering suspicion about the buildings that housed them. Until the latter half of the nineteenth century, medical practitioners affiliated with either hospitals or asylums were treated with skepticism by a populace that was not oblivious to the highly publicized grave-robbings committed by some of their peers or the autopsies performed on unwilling subjects.[6] In the mid-1850s, for example, the Toronto Asylum was plagued with many charges of abuse and corruption. A number of employees claimed that the steward had impregnated a female patient, while one former attendant, James Magar, charged that he had "known the bodies of the dead to be dissected for the information of Doctors not connected with the Asylum, and their brains kept after the body was interred."[7] Such scandals easily led to the image of the doctor who sacrificed patients in the pursuit of medical knowledge and helped to foster suspicion of all medical establishments.

Moreover, there were other, more flagrant reasons as to why people feared institutionalization in a medical establishment. Because of their unsanitary conditions and the fact that few people left them healed, hospitals were not perceived as therapeutic institutions. Instead, they were seen as places where the most unfortunate went to die and thus were avoided by all except for the very poor.[8] This view of hospitals imbued attitudes towards asylums. Even as late as the 1860s, Wolfred Nelson, inspector of asylums and prisons for the Province of Canada, remarked that "very erroneous views are generally entertained in regard to Asylums" and that they were often viewed with "distrust and alarm."[9] Consequently, institutional officials hoped to dispel negative publicity by advocating that people view their asylums first-hand and see for themselves the progress that had been made in them.

As a means of gaining society's confidence and alleviating skepticism, superintendents and other government officials encouraged visiting in their annual reports, which were reprinted in local papers. The early annual reports of the Provincial Lunatic Asylum at Toronto repeatedly emphasized that the institution was open to visitors from 12 o'clock until 3 and that it was "as open to the public as is compatible with the welfare of the patients and the duties of their attendants."[10] Such promotion was apparently effective since, in 1850, 1,400 visitors reportedly passed through the asylum during that year alone.[11] Even three decades later, in 1880, officials in the province could still be found encouraging the practice in newspapers, including Richard Maurice Bucke, superintendent of the London Asylum, who wrote a letter to the London *Free Press* publicizing that "the Asylum is always open to inspection by the whole public."[12]

As a way of alleviating social stigma, institutional tourism represented an excellent opportunity to educate the broader society on the causes and contemporary treatment of insanity. In their annual reports, officials often referred to the impressions of visitors, thereby highlighting the importance that was granted to public opinion. The chairman for the Provincial Lunatic Asylum in Toronto reported in 1852. that "Large numbers of visitors have … from time to time, been attended through the building, and these have witnessed the condition of the apartments, the appearance and happiness of the patients, the kindly, but effective discipline, which prevails amongst the afflicted and their attendants. The result has been, so far as is known, a universal satisfaction to visitors, many of whom had been acquainted with similar Institutions in Europe, or the United States."[13] Moreover, many believed that the successful treatment of insanity was dependent upon early committal to an asylum and that the longer loved ones waited, the less likelihood of a cure being achieved. Thus, as Wolfred Nelson pointed out, the "attainment

of successful results" was contingent upon the community's "countenance and good opinion."[14]

Mistrust or suspicion was not the only problem with which asylum officials had to contend while negotiating their relationship with the public. As the nineteenth century progressed, asylum expenditure grew, and superintendents were increasingly pressured to justify their efficacy in treating insanity. According to historian S.E.D. Shortt, asylums in Ontario consumed almost 16.5 per cent of the provincial budget in the 1870s, a share that stabilized at more than 19 per cent in the late 1880s. In 1893 this represented twice the combined expenditure on penal institutions, general hospitals, houses of refuge, and orphanages.[15] As James Moran has noted, the "difficulty in raising funds to construct and maintain the province's public asylums" was a persistent problem.[16] As heads of costly institutions, not only were superintendents compelled to highlight their success rates to portray the therapeutic treatments of their institutions as effective, but they also became even more aware of their need for public support.

The dependence of institutions on public funds made many feel particularly vulnerable and pressured to appease taxpayers, thereby placing asylum superintendents in a difficult situation: at what cost did their efforts to win public support through the practice of visiting endanger the mental improvement of patients? While refusing (at least in theory) to open the doors of the Toronto Asylum to the masses, Superintendent Daniel Clark admitted, much to his chagrin, that many people felt they had a right to tour asylums. "It is a public Institution," he lamented, "and it is the privilege of the British subject, if he should happen to be 'a free and independent elector' to look upon an Asylum to the support of which he has contributed his mite of taxes, as a huge menagerie, erected for the purpose of gratifying his morbid curiosity."[17] Although some may have been opposed to the practice, few institutions could afford to, or had the power to, keep the public out entirely. As the superintendent of the Maiden Lunatic Asylum explained, "Public opinion is all powerful; and by its help only we can carry into practise the most enlightened principles of management; and by the spread of enlightened principles, only, can we hope for that liberal pecuniary support from the Parliament, which is absolutely essential to the welfare of our asylums."[18] [...]

VISITORS TO ASYLUMS

[...] By the mid-nineteenth century, visiting was far from an uncommon or marginal pastime: thousands of urban and rural dwellers alike flocked to asylums annually. In fact, as the century progressed, the activity became so popular that institutions were frequently overwhelmed on holidays, by the "crush and confusion resulting from so many persons being admitted."[19] Thus, while harsh criticism of visiting was voiced and administrators complained of troublesome visitors, few could actually enforce a closed-door policy, and there do not appear to have been any publicly funded asylums in Ontario that could keep the public out entirely. Even if officials were opposed to asylum tourism, they usually had to tolerate the public's presence, and while Clark was officially against sightseers, the practice continued at the Toronto Asylum well into the late nineteenth century, as it did at all other public asylums in Ontario.[20]

Although historians have tended to agree with the attitudes expressed by Clark, the records left by visitors suggest that their motives and experiences were diverse and defy being reduced to voyeurism. Like many other Victorian pursuits, visiting was undeniably rooted in a fascination with those considered deviant and related to the desire to observe or witness the unfamiliar. It was part of the broader "spectacularization" of modern life in the nineteenth century, where "reality seemed to be experienced as a show—an object to be looked at rather than experienced in an unmediated form."[21] However, this phenomenon should not inevitably lead one to conclude that all visitors were merely interested in catching a peep show of the insane. Many visitors certainly treated asylum as human menageries where patients were spectacles to be gawked at and regarded these institutions as entertainment venues that differed little from the circuses and "freak" shows that frequently appeared in their towns and cities. At the same time, although asylum tourism was for many an opportunity to engage in sheer voyeurism, the incentives behind this practice were complex and illuminate the ideological currents and contradictions pervading Victorian culture. Voyeurism was inherent in visiting, yet for a large number of people, institutional tours were a source of self-improvement, "scientific" education, and community pride. Moreover, while its ramifications or effectiveness may be questioned, visiting nevertheless fostered greater exchange and dialogue between the public and the institutionalized and thereby served as an important means through which notions regarding the insane were constructed and defined at the lay level. Thus, by analyzing asylums not as mere physical structures but as tourist sites where popular representations of the "mad" were formed, we can understand these institutions as virtual civic monuments closely connected to the world beyond their walls.

Both Clark and Bucke tended to see all visitors as a homogeneous group, respectively as either voyeurs or responsible citizens. However, those who engaged in asylum tourism were not only guided by an array of incentives but were also from a wide range of social and cultural backgrounds that transcended the lines of gender, class, ethnicity, and age. Local farmers, female leisure travellers, and male bankers visited insane asylums, and children of all ages were exposed to their interiors. As one man remarked on his tour through the Toronto Asylum, "There was a party consisting of a Lady, Gentleman, and a little Girl going over the establishment, and, as I entered I enjoined them."[22] Visitors lived in the communities connected to these institutions or travelled from other regions and countries, some as far away as Mexico, England, and Germany. In terms of sheer numbers alone, the visitors who recorded their experiences were predominantly of a privileged social stature. Reflecting the cultural and political context of the nineteenth century, the majority of records that exist today were written by white, middle-class males, but, while particular voices dominate the written sources, such individuals did not exercise a complete monopoly over asylum tourism. The fact that many accounts were recorded by a wide range of people who did not fit a particular socio-economic profile is significant, and it thereby provides a more nuanced understanding of community attitudes towards asylums. In addition, while the predominant voice in travel narratives might be middle-class and male, since it was not uncommon for visitors to comment upon members of their tour group, their observations often shed light on the experiences of others. [...]

VISITORS' MOTIVES

The public enthusiastically responded to the promotion of asylum tourism and sought to see both the interiors of these institutions and their inhabitants for a variety of reasons that often transcended spectatorship. But this is not to imply that visitors can simply be divided between voyeurs and the well-intentioned, as all who entered into these institutions were voyeurs to a certain degree. Visitors often presented themselves as urban reformers investigating the conditions of institutions, yet, as Judith Walkowitz has argued, "the 'zeal for reform' was often accompanied by 'a prolonged, fascinated gaze' from the bourgeoisie."[23] In order to comment upon the approaches employed in asylums, visitors had to study the institutionalized, but as the power dynamic between these two groups was unequal in that the institutionalized had not made an active "choice" to be viewed by the public, patients were spectacles because of the very nature of such interactions.[24] At the same time, in spite of the fact that there was always a certain power imbalance inherent in these interactions, some visitors were much more inclined than others to view institutional tours as pure amusement and folly. For such individuals, visiting seems to have represented an alluring form of transgression, an opportunity to cross over into the nether world of "abnormal" society and to be risqué by watching, and in many cases ridiculing, the confined.

Visitors mocked patients, taunted them with tobacco, provoked outbursts, and delighted in being able to watch them without necessarily being seen themselves. While some defenders claimed that visiting served an important educational function, others believed these institutions merely offered free, "real-life" amusement. Although the nineteenth century has been characterized as a period in which treatment of the insane was reformed and, in many ways, humanized, a large number of individuals at the lay level continued to perceive asylums as little more than human menageries, in which visiting was an opportunity to gaze at the confined.

The tendency to regard custodial institutions for their entertainment value paralleled many other aspects of nineteenth-century culture. Indeed, the headline for one newspaper article reads like a circus playbill: "The Unsound of Mind. How They are Kept at the London Asylum. A Trip Through the Corridors and Rooms. The Eccentricities of the Patients. Exciting Experiences, Sad Scenes and Amusing Incidents."[25] Until the latter half of the nineteenth century, public executions, "freak" shows, and medical exhibitions encouraged both treatment of the body

as an object to be displayed and the perception that the mental and physical suffering of others could constitute a source of amusement. As Vanessa Schwartz has illustrated in her wonderful monograph *Spectacular Realities,* even in death the body was displayed for the purpose of public consumption and popular entertainment. The morgue visiting she documents in Paris was not as common in Ontario, but the popularity of public executions in Canada is a similar phenomenon that certainly attests to the continent's fascination with the human spectacle. For example, when a man sentenced to be hanged committed suicide, city officials in Toronto displayed his body to the public in the morgue in order to appease the thousands who had hoped to witness his execution.[26] Similarly, society's obsession with the physical suffering of others was highlighted in Montreal when tickets to see the last rites being given to a condemned murderer were sold to the public by the sheriff and thousands gathered to watch his hanging.[27] Alongside such popular practices as public executions, visiting can clearly be seen as one element in a rather impressive roster of nineteenth-century voyeuristic, and at times sadistic, pastimes.

Generalizations about the insane were frequently made by voyeuristic visitors, who tended to relay what they perceived as "humorous" anecdotes of female hysterics and childlike men. One journalist, on his tour of the Toronto Asylum under Dr Scott, described the patients he or she saw: the "religious mad ... who will bore you on some knotty point," those "truly pitiable objects" who were suffering from melancholy, with their "downcast head and look," and others with "much vivacity of manners, loquaciousness of speech, and fondness for narrative." The writer also portrayed one individual who "strutted about attired most ludicrously, fancying herself a Queen."[28] Such visitors saw institutions for the mentally ill primarily as sources of entertainment, and presented the insane as parodies, as characters who could easily have stepped out of a Hogarth print. One popular writer, Susanna Moodie, toured the Toronto Asylum with her daughter and son-in-law, entering areas where "strangers have seldom nerve enough to visit," and proudly relayed her sensationalist impressions and experiences to an undoubtedly dazzled audience.[29]

In spite of the efforts of many asylum superintendents, onlookers motivated by a "perverse" curiosity generally were not prevented from passing through their institutions. As was discussed above, many did struggle with the ways in which such visitors could be kept out. At the same time, though, others were untroubled by the potential presence of visitors who were unsympathetic to the plight of the incarcerated. Dr Sippi, who served as bursar at the London Asylum from 1893 to 1897, complained that the thousands who came through the institution were motivated merely by "idle" and harmful curiosity. However, Bucke refused to stem the flow of tourists, and throughout his career he remained adamant that visitors be allowed into the asylum.[30] Similarly, prior to Daniel Clark's superintendence, the Toronto Asylum was well known amongst many not necessarily for its treatment of the mentally ill but for its receptivity to strangers. After providing a lengthy and rather lurid portrait of the patients in the asylum, one journalist claimed of the superintendent: "Dr. Scott appears to be very attentive to visitors, and gives all information in his power that the most prying could desire." In this institution, the author noted, people could acquire intimate details of patients from asylum personnel, in spite of the fact that some of the lunatics treated visitors "as if they were intruding."[31] Scott may have been oblivious to his visitor's insensitivity, but he clearly was not uncomfortable with members of the "prying" public touring his institution.

As all historians who enjoy peeking into the lives of earlier generations are professional voyeurs in a sense, it is not surprising that the basest of visitors' motives have captured the attention of scholars. However, when visitor narratives are critically examined and situated within their broader cultural context, it becomes apparent that a number of factors stimulated institutional tourism and that focusing on spectatorship obscures the complexities of the practice. In particular, the growing number of people who flocked to asylums in the nineteenth century was related to the socio-economic environment. Urbanization, immigration, and industrialization are traditionally seen as the benchmarks of the nineteenth century, and along with these changes arose an increased anxiety amongst many.[32] Consequently, those who toured asylums often did so in search of a sense of stability and security and as a means of negotiating or mediating the changing urban landscape of the time. In addition, the nineteenth century was an era of reform, a period in which approaches to insanity were being transformed. Moral therapy,

as advocated by Philippe Pinel of the Bicêtre in the late eighteenth century and by William Tuke of the Quakers' York Retreat for the insane in the nineteenth, infiltrated the programs of Ontario asylums. As a result, many people wanted to see first-hand the "progress" that had been made in the sphere of health care reform. One journalist in the London *Free Press* highlighted the importance of visiting in this regard and wrote, "Knowing that a great moral and social problem was being worked out at the Asylum, in the success of which humanity's best instincts are interested, to visit it was part of our programme."[33]

In the accounts written by members of the public, there is a strong sense that they believed themselves to be conducting inspections on their tours of asylums. The majority of visitors critiqued the cleanliness and efficiency of institutions, the appearances of patients, and the approaches of superintendents, and also expressed their approval or disappointment with the institution. Consequently, their judgments resonate throughout their writings: "[We] saw nothing to complain of, but on the contrary, plenty to admire" and "beautifully clean and well kept" were typical evaluations of institutions made by visitors.[34] One visitor to the London Asylum noted, "A look through the building is always instructive and while the demented state of the inmates cannot but excite pity, the visitor will be pleased to see the manner in which the unfortunates are cared for."[35] Another visitor to the Toronto Asylum for the annual Christmas feast remarked, "The terrors associated with lunatic asylums made many conceive of them only as abodes of unmitigated wretchedness. The cell, the whip, the strait-jacket, the filth, the food flung to the poor creatures as if they were dogs, are the prevalent notions connected with them; but here we found an Elysium in comparison with those we have read of, and those we have known. The insane were wont to be governed by the law of brutality; now it is the law of kindness, and the influence of it was fully perceived here on Friday last."[36]

Visitors thus frequently claimed that misconceptions were rectified by visits to asylums and that by seeing such institutions and the people inside them, they could understand new approaches to mental illness. Officials of institutions themselves encouraged people to play a role as unofficial visitors, and annual reports frequently referred to the impressions of casual visitors, thereby granting legitimacy to the efforts made by the public.[37] For example, many superintendents believed the public could gain a better understanding of both insanity and contemporary therapeutic practices merely through custodial tourism and observation. One official in the United States expressed great faith in the people's potential to be astute visitors, and his views were undoubtedly shared by many of his Canadian counterparts. He wrote: "The public, generally, have wrong impressions in relation to the inmates of a Lunatic Asylum. They suppose them to be either idiots, or completely mad, and in both cases incapable of appreciating kindness. If this was true, moral treatment certainly would prove of little avail. But one visit to a well conducted Institution of this kind would be sufficient to correct this error."[38] Moreover, if any lay visitor was an "untrained observer" unsure of how to evaluate custodial institutions, he or she could always consult John S. Billings and Henry M. Kurd's *Suggestions to Hospital and Asylum Visitors* to "learn how to critically inspect [asylums] with a reasonable chance of seeing what is wrong and learning how to value what is praiseworthy," and to learn *"what* to see and *how* to see it."[39]

Even if some Canadians feared that insanity was increasing in the nineteenth century, most looked upon the institutions established to deal with this problem not as shameful or demonstrative of social degeneration, but instead, as symbols of progress. As visitor narratives illustrate, asylums were prominent sources of civic pride. Fairs, exhibitions, and holidays—events that are often associated with enhanced expressions of community pride—were particularly popular days for visiting. The London Asylum, for example, drew over 1,700 visitors in just three days during the fall fair in 1877,[40] and it was invariably described as one of the most beautiful spots around London.[41] This sense of civic pride is further evinced by the fact that residents drew the attention of visitors to their asylums, seeing them as important sites of interest and as community landmarks. Hosts and guides often insisted that travellers tour their institutions (occasionally to the chagrin of the tourist), and one newspaper reporter noted that "the average Londoner never fails to ask you with a conscious pride, 'Have you been out to the Asylum yet?' And if you reply in the negative," the author further noted, "you are told, with no little *empressment,* 'You must go!'"[42] Another writer further propounded, "Such institutions, which are amongst the last results of civilization, are an honour to the country which founds and maintains them; they are a credit and

ought to be the pride of the PEOPLE to whose wise liberality their existence is due."[43]

In addition to civic boosterism, asylum tourism represented an educational opportunity for many visitors, and in this regard, the incentives behind institutional tourism were inextricably tied to the nineteenth-century impulse towards self-education and self-improvement. John C. Burnham has examined nineteenth-century popular interest in science in relation to the rise of the commercial museum in the United States and has made a number of arguments that are relevant to the phenomenon of institutional tourism.[44] In many ways, asylums constituted living museums that encouraged the diffusion of knowledge through tourism and observation, and even Clark, the staunch opponent of visitors to the Toronto Asylum, supported tours by "professional men having scientific objects in view."[45] Visiting encouraged the public to examine the institutionalized and thus reason with the "experts" about the causes of mental disease, and as one visitor remarked, "a look through the [London Asylum] building is always instructive."[46] Although this particular visitor was touring the Kingston Penitentiary, his belief that information could be obtained "with the evidence of our own eyes"[47] was undoubtedly shared by many asylum visitors as well.

Since education in the nineteenth century was guided by faith in empiricism and the notion that knowledge could be acquired through observation, many people viewed asylums as sites where "scientific" knowledge could be learned. By simply touring the Toronto Asylum and seeing the patients, for example, one writer felt that visitors were given "an idea of the peculiar but lamentable circumstances that conspired to create insanity,"[48] and many felt their tours had enhanced their knowledge of medical practices. After visiting asylums, people often remarked on how the experience contrasted with prevalent assumptions or popular belief, and one writer commented that the most effective way to establish an understanding of asylum management "was to present to their own eyes, to let them see for themselves what had been done, and how it had been done."[49] Embedded as they were in the nineteenth-century culture of looking or visual display, it is clear that when many visitors described different forms of insanity or the impact that institutionalization had on humans, they were expressing a belief in their right to participate alongside other "experts" in current debates, as well as the idea that seeing or observing could foster understanding.

For those interested in contemporary approaches to deviant behaviour, visiting furthermore represented a "safe" opportunity that allowed for the study of the insane in person. One visitor to the Toronto Asylum remarked that the patients were "under such good management [...] even a stranger or a child would be unmolested by the worst of them."[50] Visitors often spoke directly to patients, inquiring into the conditions of the respective institution and the causes behind their mental illness, and frequently recorded their conversations with them.[51] Nevertheless, although the desire to better comprehend the mentally ill permeated the writings of asylum visitors, this was not necessarily accompanied by a desire to *freely* mix with them. Through asylum tourism, the public could get close to those deemed mad, yet still maintain a clear boundary between "normal" and "other." Consequently, many who would have felt threatened had they met the institutionalized in the public realm felt comforted by the fact that, in many ways, institutional tours were orchestrated affairs which were not without certain restrictions and parameters. While many sought to understand the plight of the mentally ill, "sane" citizens could feel unthreatened in the controlled context of visiting and could be assured that employees would intervene if the institutionalized became unruly. Asylum attendants stepped in when necessary, barred windows and doors often separated the institutionalized from visitors, and violent cases were frequently restrained or removed from their presence altogether. The lines could become somewhat blurred at asylum social events such as dances, lectures, or athletic games, yet there was always a clear demarcation between the institutionalized and the visitor.

For many visitors, engaging themselves with the work being done for those suffering from mental illness was closely linked to the ideals surrounding philanthropic pursuits and the notion of "Christian duty." Special events at asylums often attracted members of the public, and the writings surrounding such occasions as concerts, fairs, or dances suggest that citizens were expected to attend as part of their civic duty. However, while events such as sports games were open to all, other events such as dances or holiday parties could be more exclusive affairs in which the invited guests were usually of a certain

socio-economic profile (generally, prominent members of the middle class), and the moral obligation in attending such social functions was even more prominent. At the Toronto Asylum in 1847, Superintendent Telfer believed that interaction between asylum patients and the outside world was conducive to the welfare of the former, and he accordingly secured by invitation "the attendance of some of the citizens and their families, whom it was reasonable to conceive, would, each and all, be anxious, so far as in them lie, to aid in a work which promised a wide field, not only for 'the good Samaritan,' but for many good Samaritans."[52] While perhaps attending out of a sense of obligation, one newspaper reporter described the London Asylum Ball as a charitable event that was nevertheless enjoyable to all: "One of the most pleasant events in connection with the routine of Asylum life is the annual ball. For years it has been looked forward to with pleasant anticipation by not only the members of the staff and attendants but many in the city, who have either participated in its festivities, and they desired to be present again, or, having heard of its usually pleasant character, were anxious to be among the fortunate invited." [53] Moreover, a number of visitors speculated that such social events had salutary effects on all participants by revealing the efficacy of kind, gentle treatment, and that they could even transform those who had been drawn to asylums out of "morbid curiosity" and generate compassion and empathy for those afflicted with mental illness.[54] Indeed, whereas many initially thought the lunatic ball to be held in Toronto in 1847 was a "strange and cruel hoax," they found that not only was the evening enjoyed by patients and visitors alike, but that they themselves had broadened their knowledge of insanity and its treatment by interacting with the people in the asylum.[55]

The motives behind institutional tourism reveal that not every "free" member of society would experience his or her visit to an asylum in the same way. For some, spending their leisure time visiting was an opportunity to ridicule the suffering of the confined; for others, it was a means to improve oneself, the confined, or society at large. Nevertheless, whether it was for amusement, education, or reform, the practice reveals a society that privileged the visual and upheld the value of the spectacle in a variety of different contexts and for a variety of different purposes. More importantly, the phenomenon of visiting demonstrates that a substantial number of people in nineteenth-century Ontario sought a closer relationship to the asylums around them and actively endeavoured to better understand the people housed within them, thereby rendering these institutions important and familiar sights in the urban landscape.

Many people in the nineteenth century were fascinated by the growing number of asylums found in Ontario and felt compelled to spend their leisure time inspecting them. Individuals embarked on tours that took them through the corridors, rooms, arid grounds of asylums, allowing them not only to view the conditions the incarcerated experienced but to observe the patients themselves. The public not only read about asylums in contemporary newspapers, periodicals, and fiction, but they also toured and inspected these institutions themselves. Their interiors, therapeutic practices, and inmates were described, analyzed, and recorded in letters, diaries, and articles by people who were not members of the medical elite but who simply believed that asylums represented something remarkable in society. Asylums were important sites that were visited by thousands of people and, in contrast to traditional interpretations, were deeply embedded within the broader culture of the nineteenth century.

The popularity of visiting was maintained throughout the century, and even those superintendents who strongly opposed the practice found it very difficult to entirely exclude casual visitors and to disregard the advantages that institutional tourism offered. Some superintendents wanted to keep casual visitors out of their establishments and sought to bar their entry, yet sightseers continued to be a presence in asylums in spite of these employees' wishes. Visiting did not entirely dissolve boundaries, but its pervasiveness reveals that the asylum walls were frequently penetrated by those on the outside, and that the desire of some superintendents to remove the mentally ill from all contact with the "free" world did not automatically materialize into practice. Officials of institutions could voice their opposition to the practice, but the efforts to abolish visiting usually did not amount to more than being able to set certain parameters, such as restricting the hours in which the institution could be seen by the public. The thousands of people who toured Ontario's asylums reveal that these institutions were not as isolated from society as many have thought, and it is these moments of interchange that allow us to better understand popular perceptions of the insane and the asylum, as well as the impact the general public had upon the development of these institutions. While attitudes of both the public and asylum officials varied, the practice of visiting nevertheless illustrates that the relationship between asylums and the larger community beyond their walls was at times characterized by interaction and fluidity, rather than unilateral segregation and alienation.

Notes

1. E. Katharine Bates, *A Year in the Great Republic* (London: Ward and Downey, 1887).

2. Archives of Ontario, MU 840 1-D-4, Diary of Thomas Dick (1867-1905).

3. The terms "insane" and "lunatic asylum" are used in this article as part of the lexicon surrounding mental illness in the nineteenth century. Their usage is not meant to be disrespectful of those suffering from mental illness in any way.

4. This article stems from a broader study. See my "'As in a Menagerie': The Custodial Institution as Spectacle in the Nineteenth Century" (PhD dissertation, York University, 2004).

5. Jennifer A. Crets, "'Well Worth the Visitor's While': Sightseeing in St. Louis, 1865-1910," *Gateway Heritage* 20, no. 3 (Winter 1999-2000): 18; Patricia Allderidge, "Bedlam: Fact or Fantasy?" in W.F. Bynum, Roy Porter, and Michael Shepherd, eds., *The Anatomy of Madness: Essays in the History of Psychiatry,* vol. 2, (London and New York: Tavistock Publications, 1985), 24. Similarly, many historians have provided only cursory references to visitors. See, for example, Pamela Michael, *Care and Treatment of the Mentally Ill in North Wales,* 1800-2000 (Cardiff: University of Wales Press, 2003), 88.

6. See, for example, R.D. Gidney and W.P.J. Millar, "'Beyond the Measure of the Golden Rule': The Contribution of the Poor to Medical Science in Ontario," *Ontario History* 86 (1994): 219-35.

7. "Report of the Medical Superintendent of the Provincial Lunatic Asylum at Toronto," *Journals of the Legislative Assembly* (1856), appendix OO.

8. On public views of North American hospitals, see: Judith Walzer Leavitt, "Politics and Public Health: Smallpox in Milwaukee, 1894-1895," in Judith Walzer Leavitt and Ronald L. Numbers, eds., *Sickness and Health in America: Readings in the History of Medicine and Public Health,* 2nd ed. (Madison:

University of Wisconsin Press, 1985), 374. Only in the early twentieth century, with technological and therapeutic changes, would hospitals be transformed into "respectable" and curative institutions used by the middle class. See, for example, Charles Rosenberg, "Community and Communities: The Evolution of the American Hospital," in Diana Elizabeth Long and Janet Golden, eds., *The American General Hospital: Communities and Social Contexts* (Ithaca: Cornell University Press, 1989), 3-17; and Joel Howell, *Technology in the Hospital: Transforming Patient Care in the Early Twentieth Century* (Baltimore: Johns Hopkins University Press, 1995).

9. "Separate Report of Wolfred Nelson for 1861," in *Second Annual Report of the Board of Inspectors of Asylums, Prisons, &c 1861,* Canada (Province), *Sessional Papers,* no. 19 (1862).

10. "Report of the Medical Superintendent of the Provincial Lunatic Asylum at Toronto," *Journals of the Legislative Assembly of the Province of Canada* (1852), appendix J.

11. "Report of C. Widmer, Chairman," *Journals of the Legislative Assembly for the Province of Canada* (1851), appendix J; ibid. (1850), appendix C.

12. London *Free Press,* 8 June 1880.

13. "Report of C. Widmer, Chairman," *Journals of the Legislative Assembly for the Province of Canada* (1852), appendix J.

14. "Report of the Inspector of Asylums and Prisons for the Province of Canada," *Sessional Papers,* no. 19 (1862).

15. S.E.D. Shortt, *Victorian Lunacy: Richard M. Bucke and the Practice of Late Nineteenth-Century Psychiatry* (Cambridge: Cambridge University Press 1986), 26.

16. James E. Moran, *Committed to the State Asylum: Insanity and Society in Nineteenth-Century Quebec and Ontario* (Montreal: McGill-Queen's University Press 2002), 49.

17. "Report of the Medical Superintendent of the Asylum for the Insane, Toronto, for the Year Ending 30th September, 1876," Appendix to "Report of Inspector of Asylums, Prisons, and Public Charities for the Year Ending 30th September, 1876," in Ontario, *Sessional Papers,* 1877, ix, part I, no. 2 (Toronto: Hunter, Rose, & Co., 1877): 208.

18. "Report of the Medical Superintendent of the Maiden Lunatic Asylum," appendix to "Report of Inspector of Asylums, Prisons, and Public Charities for the Twelve Months Ending 30th September, 1869," Ontario, *Sessional Papers,* 1869, ii, no. 4 (Toronto: Hunter, Rose & Co., 1869): 60.

19. Archives of Ontario, MS 717, Journal of the Superintendent for the Kingston Asylum, 21 September 1882, 157-8.

20. For example, E. Katharine Bates claimed to have toured the Toronto Asylum with Clark, whom she described as "most kind and good-natured" and relying chiefly on "moral control." See Bates, *A Year in the Great Republic,* 26-7

21. Vanessa Schwartz, *Spectacular Realities: Early Mass Culture in Fin-de-Siècle Paris* (Berkeley: University of California Press 1998), 11.

22. Archives of Ontario, John Symons Family Papers, F 786-2.-0-1, box 2, Manuscript book of travels through the United States and Canada West (1852).

23. Judith Walkowitz, *City of Dreadful Delight: Narratives of Sexual Danger in Late-Victorian London* (Chicago: University of Chicago Press 1992), 16.

24. However, this is not to say that the institutionalized passively allowed themselves to be gawked at. Rather, as my dissertation argues, the insane often actively resisted being treated as compliant exhibits and used the presence of strangers to their own benefit.

25. London *Free Press,* 22 November 1880.

26. Toronto Reference Library, Mickle Family Diary, S 27, William Mickle to father, February 1864.

27. Montreal *Pilot,* 1 May 1845.

28. *Bathurst Courier,* 16 August 1850.

29. Susanna Moodie, *Life in the Clearings Versus the Bush* (1853), reprint (Toronto: McClelland and Stewart, 1989), 272.

30. University of Western Ontario Archives, Diary of Dr Charles Sippi, bursar of the London Insane Asylum, 20 September 1893, 20 September 1894.

31. *Bathurst Courier,* 16 August 1850.

32. Pioneering works that correlate the rise of the asylum with social anxiety are David J. Rothman, *The Discovery of the Asylum: Social Order and Disorder in the New Republic* rev. 2nd ed. (Boston: Little, Brown, and Co. 1971), and Michael Katz, Michael J. Doucet, and Mark J. Stern, *The Social Organization of Early Industrial Capitalism* (Cambridge and London: Harvard University Press, 1982).

33. London *Free Press,* c. end of June 1878.

34. *British Whig,* 12 April 1848; Bates, *A Year in the Great Republic,* 26.

35. *London Advertiser,* 1 July 1880.

36. *British Colonist,* 29 December 1846.

37. For example, one annual report for the Toronto Asylum stated, "It has been the desire of the Directors to have the Asylum as open to the public as is compatible with the welfare of the patients and the duties of their attendants. Large numbers of visitors have therefore, from time to time, been attended through the building, and these have witnessed the condition of the apartments, the appearance and happiness of the patients, the tender, but effective discipline, which prevails amongst the afflicted and their attendants. The result has been, so far as is known, a universal satisfaction to visitors." See "Report of C. Widmer, Chairman," *Journals of the Legislative Assembly for the Province of Canada* (1852), appendix J.

38. *Annual Report of the Alms House Commissioners, Comprising Reports from the Several Departments Embraced in the Institution* (New York, 1848), 62.

39. John. S. Billings and Henry M. Hurd, *Suggestions to Hospital and Asylum Visitors,* intro. S. Weir Mitchell (Philadelphia, 1895), 5-6.

40. University of Western Ontario Archives, E 16, Black Box 3; R.M. Bucke, Medical Superintendent's Journal.

41. See, for example, *London Advertiser,* 1 July 1880.

42. London *Free Press,* c. end of June 1878.

43. *Sarnia Canadian,* 24 July 1878.

44. John C. Burnham, *How Superstition Won and Science Lost* (New Brunswick, NJ: Rutgers University Press, 1987).

45. "Report of the Medical Superintendent of the Asylum for the Insane, Toronto, for the Year Ending 30th September, 1876," 208.

46. *London Advertiser,* 1 July 1880.

47. *British Whig,* 12 April 1848.

48. *Bathurst Courier,* 16 August 1850.

49. *London Free Press,* 9 June 1898.

50. *Bathurst Courier,* 16 August 1850.

51. For example, see John MacGregor, *Our Brothers and Cousins: A Summer Tour in Canada and the States* (London: Seeley, Jackson and Halliday 1859); and George Moore, *Journal of a Voyage across the Atlantic* (London: Printed for Private Circulation, 1845).

52. *British Colonist,* 8 January 1847.

53. *London Free Press,* 21 January 1881. This particular ball was deemed "the greatest assemblage in the history of the institution" and attracted 125 people from the city.

54. *British Colonist,* 8 January 1847; see also Toronto *Globe,* 9 January 1847.

55. *Toronto Examiner,* 13 January 1847; see also *British Colonist,* 29 December 1846.

■ Article 3: Awakening a Demand for Schooling: Educational Inspection's Impact on Rural Nova Scotia, 1855–74

Robert Lanning

Nova Scotia's Education Act of 1864 was central to the province's public schooling. Voters had often petitioned governments for wider access to schooling; educators and politicians had come to expect a free school system; and earlier legislation had improved educational provision. But the Act of 1864 had greater uniformity of purpose and was far more advanced administratively than any of a dozen earlier attempts.

The resulting school system was to be centrally organized and managed. State funding was increased, and financial support of schools through local taxation encouraged by offering bonuses to compliant communities. Classification and examination of pupils were regularized, and the Executive Council given authority to oversee matters as the Council of Public Instruction. Crucially, the Act also established a system of inspection[1] through a locally-based inspectorate—a system for producing the knowledge and attitudes necessary for compliant citizenship and social progress.

As early as 1851, William Dawson, the first Superintendent of Education,[2] suggested clerks of each county's Board of School Commissioners might conveniently and cheaply combine their duties with school inspection. Inspection would have a two-fold

Source: Robert Lanning, "Awakening a Demand for Schooling: Educational Inspection's Impact on Rural Noval Scotia, 1855-74," © *Historical Studies in Education/Revue d'histoire de l'éducation* 12, nos. 1&2 (Spring & Fall, 2000): 129–142. Reprinted with permission.

purpose.[3] First, it would be "of great service in stimulating teachers, trustees and people" who had yet to appreciate the value of schooling for their children and its necessity for social progress. In 1854 Dawson's successor, Alexander Forrester,[4] stressed "stimulation" as one of the few tools at the disposal of superintendents to create an appetite for education:

> The primary business of the school is not so much to impart knowledge as to awaken a demand for it, to furnish the means of meeting that demand. If there is no felt want of a thing, no effort will be put forth to get it.[5]

Inspection's second purpose was "collecting educational information" with which the system could be evaluated. Information gathering was haphazard for most of the period between 1851 and 1864. Both Dawson and Forrester in turn made annual tours of the province, which in 1854 was divided into eastern and western districts each assigned one inspector. (Few inspection reports survive beyond the summary comments and data contained in Forrester's Annual Reports.)

A rationale for an inspectorate in a public system of education is suggested in Bruce Curtis's *True Government by Choice Men?* Examining intellectual, political, and administrative preconditions for common schooling and inspection in Canada West, Curtis shows how core interests of the middle class, growing in size and substance, and deriving local power from the political centre, were diffused and supervised by school inspectors. Curtis characterizes inspection as the "development of connections between central authorities and local sites that centred upon knowledge/power relations."[6] The first corps of inspectors in Canada West exercised a certain moral and ideological imperative in its work of information gathering, evaluation of the knowledge-producing and disciplinary functions of schooling, and overseeing relations between social classes. Curtis had earlier forged a convincing argument against the "voluntarist" model of educational reform in Canada and the United States which saw mass schooling as a triumph of local over central (state) interests, and saw inspectors as benevolent overseers. Curtis argued mass schooling was in fact a well-organized political incursion of dominant cultural interests upon the everyday lives of agricultural

families, on the children of an embryonic industrial labour force, and on the offspring of the commercial middle class.[7] In what follows I have used Curtis's analysis of Canada West to make sense of Nova Scotia's early history of education and inspection.

Education in Nova Scotia was a distinctly rural activity. Census data for 1861 show 87% of the province's population (330,857 in total) lived on farms or in towns of less than 3000 people; two-thirds of the population lived outside villages (defined as a minimum population of 2000). The political and commercial centre of Halifax, with more than 25,000 people, was the only city in the province that exceeded 5000. Nova Scotia's economy was based in agriculture and natural resources. In 1861, more than half of the labour force were farmers (43%) or farm labourers (10.5%), and through most of the 19th century agriculture grew in importance in the provincial economy. The 1854 Reciprocity Treaty with the United States and the boost in trade during the American Civil War contributed to consolidation and expansion of the agricultural sector. The growth of industry and shipping encouraged migration from rural areas, and contributed to the 18% growth of Halifax between 1861 and 1871—almost equivalent to the population increase for the entire province. Between these census dates the rural proportion of the population remained virtually unchanged (though the agricultural sector declined by about 10%). During the same period, the commercial sector increased significantly, and the comparatively small proportions of the industrial and professional occupations doubled.[8]

Securing a financial base for schooling meant overcoming rural poverty and general doubt of the value of schooling. One task for an agency of inspection was to convince the public that education was vital to economic and cultural progress. But efforts by locally-based inspectors inevitably disrupted familiar rural cultural patterns and generated spontaneous resistance to schooling. The additional function of inspection, then, was to *manage* disruption, challenging the rooted values of agricultural families in the name of the "common interest" of progress.

As represented by inspectors and their superintendents, middle and upper class interests had a future-oriented, enterprising outlook—one that viewed individual success and national progress as integrally related, especially in the new features of industrial and commercial economy. Class values required stabilizing and reproductive social forces under the authority of economically powerful and culturally authoritative groups. The forms of communication at their disposal were crucial in securing their interests since they transmitted the formative goals of dominant social interests into new areas of social life[9]—even if these interests were described as "common" to all Nova Scotians. A major instrument of communication during Forrester's tenure, the *Journal of Education and Agriculture*, treated educational and agricultural intelligence as linked activities. [...]

Toward the Development of Mass Schooling in Nova Scotia

The Nova Scotia legislation of 1808 was the first to encourage school construction and hiring of teachers through a combination of freehold tax assessments and periodically increased government grants. The state tried other forms of encouragement in Education Acts up to the Act of 1866, which finally established compulsory, tax-supported free schools and eliminated education by subscription. Generalized resistance to assessment delayed full systematization of schooling.

Most of the Acts increased numbers of school buildings, teachers, and pupils. The intention was to increase availability of schooling generally, but those who had money benefited most. As in jurisdictions such as Upper Canada/Canada West, dominant classes only slowly saw the necessity of schooling as a means of political socialization.[10][...]

Reluctance to support taxation did not mean complete lack of interest in education. Petitions from hundreds of people around the province to the House of Assembly throughout the 1850s to the mid-60s demanded that schooling be more widely available—without "excessive" financial burden.[11]

During his tenure as Superintendent of Education and Head of the Normal School in Truro, Forrester repeatedly called for province-wide assessment and a system of inspection. Before the Act of 1864, he issued a ten-point appeal to the public outlining the rationale and value of a school system funded through universal taxation, and distributed petitions around the province to gather support. Taxation would equalize access to schooling for all, regardless of property. "This principle," he argued, "is in consonance with the purest equity, and the strictest justice;" and compatible "with the true principles and ends of civil government."[12] Taxation would increase the number of schools and teachers, and universally improve the quality of education. Forrester repeatedly cited the success of Egerton Ryerson in founding such a system in Canada West. Like Ryerson, he saw such legislative measures as "just taxation" producing more than administrative benefits. A school system founded on that basis "will tend to diffuse a spirit of unity and mutual affection among the inhabitants," linking "every man to his fellow men in the obligation of the common interests."[13] Ironically, by the time the Education Act of 1866 entrenched universal assessment, Forrester, arguably the most dynamic force in the establishment of mass schooling in the province, was no longer Superintendent of Education, holding only the position of Normal School principal.

Forrester knew the value of inspection and annually so reminded his political masters. His vision of inspection, put into practice by his successors, was a centrally-organized and managed body of state agents taking educational ideas into the field and reshaping everyday life to conform to the new social institution throughout the province. But in 1857 he "despair[ed] of ever being able to make out an accurate and full tabular statement of all educational statistics, without the appointment of a well-equipped staff" of inspectors. For example, the quality of official knowledge was limited by incomplete reports from trustees. Inspectors could solve this problem by organizing meetings of teachers and parents to press for "harmony" and "uniformity of action."[14] Reporting on a number of visits in 1859, he wrote that the "grand desideratum to give full effect to these visitations is a thorough system of local inspectorship."[15]

The Education Act of 1864 assigned one inspector to each of the 18 counties in the province and a committee of school commissioners to Halifax.[16] Forrester argued in his Report of 1859 that inspectors should be men of "superior Scholarship, and educational enthusiasm, and of considerable practical experience."[17] Thomas Harding Rand,[18] who succeeded Forrester, complained there were not enough qualified men to choose from, but managed to appoint thirteen "classical scholars" and five "good English scholars."[19] Among the 46 men who served as inspectors from 1864 to 1874, eleven were clergy, four members of the bar, and two medical doctors. Inspectors' reports show many others were men with teaching experience, some educational careerists.

Inspection was not a position that men of higher education or professional qualifications held for long periods of time. The average term was about four years. Only two who served in this first decade remained inspectors in 1874. It was a time-consuming and burdensome occupation. Inspectors spent 4 to 5 hours travelling to each school and back, spending only an hour to a half-day actually in the school. As the system developed their workloads increased. In 1865 there were 854 schools in 18 counties; in 1874 the same number of inspectors evaluated 1491 schools—a 75% increase.[20] Each inspector had also to act as clerk to the county Board of School Commissioners, to serve on committees to revise school boundaries and on examination committees, and to lecture on educational subjects in each school section. In 1866 (the earliest year for which complete figures are available), remuneration was based on a percentage of the average of teachers' salaries in each county,[21] plus $1.50 for each semi-annual visit to a school. Thus the average annual salary of inspectors for 1866 was about $422, a little more than one-third the salary ($1200) of the Superintendent of Education. By 1874, the average salary among inspectors had increased to $658.

Taxation as Cultural Conflict

The state's imposition of financial obligation to support schools was a sustained assault on the preservationist attitude of the rural population. Partial assessment in the 1864 Act was intended by the government leader, Charles Tupper, to "render that system as gradually acceptable to the people as it is possible."[22] After the House of Assembly began debating revisions to the Education Act to include compulsory taxation, the demands of petitioners for education changed. In December 1864, for example, 359 residents of King's county signed a request for repeal of the legislation. Such taxation, they wrote, was "at variance with the wishes of your petitioners and in its details, expensive, ridiculous and in many instances oppressive. [...]"[23] Their poor economic situation would be made worse by the Act.

Legislative requirements for education finance provided a convenient avenue by which political and cultural groups encroached upon rural life. Rural resistance to taxation was thus a barometer of rural values and of rural commitment to general progress and improvement. Although government grants to

school sections increased by a third in 1865,[24] the legislation required each section raise an additional amount equal to two-thirds of their grant. Any money required for buying, leasing or building a school house "shall be levied on the real and personal property [...] of the residents."[25] The amount of money raised locally could positively or negatively affect physical facilities, quantity of the educational apparatus purchased for the school, and calibre of teachers hired. Teachers, school buildings, and apparatus—all were perennial sources of inspectoral complaint.

Inspectors' evaluations of local commitment to education were based on an assessment of the quality of education in these areas. In a clear presentation of cultural differences over the value of education, J.B. Calkin, inspector for King's County, scolded parents whose attempts at "improvement" he considered self-serving. Some parents, he wrote,

> will do more to improve their stock, their grains and their roots, than to elevate the tone of society around them; take more interest in the architecture of a stable than of a school house, more pride in a well-groomed horse than a well-educated son.[26]

There is no evidence the state used the courts to enforce assessment legislation. A slower means of "awakening demand"—pressure applied by inspectors—was more desirable and enduring. Inspectors not only policed conformity to law, but evaluated "backward" social values and inappropriate cultural priorities.

Quality of school houses and choice of locations for them showed an under-developed appreciation of the merits of environments specifically suited to educational activity. In the first issue of the *Journal of Education and Agriculture* (1858), Forrester set out criteria for more appropriate sites for buildings and playgrounds.[27] In 1862, he still judged fewer than one-third of school houses acceptable.[28] Special government funding for poor school sections after 1864 did not alleviate the problem. Inspectors continued to chastise the population for unsuitable locations, playgrounds, and outhouses, and "deplorable" structures.[29] The Annual Report of 1866 considered only half the school houses in the province "in good repair;" 26% of the buildings were on unsuitable sites, and one third "without sufficient ventilation." Rev. D.O. Parker, the inspector for Queen's county, argued neat [and] comfortable school houses are a demand of our nature [and buildings] repulsive in all their surroundings with a vitiated atmosphere within [were] poisoning the blood, stupefying the mind and blunting the moral sensibilities.[30]

Inspectors praised or criticized residents of some school sections for their willingness (or lack of it) to raise sufficient funds for the best trained teachers. The Normal School operated from 1855, but graduation from that institution was not required for teaching licenses. The shortage of teachers adequately trained in modern pedagogy was blamed on the "cheapness" of local school commissioners, who often hired those with the lowest level of license and least experience in order to reduce the budget. Although some inspectors praised the work of women teachers,[31] many believed the main reason for their growing predominance in the profession was financial. But commissioners were wrong in blaming trustees for this, since statutes authorized paying women 25–30% less (depending on classification) than male teachers holding the same license.[32] Some inspectors saw this as a future risk to stability in the profession.[33]

To inspectors, appointments of better teachers demonstrated the population's interest in the highest quality of education for their children. Financial difficulty, whether from crop failure or poor fishing, was no excuse.[34]

Properly trained teachers were of little value without the right textbooks and educational tools. The well-equipped school house needed maps, globes, blackboards, ball-frames, and other apparatus. Although such educational instruments were partially subsidized by the Education Department, many school sections still could not afford them. "Good wall maps," as they were categorized on inspection forms, were considered essential. If we divided the number of "good wall maps" by the number of schools in a given year, we arrive at a figure of 2.4 maps per school in 1867, improving to 3.1 per school in 1873. For every 3.7 schools, only one ball-frame could be found in 1867, and one thermometer for every 13.3 schools. Six years later, every 3.1 schools possessed a ball-frame and a thermometer could be found in only one of every eight schools.

Inspectors consistently complained that even when equipment was available, it was poorly used.

A teacher's appropriate use of educational apparatus might be equated with the skilled labourer's use of tools. Nova Scotia's *Journal of Education* compared the teacher to the blacksmith, tailor, and carpenter, "[no] better off for [their] knowledge, unless [they] ha[ve] [...] suitable tools to work with,"[35] Inspectors adopted this analogy to impress upon the rural public, who relied on acquired worklore and effective tools in their own occupations, that skilled and knowledgeable teachers could produce desired results efficiently if the effort were mediated by proper application of the best educational tools.

Blackboards had particular statistical importance in early inspectors' reports documenting total square footage of blackboards in all schools in a county and, from 1867, the annual average square footage of all schools in each county. As inspector McDonnell noted, a teacher properly trained to use the blackboard "adopts the more modern auxiliaries in the work of education."[36] Others reported some schools had good apparatus and blackboard space, but "a majority of the teachers are unable to use them advantageously."[37] Because blackboards could be locally made with painted boards or a mixture of paint, ashes, and oil (a recipe provided by Rand's "Commentary and Explanation" section of the Education Act), inspectors viewed them as an index of the quantity of voluntary labour given to education in the community.

Rev. Armstrong complained that the parents and trustees in his county were not convinced of the value of educational apparatus, and schools without it "remain almost stationary for weeks." Edmund Outram expressed exasperation that inappropriate and poorly made furniture was still in use in many poor sections' school houses, despite the carpentry skills of local people.

> This I consider to be inexcusable in the poor sections, as the people are able to make them for themselves, but the teachers do not seem to understand the utility of this simple apparatus, nor how much time might be gained by the appliance of it.[38]

The burden of providing essentials for the school—well-trained teachers, apparatus, the school building, volunteer labour—thus in great measure fell to local residents, even in school sections formally recognized by the state as needing extraordinary financial assistance. Inspectors worried about the quality and efficiency of the pedagogy used in the classroom,[393] but the underlying concern was for the "underdeveloped" attitude of parents and others to advanced pedagogy and its financial support.

Attendance: Schooling as a Rural Value

The 1861 census included a survey of reading and writing ability. About 43% of school-aged children (5–15) could not read, and 58% could not write. Figures for adults were 22% and 33% respectively.[40] Forrester and Rand repeatedly cited high levels of illiteracy as proof of the need for a more centrally organized system of education in the face of a predominantly rural, subsistence economy that required the unpaid labour of all family members, regardless of age.[41] For the state, the solution lay in compulsory school attendance.

Petitions for educational provision notwithstanding, significant numbers saw little immediate value in forfeiting their children's labour. Popular demand for schooling among the rural population should be interpreted as recognition of the value of such immediately useful knowledge as basic literacy and arithmetic skills. The distant, abstract benefits of schooling would not have been immediately apparent to many under the harsh conditions of Nova Scotian daily life. Inspectors (and others) had to convince the population that schooling was a viable means of social mobility. Popular demand for education was not an open-ended agreement for the state to require or even pressure families to send their children to school all day, five days a week, especially in seasons when their labour was considered crucial. Parents did not anticipate they would be subjected to questioning by an inspector or a teacher when their children were absent from school.

In order to increase attendance, inspectors promoted the class interests they served, equating ignorance with idleness, poverty, and crime, and education with wealth and social stability.[42] Inspector Calkin, for example, wrote of a question he had recently posed to an acquaintance in Boston:

"You have a large immigration of the scum of all nations, what conservative element do you employ to save you from putrescence?"

"Our schools," he said, "our schools. Here we grind over the children of the vagabond and they come out to fill useful and honorable stations, and frequently they become our most worthy citizens."[43]

Inspectors took irregular attendance as proof that systematic education had yet to be accepted as either personally valuable or socially necessary.

"Dull times dispirit the working class," wrote A.S. Hunt, "and neglect of school is almost sure to follow." Children "thinly clad and poorly shod," especially in winter, publicly displayed their family's poverty—to them a sound excuse for non-attendance. Appropriate clothing and footwear for lengthy treks to and from school, and a presentable appearance of health, demonstrated a family's relative prosperity. The Inspector for Pictou County cited the logic of one citizen at a public meeting: "If you compel them to attend school you must clothe them to make them fit to come, and in some cases you must feed them too."[44]

Some inspectors suggested legislative force be tempered with an appreciation of the rural family's work requirements, R.B. Smith argued:

There are seasons in the year when it is impossible for the poor man's child to attend school. However, in the summer term exempting two weeks at seed time; four at haying time and Harvest; and a week for potato digging, the remainder of the time might be made compulsory.[45]

Most inspectors reluctantly accepted poverty as an excuse for keeping children at home, whether or not to work. Whatever the demand for children's labour, it was viewed disparagingly as "frittering away their precious time in desultory employment."[46] Parents whose children might devote more time and energy to their crops, their cattle, or fish flakes, saw in them a concrete benefit. Although inspectors feared threatening the sanctity of parental rights,[47] the quality of such parenting was open to question and justified the state's legal authority to substitute as parent. One inspector wrote:

Our schools are free to all, and if parents will not educate their children, the Government, who in many cases act as a parent, would only show a kindness and confer a benefit by compelling every parent to send his children [to school].[48]

Calls for compulsory attendance grew throughout the 1860s, but it would not be legislated until 1883.

Diffusing the Inspectoral Function

Inspectors represented the state by enforcing the Education Acts, including assessment of community and family commitment to the progress of local schools. As paid agents of the state, teachers' work in the classroom included an important contribution to one of Dawson's original purposes of inspection: collecting educational information. The Superintendent of Education and his inspectors hoped to obtain accurate information consistently through a daily register covering a wide range of pedagogical and managerial categories. An official register was in use as early as 1850[49] and underwent many changes over the years. In 1859, Forrester argued that however necessary inspection might be to accurate statistical information, the first requirement was "the construction of a register that shall embrace the time of the admission and withdrawal of the scholars, their attendance and progress."[50] A more comprehensive register was required by the 1864 Act, and the Act of 1866 emphasized the register as a legal, not merely professional requirement. Teachers were

> To call the roll morning and afternoon and otherwise keep an accurate Register in the manner prescribed by the Council of Public Instruction, on pain of liability to forfeiture of the public grants; the Register to be at all times open to the inspections of the Trustees, Visitors, Examiners, Commissioners, Inspectors and Superintendent.[51]

The register became a feature of the widening intrusion of the state, and a tool to propagate the educational goals of the state and the value-orientation of the superior classes. Teachers' work was to go beyond merely recording attendance to accounting for absence and classifying reasons given for it.[52] Inspectors admonished teachers who "encouraged" absence or lateness as neglecting their right to demand explanations from the families. Inspector Upham, for example, reproached teachers for "carelessness" and "neglect" for failure "to search out and

record the causes of absence." Two years later, he reported the same problem, noting that this function was viewed by some teachers as "a mere vexation."

> But when it is considered what is implied by [...] neglect [of the register], [he continued] we must cease to underrate its value, and conclude that he who neglects has not fully measured the extent and demands of his place.[53]

What exactly was neglected? The teacher's training and personal refinement; accuracy was important, but a neat and clean register more so. For Rev. Lawson, inspector for Lunenburg, registers "beautifully kept, reflect[ed] much credit on the care and taste of the teachers." Upham claimed want of neatness and tidiness revealed "a deficiency in early training or in natural taste."[54] The better-trained and higher classified teacher, presumably tidier and more professionally aware of the significance of the knowledge produced in the register, was more expensive to hire. For their part, teachers failed to see how such a simple instrument could overcome problems of uncommitted parents, penny-pinching local officials, and negligent visitors.

The properly kept register, it was argued, kept the school. Inspectors reproached county commissioners, clergy, and others for failure to visit schools regularly, review the register, and tackle problems of attendance and progress. D.M. Welton wrote that if the register were

> blotted, untidy and improperly kept, the school has been disorderly, poorly classified, and made little progress, and the converse [is true]. The use of the Register not only in keeping the attendance of the pupils, but also as a means of stimulating them in progress, in study and good deportment, is becoming better understood and more efficiently turned to account.[55]

In her analysis of registers in Scottish schools, Fiona Paterson[56] claims they were to make visible the efficiency of the teacher and the "institutional profiles" of individual students, and sees the register as one element in production of "a theory and practice of normality." Nova Scotian inspectors saw this educational "technology" as a means by which teachers and other community members could be evaluated on their commitments to the progress of education. The Shelburne County inspector wrote:

If no day were allowed to pass without a visit, the character of the school would soon become known, the ability or otherwise of the teacher apparent, the progress of the pupils exhibited, and an incitement given that would soon be evinced by greater diligence and more rapid improvement.[57]

The properly kept register as a knowledge-producing tool contributed much to educational intelligence in these first years of systematic inspection. But its equally important purpose was reduction of tensions by delegating inspectoral functions of information-gathering and "stimulation" to a broad range of people in the community. The well-kept register did indicate teacher competence in recording daily attendance, the neatness of the pupils, and their progress. But as vigilant and thorough recording progressed weekly, then semi-annually, then annually, cumulative evidence of success or weakness in pedagogy and in community involvement showed the inspector the degree of dedication of "Official Visitors" and others to school visitation, their presence at examinations, the policing of attendance, and the overall quality of school improvement. Inspectors thus diffused responsibility for promoting state interests as interests to be adopted by local populations.

Conclusion

Forrester's 1863 Report reviewed the growing requirements and authority of the state.

The state has a power which no society or church possesses, and is bound to use it; for her self-preservation is no longer believed to depend on the stolidity and ignorance of the industrial population, but on the enlightenment and morality of all classes. [...] What interference can there be with the liberty of the subject in demanding that parents educate their children so long as they are at liberty to send them to any teacher and bring them up in whatsoever religious belief they please?[58]

Inspection communicated changing social relations to all parts of the province and to all sectors of the population: broadly in terms of economic and political demands, more specifically in the normative prescriptions and expectations of everyday life. To much of the population schooling became something more than children learning the three Rs. As it was introduced, schooling came to mean interference with established patterns of work and family, and the necessity to re-structure everyday life in conformity to new and more powerful conventions determined elsewhere.

With increasing economic power and the corresponding legislative authority embodied in the state, the formation of the public system of education signalled its right to encroach upon local and familial terrains. The state's incursion through schooling and inspection was meant to produce positive attitudes to schooling, as valuable for individual development and for social progress. State action and the work of its local agents did not provoke organized resistance to schooling or to the scrutiny of everyday life, but they laid the ground for increased awareness of competing social interests and the relative powers behind them.

Notes

1. *Journal of Education* 1 (September, 1866): 2. For a history of the early years of this publication, see *Journal of Education* 1, 1 (October, 1951): 5–16.
2. On Dawson's career, see P.R. Eakins and J. Sinnamon Eakins, "Sir John William Dawson" in *Dictionary of Canadian Biography*, vol. 12 (Toronto; University of Toronto Press, 1990), 230–37; Susan Sheets-Pyenson, *John William Dawson: Faith, Hope and Science* (Kingston-Montreal; McGill-Queen's University Press, 1996).
3. W. Dawson, Superintendent's Annual Report [hereafter, A.R.] (Nova Scotia, Dept. of Education, 1851), 13. Superintendent's Annual Reports from 1851 to 1864 were published in the Appendices of the Journal of the House of Assembly; from 1865 Reports were also printed separately and included county inspector's reports and statistical tables. Hereafter, references will name the inspector, county, year of Superintendent's report, and page numbers.
4. On Forrester's career, see Judith Fingard, "Alexander Forrester," *Dictionary of Canadian Biography*, vol 9 (Toronto: University of Toronto Press, 1976), 270–73.
5. A. Forrester, A.R., (1862), 2.
6. Bruce Curtis, *True Government by Choice Men?* (Toronto: University of Toronto Press, 1992), 19.

7. Bruce Curtis, "Policing pedagogical space "Voluntary" school reform and moral regulation," *Canadian Journal of Sociology* 13, 3, (1988): 283–304.

8. Industrial and related occupations accounted for about 15% of the labour force in 1861, and the professions about 2%. See, Census of Nova Scotia (Halifax, 1862); Census of Canada 1870–1871, vol. 1 (Ottawa, 1873), 427; Bryan D. Palmer, *Working Class Experience: Rethinking the History of Canadian Labour, 1800–1991,* 2nd ed. (Toronto: McClelland and Stewart, 1992), 84; R. T. Naylor, *Canada in the European Age, 1453–1919* (Vancouver: New Star Press, 1987), 298–301, 385.

9. Ibid., 48, 63.

10. Bruce Curtis, *Building the Educational State: Canada West, 1836–1871* (London: Falmer Press, 1988); Alison Prentice, *The School Promoters* (Toronto: McCelland and Stewart, 1977), 66–84.

11. Public Archives of Nova Scotia [PANS], RG5, Series P, vols. 75–8.

12. A. Forrester, "Address to the People of Nova Scotia on the Support of Common Schools," (n.p., 1860), 13,15.

13. Forrester, "Address …", 12, 15. On Ryerson, see Prentice, *The School Promoters,* 124–7.

14. Forrester, A.R. (1862), 3, 10, 17.

15. Forrester, A.R. (1857), 53; A.R (1859), 249.

16. The Superintendent's A.R. included statistics, but only a summary from the Chair of the City Board of School Commissioners; thus, far less information is available for Halifax schools.

17. Forrester, A.R. (1859), 258.

18. On Rand's life, see A. Laidlaw, "Theodore Harding Rand," *Journal of Education* (Nova Scotia), Part I (March, 1944): 207–18; Part II (April-May, 1944): 235–334; M. Conrad, "An Abiding Conviction of the Paramount Importance of Christian Education" in R.S. Wilson, ed., *An Abiding Conviction: Maritime Baptists and their World* (Saint John, N.B.: Acadia Divinity College), 155–95, and "Thomas Harding Rand," *Dictionary of Canadian Biography,* vol. 12 (Toronto: University of Toronto Press, 1990), 879–83.

19. Rand, A.R (1864), 1.

20. These figures were reached by averaging the number of schools open in the winter and summer terms, excluding schools in Halifax.

21. In the previous year salary was based on a percentage of the total county grant.

22. Beck, *Politics of Nova Scotia,* 158.

23. PANS, RG5, Series P, vol. 77, petitions numbered 97–104, 107–11, and 117–20.

24. The 1866 A.R. showed that the government had steadily increased grants in relation to "money raised by the people" since 1856. For every dollar raised by the people in 1856, the province contributed 40 cents; in 1866 the province contributed 81 cents.

25. Nova Scotia, An Act for the Better Encouragement of Education (28 Victoria, Cap.29) (Halifax, 1865), 83; Beck, *Politics of Nova Scotia,* 161.

26. J.B. Calkin, King's, A.R. (1865), 114.

27. "Choosing a Site," *Journal of Education* 1,1 (July. 1858): 4.

28. Forrester, A.R. (1862), 5.

29. Rev. J. Christie, Cumberland, A.R.(1865), 88. E. Outram, Cape Breton, A.R. (1866), 65, blamed local trustees: H.C. Upham, Colchester, A.R. (1867), 13, reporting on outhouses, did "not believe that any tribe of Indians would permit their children to be so exposed as they are at some schools …"; F.J. Farish, Yarmouth, A.R. (1873), 68–9, blamed parents for not voting sufficient funds, and wrote that he had seen little improvement in his nine years service as an inspector.

30. Rev. D.O. Parker, Queen's, A.R. (1867), 36.

31. H.C. Upham, Colchester, A.R. (1868), 52; Rev. W.H. Richan, Shelburne, A.R.(1870), 41; R. Somerville, King's, and D. McDonald, A.R. (1871), 10 and 20 respectively. See also *Journal of Education* 2, 1 (June, 1859), 10–11.

32. Nova Scotia, Act to Amend the Act for the Better Encouragement of Education (29 Victoria, Cap.30) (Halifax: Queen's Printer, 1866), 61.

33. S.R. Russell, Guysborough, A.R. (1867), 32; H.C. Upham, Colchester, A.R. (1868), 51–52; L.S. Morse, Annapolis, A.R. (1873), 17.

34. Several inspectors make references to these problems in the A.R.'s for 1867 and 1868.

35. T.J. Chapman, "School Apparatus," *Journal of Education* (Oct 1870): 518; see also A.S. Hunt, A.R. (1870), 36.

36. J. McDonnell, Inverness, A.R. (1865), 74; W. Eaton, King's, A.R. (1867), 33–4.

37. C. MacDonald, Victoria, A.R. (1865), 72.

38. Rev. G. Armstrong, Annapolis, A.R. (1866), 38–39; E. Outram, Cape Breton, A.R. (1869),41.

39. On the use of blackboards and other apparatus, see Alison Prentice, "From Household to Schoolhouse: The Emergence of the Teacher as a Servant of the State," *Material History Bulletin* 20 (Fall, 1984), 22.

40. A. Forrester, A.R.(1862), 4. The Census showed that nearly 52% of the population was under 20 years of age. The age commonly identified as school age (5–15 years) on inspection forms made up about 26% of the population; the age group 6–16 years, as reported in the 1871 Census, comprised 25% of the population.

41. D. Campbell and R. A. McLean's *Beyond the Atlantic Roar* (Toronto: McClelland and Stewart, 1974), 122.

42. H.C. Upham, Colchester, A.R. (1866), 15; T.H. Rand, A.R. (1867), xxii; Rev. W.H. Richan, Shelburne, A.R. (1868), 15 and (1871), 13; J.Y. Gunn, Inverness, A.R. (1869), 31, A.S. Hunt, A.R. (1873), xxiii.

43. J.B. Calkin, King's, A.R. (1865), 116.

44. A.S. Hunt, A.R (1874), x-xi; H.C. Upham, Colchester, A.R. (1866), 12–13; P.J. Fillieul, Digby, A.R. (1867), 43; D. McDonald, Pictou, A.R. (1870), 59.

45. R.B. Smith, Colchester, A.R. (1871), 53.

46. H. Condon, Halifax, A.R. (1873), 56; see also, D.M. Welton, Hants, A.R. (1866), 31; P.J. Fillieul, Digby, A.R (1867), 43; Rev. W.H. Richan, Shelburne, A.R.(1868), 15–16; E. Outram Cape Breton, A.R. (1869), 42; Rev. G. Armstrong Annapolis, A.R. (1870), 64.

47. E. Outram, Cape Breton, A.R. (1866), 65; T.H. Rand, A.R. and Rev. W.S. Darragh, Cumberland, A.R.

48. A. Munro, Victoria, A.R. (1873), 30; In the same year, inspector Lawson proposed "a small fine … on parents of absentees." (45)

49. Campbell and MacLean, *Beyond the Atlantic Roar*, 140.

50. A. Forrester, A.R. (1859), 243–244.

51. "Explanations of the New Register," *Journal of Education* (September 1867): 144–46.

52. *Journal of Education* (Sept., 1867): 145–6.

53. H.C. Upham, Colchester, A.R. (1868), 52, and (1870), 99.

54. W.M.B. Lawson, Lunenburg, A.R. (1868), 19; H.C. Upham, Colchester, A.R. (1869), 35.

55. Rev. D.M. Welton, Hants, A.R. (1867), 25, and (1868), 10.

56. Fiona Paterson, "Measures of Schooling: registers, standards and the construction of the subject," *Journal of Historical Sociology* 1, 3 (1988): 278–300.

57. A.C.A. Doane, Shelburne, A.R. (1873), 33.

58. T.H. Rand, A.R. (1863), 5.

(1869), xvi and 67–68, respectively; D. McDonald, Pictou, A.R. (1870), 58–9.

AS LONG AS THE SUN SHINES AND THE WATERS FLOW

Treaties and Treaty-Making in the 1870s

Maureen Lux
Brock University

AS LONG AS THE SUN SHINES AND THE WATERS FLOW: TREATIES AND TREATY-MAKING IN THE 1870s

- **Introduction by Maureen Lux**

▲ **Primary Sources**

Document 1: Historical Indian Treaties

Document 2: Treaty Talks

Document 3: Treaty Six

Document 4: Treaty Six Chiefs

Document 5: Mistahimusqua (Big Bear) Cree Leader

Document 6: Herd of Buffalo in Foothills of Rocky Mountains

Document 7: Pile of Buffalo Skulls, Saskatoon, Saskatchewan, August 9, 1890

Document 8: Text of Treaty 7

■ **Secondary Sources**

Article 1: The Numbered Treaties: Similar Means to Dichotomous Ends
Derek Whitehouse

Article 2: Canada's Colony and the Colonized
Sarah Carter

Article 3: The True Spirit and Original Intent of Treaty 7
Treaty Seven Elders and Tribal Council et al.

● INTRODUCTION

Maureen Lux

Treaties and treaty-making probably marked the very first relations between Aboriginal people and newcomers to northern North America. Fairly equal power relations character-ized those early pacts for military or commercial alliance. But the most important docu-ment in the history of treaty-making, the Royal Proclamation of 1763, set out the means by which agreements regarding territory could be concluded. Although enacted by the British to create institutions for governing its newly acquired territories after the Seven Years' War, the Proclamation also attempted to keep peace with the Aboriginal nations of the interior by holding back agricultural settlers from the Thirteen Colonies. Thus the Proclamation acknowledged Aboriginal rights to the lands, while also asserting Crown title. The Crown alone could negotiate with Aboriginal people for access to their lands, while the negotia-tions were required to be conducted in a public forum.

In 1850, in a departure from previous treaties for military alliance or for small parcels of land, the Robinson Treaties with the Aboriginal people of Lakes Huron and Superior regions covered huge districts in preparation for commercial development, and created the precedent for the western Numbered Treaties beginning in the 1870s. Unlike earlier pacts, the Robinson Treaties in what would become Ontario provided for reserve lands, annual cash payments (annuities), and promises of continued fishing and hunting rights. Moreover, it was Aboriginal resistance to incursions into their lands, not royal edict, that forced treaty negotiations.[1]

The Numbered Treaties began with Treaty One in 1871 in southern Manitoba and even-tually extended to Treaty Eleven in 1921, which covered a vast segment of the Northwest Territories (see Document 1: Historical Indian Treaties). But this implies an orderly and coherent approach that was far from the case. The Hudson's Bay Company sale of Rupert's Land to the newly created Canadian government in 1869 prompted armed resistance by residents at Red River, who demanded a voice in the new order. The Red River resistance likewise highlighted the need to make some accommodation with Aboriginal peoples of the West who demanded an agreement before they would allow access to their lands.

The first seven treaties to 1877 covered the southern plains from Ontario to the Rockies, serving the government's nation-building project of railway construction and settlement. As the selection from Sarah Carter's *Aboriginal People and Colonizers of Western Canada to 1900* shows, Aboriginal leaders saw the treaties as a way to protect their interests in the land, but especially to ensure the peoples' survival and future livelihood in vastly changed circumstances. The image "Conference with the Chiefs (Treaty One) September 9, 1871" clearly shows that treaty negotiations were conducted in the oral traditions of the Aboriginal nations. The written text of the treaties, however, purported to represent the substance of the agreements. Fundamental misunderstandings emerged about what the parties thought or assumed they were doing when they made the treaties. The concerns varied from one treaty to another, but in general the Aboriginal negotiators, based on their cultural and oral traditions, understood they were sharing the land with the newcomers, not "surrendering" it. As Derek Whitehouse argues in "The Numbered Treaties: Similar Means to Dichotomous Ends" both government and First Nations negotiators understood that treaties were a viable way to meet their respective goals, however much those goals were at odds.

In Treaty Seven, as the selections from *The True Spirit and Original Intent of Treaty 7* makes clear, the surrender of land was not discussed during negotiations; elders understood that the agreement was in fact a treaty of peace. It is clear that the "spirit and intent" of the treaty agreements was not necessarily represented in the written version of the treaties, creating hardship in the immediate post-treaty period and controversy ever since.

Elders have kept their histories alive, but only recently have notions of what constitutes a historical source evolved to include Aboriginal peoples' oral tradition. As we come to understand the treaties as binding agreements made in the presence of the Creator that created a relationship between newcomers (the Crown) and Aboriginal people to share the land and its benefits, and not simply a contract that surrendered the land in return for specific obligations, we can come to realize that indeed all Canadians are treaty people.

NOTES

1. J.R. Miller, *Lethal Legacy: Current Native Controversies in Canada* (Toronto: McClelland and Stewart, 2004), 119, 124; Gerald Friesen, *The Canadian Prairies: A History* (Toronto: University of Toronto Press, 1987), 136.

QUESTIONS

1. Why would Aboriginal elders understand that the treaties were agreements to share, not cede or surrender, the land?
2. Only recently have historians begun to listen to Aboriginal accounts of treaty negotiations. Why?
3. Why were there such fundamental misunderstandings between government and Aboriginal negotiators over what was agreed upon in treaty discussions?
4. The written text of Treaty 7 (Document 8) refers to the Queen and "her Indians." What does this indicate about the Crown's view of the treaty relationship?
5. Why was it important for the government to photograph Mistahimusqua (Big Bear) in chains?
6. On the signature page of the written text of Treaty 7 (Document 8) note the prominence of North-West Mounted Police (NWMP) officers. What does this say about how Canada exerted control over the West?

FURTHER READINGS

Erasmus, Peter. *Buffalo Days and Nights*, ed. Irene Spry, 1976, reprint (Calgary: Glenbow Alberta Institute, 1999).

Miller, J.R., *Compact, Contract, Covenant; Aboriginal Treaty-Making in Canada* (Toronto: University of Toronto Press, 2009).

Morris, Alexander, *The Treaties of Canada with the Indians of Manitoba and the North-West Territories*, 1880, reprint (Toronto: Coles Publishing, 1971).

Ray, Arthur J., Jim Miller, and Frank Tough, *Bounty and Benevolence: A History of Saskatchewan Treaties* (Montreal and Kingston: McGill-Queen's University Press, 2000).

Tobias, John, "Protection, Civilization, Assimilation: An Outline History of Canada's Indian Policy," in *As Long as the Sun Shines and Water Flows*, Ian A.L. Getty and Antoine S. Lussier, eds. (Vancouver: UBC Press, 1983), 13–30.

Treaty Elders of Saskatchewan, with Harold Cardinal and Walter Hildebrant, *Our Dream Is That Our Peoples Will One Day Be Clearly Recognized as Nations* (Calgary: University of Calgary Press, 2000).

▲ Document 1: Historical Indian Treaties

Legend:
— Treaty boundary[1]
— Treaty adhesion[2]

YUKON

Treaty 11
1921

NORTHWEST TERRITORIES

Treaty 10
1906

Treaty 8
1899

MANITOBA

1908

Treaty 5

LABRADOR

NEW FOUNDLAND

ALBERTA

BRITISH
COLUMBIA

1889

Treaty 6
1876

1875

SASKATCHEWAN

1929–30

Treaty 9

1905
ONTARIO

QUEBEC

Robinson-Huron
Treaty 1850

Williams
Treaties
1923

PRINCE
EDWARD ISLAND

NEW
BRUNSWICK

NOVA SCOTIA

Pre-Confederation
Treaty

Pre-Confederation
Maritime Peace and
Friendship Treaties

Pre-Confederation
Vancouver Island Treaties
14 Treaties – 1850–54

Treaty 7
1877

Treaty 4
1874

Treaty 2
1871

Treaty 3
1873

Treaty 1
1871

Robinson-Superior
Treaty 1850

Manitoulin Island
Treaty 1862

Upper Canada
Treaties

Pre-Confederation
Treaties of Peace
and Alliance

● **Historical Indian Treaties**

Source: Adapted from Canada, Indian Treaties, MCR 4162. "The Atlas of Canada, 1991, Natural Resources Canada, 4 March 2009, http://atlas.nrcan.gc.ca/site/english/maps/archives/5theditions/historical/mcr4162; and from *Ways of Knowing: An Introduction to Native Studies in Canada* 1E. Belanger, Yale D. © 2010 Nelson Education Ltd. Reproduced by permission. www.cengage.com/permissions.

▲ Document 2: Treaty Talks

● "Conference with the Chiefs (Treaty One) September 9, 1871". This illustration, while likely romanticized, clearly shows the oral nature of treaty talks conducted in at least two, sometimes many, different languages. Hand gestures and displays of emotion, crucial to the context of negotiations, become lost in the treaties' written version.

Source: *Canadian Illustrated News*, 09 September 1871, Vol. IV, No. 11, 161. Library and Archives Canada, C056472.

▲ Document 3: Treaty Six

● Page 1 of Treaty Six signed at Fort Carlton and Fort Pitt, 23 August and 28 August, 1876. The images in Documents 2 and 3 refer to different treaties, but all treaties were negotiated using translators, and all treaties were eventually written in English. Imagine how many ways misunderstandings might make their way into the legalistic (and privileged) treaty texts.

Source: Manuscript original of western Treaty 6 (IT296) signed at Fort Pitt on September 9, 1876 by Alexander Morris, Lieutenant-Governor of the Northwest Territories, and representatives of the "Plain and Wood Cree". © Indian and Northern Affairs Canada. Reproduced with the permission of the Minister of Public Works and Government Services Canada (2009). Source: Library and Archives Canada/RG10, Indian Affairs, D-10-a, IT296, Microfilm Reel T-9940/e004156541.

▲ Document 4: Treaty Six Chiefs

● Ahtahkakoop (left front) and Mistawasis (right front) influential Treaty Six Chiefs at Fort Carlton in 1876 (front centre, Chief Flying in a Circle; left rear, Chief Osoup; right rear, Peter Hourie, interpreter). Note the Chiefs wearing their Treaty medal.

Source: Library and Archives Canada, C19258.

▲ Document 5: Mistahimusqua (Big Bear) Cree Leader

● Mistahimusqua (Big Bear) Cree leader who participated in Treaty Six talks at Fort Pitt in September 1876, but refused to sign until 1882. Here he is photographed in chains for his supposed role in the Riel Rebellion 1885.

Source: Library and Archives Canada, C1873.

▲ Document 6: Herd of Buffalo in Foothills of Rocky Mountains

What does this image and the next tell you about the pace of change on the prairies?

Source: Glenbow Archives NA-1041-15.

▲ Document 7: Pile of Buffalo Skulls, Saskatoon, Saskatchewan, August 9, 1890

Source: Glenbow Archives NA-354-30.

▲ Document 8: Text of Treaty 7

Treaty Seven Elders and Tribal Council et al.

The text following contains the articles of the treaty as presented by the treaty commissioners. As is clear from the evidence of the elders, this document does not represent the true spirit and original intent of the treaty that was made at Blackfoot Crossing. The elders say that the treaty as presented to them a year after the negotiations does not contain all of the agreements concluded between the commissioners and chiefs. Many contentious issues concerning the written treaty remain unresolved, especially issues relating to the translation. Many elders have stated that the written treaty they were given was written prior to the arrival of the commissioners, and that agreements made during the negotiations were never incorporated into the final treaty text. The elders feel that much discussion, analysis, and amendment are still required before the written treaty contains the true spirit and original intent of the agreement. In addition to the fundamental issue of whether the treaty represents a land surrender, the elders point to the careless drafting and translation of the treaty.

Elder Louise Crop Eared Wolf* cites examples of gross misrepresentations of names on the treaties as evidence of the incompetence of the translators and those who wrote the treaty. Improper translations and spellings of the Blackfoot names appended to the treaty abound. She identified over eighty errors made by the translators. Some of the worst examples include the recoding of Crowfoot's name as Chapo-Mexico instead of Issapo-maksika; Chapo-Mexico has no meaning and sounds more like an English word. The name of another leading Siksika elder, Old Sun, was recorded as Matose-Apiw, which is simply incomprehensible in Blackfoot. Stamis-cotocar, for Stami-kso-tokan (Bull Head) of the Tsuu T'ina, again has no meaning in Blackfoot, as there are no "r's" in the Blackfoot language. Natose-onistors is a misrepresentation of Natoso-nista, which was wrongly translated as Medicine Calf instead of Powerful Calf. Takoye-stamix is an incorrect representation for Sakoi-yi-stamik (Last Bull, which was also mistranslated as Fiend Bull.) Issokoi-ya-wotanni or Cougar Shield was translated as Sakoye-aowotan, which means Heavy Shield. Crop Eared Wolf points out that this latter translation is an example of a very poor understanding of the language, since even though the words are close in sound—*issokoioyi* for "cougar" and *issokoi* for "heavy"—a real Blackfoot speaker would know the difference. Also Pitah-siksinum, meaning White Eagle, is the wrong spelling and translation of Pitai-siki-namm, which means Black Eagle. Pitah-otsikin, which means "disgusting," was used to represent Pitai-tsi-kinn, which means Eagle Moccasin.

---

*Louise Crop Eared Wolf: "My comments regarding all the mispronounced Blackfoot names of chiefs of the Bloods, Blackfoot, and Piegan give enough evidence to show that the interpreter (James Bird) at the Treaty 7 peace-making agreement was not a fluent speaker of the Blackfoot language at the time. How could he have accurately explained the articles of the treaty if he was unable to master the Blackfoot terms of the names in Blackfoot. My belief is that our ancestors were not made aware of all the English terms of the treaty."

Source: From *The True Spirit and Original Intent of Treaty 7*, Treaty 7 Elders and Tribal Council with Walter Hildebrandt, Sarah Carter and Dorothy First Rider. Chapter 6, pp. 230–31. Montreal and Kingston: McGill-Queen's University Press, 1996. Reprinted with permission from McGill-Queen's University Press.

When recording the names of the Stoney chiefs on the treaty documents, the officials used the Cree language and the not Stoney-Siouan language. Chief Jacob Bearspaw is written as Mas-gwa-ah-sid, Cree for Bear's Paw, and Chief Jacob Goodstoney is written as Ki-chi-pwat, the Cree word for Big Stoney. The use of Cree to record Stoney names underlines the claim of the Stoney elders that their chief adviser, Reverend John McDougall, officially representing their position during the negotiations, was not a competent translator. McDougall knew Cree but not the Nakota-Siouan language.

The written treaty text below must therefore be read with the understanding that the Treaty 7 elders see it as something that does not fully represent what was agreed to at Blackfoot Crossing.

"THE TREATY WITH THE BLACKFEET; NUMBER SEVEN"

Articles of a Treaty made and concluded this twenty-second day of September, in the year of our Lord one thousand eight hundred and seventy-seven, between Her Most Gracious Majesty the Queen of Great Britain and Ireland, by her Commissioners, the Honorable David Laird, Lieutenant-Governor and Indian Superintendent of the North-West Territories, and James Farquharson McLeod, C.M.G., Commissioner of the North-West Mounted Police, of the one part, and the Blackfeet, Blood, Peigan, Sarcee, Stony, and other Indians, inhabitants of the territory north of the United States boundary line, east of the central range of the Rocky Mountains, and south and west of Treaties Numbers Six and Four, by their head Chiefs and minor Chiefs or Councillors, chosen as hereinafter mentioned, of the other part:

Whereas the Indians inhabiting the said territory, have pursuant to an appointment made by the said Commissioners, been convened at meeting at the "Blackfoot crossing" of the Bow River, to deliberate upon certain matters of interests to her Most Gracious Majesty, of the one part, and the said Indians of the other;

And whereas the said Indians have been informed by Her Majesty's Commissioners that it is the desire of Her Majesty to open up for settlement, and such other purposes as to Her Majesty may seem meet, a tract of country, bounded and described as hereinafter mentioned, and to obtain the consent thereto of her Indian subjects inhabiting the said tract, and to make a treaty, and arrange with them, so that there may be peace and good will between them and Her Majesty, and between them and Her Majesty's other subjects; and that her Indian people may know and feel assured of what allowance they are to count upon and receive from Her Majesty's bounty and benevolence;

And whereas the Indians of the said tract, duly convened in council, and being requested by her Majesty's Commissioners to present their head Chiefs and minor Chiefs, or Councillors, who shall be authorized, on their behalf, to conduct such negotiations and sign any treaty to be founded thereon, and to become responsible to Her Majesty for the faithful performance by their respective bands of such obligations as should be assumed by them, the said Blackfeet, Blood, Piegan and Sarcee Indians have therefore acknowledged for that purpose, the several head and minor Chiefs, and the said Stony Indians, the Chiefs and Councillors who have subscribed hereto, that thereupon in open council the said Commissioners received and acknowledged the head and minor Chiefs and the Chiefs and Councillors presented for the purpose aforesaid:

And whereas the said Commissioners have proceeded to negotiate a treaty with the said Indians; and the same has been finally agreed upon and concluded as follows, that is to say: the Blackfeet, Blood, Piegan, Sarcee, Stony and other Indians inhabiting the district hereinafter more fully described and defined, do hereby cede, release, surrender, and yield up to the Government of Canada for Her Majesty the Queen and her successors forever, all their rights, titles and privileges whatsoever to the lands included within the following limits, that is to say:

Commencing at a point on the international boundary due south of the western extremity of the Cypress Hills; thence west along the said boundary to the central range of the Rocky Mountains, or to the boundary of the Province of British Columbia; thence north-westerly along the said boundary to a point due west of the source of the main branch of the Red Deer River; thence south-westerly and southerly following on the boundaries of the tracts ceded by the Treaties Numbered Six and Four to the place of commencement; and also all their rights, titles and privileges whatsoever, to all other lands wherever situated in the North-West Territories, or in any other portion of the Dominion of Canada:

To have and to hold the same to Her Majesty the Queen and her successors forever:

And Her Majesty the Queen hereby agrees with her said Indians, that they shall have right to pursue their vocations of hunting throughout the tract surrendered as heretofore described, subject to such regulations as may, from time to time, be made by the Government of the country, acting under the authority of Her Majesty; and saving and excepting such tracts as may be required or taken up from time to time for settlement, mining, trading or other purposes by her Government of Canada, or by any of her Majesty's subjects duly authorized therefor by the said Government.

It is also agreed between Her Majesty and her said Indians that reserves shall be assigned them of sufficient area to allow one square mile for each family of five persons, or in that proportion for larger and smaller families, and that said reserves shall be located as follows, that is to say:

First—The reserves of the Blackfeet, Blood and Sarcee bands of Indians, shall consist of a belt of land on the north side of the Bow and South Saskatchewan Rivers, of an average width of four miles along said rivers, down stream, commencing at a point on the Bow River twenty miles north-westerly of the "Blackfoot crossing" thereof, and extending to the Red Deer River at its junction with the South Saskatchewan; also for the term of ten years, and no longer, from the date of the concluding of this treaty, when it shall cease to be a portion of said Indian reserves, as fully to all intents and purposes as if it had not at any time been included therein, and without any compensation to individual Indians for improvements, of a similar belt of land on the south side of the Bow and Saskatchewan Rivers of an average width of one mile along said rivers, down stream; commencing at the aforesaid point on the Bow River, and extending to a point one mile west of the coal seam on said river, about five miles below the said "Blackfoot crossing"; beginning again one mile east of the said coal seam and extending to the mouth of Maple Creek at its junction with the South Saskatchewan; and beginning again at the junction of the Bow River with the latter river, and extending on both sides of the South Saskatchewan in an average width on each side thereof of one mile, along said river against the stream, to the junction of the Little Bow River with the latter river, reserving to Her Majesty, as may now or hereafter be required by her for the use of her Indian and other subjects, from all the reserves hereinbefore described, the right to navigate the above mentioned rivers, to land and receive fuel and cargoes on the shores and banks thereof, to build bridges and establish ferries thereon, to use the fords thereof and all the trails leading thereto, and to open such other roads through the said reserves as may appear to Her Majesty's Government of Canada, necessary for the ordinary travel of her Indian and other subjects, due compensation being paid to individual Indians for improvements, when the same may be in any manner encroached upon by such roads.

Secondly—That the reserve of the Piegan band of Indians shall be on the Old Man's River, near the foot of the Porcupine Hills, at a place called "Crow's Creek."

And Thirdly—The reserve of the Stony band of Indians shall be in the vicinity of Morleyville.

In view of the satisfaction of Her Majesty with the recent general good conduct of her said Indians, and in extinguishment of all their past claims, she hereby, through her Commissioners, agrees to make them a present payment of twelve dollars each in cash to each man, woman, and child of the families here represented.

Her Majesty also agrees that next year, and annually afterwards forever, she will cause to be paid to the said Indians, in cash, at suitable places and dates, of which the said Indians shall be duly notified, to each Chief, twenty-five dollars, each minor Chief or Councillor (not exceeding fifteen minor Chiefs to the Blackfeet and Blood Indians, and four to the Piegan and Sarcee bands, and five Councillors to the Stony Indian Bands) fifteen dollars, and to every other Indian of whatever age, five dollars; the same, unless there be some exceptional reason, to be paid to the heads of families for those belonging thereto.

Further, Her Majesty agrees that the sum of two thousand dollars shall hereafter every year be expended in the purchase of ammunition for distribution among the said Indians; provided that if at any future time ammunition became comparatively unnecessary for said Indians, her Government, with the consent of said Indians, or any of the bands thereof, may expend the proportion due to such band otherwise for their benefit.

Further, Her Majesty agrees that each head Chief and minor Chief, and each Chief and Councillor duly recognized as such, shall, once in every three years, during the term of their office, receive a suitable suit of clothing, and each head Chief and Stony Chief, in recognition of the closing of the treaty, a suitable medal and flag, and next year, or as soon as convenient, each head Chief, and minor Chief, and Stony Chief shall receive a Winchester rifle.

Further, Her Majesty agrees to pay the salary of such teachers to instruct the children of said Indians as to her Government of Canada may seem advisable, when said Indians are settled on their reserves and shall desire teachers.

Further, Her Majesty agrees to supply each head and minor Chief, and each Stony Chief, for the use of their bands, ten axes, five handsaws, five augers, one grindstone, and the necessary files and whetstones.

And further, Her Majesty agrees that the said Indians shall be supplied as soon as convenient, after any band shall make due application therefor with the following cattle for raising stock, that is to say: for every family of five persons, and under, two cows; for every family of more than five persons, and less than ten persons, three cows; for every family of over ten persons, four cows; and every head and minor Chief, and every Stony Chief, for the use of their bands, one bull; but if any band desire to cultivate the soil as well as raise stock, each family of such band shall receive one cow less than the above mentioned number, and in lieu thereof, when settled on their reserves and prepared to break up the soil, two hoes, one spade, one scythe, and two hay forks, and for every three families, one plough and one harrow, and for each band, enough potatoes, barley, oats, and wheat (if such seeds be suited for the locality of their reserves) to plant the land actually broken up. All the aforesaid articles to be given, once for all, for the encouragement of the practice of agriculture among the Indians.

And the undersigned Blackfeet, Blood, Piegan and Sarcee head Chiefs and minor Chiefs, and Stony Chiefs and Councillors, on their own behalf and on behalf of all other Indians inhabiting the tract within ceded do hereby solemnly promise and engage to strictly observe this treaty, and also to conduct and behave themselves as good and loyal subjects of Her Majesty the Queen. They promise and engage that they will , in all respects, obey and abide by the law, that they will maintain peace and good order between each other and between themselves and other tribes of Indians, and between themselves and others of Her Majesty's subjects, whether Indians, Half breeds or whites, now inhabiting, or hereafter to inhabit, any part of the said ceded tract; and that they will not molest the person or property of any inhabitant of such ceded tract, or the property of Her Majesty the Queen, or interfere with or trouble any person, passing or travelling through the said tract or any part thereof, and that they will assist the officers of Her Majesty in bringing to justice and punishment any Indian offending against the stipulations of this treaty, or infringing the laws in force in the country ceded.

In witness whereof Her Majesty's said Commissioner, and the said Indian head and minor Chiefs, and Stony Chiefs and Councillors, have hereunto subscribed and set their hands, at the "Blackfoot crossing" of the Bow River, the day and year herein first above written.

(Signed) DAVID LAIRD,
Gov. of N.W.T. and Special Indian Commissioner.
JAMES F. MCLEOD,
Lieut.-Colonel, Com. N.-W.M.P.
and Special Indian Commissioner

CHAPO-MEXICO(or Crowfoot),	His x mark
Head Chief of the South Blackfeet.	
MATOSE-APIW (or Old Sun),	" x "
Head Chief of the North Blackfeet.	
STAMISCOTOCAR (or Bull Head),	" x "
Head Chief of the Sarcees.	
MEKASTO (or Red Crow),	" x "
Head Chief of the South Bloods.	
NATOSE-ONISTORS (or Medicine Calf.).	" x "
POKAPIW-OTOIAN (or Bad Head).	" x "
SOTENAH (or Rainy Chief),	" x "
Head Chief of the North Bloods.	
TAKOYE-STAMIX (or Fiend Bull).	" x "
AKKA-KITCIPIMIW-OTAS (or Many Spotted Horses).	" x "
ATTISTAH-MACAN (or Running Rabbit).	" x "
PITAH-PEKIS (or Eagle Rib).	" x "
SAKOYE-AOTAN (or Heavy Shield),	" x "
Head Chief of the Middle Blackfeet.	
ZOATZE-TAPITAPIW (or Setting on an Eagle Tail).	His x mark
Head Chief of the North Piegans.	
AKKA-MAKKOYE (or Many Swans).	" x "
APENAKO-SAPOP (or Morning Plume).	" x "
*MAS-GWA-AH-SID (or Bear's Paw).	" x "
*CHE-NE-KA (or John).	" x "
*KI-CHI-PWOT (or Jacob).	" x "
STAMIX-OSOK (or Bull Backfat).	" x "
EMITAH-APISKINNE (or White Striped Dog).	" x "
MATAPI-KOMOTZIW (or the Captive or Stolen Person).	" x "
APAWAWAKOSOW (or White Antelope).	" x "
MAKOYE-KIN (or Wolf Collar).	" x "
AYE-STIPIS-SIMAT (or Heavily Whipped).	" x "
KISSOUM (or Day Light).	" x "
PITAH-OTOCAN (or Eagle Head).	" x "
APAW-STAMIX (or Weasel Bull).	" x "

ONISTAH-POKAH (or White Calf).	His x mark
NETAH-KITEI-PI-MEW (or Only Spot).	" x "
AKAK-OTOS (or Many Horses).	" x "
STOKIMATIS (or The Drum).	" x "
PITAH-ANNES (or Eagle Robe).	" x "
PITAH-OTSIKIN (or Eagle Shoe).	" x "
STAMIX-OTA-KA-PIW (or Bull Turn Round).	" x "
MASTE-PITAH (or Crow Eagle).	" x "
†JAMES DIXON.	" x "
†ABRAHAM KECHEPWOT.	" x "
†PATRICK KECHEPWOT.	" x "
†GEORGE MOY-ANY-MEN.	" x "
†GEORGE CRAWLOR.	" x "
EKAS-KLINE (or Low Horn).	" x "
KAYO-OKOSIS (or Bear Shield).	" x "
PONOKAH-STAMIX (or Bull Elk).	" x "
OMAKSI SAPOP (or Big Plume).	" x "
ONISTAH (or Calf Robe).	" x "
PITAH-SIKSINUM (or White Eagle).	" x "
APAW-ONISTAW (or Weasel Calf).	" x "
ATTISTA-HAES (or Rabbit Carrier).	" x "
PITAH (or Eagle).	" x "
PITAH-ONISTAH (or Eagle White Calf.).	" x "
KAYE-TAPO (or Going to Bear).	" x "

Signed by the Chiefs and Councillors within named in presence of the following witnesses, the same having been first explained by James Bird, Interpreter.

(Signed) A.G. IRVINE, *Ass't Com.,* N.-W.M.P.

J. MCDOUGALL *Missionary.*

JEAN L'HEUREUX.

W. WINDER.

T.N.F. CROZIER, *Inspectors.*

E. DALRYMPLE CLARK, *Lieut. and Adjutant.* N.-W.M.P.

A. SHURTLIFF,

C.E. DENING,

W.D. ANTROBUS, *Sub-Inspectors.*

FRANK NORMAN, *Staff Constable.*

MARY J. MACLEOD.

JULIA WINDER.

JULIA SHURTLIFF.

E. HARDISTY.

A. MCDOUGALL.

E.A. BARRETT.

CONSTANTINE SCOLLEN, *Priest,* witness to signatures of Stonixosak and those following.

CHARLES E. CONRAD.

THOS. J. BOGG.

---

* Stony Chiefs.
† Stony Councillors

■ Article 1: The Numbered Treaties: Similar Means to Dichotomous Ends

Derek Whitehouse

On 2 August 1871, the Canadian government and the Indians of the North-West Territories signed the first of the Numbered Treaties. By the end of 1877 an additional six Treaties had been negotiated, effectively opening the North-West for settlement. Events leading up to the negotiations, and the negotiations themselves, provide clear evidence that dichotomy existed between the goals that the Indians hoped to achieve through the Treaty process and those the government hoped to attain. The Indians,[1] realizing that their environment was changing, sought to protect their culture from threatening forces such as non-native agricultural settlement and diminishing buffalo herds. The government, meanwhile, strove to encourage the absorption of the Indian cultures into broader Euro-Canadian society, not only because it wanted to open the North-West for settlement, but also because it believed that assimilation was in the best interest of the Indian peoples. Despite the disparity in the objectives that each party sought, both considered the Treaties to be tools that were essential to achieving their goals. Thus, in the first seven Numbered Treaties, the government and the Indians employed similar means toward very dissimilar ends.

Until recent decades, the historical analysis of Canada's past down-played or overlooked the contributions of aboriginal peoples. As James W. St.G. Walker noted of historical works such as Donald Creighton's *Canada: The Heroic Beginnings,* Indians were often presented as "not even minor actors in the Canadian drama, simply stage-props against which others work[ed] out their roles."[2]

A case in point is the work of Allan Harper. In 1947, Harper wrote that, during the Numbered Treaty process, discussion was controlled by the government and "confined to a careful explanation of the terms, answering questions, firmly rejecting exorbitant demands, and dispelling false notions about the government's assumption ofobligations."[3] Similarly, in 1932, G.F.G. Stanley argued that the negotiation of the Treaties "was confined to an explanation of the terms" by the government and that "the Indians never understood what was happening."[4] Until the 1970s, historians portrayed Canada's aboriginal peoples as passive victims of dominant outside forces.

By the 1970s, however, historians were beginning to revise the image of the Indian peoples as victims. Fur trade historians like A.J. Ray spearheaded the revisionists' efforts. Writing in 1978, Ray argued that historical analyses which assumed "that the Indians were ruthlessly exploited and cheated in all areas and periods by white[s] [...] gives us only half the story."[5] A reinterpretation of Canada's past which recognized the contributions made by the Indian peoples would result in new perceptions of Indians as active and creative agents in the historical process. Ray realized that treating the largely ignored aboriginal peoples as active participants in Canada's past was essential to the appropriate placement of the Indian in the historical record.[6]

While the process of reinterpreting Canada's past began with fur trade historians such as A.J. Ray and Donald B. Freeman,[7] historians working in other fields also reassessed the Indian perspective. Sylvia Van Kirk, for example, argued that the fur trade "was not simply an economic activity, but a social and cultural complex."[8] Consequently, when examining the role that Indian, Métis, and white women had in the fur trade, Van Kirk asserted that the "examination of the role played by women as actors upon the fur trade stage is essential to a full understanding of the complexities" of early Western Canadian society.[9] Thus, in viewing Canada's aboriginal peoples as active agents of history, historians developed new interpretations of economic, social, religious, and political interactions between white and Indian.[10]

J.R. Miller noted, however, that most efforts of historians to restore the Canadian aboriginal to the position of an active historical agent have focused upon the period preceding the 1860s. Indeed, as late as 1990, Miller argued that "studies of Indian-white relations after Confederation [...] have thus far largely proved resistant to reinterpretation."[11]

Articles by Jean Friesen, D.J. Hall, and John Leonard Taylor, however, are notable exceptions in that they demonstrate that the revisionists are no longer emphasizing the pre-Confederation period. Taylor, for example, maintained that the Numbered Treaties were the product of Indian and government interactions, and not, as Harper had argued, the result

Source: *Past Imperfect,* Vol. 3 (1994): 25–45. Reprinted with permission from Derek Whitehouse-Strong.

of the government dictating terms that the Indians had either to "accept or reject."[12] Taylor understood the Treaty process as having been an open negotiation in which the Indians introduced innovations that the government was subsequently forced to accept. If the government had not accepted the innovations, it "would have had even more difficulty getting the treaties, if [it] had been able to get them at all."[13]

Duncan Campbell Scott, Canada's Deputy Superintendent General of Indian Affairs from 1913 to 1932, attested to the underlying continuity of the government's Indian policy some thirty years after the completion of the first seven Numbered Treaties. In 1909, Scott stated that "the true and uniform policy [of the government] [...] has made the Canadian Indian believe the British sovereign is his great parent and [he] himself is a child under beneficent protection."[14] He went on to say that "the happiest future for the Indian race is [...] absorption into the general population, and this is the object of the policy of our government."[15] Toward this goal, the government believed that

> agriculture, education, and religion would, in time, provide the Indian with far more than he had lost. Eventually the settlement of the West would uplift the native from his state [of savagery or barbarism].[16]

The Canadian government genuinely believed that its goal of assimilation was in the best interest of the Indian peoples. The Numbered Treaties were intended to provide the tools which government officials thought were necessary to facilitate this assimilation: reserve agriculture, schools, and missionaries.[17]

Much of the Canadian population shared the government's desire to absorb the Indian peoples into broader Euro-Canadian society. For decades, official documents and reports, and "the works of scientists, social scientists, travellers, humanitarians, and missionaries"[18] had served to shape the perception that assimilation was not only in the best interest of the Canadian population, but also of the aboriginal peoples themselves. As a result of these varied influences, a paternalistic approach to the assimilation of the Indians was seen as both "desirable [...] and necessary. With the Indian as the ward of the state, steps could be taken to protect him from the harmful effects of white culture while teaching him its benefits."[19]

Imperialistic influences also strengthened and confirmed the idea that the assimilation of the Indian was the true and correct policy to follow. Colonies within the British Empire, historian Walter Houghton argued, had been founded

> it was said—and believed—by the generous and altruistic desire of spreading throughout the habitable globe all the characteristics of Englishmen—their energy, their civilization, their religion and their freedom.[20]

Consequently, those directing the government's Indian policy saw themselves as fulfilling this aspect of Britain's destiny. What could be better for an improvident, intemperate, and latently indolent people who were prone to privation[21] than to become active members of a nation destined to assume the role of dominance in the British Empire? The government expected that agriculture would help the Indians overcome the inherent weaknesses that it believed they shared as peoples, and thus it would aid their eventual assimilation into Canadian society. The aboriginal peoples would then become part of that which "represent[ed] man's highest achievement in the development of governmental and social institutions."[22] In order for the Indians to be assimilated, however, the government knew that the cultural identity of the Canadian aboriginals would have to be eliminated. On a cultural level, the Indian would have to adopt the traditions and practices of the white man.[23]

In 1877, the prominent American anthropologist Lewis Henry Morgan put to print a theory, the essence of which many of his era were already familiar with. Morgan asserted that all societies passed through the stages of savagery and barbarism on their way to becoming civilized.[24] Consequently, because passage from one level of development to the next was thought to be unilinear, "each step [...] was regarded as essential to the next and [thus] could not be transcended."[25] According to the unilinear evolutionists argument, it followed that because many of the Indian bands in the North-West engaged in hunting and gathering subsistence, they were in the initial, savage phase of the evolutionary path. Subscribing to Morgan's theory, the government believed that the Indians would have to pass through barbarism, a stage which was characterized by domestication and cultivation, before they could become civilized. Reserve agriculture was, therefore, to be the Indian peoples' "place of probation, a training ground in the lessons of civilization and citizenship."[26]

Besides viewing the Treaties as a means to encourage the assimilation of the Indian, government officials also intended to use the Treaties to open the North-West for settlement in accordance with its national policy.[27] The Royal Proclamation of 1763 made it illegal for anyone, save the Crown, to purchase land in "Indian Country."[28] Although this provision "did not apply to the Hudson's Bay Company lands, [it did] set out the basis" by which these lands would be settled after their transfer to Canada in 1870.[29] It was necessary, therefore, for the government to extinguish Indian title to land in the North-West before settlement could begin. Alexander Morris, the lieutenant governor of the North-West Territories from 1872 to 1876, summarized this objective during the discussions concerning Treaty One and Treaty Two. According to Morris,

> it was desirable to secure the extinction of the Indian title not only to the lands within Manitoba, but also to so much of the timber grounds east and north of the Province as were required for immediate entry and use, also of a large tract of cultivate ground west of the Portage, where there were very few Indian inhabitants.[30]

Regarding the completion of Treaty Three, he continued:

> and so was closed, a treaty, whereby a territory was enabled to be opened up, of great importance to Canada, embracing as it does the Pacific Railway route to the North West Territories—a wide extent of fertile lands, and, as is believed, great mineral resources.[31]

Extinguishing Indian title to land in the North-West so that settlement could commence thus constituted the second goal of the government's Treaty policy.

Morris' words demonstrate that pressures on land, resulting from the government's settlement policy, were the primary motivators behind the government's decision to treat. That settlement pressures were of such great import to the Canadian government can be largely attributed to the fact that, with an annual federal budget of only $19 million and with the construction of a transcontinental railway a national preoccupation, the government was seeking to devote only as many resources as were necessary to negotiating treaties with the Indians.[32] Indeed, Joseph Howe, Secretary of State for the Provinces cautioned Treaty Commissioner Wemyss Simpson to

> endeavour to secure the session [sic] of the lands upon terms as favourable as possible to the Government, not going as far as the maximum sum hereafter named unless it be found impossible to obtain the object for a less amount.[33]

In addition, Prime Minister Alexander Mackenzie pointed out that, when compared to "other countries," Canada's Treaty policy was not only "a humane, just, and Christian policy," it was also "the cheapest."[34] Only when it was so required by settlement pressures, therefore, would the government be induced to negotiate.

The requests of the Indian peoples themselves had little impact on the timing of negotiations when settlement pressures were not at issue. Indeed, some of the bands who would eventually be included under Treaty Six had requested negotiations toward an agreement a full five years before actual proceedings began. The government, however, did little to address the "[general] feeling of discontent and uneasiness," arising from the fact that they had not been treated with, "[that] prevailed [...] amongst the Assiniboines and Crees."[35] Only when the Indians threatened to disrupt survey and telegraph crews was the government finally compelled to negotiate.[36]

Settlement pressure of a different type was the key factor in the government's movement to negotiate Treaty Seven. On this occasion, it was white settlers who pressured the government for an agreement in order to allay growing concerns regarding their own safety. Father Constantine Scollen noted that

> The Blackfeet are extremely jealous of what they consider their country and have never allowed any white men, Half-breeds, or Crees to remain in it for any length of time

[...] [As such, the settlers] are anxious that a treaty be made as soon as possible, so that they may know what portions of land they can hold without fear of being molested.[37]

Consequently, it was again in the government's interest to obtain a treaty, despite the fact that, unofficially at least, the Blackfoot were not seeking such an agreement.

Humanistic, expansionistic, imperialistic, and nationalistic beliefs, values, and ideas thus shaped the Canadian government's Indian policy. Furthermore, it is clear that the government engaged in the treaty-making process for two main reasons. First, negotiations were initiated to facilitate the Euro-Canadian agricultural settlement of the North-West. Second, the Treaty concessions provided the means by which the distinctiveness, uniqueness, and heritage of the Indian could be eliminated, and what was left could be absorbed into the Euro-Canadian culture.

For the Indians, however, the Treaties served an entirely different function. Aware that the Treaties would open the North-West up for rapid settlement, the aboriginal peoples also understood that settlement was inevitable, with or without the Treaties. Consequently, the Indians sought to use the concessions that they gained under the Treaty system to ensure that their culture would survive, an end antithetical to that being sought by the government. To achieve their goal, the Indians, much like the government, expressed an interest in schools and in missionaries and "were desirous of according to the wish of their great Mother" that they "discard their former precarious mode of living and adopt the agricultural pursuits of the white man."[38] Aware that social and economic pressures were making it inevitable that their way of life was coming to an end, the aboriginal peoples sought to adopt a new way of life, one which would allow them to retain their independent cultures.

The Ojibwa and the Swampy Cree, who were among the first Indian peoples to be involved in the Numbered Treaty process, had outwardly expressed concern regarding the "influx of population" onto their lands. Indeed, Alexander Morris noted that "the Indians in Manitoba [...] had in some instances obstructed settlers and surveyors"[39] until their calls for a Treaty were met. Thus, while governmental policy dictated that Treaties were to be negotiated only when so required by settlement pressures, the Indian peoples were still able to "[rush] the government's timetable somewhat."[40]

Concerns about the influx of white settlers also affected the tribes involved in later negotiations. The Plains Cree were aware that great numbers of white settlers would soon be entering their lands. During Treaty Six negotiations, Star Blanket, the Chief of the Wood Indians, cautioned those of his people who opposed the Treaty:

[When the buffalo are gone] what then will be left us with which to bargain? With the buffalo gone we will have only the vacant prairie which none of us have learned to use. Can we stop the power of the white man from spreading over the land like the grasshoppers that cloud the sky and then fall to consume every blade of grass and every leaf on the trees in their path? I think not. Before this happens, let us ponder carefully our choice of roads.[41]

Indeed, in 1875, the Reverend George McDougall had been informed by certain Cree that "they were unanimous in their determination to oppose the running of lines, or the making of roads through their country, until an agreement between the Government and them had been effected."[42] This concern was echoed by the Plains Assiniboine who, on hearing that they would be treated with, informed Alexander Morris that "foolish men have told us that the Great Chief would send his young men to our country until they outnumbered us, and that then he would laugh at us."[43]

The Blackfoot, who in 1877 were signatories to Treaty Seven, also saw the early signs of white settlement. Unlike many of the tribes further east, however, they themselves were not seeking a Treaty. It is likely, nevertheless, that factors such as the diminishing buffalo herds and the steady increase of white settlers into their region would have eventually "disposed the Blackfoot towards making a treaty."[44] Indeed, the likes of the Reverends George and John McDougall and Fathers Scollen and Fourmond had penetrated as far south as the Bow River by 1877. This fact "not only indicates the hold the missionaries were gaining on the prairie Indians but also how much the Blackfoot hold on their native land was slipping."[45]

The Blackfoot's concern over the diminishing buffalo herds had also been voiced by the other Plains tribes who had realized, at least as early as the 1850s, that the herds were becoming more scarce.[46] From that time on, the Cree, for example, had attempted to protect the herds by calling on the government to limit the hunting of these creatures to Indians alone.[47] Yet, it was not until 1876 that "the North-West Council [considered] the framing of a law to protect the buffaloes."[48] Nothing ever came of the Council's consideration, however, and less than three years later the buffalo had disappeared from Canada. Despite attempts to protect the buffalo, the Cree had largely accepted the fact that their way of life was coming to an end. Star Blanket addressed this concern when he said:

> We have always lived and received our needs in clothing, shelter, and food from the countless multitudes of buffalo that have been with us since the earliest memory of our people. No one with open eyes and open minds can doubt that the buffalo will soon be a thing of the past. Will pass? No! They will die and become just a memory unless we find another way.... The mother earth has always given us plenty with the grass that fed the buffalo. Surely we can learn the ways that made the whiteman strong.[49]

Thus, Canada's aboriginal peoples realized that an adaptation to a new way of life was required, and, like the government, most saw agriculture as the answer.

Many Canadians were likely surprised to learn that the Indians were willing to take up cultivating the soil. Most Euro-Canadians believed that Indians resisted change and had lived in their current state for untold centuries. The Methodist missionary John MacLean described Canadian efforts to "civilize" and "uplift" the Indian peoples:

> We wish to make them white men, and they desire to become better Indians. They believe the native culture is best suited for themselves, and having developed under it, and enjoyed it so long, they care not to give it up for an untried system.[50]

The missionary John McDougall, who in 1876 was a commissioner for the government's treaty negotiations, concurred. He wrote that the

> aboriginal man with his traditions unchanged through the centuries met face to face representatives of another old but ever-changing race to negotiate in peace and friendship their future negotiations in this new land.[51]

Much of the Euro-Canadian populace thus believed that the cultures of the Indian peoples were static.

The perception that the Indian way of life was unchanging proved to be unfounded, however. In the two centuries prior to the signing of the Numbered Treaties, many aboriginal peoples had adapted to the new economies that had been created by the fur trade. That the Indians understood the concepts of dynamic economies is evident when one examines the adaptability of the Plains Cree. Prior to European contact, the Cree were primarily woodland hunters and gatherers.[52] After 1670, however, they had assumed a middleman role in the fur trade. When the fur traders themselves began to move into the interior, thus effectively bypassing them, the Cree had adapted again by moving on to the Plains and becoming buffalo hunters.[53] Although they were perhaps caught off guard by the rapidity with which they were required to adapt,[54] the Indian peoples accepted the fact that their lifestyle would have to change again. What the aboriginals were concerned with, however, was the impact that this change would have on their culture.

The desire of Beardy, the Chief of the Willow Crees, to negotiate in a place that "had been revealed to him in a vision"[55] provides clear evidence that the Indians believed the Treaties to be an important means of preserving Native culture. In Cree culture, as in almost all Plains cultures, the dream or vision was of great significance. The Plains Indian perceived dreams to be sources of powerful knowledge and insight. As scholar Joseph Epes Brown argued, the "nature of the received vision often obligate[d] the recipient to externalize the experience and thus ... share the power with the larger community."[56] To ensure that the Treaty would be negotiated successfully and that his people would achieve what they desired from these proceedings, Beardy sought to re-enact his vision. The government negotiators, however, misunderstood his intentions and assumed that Beardy was merely being difficult. Consequently, the government negotiators would only treat with the Willow Crees at the location they themselves had designated.[57]

The Indians of Treaty Six[58] realized that, in order to protect their culture from being destroyed by the inevitable incursion of white settlers onto their lands, they had to reach an agreement with the government. As a result, they took an active role in the Treaty negotiations. Entering the talks, the government was prepared to offer essentially the same concessions that had been granted under the first five Treaties. Regarding Treaty One, the government had intended only to establish reserves and grant annuities in exchange for the surrender of Indian title to their lands. The Indians, however, eventually extracted additional concessions such as the provision of agricultural and educational assistance.[59] Similarly, the Indian signatories to Treaty Three were able to obtain further allowances from the government including an increase in the allotment of land from 100 acres for each family of five to 640 acres and an increase in annuities from $3 to $5.[60]

The government had acceded to the Indians' demands as they were consistent with their goals of assimilation. For the Indian peoples to be able to cultivate those reserve lands that were to be set aside for them, they had to be provided with the implements and the knowledge necessary to undertake such a task. As Henry Prince, Chief of the St. Peter's band, asked when he was informed that the government wanted the Indians to take up agriculture but would provide them with only land and annuities, "[How could] the Queen expect the Indian to cultivate the land? They cannot scratch it—work it with their fingers. What assistance will they get if they settle down?"[61] Wemyss Simpson apparently concurred when he wrote that the aforementioned concessions were given "with a view to inducing the Indians to adopt the habits and labours of civilization."[62]

Those concessions which were granted under Treaties One through Five, however, did not fully address the apprehensions that the Plains Cree had concerning the protection of their culture. Consequently, much like the Saulteaux of Treaty One, the Cree were able to demand and receive additions

to the Treaty which the government had not originally intended to grant.[63] These new concessions, namely the granting of $1000 a year for three years, the medicine chest clause, and the pestilence/famine clause, addressed the concerns of the Plains Cree regarding their adaptation to, and survival in, their new environment.[64]

The government agreed to pay a sum of $1000 to those bands who were "settled on the reserves and [who were] engaged in cultivating the soil."[65] Consequently, only those Indians who were already considered to be in the process of becoming civilized were to receive benefits from the clause. The government therefore regarded the $1000 as further contributing to the eventual assimilation of the Indian and achieving the ultimate goal of its Indian policy.

The monetary concession itself had been made in response to Cree demands for "food in the spring" when they began to farm[66] In the spring, and especially during the initial years of cultivation, great expenditures of time and energy would have to be made in ploughing, seeding, and cultivating the land. Consequently, the Indians would have to abandon non-agricultural means of acquiring sustenance, such as hunting, gathering, and trapping, to ensure that their agricultural efforts were as successful as possible. The Indians believed that a secure source of food would assist them in their adaption to reserve agriculture and thus help them to preserve a unique and separate identity in Euro-Canadian society.

With regard to the pestilence/famine clause and the medicine chest clause, both were applicable only to those Indians who had signed Treaty Six.[67] Again, the government considered these concessions as aiding the inevitable assimilation of the Plains Cree as they addressed specific concerns that the Cree had expressed. Alexander Morris was aware that "small-pox had destroyed [the Plains Cree] by hundreds a few years before"[68] and that epidemics of scarlet fever and measles had also recently affected the region. In addition, the fact that the buffalo herds were rapidly disappearing had raised concerns about starvation at a time when adaption to a new method of subsistence, namely agriculture, was required.[69] In the words of Morris, the Indians "dreaded pestilence and famine."[70] The government regarded sustenance requirements as being specific to the Plains Cree alone, however. Indeed, with the exception of "spring provisions for several years" as provided in

Treaty Eight, these "pestilence/famine concessions," or any that were similar, were not repeated in subsequent agreements.[71]

The Indians viewed the pestilence/famine clause as a means of insuring themselves against any hardships that they might have encountered during their initial attempts to cultivate their reserve lands including both crop failure and destruction.[72] Big Child, Chief of the Carlton Indians, noted:

> It is well known that if we have plenty in our gardens and crops we would not insist on getting more provisions, but it is only in the case of extremity and from the ignorance of Indians in commencing to work the land that we speak. We are in the dark. This is no trivial matter with us.[73]

Knowing that the buffalo would soon be gone and that agriculture was to become their main means of support, the Indians were acutely aware of the dangers that could arise if they proved slow to learn proper agricultural techniques or if some disaster befell them. If either situation were to occur without the protection and assistance of the government, the Indians knew that they would starve.

The medicine chest clause addressed specific concerns held by the Cree regarding the aforementioned epidemics that had recently swept through the Plains. As a result of smallpox alone, hundreds of Plains Cree had died and many more had become seriously ill by the early 1870s. In one band alone, over fifty individuals had perished.[74] To make matters worse, during times of affliction many hunters and trappers were either killed or incapacitated to the point where they were unable to perform everyday duties. As a result, starvation and economic difficulties (the latter exacerbated by the need to destroy the property of those who had been infected) often accompanied and outlasted the epidemics. The Indians were aware that a vaccine to combat the disease did exist, but it was not readily available to them.[75] Thus, the aboriginal peoples believed that having a medicine chest on each reserve would help to ensure that both unnecessary deaths and economic hardships resulting from illnesses were minimized.

A consideration of the roles of both the Indian peoples and the Canadian government in the Numbered Treaty process, reveals that both parties sought similar terms to achieve dichotomous ends. While both the Indians and the Canadian government supported the concept of reserve agriculture as outlined in the Treaties, each saw cultivation as a way to help achieve different goals. The Indians recognized that their environment was changing and considered reserve agriculture to be the best method of adapting to a new way of life. In making this transition, however, the Indians attempted to protect their people from being assimilated into white society, thus preserving their separate identities. The government, on the other hand, saw both the Treaties and reserve agriculture as the most practical way to achieve the goals of its Indian policy. By utilizing the Treaties to open up the North-West for settlement, the government hoped to bring about that which it considered to be in the best interest of the Indian peoples: their assimilation into white society.

NOTES

1. It should be noted that many different groups of Indians were involved in the Numbered Treaty process, including various bands of Ojibwa, Cree, Assiniboine, and Blackfoot. For a brief introduction to the first seven of the Numbered Treaties, refer to Gerald Friesen, *The Canadian Prairies: A History* (Toronto. 1987). 138–146.

2. James W. St.G. Walker, "The Indian in Canadian Historical Writing, 1972–1982" in Ian A.L. Getty and Antoine S. Lussier, eds., *As Long as the Sun Shines and the Water Flows: A Reader in Canadian Native Studies,* (Vancouver, 1983), 346. Reprinted from Canadian Historical Association *Historical Papers* (1971), 21–47.

3. Allan G. Harper, "Canada's Indian Administration: The Treaty System," *America Indigena* 7, 2 (April, 1947), 145

4. G.F.G. Stanley, "The Indian Background of Canadian History" in Canadian Historical Association Report (1932), 20. Quoted in Jean Friesen, "Magnificent Gifts: The Treaties of Canada with the Indians of the Northwest 1869–76," *Transactions of the Royal Society of Canada,* Fifth Series, 1. (1962), 42.

5. Arthur J. Ray, "Fur Trade History as an Aspect of Native History" in R. Douglas Francis and Donald B. Smith, eds., *Readings in Canadian History* (Pre-Confederation) (Toronto, 1982), 151

6. Ibid., 149–151

7. See A. J. Ray, *Indians in the Fur Trade 1660–1870* (Toronto, 1974) and A. J. Ray and Donald B. Freeman *Give us Good Measure: An Economic Analysis of Relations Between the Indians and the Hudson's Bay Company Before 1763* (Toronto, 1978).

8. Sylvia Van Kirk, Many Tender Ties: *Women in Fur-Trade Society, 1670–1870* (Winnipeg, 1980), 2

9. Ibid., 8

10. D.J. Hall, "'A Serene Atmosphere'? Treaty 1 Revisited," *Canadian Journal of Native Studies* 4, 2 (1984), 322. Also note works such as J.R. Miller, *Skyscrapers Hide the Heavens: A History of Indian-White Relations in Canada,* rev. ed. (Toronto, 1991) and John Webster Grant, Moon of Wintertime: *Missionaries and the Indians of Canada in Encounter since 1534* (Toronto, 1984).

11. J.R. Miller, "Owen Glendower, Hotspur, and Canadian Indian Policy," *Ethnohistory* 37, (Fall, 1990), 388

12. Harper, "Canada's Indian Administration," 145

13. John Leonard Taylor, "Canada's Northwest Indian Policy in the 1870s: Traditional Premises and Necessary Innovations" in Richard Price, ed., *The Spirit of the Alberta Indian Treaties,* (Montreal, 1980), 6. Also see Friesen, "Magnificent Gifts" and Hall, "Serene Atmosphere."

14. Brian E. Titley, *A Narrow Vision: Duncan Campbell Scott and the Administration of Indian Affairs in Canada* (Vancouver, 1986), 27. For an analysis of the government's Indian strategy prior to the Indian Act and how their post-Confederation goals could be considered to be an extension of a somewhat continuous policy, refer to John E. Leslie and Ron Maguire, *The Historical Development of the Indian Act* (Ottawa, 1978).

15. Ibid., 34

16. Doug Owram, *Promise of Eden: The Canadian Expansionist Movement and the Idea of the West 1856–1900* (Toronto, 1981), 132

17. It should be noted that although missions were outside the purview of the government, both the government and the Indians wished to see them established on reserves. As such, although not prescribed by the Treaties themselves, the establishment of missions was integral to the objectives of both the Indians and the government.

18. L.F.S. Upton, "The Origins of Canadian Indian Policy," *Journal of Canadian Studies* 8, 4 (1973), 5. Alsosee Grant, Moon of Wintertime, 85.

19. Owram, *Promise of Eden,* 132

20. Walter E. Houghton, *The Victorian Frame of Mind: 1830–1870* (New Haven, 1957), 47

21. Marcel Giraud, *The Métis in the Canadian West* Vol. I trans. George Woodcock, (Lincoln, 1986), 349–351

22. Owram, *Promise of Eden,* 126

23. John MacLean, *Indians of Canada: Manners and Customs* (Toronto, 1889), 263

24. Abraham Rosman and Paula G. Rubel, *Tapestry of Culture,* 2nd ed. (New York, 1985), 14. See also Ixwis Henry Morgan, "Ancient Society" in Paul Bohannan and Mark Glazer, eds., *High Points in Anthropology* (New York, 1973), 30-60. Morgan's theory concerning the evolutionary development of societies was an embodiment of Social Darwinism, a theory that held that societal evolution represented progress. Historian, Laurence S. Fallis Jr., noted of intellectual thought in mid-to-late nineteenth-century Canada that the "idea of progress by making change appear to be natural, if not inevitable, made change acceptable." Laurence S. Fallis Jr., "The Idea of Progress in the Province of Canada: A Study in the History of Ideas" in W.L. Morton, ed., *The Shield of Achilles: Aspects of Canada in the Victorian Age* (Toronto, 1968), 173. The "cultural advancement" of the Indian peoples was thus held by much of the Euro-Canadian population as being in the best interest of all concerned, particularly with regard to the Indians.

25. [missing from original document]

26. Ibid., 19. See also Carter, *Lost Harvests,* 36–45 where it is noted that some Indian peoples possessed agricultural experience that pre-dated the Treaty era. Indeed, Carter notes that in "nineteenth-century Manitoba before the treaties of the 1870s, Indian participation in gardening and farming was not uncommon." Ibid., 40

27. Friesen, *The Canadian Prairies,* 184–186

28. Leslie, *The Historical Development,* 3–5

29. Richard C. Daniel, *A History of Native Claims in Canada: 1867–1979* (Ottawa, 1979), 2. As Daniel noted, the terms of the purchase agreement effectively extended the terms of the Royal Proclamation to the newly acquired North-West. Article 14 of the Imperial Order in Council that gave effect to the transfer stated that "[a]ny claims of the Indians to

compensation for lands shall be disposed of by the Canadian government in communication with the Imperial Government; and that the Company shall be relieved of all responsibility in respect to them." Ibid., 1–2

30. Alexander Morris, *The Treaties of Canada with the Indians of Manitoba and the North-West Territories, 1880* (Toronto, reprint, 1971), 26. Morris was the chief negotiator for the crown during the negotiations of Treaties Three, Four, Five, and Six. He also revised Treaties One and Two. Jean Friesen, "Alexander Morris" in Francess G. Halpenny, ed., *Dictionary of Canadian Biography* 11, (Toronto, 1982), 612.

31. Ibid., 46

32. Miller, *Skyscrapers Hide the Heavens*, 162. See also Gerald Friesen, *The Canadian Prairies*, 177–8 regarding the funding that the government supplied for the construction of the C.P.R. including "direct grants of $25 million." Also note Carter, *Lost Harvests*, 22.

33. As quoted in Daniel, *A History of Native Claims*, 6.

34. As quoted in Miller, *Skyscrapers Hide the Heavens*, 162.

35. Morris, *The Treaties of Canada*, 171

36. Ibid., 172

37. Ibid., 249

38. Ibid., 40

39. Ibid., 25–26

40. "Hall, "A Serene Atmosphere," 323. Also see John Tobias, "Canada's Subjugation of the Plains Cree," *Canadian Historical Review* 44, 4 (1983), 519–548. Tobias provides an alternate view to that of Hall. While Hall qualifies his remark with the term "somewhat," Tobias down-plays the government's role, at least with regards to Treaty One. I would argue that until settlement became a governmental priority, the Indians were able to do little to make their demands carry much weight. This is evident in the five-year interval between when the Plains Cree expressed a desire to treat and the beginning of negotiations. Again, in the above case, the government acted only when it perceived that its plans regarding settlement might be threatened.

41. Peter Erasmus, *Buffalo Day sand Nights* (Calgary, 1976), 249. Historian Olive Patricia Dickason makes note of the English spelling of Star Blanket's true Indian name, Ahchacoosacootacoopits, in *Canada's First Nations: A History of Founding Peoples from Earliest Times* (Toronto, 1992), 300. Similarly, Alexander Morris noted the spelling of Star Blanket's name as Ah-tak-ah-coop in *The Treaties of Canada*, 213.

42. Morris, *The Treaties of Canada*, 173

43. Ibid., 174

44. John Leonard Taylor, "Two Views on the Meaning of Treaties Six and Seven," in Richard Price, ed., *The Spirit of the Alberta Indian Treaties* (Montreal, 1980), 26

45. James MacGregor, *Father Lacombe* (Edmonton, 1978), 233

46. Carter, *Lost Harvests*, 35–36

47. Tobias, "Canada's Subjugation of the Plains Cree," 106

48. Morris, *The Treaties of Canada*, 241

49. "Erasmus, *Buffalo Days and Nights*, 250

50. John MacLean, *Canadian Savage Folk: The Native Tribes of Canada* (Toronto, 1896), 543

51. John McDougall, *Opening the Great West: Experiences oaf Missionary in 1875–76* (Calgary, 1970), 58

52. It should be noted that there is a historical debate concerning the western extent of the Cree borders. John S. Milloy argued for the traditionally accepted interpretation that the Cree "adopted a plains way of life in the 1790s" in *The Plains Cree: Trade, Diplomacy and War, 1790 to 1870* (Winnipeg, 1988), xiv. According to Milloy, the Plains Cree became "clearly identifiable" when they "own[ed] horses" and had "a different relationship to the buffalo herds and to the Europeans" than their Woodland Cree ancestors. Ibid., 23–26. Milloy, argued that the Plains Cree's "transition from beaver to buffalo, from forest to plain, was completed" during the 1790s. Ibid., 27. Dale Russell, however, reinterpreted the archival and secondary resources and contended that the Cree of the mid-1700s did not shift "from the forests to the grasslands. Rather, they were then, and continued to be, a parkland group." Dale Russell, *Eighteenth-Century Western Cree and their Neighbours* (Hull, 1991), 218. Russell believed that the western limits of the Cree had been placed 800 kilometres too far east by previous scholars (Ibid., 212) and that the change in the role of middleman Cree to Plains Cree was gradual and somewhat minimal as they already possessed experience at living in a Parkland environment.

53. Tobias, "Canada's Subjugation of the Plains Cree," 105

54. MacGregor, *Father Lacombe,* 231

55. Morris, *The Treaties of Canada,* 176

56. Joseph Epes Brown, *The Spiritual Legacy of the American Indian* (New York, 1992), 15

57. Morris, *The Treaties of Canada,* 176. See also Ibid., 225.

58. Tobias, "Canada's Subjugation of the Plains Cree," 106–107. It is important to note that not all members of the Plains Cree considered the final text of Treaty Six to be adequate for ensuring the protection of their culture. Big Bear and Little Pine did not sign the Treaty as they believed it would result in a "loss of autonomy" for their people and result in their being "enslave[d]."

59. Hall, "A Serene Atmosphere," 327–331. These concessions took the form of outside promises which were not adhered to by the government until 1875. That the government was willing to agree to these concessions is evident in that Treaty 3, signed in 1873, contained distinctly similar provisos.

60. Gerald Friesen, *The Canadian Prairies,* 141. See also Morris, *The Treaties of Canada,* 320–327.

61. Ibid., 327

62. *Morris,* The Treaties of Canada, 40

63. The additional concessions that were granted to the Indian signatories of Treaty Six were agreed to by the government as they were not considered to run contrary to the government's goal of assimilating Indian culture. As will be seen, these concessions were in fact considered to help facilitate that goal.

64. That these terms were introduced by the Indians is evident in the transcripts of the negotiations. For example, Morris implies as much when he states of the Treaty that "it is more than has been done anywhere else; I must do it on my own responsibility, and trust to the other Queen's councillors to ratify it." Morris, *The Treaties of Canada,* 215.

65. Ibid., 354–355

66. Ibid., 252

67. Ibid., 354–355

68. Ibid., 178

69. George Brown and Ron Maguire, Indian Treaties in Historical Perspective, (Ottawa, 1979). 36

70. Morris, *The Treaties of Canada,* 178

71. Brown and Maguire, *Indian Treaties,* 38

72. Sarah Carter has noted that there were many problems attached to farming in the North-West. "Crops were often damaged by frost and scourged by squirrels, gophers, and dogs. Grasshopper plagues occurred almost annually." Carter, *Lost Harvests,* 42.

73. Erasmus, *Buffalo Days and Nights,* 252. Dickason makes note of the English spelling of Big Child's true Indian name, Mistawasis, in *Canada's First Nations,* 300. Similarly, Alexander Morris noted the spelling of Big Child's name as Mis-tah-wah-sis in Morris, *The Treaties of Canada,* 213.

74. Ibid., 212

75. Ibid., 204–212

■ Article 2: Canada's Colony and the Colonized

Sarah Carter

'A Unique and Unenviable Place': Canadian Federal Indian Policy

When Manitoba and the North-West Territories joined Confederation in 1870, the vast majority of

Source: Sarah Carter, *Aboriginal People and Colonizers of Western Canada to 1900* (Toronto: University of Toronto Press, 1999), selections from Chapter 6 (pp. 111–130). © University of Toronto Press Inc., 1999. Reprinted with permission of the publisher.

the residents were Aboriginal people, and largely unknown to them, their lives from then on were to be greatly influenced by policies and legislation developed for nearly 100 years in Eastern Canada, and inherited from British imperial practices. The British North America Act of 1867 had given the Canadian federal government jurisdiction over Indians and Indian reserves. In Western Canada, by 1870 there had been over two centuries of European contact, but no formal challenges to Aboriginal land ownership, except within the territory covered by the Selkirk Treaty. The 1870s represents an important watershed for many reasons. The era of efforts to impose the values and institutions of the immigrants or colonists began (although not in earnest until after 1885), and this coincided with the destruction and disappearance of the buffalo economy, just after a devastating epidemic of smallpox and famine. Yet while economic security, independence, and opportunities were to a great extent diminished beginning in the 1870s, Aboriginal people, of course, continued to take action, and make decisions and adopt strategies that influenced the course of events. However, their ability and freedom to control their own lives was increasingly constrained in the last decades of the nineteenth century.

Recent approaches to many of the fundamental documents of Aboriginal and Canadian legal history stress that First Nations were 'not passive objects, but active participants, in [their] formulation and ratification.' To appreciate the meaning of many of these documents then, and the often radically different interpretations of them, it is not enough to have an understanding of the European, written perspective alone. The central policy pursued by the British following the military defeat of the French at Quebec was given expression in the Royal Proclamation of 1763, and this was to form the foundation of the principles governing relations between First Nations and the Crown. The proclamation recognized the 'nations or tribes' of Indians to the west of the British colonies as continuing to own their lands, despite the extension of the new British sovereignty and protection, and directed that the Indians be left undisturbed on these lands. These nations could not sell their lands, however, until they were brought within a colony, and then they could sell only to the Crown, and only through collective and voluntary public action. The proclamation is generally described as a unilateral declaration of the British Crown, but Aboriginal nations played an active role in its genesis, bringing their own considerations, their own power, range of choices, and perspectives, to the agreement. First Nations did not see themselves as dependent, conquered victims of a foreign power, and they proposed peaceful government-to-government relationships of equality, retaining their lands and sovereignty. Different objectives and visions are embedded within the text of the proclamation, and this is why the document is open to differing interpretations.

Beginning in the 1790s, with the arrival of the United Empire Loyalists, the British negotiated treaties with First Nations to permit the expansion of non-Native settlement, generally adhering to the principles established in the Royal Proclamation. At first these were for relatively small parcels of land in exchange for a once-for-all payment. Responsibility for Indian affairs was originally in the hands of a branch of the British military. After the War of 1812, and the decline of the strategic importance of Aboriginal people as military allies, pressure mounted to change the basis of British Indian policy. Missionaries in British North America, as well as a humanitarian lobby in Britain, urged that the Indian Department should take the lead in encouraging Aboriginal people to change their way of life. There was also the example of the United States, where, in the last decade of the eighteenth century, the federal government declared a policy designed to make farmers out of Native Americans, responding to the widely held belief that Native Americans had no choice but to give up their vast tracts of land, with the advantage that they could be taught to farm. From 1828, the British Indian Department sought to foster the creation of self-supporting, as well as self-governing Aboriginal agricultural communities in British North America. In that year the Indian Superintendent of Upper Canada proposed a new function for the department: it would take the lead in 'civilizing' the Indians by encouraging them to settle on reserves, and take up agriculture as a livelihood. Reserves, land set aside for the exclusive use of Indian bands, were now included in the treaties, and the concept of annual payments, or annuities, was introduced. To facilitate the new program, in 1830 in the colonies of Upper and Lower Canada, jurisdiction over the management of Indian affairs shifted from military to civil authorities.

These policies have been assigned 'good marks' by many historians who see in this era the genesis of a humanitarian, benevolent approach to Canada's Aboriginal people. In the British territories, in contrast to the United States (this line of argument goes), there was no hostility, no disposition to eliminate or to coerce; rather, the government played an active role in eliminating reasons for conflict, well in advance of sustained settlement. It is certainly the case that at the same time as the Americans were pursuing the policy of 'removal,' a sizeable portion of the Aboriginal population of the older provinces of Canada remained resident on reserves. Yet there are more cynical views of Britain's 'humanitarian' policy. There was concern about the spread of American 'republican' ideas, and there were good reasons to encourage Aboriginal people to look to Britain as their chief benefactor to gain their loyalty. The concept of reserves and agriculture, which should have ideally allowed Aboriginal people to subsist on a radically reduced land base, permitted a humanitarian veneer to be attached to a policy that was simply aimed at removing an obstacle to non-Aboriginal economic development and settlement.

The direction of the new policy was not entirely unwelcome in the Aboriginal communities. Conscious of the rapid changes unfolding around them, Aboriginal people were not averse to new economic accommodation. With an eye towards preparing themselves to cope with dwindling game and other resources, a number of bands of Upper Canada, even before the adoption of the 'civilizing' program, had used some of the proceeds from land surrenders to fund the establishment of farms and schools with the assistance of missionaries. Aboriginal governments were in favour of agriculture, and the maintenance of the integrity of their society and culture within an agricultural context. For a time beginning in the 1830s there was a progressive partnership in development with Aboriginal governments deciding the degree, nature, and direction of change. They rejected initiatives such as an 1846 effort to introduce the concept of reserve subdivision and individualized property-holding. These councils remained self-governing, with control over their population, land, and finances, until 1860, when responsibility for Indian affairs was transferred from the British government to the government of the United Canadas.

This self-governing status, however, and the progressive partnership, did not last. Colonial legislation of the late 1850s, the transfer of authority over Indian affairs from Britain to the colony, and Confederation radically altered the standing of Aboriginal people. The other parties, groups, or regions that became part of Confederation were consulted and negotiated with, often resulting in contentious and protracted debates. In Canada East, or Quebec, for example, there were concerns about the preservation of their language, religion, culture, and institutions. Aboriginal nations were not consulted, and they were to occupy what historian John Milloy has described as 'a unique and unenviable' place in the new nation. Through the British North America Act, and the legislation aimed at Aboriginal people combined in the comprehensive Indian Act of 1876, the federal government took extensive control of the Aboriginal nations, their land, and their finances. Traditional forms of government were replaced by government/Indian agent–controlled models of government. There was no Aboriginal participation in the formulation and ratification of this legislation; there were protests and objections raised, but these were ignored.

The Indian Act of 1876 incorporated and consolidated earlier legislation of the Assembly of the United Canadas, including the Gradual Civilization Act of 1857 and the Enfranchisement Act of 1869. These acts were based upon the assumption that it was only through individualized property that Aboriginal people could become industrious and self-reliant. With the act of 1857 the Indian Department became an aggressive and disruptive agent of assimilation. It stipulated that any Indian, if he was male, free of debt, literate, and of good moral character, could be awarded full ownership of 50 acres (20 hectares) of reserve land, and would thereby be enfranchised. He would then cut his tribal ties and cease to be an Indian. The goal of full civilization through the enfranchisement of individuals was to be accompanied by the disappearance of Aboriginal communities. In the 1860s there was even more overt encroachment on Aboriginal independence and further destruction of self-government. Enfranchisement had attracted very few qualified candidates, and the tribal governments and their leaders were seen as the obstacles. Self-government had to be abolished. This argument was accepted by the new Canadian government, and the 1869 Enfranchisement Act greatly increased the degree of government control of on-reserve systems. There was to be very little meaningful Aboriginal participation in their own governance. Although chiefs and councillors were to be elected by all male band members over the age of twenty-one, the superintendent general of Indian Affairs decided the time, manner, and place of election, and these officials were to serve at Her Majesty's pleasure, and could be removed by this same official. Band councils were also limited in their areas of jurisdiction, and faced an all-encompassing federal power of disallowance. As historian John Milloy concluded, 'For the original people there was to be no partnership, no degree of home rule to protect and encourage the development of a valued and variant culture, as was the case with French Canada.'

A significant feature of the colonial legislation, later incorporated in the 1876 Indian Act, was the effort to impose Euro-Canadian social organization and cultural values, and English common law, in which the wife was virtually the property of her husband. The act assumed that women were subordinate to males, and derived rights from their husbands or fathers. Women were excluded from voting in band elections and from partaking in band business. They had to prove to government officials that they were of good 'moral' character before they were entitled to receive an inheritance. Beginning with the 1869 act, an Indian woman who married a non-Indian man lost her status as a registered Indian, as did her children. So upon marriage to a non-Indian, the woman would no longer be eligible for residency on reserve land. Even if her non-Indian husband died, her status would not be affected—only remarriage to a status Indian man could reinstate her. On the other hand, white women who married Indian men, and their children, obtained legal status as Indians, and all could reside on reserve land. Another section of the act stipulated that, if an Indian woman married an Indian from another band, she was automatically transferred to the band of her husband, regardless of her personal wishes. This legislation entirely ignored Aboriginal marriage and residency customs, and it was to be keenly resented by women as well as men.

The Indian Act of 1876, which has been described as a 'formidable dossier of repression' and which established race-based laws and limitations in Canada, was originally passed with 100 sections, and this nearly doubled in the next thirty years, to 195. It consigned Aboriginal people to the status of minors; they were British subjects but not citizens, sharing the status of children, felons, and the insane, and it established the federal government as their guardians. Those who came under the act were not allowed to vote in federal or provincial elections, and as they were not voters they were legally prohibited from the professions of law and politics, unless they gave up their Indian status. Through the administration of this act, government agents were able to control minute details of everyday life. There were restrictions on Aboriginal peoples' ability to sell their produce and resources, on their religious freedom and amusements. Many of the clauses of the act were based upon nineteenth-century negative stereotypes of Indians as drunkards, as immoral, as incapable of

handling money. The act criminalized for Indians the consumption of alcohol. It also specifically denied Indians rights available even to complete newcomers to the country. It stipulated, for example, that 'no Indian [...] shall be held capable of having acquired or of acquiring a homestead [...]'

The Numbered Treaties

The First Nations of Western Canada were not informed about this formidable dossier of repression when they entered into treaties in the 1870s. The Indian Act was simply unilaterally imposed, and by not communicating anything about this legislation, government and Crown representatives at treaty negotiations seriously misrepresented the nature of the relationship Aboriginal people were entering into. Aboriginal people were, however, active participants in the treaty negotiations, and the agreements reached reflect the concerns and goals of both sides, although it is now increasingly recognized that these were not fully represented in the written texts of the treaties. There were eight 'numbered treaties' covering the territory of Western Canada (excluding most of British Columbia) made between 1871 and 1899. The written texts of the treaties, prepared well in advance of the sessions, but subject to some change as a result of negotiations, have generally been understood until recently to represent the meaning of these treaties, although that meaning has been open to many interpretations. They have been depicted as just and benevolent instruments through which non-Aboriginal Canada systematically extended its jurisdiction, while offering kindly and generous aid to a population greatly in need of such assistance. The treaties have also been described as tragic misunderstandings, disreputable documents, that were imposed upon a people who had no idea of what was happening. Research that has drawn upon oral history has demonstrated that a focus upon the written text alone projects narrow perceptions of the treaties. The meaning cannot be derived and interpreted from the written words alone as the written texts do not include the Aboriginal understandings. There has also been a Eurocentric tendency to look only at government/and Crown policy and diplomacy with regard to treaty-making, yet Aboriginal societies also had their policy, protocol, ceremonies, and laws. Aboriginal groups had a lengthy history of treaty-making with other First Nations for military, trade, and other purposes. There has been a focus upon the power and authority of the Crown commissioners, but what about the power and authority of the Aboriginal negotiators?

There was significant Aboriginal input with regard to the timing of the treaties, and they were responsible for the introduction of some of the clauses and terms of the agreements. Through treaties Aboriginal people sought to secure not only physical, but cultural survival; to gain assistance in the transition to new economies based on agriculture and husbandry; and to establish peaceful, equitable relations. Canada sought through treaties to acquire legal title to the land in order to complete the transcontinental railway (promised and held out as an enticement to British Columbia in 1871), which would in turn encourage immigration, establish a prosperous economy, and strengthen industry in Eastern Canada. Aboriginal title was to be removed with as little expense as possible, avoiding costly military campaigns. Canadian authorities were also concerned to stop American intrusion north of the forty-ninth parallel, as causes of potential serious international disputes escalated in the 1870s. There were also officials, such as Alexander Morris, who seriously believed that Canadians were honour- and duty-bound to 'elevate' the Aboriginal residents of Western Canada. There was a moral imperative here to export what was perceived as a superior way of life to people assumed to be inferior. It is important to keep in mind that members of a colonizing society can hold powerful convictions that they are behaving altruistically towards the colonized.

Until recently, in written histories the numbered treaties were generally presented as one of the deliberate, orderly, and wise policies pursued by the federal government to ensure the peaceful settlement and prosperous development of the Canadian West. Yet it now seems that there was no particular plan or direction; the pattern and timing of treaty-making, as well as some important clauses, were to a great extent the result of pressure brought to bear by Aboriginal people. In the 1870s Aboriginal people were interested in entering into agreements that could assist them to acquire economic security in the face of a very uncertain future. There was also a great deal of unease and anxiety about the intentions of the government, and concerns were voiced that their land might be taken without consultation. It was learned with alarm that the HBC had 'sold' their land; there had never been any recognition that this company with whom they had traded had any jurisdiction over their land. As legal scholar Sharon Venne recently wrote, 'In present circumstances, it would be tantamount to Pepsi Cola or another such company gaining title to the lands of another country merely by engaging in trading.' Great indignation over the HBC claiming to have sold their land, and then surveying and claiming tracts of land around posts in advance of treaties, was expressed at Treaty Four proceedings: 'A year ago these people [the HBC] drew lines, and measured and marked the lands as their own. Why was this? We own the land; the Manitou [or Great Spirit] gave it to us. There was no bargain; they stole from us [...]' Word of troops stationed at Red River in 1870 heightened fears of hostile intentions. The appearance of railway and telegraph surveyors in advance of treaties caused concern. In central Saskatchewan and in Alberta, the NWMP arrived suddenly in advance of treaties and, without permission or consultation, built posts. Pressure for agreements that would provide economic security was brought to bear through messages, deputations to Crown representatives, and interference with survey work.

The numbered treaties appear to be remarkably similar documents. In each of the written treaties, the First Nations agreed to 'cede, release, surrender, and yield up to the Government of Canada for Her Majesty the Queen,' large tracts of land. They were promised, however, that they could continue their vocations of hunting throughout the surrendered tract, except those tracts taken up 'from time to time for settlement.' Reserves of land were to be set aside. (The precise amount of land varied considerably from treaty to treaty. For example, in Treaties Three, Four, and Five, each family of five was allowed one section, or 640 acres [260 hectares], whereas in Treaties One and Two each family was allotted 160 acres [65 hectares].) These reserves were to be administered and dealt with for the residents by the government. Annual payments (varying from five to twelve dollars) were promised to each man, woman, and child, with bigger payments for chiefs and councillors, who were also to receive suitable suits of clothing. They were promised implements, cattle, and seed for the encouragement of agriculture. In Treaties One to Six, the government agreed to maintain schools on reserves, and, in Treaty Seven, to pay the salary of teachers. The signatories solemnly promised to strictly observe the treaty, to conduct and behave themselves as good and loyal subjects of the Queen, to obey and abide by the law, to maintain peace and good order. Closer inspection of the individual treaties, however, reveals significant differences in the circumstances and negotiating tactics of both sides, and in the written and oral accounts of proceedings. There were unique features to each of the agreements, and different understandings of these agreements emerged.

The earliest of the treaties illustrate the concern about future livelihood that was foremost in the minds of Aboriginal spokesmen, and the effective negotiating skills of Aboriginal leaders. They also indicate that verbal promises and statements were regarded by Aboriginal people as every bit as binding as those which appeared on the written text. The signatories to the 1871 Treaties One and Two were Saulteaux and the Cree of Manitoba. Their concern about future livelihood was shared by Crown negotiators, who clearly indicated that they wished to encourage an agricultural economy. Alexander Morris, who was the Queen's representative in the treaties made between 1873 and 1876 (Treaties Three to Six), felt that it was Canada's duty to make the new wards self-supporting through agriculture. Initially, however, the Crown negotiators did not intend to provide direct assistance in the transition to an agricultural economy in the way of implements, draught animals, and other necessities of a settled and agricultural lifestyle. In Eastern Canada, agriculture as well as education had received official support and encouragement from government, but specific clauses were not included in treaty terms as obligations upon the Crown. This situation changed in the numbered treaties as a result of the bargaining of Aboriginal negotiators. In Treaty One, specific requests were made for implements, cattle, wagons, and housing. The Crown commissioners orally agreed to this assistance, but the clauses did not appear in the printed versions of Treaties One and Two. Controversy soon surrounded the so-called outside promises, the clauses that related to agricultural assistance, and there was discontent over the non-fulfilment of these terms. These were 'outside' only to the non-Aboriginal negotiators to the treaties; to Aboriginal negotiators, who remembered precisely what had been promised orally, they were an intrinsic

part of the treaties. Before the Treaty One negotiations, government surveyor S.J. Dawson had warned his superiors that this would be the case, as 'though they have no means of writing, there are always those present who are charged to keep every word in mind.' Dawson cited the example of an Ojibway principal chief who began an oration by repeating almost word for word what Dawson had said two years earlier. Crown officials agreed to make these a formal part of the treaties in 1875 as a result of the pressure brought to bear by Aboriginal people. The numbered treaties that followed included the terms that provided for agricultural transition in the formal, written treaties.

Treaty Six was made at Fort Carlton and Fort Pitt in 1876 with Plains Cree and Assiniboine. This treaty exemplifies the themes mentioned above; in particular, there was concern about future livelihood. Aboriginal negotiators demanded further clauses that provided for agricultural assistance, and help in making a transition to a new life. As a result of their bargaining, novel terms were added to Treaty Six, including assistance in the event of famine or pestilence, and an additional clause providing for a medicine chest. Reflecting a concern for the future health of their people, the Aboriginal negotiators succeeded in exacting the promise that a medicine chest would be kept at the home of the Indian agent for the use and benefit of the Indians. A troubling aspect of this agreement is that, like Treaty Four, concluded in 1874 at Fort Qu'Appelle with the Cree, Saulteaux, and Assiniboine, a vast number of people, including most of the Cree and prominent leaders, were not informed of the proceedings and were not present. Chief Big Bear, a prominent Plains Cree leader, was not invited by the representatives of the Crown to the original negotiations for Treaty Six.

Studies of Treaty Six that focus upon Aboriginal perspectives reveal fundamentally different understandings of what was agreed to at these proceedings. At the heart of the difference is the certainty that the land was not surrendered, or sold; rather, Aboriginal negotiators agreed to share and to coexist as equals with non-Aboriginals. Given the nature of leadership in Plains societies, and the limits on the powers of the chiefs who entered into treaty, they would not have had the authority to sell or surrender the land. Elders maintain that the land was never sold in the treaty process, and that the wording 'cede, surrender [...]' was not included in the original treaty. They accepted the idea that the Queen wanted to make a treaty to share the land with her people, who were in poverty, and the concept of sharing was acceptable. As Harold Cardinal said in an address to Queen Elizabeth II in 1973, 'Our Treaties were agreements between two peoples from different civilizations to share their resources so that each could grow and successfully meet changes brought on by the passage of time.'

Oral histories with the people of Treaty Seven, made in 1877 with the Siksika, Blood, Peigan, Tsuu T'ina, and Nakoda (Stoney) peoples, indicate that a peace treaty was concluded, not a land surrender. They were asked and agreed to put away their weapons, live in peace and harmony, and share the land. But the emphasis on peacemaking was left unrecorded, and instead land surrender was made the most significant part of the written treaty. In the oral record there is no memory of the issue of land surrender being raised and discussed at the proceedings, and no realization that the land was ceded for ever. There is also little trace of the issue being raised in the documentary record of the treaty proceedings. Government officials were anxious to hastily conclude a treaty with the southern Alberta peoples in 1877, and did not want to raise issues such as land surrender as it could well mean that the treaty would be rejected. The Blackfoot were perceived as war-like, volatile, and dangerous as they were well armed. There was concern about potential Blackfoot alliances with the Lakota, who had defeated Colonel George Custer in 1876 and taken up residence in Canadian territory. To the south, in the spring and summer of 1877, there were numerous small battles between the U.S. military and the non-treaty Nez Percé, whose destination was Canada. The making of Treaty Seven coincided with the Nez Percé moving closer and closer to the camp of Sitting Bull, and there was great alarm about the formation of an alliance.

Research into First Nations' perspectives on Treaty Seven has revealed other factors that would have impeded understanding of the concepts embedded in the written document. In Blackfoot there is no equivalent word for 'cede,' and terms such as 'square mile' could not have been translated properly. In Blackfoot there is now a term for mile (*ni'taa'si*), but it entered the language in the early 1900s with the establishment of mission schools, as

did the term now used for square (*iksisttoyisi*). There was no word for 'Canada,' only a word for the territory of their own nation. The translators at the proceedings were not competent in all of the Aboriginal languages present, nor could they have understood the Victorian jargon of the commissioners. In the written text of the treaty, there are more than eighty examples of gross misrepresentations of the names of chiefs and headmen signatories, clearly indicating that the translators were not real Blackfoot speakers. The names of Nakoda chiefs, who spoke a Siouan language, were recorded in Cree, indicating that the translator for them, Reverend John McDougall, was not competent in their language.

Conflicting perceptions and interpretations of the treaties are at the root of many contemporary issues. Until recently the treaties have been narrowly interpreted by government and in the courts to mean the words on the written documents. Those who prepared these written documents likely did not fully understand or appreciate what the Aboriginal participants believed they had agreed to. From the government's perspective, treaties were straightforward agreements to secure title to land and resources for settlement and development. First Nations draw attention to the verbal promises and the negotiations, and ask that treaties be understood, not according to the technical meaning of the words, but in the sense that they were understood by Aboriginal people. There must be recognition of the 'spirit' of the treaties, and there should be a flexible and generous interpretation of the terms. The Supreme Court of Canada has found that courts cannot begin with the assumption that the written text of the treaties manifests a shared communication between the treaty parties. Instead, the courts must take into account the historical context and perception each party might have as to the nature of the undertaking.

An understanding of the spirit of the treaties also requires an appreciation of Aboriginal concepts, philosophies, and ceremonies. It is consistently explained by Elders of the First Nations that the Creator bestowed sacred responsibilities upon them to act as custodians of the land, and that it could therefore not have been possible for them to even consider breaking this inviolable sacred relationship and to cede, surrender, release, and yield up the land. This would be tantamount to giving up their life. According to Harold Cardinal, to the Cree the treaty relationship is rooted in the principles embodied in the term *meyo witchi towin*, meaning 'good, healthy, happy, respectful relationships among equal parties.' The parties agree to act according to the divinely inspired principles of *wak koo too win*, meaning a perpetual relationship patterned after familial concepts. The relationship with the Crown was understood to consist of mutual ongoing sharing arrangements that would guarantee each other's survival and stability. The concept of *wi taski win*, or sharing the blessing of the land in mutual harmony, provided that the sharing arrangements would be fair to each of the parties, enabling both to enjoy the prosperity of the land and *pim atchi hoowin*, or make a living. Through the pipe ceremonies conducted by First Nations when making treaties for the goals of peace and harmony, the most powerful spirits were called upon to assist in maintaining the peace agreement and accompanying commitments of promises. If the agreement was broken, the powerful spirits of the sun, water, thunder, and wind might unleash their wrath upon the attending parties. The serious consequences to breaking vows made to the spirits was a way of ensuring that peace and harmony would be preserved at all costs. The sweet-grass used in the ceremony represented an undertaking between the parties both that their relationship would be non-coercive and that it would be governed according to precepts of honesty, integrity, good faith, gentleness, and generosity. That these ceremonies took place affirms the sacred nature of the agreements and mutual commitments. As Cardinal wrote in his 1969 *The Unjust Society*, 'To the Indians of Canada, the treaties represent an Indian Magna Carta.'

The North-West Mounted Police

The fact that the non-Aboriginal settlement of Western Canada proceeded relatively peacefully, and that 'law and order' was to a great extent observed, has almost entirely to do with the strategies and actions of First Nations. These strategies, outlined above, featured the negotiation of treaties in order to ensure that resources would be shared, that independence and integrity would be retained, and that a useful partner in the creation of an enriched way of life would be obtained. Aboriginal negotiators solemnly promised that they would in all respects obey and abide by the law. Even leaders such as Big Bear, who rejected 'taking treaty'

for almost a decade, advised and adopted non-confrontational strategies. Despite persistent rumours of Indian 'uprisings' in Western Canada, there were no such events with the exception of Frog Lake (1885; discussed in chapter 7). Promises to maintain peace and good order were observed. Yet credit for the peaceful and orderly settlement of the West is generally attributed in written histories to the NWMP, as well as to the treaties, although these are traditionally perceived as entirely a British-Canadian strategy. Both are often presented as essential components of the vision of one man, Prime Minister Sir John A. Macdonald, who had a grand dream and design for a strong and stable Dominion from sea to sea. While the treaties established the foundation, it was this small force of intrepid few that introduced, and then maintained, law and order, according to many histories of the Canadian West. The force was launched in 1873, and 300 of them, dressed in scarlet to distinguish them from the American cavalry, dressed in blue, made the much-celebrated 'march west' the following year.

A great deal has been written about the Mounties. There are first-hand accounts, academic as well as popular works of history, fiction, and a 'Heritage Minute.' As historian Keith Walden has written, this vast body of literature has made mythic heroic figures of the Mounties. Most of the accounts contain a heavy cultural bias, as they describe these few men as members of a superior and more powerful yet humane culture, bringing stability and peace, law and order, to a wild and savage people in a fretful, uninhabitable land. The force is invariably depicted as having forged outstanding relations with Aboriginal people, who welcomed, appreciated, and respected them. They stopped the whisky trade; pacified warlike Indians; and explained the law to them, administering it in equal doses to white and Indian alike. They stood as sterling examples of manly attributes such as integrity, sobriety, and courage.

As Walden observed, none of this is very plausible as few of the residents of Western Canada could possibly have so willingly accepted the intrusion of outsiders into their affairs. There is an element of plausibility, however. The police were welcomed by some leaders and groups. Red Crow, Crowfoot, and other Blackfoot leaders were grateful that the American whisky trade was curtailed. Major James Walsh *did* forge outstanding relations with Sitting Bull and his people when they sought refuge across the border from 1876 to 1881. Yet the Mounties were outsiders intruding into the lives of Aboriginal people, and their actions were not always appreciated. There were indignant reactions to police posts being placed in the path of the buffalo, without the government first conferring with them about these establishments. A post such as Fort Calgary was placed at a popular camping and fording site without permission or consultation. As Walter Hildebrandt has argued, the police were sent in the vanguard of a 'new order for the white settlers' to pacify the people in what Prime Minister Macdonald called 'that fretful realm' and make the West a safe place to settle. They were more a military, occupying force than a police force. Their function was to assist in expanding British-Canadian influence, without the costs incurred in costly wars of conquest. They served in a military rather than a police capacity at occasions such as treaty negotiations. At Treaty Seven, the police brought and fired cannons, which the Blackfoot found menacing. As agents of the government they assisted in enforcing the Indian Act and related policies of the Department of the Interior and of Indian Affairs, and soon after their arrival they became vital enforcers of extremely unpopular coercive measures and laws that monitored, controlled, and restrained people. They had powers that were unprecedented in the history of police forces; not only did they introduce and enforce Canadian law, they were also given powers as magistrates and so administered the same laws. Many of the predominantly young men who made up the force were also a far cry from the exemplary models of behaviour that most of the police literature would have us believe, and this caused consternation among Aboriginal leaders. The police indulged in considerable drinking, and brawling among themselves and with the 'citizens.'

Missionary John McDougall was critical of the conduct of the police, whom he found to be fond of whisky, drinking all they could lay their hands on, while supposedly putting down the whisky trade. He also felt that some of the laws and policies the police enforced were foolish and unnecessary. Yet despite his criticisms, McDougall contributed to the 'myth of the Mountie.' In his *Opening the Great West*, McDougall wrote that 'here in the mid-summer of 1875 the fact remained that the major sense of all men in this big West was to respect the Police and obey the law. Thus without any bloodshed an immense lawless region was being justly and peaceably administered

[...]' Despite cherished non-Aboriginal origin narratives about Western Canada, the new realm was not, in the last three decades of the nineteenth century, as peaceable as McDougall described, nor was it as lawless as he described in the preceding years. As in other colonial settings, there was considerable resistance to aspects of the foreign presence that caused colonial authorities grave concern, although there was also accommodation to other aspects. Yet it remains the case that in Western Canada there simply was not the record of continuous violence and conquest that characterized not only the western United States, but many of Britain's imperial enterprises. This had as much to do with the strategies and actions of the Aboriginal residents as with the policies of government and the actions of a handful of police.

Bibilography

Borrows, John. 'Wampum at Niagara: The Royal Proclamation, Canadian Legal History, and Self-Government.' In *Aboriginal and Treaty Rights in Canada: Essays on Law, Equality, and Respect for Difference,* ed. Michael Asch, 155–72. Vancouver: University of British Columbia Press, 1997.

Cardinal, Harold. 'Treaty Eight: The Right to Livelihood.' Unpublished LLM thesis, Harvard University Law School, 1996.

Chartrand, Paul L.A.H. *Manitoba's Métis Settlement Scheme of 1870.* Saskatoon: Native Law Centre, 1991.

Flanagan, Thomas, and Gerhard J. Ens. 'Métis Land Grants in Manitoba: A Statistical Study.' *Histoire sociale/Social History 27/23* (1994): 65–88.

Francis, R. Douglas. *Images of the West.* Saskatoon: Western Producer Prairie Books, 1989.

Friesen, Jean. 'Magnificent Gifts; The Treaties of Canada with the Indians of the Northwest, 1869–76.' *Transactions of the Royal Society of Canada,* series 5, vol. 1 (1986): 41–51.

Hildebrandt, Walter. *Views from Fort Battleford: Constructed Visions of an Anglo-Canadian West.* Regina: Canadian Plains Research Center, 1994.

Milloy, John S. 'The Early Indian Acts: Developmental Strategy and Constitutional Change.' In *As Long as the Sun Shines and Water Flows,* ed. Ian A.L. Getty and Antoine S. Lussier, 56–64. Vancouver: UBC Press, 1983.

Morris, Alexander. *The Treaties of Canada with the Indians of Manitoba and the North-West Territories.* 1880. Reprint. Toronto: Coles Publishing, 1971.

Owram, Douglas. *Promise of Eden: The Canadian Expansionist Movement and the Idea of the West, 1856–1900*. Toronto: University of Toronto Press, 1980.

Sprague, D.N. *Canada and the Métis, 1869–1885*. Waterloo: Wilfrid Laurier University Press, 1988.

Stanley, G.F.G. *The Birth of Western Canada: A History of the Riel Rebellions* 1936. Reprint. Toronto: University of Toronto Press, 1975.

Tobias, John. 'Protection, Civilization, Assimilation: An Outline History of Canada's Indian Policy.' In *As Long as the Sun Shines and Water Flows,* ed. Ian A.L. Getty and Antoine S. Lussier, 13–30. Vancouver: UBC Press, 1983.

Treaty Seven Tribal Council, Walter Hildebrandt, Dorothy First Rider, and Sarah Carter. *The True Spirit and Original Intent of Treaty 7*. Montreal: McGill-Queen's University Press, 1996.

Venne, Sharon. 'Understanding Treaty 6: An Indigenous Perspective.' In *Aboriginal and Treaty Rights in Canada: Essays on Law, Equality and Respect for Difference,* ed. Michael Asch, 173–207. Vancouver: University of British Columbia Press, 1997.

Walden, Keith. 'The Great March of the Mounted Police in Popular Literature, 1873–1973.' *Canadian Historical Association Historical Papers* (1980): 33–56.

■ Article 3: The True Spirit and Original Intent of Treaty 7

Treaty Seven Elders and Tribal Council et al.

INTRODUCTION

Otsistsi Pakssaisstoyiih Pi
(the year when the winter was open and cold)

WILTON GOODSTRIKER

Among all First Nations people, there is and has always been a recording of significant events in our history. Our ancestors were just as anxious to leave a record of their story as we are today. I wish that somehow we could let them know that we have remembered, but then again, they probably knew all along that we would.

The stories have been recorded in many forms, through our winter-counts, on the land, but most importantly in the minds and spirit of our people. In these ways, the stories have been passed down from one generation to another throughout the ages.

Throughout this document, we will share the various methods that the First Nations people of Treaty 7 used to record our history.

In the winter-counts of the First Nations of the Treaty 7 area, the year 1877 is referred to as *otsistsi pakssaisstoyiih pi** (Blackfoot—the year when the winter was open and cold). Among the other nations, it is known as "the year when there was great hunger," "the year when the long rains did not come," "the year of starvation and hunger," or "the year when the first snow was late." In any event, to our people it was to be a year which was not going to be normal. To the elders, something was going to be wrong.

It was also the year that a treaty (Treaty 7) was entered into between the First Nations people of this area and the representatives of the Queen of Britain. Interesting is the fact that the treaty did not make its way onto any of the winter-counts of the First Nations people. However, the memory of that occasion is vivid among our people, and the story has been told many times among Niitsitapi (the real people) throughout the years since that time. This story is about *istsist aohkotspi* (the first time that we received gifts and money) at Soyooh

*Blackfoot is an oral language, and over the years several Blackfoot dictionaries have been produced. For consistency in this book, we will use Don Frantz's *Blackfoot Dictionary of Stems, Roots and Affixes* (Toronto: University of Toronto Press, 1995), second edition, unless otherwise noted. This choice is not intended to raise Frantz's dictionary as a final authority for usage, since each Blackfoot tribe has its own legitimate dialect and usage.

Source: Treaty 7 Elders and Tribal Council with Walter Hildebrandt, Dorothy First Rider, and Sarah Carter, *The True Spirit and Original Intent of Treaty 7* (Montreal and Kingston: McGill-Queen's University Press, 1996), pp. 3–5, 11–15, 111–119, 191–201. Reprinted with permission.

pawahko (ridge under water) or Blackfoot Crossing. In our languages there is no word for treaty; the event is simply referred to as *istsist aohkotspi* or *iitsinnaihtsiiyo'pi* (the time when we made a sacred alliance). Among our people, there are several ways to make an alliance and we will examine these closely in the hope that the reader will come to understand the complex ways of our people. The alliance process of the First Nations played a major role at Blackfoot Crossing.

The memory of a people is made accurate with the help of ceremony. This memory is a precious gift among our people.

The Story

"Sit here my child, and watch me close as I prepare the sacred smudge. I will then tell you a story. The reason I will use the smudge is so you will never forget that which I will share with you. And in time, when it is your turn to share, you will share with your children exactly as I will share with you. In this way, things will never change."—Sa'ksisakiaaksin (Laurie Big Plume)

Laurie Big Plume went on to tell me many stories. I remember one time when he told me that "The Christian story always begins with 'In the beginning.' Our story, if we were to write it down, would start with 'Before the beginning.'" I asked him at one point, "How old are our ways?" and he replied, "The ways of the White people are a child compared to our ways."

History has been documented in many ways, and in large part what we know of the past is dependent on information gained through archaeology and to some extent anthropology. Among our people, oral history is perhaps the most accurate. Our people's memory goes back to the beginning of time and in some respects beyond. Our story has come through seven ages, the last one being referred to as *i'kookaiksi* (the age when the people used tipi designs). We are still in this age and will be for as long as the people use the tipi design. This era dates back some five hundred years, and it will be the one that we will concentrate on for the purposes of this document. It is an era that saw the coming of the horse, of the immigrant nations to our land, and of new ways to a people.

One must keep in mind the history of a people when attempting to understand their perspective, their spirit and intent, in their dealings with the newcomers. This story will take you into the world of the First Nations. We will share our history, our alliance process, and our ceremony as they pertain to the treaty. Constant through the ages have been the use of ceremony and the need to document our history accurately. The latter has been done by way of marking in some way on the land, in our winter-counts, and, in all cases, in the oral history, which has been the most accurate method.[...]

Alliances have always been common to our people. There were alliances for trade, for cohabitation of territory. *Innaihtsiini* are sacred alliances of peace between individuals, families, and nations. These alliances find their beginning in the sacred ways of the Plains people, and they go back for thousands of years. Each year one would still witness these in our sacred ceremonies.[...]

STORYTELLING

Storytelling is a great gift among our people. A requirement among our people is for young children to spend much time with grandparents. It is the responsibility of grandparents to teach legends and stories and the ways of our people. In this way a closeness develops between the very young and the old. Our people do not believe in old-age homes.

I was a small child when I witnessed my first storytelling session among the old ones. Those present were my grandfather Many Fingers, Old Man Rabbit, Shot Both Sides, Low Horn, and Old Black Plume. For several days they shared stories, legends, and history. There was always great care in correcting each other when there was error found in one of the accounts. In this way, when everybody left for home, they all left with the same story to be retold at another time. For many years I have heard these stories, and they remained unchanged. It is in this way that our history and heritage have been accurately handed down through the ages. Because our languages are not written, we rely heavily on the oral traditions and on the winter-counts. Among our elders, it is only when individuals could recount stories without error that they were allowed to teach history. When young people were present at these storytelling sessions, they weren't allowed to make noise or be up walking around. From an early age, the young were taught to be careful listeners. A great deal of tenderness and gentleness was required when talking to young people. The elders would talk to the young ones in a low voice, sometimes so low and gentle that the children would think that they were dreaming. In this way a child would never forget.

The teaching of history among our people was given to everyone. Only a select few, however, were privy to sacred teaching, and throughout our recent documented history, this is the information which has been absent. The elders were very careful in the sharing of this kind of information. For the first time, and under the close authority of the elders, this document will attempt to shed some light on those areas which pertain to the events at Soyooh pawahko (ridge under water or Blackfoot Crossing).

SWEETGRASS

The sweetgrass with its three strands represents a harmony which is necessary between the Giver of Life, all that lives, and Mother Earth. It is a harmony which cannot be deliberately imbalanced or separated by man. This is common knowledge among the buffalo people, the Plains tribes. It was this understanding that our leaders and elders took with them to the talks at Blackfoot Crossing in 1877. This was the harmony which for some reason to this point has not been mentioned in the official accounts of Treaty 7. From an early age each young person is taught about this gift of the Giver of Life, and throughout one's lifetime, many times one will experience the ceremonies where it is used. It is a ceremony that played a major part in the talks at Blackfoot Crossing.

THE SACRED SMUDGE

The sacred smudge is a ceremony given to Niitsitapa (the real people) by the Giver of Life. Along with this precious gift there are spiritual laws which govern the use of the smudge: it is used only when there are very important issues to be discussed, the issues cannot be of a negative nature, and spiritual guidance is asked for so that all that will be discussed will be treated with the highest regard for honesty. The sacred smudge is often used in the teaching of sacred information so that the one being taught will never forget. The person teaching or sharing the information will also ask for spiritual guidance, so that he or she will share in exactly the same way as they were taught themselves. When using the smudge, the people present are conducting themselves with the knowledge that the Giver of Life is witness to the proceedings. The smudge is used for cleansing first of all the participants and then the area or environment where the ceremony is being conducted so that everything will be done in a clean and pure way. The ceremony is as old as time and can never change in process because it is a sacred gift to all First Nations. The ceremony itself is a prerequisite to the use of the sacred pipe.

THE STORY OF BLACKFOOT CROSSING

Many stories have been told surrounding the events which took place at Blackfoot Crossing in the fall of 1877, but seldom from the perspective of the First Nations people themselves. In many cases, vivid accounts have been solicited from our people as to the happenings during those few days in September, but noticeable is their reluctance to mention the ceremony attached to the participation of the First Nations. In some instances, the reluctance comes from their not wanting to share that which is sacred; in others, they were not privy to the information. On the part of historians and academics, the reason is oftentimes an ignorance of the complex ways of a people they simply do not know. Thus, in various published accounts, the occasions that involved ceremony are often recorded inaccurately or it is indicated that no record exists of what took place. A good example of this kind of reference is found in documents of the officials at Blackfoot Crossing. The officials simply reported that on the evening of the twentieth there appeared to be much joy and singing well into the night. In actuality, there were prayers and ceremonies in each of the camps of the various nations. This had been going on for several days, and the purpose was to seek guidance as the nations prepared to discuss important issues pertaining to their survival. By that time, all of the various nations were well informed about the deceit that their neighbours to the east and south had experienced at the hands of government and military officials. Many treaties had been entered into, and in most cases, the promises made had been broken over and over. It was common knowledge that the newcomers were not honest people. Before we go into the actual events and talks at Blackfoot Crossing, there is one more ceremony that needs mention, as it was probably the most important ceremony of this occasion. This ceremony took place in the few days prior to the actual discussions of the treaty.

There is a ceremony known to our people as *kano'tsississin* (where everybody smokes ceremony). At times it has been referred to as the "big smoke." It was one of the few ceremonies that brought together all those affiliated in some way with the sacred smudge—elders, medicine pipe holders, members of sacred societies, leaders, and war leaders. One requirement was that those in attendance would bring with them their pipes and knowledge of sacred songs and prayers. The elders conducted the ceremony. They played a key role even in the everyday lives of the people. Important decisions affecting the people were never made in the absence of or without consultation with the elders. The ceremony was, and is, held during the winter moons of our people or, if we use the new calendar moons, from September to March. It began at sundown and ended at sunrise and lasted throughout the night. One could hear the songs and prayers, which are as old as time, with each of the participants asking for guidance in whatever was going to happen. Many of the people in attendance would have their faces painted with sacred ochres to protect them from anything that would be negative in nature. Throughout our recorded history, this painting of the faces has been erroneously termed "war paint." Among our people, there is no such thing as war paint. As with all ceremonies, the sacred smudge was at the centre of all activity. Prior to any pipe being used, the first requirement was to place the sweetgrass on some coals, and in doing this, you would ask the Giver of Life to guide you in what you will say and that you will only hear good things. The pipe would then be taken and again you would ask the Giver of Life to give you courage and strength as the stone of the pipe is strong and that you will talk straight (honestly) as the stem of the pipe is straight. You would then ask the same of those who would join you in smoke.

At Blackfoot Crossing, the ceremony was initiated on the advice of Father of Many Children, who had been present at the signing of the Lame Bull Treaty of 1855. On his urging, the ceremony would give protection against the authorities' apparent disregard of the provisions in the American treaty and the subsequent starvation and hardships of the people. By this time, Father of Many Children was a respected elder and teacher among his people. Many of the participating leaders at Blackfoot Crossing were medicine pipe holders. Each of the five nations had beaver bundles as well as medicine pipes at the time.

Not surprising is the fact that in 1991 the chiefs of Treaty 7, on the advice of their elders, initiated this whole treaty review project by participating in the same ceremony. Their teaching had remained constant in the ways of their people. The songs which were heard were the same songs as those heard in September 1877. This ceremony has remained unchanged throughout the ages, and it is still very much in use today. The chiefs, in authorizing this review, felt that it was important to document the stories of their elders so that, for generations to come, those who would read the story would somehow get a much better understanding of the spirit and intent of the First Nations people with respect to their participation in Treaty 7.

These, then, were some of the ceremonies held in those few days in September of 1877. The sad note is the fact that no descriptions of them found their way into the official accounts of the time. Perhaps those who were responsible for the recording had viewed ceremony as a small detail, insignificant and not worth mention in official documents. To the First Nations people, this was the spirit of the whole process. Only ceremony could seal an accord that would last "as long as the sun would shine, and as long as the river would flow." I once asked Dan Weasel Moccasin where this expression came from. His response was, "The term 'as long as the sun shines and the rivers flow' comes directly out of the way of the pipe. The way of our people is the way of the pipe. Since then there is much sadness each time there is effort to renege on promises they feel were made to them upon a sacred oath."[...]

CHAPTER THREE

The First Nations' Perspective on Treaty 7

WHAT DID TREATY 7 MEAN TO THE FIRST NATIONS?

The leaders who accepted Treaty 7 believed that it was first and foremost a peace treaty. All the Treaty

7 First Nations were unanimous on this point: that through the agreement with the British Crown and the Canadian representatives, the First Nations would cease to war among themselves and that peace would be preserved between the First Nations and the Canadian authorities. Peace and order were essential for the protection of the settler populations that were to be ushered onto the prairies under various schemes initiated within the framework of John A. Macdonald's National Policy. The resulting stability in the newcomer settlements would help to realize the agricultural potential of the West that so many central Canadian explorers and politicians had desired. To some degree the peace process had already been set in motion with the arrival of the North-West Mounted Police in southern Alberta in 1874-75. Their presence and the stability they were able to establish by stopping the whiskey trade were much appreciated by the First Nations people of southern Alberta. Indeed, some historians say that Colonel Macleod became somewhat of a hero among the Blackfoot Confederacy for the authority he was able to establish in the aftermath of clearing Whoop-Up Country of the outlaw traders who had generated so much of the violence that had plagued the territory for the previous decade.

In fact, from the point of view of the elders, it was above all a peace treaty that the Canadian government had desired for this territory. Peace had not been of central importance in the other prairie treaties. The First Nations genuinely appreciated the peace and stability that was brought to the southern territory of the Canadian plains. In return, the First Nations agreed to end hostilities among themselves, promising not to interfere with the peaceful settlement of the newcomer agriculturalists who had been arriving to share the land. There was nothing said among the elders about this peace being in any way linked to giving up land; rather they viewed the peace as being of benefit to all the groups agreeing to the treaty.

In the view of the government, the most significant part of the written treaty involved the surrender of land—not peace. However, peace must have been prominent in the minds of the commissioners who set out to sign Treaty 7, since the tribes of southern Alberta, having had the least contact of any Aboriginal peoples with settler society up to this point, were thought to be a serious threat to settlement.

This fact was most trenchantly underlined by Father Scollen's letter warning the treaty commissioners that these southern Alberta nations were the most "warlike" on the plains. Scollen and others were also concerned about the potential alliance between Sitting Bull's Lakota at Wood Mountain and the tribes of the Blackfoot Confederacy. Thus, it was the Canadian officials, perhaps more so than the First Nations' attending the talks, who wanted to be assured of peace and who raised the issue specifically during the treaty discussions. Certainly they wanted to avoid other international incidents like the one precipitated by the arrival of Sitting Bull or the crisis produced by the Cypress Hills Massacre of 1873.

The First Nations at Blackfoot Crossing were very familiar with the treaty process. Indeed, a number of Blackfoot chiefs had signed the Lame Bull Treaty of 1855, which allowed road development into the West in return for peace with the tribes across the American plains and promised payments to those who signed. This treaty was not understood to be a land surrender but rather a peace treaty, and the tribes at the time were left to move freely over rather large territories. However, the nature of the peace agreed to under Treaty 7 was understood in different ways by the First Nations. Each nation's interpretation of the treaty—just what the peace was to achieve, and who was to benefit—depended on the historical situation that each found itself in at the treaty signing.

The Stoneys, traditional enemies of the other four nations that accepted the treaty, believed that peace meant that they would no longer be fighting with nations of the Blackfoot Confederacy and the other First Nations to whom they had been hostile at various times in the past. As understood by members of the Blackfoot-speaking nations, peace meant not only the kind of peace they enjoyed in the American territories into which their hunting territory still extended, but also the cessation of hostilities with the Stoneys and Cree, and the prohibition of the whiskey trade. But aside from these slight differences in perception, what is clear is that all the First Nations understood the agreement reached at Blackfoot Crossing to be first and foremost a peace treaty. Secondarily, it represented their agreement to share the land and its resources with the newcomers in return for a variety of compensation benefits understood to be their "treaty rights" or "treaty promises."

Blood Tribe

According to Pete Standing Alone, the Blood word for treaty, *innaihtsiini*, means that two sides must "achieve a common purpose." A treaty had to be approached with care and caution. One tried not to be aggressive when negotiating a treaty, as it was a serious undertaking and the consequence of failure might be too great. It was therefore with much gravity that Treaty 7 was pursued. Various interpretive language was used by the Blood elders to describe what the treaty meant to them and their ancestors. Fred Gladstone said that a treaty meant having peace between peoples or tribes; it was a "negotiation between two peoples." Rosie Red Crow indicated that the treaty meant that "we all agreed to be on friendly terms." Wallace Mountain Horse described the treaty process as it had affected the Bloods when they made treaty with both the Cree and the Crow peoples at various times in his memory. He reiterated that the treaty meant an agreement "not to fight anymore." Mountain Horse also discussed the significance of the role of the North-West Mounted Police in pacifying the territory of southern Alberta; this was seen as an important achievement by the Bloods. However, he lamented the fact that the recording of what was said about peace was one-sided, leaving it to look as though the land surrender was the most important issue discussed when in fact for the Bloods peace was most important. Louise Crop Eared Wolf said that the fundamental beliefs of the Bloods would not have allowed them to give away the land: "We believed and understood [that we would] share this territory amongst each other and we also believed that the land could not be given away because of its sacredness; therefore, it did not belong to us or anybody else. The earth is just put there by our creator for only our benefit and use."

Adam Delaney stressed that surrendering land is a concept foreign to the Bloods. Treaties can be made in three situations. Payments are made between in-laws when couples marry; payments can be made between spiritual persons to break a taboo; and finally, treaties are made between nations or tribes to signify peace and friendship or to end wars.

To illustrate the Blood understanding of what happened at Blackfoot Crossing, Louise Crop Eared Wolf related the story of Red Crow: "At the signing of the treaty at Blackfoot Crossing, Red Crow pulled out the grass and gave it to the White officials and informed them that they will share the grass of the earth with them. Then he took some dirt from the earth and informed them that they could not share this part of the earth and what was underneath it, because it was put there by the Creator for the Indians' benefit and use."

Peigan Nation

According to John Yellowhorn, it was the government that wanted the peace treaty, and it was at the government's initiative that the negotiations commenced. People were told that "they would have a much better life if they made the treaty." The reoccurring theme of peace was stated rather differently by Sally Provost: "It's a sign of peace to say we accept the treaty [...] they were just promising and promising, and we were going to get help for the rest of time." That was how important peace appeared to be for the government. Sally Provost also mentioned that the government wanted peace in order to "civilize the Indians." Nick Smith remembered that the main purpose of the treaty was that "we will make peace here with everyone." The "Queen's representatives will make laws for us." Unfortunately, these laws were used "to control us," and the peace that was sued for under the guise of the government "caring for" the First Nations was instead used to restrict and control them. The peace meant that the First Nations' way of life would be changed, for the officials told them, "These are the laws you will abide by." Hugh Crow Eagle remembered his grandfather saying that the treaty was for peace and friendship, "not only with the White man but also with all other tribes that we may have been fighting."

The North-West Mounted Police were considered significant not only for their past service in driving out the whiskey traders but also for enforcing the new laws that were established. Peace would be more complicated than simply not fighting: "You will no longer live the way you were used to. You will be taken care of by the Queen and her representatives. She sent them here. The Red Coat was sent here to watch and take care of you. We will make peace with everyone and we will live in harmony with one another."

For Cecile Many Guns, to make peace meant "no more fighting between anyone, everybody will be friends, everybody will be in peace." Tom Yellowhorn noted with disappointment that the Peigan's initial enthusiasm for the peace treaty grew into bitterness when the seriousness with which they took the agreement was later not reciprocated by the government. In subsequent years the Peigan were "sorry that they made this treaty." For the Peigan the ceremony of peace making was solemn, undertaken with much gravity, especially when they smoked the peace pipe: "They prayed that they would be friends." Yellowhorn thought that the government officials who signed Treaty 7 were serious as well; Macleod in particular was respected. When Macleod said that the First Nations would be thought of by the Queen as "my children," the Peigan thought a great obligation would be attached to so solemn and important a commitment. But disappointment soon followed: "They thought they were going to get money, that they'll own the land and still be free in the country. But this [disappointment] was after, when they found out that they had to stay on the reserves." Macleod had convinced the Peigan that the Queen "was going to treat them good." As Tom Yellowhorn bitterly concluded, in the wake of the treaty "they put up the Indian Act to punish Indian people and protect the White man." In fact, the Indian Act of 1876 had already been enacted.

Elder Ida Yellowhorn remembered: " Long Pipe Woman said that the Peigan leaders understood the making of the treaty as a peace treaty. She said that the leaders said that we should take the White man as our children and share our land with them."

Siksika Nation

The Siksika interpreted Treaty 7 as a commitment to peace in return for government assistance. Philip Many Bears remarked that "the police were to take care of us." For Arthur Yellow Fly, the terms of the peace treaty included "no more killing, no more whiskey trafficking, no more fighting with White men and other Native tribes." The end of warfare and violence was also foremost in the mind of Josephine Weasel Head, who remembered stories about her people deciding that they "wanted to save children from bloodshed and smallpox, also to stop the fighting between tribes." Stemming the violence that accompanied the economic exploitation in the free-wheeling days of Whoop-Up Country was foremost in the memory of Frankie Turning Robe, who stated that "whiskey trading was killing people. Crowfoot was thinking of his people when

he signed." In return for the Siksika's agreement to stop fighting, the Mounties were "assigned to watch over the Native people." There was to be "no more bloodshed between White and Indian."

For Augustine Yellow Sun, peace was agreed to in return for money, freedom to hunt, and rations: "The way I heard it is that treaty money was used to keep us from fighting." The government gave people $12 each for the peace agreement: "The treaty money was used as a token of peace to us at the treaty. Many material things were promised." The Siksika believed the agreement was honestly sought by the government: "We were a treaty people and really thought that we would be taken care of." But Jim Black noted that the Siksika were soon to be disappointed: "Fifty thousand dollars was given out—that was cheap compared to the land we were cheated out of."

To illustrate the point that the Blackfoot tribes had no intention of selling land, Reverend Arthur Ayoungman told a story about Crowfoot that had been related to him by Joe Crowfoot, the grandson of Crowfoot and a former chief of the Siksika himself. A few years after the making of Treaty 7, Crowfoot met with government officials in an evening meeting at his lodge, where a fire was going. Crowfoot took some earth in one hand and, throwing it into the fire, said that the earth would not burn. He then said that if he took money and threw it in the fire, it would burn and disappear. Finally he said that he would rather keep the earth because it will not burn. Ayoungman related the story to underline the contention of the Blackfoot tribes that the earth could not be sold.

Stoney Nakoda Nation

The understanding that Treaty 7 was a peace treaty is very strong among the Stoney. Lou Crawler Sr. recalled that it was "a peace agreement between First Nations and Europe." The nature of the agreement, according to Carl Simeon, was explained by Chief Bearspaw: "He said he [the Stoneys] will camp and live wherever he likes and he will not kill any White man." Della Soldier believed that peace was agreed to in return for land for the Stoney "and to choose more land in the future."

Morley Twoyoungmen remembered leaders of the Stoneys asking why the NWMP cannons were pointed in a threatening manner. The chiefs said, "You talk of peace while there are guns pointing at me. This is not peace … lay down your guns." Similar sentiments were echoed by John and Gordon Labelle. George Ear described the agreement as "a peace treaty between two races." Ear too recalled the request to turn away the cannons "if he [Commissioner Laird] really wants peace."

The Stoneys remembered discussions between their leader Bearspaw and Crowfoot: "Bearspaw told Crowfoot that there were only two options: one was to make war and fight back. But this would make things worse. Women and children will be killed. On the other hand, if we signed the treaty we would be without any worries and would be happy with each other. Crowfoot answered: 'Yes, that is why I want to make peace.'"

"Peace every day" would be valued by the Stoneys according to Joe Brown. "Before there was killing and stealing—because of the killing the treaty was made." The prospect of no more violence was a relief to all sides.

Lily Wesley contended that the peace that was agreed to was not a land surrender; it was meant to "stop the fighting." The stories Wesley remembered suggest that Whites feared an Indian war greatly, that many things were offered to secure peace and that "the White people were very persuasive using slick words." It was clearly the Whites who wanted the treaty most desperately. But according to Wesley, the Stoneys were deceived by the many promises given to get peace. The government ploy was to pacify the tribes initially with false promises so that they would not resist and talk back.

Lazarus Wesley stated that Queen Victoria was highly regarded by the Stoneys and that they solemnly agreed to stop the antagonistic practices that had existed up to that time. The treaty would stop horse stealing, and the parties agree "not to kill each other anymore—to have peace in the land."

In summary, the Stoney attitude was "let's shake hands; as long as we live, we will not oppose each other in any way." This was the meaning that the Stoneys believed both sides understood.

For Lazarus Wesley, the treaty was a comprehensive negotiation between nations: "Countries sign treaties so as not to have war and prevent devastation." The main point of a treaty was "to make peace, to shake hands, to make promises and agreements." In return "we will no longer fight over the land because the NWMP will protect us." Wesley remembered that

John McDougall, as he talked about the treaty prior to the meetings at Blackfoot Crossing, emphasized the peace that was to be gained by accepting the treaty. McDougall vowed: "We will be going to other tribes and tell the others about the [treaty] money to be given out, and that you will lay down your weapons and make peace and there will be no more animosity between the Indian people and the government's people. The government will look after you." The Methodist mission started at Morleyville in 1873 was originally set back in the forest so that it could be defended against attack. Only in 1875, when the NWMP arrived, was the mission church moved to its present location on the valley bench of the Bow River at the junction of Jacob's Creek.

The treaty meant money for Gwen Rider: "It was signed so they would receive money and to have peace." She, like a number of others, stressed that it was the government that wanted the treaty most and this was because "hostility existed between White and Native people."

Bill Mclean had perhaps the most detailed recollection of Treaty 7 as a peace treaty. Mclean remembered the significant role that John McDougall played in talking about the treaty prior to its signing. The missionaries talked about how a treaty would soon be made and the Stoneys would be part of it; they told the Stoneys about a "peace making." There had always been tribal wars but McDougall presented an ominous picture to the Stoneys; he talked about the government's intentions and "how White people would flood the land." Mclean felt that the missionaries had a strategic place among the tribes and acted as government agents, passing along messages the government wanted to get to the First Nations people: "The missionaries told the people when and where the treaty would be made." After reflecting on the nature of this peace making, he concluded that the treaty had been pre-written, even though it ought to have been a matter of "two parties coming together discussing an issue and coming to an agreement." Mclean, like John Snow, thought that the Stoneys had said much more in the treaty making than was recorded; the Stoneys had been able to say what they wanted "but no one wrote it down."

Elva Lefthand recalled that ancestors had talked of Bearspaw having said, " If I sign this treaty, everything I say now will have to be honoured. And there will be no more fighting. The fighting will have to stop." For the Stoneys, peace was the most important reason for accepting the treaty.

Tsuu T'ina Nation

Like the other five nations, Tsuu T'ina emphasized that the treaty was a peace treaty. Hilda Big Crow, Dick Big Plume, Louise Big Plume, Lucy Big Plume, Helen Meguinis, Clarabelle Pipestem, and Rosie Runner all echoed the words of Maurice Big Plume, who said that the treaty meant that Native people and Whites alike would "live as brothers and sisters in peace." The peace, according to Tom Heavenfire, meant that the Tsuu T'ina would be protected: "We were going to live our lives by the laws that White people brought," laws intended to "keep peace" and to "protect families."

CHAPTER FIVE

Treaty 7 in Its Historical and Political Context

INTRODUCTION

Past and present perspectives vie for prominence in the continual debate about what constitutes the history of any event. While the facts of an event remain unaltered, interpretations change and new stories come to light. Such is the case with Treaty 7. The history of Treaty 7, as Treaty 7 people understand it, has always been there, but it has not been part of the mainstream story of Canada. In most historical accounts, Treaty 7 is simply recounted as an event that paved the way to nationhood, making the West safe for settlement by Ontarians and Europeans. But the treaty has a different significance for the Treaty 7 First Nations because in their histories they emphasize issues that have little to do with nation-building. They even disagree with how the Canadian government continues to define its lawful obligations under Treaty 7.

It is only recently that non-Aboriginal Canadians have been willing to listen to what First Nations have to say about their history, and to acknowledge that official histories may have to be changed to accommodate the Aboriginal point of view.

One of the fundamental problems associated with coming to an understanding of Aboriginal-White relations has to do with the fact that Canadian intellectuals generally eschew a colonial framework and scarcely mention imperialism as a factor in the settlement of the West. Told from the point of view of the "victors," or the newcomer settlers, Canadian history emphasizes the perspective of the dominant society. Token recognition is extended to tragedies related to the history of the Aboriginal peoples—the unfortunate disappearance of the buffalo, disease, alcohol—but it is assumed that everything worked out for the best in the long run. Established historians such as Arthur Lower, Donald Creighton, and George Stanley consistently maintain that Canada's Indian policy was honourable, if at times misguided. Intentions were always good. In the long view of Aboriginal-White relations, the "partnership" forged between newcomers and Aboriginal peoples has served both sides well—it was inevitable that Canada's history in the Northwest turned out as it did. The effects of empire-building, according to the establishment historians, has on balance been to the benefit of all concerned in this spread of "civilization." In the words of George Stanley:

The gravest problem presented to the Dominion of Canada by the acquisition and settlement of Rupert's Land and the North-West was the impact of a superior civilization upon the Native Indian Tribes. Again and again, in different places and in different ways, the problem has unfolded itself at the contact of European and savage. Too often the advent of the white man has led to the moral and physical decline of the Native. In Africa, Melanesia and America, the clash of peoples in different stages of development has spelled disaster to the weaker. The European, conscious of his material superiority, is only too contemptuous of the savage, intolerant of his helplessness, ignorant of his mental processes and impatient at his slow assimilation of civilization. The savage, centuries behind in mental and economic development, cannot readily adapt himself to meet the new conditions. He is incapable of bridging the gap of centuries alone and unassisted. Although white penetration into Native territories may be inspired by motives of self-interest, such as trade and settlement, once there, the responsibility of "the white man's burden" is inevitable.[1]

However euphemistically writers like Stanley portray the process, we can no longer ignore colonialism and its imperial context as we write the history of the Canadian West. As cultural critic Edward Said notes:

The global reach of classical nineteenth and early twentieth century European imperialism still casts a considerable shadow over our own times. Hardly any North American, African, European, Latin American, Indian, Caribbean, Australian individual—the list is very long—who is alive today has not been touched by the empires of the past. Britain and France between them controlled immense territories: Canada, Australia, New Zealand, the colonies of North and South America and the Caribbean, large swatches of Africa, the Middle East, the Far East (Britain will hold Hong Kong as a colony until 1997), and the Indian subcontinent in its entirety all these fell under the sway of and in time were liberated from British and French rule.[2]

Imperial powers played a major role not only in physically neutralizing indigenous populations but in creating and sustaining negative images of Aboriginal peoples. The dissemination of these negative images helped those in power justify, to themselves, the removal of Aboriginal peoples from their traditional lands. Said has called this the "struggle over geography": "That struggle is complex and interesting because it is not only about soldiers and cannons but about ideas, about forms, about images and imaginings."[3]

After justifying their right to move into and control new territory, the European powers went wherever they could: "Scarcely a corner of life was left untouched by the facts of empire; the economies were hungry for overseas markets, raw materials, cheap labour, and hugely profitable land, and defense and foreign-policy establishments, were more and more committed to maintaining vast tracts of distant territories and large numbers of subjugated people. When the Western powers were not in close, sometimes ruthless competition with one another for more colonies ... they were hard at work settling, surveying, studying, and of course ruling the territories under their jurisdictions."[4]

The Aboriginal people of southern Alberta were not a pool of cheap labour, nor a new market to be exploited, but they did occupy valuable land and stood in the way of those who wanted to exploit coal, oil, and other minerals in and along the Rocky Mountains. The invasions and intrusions of traders, surveyors, and settlers were experienced by the indigenous people as the National Policy became the driving force behind the Canadian expansion into the Northwest. The same forces at work in other parts of the world were at work in the Canadian West. These forces were defined by Said as follows: "'Imperialism' means the practice, the theory and attitudes of a dominating metropolitan centre ruling a distant territory; 'colonialism,' which is almost always a consequence of imperialism, is the implanting of settlements on distant territories."[5] Imperialism can be exercised in a variety of ways, including force, political collaboration, economic pressure, and social or cultural co-option; it is the process of establishing and maintaining an empire. The accumulation of wealth that invariably takes place is accompanied by productions and portrayals—books, newspapers, visual images—that justify and document the need of the colonizers to dominate the land and make it bountiful in ways that those who originally occupied it have been unable to do. Thus, terms such as "inferior," "subject race," "subordinate people," "dependency," "expansion," and "authority" come into common use by the colonizer.

Those agents of colonialism who exercised power used concepts and languages that gradually became familiar to the colonized and over time became part of the culture of domination. As the agents of empire sought to exploit spices, sugar, slaves, coal, rubber, cotton, opium, tin, gold, oil, and silver, they found it difficult to maintain these huge empires. They needed "immense will and self-confidence even arrogance"[6] in order to rule the indigenous people and convincingly portray them as subordinate, less advanced, and inferior. Thus, a process of "education" began whereby the colonizers tried to persuade the colonized that what the colonizers were doing was right, that they should accept the colonizers' notions of what was best for the lands they were living on. It was, as Stanley put it, the "white man's burden" to persuade the indigenous people that the newcomers' way was the best way. The newcomers promoted the idea of a partnership, but in this partnership the colonizers would try to convince the colonized that what was being done was in their own best interests.

Thus, to understand properly what happened in the Treaty 7 area, one must acknowledge the concepts of imperialism and colonialism, for these concepts shaped the relations between Aboriginal and newcomer, and were behind the forces that permanently changed the landscape and lifestyle of the Aboriginal peoples of the western prairies. The history of Treaty 7 must be broadened to allow the voices of the colonized to be heard.

UNDERSTANDING TREATY 7

The numbered treaties, from 1 to 7, were substantially similar, but each one dealt with particular circumstances and contained distinct clauses. While there can be unanimity on the meaning of certain clauses, in general the texts of the treaties can be interpreted in a variety of ways. It is questionable whether a "mutually understood agreement" was ever arrived at between a people representing a written culture on the one hand and a people representing an essentially oral culture on the other. Indeed, many indigenous cultures throughout the world were at a distinct disadvantage as the nation-states that had been growing since the mid-eighteenth century expanded their interests. In the period from the late eighteenth century to the twentieth century, the world witnessed "the construction of the state in the image and interests of the new middle classes."[7] The expansion of these nation-states saw the subordination of classes, ethnic groups, and races to a dominant class or racial group. The interests of one particular class or group were privileged at the expense of the interests of the others. What emerged in each instance was a so-called national culture that in fact was little more than the culture favoured by those who made up the dominant group or class. By the twentieth century it was clear that the dominant class was the middle class, and its cultural forms and economic interests were favoured. In most nation-states this meant that the culture of the subordinated class, ethnic group, or race was either suppressed or expropriated as nominally part of the "national" culture. National identity and culture were "disseminated throughout the whole of society in several ways, such as the spread of literacy, the 'invention of tradition,' the standardization of 'national' language the establishment of public education, religious evangelism, promotion of economic individualism."[8] What went hand in hand with the valorizing of a national culture was the diminution of other cultures: "Local, 'unprogressive,' and particularist attitudes and practices, such as minority religion, dialect and minority languages, folk customs and traditions rooted in agrarian economy and so on, were either taken over (or tidied up) as folklore of

the 'nation' or discouraged and even prescribed as 'superstitious,' 'barbaric' or 'unprogressive.'"[9]

At times the subordinated groups were described in national narratives as "noble savages," especially when any threat from them had dissipated. What they learned from their experiences was that it was best to become assimilated within the dominant culture if they hoped to survive. Their real culture was somewhere far in the distant past: "Nostalgia could be indulged, and the 'primitive people' could be safely used as a moral, because they could not or soon would not pose any political, social or cultural problem in their own right and on their own behalf. Meanwhile the middleclass reformers of the early nineteenth century rapidly developed strategies for 'modernizing' these primitive people, along with the lower classes."[10] While the "noble savage" was idealized, the cultural practices of subordinated groups were belittled. This condemnation included "merely oral culture, communalism (if not communism) and sociability, apparently improvident and opportunistic work patterns and domestic economy, 'immoral' sexual practices, a tendency to nomadism if not outright vagabondage, 'superstitions' or false religion and an ad hoc and adaptive attitude to 'improvement' and new technology, an ad hoc practical approach to leadership, work organization and the 'moral economy' and 'irrational' or merely 'traditional' ideas of social land economic justice."[11]

The dominant middle-class society was either unwilling or unable to see Aboriginal culture as a successful and long-term accommodation to its environment. Thus, the dominant culture that emerged was a literate society directed by Christian principles. In the Canadian West, the dominant culture had a specific agenda: " Just as important were ideas of economic self-sufficiency and individualism and settled, disciplined and investment oriented work habits and domestic economy. These would be supported by a middle-class sexual morality and model of domesticity and reinforced by a more routine, 'orderly' and hierarchical pattern of leadership in work and social life; and a market-oriented, competitive attitude to labour and its rewards. Finally there should be acceptance of regular institutions of surveillance, control and policing."[12] The agents of this European culture, which was making its way across North America in a search for wealth, were not always primarily interested in controlling the indigenous populations—at least not at first. Early in the contact period, they needed the expertise and knowledge of indigenous people in order to establish their own position of strength. The need to denigrate and then to convert and civilize the Aboriginal only came once the economic advantaged had been secured. Those who at first had been important "partners" were soon to become major impediments to "civilization."

By the time the treaties were being negotiated on the prairies, the Euro-Canadian leadership were confident that they were powerful enough to secure agreements that would allow White settlements to be established and to thrive. Unknown to the Aboriginal leadership, the treaties were to privilege the written culture of the dominant society while denigrating the oral culture of the Aboriginal treaty makers. For this newly emerging middle-class power, the land had to be made "bountiful," and in its estimation the Aboriginal peoples had not succeeded in this. There were no cultivated fields or estates by which Euro-Canadians measure success. In fact, when the treaties were being negotiated, the Aboriginal peoples were viewed as an obstacle to the colonization schemes envisaged for the West by Euro-Canadian elites. The treaties were seen by people like Father Scollen, Reverend McDougall, Colonel Macleod, and Commissioner Laird as expedient means of beginning the process of assimilation through which (they believed) the Aboriginal populations would eventually disappear. It is clear that Canadian officials and religious leaders were preparing the Aboriginal population for the White settlers who they knew would be arriving in large numbers to take over the land. These agents of Euro-Canadian society showed scarcely any ability to appreciate the "communal economy and social practices"[13] of the populations with whom they came into contact. They did not approach the treaty process as equals negotiating with equals but rather as superiors with inferiors. This was a major disadvantage for the Aboriginal leadership, who came to negotiate Treaty 7 in good faith. The attitude of the Canadian treaty makers was paternalistic and condescending—they would do what they thought was best for the Aboriginal peoples, even to the extent of ignoring what the Aboriginal leaders clearly wanted to include in the treaty.

Thus, a major problem with the treaties was that ideologically and culturally the treaty makers for the Crown did not respect the Aboriginal leadership and what it represented: "the white policy-makers' idea of the nature and powers of native chiefs was in part a relic of the earlier political culture of monarchy and court government and the idea that a European monarch was treating a weaker or lesser peer, the chief, in The New World, Africa or Australia."[14] They did not respect the authority or legitimacy of the chiefs with whom they were negotiating, and perhaps they never had any intention of honouring what they were negotiating: "The treaties, circumstances and perceptions of the Canadian Government and its officers profoundly altered the political and social organization of the Native people, according to white assumptions and practices that had been formed in North America but they were also informed by models of social structure and relationships developed in Britain. To some extent, at least, the chiefs were made something like a cross between a Highland laird...[and] an idealized version of the professionalised landed gentleman and the Victorian public school ideal of the gentlemanly public official."[15]

The Aboriginal leaders were allowed to feel that they were negotiating as equals, but the Euro-Canadians did not respect their culture and they saw their nations as inferior. The Aboriginal leaders could hardly be expected to know that these men they were bargaining with in good faith had little resolution to take seriously the discussions that the Aboriginal leadership solemnized by smoking the pipe.

The power relationship between the Aboriginal government and the Canadian government was not equal, and leaders such as Crowfoot and Red Crow were aware that military force was being used to slaughter indigenous people in the United States. By accommodating the newcomers, the Aboriginal people hoped to work out an arrangement to share the land so that both sides could benefit from living side by side. They could not have known that the newcomers expected more than a commitment to share the land, that in fact they wanted to take what they could, even if it meant disregarding the treaties. The Aboriginal leadership did not know about the cultural attitudes that had long been evolving in Europe, which privileged the culture of one class above that of all others. Anything not European was subordinated, and values that were not middle class were dismissed or ignored. What happened in western Canada in the 1870s was only one incident in the global process of subjugation that was played out wherever colonial fragments of the British Empire took hold. There never was a reconciliation between what was actually discussed at Blackfoot Crossing in September 1877 and what was included in the written legal text of the Treaty 7 document. The territorial imperative of the Crown is still imposed today upon the First Nations of Treaty 7.

CONTEXT OF TREATY 7: SOME CONSIDERATIONS

A problem with understanding Treaty 7 arises out of the way in which it has been described and represented to date. Until very recently the treaty has been explained in the context of nation-building, usually in an academic discourse by male writers who are defending a linear approach. Their chosen form is the essay, which usually presumes a monological or single perspective, with a narrator arbitrarily organizing evidence to produce the Truth—a single unassailable verity. Much of the writing done about Treaty 7 assumes this tone of truth, of finality: that we (Euro-Canadians) are right and their (the Aboriginal peoples') opinions are of no consequence. This position has been allowed to go unchallenged—until only very recently—because few of these authors have considered what Aboriginal people themselves thought or think of the treaty; they either never asked, or when they have, they have selectively asked only certain people. The result has been that areas of the treaty that are clearly problematic have been glossed over and the discourse of those who hold power has allowed authors to ignore difficult issues. The consequence has been to discredit the voices of those who disagree with the "official" government line on what the treaty means.

What is clear is that there is no agreed-upon interpretation of Treaty 7; nor is there agreement on what motivated both sides to agree to the treaty. Studies based on a single perspective have failed to stop the nagging questions about the treaty. Over the years academics have come to the recognition that a dialogic (dual or multiple) perspective is needed to understand historical events such as Treaty 7. What becomes evident when a dialogical approach is used is that on some points there is agreement while on others there is divergence of opinion. One of the crucial differences between the perspectives of the Canadian government and the First Nations is that the government side has privileged the written form of representation, while the First Nations side has relied (and still does) on an oral discourse. Thus, while the Crown thought that what was written down was the final word, the Aboriginal people believed that what was said in the discussions at Blackfoot Crossing was as valid as what was written down.

Problems relating to language are at the very core of the Euro-Canadian's difficulty in understanding the Aboriginal world view. The spoken languages of Aboriginal peoples have been ignored by dominant imperial cultures, and the failure to recognize or acknowledge Aboriginal culture constitutes a form of cultural subjugation. As Sakej Youngblood-Henderson has written: "Everywhere we are born into language, everywhere it binds our consciousness. Its mystery and development reflect our particular habits, those of our linguistic heritage. Our language [or languages] contain the essential ways in which we experience and interact with our culture. Thus, our linguistic understanding [the world view in English] is our map that a particular language creates in order to navigate the larger worldview. These understandings become, then, in some sense, most of the worldview."[16]

Youngblood-Henderson argues that the noun-centred objectifying languages of the Eurocentric world view help users of these languages to reify and classify the world environment. By contrast, Aboriginal languages are verb-centred and reflect an apprehension of the world that is in a constant state of flux or change. Thus, there are very few fixed or rigid objects in the Aboriginal world view: "With the fluidity of semantic-phonemes comprising the verb sounds, every speaker can create new vocabulary 'on the fly,' custom tailored to meet the experience of movement to express the very finest nuances of meanings."[17] Youngblood-Henderson maintains that such different ways of seeing the world mean that these languages cannot be easily translated—that simply translating a word by itself does not relay with it the world view that the language as a whole contains.

The fundamental assumptions underlying European and Aboriginal languages are so radically different that simple translation is impossible. For the Aboriginal, "to see things as permanent is to be confused about everything: an alternative to that understanding is the need to create temporary harmonies through alliances and relationships among all forms and forces—this process is a never-ending source of wonder to the indigenous mind and to other forces who contribute to the harmony."[18]

To ignore Aboriginal languages and to insist on assimilation or "cognitive imperialism" is to deny and destroy the Aboriginal sacred understandings. Youngblood-Henderson concludes that "cultural and cognitive racism must be exposed and resolved. Under modern thought, at least in theory, every language describes the world completely, though each in its own way. The Aboriginal languages and worldviews must be strengthened and developed with their own contexts. Any interference is domination, both cognitively and culturally. Thus every Aboriginal language has the right to exist without conforming to Eurocentric languages or worldviews ... The failure to admit differences in worldview is also domination."[19]

Thus, a fundamental problem continues to exist in the discourse between those who have held power and those who have not or those who have represented a new way of life and the indigenous populations.[...]

Notes

Chapter Five

1. Stanley, *The Birth of Western Canada*, 194.
2. Said, *Culture and Imperialism*, 5–6.
3. Ibid., 7.
4. Ibid., 8.
5. Ibid., 9.
6. Ibid., 11.
7. Kelly, "Class, Race and Cultural Revolution," 19.
8. Ibid., 20.
9. Ibid., 21.
10. Ibid.
11. Ibid.
12. Ibid., 22.
13. Ibid., 24.
14. Ibid., 35.
15. Ibid., 36.
16. Youngblood-Henderson, "Governing the Implicate Order," 3.
17. Ibid., 8.
18. Ibid., 9.
19. Ibid., 19.

THE EARLY CANADIAN WOMEN'S MOVEMENT AND THE STRUGGLE FOR THE VOTE, 1870s–1918

Lynne Marks
University of Victoria

THE EARLY CANADIAN WOMEN'S MOVEMENT AND THE STRUGGLE FOR THE VOTE, 1870s–1918

● Introduction by Lynne Marks

▲ **Primary Sources**

Document 1: Points in the Laws of British Columbia Regarding the Legal Status of Women, 1911

Document 2: Excerpt from Nellie McClung *In Times Like These* (1915)

Document 3: Nellie McClung

Document 4: Canada Needs a Clean-up Week (1915)

Document 5: The Woman Question
Stephen Leacock

Document 6: Women's Christian Temperance Union (WTCU) Excerpts (1880, 1888, 1900, 1911)

Document 7: The Door Steadily Opens (1910)

Document 8: "A Nice Mess You Men Folks Make of Running a House" (date unknown)

■ **Secondary Sources:**

Article 1: 'When the Mother of the Race Is Free': Race, Reproduction, and Sexuality in First Wave Feminism
Mariana Valverde

Article 2: Rediscovering our Foremothers Again: Racial Ideas of Canada's Early Feminists, 1885–1945
Janice Fiamengo

● INTRODUCTION

Lynne Marks

In mid-nineteenth century Canada, women lacked many of the rights that women today take for granted. Then it was assumed that a woman's primary role was to remain in the home as a wife and mother. This role was captured in the ideal image of "the Angel in the Home." Women were expected to create warm, moral, and nurturing havens for their children, as well as for their husbands who had to venture into the "rough and tumble" public sphere to earn money to support their families. This ideal contrasted sharply with reality for the many working-class women who had to venture beyond the home to contribute to the family income. For the middle-class women who could afford to remain in the home, this "domestic ideology", as it has been called, very much limited their options. Because a woman's role was to be a wife and mother, university education was closed to women, as such education was considered damaging to women's reproductive functions and inappropriate to their future roles. Access to professions such as medicine and law was also denied. Although single women had property rights, upon marriage women lost these rights, including any wages that they might earn. All of this came under their husband's control.[1] Women also lacked the right to vote or to hold public office, as this was considered far outside their "proper sphere" of the home.

In the United States, where similar restrictions applied, women started publicly debating and organizing around these issues in the 1830s and 1840s, but this did not begin to happen in Canada until the 1870s. Some of what we would consider the first feminist struggles took place over higher education, with women first gaining access to certain Canadian universities in the 1870s and early 1880s. However, even when it became possible, only a tiny minority of women were able to attend university.

Many more women were involved in activities beyond the home through local churches, since Christian faith and practice were particularly important to women in this period. By the 1870s and 1880s women became increasingly involved in Christian women's organizations not only at the level of their local church, but also through provincial and national organizations, particularly missionary societies, but also Christian women's organizations for social reform. The 1880s and 1890s saw increasing concern about social issues among middle-class men and women, as the effects of industrialization and urbanization made poverty more visible, and as increasing immigration from non-British countries led to growing concerns about the need to maintain the white, English-Canadian nature of the nation. One example of a woman's Christian social reform group was the Young Women's Christian Association (YWCA), an organization intended to safeguard young working-class women who were coming to the cities to work by providing them with respectable boarding houses and wholesome amusements. In Quebec, middle-class francophone women became involved in the Fédération Nationale St.-Jean-Baptiste. This organization developed programs to assist poorer women and children, for example, by providing pasteurized milk to children and babies, in cities where unpasteurized milk was a major cause of high infant mortality rates.

Women involved in social reform argued that white middle-class, Christian women needed to get involved in these efforts as their innate moral and nurturing qualities, so important to their roles in the home, were also crucial if they were to help improve and "mother" the larger society, particularly poorer and non-white women and children. In this way, they used the existing ideas about women's domestic roles to justify their activity within the broader society.

Another influential women's organization was the Women's Christian Temperance Union (WCTU). The WCTU had a number of social and moral reform objectives, but its central concern was over the use and abuse of alcohol. There were very few restrictions on the sale of alcohol in this period, and drinking was seen as the cause of a number of major social problems. Because it was considered socially unacceptable for women to drink at this time, most of the problems associated with drinking were linked to men. The WCTU thus campaigned against alcohol as a major cause of wife abuse and other violence. Members argued that the free availability of alcohol led many husbands and fathers to drink away their earnings, leaving many wives and children in deepest poverty. The WCTU supported temperance education, and developed programs to encourage both children and adults to promise to not drink alcohol, but their main tactic was to call for prohibition, government legislation against the sale of alcohol. Their largely fruitless efforts to convince governments to bring in prohibition legislation helped to convince the women of the WCTU that they needed to have the franchise, the right to vote, if they were going to have any impact on government alcohol policy. In the 1880s the WCTU thus increasingly called for women's right to vote not primarily because women were equal to men and thus entitled to the vote, but because they held unique moral qualities to improve society. While there were a few women's suffrage organizations in Canada in this decade, the WCTU was the largest women's organization calling for women's suffrage in Canada until the early twentieth century.

As the 1880 WCTU excerpt reveals, these women demanded the vote so that women would be able to vote to protect their homes and families from the ravages of alcohol. Historians have called this kind of justification for women's rights "maternal feminism," in that the justification for women's right to vote, and for other rights, was on the basis of what were considered to be women's particular maternal qualities. We can see these attitudes in some of the cartoons included in the module. Sometimes women's organizations also used what have been called "equal rights feminist" arguments (i.e., it was only just and fair that women should have the same political rights as men). In a social context where there was a great deal of hostility to women gaining political rights (see Stephen Leacock's piece), it may have seemed politically safer to argue for the vote on the basis of what were seen as women's more conventional qualities of morality, purity, and maternal nurturing abilities. However, Stephen Leacock's piece shows that arguments about how women would reform society if they got the vote did not always convince opponents. Leacock, who liked his scotch, was also opposed to women's suffrage because he feared if they got the vote, prohibition would soon follow. He was right.

As we see in WCTU excerpts from 1888 and 1911, a more racist argument was also used by the WCTU, as well as by other women fighting for the suffrage. These women were almost exclusively white, primarily middle class, and were very proud to see themselves as loyal subjects of the British empire, as we see in the description of the WCTU float in Victoria. Like most white Canadians of British background, they believed themselves superior to non-British immigrants, and they felt that it was very unfair that they be denied the right to vote, while immigrant men could vote.

How historians should deal with these racist elements of the women's suffrage movement has been a subject of intense debate, as we can see in the Valverde and Fiamengo pieces. These concerns came to the fore during World War I. In the years immediately before World War I, many more women and women's organizations came to support the right to vote, including farm women's organizations, and many working-class women, who felt that acquiring the vote was important not only for women's equality and to help "clean up" society, as earlier feminists had argued, but also to increase the political clout of farmers and working people, and allow them to gain much needed reforms. The emergence of the suffrage movement is thus a complex mix of attitudes not only about gender, but also about race and class.

By 1914 when World War I began, the majority of those who supported women's right to vote, including leading advocates of suffrage such as Nellie McClung, supported women's war efforts as part of the way that Canadian women could do their part for Britain. Women's efforts in supporting the war, both in taking on non-traditional jobs so men could go and fight overseas, and in the range of volunteer work that women took on during the war, also helped to justify women's right to attain the suffrage.

In addition, maternal feminist arguments, in which women argued that granting women the right to vote would help to create a better and purer society, had increasing resonance during World War I, when there was a strong feeling that the deaths of so many soldiers in France had to lead to the creation of a better society after the war. Partly as a result of such arguments, women began to acquire the provincial franchise during the war, first in the prairie provinces of Alberta, Saskatchewan, and Manitoba in 1916, and in British Columbia in 1917.

At the federal level, some women received the vote in a way intended much more as a political ploy for Robert Borden, the prime minister, than for equality for women. By 1916 Borden came to believe that conscription (mandatory male enlistment in the armed forces) was necessary to help reinforce Canadian troops in Europe and to give Canada more credibility with British leaders. However, he had to call an election before bringing in conscription, so the election was fought primarily on the basis of this issue. To ensure his victory, Borden passed the *Wartime Elections Act* of 1917, which took the vote away from those he thought would oppose the government, including all voters who came from enemy countries and had become Canadian citizens since 1902. The Act gave the vote to women who were the mothers, wives, and sisters of Canadian soldiers fighting overseas, who he assumed would support conscription. This effort worked, and Borden's government won the election. The election divided the suffragists, many of whom opposed this measure as a blatant political ploy. But many also supported it, because they believed that conscription was necessary to help Canada win the war. Only a very few, such as Francis Marion Beynon, a Western feminist who opposed the war itself, also opposed the racism of taking the vote away from so many immigrant men.

In 1918, women were granted the federal franchise on the same basis as men. This still did not mean that all Canadian women were enfranchised. Women in Quebec did not gain the provincial franchise until 1940, because the Catholic Church hierarchy in Quebec, and some French-Canadian nationalist leaders, felt particularly strongly that if women voted in the public sphere, they would be abandoning their traditional God-given place in the home. Any threat to the home was seen as a threat to the survival of the French Canadian nation.

Other Canadian women did not receive the vote until after the Second World War. Like Chinese and East Indian men, Chinese and East Indian women did not receive the right to vote in Canada until 1947. Japanese women and men did not acquire the right to vote until 1949, and the franchise was not available to all Canadian First Nations women and men until 1960.

While 1918 did not see all Canadian women gain the franchise, the white women who had been fighting for the vote saw the granting of the franchise as a great victory. Historians looking back on these events have labelled this suffrage victory as the end of the "first wave" of the women's movement (with the second wave beginning with the women's liberation movement of the 1960s). More recently, scholars have recognized that feminist activism remained strong in the years between 1918 and the 1960s, with women struggling for increased rights on a number of fronts, including the right to be legally defined as 'persons', as well as for greater equality within family and property law and the workplace, and improved resources for women's health, including legal access to birth control. In some of these struggles, the racist assumptions of the suffragists remained. For example, many feminists in the 1920s and 1930s advocated the sterilization of people they defined as mentally challenged, who they deemed "unfit" to have children, because they believed this would improve the health of the nation. In many other ways, however, the efforts of these early feminists had a major positive impact on the lives of many Canadian women.

NOTE

1. Over the course of the nineteenth century, married women's right to property did improve, although these improvements were uneven across the country. Document 1 notes that significant inequities remained in British Columbia regarding married women's property rights in the early twentieth century.

QUESTIONS

1. What kinds of arguments did women use in arguing for the vote? Why do you think they used these arguments?
2. What is Valverde arguing about the role of racism among early feminists? What is Fiamengo arguing? In what ways do they differ, and in what ways do they agree?
3. Do you prefer Valverde's article or Fiamengo's? Whose arguments did you find more convincing, and why?
4. What do you think about Nellie's McClung's arguments in *In Times Like These?* Do you think her work here more closely reflects Fiamengo's arguments about first-wave feminists, or Valverde's? Are any of McClung's concerns still relevant today?
5. Why did Stephen Leacock not support women's suffrage? What was his belief about women's role and women's nature?
6. Look closely at the description of the WCTU float in the excerpts from the WCTU; how many things can this float tell us about the WCTU's program, membership, values, and beliefs?

FURTHER READINGS

Bacchi, Carol Lee, *Liberation Deferred?: The Ideas of the English-Canadian Suffragists, 1877–1918* (Toronto: University of Toronto Press, 1983).

Cook, Sharon Anne, *"Through Sunshine and Shadow": the Woman's Christian Temperance Union, Evangelicalism, and Reform in Ontario, 1874–1930* (Montreal and Kingston: McGill-Queen's University Press, 1995).

Forestell, Nancy, "Mrs. Canada Goes Global" *Atlantis* Vol.30, No.1 (2005), pp. 7–20.

Kealey Linda, ed., *A Not Unreasonable Claim: Women and Reform in Canada, 1880s–1920s* (Toronto: Women's Educational Press, 1979).

McKay, Ian, "The Woman Question," *Reasoning Otherwise: Leftists and the People's Enlightenment in Canada, 1890–1920* (Toronto: Between the Lines, 2008).

Valverde, Mariana, *The Age of Light, Soap and Water: Moral and Social Reform in English Canada, 1885–1925* (Toronto: McClelland and Stewart, 1991).

▲ Document 1: Points in the Laws of British Columbia Regarding the Legal Status of Women

Note on front page of pamphlet: This pamphlet was written by Mrs. C.R. Townley in 1911 when she was president of Vancouver Branch, Political Equality League. She did not use her name as she felt it might be less effective if people knew it had been written by a woman.

The British Columbia Political Equality League is an organization of men and women who, convinced of the fairness and wisdom of allowing to men and women equally a voice in the government of their country are working with the object of obtaining for the women of this province a like municipal and parliamentary franchise as that now enjoyed by men. It was formed in the early months of this year (1911). It is a Provincial Society having local branches. [. . .]

There is nothing of the "suffragette" [the term for the more radical women in Britain who were campaigning for the franchise for women—some of these women went on hunger strikes, broke windows and chained themselves to fences to bring further attention to their cause] in the sane and quiet movement that is taking place in our midst. It is rather the gradual outcome of thought and education amongst an admittedly intelligent, observant and progressive people.

With regard to any change, there are always a few narrow and determinedly prejudiced persons of both sexes who refuse to look into a question on its merits—who apparently prefer not to inform themselves lest they should be convinced—but they grow fewer daily. It is the experience of the Political Equality League that the majority of men are not opposed to suffrage for women and that practically all our loyal women are united in the desire for a voice in the government of the country they love [...]

Points in the Laws of British Columbia Regarding Legal Status of Women

The British system of law is admittedly the best and fairest in the world. Yet times and circumstances of life change and even in law there is evolution. Constant amendments to existing laws go on. Sometimes a step backward is taken, more often a forward movement. The general principle in our laws is based on justice to all [...]

In our own province there are in existence certain laws that are not suited to the social progress of this day and generation and yet that remain unchanged.

Some of these are of vital interest as intimately touching family life and the solidity of the home. They bear upon the legal status of women, the protection and care of children, property rights and the distribution of estates [...] laws of property, status and civil rights are provincial matters. [. . .]

A wife is not entitled to dower in any land in the ownership of her husband. [Dower was a woman's right to a life interest in a third of the property held by her husband. Dower rights prevented a husband from selling property without her consent. The concept of dower existed in many other British jurisdictions.] He may sell or give it away without consulting

Source: Issued by the Vancouver Branch of the British Columbia Political Equality League, UBC Special Collections.

I would like to thank Melanie Ihmels for bringing this source to my attention—L. Marks.

her. It is his absolutely. He may dispose of it by his will as he sees fit. They may have settled on land, or earned the property by working together, or the wife's money may have helped to buy it—but he may leave her penniless if he so desire. If he should die *without* a will, the widow has a one-third interest for life in all real estate owned by him at his death (provided the deeds are not made out—as they often are—in a form that bars all possible dower) [...]

With regard to guardianship of children:

The father has sole authority in the education and disposition of the child, although the mother is equally responsible with the father for the maintenance of the child.

The father has the right to arrange by will the guardianship and education of his child (even if unborn), till it shall be twenty-one years of age. No matter how unsuitable she may find this to be, the widow must abide by it. The mother may, however, petition the court for the care of the child until seven years of age if other guardian has been appointed by the father and after it is seven years old to have the right of access (go to see) to it.

These privileges are usually graciously granted her—but they are privileges, not rights. A mother has no right of possession in her legitimate child.

By going to law it is often possible to modify or rearrange matters. It is said "There is always a remedy in equity." But often this is no remedy, because of the expense entailed.

The consent of parents and guardians is necessary to the marriage of minors of either sex under twenty-one years of age—but the consent of the mothers is not needed if the father (or guardian appointed by will of the father) gives consent.

A girl of twelve years of age or a boy of fourteen years of age may be legally married in this province.

In the case of a deserted wife: The husband has the right to come and collect the earnings of their minor children. The wife may obtain an order of protection from the court to prevent this. But the very woman who needs this most, often is ignorant, or so situated by reason of distance or family cares that she cannot readily take the necessary steps.

The husband also may collect and use his wife's wages under certain circumstances.

These laws may well make men think. They are naturally of special interest to women—in whose lives "children" and "home" are the very watchwords of existence.

Though home is popularly regarded as woman's sphere in life, her children as her especial care and interest, it would seem that in reality the very roof may be sold over her head, the children she has borne be taken from her, and her little daughter of twelve years of age given in marriage without the mother's consent.

Cases influenced by these conditions come to the notice of every philanthropic society daily. Wives and families that might have been provided for are left destitute. Worthless husbands subdue their wives to their wishes by threatening to take their children away ...

The government has been approached at various times by women of the province with requests for amendments to these laws. It is not that men are against alterations, but that they have so many other political interests at heart—and these things do not restrict their personal liberty and legal status as they do that of women [...]

Ours is a progressive country. The men of British Columbia are in the main, broad-minded as its wide flung area—sufficiently free from prejudice and old world trammels to consider with dispassionate common-sense and freedom from arrogant egotism, the possibility of advanced legislation along national lines. They know too well the worth, comradeship, and good judgement of the women who have stood by them in their efforts to build up homes in a new land—who have their interest and prosperity at heart—to deny them (if they want it) the voice in their country's welfare that is eagerly pressed upon fresh-coming ignorant foreigners as soon as possible by politicians. In Australia where women have the franchise, there is admittedly the best domestic legislation in the world [...]

▲ Document 2: Excerpt from *In Times Like These*

Nellie L. McClung

This seems to be a good time for us to jar ourselves lose [sic] from some of the prejudices and beliefs which we have outgrown. It is time for readjustment surely, a time for spiritual and mental housecleaning, when we are justified in looking things over very carefully and deciding whether or not we shall ever need them again.

Some of us have suspected for a long time that a good deal of the teaching of the world regarding women has come under the general heading of 'dope.' Now 'dope' is not a slang word, as you may be thinking, gentle reader. It is a good Anglo-Saxon word (or will be), for it fills a real need, and there is none other to take its place. 'Dope' means anything that is calculated to soothe, or hush, or put to sleep. 'Sedative' is a synonym, but it lacks the oily softness of 'dope.'

One of the commonest forms of dope given to women to keep them quiet is the one referred to in a previous chapter: 'The hand that rocks the cradle rules the world.' It is a great favorite with politicians and not being original with them it does contain a small element of truth. They use it in their pre-election speeches, which they begin with the honeyed words: 'We are glad to see we have with us this evening so many members of the fair sex; we are delighted to see that so many have come to grace our gathering on this occasion; we realize that a woman's intuition is ofttimes truer than a man's reasoning, and although women have no actual voice in politics, they have something far more strong and potent—they have the wonder power of indirect influence.' Just about here comes in 'the hand that rocks!'

Having thus administered the dope, in this pleasing mixture of molasses and soft soap, which is supposed to keep the 'fair sex' quiet and happy for the balance of the evening, the aspirant for public honors passes on to the serious business of the hour, and discusses the affairs of state with the electorate. Right here, let us sound a small note of warning. Keep your eye on the man who refers to women as the 'fair sex'—he is a dealer in dope!

One of the oldest and falsest of our beliefs regarding women is that they are protected—that some way in the battle of life they get the best of it. People talk of men's chivalry, that vague, indefinite quality which is supposed to transmute the common clay of life into gold.

Chivalry is a magic word. It seems to breathe of foreign strands and moonlight groves and silver sands and knights and earls and kings; it seems to tell of glorious deeds and waving plumes and prancing steeds and belted earls—and things!

People tell us of the good old days of chivalry when womanhood was really respected and reverenced—when brave knight rode gaily forth to die for his lady love. But in order to be really loved and respected there was one hard and fast condition laid down, to which all women must conform—they must be beautiful, no getting out of that. They simply had to have starry eyes and golden hair, or else black as a raven's wing; they had to have pale, white, and haughty brow, and a laugh like a ripple of magic. Then they were all right and armored knights would die for them quick as wink!

Source: *In Times Like These,* with an introduction by Veronica Strong-Boag (University of Toronto Press, 1972 [1915]), pp. 38–55, 57–58, 84–88, 90–91, 93–94.

The homely women were all witches, dreadful witches, and they drowned them, on public holidays, in the mill pond!

People tell us now that chivalry is dead, and women have killed it, bold women who instead of staying at home, broidering pearls on a red velvet sleeve, have gone out to work—have gone to college side by side with men and have been so unwomanly sometimes as to take the prizes away from men. Chivalry cannot live in such an atmosphere. Certainly not!

Of course women can hardly be blamed for going out and working when one remembers that they must either work or starve. Broidering pearls will not boil the kettle worth a cent! There are now thirty per cent of the women of the U.S.A. and Canada, who are wage-earners, and we will readily grant that necessity has driven most of them out of their homes. Similarly, in England alone, there are a million and a half more women than men. It would seem that all women cannot have homes of their own—there does not seem to be enough men to go around. But still there are people who tell us these women should all have homes of their own—it is their own fault if they haven't; and once I heard of a woman saying the hardest thing about men I ever heard—and she was an ardent anti-suffragist too. She said that what was wrong with the women in England was that they were too particular—that's why they were not married, and, she went on, 'any person can tell, when they look around at men in general, that God never intended women to be very particular.' I am glad I never said anything as hard as that about men.

There are still with us some of the conventions of the old days of chivalry. The pretty woman still has the advantage over her plainer sister—and the opinion of the world is that women must be beautiful at all costs. When a newspaper wishes to disprove a woman's contention, or demolish her theories, it draws ugly pictures of her. If it can show that she has big feet or red hands, or wears unbecoming clothes, that certainly settles the case—and puts her where she belongs.

This cruel convention that women must be beautiful accounts for the popularity of face-washes, and beauty parlors, and the languor of university extension lectures. Women cannot be blamed for this. All our civilization has been to the end that women make themselves attractive to men. The attractive woman has hitherto been the successful woman. The pretty girl marries a millionaire, travels in Europe, and is presented at court; her plainer sister, equally intelligent, marries a boy from home, and does her own washing. I am not comparing the two destinies as to which offers the greater opportunities for happiness or usefulness, but rather to show how widely divergent two lives may be. What caused the difference was a wavy strand of hair, a rounder curve on a cheek. Is it any wonder that women capitalize their good looks, even at the expense of their intelligence? The economic dependence of women is perhaps the greatest injustice that has been done to us, and has worked the greatest injury to the race.

Men are not entirely blameless in respect to the frivolity of women. It is easy to blame women for dressing foolishly, extravagantly, but to what end do they do it? To be attractive to men; and the reason they continue to do it is that it is successful. Many a woman has found that it pays to be foolish. Men like frivolity—before marriage; but they demand all the sterner virtues afterwards. The little dainty, fuzzy-haired, simpering dolly who chatters and wears toe-slippers has a better chance in the matrimonial market than the clear-headed, plainer girl, who dresses sensibly. A little boy once gave his mother directions as to his birthday present—he said he wanted 'something foolish' and therein he expressed a purely masculine wish.

A man's ideal at seventeen
Must be a sprite—
A dainty, fairy, elfish queen
Of pure delight;
But later on he sort of feels
He'd like a girl who could cook meals.
Life is full of anomalies, and in the mating and pairing of men and women there
    are many.

Why is the careless, easy-going, irresponsible way of the young girl so attractive to
men? It does not make for domestic happiness; and why, Oh why, do some of our best
men marry such odd little sticks of pin-head women, with a brain similar in caliber to a
second-rate butterfly, while the most intelligent, unselfish, and womanly women are left
unmated? I am going to ask about this the first morning I am in heaven, if so be we are
allowed to ask about the things which troubled us while on our mortal journey. I have
never been able to find out about it here.

Now this old belief that women are protected is of sturdy growth and returns to life
with great persistence. Theoretically women are protected—on paper—traditionally—just
like Belgium was, and with just as disastrous results.

A member of the English Parliament declared with great emphasis that the women
now have everything the heart could desire—they reign like queens and can have their
smallest wish gratified. ('Smallest' is right.) And we very readily grant that there are many
women living in idleness and luxury on the bounty of their male relatives, and we say it
with sorrow and shame that these are estimated the successful women in the opinion of
the world. But while some feast in idleness, many others slave in poverty. The great army
of women workers are ill-paid, badly housed, and their work is not honored or respected
or paid for. What share have they in man's chivalry? Chivalry is like a line of credit. You
can get plenty of it when you do not need it. When you are prospering financially and
your bank account is growing and you are rated A1, you can get plenty of credit—it is
offered to you; but when the dark days of financial depression overtake you, and the
people you are depending upon do not 'come through,' and you must have credit—must
have it!—the very people who once urged it upon you will now tell you that 'money is
tight!'

The young and pretty woman, well dressed and attractive, can get all the chivalry
she wants. She will have seats offered her on street cars, men will hasten to carry her
parcels, or open doors for her; but the poor old woman, beaten in the battle of life, sick
of life's struggles, and grown gray and weather-beaten facing life's storms—what chivalry
is shown her? She can go her weary way uncomforted and unattended. People who need
it do not get it.

Anyway, chivalry is a poor substitute for justice, if one cannot have both. Chivalry is
something like the icing on the cake, sweet but not nourishing. It is like the paper lace
around the bonbon box—we could get along without it.

There are countless thousands of truly chivalrous men, who have the true chivalry
whose foundation is justice—who would protect all women from injury of insult or injustice, but who know that they cannot do it—who know that in spite of all they can do,
women are often outraged, insulted, ill-treated. The truly chivalrous man, who does reverence all womankind, realizing this, says: 'Let us give women every weapon whereby they
can defend themselves; let us remove the stigma of political nonentity under which women
have been placed. Let us give women a fair deal!' ...

This is the new chivalry—and on it we build our hope.

I hold it true—I will not change,
For changes are a dreadful bore —
That nothing must be done on earth
Unless it has been done before.

—Anti-Suffrage Creed

If prejudices belonged to the vegetable world they would be described under the general heading of: 'Hardy Perennials; will grow in any soil, and bloom without ceasing; requiring no cultivation; will do better when left alone.'

In regard to tenacity of life, no old yellow cat has anything on a prejudice. You may kill it with your own hands, bury it deep, and sit on the grave, and behold! the next day, it will walk in at the back door, purring.

Take some of the prejudices regarding women that have been exploded and blown to pieces many, many times and yet walk among us today in the fulness of life and vigor. There is a belief that housekeeping is the only occupation for women; that all women must be house-keepers, whether they like it or not. Men may do as they like, and indulge their individuality, but every true and womanly woman must take to the nutmeg grater and the O-Cedar Mop. It is also believed that in the good old days before woman suffrage was discussed, and when woman's clubs were unheard of, that all women adored housework, and simply pined for Monday morning to come to get at the weekly wash; that women cleaned house with rapture and cooked joyously. Yet there is a story told of one of the women of the old days, who arose at four o'clock in the morning, and aroused all her family at an indecently early hour for breakfast, her reason being that she wanted to get 'one of these horrid old meals over.' This woman had never been at a suffrage meeting—so where did she get the germ of discontent?

At the present time there is much discontent among women, and many people are seriously alarmed about it. They say women are no longer contented with woman's sphere and woman's work—that the washboard has lost its charm, and the days of the hair-wreath are ended. We may as well admit that there is discontent among women. We cannot drive them back to the spinning wheel and the mathook, for they will not go. But there is really no cause for alarm, for discontent is not necessarily wicked. There is such a thing as divine discontent just as there is criminal contentment. Discontent may mean the stirring of ambition, the desire to spread out, to improve and grow. Discontent is a sign of life, corresponding to growing pains in a healthy child. The poor woman who is making a brave struggle for existence is not saying much, though she is thinking all the time. In the old days when a woman's hours were from 5 A.M. to 5 A.M., we did not hear much of discontent among women, because they had not time to even talk, and certainly could not get together. The horse on the treadmill may be very discontented, but he is not disposed to tell his troubles, for he cannot stop to talk.

It is the women, who now have leisure, who are doing the talking. For generations women have been thinking and thought without expression is dynamic, and gathers volume by repression. Evolution when blocked and suppressed becomes revolution. The introduction of machinery and the factory-made articles has given women more leisure than they had formerly, and now the question arises, what are they going to do with it?

Custom and conventionality recommend many and varied occupations for women, social functions intermixed with kindly deeds of charity, embroidering altar cloths, making strong and durable garments for the poor, visiting the sick, comforting the sad, all of which women have faithfully done, but while they have been doing these things, they have been wondering about the underlying causes of poverty, sadness and sin. They notice that when the unemployed are fed on Christmas day, they are just as hungry as ever on December the twenty-sixth, or at least on December the twenty-seventh; they have been led to inquire into the causes for little children being left in the care of the state, and they find that in over half of the cases, the liquor traffic has contributed to the poverty and unworthiness of the parents. The state which licenses the traffic steps in and takes care, or tries to, of the victims; the rich brewer whose business it is to encourage drinking, is usually the largest giver to the work of the Children's Aid Society, and is often extolled for his lavish generosity: and sometimes when women think about these things they are struck by the absurdity of a system which allows one man or a body of men to rob a child of his father's love and care all year, and then gives him a stuffed dog and a little red sleigh at Christmas and calls it charity!

Women have always done their share of the charity work of the world. The lady of the manor, in the old feudal days, made warm mittens and woolen mufflers with her own white hands and carried them to the cottages at Christmas, along with blankets and coals. And it was a splendid arrangement all through, for it furnished the lady with mild and pleasant occupation, and it helped to soothe the conscience of the lord, and if the cottagers (who were often 'low worthless fellows, much given up to riotous thinking and disputing') were disposed to wonder why they had to work all year and get nothing, while the lord of the manor did nothing all year and got everything, the gift of blanket and coals, the warm mufflers, and 'a shawl for granny' showed them what ungrateful souls they were.

Women have dispensed charity for many, many years, but gradually it has dawned upon them that the most of our charity is very ineffectual, and merely smoothes things over, without ever reaching the root. A great deal of our charity is like the kindly deed of the benevolent old gentleman, who found a sick dog by the wayside, lying in the full glare of a scorching sun. The tender-hearted old man climbed down from his carriage, and, lifting the dog tenderly in his arms, carried him around into the small patch of shade cast by his carriage.

'Lie there, my poor fellow!' he said. 'Lie there, in the cool shade, where the sun's rays may not smite you!'

Then he got into his carriage and drove away.

Women have been led, through their charitable institutions and philanthropic endeavors, to do some thinking about causes.

Mrs. B. set out to be a 'family friend' to the family of her washwoman. Mrs. B. was a thoroughly charitable, kindly disposed woman, who had never favored woman's suffrage and regarded the new movement among women with suspicion. Her washwoman's family consisted of four children, and a husband who blew in gaily once in a while when in need of funds, or when recovering from a protracted spree, which made a few days' nursing very welcome. His wife, a Polish woman, had the old-world reverence for men, and obeyed him implicitly; she still felt it was very sweet of him to come home at all. Mrs. B. had often declared that Polly's devotion to her husband was a beautiful thing to see. The two eldest boys had newspaper routes and turned in their earnings regularly, and, although the husband did not contribute anything but his occasional company, Polly was able to make the payments on their little four-roomed cottage. In another year, it would be all paid for.

But one day Polly's husband began to look into the law—as all men should—and he saw that he had been living far below his privileges. The cottage was his—not that he had ever paid a cent on it, of course, but his wife had, and she was his; and the cottage was in his name.

So he sold it; naturally he did not consult Polly, for he was a quiet, peaceful man, and not fond of scenes. So he sold it quietly, and with equal quietness he withdrew from the Province, and took the money with him. He did not even say good-by to Polly or the children, which was rather ungrateful, for they had given him many a meal and night's lodging. When Polly came crying one Monday morning and told her story, Mrs. B. could not believe it, and assured Polly she must be mistaken, but Polly declared that a man had come and asked her did she wish to rent the house for he had bought it. Mrs. B. went at once to the lawyers who had completed the deal. They were a reputable firm and Mrs. B. knew one of the partners quite well. She was sure Polly's husband could not sell the cottage. But the lawyers assured her it was quite true. They were very gentle and patient with Mrs. B. and listened courteously to her explanation, and did not dispute her word at all when she explained that Polly and her two boys had paid every cent on the house. It seemed that a trifling little thing like that did not matter. It did not really matter who paid for the house; the husband was the owner, for was he not the head of the house? and the property was in his name.

Polly was graciously allowed to rent her own cottage for $12.50 a month, with an option of buying, and the two little boys are still on a morning route delivering one of the city dailies.

Mrs. B. has joined a suffrage society and makes speeches on the injustice of the laws; and yet she began innocently enough, by making strong and durable garments for her washwoman's children—and see what has come of it! If women would only be content to snip away at the symptoms of poverty and distress, feeding the hungry and clothing the naked, all would be well and they would be much commended for their kindness of heart; but when they begin to inquire into causes, they find themselves in the sacred realm of politics where prejudice says no women must enter.

A woman may take an interest in factory girls, and hold meetings for them, and encourage them to walk in virtue's ways all she likes, but if she begins to advocate more sanitary surroundings for them, with some respect for the common decencies of life, she will find herself again in that sacred realm of politics—confronted by a factory act, on which no profane female hand must be laid.

Now politics simply means public affairs—yours and mine, everybody's—and to say that politics are too corrupt for women is a weak and foolish statement for any man to make. Any man who is actively engaged in politics, and declares that politics are too corrupt for women, admits one of two things, either that he is a party to this corruption, or that he is unable to prevent it—and in either case something should be done. Politics are not inherently vicious. The office of lawmaker should be the highest in the land, equaled in honor only by that of the minister of the gospel. In the old days, the two were combined with very good effect; but they seem to have drifted apart in more recent years.

If politics are too corrupt for women, they are too corrupt for men; for men and women are one—indissolubly joined together for good or ill. Many men have tried to put all their religion and virtue in their wife's name, but it does not work very well. When social conditions are corrupt women cannot escape by shutting their eyes, and taking no interest. It would be far better to give them a chance to clean them up.

What would you think of a man who would say to his wife: 'This house to which I am bringing you to live is very dirty and unsanitary, but I will not allow you—the dear wife whom I have sworn to protect—to touch it. It is too dirty for your precious little white hands! You must stay upstairs, dear. Of course the odor from below may come up to you, but use your smelling salts and think no evil. I do not hope to ever be able to clean it up, but certainly you must never think of trying.'

Do you think any woman would stand for that? She would say: 'John, you are all right in your way, but there are some places where your brain skids. Perhaps you had better stay downtown today for lunch. But on your way down please call at the grocer's, and send me a scrubbing brush and a package of Dutch Cleanser, and some chloride of lime, and now hurry.' Women have cleaned up things since time began; and if women ever get into politics there will be a cleaning-out of pigeon-holes and forgotten corners, on which the dust of years has fallen, and the sound of the political carpet-beater will be heard in the land.

There is another hardy perennial that constantly lifts its head above the earth, persistently refusing to be ploughed under, and that is that if women were ever given a chance to participate in outside affairs, that family quarrels would result; that men and their wives who have traveled the way of life together, side by side for years, and come safely through religious discussions, and discussions relating to 'his' people and 'her' people, would angrily rend each other over politics, and great damage to the furniture would be the result. Father and son have been known to live under the same roof and vote differently, and yet live! Not only to live, but live peaceably! If a husband and wife are going to quarrel they will find a cause for dispute easily enough, and will not be compelled to wait for election day. And supposing that they have never, never had a single dispute, and not a ripple has ever marred the placid surface of their matrimonial sea, I believe that a small family jar—or at least a real lively argument— will do them good. It is in order to keep the white-winged angel of peace hovering over the home that married women are not allowed to vote in many places. Spinsters and widows are counted worthy of voice in the selection of school trustee, and alderman, and mayor, but not the woman who has taken to herself a husband and still has him.

What a strange commentary on marriage that it should disqualify a woman from voting. Why should marriage disqualify a woman? Men have been known to vote for years after they were dead! [reference to corrupt voting practices where men vote by impersonating men who have died, but whose names are still on the voters' rolls]

Quite different from the 'family jar' theory, another reason is advanced against married women voting—it is said that they would all vote with their husbands, and that the married man's vote would thereby be doubled. We believe it is eminently right and proper that husband and wife should vote the same way, and in that case no one would be able to tell whether the wife was voting with the husband or the husband voting with the wife. Neither would it matter. If giving the franchise to women did nothing more than double the married man's vote it would do a splendid thing for the country, for the married man is the best voter we have; generally speaking, he is a man of family and property—surely if we can depend on anyone we can depend upon him, and if by giving his wife a vote we can double his—we have done something to offset the irresponsible transient vote of the man who has no interest in the community.

There is another sturdy prejudice that blooms everywhere in all climates, and that is that women would not vote if they had the privilege; and this is many times used as a crushing argument against woman suffrage. But why worry? If women do not use it, then surely there is no harm done; but those who use the argument seem to imply that a vote unused is a very dangerous thing to leave lying around, and will probably spoil and blow up. In support of this statement instances are cited of women letting their vote lie idle and unimproved in elections for school trustee and alderman. Of course, the percentage of men voting in these contests was quite small, too, but no person finds fault with that.

Women may have been careless about their franchise in elections where no great issue is at stake, but when moral matters are being decided women have not shown any lack of interest. As a result of the first vote cast by the women of Illinois over one thousand saloons went out of business. Ask the liquor dealers if they think women will use the ballot. They do not object to woman suffrage on the ground that women will not vote, but because they will.

'Why, Uncle Henry!' exclaimed one man to another on election day. 'I never saw you out to vote before. What struck you?'

'Hadn't voted for fifteen years,' declared Uncle Henry, 'but you bet I came out today to vote against givin' these fool women a vote; what's the good of givin' them a vote? they wouldn't use it!'

Then, of course, on the other hand there are those who claim that women would vote too much—that they would vote not wisely but too well; that they would take up voting as a life work to the exclusion of husband, home and children. There seems to be considerable misapprehension on the subject of voting. It is really a simple and perfectly innocent performance, quickly over, and with no bad after-effects.

It is usually done in a vacant room in a school or the vestry of a church, or a town hall. No drunken men stare at you. You are not jostled or pushed—you wait your turn in an orderly line, much as you have waited to buy a ticket at a railway station. Two tame and quiet-looking men sit at a table, and when your turn comes, they ask you your name, which is perhaps slightly embarrassing, but it is not as bad as it might be, for they do not ask your age, or of what disease did your grandmother die. You go behind the screen with your ballot paper in your hand, and there you find a seal-brown pencil tied with a chaste white string. Even the temptation of annexing the pencil is removed from your frail humanity. You mark your ballot, and drop it in the box, and come out into the sunlight again. If you had never heard that you had done an unladylike thing you would not know it. It all felt solemn, and serious, and very respectable to you, something like a Sunday-school convention. Then, too, you are surprised at what a short time you have been away from home. You put the potatoes on when you left home, and now you are back in time to strain them.

In spite of the testimony of many reputable women that they have been able to vote and get the dinner on one and the same day, there still exists a strong belief that the whole household machinery goes out of order when a woman goes to vote. No person denies a woman the right to go to church, and yet the church service takes a great deal more time than voting. People even concede to women the right to go shopping, or visiting a friend, or an occasional concert. But the wife and mother, with her God-given, sacred trust of molding the young life of our land, must never dream of going round the corner to vote. 'Who will mind the baby?' cried one of our public men, in great agony of spirit, 'when the mother goes to vote?'

One woman replied that she thought she could get the person that minded it when she went to pay her taxes—which seemed to be a fairly reasonable proposition. Yet the hardy plant of prejudice flourishes, and the funny pictures still bring a laugh.

Father comes home, tired, weary, footsore, toe-nails ingrowing, caused by undarned stockings, and finds the fire out, house cold and empty, save for his half-dozen children, all crying.

'Where is your mother?' the poor man asks in broken tones. For a moment the sobs are hushed while little Ellie replies: 'Out voting!'

Father bursts into tears.

Of course, people tell us, it is not the mere act of voting which demoralizes women— if they would only vote and be done with it; but women are creatures of habit, and habits once formed are hard to break; and although the polls are only open every three or four years, if women once get into the way of going to them, they will hang around there all the rest of the time. It is in woman's impressionable nature that the real danger lies.

Another shoot of this hardy shrub of prejudice is that women are too good to mingle in everyday life—they are too sweet and too frail—that women are angels. If women are angels we should try to get them into public life as soon as possible, for there is a great shortage of angels there just at present, if all we hear is true.

Then there is the pedestal theory—that women are away up on a pedestal, and down below, looking up at them with deep adoration, are men, their willing slaves. Sitting up on a pedestal does not appeal very strongly to a healthy woman—and, besides, if a woman has been on a pedestal for any length of time, it must be very hard to have to come down and cut the wood.

These tender-hearted and chivalrous gentlemen who tell you of their adoration for women, cannot bear to think of women occupying public positions. Their tender hearts shrink from the idea of women lawyers or women policemen, or even women preachers; these positions would 'rub the bloom off the peach,' to use their own eloquent words. They cannot bear, they say, to see women leaving the sacred precincts of home—and yet their offices are scrubbed by women who do their work while other people sleep—poor women who leave the sacred precincts of home to earn enough to keep the breath of life in them, who carry their scrub-pails home, through the deserted streets, long after the cars have stopped running. They are exposed to cold, to hunger, to insult—poor souls—is there any pity felt for them? Not that we have heard of. The tender-hearted ones can bear this with equanimity. It is the thought of women getting into comfortable and well-paid positions which wrings their manly hearts.

Another aspect of the case is that women can do more with their indirect influence than by the ballot; though just why they cannot do better still with both does not appear to be very plain. The ballot is a straight-forward dignified way of making your desire or choice felt. There are some things which are not pleasant to talk about, but would be delightful to vote against. Instead of having to beg, and coax, and entreat, and beseech, and denounce as women have had to do all down the centuries, in regard to the evil things which threaten to destroy their homes and those whom they love, what a glorious thing it would be if women could go out and vote against these things. It seems like a straightforward and easy way of expressing one's opinion. [...]

Then there is the problem of the foreign woman's vote. Many people fear that the granting of woman suffrage would greatly increase the unintelligent vote, because the foreign women would then have the franchise, and in our blind egotism we class our foreign people as ignorant people, if they do not know our ways and our language. They may know many other languages, but if they have not yet mastered ours they are poor, ignorant foreigners. We Anglo-Saxon people have a decided sense of our own superiority, and we feel sure that our skin is exactly the right color, and we people from Huron and Bruce feel sure that we were born in the right place, too. So we naturally look down upon those who happen to be of a different race and tongue than our own.

It is a sad feature of humanity that we are disposed to hate what we do not understand; we naturally suspect and distrust where we do not know. Hens are like that, too! When a strange fowl comes into a farmyard all the hens take a pick at it—not that it has done anything wrong, but they just naturally do not like the look of its face because it is strange. Now that may be very good ethics for hens, but it is hardly good enough for human beings. Our attitude toward the foreign people was well exemplified in one of the missions, where a little Italian boy, who had been out two years, refused to sit beside a newly arrived Italian boy, who, of course, could not speak a word of English. The teacher asked him to sit with his lately arrived compatriot, so that he might interpret for him. The older boy flatly refused, and told the teacher he 'had no use for them young dagos.'

'You see,' said the teacher sadly, when telling the story, 'he had caught the Canadian spirit.'

People say hard things about the corruptible foreign vote, but they place the emphasis in the wrong place. Instead of using our harsh adjectives for the poor fellow who sells his vote, let us save them all for the corrupt politician who buys it, for he cannot plead ignorance—he knows what he is doing. The foreign people who come to Canada, come with burning enthusiasm for the new land, this land of liberty—land of freedom. Some have been seen kissing the ground in an ecstacy of gladness when they arrive. It is the land of their dreams, where they hope to find home and happiness. They come to us with ideals of citizenship that shame our narrow, mercenary standards. These men are of a race which has gladly shed its blood for freedom and is doing it today. But what happens? They go out to work on construction gangs for the summer, they earn money for several months, and when the work closes down they drift back into the cities. They have done the work we wanted them to do, and no further thought is given to them. They may get off the earth so far as we are concerned. One door stands invitingly open to them. There is one place they are welcome—so long as their money lasts—and around the bar they get their ideals of citizenship.

When an election is held, all at once this new land of their adoption begins to take an interest in them, and political heelers, well paid for the job, well armed with whiskey, cigars and money, go among them, and, in their own language, tell them which way they must vote—and they do. Many an election has been swung by this means. One new arrival, just learning our language, expressed his contempt for us by exclaiming: 'Bah! Canada is not a country—it's just a place to make money.' That was all he had seen. He spoke correctly from his point of view.

Then when the elections are over, and the Government is sustained, the men who have climbed back to power by these means speak eloquently of our 'foreign people who have come to our shores to find freedom under the sheltering folds of our grand old flag (cheers), on which the sun never sets, and under whose protection all men are free and equal—with an equal chance of molding the destiny of the great Empire of which we make a part.' (Cheers and prolonged applause.)

If we really understood how, with our low political ideals and iniquitous election methods, we have corrupted the souls of these men who have come to live among us, we would no longer cheer, when we hear this old drivel of the 'folds of the flag.' We would think with shame of how we have driven the patriotism out of these men and replaced it by the greed of gain, and instead of cheers and applause we would cry: 'Lord, have mercy upon us!'

The foreign women, whom politicians and others look upon as such a menace, are differently dealt with than the men. They do not go out to work, *en masse*, as the men do. They work one by one, and are brought in close contact with their employers. The women who go out washing and cleaning spend probably five days a week in the homes of other women. Surely one of her five employers will take an interest in her, and endeavor to instruct her in the duties of citizenship. Then, too, the mission work is nearly all done for women and girls. The foreign women generally speak English before the men, for the reason that they are brought in closer contact with English-speaking people. When I hear people speaking of the ignorant foreign women I think of 'Mary,' and 'Annie,' and others I have known. I see their broad foreheads and intelligent kindly faces, and think of the heroic struggle they are making to bring their families up in thrift and decency. Would Mary vote against liquor if she had the chance? She would. So would you if your eyes had been blackened as often by a drunken husband. There is no need to instruct these women on the evils of liquor drinking—they are able to give you a few aspects of the case which perhaps you had not thought of. We have no reason to be afraid of the foreign woman's vote. I wish we were as sure of the ladies who live on the Avenue. [. . .]

After one has listened to all these arguments and has contracted clergyman's sore throat talking back, it is real relief to meet the people who say flatly and without reason: 'You can't have it—no—I won't argue—but inasmuch as I can prevent it—you will never vote! So there!' The men who meet the question like this are so easy to classify.

I remember when I was a little girl back on the farm in the Souris Valley, I used to water the cattle on Saturday mornings, drawing the water in an icy bucket with a windlass from a fairly deep well. We had one old white ox, called Mike, a patriarchal-looking old sinner, who never had enough, and who always had to be watered first. Usually I gave him what I thought he should have and then took him back to the stable and watered the others. But one day I was feeling real strong, and I resolved to give Mike all he could drink, even if it took every drop of water in the well. I must admit that I cherished a secret hope that he would kill himself drinking. I will not set down here in cold figures how many pails of water Mike drank—but I remember. At last he could not drink another drop, and stood shivering beside the trough, blowing the last mouthful out of his mouth like a bad child. I waited to see if he would die, or at least turn away and give the others a chance. The thirsty cattle came crowding around him, but old Mike, so full I am sure he felt he would never drink another drop of water again as long as he lived, deliberately and with difficulty put his two front feet over the trough and kept all the other cattle away [...] Years afterwards I had the pleasure of being present when a delegation waited upon the Government of one of the provinces of Canada, and presented many reasons for extending the franchise to women. One member of the Government arose and spoke for all his colleagues. He said in substance: 'You can't have it—so long as I have anything to do with the affairs of this province—you shall not have it!' [...]

Did your brain ever give a queer little twist, and suddenly you were conscious that the present mental process had taken place before. If you have ever had it, you will know what I mean, and if you haven't I cannot make you understand. I had that feeling then ... I said to myself: 'Where have I seen that face before?' [...] Then, suddenly, I remembered, and in my heart I cried out: 'Mike!—old friend, Mike! Dead these many years! Your bones lie buried under the fertile soil of the Souris Valley, but your soul goes marching on! Mike, old friend, I see you again—both feet in the trough!' [...]

If any person doubts that the society of the present day has been made by men, and for men's advantage, let them look for a minute at the laws which govern society. Society allows a man all privilege all license, all liberty, where women are concerned. He may lie to women, deceive them—'all's fair in love and war'—he may break many a heart, and blast many a fair name; that merely throws a glamour around him. 'He's a devil with women,' they say, and it is no disadvantage in the business or political world—where man dominates. But if a man is dishonest in business or neglects to pay his gambling bills, he is down and out. These are crimes against men—and therefore serious. This is also a sore thought! [...]

Since women's sphere of manual labor has so narrowed by economic conditions and has not widened correspondingly in other directions, many women have become parasites on the earnings of their male relatives. Marriage has become a straight 'clothes and board' proposition to the detriment of marriage and the race. Her economic dependence has so influenced the attitude of some women toward men, that it is the old man with the money who can support her in idleness who appeals to her far more than the handsome, clean-limbed young man who is poor, and with whom she would have to work. The softening, paralyzing effects of ease and comfort are showing themselves on our women. [...]

The time will come, we hope, when women will be economically free, and mentally and spiritually independent enough to refuse to have their food paid for by men; when women will receive equal pay for equal work, and have all avenues of activity open to them; and will be free to choose their own mates, without shame, or indelicacy; when men will not be afraid of marriage because of the financial burden, but free men and free women will marry for love, and together work for the sustenance of their families. It is not too ideal a thought. It is coming, and the new movement among women who are crying out for a larger humanity, is going to bring it about.

But there are many good men who view this with alarm. They are afraid that if women were economically independent they would never marry. But they would. Deeply rooted in almost every woman's heart is the love of home and children; but independence is sweet and when marriage means the loss of independence, there are women brave enough and strong enough to turn away from it. 'I will not marry for a living,' many a brave woman has said.

The world has taunted women into marrying. So odious has the term 'old maid' been in the past that many a woman has married rather than have to bear it. That the term 'old maid' has lost its odium is due to the fact that unmarried women have made a place for themselves in the world of business. They have become real people apart from their sex. The 'old maid' of the past was a sad, anemic creature, without any means of support except the bounty of some relative. She had not married, so she had failed utterly, and the world did not fail to rub it in. The unmarried woman of today is the head saleslady in some big house, drawing as big a salary as most men, and the world kowtows to her. The world is beginning to see that a woman may achieve success in other departments of life as well as marriage. [...]

When women are free to marry or not as they will, and the financial burden of making a home is equally shared by husband and wife, the world will enter upon an era of happiness undreamed of now. As it is now the whole matter of marrying and homemaking is left to chance. Every department of life, every profession in which men and women engage, has certain qualifications which must be complied with, except the profession of homemaking. A young man and a young woman say: 'I believe we'll get married' and forthwith they do. The state sanctions it, and the church blesses it. They may be consumptive, epileptic, shiftless, immoral, or with a tendency to insanity. No matter. They may go on and reproduce their kind. They are perfectly free to bring children into the world, who are a burden and a menace to society. Society has to bear it—that is all! 'Be fruitful and multiply!' declares the church, as it deplores the evils of race suicide. Many male moralists have cried out for large families. 'Let us have better and healthier babies if we can,' cried out one of England's bishops, not long ago, 'but let us have more babies!' [...]

When the cry has been so persistently raised for more children, the women naturally wonder why more care is not exerted for the protection of the children who are already here. The reason is often given for not allowing women to have the free grants of land in Canada on the same conditions as men, that it would make them too independent of marriage, and, as one commissioner of emigration phrased it: 'It is not independent women we want; it is population.'

Granting that population is very desirable, would it not be well to save what we have? Six or seven thousand of our population in Canada drop out of the race every year as a direct result of the liquor traffic, and a higher percentage than this perish from the same cause in some other countries. Would it not be well to save them? Thousands of babies die every year from preventable causes. Free milk depositories and district nurses and free dispensaries would save many of them. In the Far West, on the border of civilization, where women are beyond the reach of nurses and doctors, many mothers and babies die every year. How would it be to try to save them? Delegations of public-spirited women have waited upon august bodies of men, and pleased the cause of these brave women who are paying the toll of colonization, and have asked that Government nurses be sent to them in their hour of need. But up to date not one dollar of Government money has been spent on them notwith-standing the fact that when a duke or a prince comes to visit our country, we can pour out money like water! [...]

If children die—what of it? 'The Lord gave and the Lord hath taken away.' Let us have more. This is the sore thought with women. It is not that the bringing of children into the world is attended with pain and worry and weariness—it is not that: it is that they are held of such small value in the eyes of this man-made world. This is the sorest thought of all! [...]

Women have carried many a sore thought in their hearts, feeling that they have been harshly dealt with by their men folk, and have laid the blame on the individual man, when in reality the individual has not been to blame. The whole race is suffering from masculinity; and men and women are alike to blame for tolerating it.

The baby girl in her cradle gets the first cold blast of it. 'A girl?' says the kind neighbor, 'Oh, too bad—I am sure it was quite a disappointment!'

Then there is the old-country reverence for men, of which many a mother has been guilty, which exalts the boys of the family far above the girls, and brings home to the latter, in many, many ways, the grave mistake of having been born a woman. Many little girls have carried the sore thought in their hearts from their earliest recollection.

They find out, later, that women's work is taken for granted. A farmer will allow his daughter to work many weary unpaid years, and when she gets married he will give her 'a feather bed and a cow,' and feel that her claim upon him has been handsomely met. The gift of a feather bed is rather interesting, too, when you consider that it is the daughter who has raised the geese, plucked them, and made the bed-tick. But 'father' gives it to her just the same. The son, for a corresponding term of service, gets a farm. [. . .]

There are some places, where a law can protect the weak, but there are many situations which require more than a law. Take the case of a man who habitually abuses and frightens his family, and makes their lives a periodic hell of fear. The law cannot touch him unless he actually kills some of them, and it seems a great pity that there cannot be some corrective measure. In the states of Kansas and Washington (where women vote) the people have enacted what is known as the 'Lazy Husband's Act,' which provides for such cases as this. If a man is abusive or disagreeable, or fails to provide for his family, he is taken away for a time, and put to work in a state institution, and his money is sent home to his family. He is treated kindly, and good influences thrown around him. When he shows signs of repentance—he is allowed to go home. Home, very often, looks better to him, and he behaves himself quite decently.

Women outlined this legislation and it is in the states where women vote that it is in operation. There will be more such legislation, too, when women are given a chance to speak out!

A New Zealander once wrote home to a friend in England advising him to fight hard against woman suffrage. 'Don't ever let the wimmin vote, Bill,' he wrote. 'They are good servants, but bad masters. Over there you can knock your wife about for five shillings, but here we does jail for it!'

The man who 'knocks his wife about' or feels that he might some day want to knock her about, is opposed to further liberties for women, of course.

But that is the class of man from whom we never expected anything. He has his prototype, too, in every walk of life. Don't make the mistake of thinking that only ignorant members of the great unwashed masses talk and feel this way. Silk-hatted 'noblemen' have answered women's appeals for common justice by hiring the Whitechapel toughs to 'bash their heads,' and this is another sore thought that women will carry with them for many a day after the suffrage has been granted. I wish we could forget the way our English sisters have been treated in that sweet land of liberty!

The problems of discovery have been solved; the problems of colonization are being solved, and when the war is over the problem of world government will be solved; and then the problem will be just the problem of living together. That problem cannot be solved without the help of women. The world has suffered long from too much masculinity and not enough humanity, but when the war is over, and the beautiful things have been destroyed, and the lands laid desolate, and all the blood has been shed, the poor old bruised and broken heart of the world will cry out for its mother and nurse, who will dry her own eyes, and bind up its wounds and nurse it back to life once more.

▲ Document 3: Nellie McClung

● Nellie McClung ca. 1910-1918. Nellie McClung was one of the most prominent leaders of the English Canadian women's suffrage movement. She lived most of her adult life in Manitoba and then Alberta, where she worked for women's rights and other social reform issues. She was also a noted author of both fiction and non-fiction.

Source: Glenbow Museum NA-273-2.

▲ Document 4: Canada Needs a Clean-up Week (1915)

CANADA NEEDS A "CLEAN-UP" WEEK

Most of the cities of Canada have an annual "Clean-up" Week each spring, when the winter's accumulation of rubbish and filth is raked together and destroyed. It has been found that the health as well as the appearance of the cities is improved and flies and other pests are greatly minimized by this process. Here we see our artist's conception of the "Clean-up" week which is needed in the public life of Canada.

● What are they burning? What message does this cartoon send about women's roles and abilities, in the home and the public world? What message does this cartoon send about men's role in social reform?

Source: Archives of Manitoba/ Archives du Manitoba, Arch Dale 22, N8929, 1915.

▲ Document 5: The Woman Question

Stephen Leacock

Stephen Leacock was a professor of political economy at McGill University in the first third of the twentieth century. He is best known as a popular writer of humourous fiction, the most well known of which is Sunshine Sketches of a Little Town *(1912)*

I was sitting the other day in what is called the Peacock Alley of one of our leading hotels, drinking tea with another thing like myself, a man. At the next table were a group of Superior Beings in silk, talking. I couldn't help overhearing what they said at least not when I held my head a little sideways.

They were speaking of the war.

'There wouldn't have been any war,' said one, 'if women were allowed to vote.'

'No, indeed,' chorused all the others.

The woman who had spoken looked about her defiantly. She wore spectacles and was of the type that we men used to call, in days when we still retained a little courage, an Awful Woman.

'When women have the vote,' she went on, 'there will be no more war. The women will forbid it.'

She gazed about her angrily. She evidently wanted to be heard. My friend and I hid ourselves behind a little fern and trembled.

But we listened. We were hoping that the Awful Woman would explain how war would be ended. She didn't. She went on to explain instead that when women have the vote there will be no more poverty, no disease, no germs, no cigarette smoking and nothing to drink but water.

It seemed a gloomy world.

'Come,' whispered my friend, 'this is no place for us. Let us go to the bar.'

'No,' I said, 'leave me. I am going to write an article on the Woman Question. The time has come when it has got to be taken up and solved.'

So I set myself to write it.

The woman problem may be stated somewhat after this fashion. The great majority of the woman of to-day find themselves without any means of support of their own. I refer of course to the civilised white women. The gay savage in her jungle, attired in a cocoanut leaf, armed with a club and adorned with the neck of a soda-water bottle, is all right. Trouble hasn't reached her yet. Like all savages, she has a far better time—more varied, more interesting, more worthy of a human being—than falls to the lot of the rank and file of civilized men and women. Very few of us recognise this great truth. We have a mean little vanity over our civilisation. We are touchy about it. We do not realise that so far we have done little but increase the burden of work and multiply the means of death. But for the hope of better things to come, our civilisation would not seem worth while.

But this is a digression. Let us go back. The great majority of women have no means of support of their own. This is true also of men. But the men can acquire means of

Source: 'The Woman Question' in *The Social Criticism of Stephen Leacock*, edited and introduced by Alan Bowker, University of Toronto Press, 1973.

support. They can hire themselves out and work. Better still, by the industrious process of intrigue rightly called 'busyness,' or business, they may presently get hold of enough of other people's things to live without working. Or again, men can, with a fair prospect of success, enter the criminal class, either in its lower ranks as a house breaker, or in its upper ranks, through politics. Take it all in all a man has a certain chance to get along in life.

A woman, on the other hand, has little or none. The world's work is open to her, but she cannot do it. She lacks the physical strength for laying bricks or digging coal. If put to work on a steel beam a hundred feet above the ground, she would fall off. For the pursuit of business her head is all wrong. Figures confuse her. She lacks sustained attention and in point of morals the average woman is, even for business, too crooked.

This last point is one that will merit a little emphasis. Men are queer creatures. They are able to set up a code of rules or a standard, often quite an artificial one, and stick to it. They have acquired the art of playing the game. Eleven men can put on white flannel trousers and call themselves a cricket team, on which an entirely new set of obligations, almost a new set of personalities, are wrapped about them. Women could never be a team of anything.

So it is in business. Men are able to maintain a sort of rough and ready code which prescribes the particular amount of cheating that a man may do under the rule. This is called business honesty, and many men adhere to it with a dog-like tenacity, growing old in it, till it is stamped on their grizzled faces, visibly. They can feel it inside them like a virtue. So much will they cheat and no more. Hence men are able to trust one another, knowing the exact degree of dishonesty they are entitled to expect.

With women it is entirely different. They bring to business an unimpaired vision. They see it as it is. It would be impossible to trust them. They refuse to play fair.

Thus it comes about that woman is excluded, to a great extent, from the world's work and the world's pay.

There is nothing really open to her except one thing—marriage. She must find a man who will be willing, in return for her society, to give her half of everything he has, allow her the sole use of his house during the daytime, pay her taxes, and provide her clothes.

This was, formerly and for many centuries, not such a bad solution of the question. The women did fairly well out of it. It was the habit to marry early and often. The 'house and home' was an important place. The great majority of people, high and low, lived on the land. The work of the wife and the work of the husband ran closely together. The two were complementary and fitted into one another. A woman who had to superintend the baking of bread and the brewing of beer, the spinning of yarn and the weaving of clothes, could not complain that her life was incomplete.

Then came the modern age, beginning let us say about a hundred and fifty years ago. The distinguishing marks of it have been machinery and the modern city. The age of invention swept the people off the land. It herded them into factories, creating out of each man a poor miserable atom divorced from hereditary ties, with no rights, no duties, and no place in the world except what his wages contract may confer on him. Every man for himself, and sink or swim, became the order of the day. It was nicknamed 'industrial freedom.' The world's production increased enormously. It is doubtful if the poor profited much. They obtained the modern city—full of light and noise and excitement, lively with crime and gay with politics—and the free school where they learned to read and write, by which means they might hold a mirror to their poverty and take a good look at it. They lost the quiet of the country side, the murmur of the brook and the inspiration of the open sky. These are unconscious things, but the peasant who has been reared among them, for all his unconsciousness, pines and dies without them. It is doubtful if the poor have gained.

The chaw-bacon rustic who trimmed a hedge in the reign of George the First, compares well with the pale slum-rat of the reign of George V.

But if the machine age has profoundly altered the position of the working man, it has done still more with woman. It has dispossessed her. Her work has been taken away. The machine does it. It makes the clothes and brews the beer. The roar of the vacuum cleaner has hushed the sound of the broom. The proud proportions of the old-time cook, are dwindled to the slim outline of the gas-stove expert operating on a beefsteak with the aid of a thermometer. And at the close of day the machine, wound with a little key, sings the modern infant to its sleep, with the faultless lullaby of the Victrola. The home has passed, or at least is passing out of existence. In place of it is the 'apartment'—an incomplete thing, a mere part of something, where children are an intrusion, where hospitality is done through a caterer, and where Christmas is only the twenty-fifth of December.

All this the machine age did for woman. For a time she suffered—the one thing she had learned, in the course of centuries, to do with admirable fitness. With each succeeding decade of the modern age things grew worse instead of better. The age for marriage shifted. A wife instead of being a help-mate had become a burden that must be carried. It was no longer true that two could live on less than one. The prudent youth waited till he could 'afford' a wife. Love itself grew timid. Little Cupid exchanged his bow and arrow for a book on arithmetic and studied money sums. The school girl who flew to Gretna Green in a green and yellow cabriolet beside a peach-faced youth—angrily pursued by an ancient father of thirty-eight—all this drifted into the pictures of the past, romantic but quite impossible.

Thus the unmarried woman, a quite distinct thing from the 'old maid' of ancient times, came into existence, and multiplied and increased till there were millions of her.

Then there rose up in our own time, or within call of it, a deliverer. It was the Awful Woman with the Spectacles, and the doctrine that she preached was Woman's Rights. She came as a new thing, a hatchet in her hand, breaking glass. But in reality she was no new thing at all, and had her lineal descent in history from age to age. The Romans knew her as a sybil and shuddered at her. The Middle Ages called her a witch and burnt her. The ancient law of England named her a scold and ducked her in a pond. But the men of the modern age, living indoors and losing something of their ruder fibre, grew afraid of her. The Awful Woman—meddlesome, vociferous, intrusive—came into her own.

Her softer sisters followed her. She became the leader of her sex. 'Things are all wrong,' she screamed, 'with the *status* of women.' Therein she was quite right. 'The remedy for it all,' she howled, 'is to make women "free," to give women the vote. When once women are "free" everything will be all right.' Therein the woman with the spectacles was, and is, utterly wrong.

The women's vote, when they get it, will leave women much as they were before.

Let it be admitted quite frankly that women are going to get the vote. Within a very short time all over the British Isles and North America in the States and the nine provinces of Canada woman suffrage will soon be an accomplished fact. It is a coming event which casts its shadow, or its illumination, in front of it. The woman's vote and total prohibition are two things that are moving across the map with gigantic strides. Whether they are good or bad things is another question. They are coming. As for the women's vote, it has largely come. And as for prohibition, it is going to be recorded as one of the results of the European War, foreseen by nobody. When the king of England decided that the way in which he could best help the country was by giving up drinking, the admission was fatal. It will stand as one of the landmarks of British history comparable only to such things as the signing of the Magna Carta by King John, or the serving out of rum and water instead of pure rum in the British Navy under George III.

So the women's vote and prohibition are coming. A few rare spots—such as Louisiana, and the City of New York—will remain and offer here and there a wet oasis in the desert of dry virtue. Even that cannot endure. Before many years are past, all over this continent women with a vote and men without a drink will stand looking at one another and wondering, what next?

For when the vote is reached the woman question will not be solved but only begun. In and of itself, a vote is nothing. It neither warms the skin nor fills the stomach. Very often the privilege of a vote confers nothing but the right to express one's opinion as to which of two crooks is the crookeder.

But after the women have obtained the vote the question is, what are they going to do with it? The answer is, nothing, or at any rate nothing that men would not do without them. Their only visible use of it will be to elect men into office. Fortunately for us all they will not elect women. Here and there perhaps at the outset, it will be done as the result of a sort of spite, a kind of sex antagonism bred by the controversy itself. But, speaking broadly, the women's vote will not be used to elect women to office. Women do not think enough of one another to do that. If they want a lawyer they consult a man, and those who can afford it have their clothes made by men, and their cooking done by a chef. As for their money, no woman would entrust that to another woman's keeping. They are far too wise for that.

So the woman's vote will not result in the setting up of female prime ministers and of parliaments in which the occupants of the treasury bench cast languishing eyes across at the flushed faces of the opposition. From the utter ruin involved in such an attempt at mixed government, the women themselves will save us. They will elect men. They may even pick some good ones. It is a nice question and will stand thinking about.

But what else, or what further can they do, by means of their vote and their representatives to 'emancipate' and 'liberate' their sex?

Many feminists would tell us at once that if women had the vote they would, first and foremost, throw everything open to women on the same terms as men. Whole speeches are made on this point, and a fine fury thrown into it, often very beautiful to behold.

The entire idea is a delusion. Practically all of the world's work is open to women now, wide open. *The only trouble is that they can't do it.* There is nothing to prevent a woman from managing a bank, or organising a company, or running a department store, or floating a merger, or building a railway—except the simple fact that she can't. Here and there an odd woman does such things, but she is only the exception that proves the rule. Such women are merely—and here I am speaking in the most decorous biological sense— 'sports.' The ordinary woman cannot do the ordinary man's work. She never has and never will. The reasons why she can't are so many, that is, she '*can't*' in so many different ways, that it is not worth while to try to name them.

Here and there it is true there are things closed to woman, not by their own inability but by the law. This is a gross injustice. There is no defence for it. The province in which I live, for example, refuses to allow women to practice as lawyers. This is wrong. Women have just as good a right to fail at being lawyers as they have at anything else. But even if all these legal disabilities, where they exist, were removed (as they will be under a woman's vote) the difference to women at large will be infinitesimal. A few gifted 'sports' will earn a handsome livelihood, but the woman question in the larger sense will not move one inch nearer to solution.

The feminists, in fact, are haunted by the idea that it is possible for the average woman to have a life patterned after that of the ordinary man. They imagine her as having a career, a profession, a vocation something which will be her 'life work' just as selling coal is the life work of the coal merchant.

If this were so, the whole question would be solved. Women and men would become equal and independent. It is thus indeed that the feminist sees them, through the roseate mist created by imagination. Husband and wife appear as a couple of honourable partners who share a house together. Each is off to business in the morning. The husband is, let us say, a stock broker: the wife manufactures iron and steel. The wife is a Liberal, the husband a Conservative. At their dinner they have animated discussions over the tariff till it is time for them to go to their clubs.

These two impossible creatures haunt the brain of the feminist and disport them in the pages of the up-to-date novel.

The whole thing is mere fiction. It is quite impossible for women—the average and ordinary women—to go in for having a career. Nature has forbidden it. The average woman must necessarily have—I can only give the figures roughly—about three and a quarter children. She must replace in the population herself and her husband with something over to allow for the people who never marry and for the children that do not reach maturity. If she fails to do this the population comes to an end. Any scheme of social life must allow for those three and a quarter children and for the years of care that must be devoted to them. The vacuum cleaner can take the place of the housewife. It cannot replace the mother. No man ever said his prayers at the knees of a vacuum cleaner, or drew his first lessons in manliness and worth from the sweet old-fashioned stories that a vacuum cleaner told. Feminists of the enraged kind may talk as they will of the paid attendant and the expert baby-minder. Fiddlesticks! These things are a mere supplement, useful enough but as far away from the realities of motherhood as the vacuum cleaner itself. But the point is one that need not be laboured. Sensible people understand it as soon as said. With fools it is not worth while to argue.

But, it may be urged, there are, even as it is, a great many women who are working. The wages that they receive are extremely low. They are lower in most cases than the wages for the same, or similar work, done by men. Cannot the woman's vote at least remedy this?

Here is something that deserves thinking about and that is far more nearly within the realm of what is actual and possible than wild talk of equalizing and revolutionising the sexes.

It is quite true that women's work is underpaid. But this is only a part of a larger social injustice.

The case stands somewhat as follows: Women get low wages because low wages are all that they are worth. Taken by itself this is a brutal and misleading statement. What is meant is this. The rewards and punishments in the unequal and ill-adjusted world in which we live are most unfair. The price of anything—sugar, potatoes, labour, or anything else—varies according to the supply and demand: if many people want it and few can supply it the price goes up: if the contrary it goes down. If enough cabbages are brought to market they will not bring a cent a piece, no matter what it cost to raise them.

On these terms each of us sells his labour. The lucky ones, with some rare gift, or trained capacity, or some ability that by mere circumstance happens to be in a great demand, can sell high. If there were only one night plumber in a great city, and the water pipes in a dozen homes of a dozen millionaires should burst all at once, he might charge a fee like that of a consulting lawyer.

On the other hand the unlucky sellers whose numbers are greater than the demand—the mass of common labourers—get a mere pittance. To say that their wage represents all that they produce is to argue in a circle. It is the mere pious quietism with which the well-to-do man who is afraid to think boldly on social questions drugs his conscience to sleep.

So it stands with women's wages. It is the sheer numbers of the women themselves, crowding after the few jobs that they can do, that brings them down. It has nothing to do with the attitude of men collectively towards women in the lump. It cannot be remedied by any form of woman's freedom. Its remedy is bound up with the general removal of social injustice, the general abolition of poverty, which is to prove the great question of the century before us. The question of women's wages is a part of the wages question.

To my thinking the whole idea of making women free and equal (politically) with men as a way of improving their *status*, starts from a wrong basis and proceeds in a wrong direction.

Women need not more freedom but less. Social policy should proceed from the fundamental truth that women are and must be dependent. It they cannot be looked after by an individual (a thing on which they took their chance in earlier days) they must be looked after by the State. To expect a woman, for example, if left by the death of her husband with young children without support to maintain herself by her own efforts, is the most absurd mockery of freedom ever devised. Earlier generations of mankind, for all that they lived in the jungle and wore cocoanut leaves, knew nothing of it. To turn a girl loose in the world to work for herself, when there is no work to be had, or none at a price that will support life, is a social crime.

I am not attempting to show in what way the principle of woman's dependence should be worked out in detail in legislation. Nothing short of a book could deal with it. All that the present essay attempts is the presentation of a point of view.

I have noticed that my clerical friends, on the rare occasions when they are privileged to preach to me, have a way of closing their sermons by 'leaving their congregations with a thought.' It is a good scheme. It keeps the congregation, let us hope, in a state of trembling eagerness for the next instalment.

With the readers of this essay I do the same. I leave them with the thought that perhaps in the modern age it is not the increased freedom of woman that is needed but the increased recognition of their dependence. Let the reader remain agonised over that till I write something else.

▲ Document 6: Women's Christian Temperance Union (WCTU) Excerpts

Excerpt 1

1880

[The WCTU's political effort to gain the vote] is not the clamor of ambition, ignorance, or frivolity trying to gain position, It is the prayer of earnest, thoughtful Christian women on behalf of their children and their children's children. It is in the interest of our homes, our divinely appointed place, to protect the home against the licensed evil (liquor) which is the enemy of the home, and also to aid in our efforts to advance God's Kingdom beyond the bounds of our homes.

It is only by legislation that the roots of great evils can be touched, and for want of the ballot we stand powerless in face of our most terrible foe, the legalized liquor traffic. The liquor sellers are not afraid of our conventions, but they are afraid of our ballots.

Source: Annual Report, WCTU Ontario, 1880, p. 10. Cited in Wendy Mitchinson, "The WCTU: 'For God, Home and Native Land': A Study in Nineteenth Century Feminism," in *A Not Unreasonable Claim: Women and Reform in Canada, 1880–1920s*, Linda Kealey, ed., (Toronto: The Women's Press, 1979).

Excerpt 2

1888

"[...] we are placed below all men, no matter how ignorant or wicked they may be, even the foreigner who perhaps can neither read or write, who by residing on Canadian soil one year and taking the oath of allegiance, though he may know nothing of our laws, nothing of the men who aspire to office, perhaps cannot speak one word of English, and yet he can say who shall be our legislators while we women are placed side by side with idiots, lunatics and children."

Source: From a 1888 speech by Maria Grant, Victoria WCTU, WCTU Yearbook, 1890, p. 52. Cited in Lyn Gough, *As Wise as Serpents: Five Women and an Organization that Changed British Columbia, 1883–1939* (Victoria: Swan Lake Publishing, 1988).

Excerpt 3

1900

Description of the WCTU float in the Victoria Day Parade, Victoria, B.C., 1900.

[The float was] [...] pure white, magnificently symbolizing the purity of aims actuating that great organization of Christian Women, who have become such a power in the world. In this triumphal "car" were fully forty children, representing the home upon which the labours of the parent organization exert their first and beneficent influence. In the hand of each child was a British flag, while on their dresses were pinned a maple leaf, a combination of which, although an incidental in the whole arrangement was of striking significance. A young lady was seated at each of the corners of the float, the first being engaged in tying a white ribbon around the world, the preserving commendable work of "Woman" for the past two decades. The second knelt before a golden cross representing the word "Christian", and "Temperance" was represented by a young lady grasping a goblet of pure water which she freely offered to all. There was a beautiful representation of the word "Union", in which the last young lady held in her hand a chain of 28 white links, representing the 28 departments of work under the control of the organization. The white ribbon tied into three links beautifully united the four representatives, making splendid allegory the words "Women's Christian Temperance Union". The Queen (the superintendent of the Band of Hope) sat in the centre of the float crowned by her pages who sat at her feet representing the loyal subjects. The monogram of the society was born on shields on each side and on the back of the float. Above all floated proudly the Union Jack [...] The children in the float sang appropriate hymns and the spectacle presented was beautiful indeed.

Source: *The Victoria Times,* May 25, 1900.

Excerpt 4

1911

[...] May they [young women members of the WCTU] be power in bringing about the day when the womanhood of our land shall be recognized to be citizens, and invested with the rights and privileges of citizens. To-day we stand aside and see the ignorant, debased, and even the lowest type of foreigner given the birthright denied to Ontario's pure and loyal womanhood, and we feel like crying out, "How long, O Lord, how long?" shall men of foreign birth and lowest intellect hold the balance of power in many of our elections, or votes on questions of temperance and moral reform? May every woman realize that this question of suffrage is one of intensest [sic] interest to her, and may every Union have a Franchise Department that will make itself felt in the community. Never say it is a question on which you are indifferent, it carries too momentous interests to be lightly set aside [...]

Source: Report of the corresponding secretary, Ontario Union, in report of the Annual Convention, Ontario WCTU, 1911. Ontario Archives F855.

▲ Document 7: The Door Steadily Opens (1910)

The Door Steadily Opens

● Who is in the room? What is the woman trying to do? What kind of feminist argument for woman's suffrage is expressed here?

Source: Grain Growers Guide, 21 September, 1910.

▲ Document 8: "A Nice Mess You Men Folks Make of Running a House" (date unknown)

● Aunt Suffragette to Bachelor Whitney: "A nice mess you men folks make of running a House. I've come to look after things a little." What does this cartoon suggest about women's abilities in the public sphere? What does it suggest about stereotypes about feminists in this period? Are these stereotypes similar to or different from today's stereotypes about feminists?

Source: Source and date unknown.

Article 1: 'When the Mother of the Race Is Free': Race, Reproduction, and Sexuality in First-Wave Feminism

Mariana Valverde

That the vast majority of English-speaking first-wave feminists were not only ethnocentric but often racist is by now widely acknowledged. It is also acknowledged that this led to the exclusion of native women, immigrant women, and women of colour from a movement which claimed to be based on gender, with negative political consequences reverberating into our own day.[1] Racist strategies were not confined to situations in which topics such as immigration were directly at issue: they were integral to the movement as a whole. An aspect of this pervasive racial politic that has seldom been examined is the way in which racist assumptions and strategies were implicated in the reproductive and sexual politics of the movement. Because women without children or husbands, as well as those in traditional family situations, justified their claims to political and social rights by reference to their quasi-maternal public and private roles, ideas about sexuality and reproduction had an impact on all women, regardless of individual situations. The purpose of this article is thus to undertake a critical analysis of the racial specificity of that key figure in our past, 'the mother of the race,' and of the discourses on sex and reproduction within which this symbolic figure was constructed.

While most first-wave feminists believed that women deserved political and social rights as a matter of equal justice, they also used utilitarian and organicist arguments that grounded women's cause in an affirmation of their role in biological and social reproduction. In this sense, the conceptualization of women's work in reproduction was key to feminism as a whole. While today feminists tend to analyse reproductive politics in terms of individual women's rights and collective gender oppression, at the turn of the [twentieth] century reproduction was generally seen, by feminists as well as anti-feminists,

as inextricable from racial and imperial politics.[2] Women did not merely have babies: they reproduced 'the race.' Women did not merely have just enough babies or too much sex: through their childbearing they either helped or hindered the forward march of (Anglo-Saxon) civilization.[3] Phrases such as 'race suicide,' or, in a feminist context, 'mothers of the race,' organize sexuality and reproduction under racial categories. Feminists challenged the sexist elements of the evolutionary theories of Darwin, Spencer, and other scientific and social Darwinists, but they did not, with one or two exceptions, question the fundamental racism of mainstream theories of social and biological evolution, and in many ways they reinforced racist theories of biological and social progress by adopting them for feminist purposes. [. . .]

Evolution and Race 'Degeneration'

> When the mother of the race is free, we shall have a better world, by the easy right of birth and by the calm, slow, friendly forces of social evolution.[4]
>
> —Charlotte Perkins Gilman

It was an article of faith among the Anglo-Saxon ruling classes in England, the United States, and English Canada that the ambiguous entity 'the race' was, at the turn of the [twentieth] century, in imminent peril of what was equally ambiguously known as 'degeneration.' Feminist intellectuals participated in the debate about who was responsible for degeneration and who was to take a leadership role in 'regeneration,' elaborating complex theories of women and evolution countering the misogynist assumptions of male-stream evolutionists. Feminist evolutionism, however, not only failed to question the racist presuppositions of evolutionary thought, but produced a profoundly racist form of feminism in which women of 'lower' races were excluded from the specifically Anglo-Saxon work of building a better world through the freeing of 'the mother of the race.'

Male evolutionary theorists used sexist assumptions about gender roles in their debates about the mechanisms of natural and sexual selection (mechanisms which, prior to the acceptance of Mendelian genetics in the second quarter of the twentieth century, occasioned much speculation). One of these assumptions was that women did not contribute to

Source: Abridged from *Gender Conflicts: New Essays in Women's History,* Franca Iacovetta and Marianne Valverde (eds.), (University of Toronto Press, 1992), pp. 34, 7–11, 13–26. © University of Toronto Press, 1992. Reprinted with permission of the publisher.

natural selection because conservatism was inscribed in their very eggs, while the male sperm was not only quick but 'progressive.' A popular book on heredity stated, in 1883, that 'the male element is the originating and the female the perpetuating factor; the ovum is conservative, the male cell progressive.'[5] The 'male element' was responsible for evolution, because, as it was generally believed, there was more genetic variability among men than among women. Women's bodies were mere storage bins, unable to generate new and potentially progressive mutations. Females were thus portrayed as in an analogous position to the so-called less evolved races—they were dragged along the evolutionary path rather than marching at the head. Darwin himself had drawn a parallel between women's role in evolution and that of 'lower' (that is, less evolved) races: 'It is generally admitted that with women the powers of intuition, of rapid perception, and perhaps of imitation, are more strongly marked than in man; but some, at least, of these faculties are characteristic of the lower races, and therefore of a past and lower state of civilization.'[6]

Women of all races, then, were the passive conservers of past biology. [. . .]

Feminist intellectuals challenged the misogynist consequences of evolutionary theories, but without questioning the overall shape of evolutionary argument or its reliance on racist categories. [. . .]

[Feminists argued that] European women were… more morally evolved than other women, and insofar as women's contribution to 'the race' was seen to lie in moral reform and education as well as in childbearing, then it was European women who led both their own race and the human race. [. . .]

White women's contribution to world progress was not limited to their private role in bringing up their children as good Christians and citizens. Some Protestant women participated in foreign missions with the idea that, as 'mothers of the race,' they had a particular role to play in evangelism, especially in Eastern societies, where sexual segregation, as Ruth Brouwer's study shows, was exaggerated by women missionaries in order to ensure a demand for their services.[7] Women missionaries envisioned Third World women as downtrodden victims of cultural practices more sexist than anything existing in Christian countries. A text written by a man but used by many women's missionary societies stated as a trite fact that 'we have been accustomed to speak of the disabilities of women in India,

her degraded position, seclusion and illiteracy. It is true that the women of India have been among the greatest obstacles to progress in that land.'[8] Third World women may have been mothers in their own right, and occasionally they were addressed as 'sisters': but the role assigned to them by the foreign female missionary was really that of devoted daughter, as a missionary poem entitled 'Work in the Zenana' vividly illustrates:

Do you see those dusky faces
Gazing dumbly to the West—
Those dark eyes, so long despairing,
Now aglow with hope's unrest?
They are looking, waiting, longing
For deliverance and light;
Shall we not make haste to help them,
Our poor sisters of the night?[9]

In this poem as well as in countless descriptions of widow-burning and other 'primitive' practices found in missionary and travel literature produced by women,[10] Third World women's own mothering is unacknowledged. Third World women are presented as either too victimized or too corrupt to qualify as real mothers. Rather, they need to be themselves mothered—by wiser Anglo-Saxon Protestant women.

While Canadian women saw their domestic and international mothering in primarily moral terms, some English and American feminists debated antifeminist male intellectuals on their own terrain. Claiming not just moral but even biological equality or superiority, they tried to turn the discourse of biological evolution to their own advantage. One of the most systematic attempts to build a feminist social theory by adapting evolutionism was made in the United States by Antoinette Brown Blackwell. She did not challenge the view that women's and men's bodies, and female and male social abilities, were totally different [. . .] She even admits that men have larger brains than women; but she argues that for every male superiority there is a corresponding inferiority. A chart in her 1875 book, *The Sexes throughout Nature*, shows that men are superior in size and strength, but inferior in 'endurance,' 'direct nurture,' and 'structure' (the latter meaning that women's physical structure is more complex than men's). As a whole, then, gender traits balance each other, so that although claiming equality for women would be biologically incorrect, the changes due to evolution have never and will never alter the fundamental 'equivalence' of the genders [...][11]

The feminist critique of the gender bias of evolutionism was a fairly narrow one. The same anti-feminist writers who deplored that college-educated women were not bearing children in large numbers usually also—and often more centrally—used the concept of racial degeneration to attack lawbreakers, the mentally ill, and people of colour. White feminists attacked only the gender bias of evolutionary and eugenic thought, leaving its basic framework intact. This was tantamount to creating a new hierarchy among women, with nefarious consequences for women who were stigmatized and oppressed not only through gender but also through their labelling as 'feeble-minded,' 'unfit,' or 'primitive.' Some women—of 'healthy' middle-class Protestant stock—claimed a spot higher up the evolutionary scale, but the majority of the world's women were in an ambiguous position between hapless victims of their own cultures and active agents of the dreaded process of 'degeneration.'

'Degeneration,' a term originally referring to the decay of nerve tissue, was in the 1880s and 1890s appropriated to refer to wider social processes of decadence and decay. As George Moss and Robert Nye have argued for Germany and for France, respectively, anxieties about urban crime and political upheavals were welded to fears about mad people, criminals, anarchists, and the racially 'other.'[12] There was in particular a fear about the reproductive excesses of 'degenerates,' whose numbers were perceived to be swelling at the expense of those of the more reproductively cautious middle classes.

Sometimes the term 'degeneration' was simply a synonym for 'biologically and morally inferior.' At other times, however, the term had a more specific meaning, and was used primarily to refer to Asian cultures. While Africans were regarded as 'primitive'—as not sufficiently evolved—Asians (most notably the Chinese, but also the vague category of 'Oriental') were seen as belonging to a civilization long past its prime, to a race that was overly evolved, decadent. When Roosevelt described the Chinese as 'an ancient and effete civilization,'[13] while Sir John A. Macdonald labelled them 'a mongrel race,'[14] they were saying that 'the Orient' (which since Marco Polo could hardly be regarded as primitive by Europeans) had had its glorious epoch in the long-ago past, but was now decayed and had lost its virility, just like Oscar Wilde.[15] The North American

panic about the role of Chinese men in so-called 'white slavery,' a panic in which feminists played a major role, was justified by reference to this general theory of racial evolution and degeneration. Black men were perceived as primitive, as unable to control their instincts; Chinese men, by contrast, were perceived as decadent perverts in need of opium and other drugs to fuel their flagging sexual energies. These mythological differences account for the varying modes of racist persecution: while black men were constantly suspected of impulsively raping or wanting to rape white women, Chinese men were suspected of hatching intelligent but devious plots, such as luring young white women into apparently harmless 'chop suey palaces' and opium dens, and from there into the 'white slave traffic.' The anti-Chinese and other racist agitations that took place in Canada in the 1920s were legitimized partly through sexual and reproductive myths.[16] Many of these myths were, unfortunately, not challenged but rather supported by Canadian maternal feminists.

Canadian Feminism and the Question of Racial Degeneration

A leading first-wave Canadian feminist, the magistrate and popular writer Emily Murphy, published an expose of the drug trade entitled *The Black Candle*, which raised the spectre of white women being lured to (perverted) sex through opium. This book, published in 1922, was part of a wider anti-Chinese campaign that was particularly virulent in western Canada. The book's sensationalist pictures of drugged individuals (mostly Chinese men) included a photo of a *black* man apparently in bed with a white woman. The connection between that photo and drug trafficking is not explained, but it is clear that white readers had their anti-black racism fuelled by the book, along with their anti-Chinese prejudices.[17] That Murphy's feminism was designed for white women only is equally clear, since, gender divisions aside, she believed that the 'Nordic' races were inherently superior: 'I think the proximity of the magnetic pole has something to do with the superiority of the Northmen. The best peoples of the world have come out of the north, and the longer they are away from the boreal regions in such proportion do they degenerate.'[18]

Murphy's sense of racial superiority was by no means unique. In the work and discourses of the largest grassroots feminist organization in turn-of-the century Canada, the Woman's Christian Temperance Union (WCTU), one can see that the white ribbon worn by female temperance activists was a symbol not only of the healthy pure milk they would substitute for alcohol but also of the kind of racial composition they favoured for Canada. The WCTU did not, at least in the 1880s and 1890s, exclude women of colour: in fact, there were a few local 'coloured unions' in southern Ontario (whose activities need to be researched by local historians). Nevertheless, the scant mentions of women of colour in the WCTU press are condescending and maternalistic, in keeping, with missionary societies' portrayal of 'natives' in Canada and 'heathens' abroad.

The WCTU was by no means impervious to the new, 'scientific' racism promoted in the later nineteenth century by anthropologists and writers on social evolution, and in the first few decades of the twentieth century by the eugenics movement. As early as 1889, the dominion WCTU had organized a separate department of 'Heredity and Hygiene' which evidenced some activity at least in Ontario and Quebec, where provincial department superintendents produced irregular reports. [. . .] While promoting addresses to local unions by physicians, the leaders of this department were obviously not interested in a strictly determinist view of genetics; such a view would have led to resignation and passivity, or possibly to joining the eugenic campaign for sterilization of the unfit. (The National Council of Women of Canada, a less evangelical and more state-oriented organization, put more work into investigating the 'problem' of 'feebleminded women.') The WCTU preferred to leave medical and scientific strategies to others; in its own work it promoted a cheerful validation of the ability of Christian mothers to overcome genetic obstacles.[19] In calling on women to 'uplift the race,' the WCTU was arguing that mothers (actual and symbolic) could do a great deal to shape both their children and the future of the nation—a contribution which would have been negated if a strict genetic determinist argument had been accepted. That women could shape the genetic pool was a necessary premise in the WCTU's argument for political rights: 'Governments rise and fall by votes, and until women have electoral value, their reforms, their labours, their dreams of an uplifted race, a purified country with 'protected' homes, will lack fulfillment.'[20]

The WCTU, however, did not directly challenge biological determinism. Some of their members, such as Mrs (Dr) Wickett, Wentworth County superintendent of heredity and hygiene, were firm believers in the reality of 'race suicide'. She warned that Canadian Anglo-Saxons were in peril of being overcome by the 'less moral' but more prolific French Canadians, 'and all because we women, for various reasons, shrink from the duty and the joy of motherhood.' As wealthy women pursued careers and other selfish goals, 'among the outcast, the feebleminded and the criminal, reproduction will still go on.'[21] It is clear that in Mrs Wickett's eyes not all actual mothers qualify as 'real' mothers. [. . .]

The strongest call for eugenic measures was heard at the Ontario WCTU 1911 convention, which passed a resolution asking the government to investigate the problem of 'the marriage of moral degenerates'; an editorial in the dominion journal followed this up with a call for compulsory pre-marital medical exams. Even this contribution to the panic about the prolific 'unfit' however, had a certain ambiguity absent from the work of Canada's scientific racists, in so far as the term 'moral degenerates' was not clearly race-based.[22]

WCTU leaders, then, were aware of developments in genetic and eugenic theory and occasionally endorsed these scientific discourses on race and heredity, but they seemed relatively lukewarm about them, in contrast with the enthusiasm for eugenics shown by Canada's physicians, especially public health doctors. This was not because of the quantity of racism present in eugenics: in 1906 the WCTU journal began to publish inflammatory articles on the vices of immigrant men and their relative worthlessness as voters compared with Anglo-Protestant women, and into the 1902s articles raising the spectre of Jewish control over the liquor trade used anti-Semitism to fuel the fire of prohibition.[23] If the WCTU did not prioritize its 'heredity and hygiene' departments, and even within those departments stressed hygiene over heredity, it was rather because of a conflict between scientific determinism and the WCTU's optimistic evangelism. A typical compromise is found in an editorial entitled 'The Law of Heredity.' [...] This editorial acknowledges that inherited *tendencies* are important, since it is clear that pipe-smoking fathers, for instance, often have sons who take up the cigarette habit. (Cigarettes were the second most important target of WCTU anger, after alcohol.) After painting a pessimistic picture of a father passing on his acquired tastes to his children, the writer quickly introduces a more prominent and brighter figure: a heroic mother who countered a hereditary taste for alcohol among her offspring through careful childrearing. The conclusion, that 'environment in this instance prov[ed] itself stronger than heredity,' was in keeping with the WCTU's practical work in mothers' groups.[24] Shortly afterwards, an editorial on 'Patriotism' concluded that, despite Canada's mixed genetic inheritance, a pure and Christian nation could be produced through hard work, because 'heredity doesn't' count for much in the presence of good environment.'[25]

This is not to say that the WCTU was necessarily less racist than the female and male advocates of science. The discourse of evangelism allowed ample opportunity to decry the wrongdoings of 'heathens' who insisted on selling ice-cream and candy on Sundays in defiance of Sunday observance laws, and of male 'aliens' who were allowed to vote although they did not own as much property as white Canadian women. In respect to Sunday observance, the WCTU thundered: 'Every decent Canadian citizen should make up his mind that foreign hosts that are sweeping down on this country shall obey its laws, or find it a decidedly uncomfortable abiding place';[26] and in respect to the vote, the spectre of hordes of 'Assyrians, Italians, and others' is invoked as the WCTU asks: 'Why should the ballot be given to these aliens, who own not a tithe of the property owned by Canadian women who are without the ballot?'[27]

The WCTU's form of racism, although influenced by the scientific discourse of eugenics, was primarily shaped by an older religious tradition labelling people of colour as 'heathens'—as culturally and morally inferior—and not necessarily as genetically inferior. The shopworn allegory equating Europe with light/morality and Africa with darkness/sin was the dominant trope utilized by WCTU women in their conceptualization of race and culture, as evidenced in the use of 'light' as a metaphor both of Christianity and of freedom in the missionary poem quoted above. The exercise suggested for young people by a British missionary textbook published in 1906 was one familiar to Canadian churchgoers of both sexes in this time period: 'Contrast the darkness of Africa with the light of civilization in England. Show how applicable the title "the Dark Continent" is to Africa, as inhabited by the Negro race, as the "Great Unknown Land" and as

the country that, more than any other, has been given over to the Works of Darkness.'[28]

The WCTU's approach to race, culture, and heredity was, in conclusion, somewhat contradictory, but it tended to rely on old missionary ideas about darkness and light more than on the new scientific racism. This evangelical perspective was less rigid and had the potential to view all people, whatever their race, as potentially useful members of society—as long as they followed Christian morality, identified by the WCTU with Canadian mores. Putting the missionary zeal at work, the WCTU proselytized among the black communities in Chatham and Windsor; in St Catharines there was a committee to recruit black women, and in Hamilton there was a 'coloured' local union.[29] The contradictory position in which black women found themselves in a movement characterized by metaphors of whiteness is clear in the following passage, in which a white WCTU member reports on a conversations she had with a black mother: 'With eyes flooded with tears, one [black] woman said, "Our children are precious and although their faces are black, yet we want their lives to be white. We do not know how to combat a terrible sin that is prevalent in our school."'[30] The black mother is not a 'real' mother, since she is quite unable to prevent her children from falling into sin. Again, here race marks the adult woman as a non-adult, as a tearful girl in need of guidance.

Although an evangelical perspective differs from a genetic-determinist one in not automatically precluding black women or children from being 'pure,' the fact that purity was equated with whiteness,[31] and hence indirectly with European culture, made it difficult if not impossible for Canada's women of colour to identify with the brand of feminism elaborated by the WCTU, and in general by the overwhelmingly Protestant women of first-wave Canadian feminism. First-wave feminism was envisaged as the freeing of 'the mothers of the race:' but not all adult women, even if they had children, qualified to mother either their own children or 'the race.'

The irony of the evangelical feminist theorization of race and culture may have been that, had they emphasized women's strictly biological role in reproduction, there might have arisen a potentially cross-racial sense of women's work in reproducing the human race. The heavy emphasis on women's role as moral teachers of children, however, privileged those women whose cultural and racial background marked them as more adult, more evolved, more moral, and better 'mothers of the race.' By proclaiming that 'the standard of morality is in the keeping of our women,'[32] the WCTU indirectly narrowed the scope of feminism to women from dominant cultures/races, since, as seen in the first section, women of colour were usually regarded as less moral and maternal and as more corrupted by their culture. Women of colour were largely invisible, making cameo appearances only as grateful recipients of the moral reform message, never as potential active agents of the feminist project.

Since the consequences of the racism and ethnocentrism of first-wave feminism are still being felt in the 1980s, it is important to understand not only that many suffragists were racist, but exactly how they were racist. As Canadians become aware of the shady past of the eugenics movement in Canada, it is important to note that racism was not the exclusive province of biological determinists. Different discourses (evangelism, science, tourism) produce specific varieties of racism performing distinct functions in the Canadian social imaginary. The WCTU employed both scientific and evangelical discourses on race in their conceptualization of 'the mother of the race,' but as a rule the latter predominated over the former. The feminist theorization of race, finally, was not only evident in their views on immigration but was also centrally implicated in their thoughts about what they saw as the core of women's gender identity and hence of the feminist project—biological and social reproduction.

Notes

Many thanks to my friends in the feminist history group, especially Lynne Marks, and also to Himani Bannerji.

1. Angela Davis, *Women, Race, and Class* (New York: Vintage 1983): Carol Bacchi, *Liberation Deferred? The Ideas of the English-Canadian Suffragists 1877–1918* (Toronto: University of Toronto Press 1983); Angus McLaren, *Our Own Master Race: The Eugenic Movement in English Canada* (Toronto: McClelland and Stewart 1990). My thanks to Angus McLaren for allowing me to read his book in manuscript.

2. Anna Davin, 'Imperialism and Motherhood,' *History Workshop no. 5* (1978):1–75; Lucy Bland, *Banishing the Beast: Feminism, Sex, and Morality 1885–1918*

(forthcoming 1992). My thanks to Lucy Bland for sharing her work with me.

3. See Hazel V. Carby, '"On the Threshold of Woman's Era": Lynching, Empire, and Sexuality in Black Feminist Theory,' in H.L. Gates, Jr, ed., *Race, Writing, and Difference* (Ithaca: Cornell, University Press 1986), 301–16; Jacquelyn Dowd Hall, 'The Mind That Burns Each Body: Women, Rape, and Racial Violence,' in A. Snitow et al., eds., *Powers of Desire* (New York: Monthly Review 1983). 328–49.

4. Charlotte Perkins Gilman, *Women and Economics 1898*; New York Harper & Row 1966), 340.

5. W.K. Brooks, The Law of Heredity, quoted in Cynthia E. Russett, *Sexual Science: The Victorian Construction of Womanhood* (Cambridge Mass.: Harvard University Press 1989), 94. See also Eveleen Richards, 'Darwin and the Descent of Woman,' in D. Olroy and I. Langham, eds., *The Wider Domain of Evolutionary Thought* (Dordrecht and London: Reidel 1983), 57–111.

6. Darwin, The Descent of Man, quoted in Flavia Alaya, 'Victorian Science and the "Genius" of Woman,' *Journal of the History of Ideas* 38:2 (1977): 261. This passage is also quoted by Richards, 'Darwin and the Descent of Woman'; Richards points out that Darwin explicitly rejected J. S. Mill's argument about the socialization of women in favour of biological determinism.

7. Ruth Compton Brouwer, *New Women for God: Canadian Presbyterian Women and India Missions, 1876–1914* (University of Toronto Press 1990), 97–101.

8. Canadian Council of the Missionary Education Movement, Canada's Share in World Tasks (np 1921), 90.

9. Quoted in 21 Ruth Compton Brouwer, *New Women for God: Canadian Presbyterian Women and India Missions, 1876–1914* (Toronto: University of Toronto Press 1990), New Women, 87.

10. A good example is Lucy Guinness, *Across India at the Dawn of the Twentieth Century* (London: Religious Tract Society 1902). The engravings in this book create a sharp contrast between the literally dark and frightening images of Indian 'superstitions' with the well-lit portraits of virtuous Anglo-Saxon women playing hymns at the piano.

11. Antoinette Brown Blackwell, *The Sexes throughout Nature* (New York: Putnam's Sons 1875), 58.

12. George Mosse, *Nationalism and Sexuality* (New York: Fertig 1985); Robert Nye, *Crime, Madnesss and Politics in Modern France* (Princeton: Princeton

University Press 1984); and Frank Mort, *Dangerous Sexualities: Medico-Moral Politics in England since 1800* (London: Routledge 1987).

13. Roosevelt quoted in Richard Hofstadter, *Social Darwinism in American Thought* (Philadelphia: University of Pennsylvania Press 1945), 155.

14. Macdonald quoted in Donald Avery, 'Canadian Immigration Policy and the 'Foreign Navvy' 1896–1914,' in M. Cross and G. Kealey, eds., *The Consolidation of Capitalism 1896–1929* (Toronto: McClelland and Stewart 1983), 52.

15. For an attack on Wilde, Nietzsche, impressionist painters, and other intellectual degenerates, see the influential work by Max Nordau, *Degeneration* (New York: Appleton 1895).

16. Mariana Valverde, *The Age of Light, Soap, and Water: Moral Reform in English Canada, 1885–1925* (Toronto: McClelland and Stewart 1991), chap. 4

17. Emily Murphy, *The Black Candle* (Toronto: Thomas Allen 1922). Murphy played a leading role in the passing of provincial laws allowing 'eugenic' sterilization. See Angus McLaren, 'The Creation of a Haven for 'Human Thoroughbreds': The Sterilization of the Feeble-Minded and the Mentally Ill in British Columbia,' *Canadian Historical Review* 67:2 (1986).

18. Emily Ferguson [Murphy], *Janey Canuck in the West* (Toronto: Cassel 1910), 38

19. See, for instance, the article 'Hygiene and Heredity' by the local superintendent of this department in Oxford County, Ontario, in *Canadian White Ribbon Tidings (CWRT)* 15 April 1907, 879–80; and the untitled article on hygiene by WCTU leader Dr Amelia Yeomans in ibid., 1 May 1907, 886.

20. 'Woman's Franchise,' *Woman's Journal*, Feb. 1892, 7

21. 'Race Suicide,' *CWRT*, 15 Aug. 1908, 1221

22. *CWRT*, 1 March 1911, 1861. See McLaren, Our Own Master Race.

23. An article reprinted from the Ford publication, *The Dearborn Independent*, entitled 'Aspects of Jewish Power,' claimed that governments were reluctant to implement prohibition because of the undue influence of Jews controlling the liquor traffic; *CWRT*, Dec. 1924, 256. My thanks to Lynne Marks for this reference.

24. Editorial, 'The Law of Heredity,' *CWRT*, 15 April 1907, 874–5.

25. *CWRT*, 15 June 1908, 1184.

26. Editorial, *CWRT*, 15 June 1907, 938.

27. *CWRT*, 15 March 1905, 228. Note the obviously literary reference to the ancient Assyrians, who are here typically mixed with the more plausible Italians. The WCTU women, like other reasonably educated Anglo-Saxons of their time, saw racial and ethnic groups through the filters of both learned and popular texts and images of 'the Orient.' The Thousand and One Nights imagery is seldom explicitly invoked, but it would have been employed by both writers and readers of such allegedly 'factual' pieces as the description of immigrant men's drunkenness in *CWRT*, 1 May 1905, 251–2.

28. Quoted in Lorimer, *Colour, Class and the Victorians*, 76. A similar racial hierarchy, expressed in somewhat more benevolent terms, is found in Canadian texts such as William T. Gunn, *His Dominion* (Canadian Council of the Missionary Education Movement 1917), and John R. Mott, *The Decisive Hour of Christian Missions* (New York: Student Volunteer Movement for Foreign Missions 1911). Mott's book was used as a textbook by Canadian Presbyterians.

29. A Miss Phelps, whose race is not indicated, was active among St. Catharines blacks in the early 1890s. See AO, WCTU Collection, minutes of Ontario WCTU for 1894 annual convention. The existence of a 'coloured union' in Hamilton has been pointed out to me by Lynne Marks, whose own work will shed further light on some of the issues raised in this paper. Lynne Marks, 'Religion and Leisure in Three Ontario Towns, 1880–1902 (PhD thesis in progress, Department of History, York University).

30. *CWRT*, 15 March 1904, 50. The 'terrible sin' is probably masturbation, vigorously denounced by Arthur W. Beall, the WCTU's paid sex hygiene educator for boys.

31. In its first issue, the *Woman's Journal* (July 1885, 1) declared: 'The distinctive badge of the WCTU Union is a white ribbon, denoting purity in the heart, in the home, in society.'

32. Ibid., Nov. 1885, 3.

■ Article 2: Rediscovering Our Foremothers Again: Racial Ideas of Canada's Early Feminists, 1885–1945

Janice Fiamengo

The full article includes a discussion of four early feminists: Sara Jeanette Duncan, Nellie McClung, Agnes Maule Machar, and Flora MacDonald Denison. This excerpt includes only Fiamengo's discussion of McClung.

The past decade witnessed a sea change in scholarship on the early Canadian women's movement as feminist scholars came to recognize (or were forced to see[1]) the racism of white feminist 'foremothers' and wrestled with its implications for critical practice. Whereas scholars in the 1970s and 1980s tended to celebrate the achievements of early suffrage and reform activists, often 'white-washing' (Smith, 1995: 93) their ideological impurities so that they might stand as icons of resistance, more recent scholarship by Carol Lee Bacchi, Angus McLaren, Mariana Valverde, and others has emphasized the imperialist and racist foundations of early Canadian 'feminism'.[2] Such work has been crucial in redressing the error and omissions of white feminist scholarship. Critical reassessment, however, has often shaded into outright dismissal, and in the process some of the complexities of early feminist discourse have been lost in the reductive conclusion that all first-wave feminist writing promoted a monolithic racism. Investigation of Canada's past is, as Veronica Strong-Boag has suggested, an ongoing and open-ended process of reexamination guided by current concerns and theoretical perspectives, and it is perhaps time to take another look at early feminist engagements with race. [. . .]

Recent developments in postcolonial and critical race theory, especially Homi Bhabha's emphasis on the ambivalence of colonial discourse, point the way to a nuanced reading of this complex archive.

Particularly important for my purpose is the recognition that ideological formations such as white supremacy are rarely stable or coherent (Hall, 2000: 15), John Comaroff (1977) has stressed that scholars studying colonialism's history do well to pay attention to its 'moments of incoherence and inchoateness, its internal contortions and complexities' (165), because they often provided the points where resistance came to be focused.[3] Race was always a contested subject in nineteenth- and early-twentieth-century Canada,[4] and competing understandings of race within Social Darwinism and evangelical Christianity made the term itself highly unstable.[5] Scientific debate raised unanswered questions about how profound racial differences were and whether they were primarily biological or cultural (Anderson, 1991: 40–4). Furthermore, early white feminism also contained competing claims. Although Darwinian beliefs about the superiority of the Anglo-Saxon race and evangelical emphasis on the civilizing mission often fit smoothly with white feminist self-positioning as 'mothers of the race' (Valverde, 1992: 1) and 'crusaders for Empire' (Carty, 1999:37), feminist rhetoric of equal justice for all complicated acceptance of racial hierarchy and made possible statements of empathy and solidarity with nonwhite people. [. . .]

Emphasizing the variety of white feminist conceptions of racial difference is useful because it demonstrates that white supremacy, undeniably the dominant ideology during this period,[6] was nonetheless not absolute in Canadian society before the Second World War. Recognizing the diverse positions that whites could occupy in those years is crucial in avoiding extremes of apology (everyone thought like that, so we can't judge them for it) or disavowal (they were all racist, so their work isn't worth reading carefully) in order to understand how well-intentioned individuals negotiated the racial and racist discourses of their day. In this discussion, I follow Kwame Anthony Appiah and David Theo Goldberg in distinguishing between racism and racialism, problematic as such a manoeuvre is. Because the writers considered in this paper used a racial discourse, it is necessary to attempt a distinction in order to notice where racialism does not lead to racism. Put simply, racialism is the belief that particular races share certain inherited traits (whether produced through culture or biology) that define 'a sort of racial essence' (Appiah, 1990: 5). Racism, in contrast, uses these traits

Source: Janice Fiamengo, 'Rediscovering our Foremothers Again: Racial Ideas of Canada's Early Feminists, 1885–1945' in *Rethinking Canada: The Promise of Women's History*, 5th ed., Mona Gleason and Adele Perry (eds.) (Don Mills: Oxford University Press, 2006). Reprinted with permission.

to create a physical, intellectual, and moral hierarchy. It is probably safe to say that, because racialism was a constituent part of the formation of Western subjects, few white persons could have escaped racialist thinking; as Kay Anderson (1991) has argued, by the end of the nineteenth century, most white Canadians believed 'that the mental, moral, and physical differences between "the races" were profound' (61). Just how they understood those differences in relation to their own whiteness is the question that I explore in the following pages. [. . .]

Prairie reformer Nellie McClung (1873–1951), was a tireless campaigner for temperance, women's suffrage, peace, democracy, and church reform, McClung was an effective leader who saw herself as a 'voice for the voiceless' (1935: 281).[7] Her vision of social reform developed at a time of expanding white settlement on the Prairies, racist fears about the immigration to Canada of 'foreigners', and developing international tensions between imperial powers. As previous references have indicated, Christianity and love for the British Empire (McClung once wrote 'My heart has been thrilled with what it is to be a citizen of the British empire'[8]) underpinned much of her thought: she was committed to Methodism (later the United Church) and to British justice even though a critic of their failings. Her commitment to justice was at least partly forged by the hard conditions of rural life, especially the poverty and government neglect that destroyed struggling white settler families on the Prairies. The two ideological strands of ethnocentrism and a commitment to democratic citizenship produce a complex racial ideology in which racism and antiracism are difficult to separate. Arun Mukherjee (1995) and, to a lesser extent, Mariana Valverde (1991) have highlighted the racist and imperialist assumptions in McClung's fiction and essays, showing how belief in Christian mission work led McClung to dismiss the civilizations of non-Christian peoples and to mobilize racist stereotypes, particularly her association of Chinese men and opium. Valverde notes that 'the very origins, as well as the form of McClung's feminism are shaped by ethnocentric ideas' (120). Mukherjee's discussion indicates the difficulty of defining McClung's beliefs about race as Mukherjee shows, nearly every 'politically incorrect' (20) statement can be countered with a more progressive one. Here I will concentrate on some of McClung's uncollected writings in order to consider lesser known aspects of her thought and

activism. These writings indicate that McClung struggled with the meaning of race throughout her life and showed herself capable of rethinking racist assumptions when the occasion demanded it; her sympathetic interest in racial Others highlights the progressiveness of her feminism even while she continued to rely on racial and racist discourses to frame her arguments.

The paradoxes of Christian commitment are everywhere in McClung's writing. Her belief in the ideals of Christian civilization limited her apprehension of the damage that settlement and government policies inflicted on Native peoples, yet that very commitment to Christian justice also galvanized some empathy for Native struggles. In *Clearing in the West* (1935), for example, McClung recounts how, as a child, she defended Métis and Indian rights to land and autonomy during the Riel Rebellion, arguing with her parents that the Métis had 'a grievance, a real one' (168). At the same time, her adult conception of Canada as a new country ('a great blank book' with 'no precedents to guide us' [1915:96]) dismissed the First Nations entirely. A scene from *The Stream Runs Fast* (1945) demonstrates McClung's willingness to extend membership in the British imperial family to a Native father whose son is fighting in the First World War; McClung recognizes that 'He was one of us— and one who had made a big contribution. We were all citizens of the British Empire; we were all of the great family of the Next-of-Kin' (158). Family membership in the empire is clearly negotiated on white terms in this scene. Equal citizenship meant assimilation to Britishness, an inclusive alternative to the early-twentieth-century assertion of Native biological inferiority. At the same time, McClung often characterized Native peoples using more or less benign racial stereotypes invoking inherent difference. For example, she records how she was prevented from being lost in London's streets while attending a Methodist conference by a young Native woman (also attending the conference) who had the 'blessed native instinct' for direction (1945: 224): in linking this young woman's ability to negotiate direction with a wild bird's homing instinct, she betrays a tendency to equate Native peoples with God's lesser creatures. The autobiography in which these passages occur was the last book that McClung published, making it difficult to argue, as one might be tempted, toward antiracism as she grew older. However, evidence from her papers reveals that she participated actively in antiracist causes toward the end of her life, most notably in defence of Japanese Canadians before and during the Second World War when she was nearing seventy years of age. McClung was more concerned about racial injustice than many of her white feminist contemporaries, and her belief in the God-given common humanity of all people anchored the liberating potential of her Social Gospel activism.

McClung was unusual in her stress on a multiracial vision of the country at a time when most whites took for granted that Canada would always be a white nation. At the London Methodist meeting cited above, she reacted with anger when southern American delegates refused to sit with the 'coloured people' of the African Methodist Church. 'We were seated near the malcontents, and quickly changed seats with them, wondering if they would carry their race prejudices to heaven,' she records sarcastically, reflecting that 'my soul was scorched with shame for my race' (1945: 221). From the early years of her career to the end of her life, McClung articulated a vision of Canada based on equal justice for all. 'One of my most glorious dreams,' she wrote famously for the Ottawa *Citizen* in 1915, 'is that Canada shall be known as the land of the fair deal.'[9] When she defined that phrase for In *Times like These* (1915), she listed racial justice as her first criterion of fairness: 'Canada should be a place where every race, colour and creed will be given exactly the same chance' (97). Living in a country that blended many peoples, Canadians, she believed, had an unprecedented opportunity for interracial understanding.[10] Too often, 'however, we are a pretty self-centred race, we Canadians', she lamented.[11] During the Second World War, McClung held on to the hope that a new world order might emerge from the fight against Hitler, dreaming of a regenerated society in which it would be recognized that 'all men are equal in God's sight, irrespective of race or colour. There are no superior races.'[12] The confusing elasticity of her use of the term *race* (which is sometimes synonymous with ethnicity, sometimes linked with colour, and at other times identified with nation) makes precise analysis of her meaning difficult but also seems to have enabled McClung to think flexibly about Canadian national identity. Her faith that all peoples could find a 'spiritual cement' to bind them together in communities of fellowship helped her to avoid the racist extremes of some fellow reformers.

As Mukherjee (1995) has stressed, such idealistic statements need to be considered in the context of McClung's racist and imperialist culture and weighed against her complicity with or opposition to the racism that McClung encountered in her daily life. For example, Mukherjee notes that McClung supported overseas Christian mission work, campaigned for women's suffrage with American racists, and wrote nothing about racial inequality when she travelled through the southern United States, 'Would it not seem interesting to know how McClung responded to the Jim Crow south and the racist feminism of the southern suffragists?' she asks (22). Indeed, while some of Mukherjee's queries about the extent to which McClung challenged friends and colleagues (e.g., Emily Murphy), on their racism may never be definitively answered, Mukherjee signals important future directions for work on McClung. Uncollected newspaper articles in McClung's personal papers give evidence of some of her more decisive and public antiracist stands and answer a few of Mukherjee's questions about McClung's antiracist practice.

Unlike some white suffragists, who voiced bitterness that they were denied the vote, while it was granted to ignorant men such as 'untutored Ruthenians and Galicians' [Ukrainians] (Bacchi, 1983: 53), McClung largely refused such postures of wounded racial superiority. In 1915, on the suffrage trail, she managed to avoid being drawn into racist arguments. The *Winnipeg Free Press* reported that McClung 'spoke passionately in defence of the foreign women' on the question of suffrage. 'Let it be remembered,' the newspaper quoted McClung, 'that there are far more foreign men that women in the county and there is no objection to their voting. It has even been urged that the vote should be taken from these foreign men because corrupt politicians have bought their votes. I wouldn't take away their vote, but I would remove their ignorance. There is no menace to be feared from the foreign women.'[13] In this instance, McClung does not refute the charge that 'foreign' men, mainly, it seems, Eastern and Southern Europeans, were particularly vulnerable to corrupt voting.[14] Her assumption that foreigners probably did need education betrays the paternalistic racialism of her thinking, but she does not call for exclusions, preferring a rhetoric of inclusivity and possibility. A number of newspaper articles from this period report McClung's '[s]tirring defence of foreign women'[15] during her wartime suffrage campaigns. In 1917, McClung seemed to contradict her earlier position by calling for the vote to be given to Canadian and English-born women first, as a special war measure however, she withdrew this suggestion and publicly acknowledged her error when Francis Marion Beynon criticized the idea in the pages of the *Grain Growers' Guide*.[16] While McClung likely believes that not all people understood democracy as well as the British, she rarely allowed that thinking to limit her commitment to voting rights for all citizens.

Angus McLaren has noted that racist and anti-immigrant mobilizing reached a peak during the Depression years, when economic hardship and the threat to public order caused by hordes of unemployed people exacerbated the racism of many Canadian officials, politicians, and business leaders. McClung's public statements during the 1930s on behalf of the Doukhobors in British Columbia, European Jews, and Chinese and Japanese Canadians reveal resistance to the fear-mongering of public officials and community elders, who frequently warned of racial threats to Canadians by unassimilable aliens (Valverde, 1991: 104–28). In fact, McClung was one of the few commentators to argue that the danger lay not in racial contamination by these others but in Canada's failure to fulfill its Christian obligation to people seeking refuge. Commenting on Canada's humanitarian obligation to accept Jews fleeing Hitler, she charged that 'in spite of our broad territory Canada has not been generous with the 'stranger at our gates' and insisted that 'unless we adopt a new policy [...] the verdict of history will be that the Canadian people were both short-sighted and hard of heart.'[17] She chided 'narrow racial groups of great political power', clearly naming and deploring the racism of whites.[18] 'Noted Author Bursts Bomb at City Rally' was the title of a Vancouver newspaper report for 10 October 1935, when McClung addressed a Liberal Party rally at the Empress Theatre in Vancouver to disagree explicitly with the Liberal MP's opposition to Oriental franchise. 'In my opinion every class and every creed of people should have equal rights,' McClung was reported to have said in explanation of her disagreement with Ian Mackenzie, Liberal MP for Vancouver Centre.[19] Two years later, when Japanese military aggression in China, combined with economic tensions at home, seemed to validate anti-Japanese discourse, McClung was urging Victoria

residents to maintain justice in their dealings with the local Japanese Canadian population. 'It was a time,' the *Colonist* reported McClung as saying on 9 October 1937, 'to show kindness and understanding and not blame those who are powerless to help what is being done by the militia party.'[20] These statements reveal that, although her conception of the nation was ethnocentric in its celebration of British heritage, faith in British justice led her to oppose racial exclusivity and persecution.

After the bombing of Pearl Harbor by the Japanese on 7 December 1941, McClung's insistence on fairness was even more unusual and difficult to maintain.[21] Although a few individuals and newspaper editors counselled calm and consideration for the difficult position of Japanese Canadians, 'those voices advocating either a "tolerant" or even a "moderate" attitude were quickly submerged in the wave of anti-Japanese protest' (Adachi, 1976: 201). At this time, McClung wrote some of her most notable newspaper columns on Canadian race relations, revealing a commitment to justice in troubled times.[22] Her providential view of history enabled her to understand the so-called problem of Japanese Canadians in British Columbia as an opportunity for Canadians to test their commitment to justice. 'We have in this province of British Columbia 23,000 Japanese people, many of them natives of Canada and some of the second generation.' she wrote on 3 January 1942[23]

> We have an opportunity now of showing them that we do respect human rights and that democracy has a wide enough framework to give peace and security to all people of goodwill irrespective of race or colour. I believe that all precautions must be taken at this time, but we must not sink into Hitler's ways of persecution. We must not punish innocent people. The Canadian Japanese are not to blame for the treacherous attack on Pearl Harbor, nor for the other misdeed of their misled people.

McClung went on to ask readers to remember that Canada's treatment of its citizens would be judged by history. 'A great opportunity is ours today to show a kindly spirit of watchful tolerance. Let us guard well, not only our bridges and our plants, but our good name for fair dealing. We must have precautions, but let us think of our Japanese, as human beings, not as enemy aliens.' 'Our Japanese' has a ring of paternalism but also stresses Japanese Canadian inclusion in the national family. The call to think outside racial categories and to see the full humanity of Japanese Canadians indicates the extent to which McClung could mobilize patriotic myth ('our good name for fair dealing') to oppose xenophobia. Given that, as a resident of Victoria, she believed herself to be in imminent danger of an air attack, this was no small achievement. Two weeks later, McClung returned to her theme of Canada's moral obligations. 'Last week I made a plea for the individual Japanese, that they should be treated fairly,' she reminded readers,

> [...] and I know these sentiments will be challenged, for this is a time of excitement, when prejudices run riot. But we must remember we are a Christian people. On New Year's Day we confessed our sins and asked God to guide us. If we are to merit that guidance we must not allow hate centers to develop here. [. . .] Let us, the free people, do all in our power to keep open the gates of mercy, no matter what comes. A great purpose and design for humanity is being worked out in the world now before our eyes and we must not blot our part of the pattern.[24]

McClung's insistence that God's hand was guiding history and that Canadians had a vital role to play in its unfolding show her use of a Christian narrative of good warring against evil that made the protection of racialized victims a cornerstone of Canada's wartime mandate.

Mary Hallett and Marilyn Davis, authors of McClung's biography, have suggested that outsight criticism of government policy would have been censored at this time. It certainly seems that McClung was under orders from her editor to avoid 'political' matters. In one article, she prefaced a few remarks on conscription with the injunction 'now don't be nervous, Mr Editor, I am not dealing with it in a political way.'[25] Whatever the reason, there is no record that McClung protested the internment of Japanese Canadians, which occurred shortly after these columns were published; the announcement of partial evacuation occurred on 14 January 1942; total evacuation of all persons of Japanese ancestry was announced on 26 February 1942. Rather than focusing on the internment, McClung turned her sights to the future, imagining the better Canada that should be built after the war, hoping that the Oriental franchise would be implemented immediately once the war ended as evidence that Canada would finally be 'through with racial antipathies' and characterizing the war as 'a war against all racial superiorities'.[26] Even to McClung, such statements must have seemed optimistic. As the war dragged on, many of her columns were devoted to strengthening morale: she urged all-out support for the war effort, with boosterish articles on conserving sugar, sharing food, making sacrifices, and salvaging useful materials. She continued to devote a good deal of print space to intemperance, which she occasionally targeted as one of the causes of the war. Her attention to wartime racial injustice was, in the end, weakened by her belief that God was on the Allies' side and that Canadians' moral energies should be fully concentrated on the war effort. Nonetheless, her articles on fair treatment for Japanese Canadians reveal that, unlike the majority of white Canadians in Western Canada, McClung was not swayed by wartime propaganda. Ultimately, her emphasis on Canada as a nation of immigrants and her belief in Christian democracy meant that she did not appreciate the unique situation of Native peoples; she promoted assimilation to British civilization as the answer to racial conflict. Nevertheless, her sense of her role in an unfolding Christian narrative often prompted concern for racial justice and explicit antiracism work. [. . .]

Constance Backhouse ends her study of the legal history of racism in Canada by noting that cases of resistance demonstrate that 'Those who espoused philosophies of white supremacy were not speaking in a moral vacuum' (278). Although racism was the dominant ideology in the period under consideration, it was not simply the air that early Canadians breathed, as is often asserted. Feminist reformers, like others, made choices from among a range of discourses, some of which enabled antihegemonic thinking about race. [...] [In addition to the writings of Agnes Maule Machar and Flora MacDonald Denison] McClung's [concept of the] fair deal, [...] seems to have favoured the development of inclusive understandings of race that saw difference as at least potentially an opportunity rather than a threat. [. . .] Important work remains to be done to contextualize and analyse the ideologies that frequently limited, but occasionally furthered, a racially inclusive white feminist vision in the early years of the Canadian women's movement.

Notes

1. Women of colour and Native women in Canada have been primarily responsible for prodding white feminists into this realization. As Donna Haraway has noted, to say that white women 'discovered' or 'came to 'realize' their complicity in racism really means that they 'were forced kicking and screaming to notice it' (157)! For a good example of such prodding, see Mukherjee, 'Right', on white feminist silence about Charlotte Perkins Gilman's racism.

2. McLaren see Valverde (1991), Perry (2001), Newman (1999), Gerson (1997), and Devereux (2000).

3. For an overview of scholarly interest in the tensions and contradictions of empire, see Stoler and Cooper (1997).

4. For an overview of Canadian thinking about race and national identity, particularly the relationship between Aboriginal peoples and Euro-Canadians, see Strong-Boag and Gerson, 2000: 19–32.

5. The instability of race in the late nineteenth century was exacerbated because it could mean 'different things simultaneously' (Valverde, 1992: 5). As Louise Michele Newman has suggested in her analysis of early American feminism, race often 'functioned as an absent presence' in white women's suffrage arguments (57). I deliberately keep the waters muddy by following the usage of my writers, evoking 'race' when referring to any people defined as foreign, non-Anglo-Saxon, or nonwhite in situations where power and exclusion are at issue. I intend such conceptual muddiness to signal my disbelief in any immutable or absolute basis for racial distinction following recent theorists in understanding race not as a biological given but as a historically inflected ideal produced through representation and constantly being remade in particular discursive situations. For an overview of central issues in race thinking, see Cornell and Hartmann, 1998: 15–38; for a history of race thinking, see Anderson, 1991: 15–38; for a history of race thinking, see Cornell and Hartmann, 1998: 15–38; for a history of race thinking, see Anderson, 1991: 38–44, and Bernasconl and Lott, 2000: vii–xviii.

6. See Backhouse for a study of 'the central role of the Canadian legal system in the establishment and enforcement of racial inequality' (15). For a discussion of moves to prevent the immigration of 'inferior' races, including Slavs, Jews, Southern Europeans, Orientals, and Blacks, see McLaren, 1990: 46–67.

7. For a biography that discusses McClung's activism, see Hallett and Davis (1993); for a 'scrapbook' with extensive quotations, see Savage (1979). For an analysis of McClung's fiction from a feminist perspective, see Warne (1993).

8. Unidentified clipping, Nellie McClung Papers, PABC, vol. 17.

9. Untitled clipping, Nellie McClung Papers, PABC, vol. 17.

10. Untitled Clipping, *Regina Star*, 9 November 1937, Nellie McClung Papers, PABC Vol. 17.

11. 'How Should We Celebrate July 1?' *Western Home Monthly*, July 1927, Nellie McClung papers, PABC, vol. 15.

12. 'What Holds the British Empire Together'. Unidentified Clipping: Nellie McClung Papers, PABC, vol. 14.

13. Unidentified Clipping, Nellie McClung papers, PABC, vol. 17.

14. But McClung also recorded how 'in our blind egotism we class our foreign people as ignorant people, if they do not know our ways and our language. They may know many other languages, but it they have not yet mastered ours they are poor, ignorant *foreigners*, we Anglo-Saxon people have a decided sense of our own superiority, and we feel sure that our skin is exactly the right color' (1915: 53).

15. Undated clipping, Nellie McClung Papers, PABC, vol. 17.

16. Untitled clipping, *Grain Growers'* Guide, 24 January 1917, Nellie McClung Papers, PABC, vol. 17.

17. Unidentified clipping, Nellie McClung Papers, PABC; vol. 17.

18. For a discussion of Canada's protracted unwillingness to offer refuge to European Jews, see Abella and Trooper (1982).

19. Unidentified clipping, Nellie McClung Papers, PABC vol. 17. In the federal election campaign of 1935, the Liberals opposed the newly created CCF's stand on enfranchising Chinese and Japanese Canadians, vowing to defend the white electorate.

20. 'Urges Women to Consider Local Japanese People', *Victoria Colonist*, 9 October 1937, Nellie McClung Papers, PABC, vol 17.

21. Within a week of the attack, demands were being made across British Colombia that all people of

Japanese heritage be interned, and soon newspaper editorials began to support the majority public opinion, See Adachl, 1976: 201–2.

22. Mary Hallett and Marilyn Davis (1993: 274–6) also discuss these columns.

23. 'What Did We Learn in 1941?' Unidentified clipping, 3 January 1942, Nellie McClung Papers, PABC, vol. 52.

24. Unidentified clipping, 17 January 1942, Nellie McClung Papers, PABC, vol. 52

25. Unidentified Clipping, 21 February 1942, Nellie McClung Papers, PABC, vol. 52.

26. 'That We May Not Forget,' *Winnipeg Free Press*, 14 November 1942, Nellie McClung Papers, PABC, vol. 53.

References

Abella, Irving, and Harold Trooper, 1982. *None is Too Many: Canada and the Jews of Europe, 1933–1948*. Toronto: Lester.

Adachi, Ken. 1976. *The Enemy That Never Was*. Toronto: McClelland.

Anderson, Kay J. 1991. *Vancouver's Chinatown: Racial Discourse in Canada, 1875–1980*. Montreal: McGill-Queen's University Press.

Appiah, Kwame Anthony. 1990. 'Racisms', pp. 3–17 in *Anatomy of Racism*, D. Goldberg, ed. Minneapolis: U of Minnesota Press.

Bacchi, Carol Lee. 1983. *Liberation Deferred? The Ideas of the English-Canadian Suffragists, 1877–1918*. Toronto: University of Toronto Press.

Backhouse, Constance. 1999. Colour-Coded: *A Legal History of Racism in Canada, 1990–1950*. Toronto: University of Toronto Press.

Bernasconl, Robert, and Tommy L. Lott, eds, 2000. *The Idea of Race. Indianapolis: Hackett*.

Bhabha, Homi. 1997. 'Of Mimicry and Man: The Ambivalence of Colonial Discourse', pp. 152–60, in *Tensions of Empire: Colonial Cultures in the Bourgeois World*, F. Cooper and A.L. Stoler, eds. Berkeley: University of California Press.

Carty, Linda. 1999. 'The Discourse of Empire and the Social Construction of, Gender', pp. 35–47 in *Scratching the Surface: Canadian Anti-Racist Feminist Thought*, Enakshi Dua and Angela Robertson, eds. Toronto: Women's Press.

Comaroff, John L. 1997. 'Images of Empire, Contests of Conscience: Models of Colonial Domination in South Africa', pp. 163–97 in *Tensions of Empire:*

Colonial Cultures in the Bourgeois World, F. Cooper and A.L. Stoler, eds. Berkeley: University of California Press.

Cook, Ramsay. 1985. *The Regenerators: Social Criticism in Late Victorian English Canada*. Toronto: University of Toronto Press.

Cooper, Frederick, and Ann Laura Stoler, eds. 1997. *Tensions of Empire: Colonial Cultures in the Bourgeois World*. Berkeley: University of California Press.

Cornell, Stephen, and Douglas Hartmann. 1998. *Ethnicity and Race: Making Identities in a Changing World*. Thousand Oaks, CA; Pine Forge.

Devereux, Cecily. 'Writing with a "Definite Purpose": L.M. Montgomery, Nellie L. McClung, and the Politics of Imperial Motherhood in Fiction for Children', *Canadian Children's Literature* 26:3 (2000): 6–22.

Gerson, Carole. 'Nobler Savages: Representations of Native Women in the Writings of Susanna Moodie and Catharine Parr Traill', *Journal of Canadian Studies* 32.2 (1997): 5–21.

Goldberg, David Theo, ed. 1990. *Anatomy of Racism*. Minneapolis: University of Minnesota press.

Hall, Catherine. 2000. 'Introduction: Thinking the Postcolonial, Thinking the Empire', pp. 1–33 in *Cultures of Empire: A Reader. Catherine Hall*, ed. New York: Routledge.

Hallet, Mary, and Marilyn Davis. 1993. *Firing the Heather: The Life and Times of Nellie McClung*, Saskatoon; Fifth House.

Haraway, Donna J. 1991. *Simians, Cyborgs, and Women: The Reinvention of Nature*, New York: Routledge.

McClung, Nellie. [1915] 1972. *In Times like These*. Toronto: University of Toronto Press.

——. 1935. *Clearing in the West*. Toronto: Allen.

——. 1945. *The Stream Runs Fast*. Toronto: Allen.

McLaren, Angus. 1990. *Our Own Master Race: Eugenics in Canada*, 1885–1945. Toronto: McClelland & Stewart.

Mukherjee, Arun P. 'In a Class of Her Own', *Literary Review of Canada* (July–August 1995); 20–3.

——. 1993. '"Right our [sic] of 'Herstory': Racism in Charlotte Perkins Gilman's Heriand and Feminist Literary Theory'. pp. 159–75 in *Returning the Gaze: Essays on Racism, Feminism, and Politics, Hlmani Bannerji*, ed. Toronto: Sister Vision.

Newman, Louise Michele. 1999. *White Women's Rights*: *The Racial Origins of Feminism in the United States*. New York: Oxford University Press.

Perry, Adele, 2001. *On the Edge of Empire: Gender, Race,*

and the Making of British Columbia, 1849–1871. Toronto: University of Toronto Press.

Savage, Candace. 1979. *Our Nell: A Scrapbook Biography of Nellie L. McClung.* Saskatoon: Western Producer Prairie.

Smith, Susan L. 'Whitewashing Womanhood: The Politics of Race in Writing Women's History', *Canadian Review of Comparative Literature* 22.1 (1995):93–103.

Staslulis, Daiva, and Nira Yuval-Davis. 1995. 'Introduction: Beyond Dichotomies—Gender, Race, Ethnicity and Class in Settler Societies', pp. 1–37 *Unsettling Settler Societies: Articulations of Gender, Race, Ethnicity, and Class*, Dalva Staslulis and Nira Yuval-Davis eds. London: Sage.

Stoler, Ann Lama, and Frederick Cooper. 1997. 'Between Metropole and Colony: Rethinking a Research Agenda', pp. 1–56 in *Tensions of Empire: Colonial Cultures in the Bourgeois World*, F. Cooper and A.L. Stoier, eds. Berkeley: University of California Press.

Strong-Boag, Veronica. 'Contested Space: The Politics of Canadian Memory', *Journal of the Canadian Historical Association* 5 (1994): 3–18.

Strong-Boag, Veronica, and Carole Gerson. 2000. *Paddling Her Own Canoe: The Times and Texts of Pauline Johnson (Tekahionwake).* Toronto: University of Toronto Press.

Valverde, Mariana. 1991. *The Age of Light, Soap, and Water: Moral Reform in English Canada*, 1885–1925. Toronto: McClelland & Stewart.

——, 1992. '"When the Mother of the Race is Free": Race, Reproduction, and Sexuality in First-Wave Feminism', pp. 3–26 in *Gender Conflicts: New Essays in Women's History,* Franca Iacovetta and Mariana Valverde, eds. Toronto: University of Toronto Press.

Warne, Randl R. 1993, Literature as Pulpit: *The Christian Social Activism of Nellie McClung.* Waterloo: Wilfrid Laurier University Press.

AGE MATTERS

Growing Up in the Interwar Years

Cynthia R. Comacchio
Wilfrid Laurier University

AGE MATTERS: GROWING UP IN THE INTERWAR YEARS

● **Introduction by Cynthia R. Comacchio**

▲ **Primary Sources**

Document 1: Centennial Number, *Everywoman's World,* 1917

Document 2: *The Surprise of My Life*, 1920s

Document 3: *Diary of Mary Dulhanty*, 1926–27

Document 4: *The Revolt of Youth*, 1926

Document 5: *Freedom to Play*, 1930s–40s

■ **Secondary Sources**

Article 1: Making Modern Childhood, the Natural Way: Psychology, Mental Hygiene, and Progressive Education at Ontario Summer Camps, 1920–1955

Sharon Yvonne Wall

Article 2: Lost in Modernity: The "Problem of Modern Youth" in English Canada, 1920–50

Cynthia Comacchio

● INTRODUCTION

Cynthia Comacchio

As a fundamental element of personal experience, age denotes much more than merely the years counted since birth. It is a status marker and a source of power. Most societies are organized along a hierarchy of age as much as one of class, gender, and "race." Like those identifiers, age is socially constructed in ways that are locally, culturally and historically specific. What it means to be a child, an adolescent, an adult, or an elder, changes over time, according to the social needs and aspirations of particular historical moments. Further, although it is at no point unimportant, age is most visibly and consistently at work in shaping ideas about children and youth, as well as their lived experiences. The young are subject to regulation more than any other social group. This process of age-based regulation has intensified since the late Victorian years, and certainly persists into the twenty-first century. Think in terms of the age categories that we use often and casually: what does "underaged" signify? "Coming of age"? Being "of age"? At certain points in every life, in every historical period, there are particular social understandings of the status, privilege and power that age connotes.

Although much criticized for his broad inferences made from a narrow and largely upper-class source base, French cultural historian Philippe Ariès inspired an international scholarly interest in childhood and youth in the past with his landmark study, *Centuries of Childhood* (1962). In Canada, Neil Sutherland's seminal *Children in English Canadian Society, 1880–1920* (1976) detailed how reform campaigns and related state initiatives reconceptualized childhood during these years, demonstrating the growth of public support for a "modernized" childhood as the nation's best way forward. The child welfare campaign was integral to the period's Social Gospel movement, a form of Christian activism that was mainly urban, Anglo-Protestant, and middle-class in composition. Reformers, often women, took up the child welfare cause out of personal commitment to social service and national betterment. But they also feared that childhood deprivation might lead to all manner of ill health, social unrest, even criminality. Children and youth are perceived and represented, historically and in our own times, as unfinished versions of adult citizens. They are metaphors. They materialize present concerns; they are omens for good or ill. In a young nation striving for the "progress" that modernity seemed to offer, they represented future Canada.

Material changes also influenced new understandings of children and childhood. By 1900, the childhood experience was being reshaped by changes in industrial production that reduced the demand for child labour, the enactment of protective legislation restricting ages and hours of work, and new ideas about children's socialization disseminated throughout the Western world as the "Century of the Child" opened. With their future-oriented mandate that gave new social value to children as "national assets," child welfare reformers redefined childhood as a special stage of institutionalized dependence centred on careful nurturance at home, school attendance, and supervised play.

A recognizably modern adolescence—a distinct transitional life stage between childhood and adult responsibility—took noticeable form in the Great War's aftermath. Socioeconomic developments consolidated earlier trends toward lengthening youth dependency. The most important of these were the high cost of living and the characteristically low wages for inexperienced youth that made their independence problematic, while also keeping some contribution of those wages important to many families, as well as the decline of formal apprenticeship and domestic service. The concurrent expansion in part-time and casual labour markets, in the burgeoning consumer and leisure sectors nonetheless opened up new possibilities for adolescents, often providing significant "pocket money" for those now legally obliged to stay in high school and financially obliged to live at home—at least for those in better-off working and middle-class households that did not need the young worker's entire pay packet to survive. New ideas and attitudes, including rising material expectations fuelled by a consumerism pushing new products, services, and lifestyles—even youth itself—urged on the young to "something better" than what their parents and grandparents had. The age of school leaving was raised to 16 years in most provinces by 1930; by mid-century, the primary occupation of youth became high school.

The interwar years also saw a modern, generationally defined youth culture develop within the context of a technology-led and increasingly commercialized popular culture. As a safe, adult-supervised antidote to dance halls, "speakeasies," and jazz parties, concerned Canadians insisted that citizenship training be part of every high school curriculum. They also wanted it to be incorporated into extracurricular clubs and activities, and to serve as the basis of youth organizations. Most of the latter, like the early twentieth-century Boy Scout and Girl Guide movements, upheld a strong ethic of community service premised on middle-class Christian values. As well as being age defined, many of these clubs were emphatically gender defined and racially exclusive. Although popular among urban middle-class youth, they did not attract the "problem youth" who were their real object as much as did the notorious commercial venues and activities that were the focus of many anxious discourses about the so-called "problem of modern youth." While the Great Depression may have somewhat dampened the "flaming youth" who were the hallmark of the "Roaring Twenties," by the 1940s, the "teenager"—a term only widely adopted during the Second World War—was well on the scene. The 1950s, in effect, "institutionalized" adolescence as most young Canadians spent the better part of their time in school, and as fashion, music, TV, film, "drive-in" theatres and restaurants, and other postwar products and services, deliberately addressed the teenage consumer.

QUESTIONS

1. What does the depiction of the child in military uniform on the front cover of the *Canadian Home Journal* suggest about attitudes regarding children and the nation in 1917?
2. Diaries and oral histories are in many ways ideal sources where the history of children and youth is concerned. What do such sources reveal about individual childhoods and childhood and youth in general? What can they *not* tell us?
3. What hints do we get, in Mary Dulhanty's summaries of the retreat sermons, about attitudes of the time toward youth culture—bobbed hair, short dresses, dancing?
4. The poem "The Revolt of Youth," is clearly meant to poke fun at the contemporary "critics" of youth, but in satirical fashion, it also indicates some of their concerns. What does the author suggest are the main charges against the youth of the day?
5. The articles by Wall and Comacchio discuss children and youth during much the same period. What do they suggest are the reasons for intensifying public concern about the young during the years from 1920 to 1950?

WORKS CITED/FURTHER READING

Baillargeon, Denyse, *Babies for the Nation: The Medicalization of Motherhood in Quebec, 1910–1970,* (Waterloo: Wilfrid Laurier University Press, 2009).
Comacchio, Cynthia R., *The Dominion of Youth: Adolescence and the Making of Modern Canada,* (Waterloo: Wilfrid Laurier University Press, 2006).

Gleason, Mona, *Small Matters: Canadian Children in Sickness and Health, 1900–1940*, (Montreal and Kingston: McGill-Queen's University Press, 2013).

Sutherland, Neil, *Children in English Canadian Society, 1880–1920: Framing the Twentieth-Century Consensus*, (Toronto: University of Toronto Press, 1976; reissued by Wilfrid Laurier University Press, 2000).

Sutherland, Neil, *Growing Up: Childhood in English Canada from the Great War to the Age of Television*, (Toronto: University of Toronto Press, 1997).

Strong-Boag, Veronica, *Fostering Nation? Canada Confronts Its History of Childhood Disadvantage*, (Waterloo: Wilfrid Laurier University Press, 2011).

Wall, Sharon, *The Nurture of Nature: Childhood, Antimodernism, and Ontario Summer Camps, 1920–55*, (Vancouver: University of British Columbia Press, 2009).

▲ DOCUMENT 1: "CENTENNIAL NUMBER," 1917

Boasting "over 130,000 subscribers," *Everywoman's World*, published in Toronto, was the most popular mass circulation women's magazine in Canada in the early twentieth century. The "Centennial Number" actually celebrated the half-century since Confederation in 1917, but that year also saw mounting public concern about the ongoing casualties of the Great War and a conscription crisis that divided the nation.

Source: Front cover, "Centennial Number," *Everywoman's World*, (July 1917). http://www.canadiana.org

▲ DOCUMENT 2: *THE SURPRISE OF MY LIFE*, 1920s

The voices of children themselves are mostly unrecorded, or at least seldom pre-
served, which makes such historical evidence as the first diary of seven-year-old
Claire Brodbinger (later Drainie Taylor) a rare and special artifact. Claire grew
up in a middle-class Jewish-Canadian family in Regina, Saskatchewan, in the
1920s. She later gained renown as a radio/television actress and scriptwriter. The
spelling and sentence structure are copied intact from the original.

September 1924

Dear Diary: You are my frist one. My frend Minny Davidner gave you to me for my
brithday. I am 7. My name is Claire Pearl Wodlinger. My muthr is Rose and my fathr is
Hymy and my big bruthr is Jim and my litle one is David and my babe sisstr is Dorthy and
that's all. I go to Centrl Scool. I am in grade 2. My best things I licke are speling, riting and
reeding and not verry much arthmutic. My best thing at reecess is the maypol for swinging
and if I haf muny for jah-brakrs. The dog of the candy stor lady has one blou eye and one
is broun. If my best frend has a penny she givs me a jah-brakr. Her name is Mary Elen
Hays. She has a litle bruthr to and he is Davids best frend. His name is Billy. Grampa Hays
is very cross in the gardn. MaryElen issnt afrade of him but I am. Goodby.

September 1924

Dear Diary: My mothr sais you shood tell everthing to yore diary even if it is bad, And also
if you think something. The bad thing I did was I toled Minny I was gowing to haf a party
and she came but I didnt haf one and she brout me this diary and I took it withowt a party.
And she had on a party dress. My mothr was mad wen I toled her but Minnys mothr sed
I could keep the diary becus it was a mistaik and I rote in it anyway. And anyway Minny
isnt my best frend. But I haf to taike her to a moving pitchr of Harld Loiyd and isecreem
next Saterday for beeing bad. My other best pressant is a book The Tale of Henriette Hen.
My Unkle David gave it to me. I think I can reed most of it by myslef so it is my frist book.
Yore suppost to rite all spechel things in a diary so if Im to bissy I dont haf to rite somthing.
So some dais I wont. Mommy sais I can spell eny way I thinnk. Goodbye.

September 1924

Dear Diary: Dad got very mad at Jim today and a litl bit mad at me but David was to yung
so Dad sed it wasnt his fawlt. What the trubble was we startd a fire on the grass on the
mptee lot. Jim just wantd to start a litl fire but it went so fast in a big surcol and we got
scard and ran for Dad. And he got the fire indjun becaus he culdnt stop it. The fireman
sed the grass was so dry becaus no rain but Daddy spnked us for plaing with machs. My
stumak aked becaus I was so scard and I fergot to pull my litl bruthr away from the fire.
He ran away by hiself so I was lucky abowt that. I put this in here becaus it is speshel
but I dont like it. I cant go to sleep becaus wen I close my eys I see the fire berning the

---

Source: Claire Drainie Taylor, "Swift Current," in *The Surprise of My Life: An Autobiography*
(Waterloo: Wilfrid Laurier University Press, 1998), 9–16.

grass and making it blak and are fense to. Jim and I wont play with machs any more in are liffe. Goodby.

October 1924

Dear Diary: Daddy took Jim and me for a long wak all the way down Cenrtl Avenu to the stashun. We wasched the trane com in. The injun is verry big and blak and a mownten of steam. It made so mutch noys I hided behind Daddy but he wusnt afrade. Nobody got of. Daddy sais nobudy gets of in Swift Current they just get on. But we saw a trane man in a uniform and he was kullerd brown but he takkd to Daddy the way we do. He was a negrow. Daddy sed negrows dont live in Swift Current but they are just the same as peepl but thare skin is darkr. We were gettin cold so he took us to the Carlton Tea room for isecreem. Daddy sed we wont be abl to do that eny more this yeer becaus wintr is in the ayre. The Carlton has chares with thin wire legs and tabls to. And the seeling has tin flowrs in it. If you sit on a stul at the cownter if feels cold and smoothe. I like it most in Swift Current and the liberry. Goodby.

December 1924

Dear Diary: Mummy let me wasch her give a villin leson to a boy. If I kepped verry still and verry quite. His name is Oscar and he is 11. I like him. He is small and his hands to and his voiss but I like to hear him takk. But mostly he plays or Mum tells him things and then he plays some more. Like my pyano lesons onlie on the villin. My Mother is the best villin player in Swift Current and if they have a consert she plays on a stage and wares a pretty dress. And she plays for us after suppr somtimes only if we want to sing she plays sheet musick on are pyano. She even plays for dancis somtimes and Daddy stais home and wasches us. I think Mummy gets som muney for that. Becaus she gets us treets the next day. Are best treet so far was when she brot a choclot bar and we each got a scware. It was yummy. And one time chickletts which are gum. Goodby.

February 1925

Dear Diary: It was Valentine's day at our school. We make them in art. I made 14 for my frends but I onlie got 10. Mary Elen gave 18 and she got 20. But she is very nice. Now she thinks she should have sent 2 more. Enyway I dont have to wurry abowt that. We had a spelling bee and I came sekond. I got watch rong becaus it has a "t." Edith Muggelston came first. She is a good reeder and so am I. She is Sweedish so she has nice strate white hair and a very rownd voise. If we have vissiters to our class Miss Hutchinson asks me to stand up and reed or eyether Edith. Goodbye.

July 1925

Dear Diary: Did you miss me? I broke my arm on a rock playing catch. So my arm was in a cast and I coudnt rite. It hurt a lot but I got to sleep in my mothers bed. I had to stop my pyano lessons but I didn't mined that and enyway Daddy didnt have muney to pay for them. Then David broke his arm so I had to go back to my owne bed. One day I neerly got drounded becaus my arm was still in a sling and I was onlie suppost to go in the water to my nees so I was afrade to tell my Mom and Dad. You see I slipt in the mud and when I got upsidedown in the water I new I was drouning and I felt so sad. I remembered all the lies I toled and beeng mean to David and Doro. I woke up on a bentch in the bath howse. I heurd one girl say were her eyes out of her head and sombody sed no but they were bullging. And a lady sed was she strugling and anuther girl sed no. They took of my wet bathing sute and put my dress on and I didnt have enything on underneeth. They wakked home with me but I sed I was fine so they woudnt come to are howse. I lied to my Mother and sed I lost my sute cause it got muddy by mistaik. I ate my supper and I went to bed erly. I didnt feel good Droudning is very scary. Goodbye.

September 1925

Dear Diary: Well I didnt have a party for my aith birthday but I got Grimms Fairy Tales and thats good. From my Unkle David. Mary Ellen my best frend has a diary to and she showd it to me so I showd her mine but maibe I wont agen. Its suppost to be privit if you want to say somthing if you dont want somebody to nowe abowt it. Mary Ellen puts in all day things and what time like 5.30 set the tabel. 6 o'clock ate diner but I think she means supper—dinner is on Sunday. 7 o'clock played hopscotch with Claire. My Mother sais Mary Ellen is verry orgenised like her Mother. Mommy sais Mrs. Hayes can do anything and her name is Ruth. She is Mothers best frend. So there are 3 best frends in there famly and also 3 in are famly. Isnt that funny. She can even drive thare car. It is a Star. They have a buntch of flowrs like sweet pees and bachler buttens becaus Mom sais Grampa Hayes lives in the gardn. My Grampas live in Selkurk. And my Grammas to. Mary Ellen has no Gramma but the best thing they have the books of Nowledje. I am aloud to look at them at thare howse but not to borro. 8 o'clock I'l go to bed now. I forgot to tell you wut I call my Grampas and Gramas Baba and Zada. Good night.

December 1925

Dear Diary: We all got to go to a Honnica party. On top of Levines store. Us, Davidners Klings, Levines and some uthr famlys who go to Elmwould School. It was all dekrated blou and white and candls to. I got Anderson's Fairy Tales and I like them. For Crissmas I got skaits from Santa onlie thay are black with rust on them. And a Jap orange and nuts in my stoking. Mommy took me to the skaiting rinck and it was nice and cold and noysie and musick but I cept falling down and Mom cept holding me up but I coodnt skait. My Mother is a very good skaiter but not my fahter. It herts my ankels. Jim can skait and David on bob skaits. Daddy and I are the only ones. Goodbye. And Dorthy. Goodby agane.

March 1926

Dear Diary: We can't go to school or even outside. There is a teribble blisserd going on and some people get lost in the snow and then they freeze to deth. Our house is cold and Jim and I are to big for Docter Dentens sleepers so we sleep in our long underware and sox. And pijammas on top. Mom dosnt like it but she lets us. Doro and David can ware them cause thare small till they get to big. They have feet and they are soft and cosy and they smell nice. We have a bath on every Sat. night and then we get cleen underware. And I get a cleen vest with long garters for sholding up my stokings. They are very hard to put on over the underware and I always get bumps. But I'm lurning to do up the garters myself. For my cleen middy blows I have to butten on the navy bloue kollar and sometimes I get mad at it but then Mummy or Daddy helps me. My navy bloue skurt is pleetd with a vest on it that goes over my head sown on. It takes me a long time to dress in winter. And poor Mommy has to do a hole lot of washing or if we have a made they both do it. In a big coppr boyler on the stove and a long stick for mooving the close around. And blooing for making the close white. Isnt that funny? Goodbye. I forgot to tell you when you bring the close in of the line and they are frosen stiff I love the smell of them. I gess its the best smell in the world so far.

March 1926

Dear Diary: It got a little warmer so we tryed to go back to school but we had to come home agen. Here is why. I got stuck in the mud on the emtee lot and my foot came out of my galosh and I was balluncing on one foot and Jim was tring to get my gulosh on and he coodnt and we both fell over in the mudd and slush. It was so slippry and mukky we coold hardly get up. Mother was very mad at us because she toled us not to go throu the emtee lot even if it is a short cut. But I gess we lookd funny because after she got mad she started to lagh reely hard. So Jim and I got a xtra bath on a Wensday. The mudd is stikky as glu. So then we playd our new records. Mine is called Maid of the Mountain. It is so big you have to wind the victrola 2 and a half times. My Dad brout it to me from Winnipeg. And Valencia for Jim but its just one time winding and a cupple more turns. Mommy got a beutiful evning dress with beads and some tafeta lamp shades for there bedroom. And he brout some good things to eat. 1. corn beef. 2. rye bread. 3. hallva thats like fudje but not brown. 4. musslinnas there black salty ollivs. 5. Winnipeg gold eyes. Thats a good kind of fish. And we all got to taste everthing. We had fun like a picnick but in the dining room. Swift Current dosnt have those things. But Dad says Winnipeg has everthing. It is a city in Canada near Selkirk. But we have the same king and Queen. Bye now.

▲ DOCUMENT 3: *DIARY OF MARY DULHANTY, 1926–27*

At the age of 17, Mary Dulhanty, born in Springhill, Nova Scotia, kept a diary chronicling about six months (December 1926–June 1927) of her time as a student in the Commercial program at a Catholic girls' school, Mount Saint Vincent Academy, in Halifax. Her father, who died in 1923, worked for the Canadian National Railways, but evidently left her widowed mother enough money to permit Mary, the youngest of four children, to attend the Academy as had her two older sisters. It was run by the Sisters of Charity. In this excerpt, she comments on the Lenten retreat (usually several days to one week of intensive prayer, meditation and sermons) that she is attending at the school. The spelling and grammar are copied intact from the reprinted diary excerpt.

Retreat Thursday February 3/26[7] Diary dear nothing very exciting. But we are going on Retreat tonight. Holy Hour this after noon. We are having Father Knox. ... ... Father Knox is some speaker. Spoke on or rather the main subject to-night was Liquor. Sez Kathleen Norris is one of the good Catholic writers. First time I knew it. But I shall take more notice of her books now. I do not like them much. Our programme by the way runs like this. Mass seven thirty and eight on Sunday. Nine thirty lecture afterward we go to the Chapel. Lecture eleven fifteen. Dinner twelve thirty. Rest until three. Pond at three. Lecture at four. Rosary at five, supper at six. Benediction at seven. Seven fifteen lecture. Then Chapel for our night prayers & bed. The lecture Friday morning was about disobeying parents and our superiors. Sez parents are more than half to blame.

... There is so much to be done at home. The kids have never been taught and not only the kids but the youths. It is a crime. I hope Father Penny gets some kind of a Sunday School organized. I have just come from another lecture. About bobbed hair and short dresses. He sez it is not the bobbed hair that is the sin it is the cutting and where it is cut that is the sin. If you must have your hair cut have it done but [by] one of your own sex. He sez girls are very delicate about people touching their necks or bodies but the[y] let any barbar maul all over their necks. If when you meet a priest you are ashamed of your short skirts why are you not ashamed and embarresed before other people. We also had a short lecture on confession. We are to go to confession at four and if we are not thru by then we are to go after lecture tonight. ... We are to go to him tomorrow in the Confessional to ask advice if we wish. His morning lectures are always the best. Diary I spend much of my spare time with you. I hope that these notes will some day be of use to me. I wish Margaret and Jane and Mom were here to make the Retreat with me. I wonder if Mom has ever made one. He sez dancing in itself is not a sin but that more than one half of the dances of today cannot be executed without the ocassion of sin. When a girl goes to a public dance in a damndable one piece dress with practically nothing else on, it is the essence of nudity and a sure occassion of sin. [Marginal notation: He sez you cannot judge a person by what she has on but you can by what she has not.] I just seem to begin to realize what life is and what is it doing or what the people of the present day are doing. The sisters all tell us not to judge our past by our present. If I did God help me. But Oh God that You will give me the strength to live a good Catholic girls life, that God I am not worthy of your notice. I seem just to begin to notice what I am and what I have been doing. Oh how I wish that Jean could come here. She has such an influence over boys if only it is the right kind Jesus, Mary and Joseph pray for her.

Source: Jann E. Cleveland and Margaret Conrad, "Mary Dulhanty (1909–1999)," in Kathryn Carter, ed. *The Small Details of Life: Twenty Diaries by Women in Canada, 1830–1996*, (Toronto: University of Toronto Press, 2002), pp. 325–6; 341–4. Reprinted with permission of the publisher.

▲ DOCUMENT 4: "THE REVOLT OF YOUTH," 1926

The "Roaring Twenties" saw the emergence of a "modern" adolescence as young Canadians came to be seen as much different than, and inadequate in comparison to, their parents and elders. The interwar years were punctuated by periodic waves of public anxiety—what historians call "moral panic"—about "the problem of modern youth," and especially their "new morality" and seeming potential for delinquency. Public discourses, ranging from parliamentary debates through popular magazines and daily newspaper columns, gave much consideration to this seemingly vast "problem."

Critic, with judgement crass
And too much haste, you say
That youth, on the primrose way
Steps on the gas.
Your ill-aimed cross-bow bolt
Quite misses youth's revolt.
Your missile hits
No bull's eye of this truth.
That ever flaming youth Is a thing of opposites.

Its constant paradox
At your mad "magpie" mocks.
Wild youth, as ever thus,
Will not be bound by us …
Our elder, sage, advice,
Our virtue, or our vice …

Youth's not its grandsire's model.
Look! It's the old that toddle
Or Charleston fast and faster …
Critic, we must not forget
Sinners such as I and you,
Are unto the younger set,
Samples horrible to view.
They will not imitate.
This is your logic's joker,
Our degenerate state,
Or touch us with a poker …

Source: Unsigned editorial, "The Revolt of Youth: To a Critic of Contemporary Adolescence," *The Toronto Star*, November 16, 1926.

▲ DOCUMENT 5: *FREEDOM TO PLAY*, 1930s–40s

Most of what we know about growing up in the past comes from memory, the recollections of adults looking back on their early years. This oral history about childhood pastimes demonstrates some of the ways in which rural children "made their own fun." Peggy Sherman grew up in Fort Saskatchewan, Alberta, during the 1930s–40s.

… In summer we went on picnics, and it didn't seem to matter where we went as long as we took something to eat. We picked berries. Always on Saturday we picked flowers for the house—tiger lilies, roses, etc., as they came along. We played soft ball, "work-up" it was called. All you needed was a pitcher, catcher and batter. If there was a fourth you had a fielder. We often played on the corner lot just outside our yard, and you know how noisy we could be. Sunday evenings it used to upset Mother that we were out there making so much noise. She'd say, "Why don't you come in and we'll sing some nice hymns?" She'd play the piano and we'd have some kids come that never came to Sunday School. I remember singing "You in Your Small Corner and I in Mine." And after singing we would always have some cocoa or something. We played marbles and jacks. Everybody had their tin of marbles, we called them alleys and they were made of glass. And there was hopscotch. We used pretty pieces of broken pottery for our toss for playing hopscotch.

Our house was just on the brow of a hill that went down to the river road and then on down to the river. In winter we had our choice of which of four hills we wanted to slide down. When we didn't want to wait for somebody to come back up with the sleigh, well, my father had a big box of shingles left over from shingling the roof—so we used those shingles to slide on down the hill. We went skating practically every night, home by nine o'clock. We played fox and goose and made angels in the snow.

I played with dolls. I can't remember for how long, but I had one beautiful baby doll that I just adored. We played house a lot too. We'd just take sticks and lay them out on the lawn. On rainy days we'd pull the dining room table apart, but we didn't put in a board. We'd stand up in the space and play store. We played rummy and other kinds of card games, crokinole, snakes and ladders, checkers, and parcheesi. We made our own valentines, and that was always a big deal. We read a lot. When we went home for lunch we'd read until the food was on the table. We were usually given books as Christmas and birthday presents.

Source: Norah L. Lewis, ed., *Freedom to Play: We Made Our Own Fun* (Waterloo: Wilfrid Laurier University Press, 2002), pp. 55–56.

ARTICLE 1: MAKING MODERN CHILDHOOD, THE NATURAL WAY: PSYCHOLOGY, MENTAL HYGIENE, AND PROGRESSIVE EDUCATION AT ONTARIO SUMMER CAMPS, 1920–1955

Sharon Yvonne Wall

Campers at Camp Tanamakoon, c. 1930s. Algonquin Park Museum Archives #3153 (George May).

In a radio broadcast of April 1947, Dr. J.G. Althouse, Ontario's Chief Director of Education, praised the summer camp for all it had to offer the children and youth of the province. In his comments he lauded the camp's natural setting, commended the simplicity of its programming, and extolled the old-fashioned self-sufficiency it engendered. In a sentence, he summed up what many regarded as the camp's most vital attribute. At summer camp, he explained, "The complications of our modern way of life are largely removed."[1] In his understanding of camp life as offering a possible flight from modernity, Althouse was not alone. Camp administrators from the late 1920s through to the early postwar period promoted the summer camp as both a much-needed escape from modern, urban living and the pathway to a world of natural, pre-modern simplicity.

Source: "Making Modern Childhood, the Natural Way: Psychology, Mental Hygiene, and Progressive Education at Ontario summer camps, 1920–1955," *Historical Studies in Education*, (Fall 2008), pp. 73–110.

Idealizations such as these were meant to convince the public, but they shouldn't fool the historian as to the camp's very real implication in modernity. Summer camps were situated in the seemingly constant world of nature, but their administrators also prided themselves on keeping abreast of the most recent psychological and educational trends. While the notion that outdoor living was good for one dated back at least as far as the mid-nineteenth century, during the middle decades of the twentieth century, this idea was elaborated and refined by those influenced by the emerging discipline of psychology. During these years, promoters of camp life regarded it as providing the ideal environment for fostering psychological health and well-being. They also argued that the camp was unique in its ability not only to preach the ideals of progressive education, but, more importantly, to apply them.

In essence, the summer camp had a dual face. What many people saw when they looked at the camp was a retreat from the modern world. ... This paper explores the impact of educational psychology and progressivism on the Ontario summer camp. As its source base, it relies on the records of a variety of camps across the province. One set of these were private camps founded by urban middle-class individuals, designed to turn a profit by serving an elite clientele. A second set were agency camps founded by groups like the YMCA, religious organizations like the Canadian Girls in Training (CGIT), and the Ontario government, all of which served a mainly middle-class (but also partly working-class) clientele. A third group were "fresh air" camps run by churches, charities and other non-profit organizations which offered subsidized camp holidays to the poorest sector of Ontario's working-class. Due to its prominence as the largest fresh air camp in the province, Bolton Camp, situated just outside Toronto, was chosen as a case study of the fresh air experience. These three types of camps represent a cross-section of the Ontario camp community during these years. An examination of their diverse settings reveals that, at all manner of camps, reliance on emerging psychological and educational expertise shaped thinking about the benefits of camp, about the nature of "the child," and about "childhood" as a category of experience. At the same time, the class background of campers shaped the application of psychological ideas in different ways at different Ontario camps as actual children were encountered and managed. As far as camps' educational missions were concerned, they were possibly more successful than schools in delivering progressive education, although there were also limits to the progressive experiment.

Modern Theories in a Natural Setting

The emergence of the summer camp took place amidst important changes in thinking concerning child development in North America. In the late nineteenth century, emerging notions of children as dependent and in need of protection resulted in the introduction of public and later, compulsory, schooling, the establishment of separate children's institutions, and struggles to eliminate child labour.[2] Into the twentieth century, the modern notion of childhood that these changes implied was further bolstered by the force of scientific and professional expertise. Common sense understandings of children as living a distinct stage of the human experience were solidified by explicit theories of child development emanating from newly established departments of psychology.[3]

The emergence of psychology as a distinct discipline was closely tied with what was known, in North America, as the mental hygiene movement. National committees for the promotion of mental hygiene were established in both the U.S. and Canada in 1909 and 1918 respectively.[4] ... With the help of funding from the Canadian body, the first Canadian Department of Psychology was established at the University of Toronto in 1926.[5] Initially, the discipline, like the movement, endorsed a largely hereditarian view of mental deficiency, a stance which limited the scope for professional intervention. As hereditarian views were increasingly discredited, however, this situation changed. According to the new wisdom, personalities were not born—they were made. Imbued with modern optimism regarding improvement and perfectibility, psychologists now emphasized the importance of environment, and the child and the earliest environments of childhood became the focus of much psychological investigation. At the same time, a focus on "normal" child development replaced the older concentration on the pathological.

In Canada, one of the psychologists who became prominent in this period was Dr. William E. Blatz. In his work, Blatz drew on each of the two dominant trends in contemporary psychology, behaviourism and Freudianism, as would the summer camp itself. On the one hand, Blatz sought to counter the "inefficiency" of most family homes; at his Institute for Child Study, for instance, the day nursery incorporated the same habit-training, unbending routine and detailed record-keeping favoured by the behaviourists and much of contemporary child-rearing advice literature.[6] We should "take them all away if we could," was his comment on the advisability of removing children from the parental home, revealing, like American psychologist, John Watson, an unabashed confidence in the expert approach.[7] On the other hand, Blatz was also influenced by Freudian ideals. He rejected the use of coercion of any kind, objected to interference with children's natural inclinations, and favoured "free-choice learning," as an important counterpart to daily habit-training. Widely known for his role in overseeing the upbringing of the Dionne quintuplets, Blatz was less well-known for his involvement with summer camps. For a time, during the interwar years, Blatz served as on-site psychologist at the two well-known private camps run by Taylor Statten in Algonquin Park. In 1942, his connection with camping was formally recognized when the Ontario section of the (then) American Camping Association enlisted him to deliver lectures and stimulate discussions with groups of counsellors.[8] ...

Just how "natural" the camp was thought to be was the crux of its appeal not only to modern psychologists, but to many North Americans. Indeed, summer camps were not unique to Ontario; they appeared in other Canadian provinces and proliferated throughout the New England and later, other states ...[9] To most observers, Canadian or American, what was most striking ... about this recreational innovation was not its connection to modern-day psychological or educational theory, but its wonderfully natural setting ... In contrast to early nineteenth-century views, camp literature constructed nature as an unquestionably positive and life-giving force, a realm to be sought out and embraced, never feared. The backdrop for this highly romantic view of nature was, of course, the population shift from countryside to city, which had occurred by these years. In Ontario, as early as 1921, the urban population already stood at 58 percent. By 1951 the number had risen to 72.[10] As a predominantly urban society, many Ontarians now looked back longingly on a time of presumably closer connection to the natural world. If not seriously interested in re-visiting their pioneer days, modern urbanites yet sought ways to "reconnect" with the natural world. In this regard, summer camp was only one among many nature-based recreations that had been attracting the attention of urban Ontarians from the late nineteenth century onwards.[11]

Like promoters of other wilderness and nature-based experiences, administrators at private, agency and fresh air camps in Ontario worked to instill images of camp life as the healthy antithesis of modern urban living. In glossy promotional brochures and in the pages of staff manuals, they depicted contact with trees, grasses, lakes, and sunshine as the ideal context for physical, emotional and spiritual health. Private camp literature extolled camp for providing well-to-do youth with "fresh strength with every contact with Mother Earth," while Fresh Air Fund promoters insisted that, for working-class children, "a good dose of outdoors cures almost anything."[12] These were not simply recreational choices, the literature seemed to insist; affiliation with the natural world was a prerequisite for healthy human development. "Every child has an instinctive yearning to get back to the natural and to the simple fundamentals of the green earth," one promoter of fresh air camps asserted in the pages of the *Toronto Star*. Another described "the inner longing for the country" that presumably resided within every youthful soul.[13] Summer camp, then, was no superfluous luxury. In Camp Ahmek's 1939 private camp counsellor handbook, the language of necessity was used to describe its origin:

> If the camp had not been invented, we should now have to create it, such need there is today of the steadying offices of direct contact with the earth: the constancy of evening and morning, the sureness of brooks and tides, the firmly planted trees, the upholding hills. Is it not well for us all early to find a close relationship with the earth, our long home? ... A camping experience may be valuable if it does nothing more than to help a child enjoy being a first-hand part of roads and trails, fire and water, sunrise and dusk.[14]

This belief in nature's powerful, yet subliminal influence was the backdrop against which all summer camp projects were launched. ... [W]hatever the camp's goals, whether to shape upper- or working-class youth, to "toughen up" boys, or socialize girls,

they were more likely to be achieved in a natural setting, so the thinking went. Nature, so it seemed, wiped children clean of negative influence, creating just the conditions for ambitious educators to imprint their new messages on the childish slate.

"As Far Removed as a South Sea Island"

... At the turn of the century, when the first camps in the province were being established, the camp was understood in different terms. Indeed, the common wisdom within the camping movement was that, before the 1930s, camp objectives were conceptualized from a primarily recreational perspective. ...[15]

According to this narrative, camp objectives became more sophisticate and "educational" in the inter-war years. Particularly from the 1930s onwards, the camping movement articulated its goals in the language of educational psychology. This was no accident; camp directors had both direct and indirect connection to educational circles and to the emerging psychological discipline. Taylor Statten, founder of Camps Ahmek and Wapomeo in the early 1920s, and perhaps the most prominent individual in Ontario camping, conducted a twenty-year career with the YMCA, first as Secretary of Boys' Work for the Toronto Y, and later as National Boys' Work Secretary. Statten became widely known in Canada as a captivating public speaker and for his part in the development of the Canadian Standard Efficiency Test (CSET) for adolescent boys. He was also brought on staff at Pickering College in the 1920s as "Director of Character Education" and, according to his biographer, as the first vocational guidance counsellor in Canada.[16] Mary Hamilton, founder of Tanamakoon in Algonquin Park in 1925, was head of physical education and later, principal, at Toronto's Margaret Eaton School, a private institution which played an important role in providing female physical education teachers across Toronto in the inter-war years. Perhaps even more so than other camp directors, Hamilton's founding of Tanamakoon was envisioned as an extension of her work at the school; uniquely, she added camp counsellor training to the school's physical education course and arranged for students of physical education to apply their skills as new counsellors at Tanamakoon during the summer.[17] Finally, Dr. Mary Northway, among the first cohort of girls to attend summer camps in the 1920s, later became staff and finally, director of her own canoe-trip camp in the 1940s, while also pursuing an academic career in child psychology at the University of Toronto as one of the favoured doctoral students of William Blatz. These are just several examples; many more could be given to underscore the fact that the summer camp in Ontario was deeply connected to the world of education and academic psychology.[18]

Operating within these milieus, camp directors were influenced by the dominant educational psychology of their time. In particular, camp literature echoed psychology's focus on the environment, something which came easily in a context where uniqueness of setting was the primary selling point. Camp administrators of all types shared the belief that human beings were capable of change and that their environment was the key factor in effecting it. While proponents of mental hygiene were "dazzled by the school's potential"[19] as a site for the observation (and alteration) of child behaviour, outdoor educationalists were even more hopeful of the camp. Camp was not only a distinct place in the geographic sense, it was also considered to provide a fundamentally new environment, with all the connotations of experimentation and potential progress this conjured up. In this lay its power, as promoters agreed. In the literature of fresh air camps as early as 1924, poor working-class children were described as "building for the days to come under a very great handicap indeed. One word explains it all and that word is 'environment.'"[20]

Though camps catered to distinct portions of Ontario's youth, they shared an understanding of what made the camp environment so valuable: first, its fundamentally "natural" character, and second, its isolation. Isolation entailed not only distance from consumer culture, but also from competing educational influences, including the home. The authors of *Camping and Character* stated openly in 1929 that it was the setting in which "erratic parental discipline can be avoided and … mental hygiene methods … carried out without prejudice or interference."[21] Clearly, when seen in light of the psychological aims of the movement, this physical removal took on added importance. Isolation was what every psychologist sought, the necessary condition for the controlled experiment. For those who favoured the natural history model, camp seemed to offer a nice balance of the two.[22]

Psychologist and camp director Mary Northway, elaborated on the camp's usefulness for child study in 1940:

The summer camp offers an ideal field for research for the social psychologist. It is an isolated, constant, temporary group, as far removed from the ordinary roads of social intercourse as a south sea island. Camp suddenly comes into existence when a group of individuals, cut off from the ties of their normal societies, are thrust together in one geographic community, and a new society is created. While camp lasts, it is an isolated community; and it may be considered a society in miniature.[23]

It would be a mistake however, to see the two essential aspects of the camp environment—nature and isolation—as unrelated. As camp educators saw it, it was precisely the combination of the two which made the camp superior to other children's institutions. Camp isolated children more completely than either schools or clinics. And yet, while the camp seemed to offer "complete environmental control," it was also thought to present opportunities for "personal fulfilment of emotions and interests."[24] In short, camp was meant to be both fun and psychologically beneficial. According to a 1933 report from Bolton (fresh air) Camp, in terms of fostering healthy "self-development," camp offered children, "greater opportunity … than if they were at the most expensive Summer Hotels."[25] The clear implication was that "over-civilized" luxury and comfort prevented honest connection with the natural world. Summer camp, by contrast, offered life-changing experiences of direct contact with nature. The healthiest modern children, then, would be shaped in this seemingly pre-modern setting.

… In effect, camp was to act as a way station between childhood and adulthood, a space in which children could achieve "emancipation" from parents. Especially at private camps where children, sometimes as young as four years old, spent the eight weeks of summer, increased independence was an inevitable by-product. … Camp was meant to build confidence, helping children to think for themselves and stand on their own feet. As in the wider world of psychology, shy children were regarded as in particular need of improvement. Staff were instructed to use "careful observation" to root out the "timid or seclusive[sic]" camper, while camp bulletins glowed with reports of "happier and more self-confident" children of those previously "quiet and withdrawn."[26]

At camp, as elsewhere, the ultimate test of the healthy personality was the ability to work well with others and especially one's peers. Though clearly ordered by adults, camp was regarded as a world made for children, a mini-community in which their needs were paramount and in which they were to learn, above all, from each other. There, children neglected, coddled, or perhaps without siblings at home were forced to live alongside others on an on-going basis, a matter for praise in the camp literature. Mary Northway stressed in 1939: "It is highly important that a child learn to be at home with his own contemporaries. Acceptability by older people or by younger children in no way makes up for failure to get along with one's own age group."[27] This focus on "peers," what historian Howard Chudacoff describes as an emerging "age consciousness," was echoed throughout the camp movement.[28] On a practical level, age grouping of campers became pedagogical imperative. ...

Typically, peers were understood to be children of the same age; at summer camp, peers were also grouped by class. While a degree of overlap always existed, generally speaking, camps of different types were established for children from different economic backgrounds, a reality which also shaped the nature of psychology's impact at camp. At private camps with typically hefty fees, resources were available to hire on-site psychologists and to undertake extensive psychological testing. Lower camper-to-staff ratios also allowed counsellors and other staff to pay more careful attention to individual campers and to apply principles of child psychology to their work. Parents of these middle- and upper-class campers might also have played a role. In the inter-war years, parents of this sort were more likely to seek out the camp for its socializing potential than, say, parents of the poor, who appreciated fresh air camps mainly for providing out-of-city holidays and a break for overworked mothers. ...

In a number of cases, private camp directors and staff were, themselves, trained psychologists who looked to the world of camping as a summertime outlet for their expertise. The case of Mary Northway has already been mentioned here. Her accomplished academic career, in fact, drew on her lifelong interest in camping. Her doctoral research was a case study of children's social relationships at camp, researched at Glen Bernard, the camp of her own childhood and youth. Upon completion of her dissertation in 1938, Blatz took her on as lecturer at the prestigious

Institute of Child Study. Northway's training clearly influenced her approach to campers, for instance, her Watsonian belief that she was working with "the most powerful and plastic material in the world, namely, children."[29] In her eyes, good camp workers were produced by combining experience with children and "technical knowledge of child development." Elsie Palter provides another example of a trained psychologist turned camp director. After founding Camp Kawagama with her husband in 1945, she prided herself on keeping a psychological profile of every camper who passed through the camp gates ...[30]

Of all private camps in Ontario, Camp Ahmek stands out for its early, most intensive and thoroughgoing application of psychology to the realm of camping. Indeed, one might regard the Ahmek administration as one of the "early adopters" of ideas that would become widely accepted elsewhere in later years.[31] Established by Taylor Statten in 1921 on the shores of Canoe Lake in the southwestern corner of Algonquin Park, Ahmek was located so as to attract the interest of the wealthier classes. It also attracted the interest of two social scientists, Hedley S. Dimock and Charles E. Hendry, who undertook observational studies at the camp, resulting in a number of publications over the years.

The most widely read of these publications was *Camping and Character*, what some would come to think of as the "North American bible of camping." Ultimately, the (over three hundred page) 1929 study amounted to the camp's public statement on the fruitful union of psychology, education and camping and was tellingly sub-titled "An Experiment in Character Education." While admitting to difficulties in the precise measurement of "character," the authors nonetheless expounded on the importance of applying "the most rigourous scrutiny and techniques" asserting, "the summer camp must participate in th[e] endeavor to develop and apply more scientific methods to test its results." Indeed, in a chapter on "Appraising the Results," life at camp read like a formal psychology experiment, complete with references to "measuring devices," "empirical judgements," and "standard deviations," replete with charts and graphs.[32]

Dimock and Hendry gathered information for their study in a number of ways. First, there were the medical exams, two or three "tests of proficiency" in camping skills, and other tests assessing campers' general intelligence, knowledge and values. More covertly, counsellors rated campers according to the camp's "Behaviour Frequency Rating Scale" which included fifty-four different aspects of behaviour. Children were also the subject of more descriptive "behaviour observation reports," and "weekly progress reports" on their general conduct and camping skills. Finally, parents were asked to assess their child's social, emotional, and psychological progress before and after camp, another way of furthering the parent education goals of mental hygiene.[33] Clearly, record-keeping and analysis were central to this project. ...[34] What solidified and further facilitated psychology's impact at Ahmek was the establishment of the camp's own "Department of Psychology" in 1930. Like the many child guidance clinics springing up across North American cities after World War I, the Department allowed a set of *bona fide* professionals to hone their strategies for the measurement and recording of psychological data at camp.[35]

What sort of "character," one might wonder, did these professionals set out to measure? The list of items on the "Behaviour Observation Scale" gave some indication. Rather than the older nineteenth-century focus on sobriety, thrift, and Sabbath-observance, or on a list of "immoral" habits, the scale aimed at detecting defective personalities and indications of "maladjustment." Counsellors were expected to rate campers in terms of "resourcefulness," "initiative," "leadership" and "friendliness," as well as 'stubbornness," "timidity," "fearfulness," and "overbearing attitude." While "character" could be detected in such things as the willingness "to observe rules and regulations" and to "contribute well-considered suggestions to the ... group," lack of adjustment was apparent in tendencies to "blush easily," to "grouch [and] find fault," and to "seek the limelight." In essence, character and well-adapted personalities were one and the same. ... With their focus on the child's "fundamental urges, drives or motives," such laws implied, as many psychologists were doing, that there were really no "bad" children, simply those who used maladaptive means to achieve their emotional ends.[36]

Ultimately the "psychological gaze" at Ahmek was broad indeed. The typical child was evaluated and assessed at every turn, whether by formal testing or simply while enjoying the life of camp.

In addition, more difficult, misbehaving youth could expect individual visits to the camp psychologist, a scenario which allowed the gaze to become even more personal and direct. ... At Ahmek and other private camps, administrators developed a psychological critique not only of their campers, but also of the well-to-do family and home life. While private campers were frequently viewed as the leaders and up-standing citizens of the future, administrators also worried about the potential problems inherent in conditions of privilege. ... Put another way, "spoiling" was regarded as the ever-present danger in privileged families. ... This type of indulgence, many agreed, was leading to the "postponing of independence" and the development of undisciplined personalities, unfit for leadership roles.[37]

Overall, wealthy parents were accused of giving too much in a material sense, but when it came to the question of proper love and attention, they were often faulted with a lack of generosity. In *Camping and Character,* absentee parents drew special attention. Mothers, in particular, were charged with neglect of their duties, too often leaving children in the hands of alternate care-givers. In the case of "problem camper Ezekiel" it was stated, "His crudeness of dress and eating habits are largely accounted for by his home situation, where the responsibility is divided between the mother, maids, and a sister. This probably means that he does just about whatever he wants." Another mother who came in for criticism was described as "a woman of culture ... away from home considerably," and who was in the habit of leaving her boys with either the housekeeper or their grandmother. Wealthy fathers, for their part, were blamed for being overly absorbed in business success and in out-of-town travel, and for giving children poor role models in their pursuit of social prestige. ...[38]

As the objects of this intensifying gaze, children at private camps responded in various ways. Reactions to on-site psychologists were sometimes distinctly negative. In this respect, the experts at Ahmek encountered some challenging cases, campers like "Freddy" who left his psychological assessment "in a humiliated ... but rebellious mood" and "Ezekiel," who, only hours after his session to improve his attitude was found "flick[ing] a large sticky piece of chewing gum into the camp mother's coiffure."[39] Even those not in any way singled out for observation sometimes bristled at the psychologist's presence. Indeed, while completing their field-work, the authors of *Camping and Character* were felt, by some, to be hindering children's full enjoyment of camp. "[T]he two men 'got in the way' of campers doing their daily activities," states one history of the camp. "There were forms to be filled out and evaluations to be made every day which interrupted the normal flow of the programme. From a campers' point of view, the two men were 'outsiders' and did not appear to be the type of people to easily fit into a camp situation."[40] ...

At agency camps run by youth organizations and religious groups, psychology also had its influence. Due to their relatively low fees, these camps did not have the resources to develop departments of psychology, but camper populations were small enough to allow for a fair bit of individual attention. At the YMCA's Camp Pine Crest, this translated in 1940 into "hundreds of hours" of "personal counselling," provided not by trained psychologists, but, nonetheless, by counsellors and, in some cases, the director. Administrators showed great faith in the value of this talk therapy, with camp reports detailing the progress of individual campers upon receiving the personalized attention of staff.[41] Campers were praised for learning to share in cabin clean-up, for accepting an outcast camper, or just generally, for getting along with others. Administrators at agency camps, like those at private camps, stressed the importance of detailed record keeping as a way of counting their successes (or failures). As at Ahmek, information for records was solicited from parents, counsellors and other staff. At the Y's Tapawingo for girls, in 1951, at least some campers went through extensive "intake interviews" which included questions about parent-child relationships, children's work habits and interests, as well as attitudes towards "race and religious prejudice, snobbishness, boys, and sex."[42] ... At the same time, these camps tried to balance Watsonian-style record keeping with a more Freudian interest in the individual child. Canoe trips, for instance, were to be planned "to fit *the campers*," while those keeping reports on the camp were expected to remember that "the most vital part of a camp concerned [the] boys, and what effect the camp had on their lives."[43]

This situation was both similar and different at fresh air camps in the province. Certainly, there was no question of on-site psychologists or departments of psychology at camps of this sort. Even if the hiring of professionals had been feasible (which it was not), with thousands of campers each summer (compared to, perhaps, two hundred at the typical private or agency camp), it would have required a small army of psychologists to offer the same level of attention. Furthermore, the short ten- to twelve-day stays typical at such camps allowed little time for observation, let alone diagnosis and treatment. Finally, one wonders to what degree psychological assessment was thought appropriate for working-class children. The actions of misbehaving poor children—boys in particular—did not go unnoticed, but were more likely to win them the label of delinquent, rather than neurotic, with the goal being to "reform" them at the hand of social workers rather than to "treat" them at the hand of psychologists.

Still, even at the low-budget, charity-run Bolton Fresh Air Camp, psychological theories had their impact and these years saw an increasing interest in campers' emotional and psychological well-being. While fresh air camps had initially recommended themselves to the public for their health benefits, concerted efforts were made in the late 1930s to convince the public that their mandate went far beyond providing nutrition and combating disease. "In terms of physical health [a camp holiday] means much," it was declared as early as 1931, "but no one will ever be able to estimate the benefits to mental health this outing ... means."[44] Though camp promoters were not the first to make such claims, their emphasis on using nature as a tool in early personality development, rather than simply as a fresh air tonic, was unique. ...

Ultimately, camps of all types contributed to the broader cultural transformation of the meaning of childhood. Crucial to this way of thinking was that children were not just smaller versions of adult psyches. "Children are neither vegetables nor miniature men," Mary Northway asserted in 1939, while of director Mary Edgar, it was said, "she felt very strongly that children should be children."[45] These seemingly banal statements spoke volumes concerning the shift in conceptions of childhood. They highlighted the notion that children had needs, interests, and abilities distinct from those of adults, beliefs not so firmly held by previous generations.

In theory then, childhood was constructed as a category beyond class. Thus, while adults who enjoyed material comforts and holiday pleasures were to count themselves "lucky," all children were understood to be "deserving" of their rightful portion of good times. In this modern view, the condition of childhood denoted not only satisfaction of needs, but also the creation of good memories. Childhood was a time not only to *be* happy, but one to look back on with fondness, much as an idealized conflict-free past figured in anti-modernist thinking about collective experience. Child-hood was to function as "the good old days" of every individual, the time before "now" when all was placid stability and calm. Again, compared with the outlook of earlier generations, this signalled a paradigm shift of somewhat radical proportions.

Psychology and the Camp in Depression, War, and Cold War

Psychology impacted the summer camp throughout this period, but time also played a role in influencing the nature of its impact. The idea of camp as isolated from the rest of society, though never wholly true at any time, was shown to be even less so in the years of worldwide depression and war. The hard times of the 1930s for instance, had distinct, if varying, effect on camps in Ontario; private camps saw their enrol-ments drop, while fresh air camps felt increasing pressure to accommodate children from needy families.[46] During World War II, state-organized mass mobilization of labour, resources and funds devoted to the war effort all had their impact, the most sig-nificant results being labour shortages and the challenges of fund-raising.[47] Along with these, the imperative to ration, conserve, and contribute to the war effort shaped camp programming. Finally, the general affluence of the post-war period altered thinking about recreation and leisure and also made camp holidays accessible to many more Canadians.

In each of these periods, apart from these gen-eral impacts, ideas about the psychology of camping were also affected. For its part, the Depression seemed to deepen the feeling that camp could offer escape from society, with the presumed isolation of camp life and its psychological benefits taking on added appeal. ... Private camps also spoke of being isolated from the Depression at camp; however, for those who lived their whole lives isolated from real economic insecurity, these statements could take on an air of complacency. One camper, looking back on the 1930s at Ahmek, sounded almost smug about how easily the troubles of the world could be forgotten at camp. "I never felt in those days ... that the camp ever suffered from the Depression. You never had the feeling that the world was down, down, down. Once you hit Canoe Lake ... we[sic] were all having the greatest time in the world, the outside world was shut off and camp carried on in a very upbeat situa-tion."[48] As positive as such experiences must have been for young campers, the comforts (and potential mental health benefits) of such camps were access-ible to only a privileged few, even in good times, and even more so during the Depression.

World War II presented camp administrators with different challenges. Though steering poor children away from criminal activities had always been a con-cern of fresh air camp promoters, it was in the war years, and immediately after, that references to juvenile delinquency increased. These concerns fit with what has already been documented about worries over family life during wartime, especially the perceived connection between married women's paid labour and increasing rates of juvenile delinquency. Camp literature and fund-raising appeals showed similar concern for absent fathers and mothers "exhausted by factory work." The children were the real concern, too often, it was said, packed into "crowded day nurseries" or, worse, left unattended and "roaming the streets." ... At camp, it was assumed these potential delinquents would make "fine contacts," form "new interests" and catch glimpses of "a better way of living" that would set them on the right path.[49]

While fresh air camps focused on the trouble working-class children might be causing around them, private camps gave more thought to the war's potentially harmful psychological effect on campers themselves. At the Taylor Statten camps, the war strengthened the citizenship-building mandate, but also caused debate over whether impressionable young minds should be exposed to the realities of military conflict. ... This all fit well with the notion of childhood as a protected time, the idea that "children should be children," and that certain types of know-ledge were not suitable for their consumption. Still, camps differed on the question. ...

As the world seemed an increasingly changing and unpredictable place in these years of Depres-sion, war and, later, the Cold War, camp was looked to as a place to provide children with the sense of security that urban life, presumably, could not. ...

... In post-war years, fostering security was deemed no less—and perhaps more—important at camp, as it was in the political, economic and domestic realms. At the level of childhood, fostering security now meant more than just the filling of material needs; providing children with positive experiences was also crucial. Under the influence of Freudian thinking, popularized during the post-war years, childhood experiences were understood to have lasting importance. In 1949, a Fresh Air Fund appeal posed the rhetorical question, "How much of later success in life has its roots in childhood!"[50] As if in response, a private camp brochure stated unequivocally in 1950, "The happiest adults are those who had happy and fruitful childhood experiences."[51] Starting from such premises, camps saw themselves providing not only happy experiences for young campers, but also lifelong emotional and psychological stability.

Once at camp, campers of the 1950s were subject to administrators with increasingly psychological aims. One place this was apparent was in the pages of camp manuals, where the language was increasingly psychologized. In 1950 at Ahmek, it was argued that children should use arts and crafts projects "to express their innermost feelings," while a CGIT camp manual of the same year advised using sports— "especially those using balls"—as a way of "releasing hostility."[52] ...

As in earlier decades, campers' parents and home life came in for criticism in post-war years. If post-war families put great stock in the value and comforts of home, and if educators continued to regard it as a key influence in a child's life, camp enthusiasts reflected the expert view that the home was not, by itself, enough. As was typical of this era, mother-blaming was common. In Mary Northway's writings, some middle- and upper-class mothers were accused of "protecting [the child] as a little god" ...[53] In effect, the home was reconceptualized as only one in a constellation of factors which promised to turn out the properly socialized child. As the province's Chief Director of Education claimed in 1947, "It is wholesome ... for boys and girls to get away for a time from their home, no matter how good that home may be."[54] Others agreed that extra-familial institutions had distinctive roles to play. ... Clearly, as in the wider society, the mental hygiene point of view now permeated the articulation of camp goals,

the planning of camp programming, and thinking about the camper one hoped to change.

"Like Progressive Schools in the Outdoors"

From the late 1920s onward, camp life was influenced not only by psychological, but also educational expertise. As early as 1929, *Camping and Character* was proclaiming that efficient camp programming required "the most critical consideration of educational technique."[55] Ten years later, Camp Ahmek's "Talks to Counsellors" stated: "The whole life of the camp is the curriculum. The process of living, the interaction of persons within activities of many sorts ... constitute the educative process."[56] By 1936 CGIT literature preached a similar message, that camping was "a necessary part of the modern girl's education."[57] By the post-war period the influence of educational theory at camp was widespread and, accompanying it, a keen sense of the movement's progress ... Though its relationship to formal education was conceptualized as auxiliary or complementary, by the closing months of World War II it was proudly proclaimed that "the best summer camps are like progressive schools in the outdoors."[58]

As much as camp administrators felt like they were embarking on a unique pedagogical journey, by the 1930s, ideals of progressive education were the much talked-about fashion in educational circles throughout North America. In particular the ideas of John Dewey, American philosopher and educator, were taken up by numerous others and formed the basis for what became known as "progressive" education. Among the key aspects of Dewey's approach was the call to respect each child as an individual, with varying and specific needs. ... [H]is new approach promised "education for the whole child," that would unfold in an organic and child-centred way. In this respect, the "field trip"—an adventure out into the "real world"—might be more useful than the typical teacher-led lesson. ...[59] Education defined in this way clearly fit well with the aims and perspective of the mental hygiene movement. ...

... Camp administrators were influenced by these new trends and regarded their own work as part of the progressive movement in education. At many camps, for instance, much was made of the shift from regimented programming to a free and open system of activities, increasingly to be chosen by campers themselves. Camps self-consciously promoted this notion of their work and of how far it had come since the "old days" of camping ... This perspective seemed to hold sway equally at fresh air and agency camps. In 1947 Bolton administrators proudly declared, "There is nothing institutional about Bolton Camp. Every activity is planned for the utmost enjoyment of each individual child. ... Every child is treated as a guest and there is no regimenting. Each can do what he likes best."[60]

Along with the new-found antipathy for regimentation, the adoption of a child-centred approach transformed attitudes towards competition and punishment at many camps. In the 1920s, children had been encouraged to work at their camp skills by the awarding of all manner of prizes, badges, and trophies. Even girls, generally discouraged from competing and from developing an active physicality in school-based physical education programmes, were not entirely excluded from competition at camp, even if they were treated more carefully than boys.[61] ... From the perspective of the progressive educator, however, competition was regarded as an artificial way of encouraging interest, and awards, as behaviourist crutches. Echoing the progressive educator's love of education for its practical application, camps now sought to have children "do things because they wanted to" and not simply to achieve recognition or "points." ... Overall, camps were less concerned with skill acquisition than with socialization, now the camp's highest goal: "The experience of campers in social relationships is what influences or educates them," Camp Ahmek's 1939 handbook stated, "not the activities of swimming, canoeing, dramatics ... as such."[62] Under the new system, corporal punishment—still freely resorted to in formal educational settings, but increasingly under fire from modern psychology—was officially frowned on and forms of positive reinforcement advocated in their place. As Taylor Statten optimistically suggested to counsellors in 1939, "I hope we shall be able to go through the entire season without using the word 'don't.'"[63]

The influence of new pedagogical theories was experienced not just in a negative sense (discouraging regimentation and competition), but also in a positive one—encouraging a hands-on and direct approach to learning. Camps took great pride in the fact that, as they saw it, children learned much more at camp than "within the four walls of any school," as YMCA promotional literature put it.[64] ...

Progressive education at camp also meant the training of a new kind of "teacher"—the counsellor. Of all leaders, it was agreed that the counsellor was "the most vital single factor in the camp situation" and, as some put it, "the most important man in camp."[65] Except for a half-holiday per week, counsellors were expected to be on the job every moment of the day not only getting campers out of bed in the morning, monitoring their bodies and behaviours, and teaching them camp skills, but also acting as living, breathing examples of health, fitness, right values and attitudes. All told, counsellors were expected to show the understanding of a psychologist, the loving guidance of a parent, but also, as one source put it, "something of the detachment of a doctor."[66]

... In the final analysis, camp administrators saw themselves as the most truly progressive educators, those who had grasped the genius of "the natural." This "natural-ness" described both its setting (in wilderness and rural contexts) and its structure (child-centred and holistic). By contrast, traditional education was deemed doubly artificial: set in the constructed spaces of urban society and organized in a constructed and artificial manner. ... Even in their "modern-ness," then, camp enthusiasts revealed their anti-modern tendencies.

Assessing the Impact of Progressive Education at Camp

One of the early conclusions of Canadian historians of progressive education is that, quite simply, the movement failed to have significant impact. ... My assessment of the camp experiment with progressive education leads to similar conclusions. Camp programmes revealed a complex mix of success and failure in the experiment with progressive education.

Admittedly, camps, like schools, did not always live up to educational ideals. For one, the freedom of programming was sometimes exaggerated. Fresh air camps for the poor, with their often large numbers and low staff/camper ratios, were particularly susceptible to on-going regimentation. While fresh air literature painted a picture of the "free and easy" life of camp, this was clearly an exaggeration.[67] In fact, along with its admiration for freedom, promotional literature revealed an abiding respect for efficiency and order. "At the fresh air camps there is a definite routine," *The Toronto Star* noted appreciatively as late as 1949. "Certain activities take place at a certain time. Meals are served at a definite hour. There is a rest period every day which every child ... must observe."[68] At these camps with large camper populations, a degree of regimentation was no doubt a necessity. For instance, teaching children camping and sporting activities "in shifts of one hundred at a time," as at one fresh air camp on Georgian Bay, clearly did not allow for either individual attention or a free and easy approach.[69] ...

... Youthful counsellors, as already noted, were not always the wise and willing teachers of progressive ideal. At times, some acted more like disgruntled workers than as dedicated instructors or psychologists in training. A 1931 study of Ahmek noted that counsellors were not always enthusiastic, for instance, about the "great amount of "clerical work" or record-keeping demanded by the camp."[70] In 1938 a final report from the camp indicated "a certain feeling of tension among staff members," that some felt that "much fun ha[d] departed" from camp life and were ready to "pack [their] trunk[s]."[71] At the Y's Camp Pine Crest, reports likewise complained of counsellors who were "not at all qualified," who lacked "personalized interest" and who weren't overly interested in the details of "campers' routine."[72]

From the perspective of campers, relationships with counsellors were sometimes more distant than warm. In part, this distance was built into the structure of camp, where counsellors did not always share cabins with campers, an arrangement said to foster independence and co-operation among campers.[73] "When I was in intermediate camp," Shirley Ford remembered of 1930s Glen Bernard, "our counsellor came into the cabin the first day and said, 'Hi, I'm so-and-so,' and we didn't see her again for weeks."[74] Bolton fresh air camper, Mary Murphy, also confided that she had few memories of her counsellor, in her view, "because they weren't that personal with you."[75] In their defence, one might add that counsellors were often warned to keep their distance from campers, due to fears of encouraging "crushes" and, in the worst-case scenario, homosexuality. Here, it was thought, camp had some developmental hazards as well as benefits.[76]

In some cases, children themselves sometimes could find camp a less than agreeable experience, whatever the belief that learning was to be an organic and enjoyable process. Indeed, for some, psychological health was more threatened than enhanced by the camping experience. No matter how good the camp, separation from parents and home—for private campers, sometimes as long as two months—could be traumatic. Ahmek reported that each year at its camp saw two or three cases of "hysterical homesickness," campers like fourteen-year-old "Tom" who rarely slept through the night. "I would trade you places any day," he was said to have written home to his brother. "I was sick the other night and it was heckish. ... When you see the Pirate Ship in the camp book it looks big but it is small. So is the theatre. ... I am in the Intermediate section and it's not much good. ... I hope Mom and Dad come home ... so I will be able to go home. I will tell you straight that I will not come back here any more."[77]

Even those campers who generally took to camp life, sometimes found homesickness a persistent problem and one of the psychological challenges of camp. Ruth-Ellen Soles cried herself to sleep the first night of every camp season. "I did until I was eighteen," this 1950s Kawagama camper explained. "It became a ritual."[78] According to a 1957 study of homesickness at fifteen camps, this was one of the most common manifestations, as were sleep and digestion problems. In many of these cases, homesickness was accepted as a natural reaction, even a healthy part of growing up. ...[79]

Apart from painful separation from family and friends, certain campers experienced the peer group in a mainly negative fashion. The bed-wetter, the physically uncoordinated, or the fearful child could all find camp to be a miserable experience. Peer group adjustment was clearly not always smooth. At Glen Bernard Camp it was noted in the 1930s that bullies could be "cruel and cutting," and that, generally, "In a community such as this, one or two people actually develop the role of the scapegoats of the group."[80] While scapegoating also occurred at school, at camp there was not even the chance of daily reprieve.

The freedom so valued by the progressive educator could lead to other uninvited behaviours at camp. Pranks and practical jokes were common at many camps. ... Other sorts of camper activities and responses were considered more problematic. Camp Ahmek literature referred disapprovingly to the misuse of equipment, night-time "tent feeds," "dangerous risk-taking," and to lack of cleanliness and punctuality as general problems. ... Whatever the rhetoric of progressive pedagogy, clearly, a certain level of regimentation was still seen as indispensable.[81]

For their part, staff did not always choose the most progressive approaches in dealing with misbehaving children. Interviews revealed at least two cases of counsellors hitting children, and one camper being shut up alone in her cabin for "about a day and a half."[82] ...

If camps were not the utopian worlds and controlled laboratories their administrators envisioned, neither did they fail entirely at their educational mission. As with other social institutions, a gap between goals and reality was always apparent, but in terms of the camp setting this did not necessarily entail the "triumph of formalism." In part, this can be read from children's own reactions. For every child who regretted the experience, there were many more for whom camp was a special and long-remembered treat, one they would no doubt look back on in adulthood as "educational." ...[83] True enough, many campers showed an excitement, delight, and, sometimes, devotion rarely expressed in connection with institutions of formal education. "Hysterical homesickness" and major behavioural problems appear to have been a minority problem, with many children preferring camp life to school. According to Geraldine Sherman, post-war Kawagama camper, "The most eager campers were those who most hated school." [84]

What we know of camp programming and organization further suggests that the summer camp was at least partly successful in its experiment with progressive education. Camps were often more regimented than their literature admitted, but, for many campers, they also offered the most freeing and relaxed atmosphere of any childhood experience. For such campers, it is not the bells and the bugles which are now remembered, but rather the liberty to experiment with new activities and the general feeling of independence this engendered. Some experienced this particularly in terms of the distance from parental control; others, like Wapomeo camper, Joan Moses, found simply that the pace of camp life was to their liking. "Being a senior girl—from 14 on," she recalled, "we had our own little island across the way from the main girls island. ... The counsellors had their own separate cabins and we had the cabin to ourselves. There were no inspections and if you didn't make your bed the whole summer, that was your problem—and some

didn't!"[85] In Moses' experience, camp was very much a world unto itself, where the peer culture of youth dictated the pace as much as the camp administration.

This type of behaviour was not permitted at every camp, nor for all ages of campers. For some campers it was time spent away from camp, canoe-tripping, that offered the widest scope for autonomy. Out on canoe trips, one was removed not only from parental control, but from that of most of the camp administration. With only several counsellors—perhaps not much older than themselves—and two or three guides, campers paddled their way through adventure and adversity, with a sense of freedom and independence likely both physical and psychological. Merle Storey looked back on her experience with a bittersweet nostalgia:

> I remember struggling across the portages with the unaccustomed weight of a pack on my back, welcoming the sight of the end of the portage where a canoe was waiting to be loaded, paddling down the silent lakes with only the sound of our own voices echoing across the water and gathering around the campfire at night with the dark forest beyond. It was an unforgettable experience.[86]

While demanding its own kind of discipline, in a sense, tripping eliminated the need for formal regulations, the ultimate goal of the progressive educator. ... [O]ther aspects of activity planning helped to imbue camps with a more child-centred tone than most schools. Indeed, in contrast to the school, with its concern for well-roundedness and facility with every subject, camp programming frequently allowed children to focus on those activities of most interest to them. This scenario was less likely to be found at larger camps, where moving large numbers of children from activity to activity did not allow for the same individual freedoms. Even there, however, the structuring of programming—involving hands-on "doing" and active physicality, rather than abstract thinking, as well as the general novelty of setting and activities—appears to have made a trip to camp an enjoyable and sought-after privilege for many. More than this, camp provided its own kind of education—about the natural world, about the regions in which children camped and travelled, about physical ability and stamina, and about getting along with others. School educators might well have been envious of this relative success.

CONCLUSION

As the authors of *Camping and Character* saw it, the application of psychology to the realm of outdoor education heralded the emergence of "the modern summer camp." In this view, to be modern was to grasp the importance of the camp as the tool of social science and education, to understand the parameters and importance of child psychology, and to enthusiastically apply the insights of progressive pedagogy. This striving to "be modern" might seem at odds with the camp's natural ethos and simple life rhetoric. In fact, this two-sidedness, the pull of the modern and the anti-modern were both essential aspects of the camp phenomenon. In the eyes of camp promoters and administrators, successful modern living entailed regular trips back to the natural (read: pre-modern) world. ... As administrators agreed, camp was "a new type of education ... made necessary by modern conditions."[87] Ultimately, whatever the anti-modern aspects that inspired its birth, when it came to its vision of childhood and education, the summer camp had its face not backwards towards the past, but toward a future where children would be increasingly analysed, understood and shaped by the tenets of psychological and educational expertise.

NOTES

1. Ontario Camp Leadership Centre files in possession of Dorothy Walter, Toronto, Ontario, Dr. J.G. Althouse, Transcript of CKEY Broadcast, 25 April 1947, 1.

2. In Rooke and Schnell's view, Victorian childhood was defined by four essential factors: segregation from, and also protection by, adult society, as well as social and economic dependence. Patricia T. Rooke and R. L. Schnell, "Childhood as Ideology," *British Journal of Educational Studies* 27 (February 1979): 7–28. On child labour, see Lorna Hurl, "Restricting Child Factory Labour in Late Nineteenth-Century Ontario," *Labour/Le Travail* (Spring 1988): 87–121; Dominique Jean, "Le Recul de travail des enfant au Quebec entre 1940 et 1960: Une Explication des Conflits entre les Familles Pauvres et L'Etat Profidence," *Labour/Le Travail* 24 (Fall 1989): 91–129; John Bullen, "Hidden Workers: Child Labour and the Family Economy in Late Nineteenth-Century Urban Ontario," *Labour/Le Travail* 18, (Fall 1986): 163–87. In the American context, see Viviana A. Zelizer, *Pricing the Priceless Child: The Changing Social Value of Children* (New Jersey: Princeton University Press, 1994).

3. On psychology and child development theories, see Steven Schlossman, "Philanthropy and the Gospel of Child Development," *History of Education Quarterly* 21, no. 3 (1981): 275–99.

4. As Sol Cohen explains, these bodies were constituted by "reform-minded academicians, social workers, physicians and psychiatrists" Sol Cohen, "The Mental Hygiene Movement, The Development of Personality and the School: The Medicalization of American Education," *History of Education Quarterly,* 23 (Summer 1983): 136–7.

5. A department of psychology also emerged at McGill University in the 1920s. Mona Gleason provides one of the most informative accounts of the rise of academic psychology in this country; Gleason, *Normalizing the Ideal: Psychology, Schooling, and the Family in Postwar Canada* (Toronto: University of Toronto Press, 1999), 19–36. On the mental hygiene movement, see Schlossman, "Philanthropy and the Gospel of Child Development"; Cohen, "The Mental Hygiene Movement"; Theresa R. Richardson, *The Century of the Child: The Mental Hygiene Movement and Social Policy in the United States and Canada* (Albany: State University of New York Press, 1989), 112–27; Hans Pols, "Between the Laboratory and Life: Child Development Research in Toronto, 1919–1956," *History of Psychology* 5, no. 2 (2002): 135–62; Brian J. Low, "The New Generation: Mental Hygiene and the Portrayals of Children by the National Film Board of Canada, 1946–1967," *History of Education Quarterly* 43, no. 4 (2003): 540–70; Brian J. Low, "The Hand that Rocked the Cradle: A Critical Analysis of Rockefeller Philanthropic Funding, 1920–1960," *Historical Studies in Education* 16, no. 1 (2004): 33–62; Neil Sutherland, *Children in English-Canadian Society, 1880–1920: Framing the Twentieth-Century Consensus* (Toronto: University of Toronto Press, 1976, reissued by Wilfrid Laurier University Press, 2000), chapter 1. On forced sterilization of the "feeble-minded," see Angus McLaren, "The Creation of a Haven for "Human Thoroughbreds": The Sterilization of the Feeble-Minded and the Mentally Ill in British Columbia," *Canadian Historical Review* 67, no. 2 (1986): 127–50 and also his monograph, *Our Own Master Race: Eugenics in Canada, 1885–1945* (Toronto: McClelland and Stewart, 1990).

6. Miller, "Psychology and the Child," 57–80; John Cleverley and D. C. Phillips, *Visions of Childhood: Influential Models from Locke to Spock* (New York: Teachers College Press, 1986), 114–24. On the Canadian setting, see Veronica Strong-Boag, "Intruders in the Nursery: Childcare Professionals Reshape the Years One to Five, 1920–1940," in *Childhood and Family in Canadian History*, ed. Joy Parr (Toronto: McClelland and Stewart, 1982), 160–78; Nora Lewis, "Creating the Little Machine: Child-rearing in British Columbia, 1919–1939," *BC Studies* 56 (Winter 1982–83): 44–60; Katherine Arnup, "Raising the Dionne Quintuplets: Lessons For Modern Mothers," in the special issue of *Journal of Canadian Studies* 29, no. 4 (Winter, 1994–95): 65–84 and other articles; Katherine Arnup, *Education for Motherhood: Advice for Mothers in Twentieth-Century Canada* (Toronto: University of Toronto Press, 1994), 84–116; Cynthia Comacchio, *Nations are Built of Babies: Saving Ontario's Mothers and Children* (Montreal/Kingston: McGill-Queen's University Press, 1993).

7. Jocelyn Motyer Raymond, *The Nursery World of Dr. Blatz* (Toronto: University of Toronto Press, 1991), 42. On John B. Watson and behaviourism, see Peter J. Miller, "Psychology and the Child: Homer Lane and J.B. Watson," in *Studies in Childhood History: A Canadian Perspective,* eds. Patricia T. Rooke, R.L. Schnell, (Calgary: Detselig Enterprises Ltd., 1982), 73; Ann Hulbert, *Raising America: Experts, Parents and a Century of Advice About Children* (New York: Alfred A. Knopf, 2003).

8. For biographical information on Blatz, see ... note 16. For Blatz's camping involvement: Hedley S. Dimock and Charles E. Hendry, *Camping and Character: A Camp Experiment in Character Education,* (New York: Association Press, 1929), 159; Trent University Archives [hereafter TUA], OCA Papers, 78-006/1/1, 'Second Annual Report of the Committee on Education and Research of the Ontario Section of the American Camping Association," April 13, 1942.

9. Existing histories of Canadian summer camps are sparse, although a smattering of articles has appeared on the subject. See the collection of articles in Bruce W. Hodgins and Bernadine Dodge, eds., *Using Wilderness: Essays on the Evolution of Youth Camping in Ontario* (Peterborough: Frost Centre for Canadian Heritage and Development Studies, 1992). See also Susan L. Forbes, "'Nothing But a Rag Between You and the Sky': Northway Lodge Girls' Camp and the Wilderness Experience," paper given to the Canadian Historical Association Conference, Edmonton, May 24–29, 2000; Anna H. Lathrop, "'Strap an Axe to Your Belt': Camp Counselor Training and the Socialization of Women at the Margaret Eaton School (1925–1941)," *Sport History Review* 32, no. 2 (2001): 110–25; and Sharon Wall, "Totem Poles, Teepees and Token Traditions: 'Playing Indian' at Ontario Summer Camps, 1920–1955," *Canadian Historical Review* 86, no. 3 (September 2005): 513–44. On the history of summer camps in the American setting, see Leslie Paris, "Children's Nature: Summer Camps in New York State, 1919–1941" (Unpublished Doctor of Philosophy dissertation, University of Michigan, 2000); Leslie Paris, "The Adventures of Peanut and Bo: Summer Camps and Early Twentieth Century American Girlhood," *Journal of Women's History* 12 (Winter 2001): 47–78; Susan A. Miller, "Girls in Nature/The Nature of Girls: Transforming Female Adolescence at Summer Camp, 1900–1939" (Unpublished Doctor of Philosophy dissertation, University of Pennsylvania, 2001); Michael B. Smith, "'And They Say We'll Have Some Fun When It Stops Raining': A History of Summer Camp in the United States" (Unpublished Doctor of Philosophy dissertation, Indiana University, 2002); Michael Smith, "The Ego Ideal of the Good Camper and the Nature of Summer Camp," *Environmental History* (Jan. 2006), http://www.historycooperative.org/journals/eh/11.1/smith.html (accessed August 18, 2007); Nancy Mykoff, "A Jewish Season: Ethnic American Culture at Children's Summer Camp, 1918–1941" (Unpublished Doctor of Philosophy dissertation, New York University, 2002); and Abigail Van Slyck, *A Manufactured Wilderness: Summer Camps and the Shaping of American Youth, 1890–1960* (Minneapolis: University of Minnesota Press, 2006).

10. "Urbanization," *The Canadian Encyclopedia* (Edmonton: Hurtig Press, 1988), 2235.

11. On changing views of nature, see Roderick Nash, *Wilderness and the American Mind* (New Haven: Yale University Press, 1973); Elizabeth McKinsey, *Niagara Falls: Icon of the American Sublime* (Cambridge: Cambridge University Press, 1985); William Cronon, ed., *Uncommon Ground: Toward Reinventing Nature* (New York: W.W. Norton and Company, 1995); Max Oelschlaeger, *The Idea of*

Wilderness: From Prehistory to the Age of Ecology (New Haven: Yale University Press, 1991); and Peter Schmitt, *Back to Nature: The Arcadian Myth in Urban America* (Baltimore: John Hopkins University Press, 1990). On nature-based recreation and its therapeutic effects in the Canadian context, see Roy I. Wolfe, "The Summer Resorts of Ontario In the Nineteenth Century," *Ontario History* 54, no. 3 (1962): 149–61; George Altmeyer, "Three Ideas of Nature in Canada, 1893–1914," *Journal of Canadian Studies* 11, no. 3 (1976): 21–36; Douglas Cole, "Artists, Patrons and Public: An Enquiry into the Success of the Group of Seven," *Journal of Canadian Studies* 13, no. 2 (Summer 1978): 69–78; G. Wall and J. Marsh, eds., *Recreational Land Use: Perspectives on its Evolution in Canada* (Ottawa: Carleton University Press, 1982); Bruce W. Hodgins and Margaret Hobbs, eds., *Nastawgan: The Canadian North by Canoe and Snowshoe* (Weston: Betelgeuse Books, 1985); Bruce W. Hodgins and Jamie Benidickson, *The Temagami Experience: Recreation, Resources, and Aboriginal Rights in the Northern Ontario Wilderness* (Toronto: University of Toronto Press, 1989); Patricia Jasen, *Wild Things: Nature, Culture, and Tourism in Ontario, 1790–1914* (Toronto: University of Toronto Press, 1995); Jamie Benidickson, *Idleness, Water, and a Canoe: Reflections on Paddling for Pleasure* (Toronto: University of Toronto Press, 1997); Karen Dubinsky, *The Second Greatest Disappointment: Honeymooning and Tourism at Niagara Falls* (Toronto: Between the Lines Press, 1999); and Tina Loo, "Of Moose and Men: Hunting for Masculinities in British Columbia, 1880–1939," *Western Historical Quarterly* 32, no. 3 (2001): 296–319. On the creation of provincial parks during this same period, see K. Morrison, "The Evolution of the Ontario Provincial Park System," in *Recreational Land Use*, eds. Wall and Marsh, (Ottawa: Carleton University Press, 1982), 102–119; Gerald Killan, *Protected Places: A History of Ontario's Provincial Parks System* (Toronto: Dundurn, 1993).

12. TUA, Ronald H. Perry Fonds, 82-016/2/8, "The Summer Camp: Recreation or Education," *Canoe Lake Camp Echoes* 4, no. 2 (April 1931), 13; "Come On! Kick in and Smile! Give Kids the Break You Got," *Toronto Daily Star* [hereafter *TDS*], August 28, 1930, 25.

13. *TDS*, June 24, 1920, 5; "Reminiscent Army Man Defines Joys of Childhood," *TDS*, July 2, 1943, 18.

14. Abbie Graham, quoted in Hedley S. Dimock and Taylor Statten, *Talks to Counselors*, (New York: Association Press, 1939), 18.

15. TUA, OCA papers, 72-007/2/9, Irwin Haladner to staff members, "Letter #1," May 1952. See also TUA, OCA Papers, 78-006/25/40, Charlie F. Plewman, "The Days Leading up to the Formation of the Ontario Camping Association" part of poster "Today: Tomorrow's Yesterday," c. 1967.

16. The C.S.E.T. programme was used by groups of 'Trail Rangers' (boys, twelve to fourteen years of age) and Tuxis boys (sixteen to seventeen years of age) and was designed to develop boys' intellectual, spiritual, physical and social capacities. C.A.M. Edwards, *Taylor Statten* (Toronto: The Ryerson Press, 1960); M. Lucille Marr, "Church Teen Clubs, Feminized Organizations?: Tuxis Boys, Trail Rangers, and Canadian Girls in Training, 1919–1939," *Historical Studies in Education*, 3, no. 2 (1991): 249–67.

17. On Mary Hamilton and the History of Camp Tanamakoon, see Mary G. Hamilton, *The Call of Algonquin: Biography of a Summer Camp* (Toronto: The Ryerson Press, 1958), 16. Lathrop, "'Strap an Axe to Your Belt' ..."; John Byl "Mary G. Hamilton: Committed, Dedicated Pioneer Made a Difference," Canadian Association for the Advancement of Women and Sport and Physical Activity http://www.caaws.ca/e/milestones/women_history/mary_hamilton.cfm (accessed August 4, 2007).

18. For biographical information on Mary Northway see TUA, Northway Family Fonds, 90-016/1/1, 'Fonds Level Description—Northway Family'; Curriculum vitae: Mary Northway, 1979. Northway is also mentioned by Raymond as a significant part of Blatz's work at the Institute and, indeed, as integral to the publication of Blatz's final study, *Human Security*. See Raymond, *Nursery World*, 144, 210–16, 220. Northway's dissertation was not only published but also translated into six other languages.

19. For just a few other examples, A.L. Cochrane and A.S. Clarke—founders of the first boys' camps in Temagami in 1903—both held positions at private boys' schools, Cochrane at Toronto's Upper Canada College (UCC), and Clarke, at the Gunnery School, a Connecticut preparatory school. Mary S. Edgar, who founded Glen Bernard Camp near her home

town of Sundridge in 1922, was involved in the YWCA, the CGIT and the Girl Guides. Because of her educational contributions to the world of camping, Edgar was named honorary trustee at Havergal girls' college, where she attended as a student in former years. For more on the life of Cochrane, see Upper Canada College Archives [hereafter, UCCA], Ann Hall, "Arthur Lewis Cochrane: A Biographical Sketch," unpublished paper, Queen's University, Kingston (1964): 36–37. For biographical information on A.S. Clarke and the history of the Keewaydin Camp, see Brian Back, *The Keewaydin Way: A Portrait, 1893–1983* (Temagami: Keewaydin Camp Ltd., 1983). For biographical information on Edgar, see TUA, Northway Family Fonds—Additions, 90-016/1/34, Mary Northway, "Mary S. Edgar, 1889–1973," *Canadian Camping Magazine*, (Summer 1973); TUA, OCA Sound/Tape collection, 83-002/5/8, Barbara Gilchrist, interview by Jack Pierce, November 6, 1986.

20. Cohen, "Mental Hygiene Movement," 129.
21. "Have Alley as Playground, No Trees or Grass in Sight," *TDS*, July 5, 1924, 1.
22. Dimock and Hendry, *Camping and Character*, 145. 23 Ibid., 146.
23. Mary L. Northway, *Appraisal of the Social Development of Children at a Summer Camp* (Toronto: University of Toronto Press, 1940), 12.
24. Dimock and Hendry, *Camping and Character*, 145.
25. Family Services Association of Toronto, Archival Collection, [hereafter, FSATA] "The Gateway to Health and Happiness: Bolton Camp Speaks Again, 1933," 15.
26. Dimock and Statten, *Talks to Counselors,* 20; "You're Tanned and Peppy, What About Poor Kiddies," *TDS*, July 21, 1948, 7; "Fresh Air Fund Needs $417 Daily to Help 5,000 Children Left," *TDS*, August 31, 1950, 8; "Fund Helps Kiddies Escape Mental, Physical Collapse," *TDS*, July 7, 1947, 4. In 1937, the Project on Shy Children was initiated by University of Toronto psychologists. See Pols, "Between the Laboratory and Life," 148–50. On shyness as presented in postwar NFB films, see Low, "The New Generation," On the school's new approach to shy students, see Cohen, "The Mental Hygiene Movement," 131.
27. TUA, Northway Family Fonds—Additions, copy of Mary Northway, "Socialization," *The Camping Magazine* 11, no. 8 (1939): 4.

28. In 1958 Mary Hamilton reiterated Northway's sentiments, stating, "The camp is a child's world and it is very important that the child should feel at home with her own age group. The fact that she gets along at home, does not necessarily mean she can get along with her own contemporaries." Mary G. Hamilton, *The Call of Algonquin: Biography of a Summer Camp* (Toronto: The Ryerson Press, 1958), 101. On age consciousness, see Howard Chudacoff, *How Old Are You?: Age Consciousness in American Culture* (Princeton: Princeton University Press, 1989).
29. On staff—camper ratios see TUA, OCA "1949 Directory of Member Camps"; TUA, OCA Papers, 82-009/2/2, "Northway Lodge: A Pioneer Camp for Girls," Brochure, 1941.
30. Mary Northway, "Socialization," 3.
31. On Palter's role at Camp Kawagama, see Geraldine Sherman, 'The Girls of Summer,' *Toronto Life* (September 2001): 100. Adult camp alumni from Kawagama have claimed that whenever one of her campers attained a degree of fame or notoriety—of good or bad variety—Palter returned to her original box of index cards, "well into old age," to verify the accuracy of her original impressions.
32. Everett Rogers lists five categories of response to the presentation of new ideas: the innovators, the early adopters, the early majority, the late majority and the laggards. Everett M. Rogers, *Communication of Innovations: A Cross-Cultural Approach* (New York, 1971), referenced in Cohen, "The Mental Hygiene Movement," 138.
33. Dimock and Hendry, *Camping and Character*, 256–7, 277.
34. According to Cohen, interwar parent education programmes, another offshoot of the mental hygiene movement, sought to change parents' "pre-scientific" views and educate them as to the importance of personality development. Involving parents in studies and questionnaires was one way of drawing them in to the mental hygiene perspective. Cohen, "Mental Hygiene Movement," 129.
35. Dimock and Statten, *Talks to Counselors,* 86–7.
36. TUA, Ronald H. Perry Fonds, 82-016/2/8, *Canoe Lake Camp Echoes* 4, no. 3 (May 1931): 42; 4, no. 1 (February 1931): 40. On the host of methods for information gathering at Ahmek, see Dimock and Hendry, *Camping and Character,* 256–7, 263–88; Dimock and Statten, *Talks to Counselors,* 24–26.

37. TUA, Ronald H. Perry Papers, 82-016/2/8, Dimock, "Camping and Character Growth," 10–12. These laws received further elaboration in later editions of *Camping and Character.*

38. Hamilton, *Call of Algonquin*, 168.

39. For discussions of parents see Dimock and Hendry, *Camping and Character*, 167, 183–4, 189. For the evolution of fatherly roles in these years, see Cynthia Comacchio, "'A Postscript for Father': Defining a New Fatherhood in Interwar Canada," *Canadian Historical Review* 78, no. 3 (September 1997); and Robert Rutherdale, "Fatherhood and Masculine Domesticity During the Baby Boom: Consumption and Leisure in Advertising and Life Stories," in Edward-Andre Montigny and Anne Lorene Chambers, eds., *Family Matters: Papers in Post-Confederation Canadian Family History* (Toronto: Canadian Scholar's Press, 1988), 309–30; Chris Dummitt, "Finding a Place For Father: Selling the Barbecue in Postwar Canada," *Journal of the Canadian Historical Association* 9 (1998): 209–23.

40. Ibid., 169.

41. Donald Burry, "A History of the Taylor Statten Camps," (Unpublished Master of Science in Physical Education, University of Saskatchewan, 1985), 23.

42. TUA, Camp Pine Crest Fonds, 78-009/2/1, Camp Pine Crest, "Annual Report," 1940.

43. TUA, OCA Papers, 72-007/2/5, Toronto YWCA, "Camp Tapawingo," 1951.

44. TUA, Camp Pine Crest Fonds, 78-009/2/1, Rix Rogers, Camp Pine Crest, "Out-Trip Department—1951 Report." Emphasis in original; TUA, Camp Pine Crest Fonds, 78009/2/1, Camp Pine Crest, "Annual Report," 1940.

45. "Mother Fights for Health, Her Children Get Holiday," *TDS*, August 5, 1931, 2.

46. Northway, "Socialization," 3. TUA, OCA Sound/Tape collection, 83-002/5/8, Barb Gilchrist, interview by Jack Pearse, November 6, 1986[;] Sutherland, "Triumph of 'Formalism'"; For other accounts of the failure of progressive education, see also Robert Stamp, "Education for Democratic Citizenship"; Mann, "G.M. Weir and H.B. King"; Patterson, "Canadian Experience with Progressive Education"; Callan, "John Dewey"; Tomkins, *A Common Countenance;* Gleason, *Normalizing the Ideal*, 119–39[;] Paul Axelrod, "Beyond the Progressive Education Debate: A Profile of Toronto Schooling in the 1950's," *Historical Studies in Education* 17, no. 2 (2005): 227.

47. On falling enrolments at private camps, see Brian Back, *Keewaydin Way;* Donald Burry, "A History of the Taylor Statten Camps" (Unpublished Master of Science in Physical Education, University of Saskatchewan, 1985), 38–39, 39–40. On the pressure on fresh air camps, see "Star Fresh Air Fund Faces Certain Deficit Unless Cash Donated," *TDS*, August 27, 1931, 23; "Fresh Air Treasurer Needs $3000 badly," *TDS*, August 31, 1931, 16; NWA, "New Interests at Bolton Camp in 1935," 1; FSATA, Minutes, Bolton Camp Committee, March 20, 1930.

48. On general labour shortages at camp, see TUA, OCA Papers, 78-006/1/1, Minutes, OCA Open Meeting, January 25, 1943. On the challenges of wartime fund-raising for fresh air camps, see "Fund Again to Give Holiday to City's Underprivileged," *TDS*, June 7, 1943; "First Holiday in 15 Years, Mother 'Happy as a Lark,'" *TDS*, August 31, 1944.

49. Dan Gibson to Donald Burry, December 20, 1984, quoted in Burry, "A History of the Taylor Statten Camps," 40.

50. Camp Fire, Fresh Air, "God's Gift to Boys," Judge sees Big Need," *TDS*, August 19, 1948, 1.

51. FSATA, "Bolton Summer Camp: Tomorrow Belongs to the Children," Brochure, 1949.

52. TUA, Adele and Harry Ebbs Papers, 80-014/1/8, "The Taylor Statten Camps," Brochure, c. 1950.

53. TUA, Adele and Harry Ebbs Papers, 80-014/1/8, "The Taylor Statten Camps," Brochure, c. 1950; UCA/VUA, Canadian Girls in Training Collection [CGIT], 85.095C – box 14 –file 1, CGIT Camp Manual, 1950, 44–45.

54. Northway, "Socialization," 3–5, 30.

55. Ontario Camp Leadership Centre [hereafter OCLC.], files in possession of Dorothy Walter, Toronto, Ontario, Copy of Address over C.K.E.Y. Broadcast, by Dr. J.G. Althouse, April 25, 1947, 3.

56. Dimock and Hendry, *Camping and Character,* 5.

57. Dimock and Statten, *Talks to Counselors*, 33.

58. Margaret Rieder Paisley, "A Chat About Camps," *The Torch* 12, no. 2 (April/May 1936): 32.

59. Archives of Ontario [hereafter, AO], Legislative Press Clippings, MS-755, Reel 86, "For Children's Welfare," *Globe and Mail*, July 14, 1944.

60. Dewey's thoughts on education are summed up in *The School and Society* (1900) and *Democracy and Education* (1916). For discussions of experimentation with progressive education in Canadian schools, see Gleason, "Psychology in Postwar

Schools," chapter 6 in *Normalizing the Ideal*, 119–39; R. S. Patterson, "The Canadian Experience with Progressive Education," and Eamonn Callan, "John Dewey and the Two Faces of Progressive Education," both in *Canadian Education: Historical Themes and Contemporary Issues,* ed. E. Brian Titley (Calgary: Detselig Enterprises, Ltd., 1990), 95–110; Neil Sutherland, "The Triumph of "Formalism": Elementary Schooling in Vancouver from the 1920's to the 1960's," *B.C. Studies* 69–70 (Spring/Summer 1986): 175–210; Robert Stamp, "Education for Democratic Citizenship, *The Schools of Ontario, 1876–1976* (Toronto: University of Toronto Press, 1982), 164–82; Jean Mann, "G.M. Weir and H.B. King: Progressive Education or Education for the Progressive State?" in *Schooling and Society in Twentieth-Century British Columbia*, ed. J. Donald Wilson and David C. Jones (Calgary: Detselig Enterprises Ltd., 1980), 91–11; see also Sutherland, chapters ten to thirteen in *Children in English-Canadian Society*. For discussion of progressive education in the American context, see Cohen, chapter five in *Challenging Orthodoxies*.

61. 99 FSATA, "Bolton Summer Camp," First Appeal brochure, 1947.

62. On the physical education of girls, the opening up of new programmes and debates over competition, see Veronica Strong-Boag, *The New Day Recalled: Lives of Girls and Women in English Canada, 1919–1939* (Toronto: Copp Clark Pittman, 1988): 31–32; Helen Lenskyj, "Femininity First: Sport and Physical Education for Ontario Girls, 1890–1930," *Canadian Journal of History of Sport* 13, no. 2 (December 1982): 4–17; Helen Lenskyj, "Training for "True Womanhood": Physical Education for Girls in Ontario Schools, 1890–1920," *Historical Studies in Education* 1, no. 2 (Fall 1990): 205–23; M. Ann Hall, "Rarely Have We Asked Why: Reflections on Canadian Women's Experience in Sport," *Atlantis* 6, no. 1 (1980): 51–60. It should be noted that camp programmes for girls and boys were never identical. Girls were always treated more carefully at camp, though, especially at canoe-tripping camps they were also exposed to numerous challenges and were given the chance to hone their less traditionally "feminine" skills. See Author, 2003. See also Lathrop, "'Strap an Axe to Your Belt'"; Susan L. Forbes, "'Nothing But a Rag Between You and the Sky'." For the treatment of girls at American camps see Paris, "Children's Nature"; Miller, "Girls in Nature/

63. Dimock and Statten, *Talks to Counselors*, 39. Similar statements were made at other camps: "swimming instruction," according to a Bolton report, "involved a great deal more than the skill of swimming. The qualities of courage, perseverance and self-confidence are all part of the learning process." FSATA, "Bolton Camp: Report of Operation, 1937," 3.

64. Statten, *Talks to Counsellors*, 8.

65. TUA, Camp Pine Crest Fonds, 78-009/2/1, "Interim Report to the Camp Pine Crest Commitee," September 22, 1952.

66. Hamilton, *Call of Algonquin*, 57.

67. Dimock and Statten, *Talks to Counselors*, 27, counsellor duties, 27–34. To help ensure a supply of staff with this level of skills, efforts were made towards establishing a standardized system of "teacher training." In 1925, the Margaret Eaton School of Physical Education in Toronto offered one of the first institution-based courses in counsellor training. In 1941 it merged with the University of Toronto's to form the School of Physical and Health Education. Hamilton, *Call of Algonquin*, 169–170. Underscoring its own belief in the educational value of camping, in 1949, the provincial government set up its own counsellor-training camp at Bark Lake in Haliburton. OCA, *Ontario Camp Bulletin* Edition 2, 1946; TUA, Adele and Harry Ebbs Papers, 80-014/1/5, "season of 1947—Programme of Staff Training," 1947; OCA Papers, 72-007/2/8, Camp Responses to Ontario Camping Association, "Confidential Camp Counsellor Survey" 1952; Hamilton, *Call of Algonquin*, 86, 89.

68. "City Mission Carries on Fresh Air Work 46 Years," *TDS*, July 16, 1940; "Every $7.50 You Send in Sends a Poor Child Away," *TDS*, July 29, 1925, 1; "Fresh Air Fund Donations buy Shares In Happiness," *TDS*, June 5, 1926, 17.

69. "Children Get New Outlook by Miracle of Fresh Air," *TDS*, June 6, 1949, 5.

70. "Lions Party At Beausoleil Camp Closes Spot Where Lads Had Fun," *TDS*, August 20, 1940, 9.

71. Dimock and Hendry, *Camping and Character*, 156, 279–80.

72. TUA, Ronald H. Perry Papers, 82-016/3/2, "1938 Final Report—Canoeing."

73. TUA, Camp Pine Crest Fonds, 78-009/2/1, Camp Pine Crest, "Report on Lumberman Section,

June 30–August 25, 1949"; TUA, Camp Pine Crest Fonds, 78-009/2/1, Camp Pine Crest, "Director's Report," 1949.

74. n.a., *Fires of Friendship: Eighty Years of the Taylor Statten Camps* (Taylor Statten Camps: 2001), 29. This was also the practice at Glen Bernard, and, more than likely, other camps as well. Shirley Ford, interview by author, June 20, 2000.

75. Shirley Ford, interview by author, June 20, 2000.

76. Mary Murphy, interview by author, June 7, 2000.

77. On the danger and frequency of "crushes" and same-sex affection at camp, see Taylor Statten Camps, *Talks to Counsellors*, 1928, 2; Dimock and Statten, *Talks to Counselors*, 31; TUA, OCA Papers, 98-019/13/10, "Notes from the Course in Camp Education, Margaret Eaton School," 10 February–17 March 1937, 2; TUA, Northway Family Fonds—Additions, 90-016/1/25, Mary Northway, "What Are the Camps Achieving," *The Camping Magazine* 9, 8, (1937).

78. Dimock and Hendry, *Camping and Character*, 180.

79. Ruth-Ellen Soles, quoted in Sherman, "Girls of Summer," 102.

80. Paris, "Children's Nature," 164. See also Paris, "'Please Let Me Come Home': Homesickness and Family Ties at Early-Twentieth-Century Summer Camps" in *The American Child: A Cultural Studies Reader*, eds. Caroline Levander and Carol Singley (New Brunswick, NJ: Rutgers University Press, 2003). The 1957 study was carried out by Dr. Taylor Statten, psychiatrist and son of the well-known Taylor Statten, who founded Camp Ahmek. TUA, OCA fonds, 72-007/5/16, Dr. Taylor Statten, "Homesickness," April and June 1957.

81. Northway, *Appraisal of Social Development*. 55.

82. TUA, Adele and Harry Ebbs Papers, 80-014/1/5, "Season of 1947—Programme of Staff "Training," 1947.

83. Norman Gulko, interview by author, June 16, 2000; Bert Danson, interview by author, June 12, 2000; Shirley Ford, interview by author, June 20, 2000.

84. TUA, Camp Pine Crest Fonds, 78-009/2/1, Camp Pine Crest, "Annual Report," 1940.

85. Sherman, "Girls of Summer," 101.

86. Merle S. Storey, quoted in *Fires of Friendship*, 37.

87. Snedden, quoted in Dimock and Hendry, *Camping and Character*, 328.

ARTICLE 2: LOST IN MODERNITY: THE "PROBLEM OF MODERN YOUTH" IN ENGLISH CANADA, 1920–50

Cynthia Comacchio

The years immediately succeeding the Great War heralded a "new day" and the dawning of a "new generation." For contemporaries who were disturbed by ... modernity's promises, modern youth were further characterized as a "lost generation." Although the term signified a cultural movement of writers and artists, many of whom had come of age during the war, those concerned about the young applied the notion of generational "lost-ness" much more broadly.[1] By the 1920s, ... [c]ontemporary discourses about a multitude of "modern problems" consistently revealed a subtext of anxiety about the future. ... [A]dolescence came to be regarded as a social problem primarily because its constituents were coming of age in the modern age. Their specific life-stage coincided with a historic moment that marked them as generationally distinct, but also distinctly disadvantaged, lost, fundamentally "maladjusted."

... Carried along in an international tide of violence, working-class unrest, the undermining and collapse of political and social institutions, the proliferation of radical ideas, and the apparent loosening of moral standards, the generation born into the prewar world came of age in one that had changed irrevocably from that time not so long past.[2] The young were not merely confronting problems peculiar to their location in their personal life-histories, and in history. They were a problem in and of themselves because they were young in dangerous times—and consequently "dangerous" for being young.[3] Despite the absence of any proven direct causal relationship, youth experts increasingly associated adolescent maladjustment with the pressures of modernity,

adding their "science" to popular ideas about the "lost generation." Young Canadians were seen to be incapable of navigating a wholesome, socially approved accommodation to the complexities of the modern age.

... [M]aladjustment could manifest in any number of ways, from broad-spectrum delinquency and promiscuity, often the same "problem" where girls were concerned, through anorexia, depression, and, at its extreme, suicide. It was age-determined, but also a gendered condition with its own racial and class dimensions. In the shaky aftermath of the Great War, these worries were not so much about the medical and psychological problems relevant to the adolescent years, as about middle-class ideals regarding how adolescence should be managed as a healthy transition to adulthood. Within the context of emergent theories that conceptualized adolescence as a troubled, and troublesome, life-stage, the young could not be left to work out a healthy self-individuation on their own, nor to do so within their uninformed families, and especially not within their suspect peer group. They became the cardinal symptoms of a widening urban pathology, just as doctors, psychologists, educators and social workers were increasingly inclined to consider the life stage as resembling a psychotic episode.[4]

The modern era's most important study on adolescence actually predated the war, gaining influence in professional circles and among the educated public, with scarce contestation, through the first half of the twentieth century. In his multivolume work, *Adolescence: Its Relation to Physiology, Anthropology, Sociology, Sex, Crime, Religion, and Education* (1904), American psychologist Dr. Granville Stanley Hall defined the contours of the modern experience. A pioneer in child development studies, Hall worked within the recapitulation paradigm borrowed from evolutionary theory and cultural anthropology. Recapitulationism correlated individual human development with the larger process of human evolution. Childhood and adolescence reflected the prehistoric state of humanity, the primitive and savage. Each succeeding stage of "normal" development, successfully negotiated, would bring the young closer to the evolutionary apex represented by modern adulthood. Finding resonance within a context of conflicting and even contradictory ideas about modernity, Hall's theories affirmed that adolescence constituted

Source: Cynthia Comacchio, "Lost in Modernity: 'Maladjustment' and the "Modern Youth Problem" in English Canada, 1920–50." Reprinted with permission of the Publisher from *Lost Kids: Vulnerable Children and Youth in Twentieth-Century Canada and the United States* edited by Mona Gleason, Tamara Myters, Leslie Paris and Victoria Strong-Boag. © University of British Columbia Press 2009, pp. 53–71. All rights reserved by the Publisher.

the critical gap between primitive childhood and the "more perfect form" of civilized adulthood.[5]

In focusing on the moral, sexual and psychological upheaval that he related exclusively to the onset of biological puberty, Hall produced an enduring portrayal of "normal" adolescence as an episode of "physical and mental anarchy" during which the young demonstrated a "peculiar proneness to be either very good or very bad."[6] He was clearly referring to good and bad judgment and behaviour rather than the quality of mental and physical health. Consequently all responsible adults had to work toward "the stabilization of youth during this important period."[7] Hall's theory of adolescence was not "modern" in the sense of diverging greatly from its antecedents, many of which were medical in origin, most also asserting that puberty entailed interrelated physiological and emotional changes. More synthetic than innovative, moralistic than scientific, homiletic than analytical, his study was nonetheless the first comprehensive multidisciplinary treatment of the subject. What made Hall's ideas inaugural and uniquely tenable was their introduction at a notable historical conjuncture. Socioeconomic transformation had prepared a receptive audience for "scientific" theories that explained current ills and suggested ways to resolve or at least to regulate them.[8] While psychologists, doctors and other experts upheld a definition of adolescent health that encompassed much more than the physiological changes associated with puberty, they returned always to these as the roots of maladjustment. In this manner, the biological process of puberty became conflated with the sociocultural experience of adolescence. Early twentieth-century experts were agreed upon one notion: that modern youth comprised a "problem" of alarming scope and potential.

Particularly during the interwar years, public and professional discourses alike gave signal importance to the "hectic modern times" that rendered adolescence "characteristic of and created by our form of civilization."[9] In the popular parenting manual *Normal Youth and Its Everyday Problems* (1932), whose very title captures the central paradox in modern theories about adolescence—that the experience is *normally* troubled—Dr. D.A. Thom acknowledged that there were "no specific psychological principles applicable to the adolescent period." Yet he managed to locate "certain physiological factors

and psychological situations that are not met elsewhere, or are met here for the first time, or are met more frequently here than at any other time," so that adolescence was inevitably a stage "when all of life seems to be dominated by the intensity of the individual's own feelings."[10] The boundaries between mental and physical health and what was considered proper social functioning were nowhere as ambiguous as in discussions about adolescence. The period's pre-eminent Canadian paediatrician, Dr. Alan Brown, lamented that "the importance of an early recognition of mental disturbances arising during the period of adolescence" demanded a far more "comprehensive" approach than was available in most medical schools. He called for the "most valuable assistance" that psychologists could provide to physicians in a productive collaboration on behalf of the young.[11] In the interest of their safe passage to adulthood, in the midst of a sociohistorical swirl, the minds and bodies of youth became objects for much keener examination and regulation than had been accorded to earlier generations.[12]

Such contemporary studies did not simply expand the knowledge base about adolescence: they operated in a fundamentally political manner, interacting with contemporary public concerns about the national importance of childhood and youth, the cultural implications of modernity, the maintenance of civil order, and the training of a citizenry to meet certain desired ends. In these modern times, individual age, and the age-group, became useful categories for sorting and classifying human beings, identifying status and role, civic rights and duties, and also—perhaps most important—for defining the appropriate means and methods of regulation. The study of adolescence thus gave rise to numerous attempts to "manage" the actual members of that life-stage. Such campaigns were not ... a modern phenomenon either, as the complex schooling, apprenticeship, inheritance and marriage laws of earlier times demonstrate. What is different—modern—about early twentieth-century approaches is the extent and uniformity of theorizing about, and surveillance of, young people, as reflected in public discourses, professional studies, government surveys and all manner of reform campaigns ... Nor were such broadening, at times escalating, anxieties about young people contained at the discursive level. In Canada as elsewhere, they took form in an intricate network of state policies and legislation designed to address such related "problems" as those of youth recreation, labour, schooling, vocational training, "social hygiene," and juvenile corrections—to name the most prominent—that comprised the multifarious modern youth problem.[13]

Although the "storm and stress" model did not go entirely unchallenged even in Hall's own time, its imprint on the body of twentieth-century theories of adolescence has been remarkably tenacious. While there is no obvious link between his ideas and those of Sigmund Freud, Hall also did much to introduce North Americans to the Freudian approaches that would so influence modern psychology. Freud's biological view of the psyche clearly fits with Hall's own biological determinism: both the psychoanalytic and the recapitulation approaches depict adolescence as "phylogenetic," involving a staged process of psychosexual development that is genetic, and therefore not greatly affected by environment. Most important, like Hall, Freud stressed the critical relationship between the physiological manifestations of puberty and the growth of the psyche, thereby reinforcing the "storm and stress" perspective on sexual maturation.[14]

Hall's ideas did much to shape North American perceptions of youth as a social problem of distinctly modern proportions. Along with those of other American experts and reformers who specialized in youth issues ... his writings were cited in Canadian publications, both professional journals and newspapers and mass-distribution magazines, whether Canadian-produced or those of American origin that enjoyed a wide Canadian readership. ... Canadian medicine, psychology and sociology were increasingly affected by these new ideas about the nature of adolescence and its social impact.[15] Physicians and psychologists drew a direct line of causation between the "rapid physical and mental growth" of the teen years and their characteristic "emotional confusion," while also faulting the socialization of adolescents which found them, without adequate preparation, thrust into the "hostile world" of adult customs. Anxiety and alienation were the inevitable, indeed the "natural" outcome. As one Canadian doctor declared, it was "not to be wondered that so many ... break down physically or mentally, but the wonder is that so many survive the ordeal with the little health supervision and health knowledge they receive."[16]

If biology were destiny, the worried public needed to understand that destiny could be positively affected by intervention, regulation, and management of the problem, in this instance, the adolescent. A number of contemporary sociological surveys also highlighted the complications of coming of age in a time of rapid change, emphasizing the generational conflict inherent in the relations of modern youth with their less-than-modern parents.[17] In his 1936 study of the traditional Catholic rural community of St. Denis, Quebec, Horace Miner contended that "every phase of life" had been touched by the "cultural changes" of the previous generation or two.[18] McGill sociologists Charles Young and Carl Dawson made similar observations about immigrant communities in western Canada. While they emphasized environment—the changes in the family's outer world and how this affected changes within—they nonetheless assumed adolescent angst to be a "normal" feature of the life-stage, although in these instances exacerbated by generational tensions between old and new-world cultures.[19]

Already by the Great War years, extended compulsory schooling and child protection legislation, child study, "child-saving" through new social agencies and family courts, and state-supported campaigns to supervise the health and upbringing of infants and school children denoted a childhood that was being modernized by means of science and state regulation. The stage was set to support arguments, policies and initiatives aimed at following these newly supervised children into the adolescent vortex, where they stood in danger of squandering all efforts previously extended on their behalf and in the nation's interest. If modernity were complex, tantalizing yet worrisome, what better means to realize its benefits than through youth, modern citizens-in-the-making?[20] The challenge lay in the fact that the young also appeared the most inclined of all age groups to embrace the modern age's darker elements. And, generationally speaking, these young Canadians were also the first to have to contend with modern evils. In the interests of their safe passage to adulthood, in the midst of a sociohistorical swirl, the minds and bodies of adolescents became objects for much keener examination and regulation than ever before in history.

... [C]lass, race and gender remained key signifiers of what made the young a "problem" or at least what made some young Canadians more a problem than others. The so-called "normal" psychological patterns of adolescence were themselves abnormal in reference to the only standard that mattered, that of the mature adult, with the white adult male standing tall at the evolutionary pinnacle. In 1920, psychologist Dr. C.K. Clarke, founder of the Canadian Mental Hygiene Association, and Dean of the University of Toronto Medical Faculty, admonished an audience of 800 teachers that "upon them fell the duty of saving the race" from the "deplorable depravity" of Canadian youth. Clarke had discovered girls as young as 13 suffering from venereal diseases, some becoming unmarried mothers, others "commencing lives of shame," with little to tell the difference between these paths. He had also seen boys who had acquired habits associated with "only the most hardened moral perverts." Reflecting the eugenic ideas popular among educated Canadians during the interwar years, he saw the source as "organic": the "moral depravity" of many of these young people was largely attributable to feeblemindedness. He might well have made class and race the primary cause, as he contended that feeblemindedness disproportionately affected the families of workers and immigrants.[21]

Clarke's characterization of troubled and consequently dangerous youth shared, and undoubtedly reinforced, the racialized profiles that underpinned many of the period's discourses of anxiety. Not only were the "foreign-born" felt to be more inclined to deviance at all ages, "aliens" provided the settings most conducive to it. The *Toronto World* reported in 1918 that "aliens" owned most of the city's licensed pool-rooms: a reporter who visited 14 pool-rooms in the Queen-Bathurst district "found himself as in a strange country ... a stranger among the elect ... No one spoke either French or English." Worst of all, in his view, "the preponderance of youth was noticeable."[22] Moreover, the "foreign" neighbourhoods, with their crowded and substandard housing, harboured any number of "crime-producing tendencies." Young people inevitably strove to "escape as often as possible from their cramped quarters. ... They drift to sidewalks, to gatherings under street lights, or to shops and dance-halls, anywhere where they may find space and light, and if the weather is cold, warmth." If they justifiably ventured out to seek light, warmth and companionship, they invariably found

"opportunity for mischief that sometimes degenerates into serious misdemeanour."[23]

Nor was this evidence of maladjustment among "foreign" youth merely an urban phenomenon. Sociologist Charles Young claimed to have personally observed much fighting in the Ukrainian settlements of the west, most of it resulting from "the capers of the young males," usually touched off by drinking. The situation was decidedly worse for Ukrainians in urban areas, where he thought he saw definite signs of the breakdown of parental authority and "misbehaviour among large numbers of the younger generation." In particular, the young men, "surer of foot, more accustomed to the ways of the new world and slightly contemptuous of the old" had "gone their own way," in many instances making "a sorry mess of things." Their gangs and wild parties were largely responsible for incidents of disorder in the Ukrainian communities. Settlement teachers reported that "the imperfectly assimilated adolescent," who knew little English and lacked "character training" opportunities, all the while "shut off" from the traditional prohibitions of the older generation, was becoming "a serious menace." According to Young, national duty demanded that "inclusive programmes" be implemented to prevent the social disorganization that immigrant communities were evidently suffering due to the generational clash and the youthful [male] propensity for inflammatory action.[24]

If adolescence were a dangerous passage for all, young women, as Clarke's views suggest, were thought to be predisposed by "nature" to an inestimable variety of potential physical and mental health complications. Stanley Hall saw women as perpetually adolescent, their psychological formation never completed, never approaching the evolutionary summit claimed by adult men. ... . He insisted that feminists persistently ignored" the central importance of reproduction in women's lives," much to their physical and emotional detriment in adolescence, and what could only be their further deterioration in adulthood.[25] Although Hall actually acknowledged that gender roles are in part socially constructed, he warned that, because they are fundamentally biologically determined, their modification could not be countenanced in the long term: "nature decrees with advancing civilization that the sexes shall not approximate but differentiate". ... Caught up in such modern trends as urban living and employment, best left to men, young women were pushing beyond their natural limitations and resisting their naturally evolving womanly specialization, which actually resembled their traditional roles as wives and mothers. They were "fired" with ambitions that they could not safely and effectively attain, and therefore condemned to the unhealthy condition of what Hall termed "a suppressed semi-erotic state with never-culminating feeling." Unable to "fix their attentions properly" on womanly things, they were "lapsing into mannish ways, methods and ideals."[26] Paradoxically, even as they became mannish, modern young women seemed to be transforming themselves into "mere figurines" and "grow[ing] dollish" by resorting to commercial amusements and shopping to pass their time, rather than taking up their ordained vocation in homemaking.[27]

The "girl runaway" was a hot subject in the press during the 1920s, fuelling public worries about the seemingly new propensity for dangerous adventuring among young women. In 1925, the *Globe*'s regular "Homemaker Page" featured a detailed interview with Mary E. Hamilton, "New York's best-known policewoman," who estimated that some 5,000 girls "disappeared" in the United States every year.[28] Hamilton's view of the "girl runaway" situation was true to Hall's theories: she believed that the young were simply "apt to go to extremes, emotionally and mentally" simply because of the fragile condition that was adolescence. Hurt feelings, a desire to be alone, rebellion against authority, boredom, love of adventure, and a "desire to see the world" were the principal motives.[29]

Running away was the ultimate show of adolescent rebellion, an extreme form of individuation, and therefore maladjustment. In one reported instance, two fifteen-year-old Toronto girls left home to "be in the movies." One of the girls claimed to have two sisters who were actresses and "to this influence the police ascribe[d] the determination of the two girls to leave home." They were ultimately tracked down by police, after several days' search, at the Metropole Hotel in Detroit.[30] ... Another two girls, aged 14 and 15, escaped from the Ursuline Academy at Chatham, Ontario, only to be "picked up" by police after a few nights in Windsor, and returned to their school. The runaways confessed to have been "looking for adventure, which they expected to find in Detroit." Penniless and hungry when found, the girls said that they would go back gladly.[31] Some parents felt the need to "turn in" their seemingly intractable offspring when they were unable to deal with them, at times sparking serial escape attempts by those confined against their will. Such was the case of sixteen-year old Kathleen, committed to the Orillia, Ontario industrial refuge by her father, who reportedly felt assured that a year's confinement would "cure his daughter of all her waywardness." After her first successful escape, she spent the months from May to September in "the north," where she was taken in by a sympathetic family. Something appears to have gone awry in that arrangement, because she was soon sent to live with an aunt; the aunt quickly asked to have her recommitted because she had run away to Buffalo and "was not doing at all well." The hapless Kathleen once again fled the refuge within days of her involuntary return, but was located two days later, suffering from exposure.[32]

The new day's "revolution in morals" was so closely associated with the "flaming youth" of modernity that the hapless flapper came to be its emblem, a sort of folk devil for the times.[33] American psychologist W.I. Thomas was one of many experts who stirred controversy on the subject of the sexual proclivities of modern young women. In his "shocking" and widely circulated 1923 study, *The Unadjusted Girl, with Cases and Standpoint for Behaviour Analysis*, Thomas proclaimed the adolescent girl's "lack of adjustment" was outright "demoralization" due to a "sexual delinquency" attributed unequivocally to "today's unrest." Yet, echoing Hall and ignoring Freud, he insisted that "the sex passion" played an insignificant role in female sexual delinquency. He claimed to have 3000 documented cases revealing that girls had "usually become wild before the development of sexual desire," and that "their casual sexual relations do not usually awaken sex feeling." It appeared instead that these "demoralized" young women, evidently "unadjusted" to society's expectations of womanhood, deployed sexuality as "their capital," as "a condition of the realization of other wishes."[34] Put simply, the sexuality of adolescent girls was pathological, in no way related to healthy adult sexuality of the kind involving marriage and procreation.

Although the modern girl, the flapper, was possibly the most frighteningly maladjusted of adolescents, it was also considered that all young people who failed to learn sexual self-control during adolescence were "on the road to becoming sexual perverts." As warned by Dr. Thom, heterosexuality had to be "accomplished" during those critical years, or it would "never be accomplished in a normal way," but only by means of "some technical interference … only after much conflict, failure and illness."[35] Given the magnitude and intensity of public anxiety about adolescent sexuality, the sexual regulation of the young was easily the issue that drew the most attention from youth-watchers during the first half of the twentieth century, and one that would remain a constant and remarkably consistent theme despite changing generational and historical contexts.

During these years, Hollywood and advertising agencies were ever more intently selling the freshly coined "sex appeal," euphemistically and provocatively labelled "IT," as a package wrapped in, and entirely dependent upon, youth and beauty. Experts were quick to pick up on the health repercussions of the exacting new physical standards that "sexiness" entailed, especially for young women. Visiting Montreal families during the Depression, a McGill University social worker was struck by the extent to which adolescent girls were affected by "the idea" that they were not attractive by current standards, and how this notion undermined their social confidence. One of her cases, Anne, from a middle-class Anglophone family, had become so self-conscious about her height that she had withdrawn almost entirely from the company of her peers, believing that she was "not one of them."[36] A familiar theme in autobiographies, memoirs, and diaries is the sense of confusion about the body that often accompanied the attainment of puberty by young women, for whom its other manifestations were crowned by menstruation. Growing up in Winnipeg in the 1920s, and the last of her friends to develop physically, Lillian Allen was "terribly scared" when it happened to her at age 13. Her very religious father, finding her in bed with "periodic pains," would ask her "What have you done that God is punishing you?", thus inspiring in her a lasting "fear complex" about her own feminine body.[37]

… Awareness of both a certain socially decreed physical ideal and the degree to which the individual falls short of its achievement is central to the process of self-formation that takes place during adolescence. … During her own life history, at any time in history, young women do not stand alone before their mirrors. Reflected back to them are the ideals that are conceptualized, disseminated, and constructed as "the norm." The on-going medicalization of women's bodies provided women with a scientific vocabulary to describe their bodily concerns and functions. But modern medicine, technology and popular culture, as well as informing, also allowed for an increasingly pervasive understanding of what constituted the ideal body and, consequently, that which deviated from it. Ultimately, idealized body types are made to correspond to ideal moral types, the acknowledged "good citizen": hence the healthy, beautiful citizen is the good citizen, an application especially pertinent to young women in their specialized social role as future mothers.[38]

Although the science of nutrition did not become established until the 1930s, doctors early recognized the importance of nutrition to guard against chlorosis [anemia] in adolescent girls in order to ensure that it would not do "permanent damage to the future wife and future mother."[39] With its new emphasis on the straight, angular, androgynous "flapper" physique for women, the 1920s brought "slenderizing" and "slimming" into the popular consciousness more than ever before. During the 1930s, in light of public health concerns about Depression-induced deprivation, health professionals were worried about the findings of dietary surveys that consistently showed adolescent girls to have the poorest diet of any family member in every economic class. They attributed this not to ignorance about nutrition nor to lack of adequate food, especially for those families on relief, but to "the urge for slenderness and the compulsion to do as the group does."[40] It appeared that new pressures exerted by the increasingly commercialized popular culture of the day, especially the movies, the dance hall and mass circulation magazines, and fortified by the newly important, high-school based peer culture, were pushing a dangerous obsession with thinness among the nation's prospective mothers at the crucial point of their physiological development.[41] Whether the problem was poor eating habits or actual eating disorders, clearly a broad spectrum of "maladjustments," most important is the fact that they were all considered to an outcome of age compounded by the matter of gender. Adolescent girls were prone to such maladjustments because they were uniquely vulnerable to social pressures as well as to psychological disorders: the two were often intertwined.

Anorexia nervosa, a "feminine" problem, was also an adolescent one. It was believed to materialize "following some emotional disturbance." The sufferer typically showed symptoms of "an active morbid or fanatic aversion to eating high caloric foods; perverse habits of eating, often pretending to eat and throw food away" and, ominously, amenorrhea [absence of menstruation] was a "constant finding."[42] Removal from the home, where, it was surmised, there were almost invariably troubled relations with parents—especially mothers—to a hospital under close regulation and constant surveillance by a team of nurses, physicians and psychologists, had come to be the favoured remedy by the Second World War.

If girls were seen to be inclined to promiscuity and self-starvation to assuage their adolescent angst, or at least to draw attention to it, among boys, besides the gang membership, "hooliganism" and petty criminality classified as delinquency, suicide was the extreme manifestation of maladjustment. Because they were perceived to be "naturally" more impulsive than girls, more aggressive, violent and given to immediate action, experts reasoned that self-annihilation was a problem—a tragic solution—that afflicted adolescent boys more than girls. The suicides of a number of teenage male immigrants who came with the British "home children" to work on Canadian farms during the 1920s sparked a public outcry, both here and overseas, sufficient to bring about an investigation into their treatment and living conditions.[43] A full courtroom and detailed press coverage greeted the 1923 inquest into the suicide by hanging of 16-year-old Charles Bulpitt, sent to a Goderich, Ontario, farm despite his London upbringing, a tragic mismatch that was common fate among the young immigrants.[44] Within days of young Bulpitt's death, John Payne, another juvenile immigrant working on a farm in Emily Township in eastern Ontario, killed himself by ingesting the common household poison Paris Green, which induced an agonizing death. It was felt that the Bulpitt case had inspired Payne, whose personal history was very similar, to consider suicide.[45] ...

If such tragic deaths stirred public compassion about the plight of disadvantaged youth, the central fact of the victims' isolation from home and family helped to explain their recourse to self-destruction. The complicated emotions of adolescence formed part of that story, but not its key element. Young suicides who were better positioned in terms of class, family, and conceivably prospects, provoked more deeply psychological discussion to ease the public bafflement about their demise. Before the first week of 1945 had closed, the *Toronto Star* reported the suicide of a "promising young man," a resident of the city's solidly middle-class Forest Hill Village. The seventeen-year-old was found shortly after midnight in a parked car not far from his home, shot in the temple, a .22 calibre revolver on the seat beside him. President of the student council of Northern Vocational School where he was in his graduating year, he was described by family, friends and teachers as "among the most popular students at school." Police investigation revealed that he was "believed to have been depressed since receiving his report card" the previous week. Stunned by the outcome, the school's principal and the Toronto Board of Education's superintendent both observed that he had always done well academically and could readily have improved his disappointing score on the final examinations to achieve matriculation that year. Active in extracurricular activities, and as student council president, "he did not appear depressed or despondent to his teachers or classmates."[46]

In a plaintive editorial under the declarative heading "Nobody Really Knew Him," a *Toronto Star* columnist interpreted the "schoolboy suicide" as "a tragic reminder of the inadequate mental hygiene services" and health supervision in the nation's high schools, "something for which welfare and parents organizations [had] agitated for some time without success." In the editor's view, "had there been such a service, this boy's suicide might have been prevented and his life made happier":

> No one among those with whom he mingled really knew this lad. What loneliness and torture he must have experienced as he approached the fatal moment! ... His case should serve as a severe warning to health and school authorities; to parents and all who care about the happy development of children. The science of psychology is far enough developed today to provide the means of preventing some of these tragedies ...[47]

The conclusion drawn, the warning issued, were those that had underlain discussions about "lost youth" for a quarter century by this time: "it is costly to neglect the youth of the nation." For, as one psychologist had observed nearly forty years earlier, "Suicide accompanies civilization and education as an unerring index of maladjustment in society and defects in education."[48]

At the beginning of the twentieth century, Granville Stanley Hall contended that to study the changing meaning of adolescence was to gain understanding of the nature of modernity: "Other oracles may grow dim," he argued, "but this one will never fail."[49] Age became an important modern instrument for assessment and classification, standardization and regulation, as the social sciences, medicine and psychology expanded their influence over the population. Modernity's dangers were perceived to be peculiarly dangerous to the young, thus endangering the nation's future that they embodied. Much like the larger youth problem in its vagaries, the problems of the young as individuals were encoded in the decidedly non-specific term "maladjustment."

The "maladjustment" classification newly favoured by doctors, psychologists, social workers and educators had the dual benefit of being sanctioned by modern science and yet so embedded with facile popular assumptions that it could be easily and broadly applied. As it came to be the catch-all diagnosis for a myriad of adolescent mental and physical health concerns, it reinforced the Hall model of adolescence as a "normally" volatile life stage, feeding social constructions about "typical" teenage behaviour, individual and generational. It made "patients" of virtually all adolescents, openly maladjusted or just assumed to be, treated or left untreated, on their own and as a cohort, thereby medicalizing the adolescent experience. And the effects have been enduring, as witnessed in the manner in which the universal designation of "maladjustment" continues to support the paradox at the heart of modern adolescence. Normalizing maladjustment inflates concerns about the problems of youth, and of youth as a social problem; at the same time, it allows for ready dismissal as mere "teenage angst" what might well have been—and continue to be—very real problems tending toward self-destructive practices and even suicide. ...

NOTES

1. The "Lost Generation" concept is associated with Ernest Hemingway's 1926 novel, *The Sun Also Rises*, although Hemingway himself attributed the phrase to Gertrude Stein. For contemporary views, see the essays in V.F. Calverton, Samuel D. Schmalhausen, eds. *The New Generation: The Intimate Problems of Modern Parents and Children* (New York: The Macaulay Company, 1930), especially the introduction by Bertrand Russell, 17–24; also Karl Mannheim, "The Problem of Generations," (1927) in Mannheim, *Essays on the Sociology of Knowledge* (London: Routledge and Keegan Paul, 1972; originally published 1952), 320. For an overview of the "sociology of generations," see June Edmunds, Bryan S. Turner, "Introduction," 2–3, and Turner, "Strategic Generations: Historical Change, Literary Expression, and Generational Politics," 15, in Edmunds, Turner, eds. *Generational Consciousness, Narrative, and Politics* (Lanham, Md.; Rowman and Littlefield, 2002).

2. Robert Wohl, "Heart of Darkness: Modernism and Its Historians," *Journal of Modern History* 74, 3 (September 2002): 576; 614–15. See also the classics by Marshall Berman, *All That Is Solid Melts Into Air* (New York: Simon and Schuster, 1982), and William R. Everdell, *The First Moderns* (Chicago: University of Chicago Press, 1997), as well as the expansive synthesis by Peter Watson, *A Terrible Beauty: The People and Ideas that Shaped the Modern Mind* (London: Phoenix Press, 2000), especially ch. 16, 273–99. Allan Levine discusses "the modern' in Canada within a North American context in A. Levine, *The Devil in Babylon: The Fear of Progress and the Birth of Modern Life* (Toronto: McClelland and Stewart, 2005).

3. Contemporary commentaries include T.R. Robinson, "Youth and the Virtues," *Social Welfare* (October 1928): 9; H. Dobson, "Youth: Scapegrace or Scapegoat," *Social Welfare* (July 1929): 228; Editorial, "Hygiene of Recreation," *Canadian Practitioner* (June 1924): 309. These anxieties are also discussed in Cynthia Comacchio, *The Dominion of Youth: Adolescence and the Making of Modern Canada, 1920–50* (Waterloo, ON.: Wilfrid Laurier University Press, 2006), especially ch. 1, 17–44. Among the seminal works on the historical experience of adolescence are J. Kett, *Rites of Passage: Adolescence in America* (New York: Basic Books, 1977); J. Springhall, *Coming of Age: Adolescence in Britain, 1860–1960* (London: Oxford University Press, 1986); J. Modell, *Into One's Own: From Youth to Adulthood in the United States* (Berkeley, Ca.: University of California Press, 1988); R. Wegs, *Growing Up Working*

Class: Youth in Vienna, 1870–1920 (Philadelphia, Penn: University of Pennsylvania Press, 1989); D. Linton, *Who Has the Youth Has the Future* (Cambridge, Mass.: Harvard University Press, 1990); H. Hendrick, *Images of Youth* (London: Oxford University Press, 1990); J. Neubauer, *The Fin-de-Siecle Culture of Adolescence* (New Haven, Conn.: Yale University Press, 1992); M. Childs, *Labour's Apprentices* (Montreal/Kingston: McGill-Queen's University Press, 1993).

4. E. H. Erikson, *Identity, Youth and Crisis* (New York: W.W. Norton, 1968), 102, describes the development of this perspective on adolescence.

5. G. Stanley Hall, *Adolescence: Its Psychology and Its Relation to Physiology, Anthropology, Sociology, Sex, Crime, Religion and Education,* v. 1 (New York: D. Appleton and Company, 1904), vii, 614. Hall was Professor of Psychology at Johns Hopkins University; in 1888, he became president of newly established Clark University in Worcester, Massachusetts. He is considered one of the founding fathers of experimental psychology, and child psychology in particular, as well as the leading American figure in the child study movement. See N. Lesko, "Denaturalizing Adolescence: The Politics of Contemporary Representations," *Youth and Society* 28, 2 (December 1996): 144–7; Rolf E. Muus, *Theories of Adolescence,* 5th ed. (New York: Random House, 1988), 17–21; Kett, *Rites of Passage,* 218-9. The definitive biography remains D. Ross, *G. Stanley Hall: The Psychologist as Prophet* (Chicago: University of Chicago Press, 1983), 332–3. On early child pyschology in Canada and the United States, see T.R. Richardson, *The Century of the Child* (Albany, NY: State University of New York Press, 1989).

6. G. Stanley Hall, *Youth: Its Education, Regimen and Hygiene* (New York: D.E. Appleton: 1907), 135; H.P. Chudacoff, *How Old Are You? Age Consciousness in American Culture* (Princeton, N.J.: Princeton University Press, 1989), especially ch. 4, 65–91. Hall's 1907 volume is the popularized, condensed version of the 1904 multivolume study.

7. Dr. D.A. Thom, *Normal Youth and Its Everyday Problems,* (New York: D. E. Appleton, 1932), ix; also Dr. A. Goldbloom, "Problems of the Adolescent Child," *Canadian Medical Association Journal* 43, 4 (October 1940): 336–9; Hall, *Adolescence,* 1, xvi–xvii.

8. Theories about adolescence were circulating long before Hall's work: it is clear that he was inspired not only by Darwinian biology but also by the ideas of French Enlightenment *philosophe* Jean-Jacques Rousseau and the German Romantic school of *Sturm und Drang*; see Kett, *Rites of Passage,* 221; Sutherland, *Children in English Canadian Society,* 6–13; Thom, *Normal Youth and Its Everyday Problems,* ix.

9. Thom, *Normal Youth and Its Everyday Problems,* 18.

10. Thom, *Normal Youth and Its Everyday Problems,* 19.

11. Dr. A. Brown, "Toronto as a Paediatric Centre," *Canadian Medical Monthly* 5, 6 (June 1920): 205. H. Prescott Munro, *A Doctor of Their Own: The History of Adolescent Medicine* (Boston, Mass.: Harvard University Press, 1998), 14, notes that this "cross-training" in medicine and psychology was actively promoted by the Commonwealth Fund during the 1930s.

12. Lesko, "Denaturalizing Adolescence," 150. On this model and its context, see also A. James and A. Prout, *Constructing and Reconstructing Childhood: Contemporary Issues in the Sociological Study of Childhood* (London: Falmer, 1990).

13. Tamara Myers provides full treatment of girl delinquency in *Caught: Montreal's Modern Girls and the Law, 1869–1945* (Toronto: University of Toronto Press, 2006).

14. As President of Clark University, Hall invited Freud to give a lecture series in 1909, and personally wrote the preface to the American edition of Freud's *A General Introduction to Psychoanalysis* (New York: Liveright, 1920); see Muus, *Theories of Adolescence,* 45.

15. Harvey Graff, *Conflicting Paths: Growing Up in America* (Cambridge, Mass.: Harvard University Press,1995), 302.

16. Dr. D.V. Currey, A.G. Nicolle, P.H.N., "Development of a Health Program in the Secondary School," *Canadian Public Health Journal* 31 (April 1940): 176; also, Editorial, "School Health Supervision in Secondary Schools," *CPHJ* 31 (April 1940): 199. See the psychiatrists' viewpoint on the "mental, social and moral difficulties" of adolescence in Dr. W.T.B. Mitchell, "The Clinical Significance of Some Trends in Adolescence," *CMAJ* 22, 30 (February 1930): 182–7. Similar views are found in Thom, *Normal*

Youth and Its Everyday Problems, ix; also, Goldbloom, "Problems of the Adolescent Child," 336–9. On newspaper and magazine circulation, see Russell Johnston, *Selling Themselves: The Emergence of Canadian Advertising* (Toronto: University of Toronto Press, 2001). *The Saturday Evening Post* had the highest circulation of any magazine in Canada.

17. The interactionist approach to family sociology was imported to Canada by the University of Chicago-trained Carl Addington Dawson, who was instrumental in establishing sociology at McGill University. With Warner Gettys, Dawson produced an influential textbook, *An Introduction to Sociology* (New York: Ronald, 1929), 61, 77–9, in which they catalogued modernization's undermining impact on families. Ostensibly targeting the relations of industry and community during the economic crisis of the 1930s, McGill's Social Science Research Project discussed family as an integral player in these interactions. See M. Shore, *The Science of Social Redemption: McGill, the Chicago School, and the Origins of Social Research in Canada* (Toronto: University of Toronto Press, 1987), xvi, 118, 227–30.

18. Horace Miner, *St. Denis, a French-Canadian Parish* (Chicago: University of Chicago Press, 1939), 233; 268. Miner was also University of Chicago-trained. The parish consisted of 700 people in 120 households. Among the most notable developments was the growing number of youth who left the family farm and the community itself for urban employment, especially among those who came of age in the mid-1930s. Twenty-four percent of that generational cohort [15 to 24 years] had emigrated by 1947.

19. See Charles H. Young, *The Ukrainian Canadians: A Study in Assimilation* (Toronto: Thomas Nelson and Sons Ltd., 1931); Carl Dawson, *Group Settlement: Ethnic Communities in Western Canada* (Toronto: Macmillan, 1936). Dawson mentored both Young and Miner.

20. G.S. Hall, "Child Study and Its Relation to Education," *Forum* 29 (1900): 689; see also Lesko, "Denaturalizing Adolescence,"139.

21. Cited in Editorial, "A Deplorable Depravity of Young Girls and Boys," *Globe and Mail*, 3 April 1920.

22. Editorial, "Many Aliens Hold Licenses in City," *Toronto World*, 1 January 1918.

23. Editorial, "A Deplorable Depravity of Young Girls and Boys," 3; see also A Juvenile Court Probation Officer, "As the Twig is Bent: What Are We Doing to Keep Children from the Reformatory?", *Chatelaine* (March 1928): 3–6; R. Coulter, "Not to Punish But to Reform: Juvenile Delinquency and the Children's Protection Act," in R.B. Blake, J. Keshen, eds. *Social Welfare Policy in Canada* (Toronto: Copp Clark, 1995), 137–52; Bryan Hogeveen, "'The Evils with Which We are Called to Grapple': Élite Reformers, Eugenicists, Environmental Psychologists, and the Construction of Toronto's Working-Class Boy Problem, 1860–1930," *Labour/Le Travail* 55 (Spring 2005): 37–68.

24. Young, *Ukrainian Canadians*, 282-3. See also W. Burton Hurd, "The Decline in the Canadian Birth Rate," *Canadian Journal of Economics and Political Science* 3, 1 (February 1937): 40–57.

25. Hall, *Adolescence*, 2, 566; 624; also 572; 646; on menstruation, see Hall, *Adolescence* 1, xiv; 472, 494.

26. Hall, *Adolescence*, 2, 617.

27. Hall, *Adolescence*, 2, 617.

28. The Homemaker's Page, "Among Ourselves: Runaways," *Globe and Mail*, 25 September 1924.

29. "Among Ourselves: Runaways, " 16.

30. "15-Year-Old Toronto Girls Run Away to Join Movies," *Globe and Mail*, 4 March 1920.

31. "Seeking for Adventure; Glad to Go Back Home," *Globe and Mail*, 19 January 1920; see also Editorial: "Runaways," *Toronto World*, 2 March 1918.

32. "Girl Returns After Escape from Refuge," *Globe and Mail*, 4 March 1920. The difficulties of "delinquent girls" have been thoroughly examined by Joan Sangster, *Regulating Girls and Women: Sexuality, Family, and the Law in Ontario, 1920–1960* (Don Mills, ON.: Oxford University Press, 2001); see also Sangster, "Incarcerating Bad Girls: The Regulation of Sexuality through the Female Refuges Act in Ontario,1920–45," *Journal of the History of Sexuality* 7, 2 (1996): 239–75.

33. The terms "folk devil" and "moral panic" are attributed to Stanley Cohen, *Folk Devils and Moral Panics* (Oxford: Basil Blackwell, 1990; originally published 1972). For contemporary views about these fears, see Lorine Pruette, "The Flapper," in Calverton, Schmalhausen, eds. *The New Generation*, 572–90. Pruette was a Columbia-trained psychologist and author of a biography of G. Stanley Hall, whose views on women she disputed. See also

E. McLaughlin, J. Muncie, and G. Hughes, "Introduction," in McLaughlin, Muncie, Hughes eds. *Youth Justice: Critical Readings* (London: Sage, 2002), 19-21; John Clarke, "The Three Rs–Repression, Rescue and Rehabilitation: Ideologies of Control for Working-Class Youth," in McLaughlin, et al. eds. *Youth Justice*, 121-37.

34. W.I. Thomas, *The Unadjusted Girl, with Cases and Standpoint for Behavior Analysis* (Boston, Mass.: Little Brown and Company, 1923), xi–xvii; 109; G. Pringle, "Is the Flapper a Menace?" *Maclean's* (15 June 1922): 19. G. Pringle, "Is the Flapper a Menace?" *Maclean's* (15 June 1922): 19.

35. Dr. Thom, *Normal Youth and Its Everyday Problems*, 69-70.

36. Inez LePage, "Group Organization and the Development of the Adolescent Girl," unpublished MA thesis, Sociology, McGill University, Montreal (1932): 27.

37. University of Manitoba Archives, Lillian Beatrice Allen papers, MSS 45, Box 14, file 1, typescript, undated, "Growing Up," 21–23. Allen was born in Winnipeg, 9 November 1904. She was the only daughter of Frank Allen, the first physics professor at the University of Manitoba. She earned a Masters degree in home economics at the University of Syracuse in 1947 and lectured at Manitoba's Faculty of Agriculture and Home Economics.

38. J. Brumberg, *The Body Project: An Intimate History of American Girls* (New York: Random House, 1997), xvii; 96; Brumberg, "Chlorotic Girls, 1870–1920: A Historical Perspective on Female Adolescence," *Child Development* 53 (1982): 1468–77; for Canada, see Wendy Mitchinson, *The Nature of Their Bodies: Women and Their Doctors in Victorian Canada* (Toronto: University of Toronto Press, 1991).

39. Editorial, "The Care of Growing Girls," *Canada Lancet* (September 1907): 93.

40. Dr. J.F. Webb,. "Horizons in Child Health Supervision," *Canadian Public Health Journal* 50, 12 (December 1959): 491–5.

41. E.W. McHenry, "Nutrition and Child Health," *Canadian Public Health Journal* 33, 4 (April 1942): 152–7; Canadian Council on Nutrition, "A Dietary Standard for Canada," *Canadian Nutrition Notes* (1949): 60.

42. R.F. Farquharson, H.H. Hyland, "Anorexia Nervosa: The Course of 15 Patients Treated from 20 to 30 Years Previously," *Canadian Medical Association Journal* 94, 2 (February 1966): 411-14. This study returns to 7 teenage patients treated for anorexia between 1932 and 1937, and 8 patients treated between 1936 and 1943.

43. "Lonely 'Home' Boy, Licked by Farmer, Hanged Himself," *Globe and Mail*, 23 January 1924; "London Wants Probe into Tragic Deaths of Immigrant Boys," *Globe and Mail*, 31 January 1924; "Two Months in Prison for Bulpitt's Employer," *Globe and Mail*, 1 February 1924; "Farmer Sent to Jail for Assaulting Boy Who Hanged Himself," *Globe and Mail*, 2 February 1924. See also National Library and Archives, MG 28 I 10, Canadian Welfare Council, v. 6, file 33, 1928, Charlotte Whitton, Letter to Miss Gladys Pott, Society for Overseas Settlement of British Juveniles, 16 August 1928, 2. Whitton was the Council's Executive Secretary; in this letter criticizing the juvenile immigration scheme, she refers to the "suicides of recent years."

44. "Urge a Readjustment–Children's Aid Staff," *Toronto Star*, 28 February 1924; also "Seek to Guard Young Who Come to Ontario, *Toronto Star*, 8 May 1924.

45. "Funeral of Home Boy Moves Many to Tears," *Globe and Mail*, 28 January 1924; "Farmer Exonerated at Omemee Inquiry into Boy's Suicide," *Globe and Mail*, 3 February 1924.

46. "High School Student Found Dead in Car," *Toronto Daily Star*, 9 January 1945.

47. Editorial, "Nobody Really Knew Him," *Toronto Daily Star*, 10 January 1945; also "Studies Not Cause for Boy's Suicide," *Toronto Daily Star*, 12 January 1945. The *Globe* was not as interested in the story, running only one short report, "Boy Self-Slain in Parked Car," 9 January 1945.

48. James Gibson Hume, "The Significance of Suicide", *Philosophical Review* 19 (1910): 179–80; cited in Classics in the History of Psychology, developed by Christopher D. Green, York University, Toronto, Ontario, http://psychclassics.yorku.ca/. Hume (1860–1949) was Professor of Philosophy at the University of Toronto, 1891–1926.

49. G.S. Hall, "Child Study and Its Relation to Education," 689.

A NATIONAL CRIME
Residential Schools in Canada, 1880s to 1960s

Maureen Lux
Brock University

A NATIONAL CRIME: RESIDENTIAL SCHOOLS IN CANADA, 1880s TO 1960s

● **Introduction by Maureen Lux**

▲ **Primary Documents**

Document 1: Report on Industrial Schools for Indians and Half-Breeds
Nicholas Flood Davin

Document 2: Anglican Indian School, Siksika (Blackfoot) Reserve

Document 3: Students Filling Mattresses with Straw, Kanai (Blood)
Anglican School

Document 4: The Story of a National Crime: Being an Appeal for Justice
to the Indians of Canada
Dr. Peter Henderson Bryce, M.A., M.D.

Document 5: School Boys from Tsuu T'ina (Sarcee) Reserve, 1920

Document 6: Schoolchildren at the United Church School on the
Stoney Reserve, Morley, Alberta, ca. 1950

Document 7: Bed-time Prayers at Girls' Dormitory, Old Sun School,
  Siksika (Blackfoot) Reserve

■ **Secondary Documents**

Article 1: The Tuition of Thomas Moore
John Milloy

Article 2: The Charge of Manslaughter: Disease and Death, 1879–1946
John Milloy

Article 3: You Ain't My Boss: Resistance
J.R. Miller

● INTRODUCTION

Maureen Lux

In June 2008 Prime Minister Stephen Harper stood in the House of Commons to deliver a most unusual speech:

> Mr. Speaker, I stand before you today to offer an apology to former students of Indian residential schools. The treatment of children in Indian residential schools is a sad chapter in our history. [...]
>
> The government of Canada built an educational system in which very young children were often forcibly removed from their homes, often taken far from their communities. Many were inadequately fed, clothed and housed. All were deprived of the care and nurturing of their parents, grandparents and communities. First Nations, Inuit and Métis languages and cultural practices were prohibited in these schools. Tragically, some of these children died while attending residential schools and others never returned home. The government now recognizes that the consequences of the Indian residential schools policy were profoundly negative and that this policy has had a lasting and damaging impact on aboriginal culture, heritage and language. [...]
>
> The government of Canada sincerely apologizes and asks the forgiveness of the aboriginal peoples of this country for failing them so profoundly. We are sorry. [...][1]

The apology and the limited financial compensation for survivors went some way to acknowledge the damage done to many generations of Aboriginal people and their communities. But the formal apology, coming 128 years after the residential school system began, and more than a decade after the worst abuses were widely known, made many wonder whether government efforts were not too little, too late. The Christian churches that managed the schools on the government's behalf had already apologized a few years before, although the Catholic Church issued a Papal apology only in 2009.

The residential schools' tragic legacies—the loss of language and history, damaged lives, and corroded communities—were not unforeseen or unintended consequences, but rather were the *raison d'être* of the schools. Indeed, the foundation of the residential school system rested on what was called in the late nineteenth century "aggressive civilization," or the forced assimilation of Aboriginal people into Christian, capitalist Canadian society by actively repressing their languages, cultures, religion, and medicine. To that end, residential schools, which removed children from their parents' influence, forced them to speak English (or French in Quebec), and indoctrinated them in the Christian faith that denigrated Aboriginal spirituality, became the centrepiece of government policy. For nearly a century, from the 1880s to the closure of most of the schools in the 1960s, the moral authority of the Christian churches joined forces with the legislative and financial power of the state to create and perpetuate the school system. It is important to note that some students had a positive experience at residential schools, and not all Aboriginal children attended the schools. As for the numbers of children enrolled, the *Report of the Royal Commission on Aboriginal Peoples* notes that the records do not allow a precise accounting, but "the impact of the system was felt not only by the children who attended schools but by the families and communities that were deprived of their children and had to deal subsequently with children who returned damaged from the schools. In that sense, communities, parents and, indeed, children later born to former students of the residential schools were all 'enrolled'."[2] At its height in 1931 there were 80 schools in the Northwest Territories and every province except Prince Edward Island, New Brunswick, and Newfoundland. The question must be, why? How did Christian stewardship and state responsibility become so perverted as to create such a tragic end?

In 1879 Canadian Prime Minister John A. Macdonald sent Nicholas Flood Davin, failed Conservative candidate and journalist, to investigate the American Indian Industrial schools and to report on the advisability of establishing such schools in Canada. Davin's confidential 1879 *Report on Industrial Schools for Indians and Half-Breeds* (excerpted here) recommended the establishment of Industrial schools. Davin's consistent and objectionable (to our twenty-first-century ears) references to "race" sheds some light on Victorian perceptions of Aboriginal peoples and the notions of racial superiority that influenced the establishment of the residential school system. As Davin noted, "[...] if anything is to be done with the Indian, we must catch him very young. The children must be kept constantly with the circle of civilized conditions."

As historian John Milloy explains in "The Tuition of Thomas Moore," the state policy of assimilation that attempted to make Aboriginal peoples strangers in their own lands found a most accommodating partner in the Christian churches. But the school system, always underfunded, increasingly forced the churches to economize on food and clothing, while the children spent less time in the classroom and more time working in the fields, barns, kitchens, and laundries to maintain the schools. Despite ample evidence that the "circle of civilized conditions" was creating appalling conditions, those responsible, the churches and government, each blamed the other.

In "The Charge of Manslaughter: Disease and Death, 1879–1946," Milloy examines the dreadful conditions in some of the schools. Rising concerns over costs and the alarming state of the children's health led government and the churches to lower their expectations. The original distinction between Industrial schools (intended to teach trades to older students) and the less expensive boarding schools (for younger students) had become negligible, and after 1923 all were simply known as residential schools.

One of those intimate with the dangerous condition of the schools and the subsequent deterioration in the children's health was the department of Indian Affairs medical officer, Dr Peter Bryce. In the excerpt of his 1922 pamphlet *The Story of a National Crime: Being an Appeal for Justice to the Indians of Canada,* Bryce recounts how the department, especially Departmental Accountant and later Deputy Minister Duncan Campbell Scott, actively suppressed his 1907 report on the conditions of the schools, and ignored his recommendations to ameliorate the children's misery. It is important to note, however, that Bryce's condemnation of the government was motivated not only by the deplorable state of health, but also by his own resentment at being passed over in 1919 for a position in the new federal Department of Health.

School children, their parents, and communities were not passive victims of the assimilationist policies pursued by state and church in the residential schools. Granted, the power relations were hardly equal and the Indian department had considerable resources to force children into school and keep them there. Amendments to the *Indian Act* in 1894 and again in 1920 legislated compulsory attendance at school; police charged parents who refused to comply, and rounded up and returned children who made a run for home. Besides sheer compulsion, there were also the concerted efforts of school principals, Indian Agents, and missionaries to coerce parents and communities to surrender their children. Nevertheless, children and their parents accepted what they could not change, but resisted when and where they could. As historian J.R. Miller explains in "You Ain't My Boss," children and their communities resisted their maltreatment, but their voices were rarely heard beyond the local school. But perhaps ironically, when concerted Aboriginal political action emerged as a national force in the 1960s it was often residential school graduates who were the most effective leaders. The schools themselves created those who mounted the most effective forms of resistance.

Even after the end of the church–state educational relationship in 1969 and the closure of most schools, the story of neglect and abuse was still not widely known beyond the Aboriginal communities that continued to struggle with its legacy. As John Milloy explains, what finally broke the silence was "[…] ironically, the deepest secret of all—the pervasive sexual abuse of the children."[3] In the 1980s, harrowing reports of sexual abuse of non-Aboriginal children at orphanages in Newfoundland and Ontario prompted a public dialogue that eventually listened to Aboriginal revelations of similar abuse. In British Columbia, police uncovered widespread sexual abuse by priests at Williams Lake school; in 1990, Phil Fontaine, chief of the Assembly of Manitoba Chiefs, spoke out about his mistreatment at the hands of priests at Fort Alexander school in Manitoba: "I think what happened to me happened to a lot of people. It wasn't just sexual abuse, it was physical and psychological abuse. It was a violation."[4] Revelations of abuse continued and lawsuits mounted, but it was the aftermath of the failed Meech Lake Accord and the clash between police and Mohawks at Kanestake (Oka) that prompted the establishment of the Royal Commission on Aboriginal Peoples in 1992. With a mandate to explore the relationship among Aboriginal peoples, the government, and Canadian society, and to propose solutions to the problems that plagued the relationship, the Royal Commission reported in 1996. One of its priorities was to investigate the history of the residential schools, and the Commission recommended a public inquiry to allow survivors to tell their stories and begin the healing process. Further, the Commission recommended a compensation package for victims and a government apology. After much prompting and pressure by Aboriginal and non-Aboriginal groups, the apology came 12 years later, while the public inquiry, the Truth and Reconciliation Commission, has yet to begin its work. For very many former students all of this comes far too late, but the opportunity for public debate of this sad history may go some way to honour their memory.

NOTES

1. Prime Minister Stephen Harper's statement of apology, 11 June 2008.
2. Royal Commission on Aboriginal Peoples, *Looking Forward, Looking Back,* Vol. 1, Part 2, Chapter 10, "Residential Schools," n. 15.
3. John Milloy, *A National Crime: The Canadian Government and the Residential School System,* 1879–1986 (Winnipeg: University of Manitoba Press, 1999), 298.
4. *The Globe and Mail,* 31 October 1990, quoted in J.R. Miller, Shingwauk's *Vision: A History of Native Residential Schools* (Toronto: University of Toronto Press, 1996), 328.

QUESTIONS

1. Why was the nineteenth-century policy of "aggressive civilization" actively pursued into the late twentieth century?
2. How was it that the worst abuses of the residential schools did not become the subject of public debate for more than a century? Has there been a public debate?
3. Prime Minister Harper's apology to Aboriginal people is similar to the government's 1988 apology to Japanese Canadians for their internment during World War II. Why

did it take another two decades for an apology to Aboriginal Canadians? Do government apologies create the impression that past wrongs have somehow been corrected or forgiven?

4. What does Davin's 1879 Report tell us about late nineteenth century views of Aboriginal people? What does it say about their views on education? Why were there no plans to train Aboriginal teachers for the schools?

5. Peter Bryce, a physician and powerful public health expert, was eventually drummed out of government service for his public criticisms of the residential school system. What impact would criticisms by the children and their parents have had on the schools?

FURTHER READINGS

Barman, J., Y. Hebert, and D. McCaskill, eds., *Indian Education in Canada, Volume One: The Legacy,* (Vancouver: University of British Columbia Press, 1986).

Dyck, Noel, *Differing Visions: Administering Indian Residential Schooling in Prince Albert, 1867–1967,* (Halifax: Fernwood Publishing, 1997).

Haig-Brown, Celia, *Resistance and Renewal: Surviving the Indian Residential School,* (Vancouver: Tillacum Library, 1988).

Miller, J.R., *Shingwauk's Vision: A History of Native Residential Schools,* (Toronto: University of Toronto Press, 1996).

Milloy, John, *A National Crime: The Canadian Government and the Residential School System, 1879–1986,* (Winnipeg: University of Manitoba Press, 1999).

Royal Commission on Aboriginal Peoples, *Looking Forward, Looking Back,* Volume 1, Part 2, Chapter 10, "Residential Schools," accessed from http://www.collectionscanada.gc.ca.

The following are memoirs by former students or based on interviews with students. See, for example, Celia Haig-Brown, *Resistance and Renewal: Surviving the Indian Residential School* (Vancouver: Tillacum Library, 1988); Isabelle Knockwood with Gillian Thomas, *Out of the Depths, The Experiences of Mi'kmaq Children at the Indian Residential School at Shubenacadie, Nova Scotia* (Lokeport, Nova Scotia: Roseway Publishing, 1992); Basil H. Johnston, *Indian School Days* (Toronto: Key Porter Books Limited, 1988); G. Manuel and M. Posluns, *The Fourth World* (Don Mills: Collier-Macmillan Canada Ltd., 1974); Linda Jaine, ed., *Residential Schools: The Stolen Years* (Saskatoon: University [of Saskatchewan] Extension Press, 1993); Geoffrey York, *The Dispossessed: Life and Death in Native Canada* (Toronto: Lester & Orpen Dennys, 1989); Assembly of First Nations, *Breaking the Silence, An Interpretive Study of Residential School Impact and Healing as Illustrated by the Stories of First Nations Individuals* (Ottawa: First Nations Health Commission, 1994).

▲ Document 1: Report on Industrial Schools for Indians and Half-Breeds

Nicholas Flood Davin

Ottawa, 14th March, 1879
To the Right Honourable
The Minister of the Interior

SIR,—I have the honour to submit the following report on the working of Industrial Schools for the education of Indians and mixed-bloods in the United States, and on the advisability of establishing similar institutions in the North-West Territories of the Dominion.

In accordance with your directions of the twenty-eighth of January, I went to Washington. His Excellency Sir Edward Thornton, the Honourable Carl Schurtz, Secretary of the Interior, and the Honourable E. A. Hayt, the Commissioner of Indian Affairs, secured for me every facility for becoming acquainted with the establishment, cost and practical value of industrial schools among the Indian populations of the United States.

The industrial school is the principal feature of the policy known as that of "aggressive civilization." This policy was inaugurated by President Grant in 1869. But, as will be seen, the utility of industrial schools had long ere that time been amply tested. [...] After eight years' experience of the partial carrying out of these recommendations, the Board pressed for a still more thorough policy; they urged, among other things, that titles to land should be inalienable from the family of the holder for at least three generations. From 1869 vigorous efforts in an educational direction were put forward. But it was found that the day school did not work, because the influence of the wigwam was stronger than the influence of the school. Industrial Boarding Schools were therefore established, and these are now numerous and will soon be universal. [...]

The Indian character, about which some persons find such a mystery, is not difficult to understand. The Indian is sometimes spoken of as a child, but he is very far from being a child. The race is in its childhood. As far as the childhood analogy is applicable, what it suggests is a policy that shall look patiently for fruit, not after five or ten years, but after a generation or two. [...]

[...]

The Indian is a man with conditions of his own, which make civilization a puzzle of despair. He has the suspicion, distrust, fault-finding tendency, the insincerity and flattery, produced in all subject races. He is crafty, but conscious how weak his craft is when opposed to the superior cunning of the white man. [...]

The first and greatest stone in the foundation of the quasi-civilization of the Indians, wherever seen, was laid by missionaries, men who had a supreme object and who did not count their lives dear unto them. Schools are scattered over the whole continent, wherever Indians exist, monuments of religious zeal and heroic self-sacrifice. These schools should be utilized as much as possible, both on grounds of efficiency and economy. The missionaries' experience is only surpassed by their patient heroism, and their testimony, like that of the school teachers, like that of the authorities at Washington is, that if anything is to be done with the Indian, we must catch him very young. The children must be kept constantly within the circle of civilized conditions. [...] The plan now is to take young children, give

Source: Nicholas Flood Davin, *Report on Industrial Schools for Indians and Half-Breeds* (14 March 1879), Library and Archives Canada, MG26A, Sir John A. Macdonald Papers, Vol. 91, 35428-45.

them the care of a mother, and have them constantly in hand. Such care must be *pari passu* with religious training.

[…]

The recommendations I venture to submit are as follows:—

(1.) Wherever the missionaries have schools, those schools should be utilized by the Government, if possible; that is to say, a contract should be made with the religious body controlling the school to board and educate and train industrially a certain number of pupils. […]

(2.) Not more than four industrial boarding schools ought to be established at first. […]

(3.) An industrial boarding school should be established somewhere in the fork of the North and South Saskatchewan, near Prince Albert, in connection with the Episcopalian Church. The land is wonderfully fertile. There are a good many Indians in the neighbourhood. There are Bands of Indians near Carlton and near Dutch Lake. There is plenty of fish and timber.

(4.) In no place could an industrial boarding school in connection with the Methodist body be more properly placed than near Old Bow Fort. The Blackfeet and Stoneys, wild but noble types of Indians, would thus be reached. […]

(5.) At Qu'Appelle it might well be thought we should find an appropriate site for an industrial boarding school to be conducted by Roman Catholics.[…]

(6.) An industrial boarding school, in connection with the Presbyterian Church, should be established on Riding Mountain. […]

The importance of denominational schools at the outset for the Indians must be obvious. One of the earliest things an attempt to civilize them does, is to take away their simple Indian mythology, the central idea of which, to wit, a perfect spirit, can hardly be improved on. The Indians have their own ideas of right and wrong, of "good" Indians and "bad" Indians, and to disturb this faith, without supplying a better, would be a curious process to enlist the sanction of civilized races whose whole civilization, like all the civilizations with which we are acquainted, is based on religion. […]

(7.) Some distinction should be made between the treatment of parents who send their children regularly to the day-school, and of those who are either careless whether their children go to school or not, or who are wholly opposed to their children attending school, as some are. To the first, an additional ration of tea and sugar might be given.

(8.) Where practicable, some inducement of a special nature should be held out to the child.

(9.) As Bands become more amenable to the restraints of civilization education should be made compulsory.

(10.) The character of the teacher, morally and intellectually, is a matter of vital importance. If he is morally weak, whatever his intellectual qualifications may be, he is worse than no teacher at all. If he is poorly instructed or feeble in brain, he only enacts every day an elaborate farce. […]

(11.) In order to secure that the education given would be efficient, there ought to be competent inspection. […]

(12.) Where boys or girls, whether Indians or half-breed, show special aptitudes or exceptional general quickness, special advantages should be offered them, and they should be trained to become teachers and clerks in connection

with the Department, as well as fitted to launch out on commercial and professional careers.

(13.) The salary of a teacher must be such as will induce good men to offer
themselves. The teacher should be paid according to his qualifications. [...]

I have the honour to be,
Sir,
Your obedient servant,
Nicholas Flood Davin.

▲ Document 2: Anglican Indian School, Siksika (Blackfoot) Reserve

ALL ONE IN CHRIST JESUS

● Anglican Indian School, Siksika (Blackfoot) Reserve, Alberta, ca. 1901–1910. Who might have taken this photograph? Why?

Source: Glenbow Museum, NC-5-1.

▲ Document 3: Students Filling Mattresses with Straw, Kanai (Blood) Anglican School

● Students filling mattresses with straw, Kanai (Blood) Anglican school, ca. 1916. What does this tell you about the kinds of work schoolchildren did? What does it tell you about the living conditions at the school?

Source: Glenbow Museum, NA-1400-31.

▲ Document 4: The Story of a National Crime: Being an Appeal for Justice to the Indians of Canada

Dr. Peter Henderson Bryce, M.A., M.D.

The Story of a National Crime Being a Record of the Health Conditions of the Indians of Canada from 1904 to 1921

I. By Order in Council dated Jan. 22nd, 1904, the writer was appointed Medical Inspector to the Department of the Interior and of Indian Affairs, and was entrusted with the health interests of the Indians of Canada. [...]

For the first months after the writer's appointment he was much engaged in organizing the medical inspection of immigrants at the sea ports; but he early began the systematic collection of health statistics of the several hundred Indian Bands scattered over Canada. For each year up to 1914 he wrote an annual report on the health of the Indians, published in the Departmental report, and on instructions from the minister made in 1907 a special inspection of thirty-five Indian schools in the three prairie provinces. This report was published separately; but the recommendations contained in the report were never published and the public knows nothing of them. It contained a brief history of the origin of the Indian Schools, of the sanitary condition of the schools and statistics of the health of the pupils, during the 15 years of their existence. Regarding the health of the pupils, the report states that 24 per cent of all the pupils which had been in the schools were known to be dead, while of one school on the File Hills reserve, which gave a complete return to date, 75 per cent. were dead at the end of the 16 years since the school opened.

Recommendations of school report 1907

Briefly the recommendations urged, (1) Greater school facilities, since only 30 per cent. of the children of school age were in attendance; (2) That boarding schools with farms attached be established near the home reserves of the pupils; (3) That the government undertake the complete maintenance and control of the schools, since it had promised by treaty to insure such; and further it was recommended that as the Indians grow in wealth and intelligence they should pay at least part of the cost from their own funds; (4) That the school studies be those of the curricula of the several Provinces in which the schools are situated, since it was assumed that as the bands would soon become enfranchised and become citizens of the Province they would enter into the common life and duties of a Canadian community; (5) That in view of the historical and sentimental relations between the Indian schools and the Christian churches the report recommended that the Department provide for the management of the schools, through a Board of Trustees, one appointed from each church and approved by the minister of the Department. Such a board would have its secretary in the Department but would hold regular meetings, establish qualifications for teachers, and oversee the appointments as well as the control of the schools; (6) That Continuation schools be arranged for on the school farms and that instruction methods similar to those on the File Hills farm colony be developed; (7) That the health interests of the pupils be guarded by a proper medical inspection and that the local physicians be encouraged through the provision at each school of fresh air methods in the care and treatment of cases of tuberculosis.

Source: Dr. Peter Henderson Bryce, M.A., M.D., *The Story of a National Crime: Being an Appeal for Justice to the Indians of Canada*. Ottawa: James Hope and Sons, 1922.

II. The annual medical reports from year to year made reference to the unsatisfactory health of the pupils, while different local medical officers urged greater action in view of the results of their experience from year to year. As the result of one such report the Minister instructed the writer in 1909 to investigate the health of the children in the schools of the Calgary district in a letter containing the following:—

> "As it is necessary that these residential schools should be filled with a healthy class of pupils in order that the expenditure on Indian education may not be rendered entirely nugatory, it seems desirable that you should go over the same ground as Dr. Lafferty and check his inspection."

Recommendations based upon examination of 243 school children

These instructions were encouraging and the writer gladly undertook the work of examining with Dr. J.D. Lafferty the 243 children of 8 schools in Alberta, with the following results:—

> (a) Tuberculosis was present equally in children at every age; (b) In no instance was a child awaiting admission to school found free from tuberculosis; hence it was plain that infection was got in the home primarily; (c) The disease showed an excessive mortality in the pupils between five and ten years of age; (d) The 10,000 children of school age demanded the same attention as the thousand children coming up each year and entering the schools annually.

Recommendations, made in this report, on much the same lines as those made in the report of 1907, followed the examination of the 243 children; but owing to the active opposition of Mr. D. C. Scott, and his advice to the then Deputy Minister, no action was taken by the Department to give effect to the recommendations made. [...]

The writer had done no regular inspection work since Mr. D. C. Scott was made Deputy minister in 1913, but had in each year up to 1914 prepared his medical report, printed in the annual report of the Department. [...]

Thus we find a sum of only $10,000 has been annually placed in the estimates to control tuberculosis amongst 105,000 Indians scattered over Canada in over 300 bands, while the City of Ottawa, with about the same population and having three general hospitals spent thereon $342,860.54 in 1919 of which $33,364.70 is devoted to tuberculosis patients alone. The many difficulties of our problem amongst the Indians have been frequently pointed out, but the means to cope with these have also been made plain. [...]

The degree and extent of this criminal disregard for the treaty pledges to guard the welfare of the Indian wards of the nation may be gauged from the facts once more brought out at the meeting of the National Tuberculosis Association at its annual meeting held in Ottawa on March 17th, 1922. The superintendent of the Qu'Appelle Sanatorium, Sask., gave there the results of a special study of 1575 children of school age in which advantage was taken of the most modern scientific methods. Of these 175 were Indian children, and it is very remarkable that the fact given that some 93 per cent. of these showed evidence of tuberculous infection coincides completely with the work done by Dr. Lafferty and the writer in the Alberta Indian schools in 1909.

It is indeed pitiable that during the thirteen years since then this trail of disease and death has gone on almost unchecked by any serious efforts on the part of the Department of Indian Affairs, placed by the B. N. A. Act especially in charge of our Indian population, and that a Provincial Tuberculosis Commission now considers it to be its duty to publish the facts regarding these children living within its own Province.

▲ Document 5: School Boys from Tsuu T'ina (Sarcee) Reserve, 1920

● School Boys from Tsuu T'ina (Sarcee) Reserve, 1920; note the bandages on the boys' heads, likely covering 'scrofula' sores or tuberculosis of lymph nodes of the neck. One-quarter of the boys have their heads bandaged. If these are the 'healthy' boys, what might this say about the other children in the school?

Source: Glenbow Museum, NA-192-13.

▲ Document 6: Schoolchildren at the United Church School on the Stoney Reserve, Morley, Alberta, ca. 1950

● Class in session at the Residential School on the Stoney Reserve, Morley, Alberta. Note the pictures of the Royal Family on the wall. Why would all the children be dressed in their coats?

Source: Glenbow Museum, NA-5719-4.

▲ Document 7: Bed-time Prayers at Girls' Dormitory, Old Sun School, Siksika (Blackfoot) Reserve

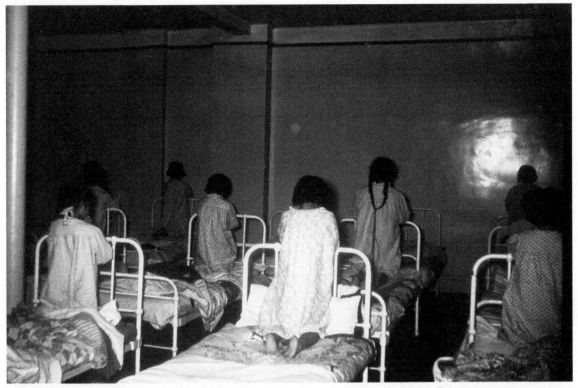

● Bed-time prayers at the girls' dormitory, Old Sun School, Siksika (Blackfoot) Reserve, ca. 1955. Note the ordered beds in the crowded dormitory. Who might have taken this photo? Why?

Source: Glenbow Museum, NA-4817-22.

Article 1: The Tuition of Thomas Moore

John Milloy

In its *Annual Report* of 1904, the Department of Indian Affairs published the photographs of the young Thomas Moore of the Regina Industrial School, "before and after tuition." The images are a cogent expression of what federal policy had been since Confederation and what it would remain for many decades. It was a policy of assimilation, a policy designed to move Aboriginal communities from their "savage" state to that of "civilization" and thus to make in Canada but one community—a non-Aboriginal one.[1]

At the core of the policy was education. It was, according to Deputy Superintendent Duncan Campbell Scott, who steered the administration of Indian Affairs from 1913 to 1932, "by far the most important of the many subdivisions of the most complicated Indian problem."[2] In the education of the young lay the most potent power to effect cultural change—a power to be channelled through schools and, in particular, through residential schools. Education would, Frank Oliver, the Minister of Indian Affairs, declared in 1908, "elevate the Indian from his condition of savagery" and make "him a self-supporting member of the State, and eventually a citizen in good standing."[3]

The pictures are, then, both images of what became in this period the primary object of that policy: the Aboriginal child, and an analogy of the relationship between the two cultures—Aboriginal and White—as it had been in the past and as it was to be in the future. There, in the photograph on the left, is the young Thomas posed against a fur robe, in his beaded dress, his hair in long braids, clutching a gun. Displayed for the viewer are the symbols of the past—of Aboriginal costume and culture, of hunting, of the disorder and violence of warfare and of the cross-cultural partnerships of the fur trade and of the military alliances that had dominated life in Canada since the late sixteenth century.

Source: John S. Milloy, *A National Crime: The Canadian Government and the Residential School System, 1879–1986.* Winnipeg: University of Manitoba Press, 1999, pp. 3–9. Reprinted with permission.

Those partnerships, anchored in Aboriginal knowledge and skills, had enabled the newcomers to find their way, to survive, and to prosper. But they were now merely historic; they were not to be any part of the future as Canadians pictured it at the founding of their new nation in 1867. That future was one of settlement, agriculture, manufacturing, lawfulness, and Christianity. In the view of politicians and civil servants in Ottawa whose gaze was fixed upon the horizon of national development, Aboriginal knowledge and skills were neither necessary nor desirable in a land that was to be dominated by European industry and, therefore, by Europeans and their culture.

That future was inscribed in the photograph on the right. Thomas, with his hair carefully barbered, in his plain, humble suit, stands confidently, hand on hip, in a new context. Here he is framed by the horizontal and vertical lines of wall and pedestal—the geometry of social and economic order; of place and class, and of private property the foundation of industriousness, the cardinal virtue of late-Victorian culture. But most telling of all, perhaps, is the potted plant. Elevated above him, it is the symbol of civilized life, of agriculture. Like Thomas, the plant is cultivated nature no longer wild. Like it, Thomas has been, the Department suggests, reduced to civility in the time he has lived within the confines of the Regina Industrial School.

The assumptions that underlay the pictures also informed the designs of social reformers in Canada and abroad, inside the Indian Department and out. Thomas and his classmates were to be assimilated; they were to become functioning members of Canadian society. Marching out from schools, they would be the vanguard of a magnificent metamorphosis: the savages were to be made civilized. For Victorians, it was an empire-wide task of heroic proportions and divine ordination encompassing the Maori, the Aborigine, the Hottentot, and many other indigenous peoples. For Canadians, it was, at the level of rhetoric at least, a national duty—a "sacred trust with which Providence has invested the country in the charge of and care for the aborigines committed to it."[4] In 1880, Alexander Morris, one of the primary government negotiators of the recently concluded western treaties, looked back upon those agreements and then forward, praying: "Let us have Christianity and civilization among the Indian tribes; let us have a

● Thomas Moore, as he appeared when admitted to the Regina Indian Industrial School (Saskatchewan Archives Board, R-82239 [1]). [Source: Saskatchewan Archives Board R-A8223-1]

● Thomas Moore, after tuition at the Regina Indian Industrial School (Saskatchewan Archives Board, R-82239 [2]). [Source: Saskatchewan Archives Board R-A8223-1]

wise and paternal Government...doing its utmost to help and elevate the Indian population,...and Canada will be enabled to feel, that in a truly patriotic spirit our country has done its duty by the red men."[5]

In Canada's first century, that "truly patriotic spirit" would be evident in the many individuals who devoted their "human capabilities to the good of the Indians of this country." In the case of Father Lacombe, Oblate missionary to the Blackfoot, for example, the "poor redman's redemption physically and morally" was "the dream of my days and nights."[6] According to Canada's first Prime Minister, Sir John A. Macdonald, the nation, too, dreamed of discharging its benevolent duty. A national goal, he informed Parliament, was "to do away with the tribal system and assimilate the Indian people in all respects with the inhabitants of the Dominion, as speedily as they are fit to change."[7] With the assistance of church and

state, wandering hunters would take up a settled life, agriculture, useful trades and, of course, the Christian religion.

Assimilation became, during Macdonald's first term, official policy. It was Canada's response to its "sacred trust" made even more alluring by the fact that supposedly selfless duty was to have its reward. The Deputy Superintendent General of Indian Affairs, L. Vankoughnet, assured Macdonald in 1887 that Indian expenditures "would be a good investment" for, in due course, Aboriginal people, "instead of being supported from the revenue of the country,...would contribute largely to the same."

Education, as Scott indicated, was the most critical element of this assimilative strategy. Vankoughnet, in his memo of 1887 to the prime minister, was doing no more than reflecting the common wisdom of the day when he wrote:

Give me the children and you may have the parents, or words to that effect, were uttered by a zealous divine in his anxiety to add to the number of whom his Church called her children. And the principle laid down by that astute reasoner is an excellent one on which to act in working out that most difficult problem—the intellectual emancipation of the Indian, and its natural sequel, his elevation to a status equal to that of his white brother. This can only be done through education....Only by a persistent continuance in a thoroughly systematic course of educating (using the word in its fullest and most practical sense) the children, will the final hoped and long striven for result be attained.[8]

"That most difficult problem" was to be solved not only through "persistent" tuition but also, more specifically, by residential school education, which, initially, took two forms: "boarding" schools, which were situated on or near a reserve, which were of moderate size and which taught reading, writing and arithmetic, agriculture, and the simple manual skills required by farmers and their wives; and "industrial" schools, such as Thomas's Regina Industrial School, which were large, centrally located, urban-associated trade schools and which also provided a plain English education. "It would be highly desirable, if it were practicable," the Department wrote in its *Annual Report* of 1890 "to obtain entire possession of all Indian children after they attain to the age of seven or eight years, and keep them at schools...until they have had a thorough course of instruction." The Department was confident that if such a course were adopted "the solution of the problem designated 'the Indian question' would probably be effected sooner than it is under the present system" of day schools.

By 1890, the government had been committed for just over a decade to the development of a system of residential schools of "the industrial type."[9] That commitment had sprung from the recommendations of the now-famous *Davin Report* of 1879. Nicholas Flood Davin, a journalist and a defeated Tory candidate, had been rewarded for his electoral effort by Macdonald with a commission to "report on the working of Industrial Schools...in the United States and on the advisability of establishing similar institutions in the North-West Territories of the Dominion." Senior American officials who Davin visited, Carl Schurtz, the Secretary of the Interior, and E.A. Hayt, the Commissioner of Indian Affairs, evinced the greatest confidence in the efficacy of the industrial school, which was, Davin was informed, "the principal feature of the policy known as that of 'aggressive civilization,'" their policy of assimilation. Day schools had proven a failure "because the influence of the wigwam was stronger than the influence of the school." Indeed, support for this thesis came, he claimed, from Cherokee leaders he met in Washington. They described the "happy results of Industrial Schools" and convinced him "that the chief thing to attend to in dealing with the less civilized or wholly barbarous tribes, was to separate the children from the parents."

Next on Davin's agenda was a trip to the school at the White Earth Agency in Minnesota. He was obviously impressed. The school was 'well attended and the answering of the children creditable....The dormitory was plainly but comfortably furnished, and the children...were evidently well fed." The whole reserve had an air of progressive development, traceable, in the opinion of the agent, to the school. Subsequent meetings in Winnipeg with "the leading men, clerical and lay, who could speak with authority on the subject" must have confirmed his American observations, for Davin's report gave unqualified support to the "application of the principle of industrial boarding schools." He submitted, as well, a detailed plan for beginning such a school system in the west that he probably worked out with those authorities—Bishop Taché, Father Lacombe, the Honourable James McKay and others.[10]

While the *Davin Report* may properly be credited with moving the Macdonald government to inaugurate industrial schools in the 1880s, it is far from being, as it is often characterized,[11] the genesis of the residential school system in Canada. Indeed, when Davin submitted his report, there were already in existence in Ontario four residential schools, then called manual labour schools—the Mohawk Institute, and the Wikwemikong, Mount Elgin, and Shingwauk schools; and a number of boarding schools were being planned by missionaries in the west.

Furthermore, the report does not answer the most important questions about the beginning and intended character of the residential school system.

Why did the federal government adopt a policy of assimilation? What was the relationship between that policy, its ideology and structures, and education, particularly residential schools? Not only are the answers to such central questions not in the *Davin Report*, but neither are they found in any single report in the early years after Confederation. Indeed, to discover the roots of the Canadian residential school system, we must make recourse to the history of the pre-Confederation period of Imperial control of Indian affairs. It was in that earlier era that the assimilative policy took shape with the design of programs for the "civilization" of the Indian population of Upper Canada. The policy was then given a final legislative form, in the first decade after Confederation, with the determination of the constitutional position of Indian First Nations expressed in two early Indian acts: 1869 and 1876.

The Imperial policy heritage of the 1830s, 1840s, and 1850s, supplemented by federal legislation and programming in the first decade of Confederation, was both the context and the rationale for the development of residential schools, which in turn constituted part of the most extensive and persistent colonial system—one that marginalized Aboriginal communities within its constitutional, legislative, and regulatory structure, stripped them of the power of self-government, and denied them any degree of self-determination. As a consequence, Aboriginal people became, in the course of Canada's first century, wards of the Department of Indian Affairs and increasingly the objects of social welfare, police, and justice agencies.

The result of the federal government's colonization of First Nations was sorrowful, indeed. When, in 1946, a joint committee of the House of Commons and Senate met "to examine and consider the Indian Act"[12] and the record of federal administration of Indian affairs, the members found not only a policy that had remained largely unchanged since the Confederation era—"an unwritten heritage of the past"[13]— but also one that had clearly fallen far short of its goal and showed no sign of imminent success. By every indicator—health, employment, income, education, housing—Aboriginal people, far from being assimilated, were still separate and second-class citizens. What unfolded before those parliamentarians was a complex social, economic, and political tapestry with a single unifying thread—growing Aboriginal poverty.

One of the darkest hues in that tapestry came from the fact that the main thrust of the colonial system's assimilative strategy had concentrated on the young, on the thousands of Thomas Moores, boys and girls, Indian, Métis, and Inuit, across the land. They were the vulnerable future of communities and of Aboriginal culture, and they had been removed from their homes and placed in the care of strangers, many of whom were hostile to their culture, beliefs, and language. For the sake of civilization, in the discharge of a national duty, they were placed in the residential schools. For those children and their communities and, indeed, for all Canadians, the consequence of those schools, of Thomas Moore's tuition, has been truly tragic.

Notes

1. For a review of Canadian policy see: J.L. Tobias, "Protection, Civilization, Assimilation: An Outline History of Canada's Indian Policy," in *As Long as the Sun Shines and Water Flows*, edited by I. Getty and A.S. Lussier (Vancouver: University of British Columbia Press, 1983); J.R. Miller, *Skyscrapers Hide the Heavens: A History of Indian/White Relations in Canada* (Toronto: University of Toronto Press, 1989); and O. Dickason, *Canada's First Nations: A History of Founding Peoples from Earliest Times* (Toronto: McClelland and Stewart, 1992).

2. *Annual Report of the Department of Indian Affairs* [hereinafter referred to as the Annual Report] 1911, 273.

3. N.A.C. RG 10, Vol. 6039, File 160-1, MR C 8152, F. Oliver to Joint Church Delegation.

4. *Annual Report* 1891, x.

5. A. Morris, *The Treaties of Canada with the Indians of Manitoba and the North-West Territories* (Toronto: Belfords, Clarke and Col. 1880), 278.

6. N.A.C. MG 27, I C4, E. Dewdney Papers, A. Lacombe to E. Dewdney, 25 November 1889, 2, 189–192.

7. As quoted in M. Montgomery, "The Six Nations and the Macdonald Franchise," *Ontario History* 57 (March 1965): 13.

8. INAC File 1/25-1. Vol. 15, L. Vankoughnet to Sir John A. Macdonald, 26 August 1887.

9. *Annual Report* 1890, xii.

10. *The Davin Report,* 1–17.

11. See for example: J. Barman, Y. Hébert, and D. McCaskill, "The Legacy of the Past: An Overview," in *Indian Education in Canada*, edited by J.

Barman, Y. Hébert, and D. McCaskill, vol. 1: *The Legacy* (Vancouver: University of British Columbia Press, 1986), 6.

12. J. Leslie and R. Macguire, eds., *The Historical Development of the Indian Act* (Ottawa: Depart-

ment of Indian and Northern Affairs Canada, 1979), 133.

13. J. Taylor, *Canadian Indian Policy during the Inter-War Years, 1919–1939* (Ottawa: Indian and Northern Affairs Canada, 1983), 4.

■ Article 2: The Charge of Manslaughter: Disease and Death, 1879–1946

John Milloy

The provisions of the 1911 contract and the discussions during the negotiating sessions make it clear that there was a crisis in conditions, sanitation, and health in the schools. Neither the Department nor the churches could have pretended otherwise. Dr. P. Bryce's first report was published in 1907 just as the discussions were about to get under way, and another report, by F.H. Paget, a Departmental accountant, which was highly critical of the condition of school buildings, came to hand in 1908. The Honourable S.H. Blake, a lawyer conducting a review of Anglican mission work, who was an influential force in the negotiations, characterized the situation in the schools for the Minister, Frank Oliver, in the most blunt fashion: "The appalling number of deaths among the younger children appeals loudly to the guardians of our Indians. In doing nothing to obviate the preventable causes of death, brings the Department within unpleasant nearness to the charge of manslaughter."[1]

The residential school system began its drift to that "unpleasant nearness" right from its inception. The "appalling number of deaths among the younger children" was the result of removing children, as Blake explained to the minister, from a healthy "out of door life" to the confines of badly constructed schools made worse over time by neglectful and inadequately funded maintenance programs. Perhaps even more pertinent, careless administration of health regulations, a lack of adequate medical services and

the effect on children of the harsh and alien routines of education added their deadly weight.

In those hundreds or thousands of deaths (extant records do not allow an accurate count)[2] the churches, Department and government shared complicity.[3] The disease and deaths and the cause of them were known to all. Indian Agent MacArthur commented, in 1910, in view of the situation at Duck Lake, where he estimated that, in the past, nearly fifty percent of the children sent to the school died: "[No one] responsible can get beyond the fact that those children catch the disease while at school" confined for months on end "in a building whose every seam and crevice is, doubtless, burdened with Tuberculosis Baccilli."[4] To those entering the circle of civilization for the first time, the all-too-common conditions could be a shock. For the new Principal of Red Deer school, Dr. J.P. Rice, arriving in 1903 from his comfortable Toronto parish, "the sight of the ragged ill-kempt and sickly looking children was sufficient to make me sick at heart." Enrollment was down due to deaths, the removal of children by their parents, and because the "sanitary conditions of the buildings are exceedingly bad."[5]

It all began with the buildings. Those many schools that were opened by the churches in advance of government grants were routinely "erected on very primitive plans"[6] by amateurs without the guidance of professional architects.[7] They often received grants sight unseen, without any Departmental inspection, and despite the fact that senior officials, like Scott, admitted that they were "intensely apprehensive" about the quality and safety of church-built structures.[8] This was such a common concern that Hayter Reed, when drafting the 1894 regulations, included a proposal that the Department, before any grant was authorized, should have the right to inspect the plans or, if already built, the school premises.[9] Such a regulation, had it been adopted and enforced, may well have been useful for when schools were finally visited; the Department discovered, in some instances, that their decision to proceed had not been wise.[10]

Source: John S. Milloy, *A National Crime: The Canadian Government and the Residential School System, 1879–1986*. Winnipeg: University of Manitoba Press, 1999, pp. 77–107. Reprinted with permission.

The Department's own record was not a great deal better, however. Benson, in a general assessment of the school system in 1897, pulled no punches: "The buildings have been put up without due consideration for the purpose for which they would be required, hurriedly constructed of poor materials, badly laid out without due provision for lighting, heating or ventilating."[11]

From the outset, schools had been built with an eye to economy. E. Dewdney, who supervised the construction of the first three industrial schools in the west, insisted that they be of the "simplest and cheapest construction." Putting them near railway lines would facilitate the acquisition of construction materials and supplies. In the course of time, he reasoned, with the growth of settlement, construction costs would drop and the schools could be upgraded.[12] That was, it turned out, a foolish assumption. The trains, when they came, brought settlers, but certainly no federal funds for reconstructing schools.

[...]

It is important (and it illustrates the range of problems, rooted in construction deficiencies, siting, and short budgets) to give some indication of the degree of crisis that existed in the fabric of the residential school system as a whole. Moreover, it is important to give an indication of how conscious officials in the Department were, or could have been, of the situation.

A single report, submitted in 1908 by F.H. Paget, an accountant with the Department, gives some sense both of the scope of the problem and of senior Departmental staff's awareness of it. The report was commissioned by the Department during the negotiations for the contracts when information on the condition of the system was vital. It amounted to a review of a cross-section of nearly one-third of the system including both industrial and boarding schools.

[...]

Paget's report revealed that the schools ran the gamut from good to deplorable. The majority—fifteen out of the twenty-one—were in the latter category. He was impressed with the Qu'Appelle School, which was rebuilt after its fire "with all the modern conveniences." Lacombe's High River School "was splendidly conducted,...neat and clean." He was impressed most with the Duck Lake Boarding School, despite what Indian Agent MacArthur said only two years later about its historic fifty-percent death rate: "Excellent order, neat and clean throughout, [and] very much a self-contained institution, all clothing being made, and meats, roots, grains and vegetable raised."

All of this was overshadowed by Paget's descriptions of schools that did not pass muster. Not surprisingly, Regina and Red Deer topped the industrial school list. Red Deer was "not modern in any respect." Regina was a sorrowful school: "Driving up it looked more like a deserted place than a Government Institution," The "building is old and the floors are worn, the plaster broken and marked in places and the paint worn off." The children "did not have that clean and neat appearance that was in evidence at other schools."

[...]

Finally, the report indicated what was by 1908 a commonplace, the connection between the condition of the schools and the ill health of children, particularly through tubercular infection. Though Paget covered much of the same ground as Bryce's report of the year before had, he had not been directed to check the doctor's findings. He was, however, certainly familiar with Bryce's report and even referred to it obliquely in his description of Old Sun's Boarding School, which he "found to be all that had been said of it by others in regard to being unsanitary and the building unsuitable in every way for such an institution." In addition, he brought forward similar observations of other schools.[13]

The Department, of course, was fully aware, before either the *Bryce Report* or the *Paget Report*, of the plague of tuberculosis affecting the Aboriginal population and the fact that it had insinuated itself into the schools. The tubercular epidemic, which had moved across the country with the tide of settlement, was the result of white presence coupled with the Aboriginal community's lack of immunity to infectious diseases. It was also, however, a consequence of the process of colonization, of the forces that marginalized communities, divorcing them from their traditional life ways. Confinement to reserves and overcrowded European-style lodgings of the lowest quality provided the fertile ground with malnutrition, lack of sanitation, despair, alcoholism, and government parsimony, from which the infection ran its mortal course through communities.

The impact of tuberculosis, statistically expressed, was out of all proportion to the size of the Aboriginal population. A study by Bryce revealed that the rate of tubercular infection for Indians was one in seven "and the death rates in several large bands 81.8, 81.2, and in a third 86.1 per thousand." The "ordinary death rate for 115,000 in the city of Hamilton was 10.6 in 1921."[14]

The tubercular bacilli infested the body in a multitude of manifestations. "Contracted in infancy [it] creates diseases of the brain [tubercular meningitis], joints, bones and to a less degree the lungs [pulmonary tuberculosis or consumption] and ...if not fatal till adolescence it then usually progresses rapidly to a fatal termination in consumption of the lungs."[15] It was signalled by a wide range of symptoms: head and joint aches, pain in breathing, and glandular swelling and eruption (scrofula) being some of the more common ones. In its most contagious phase, that is, consumption, coughing and spitting blood or sputum spread the infection to others; and fever, weakness, and wasting led to death.

One mode of transmission that particularly affected the children in the schools was drinking milk infected with bovine tuberculosis. Industrial and boarding schools kept cows, and the children routinely drank unpasteurized milk. As with the school buildings, the outbuildings for livestock were often a problem. The principal of St. George's School in Lytton, for example, was told by the Department of Agriculture that he would have to pull down his barn because it was a log structure and could not be disinfected. The school had lost eighteen head of cattle in the previous three years.[16]

Not only was it impossible to isolate the schools from the epidemic, but, as well, the schools themselves were expeditors; they aggravated the problem by simulating in an exaggerated fashion many of those problematic conditions that affected reserve communities.[17]

[...]

The root of overcrowded dorms and classrooms, as with the deteriorating condition of school buildings, could be traced back to funding arrangements and particularly to the per-capita system. The critical need that principals had to maintain high enrollments to qualify for the full grant that had been assigned to their school led to practices that contributed directly to the health problem. Pushing enrollments to and past the point of overcrowding was one of these. The Crowfoot School in 1909 provided a striking example

of this. In that year, Duncan Campbell Scott, then the Department's Chief Accountant, had before him a request from the principal for more students and information supplied by Benson that the dormitories were overcrowded and the ventilation was poor. Scott told the deputy superintendent, rather angrily, that of the fifty-two pupils that had been in the school since it had been in receipt of grants eight years earlier, eight had died, seven of those in the school and the other within a month of leaving. Of the thirty-nine children in the school who had been examined in the previous few months by Dr. J.D. Lafferty, twenty-two were infected with tuberculosis in the lungs:

This is what we have to show for an expenditure of $15,611. The outlook for the remaining pupils in attendance is not very bright and there is very little hope that the graduates of the School will attain maturity and be able to exercise any civilizing influence....The accommodation at the School is inadequate for the number of pupils in residence, and the unhealthy pupils should be discharged.[18]

Principals, of course, were contending with problems flowing directly from just the sort of funding that Scott referred to. As the per-capita ceiling remained stubbornly unchanged at $72 until 1911, they could increase their grant only by having their authorized student number raised. Annually, the Department was besieged with such requests. Additionally, principals had to strive to recruit up to the maximum number authorized, which might already have been a figure that permitted the overcrowding of the living spaces of the school, as was evident in the case of Crowfoot and many other schools.

The pressure that principals worked under to secure adequate funds meant that there was a tendency to be less than careful about the condition of the children they brought into the school. In 1907, the Anglican bishop of Caledonia wanted to turn over Metlakatla to government control because of the anxiety, and perhaps the moral disquiet, that he felt over recruitment. He admitted candidly: "The per capita grant system encourages the taking in of those physically and intellectually unfit simply to keep up numbers."[19]

[...]

Of course, neither the principals nor the churches were solely responsible for the schools. If school administrators were driven into excess by funding needs and led there by missionary zeal, they were not restrained in any effective way by the Department. The 1892 and 1894 Orders-in-Council and the 1911 contracts established the government's responsibility for providing medical services to the schools and the Department's right to inspect the schools was made a condition of the grant. Regulations were issued in 1894 and retained, throughout the period, stipulating that children had to have a medical certificate signed by a doctor before admission.[20]

Unfortunately, the implementation of those regulations left much to be desired. There was no regular inspection of the schools nor any guarantee that forms were being filled in or doctors consulted. In 1909, the Departmental secretary sent out new admission and certificate-of-health forms, which he thought were "sufficiently stringent to guard against tubercular children being taken into the school." They were not enough, however, to keep Louise Plaited Hair out of St. Mary's Boarding School on the Blood Reserve. Her form was signed by Dr. O. Edwards and accepted without question by the Department, in 1911, despite the fact that there was evidence that she had contracted tuberculosis. To a question that asked if there were signs of scrofula or other forms of tubercular disease, Edwards had written, "Glands on right neck slightly enlarged."[21]

According to Scott, when he reviewed the situation with other senior officials in 1925, Louise represented hundreds who had been admitted despite the regulations. The "indiscriminate admission of children without first passing a medical examination" continued. It was not only the principals, he realized, but "our own officers who are picking up orphans, delinquents and others, that are causing the difficulty, as occasionally no application forms are forwarded." There had to be, as well, "more careful checking of the medical officers' remarks in the case of all applicants."[22]

The administrative difficulties identified in Scott's review encompassed more, however, than lax implementation of regulations by officials or attempts to evade those regulations by principals desperate to keep up enrollments. The system simply did not have the medical support that the Department was pledged to provide and that was required to properly protect the children and attend to their health needs.[23] That tragic omission had to be laid on the Department's doorstep.

The scope of this tragedy was measured in 1907 by Dr. P.H. Bryce, then the "Medical Inspector to the Department of the Interior and Indian Affairs." He had been appointed to that position in 1904 after a career in public health with the Ontario government. In February 1907, the Deputy Superintendent, F. Pedley, directed him to inspect the schools in the west, reporting particularly on "the sanitary conditions at each of these schools."[24] After visiting thirty-five schools, he submitted his report in November. It was printed and distributed to members of Parliament and to the churches.

[...]

The impact of the report lay not in his narrative of the disease nor in its scientific tone. It was the statistical profile of the extent of the white plague among the children that projected the stunning gravity of his findings.[25] It was the stuff of headlines. The *Ottawa Citizen* on 16 November ran its story of the report under the banner: "Schools Aid White Plague—Startling Death Rolls Revealed among Indians—Absolute Inattention to Bare Necessities of Health."

The article published by *Saturday Night* on the twenty-third of that same month screamed just as loudly. The report should "startle the country" and "compel the attention of Parliament....Indian boys and girls are dying like flies in these situations or shortly after leaving them....Even war seldom shows as large a percentage of fatalities as does the education system we have imposed on our Indian wards." It revealed "a situation disgraceful to the country."[26]

Bryce's statistics were based upon questionnaires that he distributed to all thirty-five schools eliciting the health history of the children who were then, or had been, in the schools. He received only fifteen replies, all from boarding schools founded between 1888 and 1905. Nevertheless, he was convinced that he had "valuable information and food for thought." The information related to the history of 1,537 children. Of these, twenty-four percent had died. Invariably, the cause of death is given as "consumption or tuberculosis," and just as regularly, whenever an answer was given to the question "Condition of the child on entry?," it is "given as good."

The situation was even worse, however, than his initial calculations suggested. The death rate inevitably moved beyond the twenty-four percent mark. Close analysis by Bryce of some of the returns revealed "an intimate relationship between the health of the pupils while in the school and their early death subsequent to discharge." For example, of the thirty-one pupils who had been discharged from the File Hills Boarding School, fifteen left in coffins. An additional seven died from within a few months to three years after returning home. In total, seventy-five percent of those on the discharge roll were actually dead. When the File Hills ratios are applied to Bryce's sample of 1,537 children, it results in an increase from twenty-four percent to forty-two percent as the percentage of those children who died from their school experience. Assuming that these ratios were constant, and projecting them throughout the system in 1907, when there were 3,755 students in the schools, would mean that some 1,614 of those children would die prematurely. And every year more children came into the schools and more became infected.[27]

[...]

With the *Bryce Report* in hand and corroborative comments from local agents, it is not surprising that the Church and Department negotiations turned to the question of the tuberculosis epidemic in the negotiations that took place between 1908 and 1910. In fact, the *Report* had carried recommendations for the reform of the school system. These urged the government to press on with residential education with the stress on reserve-based boarding schools, to place the management of the schools wholly in Departmental hands, relegating the churches to an advisory capacity, and to insure that "the health interests of the pupils be guarded by a proper medical inspection and that the local physicians be encouraged through the provision at each school of fresh air methods in the care and treatment of cases of tuberculosis."[28] Bryce's recommendation of "fresh air methods" was shorthand for sanatoria. This would have been a very expensive approach to the problem necessitating considerable remodelling of buildings and high levels of medical staffing.[29]

Not surprisingly, perhaps, the contract took a different approach,[30] with regulations aimed at improving the medical screening of children entering the schools, ending overcrowding and suggested revisions to the funding system to facilitate better maintenance and improvements in the vital areas of ventilation, health and sanitation. That focus was laid out in a memorandum of agreement sent by the Departmental Secretary, J.D. McLean, to the church representatives who had met with Oliver in November 1910. The contract embodied the conditions upon which the increased grant was to be paid.

"Those conditions require that the school buildings shall be sanitary and that the school management shall be such as to conduce to the physical, moral and mental well-being of the children." The revised per-capita rates were designed to assist in that.

[...]

Unfortunately, the concern for the children reflected in the contract did not give any priority to the improvement of the condition of the schools. By the end of the First World War, it was "business as usual," business as it had been since the 1880s. In 1918, Duncan Campbell Scott briefed the Superintendent General, Arthur Meighen, on the state of Indian education. He reviewed the contract system, pointing out that one of its central purposes had been to deal with the "inadequate" buildings, which "were unsanitary and ... were undoubtedly chargeable with a very high death rate among the pupils." For a few years after 1911, "until the outbreak of the war," the Department, he continued, "had been able to do its share" toward improving conditions. Then, "as the war continued[,] all new projects were abandoned."[31]

While the Department was able to hold the line on per-capita rates, and even managed a $10 advance in 1917, it lost ground in its attempt to fund improvements in the physical condition of the schools. Increasingly, the "circle of civilized conditions" was a crumbling edifice. If it had been Blake who briefed Meighen in 1918, he may well have added to Scott's commentary a sobering reflection; because the Department was still, a decade later, "doing nothing to obviate the preventable causes of death," it continued to be "within the unpleasant nearness to the charge of manslaughter."[32]

[...]

The Department, too, had it within its power to make a greater effort, if not through improved funding, at least through its authority. It could have insisted that its officials carry out inspections and that the churches follow regulations directed to the care of the children. It did not do so. The Departmental watch dog was far from vigilant; it rarely barked and, despite the conditions over which Bryce, Paget, Corbett, local doctors, and even senior Departmental officials had shaken their heads,[33] it certainly did not bite. Grants were not withdrawn, schools were not forced to close or principals to resign. The Orders-in-Council of 1892 and 1894 and the contracts of

1911 were in fact administrative fictions. They constituted powers, authorities, and agreements that did not facilitate effective, efficient, or even what seemed the most constant, goal—economical management.

The reality was that, from the moment the school system was launched in the 1880s and 1890s, it drifted without a firm hand, without concerted intervention. And this was despite the knowledge that many children were held in dangerous circumstances and that the death rate was not only of tragic proportions but was, in addition, undercutting the whole purpose and strategy of the system. Many, many children—perhaps as high as fifty percent according to Scott's estimate—would not "attain maturity and be able to exercise any civilizing influence" in their communities.[34]

A significant cause of this lay with personnel in the Department and in the churches involved directly in the management of the system. These many men and women failed to act decisively in the face of the suffering and death of so many children. They were not alone, however. They were joined in complicity and insensitivity by non-Aboriginal society as a whole. The devastation that the white plague brought to the children in the schools and through their deaths to their parents and communities drew out the fundamental contradiction between the persistent cruelty of the system and the discourse of duty, of the "sacred trust with which Providence has invested the country in the charge of and care for the aborigines committed to it."[35]

It was a contradiction that the country was not prepared to face, and did not in fact face, throughout the rest of this period to 1946. The editor of *Saturday Night* seemed to sense this contradiction from the very moment of the publication of the 1907 *Bryce Report*:

> His report is printed, many people will scan the title on the cover, some will open it, a few will read it and so the thing will drift along another year. And so with the next year and the year after. So will be the course of events…unless public opinion takes the question up and forces it to the front. Then Parliament will show a quick interest, pigeon holes will give up their dusty contents, medical officers will have a wealth of suggestions and the scandalous procession

of Indian children to school and on to the cemetery may possibly be stopped.[36]

Of course, none of those conditions was fulfilled. There was no "public opinion," Parliament showed no interest, quick or otherwise, and the children continued to go to the schools and to the schools' cemeteries, as Bryce's pamphlet in 1922 revealed.

In 1922, the issue of Aboriginal people had long since been swept into the darker reaches of national consciousness. The deaths, and the condition of the schools pricked no collective conscience, wrought no revolution in policy, or even any significant reformulation. Sir George Murray's comment in 1830 about the old Imperial policy was just as true nearly one century later. This federal policy "was persisted in…as a matter of routine, [rather] than upon any considered grounds of preference."[37] There was no reconsideration, no second thoughts, no questioning of the assumptions of assimilation or of residential schools as an appropriate method of achieving that end. There appeared to be no thought or reaction at all.

The "routine" of residential education after the industrial school era, in the years after 1923 through to 1946, simply persisted. Unlike so many children, the school system survived the tubercular infection. It even grew, if more slowly than in the initial decades in the life of the system. In 1923, there were seventy-two residential schools. That number grew to a high of eighty in 1931.[38] The number then gradually fell through closures, many because of fires, to seventy-five in 1943.

The much slower rate of growth after the First World War did not indicate any waning in the enthusiasm for expansion. Churches continued to push to open schools in the few remaining untapped educational areas.[39] There were simply not that many areas left. Departmental cooperation continued. Scott, himself, led the way in moving the system into one of those areas—the east, Quebec, and Nova Scotia. The first school commissioned in Quebec was the Anglican Fort George School followed by Fort George Roman Catholic School, and in Nova Scotia the first and only school was the Roman Catholic Shubenacadie School. Scott was particularly dedicated to this latter project: "When we have this school established," he wrote to the Catholic church in 1926, sounding more like Vankoughnet than himself, "one of the desires of my official life will have been accomplished."[40]

As well as there being but limited horizons by the 1920s, finance continued to be a restraint and a detrimental factor in the condition of existing schools. Wartime reductions, which had blighted the program of improvements of 1911, ushered in yet another era of underfunding. Initially after the war, there were advances in the level of per capitas. A $10 increase was authorized in 1919.[41] Other increases followed in 1921, 1924, 1926, and 1931, moving the average per capita to $172.[42] These increases were never enough, however, to satisfy the churches' appetites for government funds nor to prevent them from again "encountering huge deficits."[43]

With the Depression, the situation got worse because, as the minister responsible for Indian Affairs, T.G. Murphy, phrased it, the "financial condition of the country [was] such that economies" were then "imposed on" the government.[44] In 1932, it was "found necessary ... to make a flat decrease in per capita grants." Other cuts followed.[45] In 1938, the Committee of Churches Cooperating with the Department of Indian Affairs calculated that between 1932 and 1938 the reductions amounted to a $840,000 loss to the churches.[46]

The Department put the best public face on the situation.[47] Privately, senior staff knew that the per-capita average, claimed to be still about $180 in 1938, was "exceptionally low" and inadequate particularly in relation to the funding available to other residential child-care facilities. R. Hoey, the Department's Superintendent of Welfare and Training, supplied H. McGill, the Director of Indian Affairs, with revealing comparative figures. The government of Manitoba provided per-capita grants of $642 and $550 respectively to the Manitoba School for the Deaf and the School for Boys. Private institutions in that Province were also more generously funded. The Knowles School for Boys in North Kildonan was sponsored by the Community Chest at $362 per boy. The Catholic Church provided St. Norbert's Orphanage with $294 and St. Joseph's Orphanage with a $320 per-capita grant. Finally, an international comparison was not in the Department's favour either. The child Welfare League of America estimated that the average per-capita grant in the United States of large child-care institutions was $541, with the smaller ones running only as low as $313.[48]

The Second World War pulled the country out of the deep economic trough of the Depression, but it brought no benefits to the school system. Wartime military expenditures meant reductions "to almost every appropriation"[49] for the Department and a building freeze. In the face of this, Hoey realized that it would be "exceedingly difficult to secure the funds necessary ...at any time during the years that [lay] immediately ahead."[50]

The persistence of underfunding undercut the maintenance and repair of buildings. Under the terms of the 1911 contracts, the Department had been charged with that expense, and, even after the contracts lapsed, it agreed to continue.[51] Indeed, in the relatively optimistic days following the First World War, the policy of the Department was to buy up the church schools and then to be responsible for all capital costs including repairs and new construction.[52] Scott went so far as to propose that the cost of purchasing all the church-owned schools be placed in the supplementary estimates in order that the whole matter "may receive the careful consideration of the government."[53] This would have meant acquiring forty-three of the seventy-five schools then operating in 1922.

The Department's promise and Scott's proposal remained good intentions only. In the early years of the Depression, expenditures (combining the per-capita grants and capital funds) fell from an average of $28,000 per school to $16,000.

By the Second World War, the Department was so far behind that Hoey and P. Phelan, Chief of the Training Division, estimated that they had less than half the funds necessary to meet repair commitments.[54] McGill admitted, in fact, that they had "been experiencing for the [previous] 10 or 12 years the utmost difficulty in securing the funds necessary to keep [the] schools in a state of repair."[55] They were not, he concluded, being maintained "in a reasonable state."[56]

As in the industrial school era, the net result of underfunding could be seen both in the condition of the schools and in the care given to the children. The building stock was in poor shape at the outset. A Departmental survey in 1922 concluded that of the seventy-five schools the great majority were not "modern up to date buildings in good condition," nor were they "adequate for the purpose of Indian education." A smaller number were condemned as "dilapidated and inadequate."[57]

Needless to say, the condition of the system was not improved by the reductions in funding in the 1930s and the wartime freeze. In 1931, one of the system's flagship schools, Shingwauk, was condemned.[58] Long lists of repairs from every corner of the system were submitted and ignored, as were pleas for urgent assistance.[59]

Bad and badly maintained buildings continued to translate into bad health.[60] However, the extent of the tuberculosis problem in the schools in the 1930s and 1940s is hard to assess. There were no reports of the scope or calibre of the Bryce or Corbett reports. Routine agents' reports, which are the most common documentation, are of limited value because agents were not trained medical observers. In many cases, however, the condition of the children was sorrowfully obvious even to such amateurs.[61]

It was obvious, too, from those reports that the Department's administrative system regarding health certificates was still far from watertight. Dr. C. Pitts, who attended the children at Lejac School in British Columbia, certainly held that position. He had special knowledge of the school system because his father was a long-serving principal, and he had friends who were school doctors. He went so far, in 1935, as to suggest that the regulations were a farce and their enforcement a practical impossibility: "As for the general medical examination...this is not done in any other school that I have any knowledge of....Where is the point of this [examination], when I know that were I to apply the standards of health to them that is applied to children of the white schools that I should have to discharge 90% of them and there would be no school left."[62]

An equally serious impediment to any attempt to care for the health of the children was the inability of the Department to acquire funds to underwrite attacks on tuberculosis in the schools. Only at the end of the 1930s did funding for sanatoria treatment appear, and that was largely owing to pressure from the Canadian Tuberculosis Association. No special funds were set aside especially for the schools, however.[63]

The 1920s, 1930s, and 1940s had more in common with the previous Industrial era than underfunding, the woeful condition of the buildings, and the infection and death of children from tuberculosis. Connected to each of these issues, nested in reports on them, is another persistence: abundant evidence of the failure of the churches and the Department to adequately parent these children, to operate institutions that were above reproach as homes and as schools. In part, this was again due to the issue of finance. Whenever correspondence turned to the per capitas or maintenance funds, someone was bound to point out that this affected the children, that it would "render almost superhuman the task of feeding, clothing and treating the children in the manner required by the Department."[64] And there were numerous reports from schools confirming this. Principals were forced to meet budget shortfalls, as the Principal of Christie School in British Columbia, Victor Rassier, O.S.B., had had to do, "by economizing to the bone in every department."[65] And Agent J. Smith at Kamloops School stated: "If the children are to be kept they ought to be reasonably clothed and fed, and this is utterly impossible to do from the present per capita grant."[66]

But the failure to care properly for the children was rooted in more than the issue of funding, and in more than just the difficulties of building and managing the system. The "manner required by the Department [for] feeding clothing and treating the children,"[67] a standard of care, was both an ill-defined and a rarely achieved goal. Bryce, Paget, and Corbett stand as witnesses to the inherent structural flaws in the system. The Reverend Thompson Ferrier comes forward to add to their witness the human failings and the resultant suffering of the children who were neglected by Departmental-church "parents," cruel or incompetent, who presumed that they should and could supplant the childrens' natural Aboriginal parents but who did not consistently carry out their parenting responsibilities.

In July 1925, just three years after Bryce's *Story of a National Crime* was published, Ferrier, who had then been in charge of Methodist industrial and boarding schools and hospitals for twenty-five years, set down on paper his memory of a cross-country tour of those schools when he first took up his position. Only Coqualeetza School in British Columbia was, in his opinion, in good order. The others were not circles of civilized conditions:

Mount Elgin Institute at Muncey looms up in memory with its untidy yard and a lot of old sheds, outbuildings and dilapidated barns that had passed their day all unconscious of their need of repairs and paint. The main building had accommodation for about one hundred pupils who were receiving such harsh treatment as to call forth numerous complaints from the Indian people and the Indian department. Several attempts were made on the part of the pupils to burn up the whole business all because it was under the management of a man who had the idea that physical strength was to take the place of what ought to be done by the heart and head in educating and training young life, who believed that it was safer to deal with the hide than the honour of the pupil and a man who took more interest in hydraulics than hygiene.

When Ferrier got to Brandon, he found ninety children who seemed to have the upper hand. They were "destructive, untrained young men and women from thirteen to twenty-three years of age. They were having their own way, smashing everything they could not eat or wear and running roughshod over a discouraged staff. It looked as though the institution had fallen into a pit and was waiting for someone to come and give it a decent burial."

At Norway House, they had a poor barn shaped building with broken doors, worn out floors, no modern conveniences of plumbing, heating or lighting, a cold shell of a place with partial accommodation for about thirty-five pupils who were obliged to live without a balanced ration as there was no garden, poultry or stock. An incompetent staff were trying to penetrate the stronghold of heathenism with the belief that the problem would never be solved. Red Deer was no better. The school comprised a miserable lot of buildings, the boys home being very dark and unsanitary. There was a stable for horses but none for stock. The management was unconscious of the great possibilities of the rich fertile land of the farm and the opportunity presented as a training school for farmers and stockmen. For many reasons the whole institution was very unpopular with the Indian people of Alberta. The office appeared to be used more for a real estate business than to make a contribution toward civilizing and educating the people.

Finally, Ferrier went to the west coast and to Port Simpson, where they "had twenty boys housed in a building and under a management that was a disgrace to the Methodist church."[68]

As had been the case with all the previous reports (Bryce's, Paget's, and Corbett's), none of the conditions described by Ferrier was news to the Department or the churches. They already had a flood of evidence, a spate that continued through to and beyond 1946, that indicated that in too many cases the children were not being adequately fed, clothed, or taught and that discipline often crossed the line into abuse. The vision of life and learning in the "circle of civilized conditions" had not become a reality. The promise that children would receive the "care of a mother"[69] and an education that would elevate the child "to a status equal to that of his white brother" remained unfulfilled.[70]

Notes

1. Anglican Archives, MSCC, Series 2-14, Special Indian Committee, 1905–1910, S.H. Blake to the Hon. Frank Oliver, Minister of the Interior, Sunday Morning, 27 January 1907, printed in *To the Members of the Board of Management of the Missionary Society of the Church of England in Canada*, by The Hon. S.H. Blake, K.C., 21.

2. Given the incomplete state of student records in the school files, it is impossible to arrive at the number of deaths from disease in the schools in any year or decade. Later in the chapter, a sense of how "appalling" the number was is given through percentages supplied in large part by Dr. Bryce. In light of the anecdotal evidence, Bryce's figures seem to have been supported generally by Departmental staff and to have applied nation-wide.

3. There is no statistical base for determining the number of children who died from disease in the schools. The Bryce Report of 1907 gives some indication of death rates when tuberculosis was most rampant (N.A.C. RG10, Vol. 4037, File 317021, MR C 10177, P. Bryce. Report on the Indian Schools of Manitoba and the Northwest Territories, Ottawa, Government Printing Bureau, 1907).

4. N.A.C. RG 10, Vol. 6305, File 652-1, MR C 8682, Agent MacArthur to Secretary, 27 December 1910. To be fair, some children came to school already infected, having contracted the disease in

over-crowded and squalid living conditions in their reserve homes.

5. N.A.C. RG 10. Vol. 3920, File 116818, MR C 10161, Dr. J.P. Rice to C. Sifton, 3 August 1903: M. Benson to Deputy Superintendent General of Indian Affairs, 9 September 1903.

6. N.A.C. RG 10, Vol. 7185, File 1/25-1-7-1, D.C. Scott to Hon. Charles Stewart, 31 October 1927.

7. N.A.C. RG 10, Vol. 4037, File 317021, MR C 10177, D. Laird to Secretary of Indian Affairs, 7 December 1907.

8. N.A.C. RG 10, Vol. 7185, File 1/25-1-7-1, D.C. Scott to Hon. Charles Stewart, 31 October 1927.

9. N.A.C. RG 10, Vol. 3836, File 68557, MR C 10146, H. Reed, Suggestions for the Government of Indian Schools, 27 January 1890.

10. N.A.C. RG 10, Vol. 6467, File 889-1 (1-2), MR C 8785, C. Perry to Dr. H. McGill, 25 May 1900. The Squamish school was a case in point. It was built by the Catholic missionary and funded in 1900 after a direct appeal to Clifford Sifton by the local member of Parliament and the Catholic bishop. It was, when inspected by the Assistant Indian Commissioner of British Columbia, C. Perry, shortly after its opening, in such ramshackle condition that Perry thought it should be closed immediately.

11. N.A.C. RG 10, Vol. 6039, File 160-1, MR C 8152, M. Benson to J.D. McLean, 15 July 1897.

12. N.A.C. RG 10, Vol. 3674, File 11422, MR C 10118, E. Dewdney to Father Lacombe, 22 July 1883; and E. Dewdney to Superintendent General of Indian Affairs, 16 April 1883.

13. N.A.C. RG 10, Vol. 4041, File 334503, MR C 10178, E.H. Paget to F. Pedley, 25 November 1908.

14. Bryce, *The Story of a National Crime*, 11. The Canadian Tuberculosis Association circulated figures that detailed the percentage of Aboriginal tuberculosis deaths by province compared to their percentage of the population. In Manitoba, of the total deaths, forty-one percent were Aboriginal, though Aboriginal people made up only 2.2 percent of the population; in Saskatchewan it was twenty-seven percent of the deaths and 1.6 percent of the population; in Alberta it was thirty-four percent of the deaths and 2.1 percent of the population; and in British Columbia it was thirty-five percent of the deaths and 3.7 percent of the population (Wherrit, *The Miracle of Empty Beds*, 110).

15. Bryce, *The Story of a National Crime*, 11.

16. Wherrit, *The Miracle of Empty Beds*, 16–17; and N.A.C. RG 10, Vol. 6462, File 888-1 (2-3, 6-7), MR C8781, Rev. A. Lett to D.C. Scott, 6 March 1922.

17. Wherrit, *The Miracle of Empty Beds*, 16-17 and 100-103.

18. N.A.C. RG 10, Vol. 6348, File 752-1, MR C 8705, D.C. Scott to Deputy Superintendent General of Indian Affairs, 23 April 1909.

19. N.A.C. RG 10, Vol. 3937, File 120048-1, MR C 10164, Bishop of Caledonia, to A. Vowell, 11 November 1907.

20. See, for example, N.A.C. RG 10, Vol. 6210, File 469-1 (1-3), MR C 7941, Deputy Superintendent General of Indian Affairs to J. Lawlor, 8 November 1894.

21. N.A.C. RG 10, Vol. 1543 [no file number], MR C 14839, J.D. McLean to R. Wilson, 2 October 1909; and D. Laird to R. Wilson, 7 March 1911 (Application for Admission attached).

22. N.A.C. RG 10, Vol. 6015, File 1-1-13. MR C 8141, D.C. Scott to W. Graham, 16 February 1925.

23. See, for example, the explanation from a field official citing the lack of doctors in remote areas as the reason for non-compliance with the medical regulations: N.A.C. RG 10, Vol. 6015, File 1-1-13, MR C 8141, Acting Agent to R. Ferrier, 9 March 1925.

24. N.A.C. RG 10, Vol. 4037, File 317021, MR C 10177, Deputy Superintendent General of Indian Affairs to J.D. McLean, 14 February 1907.

25. N.A.C. RG 10, Vol. 4037, File 317021, MR C 10177, P. Bryce, *Report on the Indian Schools,* 1907, 17–19.

26. N.A.C. RG 10, Vol. 4037, File 317021, MR C 10177. Copies of stories in the *Citizen*, 16 November 1907, and *Saturday Night*, 23 November 1907, as well as the *Montreal Star*, 15 November 1907, are in this file.

27. N.A.C. RG 10, Vol. 4037, File 317021, MR C 10177, P. Bryce, *Report on the Indian Schools*, 1907, 17–20.

28. Bryce, *The Story of a National Crime*, 4.

29. N.A.C. RG 10, Vol. 6039, File 160-1, MR C 8152, Bishop of St. Boniface et al. to R. Rogers, 24 November 1911 and 15 November 1912. Bryce's recommendations may also have been sidelined in the negotiations by political considerations. The Catholic church was opposed to many of the reforms—Bryce's and even some of those eventually included in the contracts. The schools, the church charged, were being "submitted to vexatious requirements by physicians, whose interests therein appear to have been in large measure confined to making unnecessary demands."

30. For further details on the government's approach, see N.A.C. RG 10, Vol. 6039, File 160-1, MR C 8152, F. Oliver to Reverend and Dear Sirs, 21 March 1908. See particularly Oliver's discussion of Winnipeg Resolution No. 7.

31. N.A.C. RG 10, Vol. 6001, File 1-1-1 (1), MR C 8134, D.C. Scott to A. Meighen, n.d. January 1918. The effect of the war on expenditures was dramatic. In 1914, the Department spent on average $8,684 on each boarding school and $16,146 on each of the remaining industrial schools. In 1918, those figures had fallen to $5,738 and $12,338 respectively. Total expenditures for the system fell by thirty-three percent from $811,764 to $542,568.

32. Anglican Archives, MSCC, Series 2-14, Special Indian Committee, 1905–1910, S.H. Blake to the Honourable Frank Oliver, Minister of the Interior, Sunday Morning, 27 January 1907, printed in To the Members of the Board of Management of the Missionary Society of the Church of England in Canada, by The Hon. S.H. Blake, K.C., 21.

33. See, for example, correspondence on the Chapleau School: N.A.C. RG 10, Vol. 6191, File 462-1, MR C 7926, J.D. McLean to Rev. J. Anderson, 29 December 1914; Extract of Inspection Report by W. Hamilton, 3 May 1915; and J. Sheahan, M.D., to J.D. McLean, 2 July 1917. See also the correspondence relating to St. Cyprians: N.A.C. RG 10, Vol. 6368, File 763-1, MR C 8720, Assistant Deputy and Secretary to E. Yoemans, n.d. 1911; S. Stewart to Archdeacon J. Tims, n.d. 1911; J.D. McLean to Archdeacon J. Tims, 22 January 1913; J.D. McLean to Archdeacon J. Tims, 15 February 1913; J.D. McLean to A. Gunn, 15 February 1914; and W. Graham to Secretary, 21 July 1925.

34. N.A.C. RG 10, Vol. 6348, File 752-1, MR C 8705, D.C. Scott to Deputy Superintendent General of Indian Affairs, 23 April 1909.

35. *Annual Report* 1891, x.

36. N.A.C. RG 10, Vol. 4037, File 317021, *Saturday Night*, 23 November 1907.

37. N.A.C. C.O. 42/27, G. Murray to J. Kempt (No. 95), 25 January 1830.

38. There was then one school in Nova Scotia, thirteen in Ontario, ten in Manitoba, fourteen in Saskatchewan, twenty in Alberta, sixteen in British Columbia, four in the Northwest Territories, two in the Yukon, and plans for two schools in Quebec.

39. See, for example, N.A.C. RG 10, Vol. 6040, File 160-3A, Part 1, MR C 8153, Rev. T. Ferrier to D.C. Scott, 8 July 1920.

40. N.A.C. RG 10, Vol. 6041, File 160-5, Part 1, D.C. Scott to J. Guy, 11 July 1926. See Appendix, p. 307 herein, for school list, 1931.

41. N.A.C. RG 10, Vol. 6039, File 160-1, MR C 8152, J.D. McLean to Sir James Lougheed, 24 August 1920.

42. N.A.C. RG 10, Vol. 6040, File 160-3, Part 1, MR C 8153, Rev. T. Ferrier to D.C. Scott, 6 December 1921; and Vol. 7185, File 1/25-1-7-1, R.T. Ferrier, Superintendent of Eduacation, Memorandum to File, 5 April 1932.

43. N.A.C. RG 10, Vol. 6040, File 160-3A, Part 1, MR C 8153, Joint Church Delegation to Minister of the Interior, 7 January 1921; Canon S. Gould to D.C. Scott, 23 September 1924; D.C. Scott to C. Stewart, 7 March 1927; and Memorandum to File, 8 February 1926.

44. N.A.C. RG 10, Vol. 6730, File 160-2 (1-3), MR C 8092, T.G. Murphy to Canon S. Gould, 26 April 1931.

45. N.A.C. RG 10, Vol. 7185, File 1/25-7-1, R.T. Ferrier, Memorandum to File, 5 April 1932; and N.A.C. RG 10, Vol. 6041, File 160-5 Part 1, MR C 8153, H. McGill to Rev. J. Scannell, O.M.I., 17 February 1936; and Vol. 7185, File 1/25-1-7-1, Deputy Superintendent General of Indian Affairs, Circular, 26 March 1936.

46. United Church Archives, WMS Fonds, Accession 83.058C, File 3, Memorandum of the Committee of Churches Cooperating with the Department of Indian Affairs in Indian Education, 8 February 1938.

47. N.A.C. RG 10, Vol. 7185, File 1/25-1-7-1. R. Hoey to H. McGill, 4 November 1938.

48. N.A.C. RG 10, Vol. 7185, File 1/25-1-7-1, R. Hoey to H. McGill, 4 November 1938. Hoey provided additional figures that were equally depressing. The Children's Aid Society of Alberta estimated that the minimum per-day maintenance cost for a neglected child was $1. The Ontario figure was slightly lower at seventy-five cents, Manitoba was between sixty-three and seventy-two cents, B.C. was at fifty-seven cents and Saskatchewan was at fifty cents. This worked out to an average of seventy cents. The Department's national average, using its $180 figure, was forty-nine cents, and it was supposed to cover more than just food and clothes.

49. N.A.C. RG 10, Vol. 6041, File 160-5, Part 1, MR C 8153, R. Hoey to Rev. J. Plourde, 15 October 1940.

50. N.A.C. RG 10, Vol. 6730, File 160-2 (1-3), MR C 8092, Director of Indian Affairs to Rev. T. Westgate, n.d. 1940.

51. N.A.C. RG 10, Vol. 6041, File 160-5, Part 1, MR C 8153, D.C. Scott to Charles Stewart, 7 March 1922.

52. N.A.C. RG 10, Vol. 6039, File 160-1, MR C 8152, R.F. Ferrier, Memornadum—Impression of the Interview between Church Representatives and the Superintendent General, 13 April 1922.

53. N.A.C. RG 10, Vol. 6041, File 160-5, Part 1, MR C 8153, D.C. Scott to Charles Stewart, 7 March 1922.

54. N.A.C. RG 10, Vol. 6479, File 940-1 (1-2), MR C 8794, R. Hoey to H. McGill, 16 November 1942.

55. N.A.C. RG 10, Vol. 6479, File 940-1 (1-2), H. McGill to Rev. W. Geddes, 21 November 1942.

56. N.A.C. RG 10, Vol. 6482, File 941-2, MR C 8796, H. McGill to Rev. J. Plourde, 15 February 1940.

57. N.A.C. RG 10, Vol. 6039, File 160-1, MR C 8152, R.F. Ferrier to Charles Stewart 12 May 1922.

58. N.A.C. RG 10, Vol. 6730, File 160-2 (1-3), MR C 8092, Rev. T. Westgate to Secretary, 29 October 1931. It did not, however, close.

59. See, for example, the plight of the Catholic Sturgeon Lake School in: N.A.C. RG 10, Vol. 6041, File 160-5, Part 1, MR C 8153, Bishop J. Guy to Secretary of Indian Affairs, 10 October 1936; and R. Hoey to Father Plourde, 16 October 1940.

60. See, for example, the reports in 1927 from Dr. P. Wilson and C. Perry on St. George's, Lytton, in which overcrowding and defective plumbing, ventilation, and sanitation are charged with the death of thirteen children from mumps and influenza (N.A.C. RG 10, Vol. 6462, File 888-1 (2-3, 6-7), MR C 8781, Dr. P. Wilson to H. Graham, 23 February 1927; and C. Perry to Secretary, 6 May 1927).

61. N.A.C. RG 10, Vol. 6452, File 884-1 (1-3), MR C 8773-8774, Extracts of a Report by C. Perry attached to W. Ditchburn, 16 June 1930.

62. N.A.C. RG 10, Vol. 6443, File 881-1 (1-3), MR C 8767, C. Pitts, M.D., to R.H. Moore, 22 October 1935.

63. See: Wherrit, *The Miracle of Empty Beds*, 107 and 111–14, for a discussion of these events; and INAC File 961/23-5, Vol. 1, G.H. Berry to Major D.M. Mackay. This Inspection Report notes the opinion of Dr. R.N. Dick, who claimed that the children's health, at Kuper Island School, was threatened by budget restrictions.

64. N.A.C. RG 10, Vol. 6041, File 160-5, Part 1, MR C 8153, Rev. U. Langlois, O.M.I., to H. McGill, 28 April 1936.

65. INAC File 951/23-5, Vol. 1, V. Rassier, O.S.B., to The Secretary, 15 April 1934.

66. N.A.C. RG 10, Vol. 3918, File 116659-1, MR C 10161, J. Smith to Assistant Deputy and Secretary, 8 February 1918. For additional examples see: N.A.C. RG 10, Vol. 6327, File 660-1 (1-3), MR C 9807, M. Benson to Deputy Superintendent General of Indian Affairs, 23 December 1903; and N.A.C. RG 10, Vol. 6205, File 468-1 (1-3), MR C 7937, M. Benson to Deputy Superintendent General of Indian Affairs, 26 November 1902.

67. N.A.C. RG 10, Vol. 6041, File 160-5 Part 1, MR C 8153, Rev. U. Langlois, O.M.I., to H. McGill, 28 April 1936.

68. N.A.C. RG 10, Vol. 6040, File 160-3A, Part 1, MR C 8153, Rev. T. Ferrier to C.E. Manning, 1 July 1925.

69. *The Davin Report*, 12.

70. INAC File 1/25-1, Vol. 15, L. Vankoughnet to Sir John A. Macdonald, 26 August 1887.

■ Article 3: You Ain't My Boss: [1] Resistance

J.R. Miller

My grandmother was very, very upset. I distinctly recall the third time—my final year at the Baptist Mission school—when these missionaries came again to take me away, I was at that time living with my grandmother and my aunt ... who was a blind person. They in a sense were my immediate family ... When these missionaries came to the door and they said, 'Well, we have permission to take [named deleted] to this Whitehorse Baptist Mission school,' and they came to physically take me out of my home, I hung on to my grandmother's legs. I was crying, of course, and my grandmother was very angry. She was quite old—in her sixties, probably. I remember her taking her tut as we called it, walking cane—and beating this missionary, this white missionary over the backside, and saying, 'You leave my grandson alone. You are not taking him anywhere.' And my aunt Pat came out— and she was blind then, too—and saying the same thing, supporting her mother. And saying that you cannot take this child from this home no matter what permission you have. They didn't produce any written document at the time ...

My grandmother stood by me, and she was able to drive these white missionaries out of our home. And they finally left in defeat. And this is one Indian child who didn't get to go to the Whitehorse Baptist Mission school forever after.[2]

It is hardly surprising that the excesses that occurred in many residential schools provoked protest and resistance, from both parents and students. In due course, the same grievances would lead to collective recriminations and pressure for change that were transmitted through Indian political organizations. During the first six decades of the modern residential school system, however, opportunities to combine voices of protest were usually limited to the family or the band in the case of adults, and to the level of

a dormitory among the student body. Though limited in scope for a long time, the forms that Native resistance took were surprisingly numerous. Among parents and family friends the reactions ranged from complaints, to withholding of cooperation, to violent retribution, to defiance of the underlying assimilative thrust of Indian Affairs policy. Within the ranks of the students themselves, there was a similarly large number of ways in which children and young adults could make their objections known. They could and did complain loudly to their families; they could disturb the schools' routine with behaviour that ranged from a lack of cooperation to outright disruption. When pushed too far to be satisfied by these modest responses, they had available more serious sanctions, such as desertion and destruction. Residential school children and parents protested and resisted in many ways.

The effectiveness of both students' and parents' protests depended on a series of particular, often local, circumstances. Headquarters staff of both government and the missionary organizations were usually inclined to discount complaints from Natives themselves. A Presbyterian group that visited a number of schools in Manitoba and Saskatchewan in 1913 reported dismissively that the complaints about the troubled Crowstand school on the Cote reserve near Kamsack were 'of a stereotype character' and tiresomely familiar.[3] Bureaucrats in the secular realm were usually even less inclined to pay attention to Natives' complaints than were those in the ecclesiastical. However, there were a series of circumstances that could force either or both to be more responsive. A principal who was already under a cloud with his superiors sometimes found it desirable to counteract, if not always to accede to, Indians' complaints. The Indian Affairs department was more inclined to seek a solution to protests if its officials were convinced that ignoring the objections would lead to political complications for which their elected masters might hold them responsible. Missionary bureaucrats were often anxious to conciliate parental opinion in situations where their schools were in competition with institutions of another denomination. Denominational rivalry was an especially sharp goad to action where the competition was between a Roman Catholic and a non-Catholic school. There were few threats more effective than removal of one's children from their school.

Source: J.R. Miller, *Shingwauk's Vision: A History of Native Residential Schools.* Toronto: University of Toronto Press, 1996, pp. 343–374. © University of Toronto Press Inc., 1996. Reprinted with permission from the publisher.

These factors sometimes created circumstances in which protests from parents could have limited effect. Such situations at times allowed Native communities and families to influence, if not control, the way in which individual schools treated their children. What emerges from a survey of the interaction of both schoolchildren and their adult communities is a picture not simply of authority and submission, but of a subtle and shifting interplay of forces. Influence and power could in some instances flow in favour of the Aboriginal constituency, in spite of the apparent dominance of government and church. Although too much should not be made of this phenomenon—it would be misleading to suggest, for example, that Native groups were able to force schools to operate as they wished—it is important to understand that protests and resistance could and did have some effect.

The simplest form of parental protest was a complaint lodged with either a missionary or an official of the Indian Affairs department. The Anglican bishop of Caledonia, for example, reported to Ottawa as follows: "'My child might as well be dead" said one mother bitterly when she found she could not get her child back for eight years.' That was one argument the cleric used to support the government's proposal to place more emphasis on day schools at the expense of industrial schools during the first decade of the century.[4] Complaints about the Anglican T.E. Clarke, principal at Battleford, led the Indian commissioner to dispatch the Department of Indian Affairs inspector to investigate, although dismissal of the principal in this instance did not come for another two years.[5] The Ojibwa whose children attended Wikwemikong in the 1890s proved unable to get the government official to force the missionaries to do anything about their complaints concerning excessive instruction in catechism, though the inspector was prepared to act on a father's fear that it was 'dangerous and indecent for his girl to get on the swing.'[6] And when Mr and Mrs Badger took their objections about mistreatment of their children at the Anglican school at Onion Lake to the DIA, they did get the satisfaction of having the agent report to the Indian commissioner, who quickly issued orders that the overwork and 'the ear-twisting for punishment should be dropped, the latter absolutely.'[7]

Sometimes principals responded to parental criticism themselves, although not always with an eye to correcting the conditions that had given rise to the complaints. Missionary supervisors of schools were often more interested in counteracting public criticism than in resolving the difficulty. The beleaguered Principal Clarke of Battleford, anticipating criticism of his regime at the next diocesan synod and cognizant of the likelihood that Ahtahkakoop (Star Blanket) would attend as a delegate, went to considerable trouble to ensure that friends of his school and of the DIA would be in attendance to counter the critics.[8] Missionaries sometimes found that efforts to involve Native leaders in the deliberations of their organizations provided occasions for criticism, such as the time Chief Rattlesnake told the annual convention of Presbyterian workers in Manitoba and Saskatchewan that he 'wanted [the] children to be taught so that they could help the older Indians. Children [were] not learning fast enough.'[9] On the other hand, the principal of Lestock school interpreted 'a large and representative delegation' that objected to an anticipated cancellation of 'the monthly holiday' as proof that the sisters had blabbed to their charges, and complained to his superior in Ottawa.[10] Other forms of complaint that could have some effect were to the church superiors of those in charge of a school to which parents objected. Two Presbyterian worthies from head office in Toronto collected quite a number of objections to overwork, discipline, and inadequate care at several mission locations, including two boarding schools, on the west side of Vancouver Island.[11] Indians at Sandy Bay reserve in Manitoba forwarded their complaints about the Anglican Elkhorn school through the rural dean and the field secretary of the church's principal missionary organization.[12] And, finally, the disgruntled Ojibwa of Couchiching reserve near Fort Frances, Ontario, demanded a meeting with the Oblate provincial to pursue objections to the way the school in their region was being run.[13]

The aggrieved Couchiching band was engaging in another common form of protest against residential school conditions—the formal petition directed either to Indian Affairs or to church officials. Not all such petitions were critical; there were rare petitions in favour of missionaries. For example, the chief and head men of a band whose children attended the Crowstand school, where the principal had resigned because he could not secure adequate housing for his ailing wife, sent a message to the Presbyterian committee in Winnipeg asking 'that your resignation be not accepted and that a house be built for your accommodation.'[14] By far the majority of formal protests, however, criticized school leadership.

In this case, too, there was a familiar pattern of denial on the part of those who were accused of contravening the wishes of parents. A request that the principal of the Alberni school be removed in 1905 because he did not provide adequate supervision of the senior girls met a rejoinder that the letter came from 'the father of the only illegitimate child born of a girl in this Mission in recent years.'[15] Ojibwa in the Shoal Lake area of northwestern Ontario became quite expert in petitioning the Presbyterian officials about aspects of boarding-school administration to which they objected. In 1902 the leading men objected to the administration of the matron, who was perceived to be too strict, with the result that the woman tendered her resignation. She particularly objected to the fact that a contract between the Indians and her church limited what the missionaries could do and required that the children be 'well-treated.'[16] A few years later, the local Indian leadership had to protest again, this time against removal of the missionary who had tried to enforce their wishes in the operation of the school. Chief Red Sky threatened that if the Presbyterians removed this man, 'I will ask the Indian Agent to send the children to another school for we won't have them here at all.'[17] This threat proved unavailing, and the Indian parents found themselves petitioning against excessive corporal punishment the next year.[18]

[...]

A particular source of grievance to parents that might cause them to withhold their children was sickness and mortality at the schools. In northern Manitoba, Native people were 'dumb to entreaties' to send their children to the Methodists' Brandon or Norway House schools. 'Some years ago children were sent to Red Deer. Two have returned, two are at Brandon and will return this summer. The rest, the majority died. Seven were sent to Norway House this past summer. Two are already dead. These things completely knock the attempts re Brandon or Norway House in the head. They just sit right down on a fellow. And one must shut up because there is at least a degree of justice on their side.'[19] The most striking example of withholding children because of a school's bad reputation, particularly for health, was the Presbyterians' Regina school. Parents had

always had problems with the institution, and with its aggressive efforts to fill it with students. One mother even wrote another warning: 'You better bring here your children at once or they will be taken to Regina. They are taking children of[f] the Reserve to Regina. 19 children have been taken from the Reserves to the Regina School.'[20] Problems at the Regina school worsened steadily thanks to incompetent leadership and serious health problems that alienated parents from the institution. The trouble, noticeable early in the century, neared a crisis point towards the end of the decade.[21]

Regina's unhappy experience pointed up several aspects of residential school operations that gave parents at least a narrow area in which to protest effectively. First, when a school was located in a region with numerous institutions, parents had a certain amount of choice. A defective school could be taught a lesson by withholding students. In the southern prairies there were at least a dozen schools serving four denominations in the early decades of the twentieth century, and there were even instances where the same denomination had an industrial and a boarding school within a fairly short distance. The Presbyterians, unfortunately for Regina, operated boarding schools at File Hills in Saskatchewan and at Birtle, Manitoba, in addition to the unpopular industrial school at Regina. A veteran missionary contended 'that the feeling against sending children to the far away Industrial Schools is becoming stronger with the Indians themselves. Many of the old people say, that the worst element on the reserve is to be found among returned graduates who in a year or two, drift down sadly.'[22]

Regina was in bad odour with parents for many reasons. It was distant, run by an unpopular principal, had a reputation for overworking children, and experienced a lot of sickness and death among the students. A missionary on a reserve near the Birtle school reported to Presbyterian head office that 'some of the parents intimate that they will send their children to Birtle when they are bigger. The Regina is looked upon with disfavour. It is a long way off and of the seven who were sent there only one is alive to-day, all the rest dying of tuberculosis. The parents are really afraid to let the children go.'[23] A meeting with a group of parents in the chief's house on Muscowpetung reserve resulted in a list of reasons that explained why, although all wanted education for their children, 'some graduates absolutely refuse to send their children from home any more':

(a) The secrecy observed by most schools as to sickness among the pupils.
(b) The use of the pupils for work about the farm and the school when they should be in the classroom.
(c) The breaking up of their home circle.[24]

As long as there were other schools in the region, parents enjoyed some latitude in seeing that their children were educated without sending them to a distant and threatening institution. Even where dissatisfaction did not reign, 'parents prefer to keep their children in the schools nearest their homes.'[25]

[...]

In some cases, avoidance of schooling appeared to be part of a strategy chosen by the leaders of a particular community. Chief White Bear adhered to Treaty 4 in 1875, but he and his followers clearly were not interested in sedentary agriculture as an alternative to the buffalo economy. Instead, the band selected a reserve with rolling land, lakes, and numerous trees, and it proceeded to develop a mixed economy of hunting, fishing, selling products such as tanned hides and charcoal to townspeople, and limited gardening. As the farmer in charge of the reserve observed in 1897, the White Bear band 'try to live as they did before treaty was made with the North-west Indians.' Their strategy, which was in marked contrast to the Pheasant Rump and Ocean Man bands in the same agency, worked. White Bear lost fewer people to disease compared with these other two bands, and his people maintained themselves well on the varied sources of income.

What was instructive was that White Bear, his sons, and their followers among the leadership rigorously eschewed both missionaries and residential schools. The farmer who commented adversely on their economic activity in 1897 continued his plaint by adding, 'and they will hardly allow any one talk on the subject of education to them, and simply say that their "God" did not intend them to be educated like white people; they will not allow that there would be any benefit to be derived from having their children taught.' Tom White Bear, for example, reportedly would 'not farm or keep cattle himself, and uses all his influence to prevent other Indians from doing

so.' White Bear's son would 'not allow his children to be sent to school, says he would sooner see them dead, and on every chance he gets speaks against education and the Industrial schools provided by the Government.' In an effort to induce White Bear to cooperate on farming and schooling, Indian Affairs deposed him as chief, provoking a kind of boycott by the old chief's followers. When Ottawa noticed in 1897 that there was no chief or councillors on the White Bear reserve, the agent proposed the appointment of a 'good hardworking man, [who] has the best farm and buildings in the Agency, has had five of his children sent to school (three have died there) and does all in his power to help on the work on the reserve, and has a large following.' Eventually, Indian Affairs had to capitulate to the stubborn White Bear traditionalists. Ottawa restored the old chief not long before his death, and the reserve received the day school the leaders sought a couple of years later.[26]

[...]

The ability of parents to resist schools was not confined to the prairie region or to the period before the Great War, when problems of disease and student deaths were at their most intense. In the 1920s the Chooutla school in Yukon experienced severe financial problems because of a persistent inability to get and maintain enrolment at the authorized pupilage. In 1925, when enrolment was ten below the authorized forty, the Anglicans' head office chastised the principal, noting that a loss of 'confidence of the parents' was usually part of the explanation of such problems, along with the competition provided by day schools.[27] The venerable bishop, Isaac Stringer, conceded four years later that the continuing problem of under-enrolment owed much to illness and death at the school, not to mention the fact that 'for some time the idea has gone abroad that the children have not been well fed.'[28] Much later Clara Tizya recalled of the same era that when a girl from Rampart Landing died at Chooutla and 'they sent the body back there were many rumours about the children receiving bad treatment and this scared the parents or gave them an excuse for not sending their children to school.'[29]

[...]

The final way in which the adult community could resist the schools was to persist with the traditional practices that residential schooling was designed to eradicate through assimilation. The Ojibwa at Shoal

Lake in northwestern Ontario had inserted in the 'contract' that they signed with Presbyterian missionaries a provision 'that parents shall be allowed to take their children to their religious festivals, but only one child at a time and the child shall not remain over night.'[30] On the File Hills Colony, which was home to selected graduates from the Lebret and File Hills schools, 'fiddle dances, pow-wows and tribal ceremonies were forbidden.' Nonetheless, Eleanor Brass can 'remember as a child accompanying my parents to some secret fiddle dances held in private homes. There were numerous violin players and the dances were quite lively.'[31]

Charles Nowell used to participate in children's potlatch ceremonies when he was a boy at Fort Rupert, before going to Alert Bay school. When he was twelve, his ailing father sent for him in order to instruct him on the necessity of carrying on the potlatch tradition and to have him use his newly acquired learning—writing—to record essential traditional lore. '"I think the only way for you to remember the main positions and all the ancestors is for you to write them down, because it seems to me that everybody is forgetting all their ancestors and names," said his father. "The first thing, you will write down our ancestors till now." So I did—all our ancestors right down to him.' Soon after having his son record their ancestors, names, position in the clan, the dances and their names—all information vital to the preservation of potlatch practice—Nowell's father 'lay down to sleep' and 'he died.'[32] Nowell as an adult not only observed potlatch practices, but he also helped anthropologists to record for prosperity considerable Kwagiulth heritage.

Other adults, such as the men on a reserve in Manitoba, took action immediately to defend their practices. When the agent and DIA inspector came to the reserve and 'cut down or tore down the booth that had been erected for their dance,' the people were so angry that they boycotted the missionary's services for months afterwards.[33] The centrality of traditional Aboriginal ceremonies to both parents and students from Plains cultures was also demonstrated in the early decades of the modern residential school system by the way in which the onset of dancing provoked a rash of runaways, as at the Regina school in 1891.[34] In some cases, as with the Assiniboine Dan Kennedy, the reaction against church-government efforts to suppress traditional practices came after graduation. Kennedy, a graduate of Lebret, turned out to be one of the most energetic and persistent champions of traditional dancing.[35]

Unlike Dan Kennedy, many residential school children did not wait until after graduation to resist the oppressive program to which they were subjected. Like their parents, the pupils themselves had a variety of means to register their protest and try to change the conditions to which they objected. Even more so than the older generation, they were in a vulnerable position as inmates of institutions staffed by the object of their complaints, facilities that were sometimes far removed from countervailing home influences. However, vulnerability did not mean total incapacity or impotence. Residential school children had a range of sanctions from which to select, although their position usually led them to indirect forms of protest and complaint. They might, for example, seek outside help against the school officials, rather than tackling the situation themselves. Or they might register their objections by lack of cooperation and various forms of 'acting up.' In extreme cases they resorted to avoidance techniques that ranged from getting away from the source of the problem to a direct attack on the school. As was often the case in all sorts of institutional settings, the inmates showed an astonishing inventiveness and energy in combating and trying to reshape the forms and forces that held them.

What gave student opinion at least limited influence was the pupilage system and parents' ability in some situations to withhold their children. These background factors ensured that school authorities, if only sporadically, would make an effort to secure good opinions from the children for home consumption. Censorship could stifle negative reports, but it could not generate positive ones. To get endorsement required effort by the staff. An Oblate wrote enthusiastically from Moose Factory to the principal of the order's Fort George school that parents there 'qui ont des enfants chez vous en recoivent que d'excellentes nouvelles,' and predicted that the 'recrus seront probablement trop nombreuses dans un avenir prochain.' On the other hand, he gently chided the principal for failing to ensure that the children from Moosonee wrote home. 'Les parents des enfants à votre école ont restés surpris de ne pas reçevoir de lettres par les derniers courriers.'[36] In 1936 the official publication of the Chooutla school near Carcross, Yukon, indirectly acknowledged the influence of Native opinion when it congratulated itself on being 'full to over-flowing,' with more 'awaiting admittance.' Chooutla, 'under the popular and efficient leadership of Rev. H.C.M. Grant, its Principal, seems to be more than ever highly regarded by the Indians [sic] parents.'[37] And school officials were quick to celebrate when student opinion seemed favourable, as when Chief Starblanket's son was unexpectedly enrolled in the File Hills school, or a student of the Chapleau institution wrote a positive composition on 'Indian Education' that was published in the Toronto *Globe*.[38] These instances were merely the favourable side of the coin of student opinion. Most of the examples of parental protest and pressure noted above were the result of student complaints, sometimes transmitted surreptitiously by the pupils outside censored channels.

Within the walls of the schools themselves, disgruntled students were most likely to indicate their unhappiness with ridicule and a lack of cooperation. One practice that residential school students shared with pupils everywhere was the use of derisory nicknames for teachers and childcare workers. Among themselves, children at Shubenacadie tagged Sister Mary Leonard, the heavyset supervisor they feared, with the name 'Wikew,' which was Micmac for 'fatty.'[39] At St Philip's school a nun who was particularly hated by the students was known as 'Little Weasel' in Saulteaux.[40] At Shubenacadie during Isabelle Knockwood's time as a student, some 'boys developed nicknames for various nuns based on elaborate and obscene wordplays in Mi'kmaw.' One sister who the boys believed 'was sexually "loose" was named *Bujig'm*—a nonsense word which sounds similar to *Bijag'n*—which translates literally as "throw it in."' One of the girls would alter Latin words in hymns into ribald Micmac. For example, *Resurrecsit sicut dixit* became *Resurrecsit kisiku iktit*, changing the meaning from 'He said he would rise again' to 'When the old man got up, he farted.' What made the episode all the more delicious was that the sister presiding would stop the singing and 'patiently teach Clara the proper pronunciation. Clara would just stand there and grin. Even the holy ones had to laugh.'[41]

Non-cooperation was more overt than name calling. A former student of the Anglicans' Pelican Lake school vividly remembered an 'older boy' in one of her early classes who never participated in the work of the classroom. He simply sat stolidly at his desk ignoring everything around him.[42] At Moose Factory, Billy Diamond defied a supervisor by refusing to finish his vegetables. The future chief 'sat without eating for eight hours, the plate in front of him and the supervisor pacing behind until finally, at two o'clock in the morning, with the vegetables cold and still untouched, the supervisor caved in and sent the boy up to the darkened dormitory, where dozens of boys still lay with their eyes closed, feigning sleep while they awaited the outcome of the vegetable standoff.'[43] The Methodists' Coqualeetza school in British Columbia recorded in its register of admissions and discharges several students who were 'Discharged because of indisposition for work or study,' or 'Sent away as incorrigible,' or discharged because of an 'indisposition or inaptitude for study.'[44] The Oblate principal at Fort George also expelled a young fellow whom he described as 'unusually stubborn and would not cooperate with school authorities.'[45] Offences might range from refusal to do school work to misbehaviour in chapel; an almost unlimited number of possibilities was available. Isabelle Knockwood delighted in defying Wikew's 'Don't dare move a muscle' at bedtime by 'wiggling my toes under the blankets thinking, "You ain't my boss and I'll wiggle all I want." At the same time, I was looking straight at her wearing the Indian mask which I had discovered over the years she couldn't read.'[46] More overt were the boys at Lytton who threatened the principal to his face that they would steal food if he didn't provide them with better rations. They were pleasantly surprised when their challenge succeeded.[47]

Indeed, the favourite form of misbehaviour among students was stealing food. The young women at Kamloops school organized elaborate schemes to pilfer apples and other food that they shared in the dormitory.[48] Similar stunts were carried out at most schools at one time or another. The boys at Elkhorn in the 1940s killed one of the school's pigs by spraying it with water and leaving it to freeze to death. When the school authorities could not figure out what had killed the pig, they ordered it incinerated. The boys who leapt to dispose of the carcass in fact roasted and hid it, treating the contraband pork as snack for many days.[49] Food pranks that involved staff were fondly remembered. One woman took advantage of the assignment of clearing the staff dining room to sample delicacies with a spoon she had brought. When she found the large jar of horseradish not to her liking, she spat the condiment back in the jar and screwed the lid on.[50] A male former student of Shubenacadie told Isabelle Knockwood that boys working in the barn sometimes urinated in the milk destined for the sisters and priest.[51] A particularly wicked thrill could be obtained by directing misbehaviour at the religious practices of the missionaries. Some students conscripted into assisting with services indulged in mockery, and a former altar boy recalled how they used to mock the Mass that all were compelled to attend every morning.[52]

More daring—and more rewarding—was theft of communion wine, either by suborning a person who looked after the sacristy or through a nighttime raid.[53] Getting drunk on the stolen wine, however, gave the game away with dire consequences.[54] A man who had attended several residential schools in Ontario recalled that at Shingwauk he and another boy had made homebrew in the attic of the carpenter's workshop. They had a fright one day when the carpenter smelled something strange and noticed a leak in his shop ceiling. The artisan said that they would have to reroof the building because it was obviously leaking. The boys, who knew better, moved their illegal brew to the barn, where they later got roaring drunk on it.[55]

Another guilty pleasure for multitudes of residential school students was getting around the strict rules on segregation of the sexes. Justa Monk 'had my first sexual experience with another student, a girl I really liked, within the walls of Lejac, just a few feet from one of the brothers who was peeling potatoes at the time.'[56] In some schools, like Shingwauk, where the girls' and boys' dormitories were wings at opposite ends of the same building, contact could be made by going over the rooftop at night—a dangerous resort even if one was not apprehended.[57] Boys at Blue Quills who thought access to the latest technology was the solution to their isolation discovered that science could be their undoing, too. 'I remember one time we used walkies talkies to socialize with the girls,' recalled one, 'but we were found out because of the wiring system or the pipes. Somehow it got connected with the television and we got caught because our voices came on the television.'[58]

Where the living quarters of the sexes were completely separate, as at Spanish where the girls' school was across the road from the boys', more elaborate arrangements were necessary. There a complicated communications system was worked out, one that, ironically, relied on the daily visit of one of the Jesuits to the girls' chapel to say Mass. A boy who wanted to communicate surreptitiously with a girl would arrange for a message to be slipped into the priest's hatband. When the celebrant reached the vestibule at the girls' school, his hat would be placed on a stand, whence it would be quietly picked up and the slip of paper with the illicit message extracted. A return note could be sent back to the boy with the priest on his return after Mass. Another means used at Spanish capitalized on the fact that shoe repairs were carried out in the cobbler shop in the boys' building. A girl would sew a message into the lining of a pair of boots that was being sent across for repair. This system worked reasonably well, too, although the girls sometimes damaged the newly refurbished boots extracting the return message.[59] Some students simply arranged for regular meeting places and times with either siblings or members of the opposite sex in whom they had a romantic interest.[60] Charlie Nowell in British Columbia eventually got expelled from Alert Bay school when one of his notes to a girl whom he met regularly in the evenings was intercepted by her stepfather.[61] Peter Webster got out of Ahousaht at the age of fourteen when 'I took the blame for the pregnancy of one of my classmates.'[62]

In situations where extensive flouting of the rules about segregation of mature males and females occurred, complications generally ensued. In the early days, a small boarding school such as Alberni on Vancouver Island had considerable difficulty dealing with such a problem. Lax supervision by a trusting matron led to her dismissal, only to be replaced by new officers who upset children and parents by locking the girls in their dormitory every night.[63] At the Anglicans' Sarcee school, similar concerns led to protracted discussions over the design of dormitory windows. The local missionary wanted windows with sashes that could be opened, necessitating, in his opinion, the installation of bars on the outside of the window openings. But the Indian agent ruled that no bars were necessary, leaving the cleric with grave concerns about security.[64] As the new regime at Alberni learned a couple of years after the window debate at Sarcee, open windows led to nocturnal visits, which in the Alberni case led to nailing the windows closed.[65] In extenuation, the Alberni principal contended that 'in other schools similar difficulties have arisen and in Regina we had a share and a great deal more serious than ours.'[66] Indeed, both the Cecilia Jeffrey and the Regina schools had had encounters with the problem. Things so degenerated at the Presbyterian schools that one missionary charged 'the conduct has become almost like that of a brothel instead of a Church home,' while the principal of the File Hills boarding school stated flatly that 'I for one will never consent to send my children that I am treasuring with a mother's love where they would be exposed to such dangers.'[67]

At the Methodists' Brandon school, some of the boys obtained duplicate keys and used them to visit the girls' dormitory before they were caught.[68] When principals at Regina and Alberni responded to renewed scandal by locking the dorms from the outside or by barring the windows, they encountered objections from the Indian Affairs department, which 'objects to the bars lest the building should be a fire trap in case of accident.'[69] Concerns over the students' persistent success in violating the rules against fraternization contributed to the problems that caused closure of both Crowstand and Regina.[70] Others, such as Alberni, carried on for many decades in spite of recurrent problems. At Alberni, the staff put 'a wax stamp and a chain' across the window of the most accessible boys' dormitory, but this merely forced the amorous to take a more dangerous route 'through the window on the west side of the building, and along a ledge of the roof. There was a drop of thirty feet to the ground.'[71] Whether it was a Presbyterian school on Vancouver Island or an Anglican institution near Sault Ste Marie, adolescents found similar ways to flout the rules and get in touch with members of the opposite sex.

Sometimes there was a connection between illicit relations and what was probably the most commonly reported manifestation of student resistance—running away from school. A former administrator of the Pelican Lake school recalled an incident in which an Indian boy who lived with a family in the town of Sioux Lookout paddled across the lake to rendezvous with his girlfriend, a classmate. The following morning they were discovered in a tent not too far off from the school.[72] Although there could be many reasons for students' deserting, the reaction that flight evoked

among staff was uniformly negative. For one thing, runaways caused considerable difficulties and anxieties. Early in the century, the missionary principal of Norway House in northern Manitoba had to make a January trip 320 kilometres northeast accompanied by a Mountie to retrieve pupils who had not returned after the summer vacation.[73] At a crasser level, unauthorized absences, if detected by Indian Affairs officials, would lead to a decrease in revenue. For example, when six girls ran away from a Manitoba school 'to attend a dance on the Reserve,' it cost the Anglican Missionary Society a thirteen dollar fee to the police.[74]

[…]

Even more dramatic a form of rebellion than truancy was arson. For students who were unable to escape, often an emotionally satisfying substitute was to attack the school with fire. Once again, as with the problem of runaways, there tended to be a suspiciously high correlation between troubles at a school and a mysterious outbreak of fire. For example, at Wikwemikong in the 1880s, during a period of some tension between missionaries and parents, there were two unexplained fires early in 1885, and another fire at the girls' school in the autumn of 1888 that had definitely been set by two students.[75] At the Presbyterian school at Birtle, Manitoba, a young boy calmly went into the pantry, took matches, and proceeded to set fire to the barn on a September day in 1903.[76] Alberni home burned down in suspicious circumstances in 1917.[77] The Anglicans in the 1920s experienced arson at Alert Bay, which was full to overflowing—sometimes a sign of parental confidence in a school—and at Onion Lake, which was always in some difficulty.[78] The Onion Lake fire in 1928 appeared to be 'copycat' incendiarism: two boys at the Anglican school seem to have been influenced by a recent fire at the neighbouring Catholic school that had completely destroyed the institution. The razing of the Cross Lake school in Manitoba, also in 1928, probably was a coincidence.[79] The Oblates had a suspicious fire at Duck Lake in 1926, and two boys attempted arson at the Sioux Lookout school in 1931. The principal of the Elkhorn residential school was not very pleased when the two would-be arsonists were transferred to his school.[80] The Oblates at Pine Creek, Manitoba, in 1930 had the distinction of double arson, one boy 'having set the church on fire and another boy … tried to do the same to the School.'[81] In less than a decade after 1936, nine residential schools were destroyed by fires of various origins.[82]

[...]

Arsonists and runaways were merely the extreme of a continuum of unhappy and angry students who, like their parents, often resisted and protested as best they could against the iniquities of residential school life. From complaints, to acts of non-cooperation and defiance, to antisocial actions—these students often expressed by their words and actions what many others felt, others who often were too timid or intimidated to follow suit. What is less clear about resistance by both parents and schoolchildren is how effective their deeds and arguments were. Certainly, when a leading Blood man came to Canon Middleton and objected to his children being taught Blackfoot syllabics, the missionary was more than happy to oblige his desire for solely English instruction.[83] Often missionaries evinced concern to maintain good relations with children and parents, and they trumpeted any small victories they experienced. Kate Gillespie of File Hills was delighted when Chief Starblanket let his son attend the Presbyterian school rather than Catholic Lebret.[84]

[...]

Probably the best symbol of Native resistance to the intrusive and oppressive nature of residential schools was found in the persistence of traditional cultural practices, such as dancing among Plains peoples and the potlatch on the Pacific. That former residential school students, as noted earlier, were among the most energetic in defending the practices that assimilative education was supposed to consign to oblivion is among the most pointed ironies of the history of residential schooling. Also ironic was the fact that, by the time Native resistance led to removal of such coercive elements as the potlatch and prairie dancing bans in the 1951 amendment of the Indian Act, a dramatically new chapter in the residential school story was opening. This instalment—the conclusion, as it turned out—was the increasingly assertive and influential campaign of Native political organizations to eliminate residential schooling in Canada. The irony in this process, which stretched from the first major outpouring of Native political process in the later 1940s to the elimination of government-controlled residential schools in the late 1960s and 1970s, was that it was often former residential school students who provided the most vociferous criticism of education and the most effective political leadership. In helping to shape the generations of political leaders who emerged after the Second World War, residential schools contributed to the most effective of the many forms of Native resistance that had been spawned by these institutions.

So, anyway, after I finished sweeping—she kept following me around like this, cutting me [up], cutting my people up. All of a sudden I just swung my broom like this. 'F you!' Oh, I swore. 'Don't swear.' I said, 'F you.' I kept on. I just went wild. I just snapped. 'You f-ing, fucking...' Oh, did I ever use that F word! Did I ever swear! 'Keep quiet! Everybody's listening.' 'I don't give a damn. I don't give a fuck!' I just went completely wild. And I stood up to her like this.

She said, 'You come upstairs. I'm going to fix you.' 'You're f-ing right I will,' I said. In the meantime, even the boys came running towards the girls' side. And they're all prompting me, 'Don't be scared of her. Keep it up. Keep it up.' They took me upstairs. Those other two—that nun that made trouble for me and another nun—came running. Three of them, they grabbed brooms on the third floor. They beat me up with brooms. Brooms all over. And I grabbed ahold of her ... I grabbed her veil like this. And she was hanging on, and she had me by the hair. And another nun was hitting me all over. I just didn't care. One of them nuns, I grabbed ahold of her like this and swung like this. She landed far [away]. Oh, she landed like at the end of that wall. That's how far [away] she landed. I really went wild that time. And the other one, I grabbed her and flung her like this. And I hung on to this one. And then she told them in French to go. They went crying 'cause I made them cry.

There was me and her now. I said, 'Kill me first; I'm not giving up.' I just hung on to her. Every time she'd hit me, I'd hit her right back. Oh, I had her good. 'Let me go,' she said. I'd jerk her like this. And she'd hang on to it [her veil]. Finally, she said, 'In the name of God, please let me go, Pauline.'[85]

Notes

1. Isabelle Knockwood, *Out of the Depths: The Experience of Mi'kmaw Children at the Indian Residential School of Shubenacadie, Nova Scotia* (Lockeport, NS: Roseway Publishing 1992), 125

2. Interview, 21 June 1990, Whitehorse, with a Han male who attended Whitehorse Baptist Mission school 1951–3 (interview by Lu Johns Penikett)

3. United Church of Canada Archives [UCA], Records of the Presbyterian Church [PC], Foreign Mission Committee [FMC], Western Section [WS], Indian Work in Manitoba and the North West [IWMNW], box 7, file 155, Report of Visit to Indian Missions, 15 Aug. 1913. Other examples concern Mount Elgin in Ontario, both before the Great War (ibid., A. Sutherland Papers, box 8, file 154, T.T. George to A. Sutherland, 27 May 1908, and Sutherland to George, 3 June 1908) and during the 1940s (ibid., E.E. Joblin Papers, box 1, file 3, Notes on the Survey of the Education of Indian Children in Western Ontario, 15 Sept. 1943). In commenting on complaints made in the 1890s about the Wikwemikong schools on Manitoulin Island, the Jesuit historian noted, after conceding that Indian Affairs investigated parental complaints, that the outcome 'shows that the Indians were still capable of thinking and speaking nonsense.' Regis College Archives, Father Julien Paquin, 'Modern Jesuit Indian Missions in Ontario' (unpaginated manuscript)

4. General Synod Archives [GSA], GS 75-103, Papers of the Missionary Society of the Church in Canada [GS 75-103], Series 2-14, Special Indian Committee [Series 2-14], box 19, S.H. Blake correspondence, file Mar/08–June/09, F.H. DuVernet to S.H. Blake, 23 Mrch 1909, enclosing copy DuVernet to Secretary, Department of Indian Affairs, 23 March 1909.

5. National Archives of Canada [NA], MG 29, E. 106, Hayter Reed Papers, box 20, 1255, H. Reed to Inspector J.A. Macrae, 30 June 1892.

6. Paquin, 'Modern Jesuit Indian Missions'

7. NA, Records of the Department of Indian Affairs [RG 10], School Files, vol. 6320, file 658-1, part 1, 305595, (copy) David Laird to Indian Agent Sibbald, 28 Nov. 1906,' enclosed with Laird to Secretary, DIA, 4 March 1907. Laird continued to the Agent: 'When the children have sore necks or are tender about the throat, this sort of punishment is cruel. 'I think it would be well to call the meeting of Indians you propose, speak to them in a persuasive manner, assure them the overwork and ear-twisting will be discontinued, and tell them the Indian Commissioner [Laird] and the Department are most anxious that they should send their children to school.'

8. Reed Papers, vol. 12, file 'Rev. T. Clarke 1891-92,' 132, T. Clarke to Hayter Reed, 14 July 1891

9. Archives of the Manitoba and Northwestern Ontario Conference of the United Church of Canada, University of Winnipeg [UCA-Wpg], Minute Book of Presbyterian Workers among the Indians, Synods of Manitoba and Saskatchewan, 1909–1915, 68, Fifth Convention, Crowstand school, 23–24 July 1912

10. Archives Deschâtelets [AD], L 535 .M27L 349, William Moss, OMI, to J. Magnan, OMI, 18 April 1932. Father Moss was replaced as principal shortly after this incident. Ibid., 351, J. Magnan to A.S. Williams, 21 May 1932

11. PC, FMC, WS, Indian Work in BC [IWBC], box 1, file 16, Hamilton Cassels and Andrew Jeffrey to R.P. MacKay, 4 Aug. 1897

12. GS 75-103, Series 2-15, Papers of the MSCC [Series 2-15], Records of the Indian and Eskimo Residential School Commission [IESRC], box 21, 9, Minute of 28 Aug. 1928. In this case, since the principal at Elkhorn had already rejected similar complaints, 'No further action was considered necessary' by the central body.

13. AD, L 912 .M27C 195, Maurice Bruyere and Joe Mainville to Rev. Fr. Magnan, Provincial OMI, nd [1933]. The following year a new principal was appointed and, apparently, conditions improved for a number of years. However, by the end of 1940, the president of the Columbus Indian Mission Club on the reserve was objecting to another deterioration in conditions at the school.

14. UCA-Wpg. A.B. Baird Papers, box G, G 1393-4, A.B. Baird to Rev. C.W. Whyte. The principal's resignation (Whyte to Baird, 12 March 1897) is ibid., G 1214-18.

15. PC, FMC, WS, IWBC, box 3, file 174, A.W. Vowell to Dr John Campbell, 13 May 1905 (enclosing letter from Dan Watts, Big George, Tatoosh Jimmie George, Tyee Bob of 6 May); ibid., James R. Motion to R.P. MacKay, 27 May 1905. Swewish, who claimed to be 'chief of the Shesaht people,' later wrote to denounce the petitioners and to endorse the work of the principal. Ibid., file 75, Shewish to R.P. MacKay, 5 July 1905 (translated and typed by James R. Motion)

16. PC, FMC, WS, IWMNW, box 2, file 41, petition from Shoal Lake Reserve, 22 Sept. 1902 (enclosed with A.G. McKitrick to MacKay, 23 Sept. 1902); ibid., Maggie A. Nicoll to R.P. MacKay, 23 Sept. 1902;

ibid., file 42, same to same, 13 Oct. 1902; ibid., file 40, same to same, 25 Aug. 1902. See also ibid., box 3, file 55, J.O. McGregor and Sarah McGregor to R.P. MacKay, 27 Nov. 1903, in which a new principal and matron complained that the missionary, A.G. McKitrick, interfered with their work by insisting that the original promise 'that the children would not be taught religion' be honoured.

17. Ibid., box 5, file 95, Petition dated Shoal Lake, 4 March 1907, to Foreign Mission Society, Toronto (interpreted by Miss Mary Begg and transcribed by Miss E. Robertson, teacher)

18. Ibid., file 111, Report of the Subcommittee of Synodical Indian Mission Committee, Manitoba and Saskatchewan, July 1908. See also ibid., box 6, file 117, Agnes Sibbald to Rev. Dr J. Farquharson, 30 Jan. 1909.

19. Ibid., W.W. Shoup (Nelson House) to A. Sutherland, 17 March 1907

20. Reed Papers, vol. 19, file 'May 1891,' 619, Knatakasiwisine (Piapot Reserve) to D[ea]r Sister in law (Mrs Mistassini], 21 May 1891

21. PC, FMC, WS, IWMNW, box 1, file 24, J.A. Sinclair to R.P. MacKay, 19 April 1901; ibid., box 5, file 115, (copy) R.P. MacKay to J. Farquharson, 30 Nov. 1908; ibid., file 116, J. Farquharson to R.P. MacKay, 3 Dec. 1908

22. Ibid., box 4, file 70, Neil Gilmour (Norway House) to R.P. MacKay, 11 Feb. 1905. Gilmour was referring specifically to 'the reserves that form the Regina School constituency.'

23. Ibid., file 72, F.O. Gilbart to R.P. MacKay. 28 April 1905

24. Ibid., box 7, file 145, W.W. McLaren, report on tour of reserves and schools in southern Manitoba and southern Saskatchewan, 22 April 1912

25. Report of Deputy Superintendent General James A. Smart, in Annual Report of DIA for 1900, Canada, *Sessional Papers [CSP] (No. 27) 1901,* xxxiii. The deputy minister went on: 'equally natural is it for the teachers of boarding schools to desire to retain their pupils instead of drafting them to the higher institutions.'

26. The materials for the White Bear story, which were assembled by Mary Miller for my benefit, are found in RG 10, Black Series, vol. 3940, file 121,698-13, part 0; and Annual Reports of the Department of Indian Affairs, 1880–1906. The materials quoted are from letters written in 1897, and from the report for 1897. Concerning the resistance to residential schooling, the 1897 department report (*CSP[No. 14] 1898,* 161) was clear and revealing: 'There are twenty-five children of school age in the band, and seven of them are attending the industrial schools at Regina, Qu'Appelle and Elkhorn. It is very difficult to get the parents to allow the children to be sent away to school, more especially those Indians who are in any way connected with the deposed chief White Bear and his sons, who will have nothing to do with anything in the shape of education, and who try to live as they did before treaty was made with the North-west Indians.'

27. Archives of Yukon [AY], Anglican Diocese of Yukon Records, box 7, file 9, T.B.R. Westgate to W. Barlow, 7 July 1925

28. Ibid., I.O. Stringer to T.B.R. Westgate, 21 Oct. 1929. Westgate, the Anglican's head man in missionary work in Canada, in turn lamented to DIA that an enrolment of twenty-six in a school with a pupilage of forty meant serious financial problems for the school and the church. Ibid., T.B.R. Westgate to Secretary, DIA, 16 Dec. 1929

29. L.G.P. Waller, ed., *The Education of Indian Children in Canada* (Toronto: Ryerson Press 1965), 103–4. Mrs Tizya also recalled: 'And so, for the next 25 years, no children were sent out to the Carcross Indian Residential School and it was for this reason that we decided to bring our children out to where they could become educated. We realized that we could not do anything for our children in an atmosphere where no one else cared about his children' (104).

30. PC, FMB, IWMNW, box 1, file 33, 'Agreement' of 14 Jan. 1902 enclosed with J.C. Gandier to R.P. MacKay, same date. The first clause of the agreement provided: 'That while children are young and at school they shall not be baptized without the consent of their parents …'

31. Brass, *I Walk in Two Worlds,* 13

32. Clelland S. Ford, *Smoke from Their Fires: The Life of a Kwakiutl Chief* (New Haven, Conn.: Yale University Press 1941), 85–6 and 107

33. PC, FMC, WS, IWMNW, box 3, file 46, D. Spear to R.P. MacKay, 26 Feb. 1903. The agent's visit had occurred a little before Christmas.

34. Baird Papers, box 3, E1156-9, A.S. McLeod to A.B. Baird, 4 June 1891

35. See PC, FMC, WS, IWMNW, box 4, file 59, E. MacKenzie to R.P. MacKay, 7 March 1904; James R.

Stevens, ed., *Recollections of an Assiniboine Chief* [Dan Kennedy, Ochankuhage] (Toronto: McClelland & Stewart 1972), 103–4. See also RG 10, Black Series, vol. 3825, file 60, 511-1, J.D. McLean to Indian Commissioner, 5 Jan. 1903: 'Chief Wanduta, of the Oak River Sioux Band, has called at the Department with his son, who is a graduate of the Brandon Industrial School.'

36. AD, LCB 3445 .G46M 65, J. Cyr, OMI, to Father Labrèche, 13 Feb. 1944 [families that have children at your school have received only excellent reports, (and) recruits probably will be too numerous in the near future]; ibid., 66, same to same, 28 March 1944 [families of children at your school remain surprised at not receiving letters by the last mail].

37. AY, Anglican Yukon Records, *Northern Lights* 25, 4 (Nov. 1936): 3

38. PC, FMC, WS, IWMNW, box 3, file 55, K. Gillespie to R.P. MacKay, 20 Nov. 1903; *Globe,* 9 Oct. 1926, 'Certified by G.T. Snowden, Acting Principal,' The published letter was noted by the Anglicans' missionary body: GS 75-103, Series 2-15, box 21, 812

39. Knockwood, *Out of the Depths,* 32. The students had other, somewhat less derogatory names in their own language for other sisters.

40. Joe Severight interview, Cote Reserve, 19 Feb. 1992. Mr Severight also recalled that some boys— 'peeping Toms,' he called them—spied on two of the sisters, whose bedroom adjoined the boys' dormitory.

41. Knockwood, *Out of the Depths,* 124

42. Interview with an Ojibwa woman who in the 1940s attended Pelican Lake from age seven until about age eleven, 2 Feb. 1991, Sioux Lookout, Ont. She recalled that this boy ran away several times and was strapped for it once.

43. Roy MacGregor, *Chief: The Fearless Vision of Billy Diamond* (Toronto: Penguin 1989), 25–6. The episode clinched young Billy's role as leader of the students.

44. Vancouver, United Church of Canada Conference of BC Archives, Coqualeetza Register of Admissions and Discharges, numbers 38, 049, 89, and 90

45. AD, LCB 3346 .G46M 112, (copy) W.S. Gran to Regional Supervisor, 14 Feb. 1961

46. Knockwood, *Out of the Depths,* 125

47. 100 Verna J. Kirkness, ed., *Khot-La-Cha: The Autobiography of Chief Simon Baker* (Vancouver/ Toronto: Douglas & McIntyre 1994), 36–7

48. Haig-Brown, *Resistance and Renewal,* 89–90

49. Telephone interview with Ernest Hall, 3 Aug. 1993. I am indebted to Regina writer Jim Anderson, who first told me of this incident.

50. This anecdote was told by an unidentified woman, who said that it had been experienced by another woman, during a public session of the 'Journey to Healing' Conference, 26 Sept. 1991, Saskatoon.

51. Knockwood, *Out of the Depths,* 55. The workers knew which milk was headed for the staff dining room because it always came from the cows that gave milk of higher quality than the rest.

52. Interview, 21 Jan. 1992, Saskatoon, with male Saulteaux student who attended St Philip's, 1955–62, and Marieval 1962–5

53. Haig-Brown, *Resistance and Renewal,* 91, recounts an organized system at Kamloops for the theft and sale of eucharistic wine.

54. Joe Severight interview. Mr Severight, who attended St Philip's school in the 1930s, recalled that he and his companions were punished—after they had sobered up.

55. A male (surname Kakeegesic) who attended Chapleau, Moose Factory, and Shingwauk schools, speaking at the public session of Shingwauk reunion, 4 July 1991

56. Bridget Moran, *Justa: A First Nations Leader* (Vancouver: Arsenal Pulp Press 1994). 54. On another occasion, 'Sister Alphonse saw me kissing a girl in the priests' dining room' and 'started slapping me. I grabbed her wrists and squeezed them hard and I said to her, "You're not my teacher now,"' Ibid., 55

57. Recollection in public session at Shingwauk reunion, 4 July 1991

58. Diane Persson, 'The Changing Experience of Indian Residential Schooling: Blue Quills, 1931–1970,' in Jean Barmen, Yvonne Hébert, and Don McCaskill, *Indian Education in Canada,* vol. 1: *The Legacy* (Vancouver: University of British Columbia Press and Nakoda Institute 1986), 164

59. Interview with Miss Ann Berrigan, SFM (La Société des Filles du Coeur de Marie), Montreal, 16 Oct. 1990. Students at St Philip's school in the 1950s used a wood box as a 'drop' for messages between boys and girls. On one occasion, a staff member found a note, assembled the students, and read the message aloud to embarrass those involved. Interview, 21 Jan. 1992, Saskatoon, with male Saulteaux student of St Philip's, 1955–62, and Marieval, 1962–5

60. Interview, 15 Dec. 1987, Regina, with Joy Mann

61. Ford, *Smoke from Their Fires*, 104–5

62. Peter Webster, *As Far as I Know: Reminiscences of an Ahousat Elder* (Campbell River, BC: Campbell River Museum and Archives 1983), 42

63. PC, FMC, WS, IWBC, box 1, file 22, M. Swartout to R.P. MacKay, 22 Feb. 1899; ibid., file 23, K. Cameron to R.P. MacKay, 30 May 1899; ibid., B.I. Johnston to R.P. MacKay, 17 June 1899

64. Calgary Indian Missions Papers, box 3, vol. 1, 124–7, J.W. Tims to Mr Scott, 11 Aug. 1903

65. PC, FMC, WS, IWBC, box 3, file 72, K. Cameron to R.P. MacKay, 1 and 25 March 1905: ibid., Mrs J.R. Motion to R.P. MacKay, 29 March 1905

66. Ibid., file 75, J.R. Motion to R.P. MaKay, 17 June 1905

67. Ibid., IWMNW, box 3, file 55, A.G. McKitrick to R.P. MacKay, 14 Nov. 1903; ibid., box 5, file 74, Kate Gillespie to R.P. MacKay, 22 June 1905

68. Ibid., box 6, file 123, W.W. McLaren to R.P. MacKay, 5 July 1909. McLaren also noted of Brandon, 'The older boys too whenever they got a chance when on leave down town often frequent the redlight district of the city.'

69. Ibid., box 5, file 1095, (copy) D.M. Laird to Rev. Sir, 14 Jan. 1908; ibid., BFM, Correspondence with WFMS, box 1, file 24, (copy) R.P. MacKay to Mrs C. Clark, 5 May 1910

70. For a sample of the material on the Crowstand dormitory problems, see PC, FMC, WS, IWMNW, box 5, file 99, (copy) E. McWhinney to J. Farquharson, 8 July 1907.

71. PC, BFM, Correspondence with WMS, box 5, file 84. Helen W. Horne, assistant secretary for Indian Work, WMS to J.H. Edmison, 6 Jan. 1923; Chief Earl Maquinna George's Life Story (typescript), 25

72. Derek and Hazel Mills interview, 2 Feb. 1991, Sioux Lookout, Ont.

73. UCA-Wpg. J.A. Lousley Autobiography (manuscript), chapter 11, 2–3

74. GS 75-103, Series 2-15, box 20, minutes of 23 Oct. 1924. See also Archives of Yukon, YRG 1, Series 1., vol. 11, file 2335, part 6, (copy) John Hawksley (DIA) to Rev. Principal, Chooutla Indian School, 20 July 1932.

75. Paquin, 'Modern Jesuit Indian Missions': and 'Synopsis of the History of Wikwemikong'

76. PC, FMC, WS, IWNMW, box 3, file 53, E.H. Crawford to R.P. MacKay, 30 Sept. 1903

77. PC, BFM, Correspondence with WMS, box 4, file 61, Jessie Wilson to R.P. MacKay, 31 May 1917

78. GSA, M 75-1, Bishop Lucas Papers, box 2, Minutes of Commission, 23 Oct. 1924 re Alert Bay; GS 75-103. Series 2-15, box 21, Minutes of 6 March 1928

79. AD, LC 6201 .K26R 1, clipping from *Le Patriote*, 21 Oct. 1931

80. AD, HR 6671, .C73R 47, (copy) J. LeChevalier, OMI, to W.M. Graham, 4 May 1926, concerning Duck Lake; GS 75-103, Series 2-15, box 22, Minutes of 7 April and 30 April 1931

81. RG 10, School Files, vol. 6041, file 160-5, part 1, J. Magnan, OMI, to Duncan C. Scott, 2 Dec. 1930

82. Joblin Papers, box 1, file 3, (copy) R.A. Hoey to G. Dorey, 29 May 1944. With all these fires, missionaries might be forgiven the odd bit of paranoia. The Oblates, for example, thought that a fire at Fort Frances school had been set by an American socialist in revenge for the principal's discouraging organizing on the nearby reserve. *Missions*, no. 214, (Sept–Dec. 1921): 307–8

83. Middleton Papers, box 2, file 7, (copy) S.H. Middleton to Roberta Forsberg, 7 Nov. 1960

84. PC, FMC, WS, IWMNW, box 3, file 55, K. Gillespie to R.P. MacKay, 20 Nov. 1903

85. Interview with Pauline Pelly, former St Philip's student, 6 Sept. 1991, Saskatoon. The altercation between Pauline and the sister lasted some time, and eventually the confrontation shifted to the student's home on the reserve, because the principal followed her there. Pauline's father sternly admonished the Oblates for the behaviour of the sister and the principal.

MEDIUM AND MESSAGE

Popular Culture, Mass Media, and National Identity, 1960s–2000s

Cynthia R. Comacchio
Wilfrid Laurier University

● MEDIUM AND MESSAGE: POPULAR CULTURE, MASS MEDIA, AND NATIONAL IDENTITY, 1960S–2000S

● **Introduction by Cynthia R. Comacchio**

▲ **Primary Sources:**

Document 1: Lament for a Nation, 1965
  George Grant
Document 2: Cover Illustration, *Captain Canuck*, 1975
Document 3: Sixth Report, 2008
  CBC/Radio Canada
Document 4: "Why We Don't Have Hit TV Series," 2013

■ **Secondary Sources:**

Article 1: The Many Lives of Captain Canuck: Nationalism, Culture, and the Creation of a Canadian Comic Book Superhero
  Ryan Edwardson
Article 2: I Am Canadian: National Identity in Beer Commercials
  Robert M. MacGregor

● INTRODUCTION

Cynthia R. Comacchio

Popular culture, as the very classification suggests, belongs to "the people." Despite its assumed inclusivity, factors such as those of class, gender, "race," age, region, religion, urban or rural location, and any combination of these, clearly affect both its content and the extent and nature of public participation. Historians are understandably interested in the subject, which concerns how culture is created, disseminated, and received on the level of everyday life in the past. As such, the kind of popular culture that Canadians create and consume is integral to self, group, and ultimately national identity. The recent flourishing of cultural and communications studies, especially in critical media research, has expanded the subject area enormously, ensuring that it is interdisciplinary, multi-disciplinary, and often transnational in approach. But Canadian scholars have long been active participants in the study of popular culture and media. More than half a century ago, University of Toronto theorists Harold Adams Innis (1894–1952), Marshall McLuhan (1911–1980), and George Grant (1918–1988) left a significantly "Canadian" imprint on the scholarly study of modern media, communications, and popular culture, entwined as they are with modern technology and mass media. In particular, Alberta-born and Cambridge University-educated philosopher Marshall McLuhan (1911–1980) was an international pioneer in communications theory and critical media study. A controversial public intellectual, he is best remembered for his catchy slogans, "the medium is the message," and "the global village," both of which illustrated—well in advance of the Internet—suggested how national/regional identities are challenged by "borderless" communications technology.

By the early twentieth century, mass production was making new technologies more affordable to more Canadians, as well as more desirable, thanks to the expanding social influence of advertising and the related development of consumerism. Accelerated by the military demands of the two world wars, technology had effectively reconfigured popular culture into mass culture by the 1950s, making its experience more "democratic," and, as "mass" implies, more widespread than ever before. The historical study of popular culture and media allows us a sense of how social relations such as those hinging on economic and political issues, or those concerning gender, race, age, sexuality, and religion, operate in the everyday culture of everyday people. The question of technology, and who can access it, is also important in this context.

The history of popular culture is also the history of Canadian–American relations. Preserving and promoting what is believed to be "distinctly Canadian" has been a central issue in the larger, and largely unresolved, question of national identity, a matter explored by George Grant in his aptly named *Lament for a Nation* (1965). Sustaining cultural distinctiveness remains daunting, given American proximity, cultural commonality, technological entrepreneurship and media domination. Established in 1949 and reporting in 1952, the Royal Commission on the Arts, Letters and Sciences (The Massey Commission) opened the way to a new state involvement in cultural production and promotion and the regulation of media content. Yet, already by the end of the 1920s, Canada's fledgling feature film industry had been overtaken by Hollywood. American radio programming was being broadcast to, and enjoyed by, Canadian listeners across the land by the 1930s, sparking the instigation of the Canadian Radio Broadcasting Commission (1932–36) upon the recommendation of the Royal Commission on Radio Broadcasting (Aird Commission, 1928–29). The National Film Board of Canada was established in 1939, largely to produce documentary and educational films on Canadian subjects, by and for Canadians. Although its productions have amassed more than 5,000 international awards, the NFB did not begin to challenge the dominance of foreign films in Canadian theatres.

Similar developments can be traced in any number of areas of media and popular culture. During the Second World War, as comic books became increasingly popular among children and teenagers, trade exigencies cut off the supply of American comics, thereby opening the way to those "made in Canada." The homegrown comic book protagonists included the dashing and indestructible Nazi-fighter Johnny Canuck, and the first female super-hero—predating the American Wonder Woman by only a few months—"Nelvana of the Northern Lights." The transparently "Canadian" qualities of these two heroic wartime characters is summed up in their names alone. The reopening of the comic import gates saw the resurgence of the American DC and Marvel books; it was not until the 1970s that artist Richard Comely would unleash his Captain Canuck, but his season proved to be short lived.

The Canadian Broadcasting Corporation (CBC) expanded from radio into television broadcasting in 1952. The CBC's mandate was, and continues to be, to reflect back to us our own stories, nationally, regionally, locally, and in both official languages (via Quebec's Radio-Canada). By the 1990s, First Nations politicization, media attention to First Nations causes, and federal responses to these, brought about the first Indigenous community programming: Television Northern Canada was founded in 1992. It was superseded in 1999 by the Aboriginal Peoples Television Network (APTN). Despite the CBC's early state-funded monopoly, the Television Age that dawned in the 1950s was almost immediately identified with American TV networks, shows, and stars. The exception was Quebec, where Radio-Canada captured a unique francophone audience and "made in Quebec" television programming predominated.

In the realm of popular music, and in the context of the American rock n' roll that captured adolescent hearts in the 1950s, the first Canadian pop chart-topper and teen idol was Ottawa's Paul Anka, whose crush on his babysitter Diana inspired his hit single by that name, produced in 1957 when he was only 16. During the 1960s Canadian singer-songwriters such as Ian and Sylvia Tyson, Gordon Lightfoot, Joni Mitchell, and Leonard Cohen also acquired an international following, reassuring anxious Canadian fans that there was an identifiably Canadian popular music. Yet the rock music that revolutionized 1960s popular culture was also, by and large, the music of the so-called "British Invasion," epitomized by the Beatles, and also that of the American Billboard Top 100. By 1967, the Centennial year, an expanding, increasingly defensive, and not infrequently anti-American cultural nationalism brought about the establishment of the Canadian Radio-Television and Telecommunications Commission. In order to ensure support for Canadian popular music, the CRTC legislated that the playlists of radio stations had to be at least 30 percent Canadian: composed, performed, or produced in Canada by Canadians. The so-called Can-Con regulations were highly controversial, but they did succeed in encouraging Canadian record production and exposure for Canadian artists.

Although their own history predated Can-Con, it was not until 1970 that a Canadian song by a Canadian band—and one with a distinctly Canadian perspective—climbed the Billboard 100 to its coveted number 1 spot. Winnipeg band The Guess Who, fronted by Burton Cummings and Randy Bachman, made its mark with its "American Woman." Ironically, the song itself is a dramatic attempt to distinguish Canada from an American neighbour increasingly marred by its Vietnam involvement, and violent student protests and race riots at home. By the 1980s, bands such as the Kingston, Ontario–based Tragically Hip, and Newfoundland's Great Big Sea, featuring songs with historic and topical references to Canada, found ready national audiences without looking to make it big in the United States. With a sound that simply spoke to pop music tastes of the time and very little to their Canadian origins, singers Celine Dion, Alanis Morisette, and Shania Twain numbered among the top international performers of the mid-1990s.

Questions about national identity and cultural sovereignty, and consequently about our relations with our powerful southern neighbour, dominate our cultural history, especially in the arena of popular culture, where the borders are more permeable and the access and participation proportionately greater. The late-twentieth-century digital revolution, like the industrialization of the previous century, marked a watershed in communications and mass culture along the historic lines of the printing press, the telegraph and telephone, film, radio, television and the Internet itself. The purportedly border-free Internet carries a considerable proportion of American content, exposing the rest of the world to the kinds of "cultural domination" that have so long framed the Canadian identity conundrum. What Canadians have embraced as popular culture at various points in our history reveals a great deal about both changes and continuities in our perceptions of ourselves as citizens, as a society, and as a nation. The proliferation of digital technologies that transmit instantaneously and unremittingly around the world make McLuhan's theory that "the medium is the message" acutely relevant in our own time. Particularly since the 1960s, with the growing public appetite for television, as well as rapid advances in satellite communications, cable transmission, and internet and wireless technologies, Canadians have had to confront the complex matter of protecting a distinctive popular culture in view of not only American dominance, but also the elastic borders of the "global village" prophesied by McLuhan.

QUESTIONS

1. Why does George Grant connect the demise of Canadian cultural distinctiveness, and consequently Canadian sovereignty, with the rise of American technological entrepreneurship?
2. Historian Ryan Edwardson classifies the comic book superhero Captain Canuck as "a cultural artifact." What purposes have been ascribed to this artifact, in terms of how the images associated with him have been put to social and cultural uses?
3. What does Robert MacGregor's analysis of the Molson beer commercial phenomenon that came to be known as "Joe's Rant" suggest about the relationship of media, popular culture, and national identity?
4. Why does the government report on the CBC/Radio Canada see young Canadians as a particularly important audience in the early twenty-first century?
5. The "viewing share" chart quantifies Canadian preferences in television programming, but does it help to explain why viewers make these choices? What kind of evidence do historians need to make conclusions about this matter?

FURTHER READINGS

Ryan Edwardson. *Canadian Content: Culture and the Quest for Nationhood* (Toronto: University of Toronto Press, 2008).

Ryan Edwardson. *Canuck Rock: A History of Canadian Popular Music* (Toronto: University of Toronto Press, 2009).

Harold Adams Innis. *The Bias of Communication* (Toronto: University of Toronto Press, 1951).

L. B. Kuffert. *A Great Duty: Canadian Responses to Modern Life and Mass Culture in Canada, 1939–1967* (Montreal and Kingston: McGill-Queen's University Press, 2003).

Paul Litt. *The Muses, the Masses and the Massey Commission* (Toronto: University of Toronto Press, 1992).

Ted Magder. *Canada's Hollywood: The Canadian State and Feature Films* (Toronto: University of Toronto Press, 1993).

Marshall McLuhan. *Understanding Media: The Extensions of Man* (New York: McGraw Hill, 1964).

Peter Morris. *Embattled Shadows: A History of Canadian Cinema, 1895–1939* (Montreal and Kingston: McGill-Queen's University Press, 1978).

Paul Rutherford. *When Television Was Young: Prime Time Canada, 1952–1967* (Toronto: University of Toronto Press, 1990).

Mary Vipond. *Listening In: The First Decade of Canadian Broadcasting, 1922–1932* (Montreal and Kingston: McGill-Queen's University Press, 1992).

▲ DOCUMENT 1: LAMENT FOR A NATION, 1965

In the wake of the Conservative Party's resounding defeat at the polls in 1964, philosopher Grant argued that the Pearson Liberals' evident embrace of American science, technology and corporate capitalism would soon prove that Canadians could not sustain an indigenous culture. Ultimately, national sovereignty itself was doomed to collapse as Canada became an American satellite state …

… The confused strivings of politicians, businessmen, and civil servants cannot alone account for Canada's collapse. This stems from the very character of the modern era. … The aspirations of progress have made Canada redundant. The universal and homogeneous state is the pinnacle of political striving. "Universal" implies a world-wide state, which would eliminate the curse of war among nations; "homogeneous" means that all men would be equal, and war among classes would be eliminated. The masses and the philosophers have both agreed that this universal and egalitarian society is the goal of historical striving. It gives content to the rhetoric of both Communists and capitalists. This state will be achieved by means of modern science—a science that leads to the conquest of nature. Today scientists master not only non-human nature, but human nature itself. Particularly in America, scientists concern themselves with the control of heredity, the human mind, and society. Their victories in biochemistry and psychology will give the politicians a prodigious power to universalize and homogenize. Since 1945, the world-wide and uniform society is no longer a distant dream but a close possibility. Man will conquer man and perfect himself.

… Modern civilization makes all local cultures anachronistic. Where modern science has achieved its mastery, there is no place for local cultures. It has often been argued that geography and language caused Canada's defeat. But behind these there is a necessity that is incomparably more powerful. Our culture floundered on the aspirations of the age of progress. The argument that Canada, a local culture, must disappear can, therefore, be stated in three steps. First, men everywhere move ineluctably toward membership in the universal and homogeneous state. Second, Canadians live next to a society that is the heart of modernity. Third, nearly all Canadians think that modernity is good, so nothing essential distinguishes Canadians from Americans. When they oblate themselves before "the American way of life," they offer themselves on the altar of the reigning Western goddess. … As Canadians we attempted a ridiculous task in trying to build a conservative nation in the age of progress, on a continent we share with the most dynamic nation on earth. The current of modern history was against us …

… All the preceding arguments point to the conclusion that Canada cannot survive as a sovereign nation. … Perhaps we should rejoice in the disappearance of Canada. We leave the narrow provincialism and our backwoods culture; we enter the excitement of the United States where all the great things are being done. Who would compare the science, the art, the politics, the entertainment of our petty world to the overflowing achievements of New York, Washington, Chicago, and San Francisco? … In the mass era, most human beings are defined in terms of their capacity to consume. All other differences between them, like political traditions, begin to appear unreal and unprogressive. As consumption becomes primary, the border appears an anachronism, and a frustrating one at that.

Source: George Grant, *Lament for a Nation: 40th Anniversary edition* (Montreal: McGill-Queen's University Press, 2005), pp. 65–67, 84, 88. Reprinted by permission of the publisher.

● As Ryan Edwardson discusses in his article, the comic book series *Captain Canuck* was the creation of artist Richard Comely, with initial inspiration from Calgary teacher and cartoonist Ron Leishman.

Source: Richard Comely, *Captain Canuck* cover, no. 1, (first issue), (July 1975). Courtesy of Captain Canuck Incorporated.

▲ DOCUMENT 3: SIXTH REPORT, 2008

CBC/Radio Canada

In February 2008, the Standing Committee on Canadian Heritage, appointed by the Harper Conservative government, and chaired by Conservative Member of Parliament Gary Schellenberger, published its report on the CBC/Radio Canada. The multiparty committee was mandated to study "the role of a public broadcaster in the twenty-first century." The committee held 45 public meetings across the country, heard hundreds of witnesses, and received more than 50 written submissions.

CBC/Radio-Canada has played a major role in the development of the broadcasting system in Canada. It is at the centre of cultural, political, social and economic life in Canada. It brings Canadians closer together and allows them to share their unique experience in North America. This is a huge task for CBC/Radio-Canada, as it has to operate over a very large geographic area while reaching out to a linguistically and culturally diverse audience. The development of new communications technologies in the last 20 years has made the Corporation's work more complex. ... There is no question that the Canadian broadcasting system is facing tremendous changes that will continue to have unpredictable effects in the future. The multiplication of digital platforms, the increasing number of specialty channels and the transition to digital/HD television will all affect the future of CBC/Radio-Canada. The Committee gave special consideration to the impact of emerging technologies on the Corporation's mandate. ...

... We are asking CBC/Radio-Canada to be original, of high quality and innovative, and to represent the reality of all Canadians living in this immense land, and in many languages. There is absolutely no doubt that we must always bear in mind what a colossal task it is for our public broadcaster to satisfy these demands. ... The English-language network has seen its audience share decline for a decade now. The appearance of many specialised channels and the emergence of broadcasting by satellite in part explain the fragmentation of CBC/Radio Canada's television audiences. Nor should we forget that CBC/Radio-Canada television operates in a market in which American broadcasts exert a very strong attraction. ...

CBC/Radio-Canada's English-language television competes with all the other broadcasters for the viewers' attention. In 1993, English-language pay and specialty channels had 6.2 percentage points of the audience share; in 2004, that figure was 22.4. Conversely, CBC Television's audience share declined by 6.5 percentage points between 1993 and 2004. ...

For many northern communities, CBC/Radio-Canada plays a capital role because it is a point of contact with the rest of the world. During our hearings in Yellowknife, witnesses even indicated that the presence of a public broadcaster was an essential service. In many communities, CBC North's radio and television broadcasts are the only sources of entertainment and information the residents have. Some communities do not have a local cable network, and the cost of satellite broadcasting services is often prohibitive. ... The various Aboriginal organisations that appeared before our Committee requested a change to CBC/Radio-Canada's mandate to include explicit obligations to Canada's Aboriginal peoples. ... The Committee considers that matters should be rectified without delay. As a national broadcaster, CBC/Radio-Canada has the mandate to represent everyone in

Source: From the Report of the Standing Committee on Canadian Heritage, *February 2008, CBC/ Radio-Canada: Defining distinctiveness in the changing media landscape.* Reprinted by permission of the Office of the Law Clerk and Parliamentary Counsel.

Canada, including the Aboriginal peoples. CBC/Radio-Canada is capable of doing more to serve the Aboriginal audience. It is a network's role to bring people together and to give the First Nations a voice. Partnerships with certain Aboriginal broadcasters could be strengthened.

... The ubiquity of digital media has forever changed the Canadian broadcast environment. Over the past decade, digital technology has significantly expanded the number of platforms from which audio and video programming can be accessed and received. The new services are characterised by their personalisation and on-demand accessibility from the Internet and mobile screens. Demand for these services is driven by the estimated 16.8 million adult Canadians who made personal non-business use of the Internet in 2005. That year, nearly 64% of Canadians 18 and older used the Internet at least once a day, a figure that jumps to nearly 73% in the 18–34 demographic. ...

Because of digital media's influence, traditional broadcasting is now about content delivery across as many platforms as can be made available, and the development of a global brand to attract audiences to that content. It is in the global milieu that Canada's public broadcaster must act, competing for audiences, advertising dollars, and the public's finite attention span for news, information and entertainment.

Audiences too have changed, now expecting the content they want, when, where and how they want it. Traditional broadcast television's former stranglehold on audiences has been weakened by competition from the Internet, specialty channels, iPods, video-on-demand, and audio and video streaming, to name just a few. As audiences fragment across multiple platforms, advertisers follow, seeking to take advantage of increasingly targeted niche programming and Web sites to deliver their messages. Advertisers spent in excess of $1 billion on the Internet last year in Canada. This has significantly impacted the traditional business model of conventional broadcasters for which advertising revenues are the foundation. ... Digital and broadband properties are now part of developing a global brand and remaining relevant to audiences, particularly younger audiences. The need for CBC/Radio-Canada to meet the new standard for content delivery was repeated by witnesses throughout the study. ... Witnesses pointed to new media, particularly the Internet, as a means for CBC/Radio-Canada to renew its commitment to Canadians and better reflect both the regions and individual voices. ... It is in this sense that digital media are seen to enable a redefinition of the "public" in public broadcasting.

... CBC/Radio-Canada established its web presence at CBC.ca and Radio-Canada.ca in 1995. ... The national public broadcaster is seen to be providing a reliable Canadian presence for news, information and Canadian content in a global media environment dominated by foreign content and market influence. Traffic has more than doubled to its two main Web sites, cbc.ca and radio-canada.ca, in the past five years, and they are among the most visited Canadian news and information Web sites. ... The Committee heard from some witnesses, however, that CBC/Radio-Canada needs to go further to develop a stronger national and global brand if it is to compete in the fragmented, global media environment. ...

Known as "digital natives" or "millennials", young people between the ages of about nine and 28 have a relationship with media that is different from previous generations. If Baby Boomers were the TV generation, Generation Y are the Internet generation, and they understand and use the new media tools in a different way. This group was born into the digital era, where previous concepts of bundling and scheduling have been replaced by downloading, streaming, peer-to-peer networks and on-demand programming. Their interactions with media are characterized by multi-tasking: they commonly use several media and platforms at the same time.

... More than 60% of young people have visited a social networking site, and nearly all of these have registered and created a profile. They have an expectation of interactivity and participation in media. When speaking of putting the public back into public broadcasting, younger Canadians will therefore be an important group of participants. ... CBC/Radio-Canada's online presence will be fundamental to its relevance to Canadian audiences in the future. According to the Canadian Internet Use Survey (CIUS), an estimated 16.8 million adult Canadians made personal non-business use of the Internet in 2005, and nearly 64% of Canadians 18 and older used the Internet at least once a day, a figure that jumped to nearly 73% in the 18–34 demographic ... More recently, a July 2007 Angus-Reid poll on Canadian technology habits reported that more than half of Canadians said that their lives are better because of the Internet (52%) and that they visit news Web sites at least once a day (55%) ... Among 18–34 year olds, 40% said that the Internet strengthens their sense of community with others, as did nearly one in three adult Canadians overall. ...

The Committee agrees that CBC/Radio-Canada requires a new media presence in order to remain relevant to Canadian audiences now and in the future. Innovative new media content and services are an essential part of renewing the Corporation's role as our national public broadcaster. ... The majority of witnesses, experts, academics and public and private organisations, supported an amendment to the CBC/Radio-Canada mandate commensurate with the view that the power of new media should be harnessed to fulfil Canada's public broadcasting objectives.

▲ DOCUMENT 4: "WHY WE DON'T HAVE HIT TV SERIES," 2013

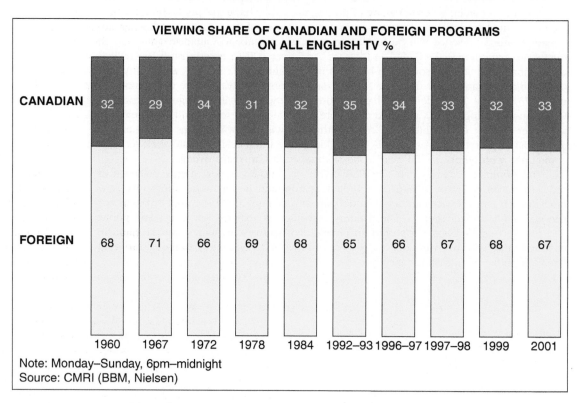

VIEWING SHARE OF CANADIAN AND FOREIGN PROGRAMS ON ALL ENGLISH TV %

	1960	1967	1972	1978	1984	1992–93	1996–97	1997–98	1999	2001
CANADIAN	32	29	34	31	32	35	34	33	32	33
FOREIGN	68	71	66	69	68	65	66	67	68	67

Note: Monday–Sunday, 6pm–midnight
Source: CMRI (BBM, Nielsen)

● In 1960, only six years after CBC-Radio Canada went on the air, two-thirds of Canadian prime-time viewing (6 pm to midnight) was dedicated to American programs. The same proportion has held from that time until the present, despite all technological advances and efforts by the federal government, especially the CRTC, to ensure both public funding and Canadian content.

Source: Canadian Media Research, Trends and Truth in Canadian Media, "60th Anniversary of Canadian TV: Why We Don't Have Hit TV Series," (18 April 2013). http://mediatrends-research.blogspot.ca/2013/04/60th-anniversary-of-canadian-tv-why-we.html. Used with permission from Barry Kiefl.

ARTICLE 1: THE MANY LIVES OF CAPTAIN CANUCK: NATIONALISM, CULTURE, AND THE CREATION OF A CANADIAN COMIC BOOK SUPERHERO

Ryan Edwardson

"Canada finally has her own honest-to-goodness comic magazine, with Canada's very own superhero—Captain Canuck!" (C.C. 1).[1] *Captain Canuck*'s 1975 release was the first Canadian comic book success since the collapse of the Second World War comic book industry. Captain Canuck, clad in a red and white suit and maple leaf emblems, used his strength—derived from a healthy diet and fitness—to fight for Canadian "peace, order, and good government." He avoided violence when possible, prayed before missions, and dedicated himself to protecting Canada and the world from evildoers. Canadian readers enjoyed the familiarity of national images, symbols, and locations infused with the action-adventure format established by American comic books. Yet, despite its popularity, the comic collapsed several times due to the economics of publishing in Canada and the problem of American cultural "dumping."

Captain Canuck is more than a comic book relic, however; it is a cultural artifact, a key item in the construction of modern Canadian cultural identity and consciousness. While in print, the comic presented popular cultural characteristics, myths, symbols, and stereotypes that legitimized the national identity and reinforced the conception of Canada as a "peaceable kingdom." Following the comic's publication run, Captain Canuck was revived by the Canadian government and incorporated as a national icon valuable for fostering national awareness and pride. It is an example of perpetual nation-building, an item of popular culture presenting national signifiers that, following its demise, was resurrected and recycled into a national signifier itself; it was fostered in a period of nationalism, empowered the national

Source: Ryan Edwardson, "The Many Lives of Captain Canuck: Nationalism, Culture, and the Creation of a Canadian Comic Book Superhero," *Journal of Popular Culture*, vol. 37, no. 2, (2003), pp. 184–201. Copyright © 2003 John Wiley and Sons. Reprinted by permission of the publisher.

identity, and later was integrated into the national myth-symbol roster.

"Nationalism," according to Ernest Gellner, "is not the awakening of nations to self-consciousness: it invents nations where they do not exist" (169). Benedict Anderson has furthered this idea, arguing that nations are imagined into existence because "the members of even the smallest nation will never know most of their fellow-members, meet them, or even hear of them, yet in the minds of each lives the image of their communion" (6). Comic books, as a visual medium, engage this act of imagination, in turn facilitating the mental construction of the nation and national identity. It is an act that may be an essential part of being Canadian. Canadian cultural historian Daniel Francis has argued (perhaps too generally but a valid observation nonetheless) that "because we lack a common religion, language or ethnicity, because we are spread out so sparsely across such a huge piece of real estate, Canadians depend on this habit of 'consensual hallucination' more than any other people" (10).

National identity, it can be argued, is also consumed into existence. Commodities can embody and popularize social identities and lifestyles—such as Nike and "Just do it" or the Body Shop and environmentalism—which are in turn confirmed through the consumption of those products (Klein). Through the consumption of commodities proposing certain myths, symbols, and values, national identities can be popularized and validated. In the area of Japanese national identity, Kosaku Yoshino has made some interesting insights into "a 'market' process whereby ideas of cultural differences are 'produced,' 'reproduced' and 'consumed'" (9). By drawing on Jean Baudrillard's argument that consumption "is a whole system of values, with all that expression implies in terms of group integration and social control functions" (81), one can see how cultural consumption provides a basis for identity construction. The material consumed carries a series of meanings that are either accepted or rejected by the consumer. [...]

[...] Consequently, in mass culture one can find mass national identity. Captain Canuck's red and white costume adorned with maple leaves signified his Canadianness, while his moralism, natural strength, and self-sacrificing persona reinforced conceptions of Canadians as polite, kind, moral, heroic peacekeepers. Distinctively national comic books, then, are vessels for transmitting national myths, symbols, ideologies, and values. They popularize and perpetuate key elements of the national identity and ingrain them into their readers—especially, given the primary readership, younger generations experiencing elements of that identity for the first time.

ALL IN THE FAMILY: CAPTAIN CANUCK'S COMIC BOOK LINEAGE

Late nineteenth-century Canadian newspapers often explored social, political, and cultural issues through comical caricatures, not only to highlight the editor's view, but to use as an aid for those lacking reading abilities. In the tradition of Miss Britannia, Canada often was cast as Miss Canada, the young daughter of the British Empire, or joined other masculine characters—including Britain's John Bull and America's Uncle Sam—as a youthful and sprightly Johnny or Jack Canuck.[2] Political parties, for example, attacked each other through newspaper cartoons that depicted Miss Canada in jeopardy, her virginal Victorian morality threatened by the older, seedy Uncle Sam. Jack or Johnny Canuck, on the other hand, embodied the "youthful" national spirit, ready to take on the world or, more often, confront Uncle Sam over an issue of trade or natural resources.

Comic books first appeared in the early 1930s, bringing together collections of reprinted comic strips. By 1938, stimulated by the popularity of Superman and similar superhero figures, they often included full-length original stories.[3] From the very beginning, the lack of a Canadian publishing industry and the cheap cost of American comic overruns ensured that the Canadian market was dominated by American comics. Stories of American heroes and villains supplied entertainment through exciting and spectacular figures, including Superman, the Flash, and Batman. They were a part of the American monomyth that "secularizes Judeo-Christian ideals by combining the selfless individual who sacrifices himself for others and the zealous crusader who destroys evil" (Land and Trimble 158). Yet Canadians share those "youthful, physically vigorous" and "morally upright" heroes, not only because their popular fiction is predominantly American in origin, but because their national, social, and economic developments have been similar. Thus, while the comics were of American origin, they engaged the imagination of Americans and Canadians by drawing on a shared North American monomyth of individualism, self-sacrifice, and personal humility. The fact that the superheroes existed in American cities like New York—or, at best, an undefined or imaginary "Anywhere, USA" metropolis—was a requisite part of reading comics in Canada.

In 1940, however, the American comics in Canada faced a challenge they were powerless to overcome: political policymaking. American comic book dominance was delivered a swift blow by Prime Minister William Lyon Mackenzie King's War Exchange Conservation Act, which limited the importation of "nonessentials"—including comic books—as a means of conserving American dollars for the war effort. Canadian companies, previously unable to compete against the "dumped" American comics, prospered in the protected market. Maple Leaf Publishing, Anglo-American, Hillborough Studios, and Bell Features and Publishing filled the Canadian demand for comic book entertainment. They produced superhero figures in mass quantities, relying on established American character types and war-inspired storylines. Out of the numerous heroes emerged Canada's first distinctly Canadian superhero, Nelvana of the North. The product of Hillborough Studios, Nelvana drew on the powers of the Aurora Borealis to fight superpowered Nazi agents. Nelvana's name came from an Inuit legend, but she was drawn as an Anglo-Saxon and clothed in a cape and miniskirt. In *Guardians of the North: The National Superhero in Canadian Comic-Book Art*, John Bell, Canada's foremost comic book historian, describes Nelvana as coming from the "same mold as the many white queens and goddesses that had appeared in popular fiction" (7). Nelvana was joined by Johnny Canuck in 1942, taking care of Nazis with his fast fists and solid jaw in adventure-packed (if slightly monotonous) comic book stories. Lacking superpowers but endowed with wit, charisma, and a strong right hook, Johnny Canuck traveled the world fighting Nazi tyranny. The war's end, however, brought the return of American comic books and the end of comic book Nazi antagonists. Canadian production quickly ended, once again unable to compete with the cheaper American material.

Until the 1970s, Canadians were limited to American comic books. There was little to ask for in the way of quality, as the comics supplied elaborate plot lines, skillful artistry, and exciting characters.

The comics were very American, however, in their symbols, figures, myths, and locations, right down to advertisements and the spelling of words. In Bell's assessment,

> what all Canadian comic-book readers of the 1950–1970 period had in common was a sense of alienation. For English Canadians, comics had become an American medium: the heroes were American, the settings were largely American, and even the alluring comic-book ads for toy soldiers and sea monkeys were American. Like U.S. television, comics seemed to contain an implicit message: Canada was a backwater bereft of heroes, bereft of guardians. For French Canadians, the medium was also dominated by the European francophone publishing houses. (*Guardians of the North* 19)

Indeed, in *Canuck Comics*, Bell notes that "Life in America, we just knew, was more exciting. Superman might visit his Fortress of Solitude in our Arctic from time to time, but never Toronto or Montreal, let alone Halifax where I lived" (13). It was a common experience for many Canadians. Reflecting on his own experience, Francis has described how

> in the universe I inhabited as a boy, there were no Canadian stars. There was no room; the skies were filled with the super novas of American history, politics, and pop culture. ... When I was looking for "role models" ... I found them on American television or in the myths of the American West or the comic books about U.S. marines in World War II. (112)

American cultural dominance increasingly came under criticism in the late 1960s, as a Canadian nationalist boom sparked an intense interest in cultural identity and concern over the lack of domestic cultural products. While American comics utilized ideas of heroism and self-sacrifice common to both Americans and Canadians, the dominance of American symbols and references drew scorn. Nationalists were especially keen to distinguish between conceptions of the American melting pot, tarnished by race riots and Vietnam violence, and the Canadian mosaic, a "peaceable kingdom" and multicultural haven of pluralism and understanding.[4] They called for cultural products reflecting distinct Canadian values, myths, and symbols.[5] Where were the

Canadian songs, movies, books, and even comic books? they asked.

"UP, UP, AND AWAY, EH?": THE BIRTH OF A CANADIAN SUPERHERO

Ron Leishman, a teacher and amateur cartoonist living in Winnipeg, Manitoba, first sketched a character he called Captain Canada in 1971. About a year later, Leishman met fellow comic book fan Richard Comely at a meeting of the Church of Jesus Christ of Latter Day Saints. They talked of creating a Canadian-themed comic book based on Leishman's Captain Canada, but the venture did not look promising. They were unable to get funding through government programs or loans, and in 1974 Leishman left to work in Alberta, followed by a two-year church mission in Belgium and France (Comely 2001).

Despite Leishman's absence, Comely did not give up on the plan. There were trademark problems with the name Captain Canada, so Comely changed it to Captain Canuck. The similarity to Johnny Canuck, however, was accidental; Comely was not aware of the national Nazi fighter until after the first issue of *Captain Canuck* was published (Comely 2001). "Canuck," the slang term for a Canadian, was distinctively national but not without its drawbacks. As one fan wrote in to the comic, "I thought it was some kind of a joke. Who would seriously think of naming a hero—even a comic book hero—'Captain Canuck'? Even if he is Canadian?" (12). The editor responded that "Canuck" was just "a casual term," and "like Yankee, it depends on how and when you say it." By placing the slang in a culturally positive context, Captain Canuck empowered the term, helping to popularize it as a valid nickname for a Canadian.

The first issue of *Captain Canuck* was published in 1975 with Comely as editor, artist, writer, publisher, production manager, and floor sweeper. Comely was, however, aided by Dave Abbott's "writing assistance," and he consulted Leishman on aspects of the comic. By the third issue, he was joined by George Freeman and Jean-Claude St. Aubin on penciling and coloring duties. Its release is regarded as the beginning of English Canada's "Silver Age" of comic book production (Bell, *Guardians of the North* 39). It was a milestone in Canadian comic book production. "Captain Canuck's very existence," Bell notes, "underscored the paucity of indigenous heroes that Canadian kids had experienced throughout the fifties and sixties" (*Canuck Comics* 39).

Captain Canuck was set in the future of the early 1990s, with Canada as the dominant world superpower—certainly a situation that could only occur in a comic book—facing evil forces seeking world domination. Tom Evans, a Mountie recruited into the Canadian International Security Organization, was of British descent, clean cut, strong and stocky, part "Indian blood,"[6] bilingual, and an ardent nationalist: a suitable candidate to protect Canada. As Captain Canuck, he literally embodied the Canadian flag, clad in a red and white costume adorned with maple leaves. Joined by the French Canadian agent "Kébec" and the super-Mountie "Redcoat," Captain Canuck was the first line of defense against super-villains seeking world domination. From futuristic Mounties to a maple-leaf-emblazoned snowmobile, Comely incorporated numerous Canadian references. Nelvana of the North may have fought superagents in the arctic while Johnny Canuck was overseas, but, in the first three issues alone, Captain Canuck's travels included dog sledding across the arctic, flying over "the magnificent Rockies," strolling "across the rooftops of scenic Montreal," and being abducted from "smog-ridden Sudbury" (Issues 1–3).[7]

Comely was "moved by the nationalism at the time" and proud of the comic's origin (Comely 2001). "We're 100% Canadian," the first issue announced, with the letters column in the third issue describing "national pride and patriotism [as] worthy attributes." *Captain Canuck* tapped into the nationalism of the period, and readers responded with great enthusiasm to having a distinctively Canadian comic: "as a Canadian I am proud to see our nation's greatness recognized," "here's to success in making *Captain Canuck* 100% Canadian," and "*Captain Canuck* has brought out the nationalistic spirit in all its readers, a pride this country now needs" (Issues 2, 3) are a few of the comments mailed in. He tried to make the comic as Canadian as possible, right down to the advertising. It was not easy, however. He contacted over 600 Canadian and 250 American companies, but had more success with the American advertisers. "Hopefully," Comely noted in the second issue, "it won't be too much longer before Canadian companies realize that it would be to their advantage to advertise in a 100% Canadian magazine like Captain Canuck." The lack of a Canadian publication industry posed problems, so distribution was handled by a U.S. company (*TIME* 1975, 10).

The myths and symbols were Canadian, but Comely's interest in conspiracy theories and his Mormon beliefs shaped the comic's content. "We're proud to say that there is nothing within that is degrading or offensive," the introduction to the first issue stated. Radical Communists bent on world domination were dealt with swiftly and with as little violence as necessary.[8] Captain Canuck prayed before missions and fought with God on his side. His abilities came from his moral character and natural health, a strong contrast to the supernatural powers of the American comic book characters. "Captain Canuck's tremendous strength and endurance come from a good wholesome diet and lots of exercise," Comely explained in the second issue. "His alertness and determination come from having a strong, clean mind." As the Canadian edition of *TIME* magazine noted in its 1975 review of the comic, "What distinguishes Captain Canuck from his American counterparts? Answer: The Canadian is polite and God-fearing and, although immensely strong, is not noted for his speed" (10). Concerned about the impact of excessive violence in society, in issue 2, Comely reprinted a four-page article on "How do movies and TV influence behaviour?" from a Mormon magazine. Comely was concerned with establishing a greater moral standard than existed in many mainstream comic books. He told *TIME* that "we need some moral fiber today and U.S. comics are tending more and more to violence and sexual innuendo … [Captain Canuck] will give thanks to God from time to time. [But] I don't want people to think I'm out to subvert them through a comic" (10).

At thirty-five cents, it was significantly more expensive than the popular twenty-five-cent American comics, yet Comely tried to provide plenty of value for the money. The early issues used a higher quality glossy paper and more complex coloring than their American counterparts. The issues contained a Captain Canuck story as well as a second feature story, often featuring two of Comely's other hero figures: "Jonn," a space commander stuck on a planet of iron-age warriors, or "Catman," a costume-clad vigilante. Occasionally there was "Beyond," a comical adventure series set in the Middle Ages. The early issues also included lessons on drawing and illustrating comic characters, a gallery for reader-submitted art, and small comic strip filler. With fewer ads, "at least 30% less than most super hero comics," issue 2 boasted, and a lower comic-to-ads ratio than the American comics, Comely offered a graphic-packed comic.

Captain Canuck was a source of inspiration for many Canadian comic book artists. Bell has noted that "the comic served to demystify the comic book business. Suddenly, the dream of creating Canadian superhero comics, which so many young artists and writers obviously harbored, became attainable" (Bell, *Canuck Comics* 39).[9] Yet *Captain Canuck* could not maintain production. Comely Comix, as the business was called, described itself as "a small struggling company with grand and lofty ideas" (C.C. 3)—an accurate claim for many Canadian publishing houses. Although "Canadian content" was fostered in television and radio through broadcasting regulations, and the arts community benefited from the Canada Council for the Arts, publishing had very little protection or domestic support.[10] The extensive coloring and higher quality paper added to the cost of production, but the biggest problem was the cost of producing a comic book in Canada. The market was small, funding sparse, distribution difficult, and printing expensive. As Comely explained to the readers in issue 2,

> I'm sure you're … aware that C.C. cost [sic] slightly more than U.S. comics. Sure, the higher quality increases the cost, but this is not the main reason. The small print runs and the fact that printing costs of comics are higher in Canada, cause our magazine to cost more than twice as much to produce than the U.S. comic magazines. I'm trying my best to bring cost down. One of the ways is to increase sales by distributing through out the U.S. as well as Canada.

Besides funding problems, the comic suffered from rigid characters, poor detailing, and unsophisticated plots with little tension or hook. In its review of the first issue, *TIME* magazine criticized its "amateurish quality" and "often clumsy artwork and story line" ("Canuck to the Rescue," 10). Issue number 3 was released in 1975, leaving the reader hanging on as Captain Canuck, badly wounded, was abducted in an ambulance by evildoers. Unfortunately, Comely Comix folded, unable to bear the costs of publishing *Captain Canuck*. It was a storyline cliffhanger that lasted for four years.

In 1979, Comely and partners, as CKR Productions in Calgary, Alberta, restarted the series at issue number 4. Comely wrote the stories, Ken Ryan was the business manager, George Freeman did the artwork, and Jean-Claude St. Aubain took care of the inking and coloring. Although this allowed Comely to focus on improving storylines, it isolated him from the aesthetic side of the comic. As of issue 5, Freeman was editing the comic with Comely as editor-in-chief.

This next generation of *Captain Canuck* maintained the focus on Canadian content. When confronted with the possibility of a Canadian civil war, for example, Captain Canuck announced that it would be stopped by "the War Measures Act! Then the Army would be everywhere!" (C.C. 6). Issue 11, set in Quebec City, had characters speaking French without translation for much of the issue, to the delight of some readers. One fan told the comic that he had "been interested in Captain Canuck over these years because of its potential to voice Canadian traditions and attitudes but never, in all that time, did I ever expect you to venture into such a sensitive area as Canadian bilingualism, especially when your magazine is so dependent on popularity for its existence" (13). Captain Canuck traveled to Halifax dockyards, Labrador ice fields, and visited his brother on a western Canadian ranch, interspersed with trips to more exotic places, including a lost South America city of gold and a multinational space station. "It is nice to see some Canadian landmarks for a change," a reader remarked, "such as Ottawa and Halifax. It is better than seeing New York and Washington all the time" (C.C. 9).

Under the new team, however, the revamped series integrated aspects of the established American comic book genre while shedding the elements that gave Comely's first three issues a grassroots feel. The religious undertone disappeared, and the conspiracy-driven plot lines were replaced by superhero supernaturalism and space-oriented themes. Captain Canuck no longer derived his strength from diet and moral cleanliness; history was rewritten, making him the product of an alien ray-beam that doubled his strength and speed (C.C. 5). Although this moved *Captain Canuck* in line with the established superhero genre, one fan complained that the change "lowers him to the level of the American super-heroes" (9). In addition, Captain Canuck became a freelance operative, serving both the Canadian government and a science-fiction-style international antiterrorist organization called Earth Patrol. Along with hoods and crooks, the Captain increasingly fought supernatural creatures and space aliens. Finally, perhaps in an attempt to spark circulation among American readers, Captain Canuck was removed from the future of the 1990s and, like most other superheroes, was relocated into the contemporary timeline—by that point, the early 1980s (13). Business manager Ken Ryan told readers that the time shift was for the best, as "a whole new lifestyle has been opened up for Captain Canuck—one that was not possible in the confines of the semi-futuristic period of the mid 1990s" (13).

The revitalized *Captain Canuck* was quite successful. In Bell's assessment, "*Captain Canuck* was transformed into one of the most accomplished alternative superhero comics ever published" (*Canuck Comics* 41). One fan confessed that "at first I only bought the comic out of Canadian pride, but now, who can resist?" (Special Summer issue 1980). In 1979, it was the bestselling comic book in Canada (C.C. 7), even though, at fifty cents an issue, it was still more expensive than many forty-cent American comics. A year later, *Captain Canuck* was the first Canadian comic to be distributed coast to coast in both Canada and the United States (10). There was even a *Captain Canuck* comic strip in the *Winnipeg Tribune*. Yet in 1981, with thirteen issues completed, Comely left *Captain Canuck*, returning to freelance design. In 1982, he released a new comic book titled *Star Rider and the Peace Machine*, but it only lasted two issues. With Comely's departure, Freeman was to take over the writing duties. Captain Canuck's time shift and the impact of Comely's departure did not have a chance to come to fruition, however, as CKR Productions only produced one more issue before financial difficulties caused it to shut down; *Captain Canuck* once again came to an end.

If Captain Canuck proved his heroism by never giving in to defeat, it reflected Comely's personal dedication to producing a Canadian comic book. In 1993, Comely and a new production staff released *Captain Canuck Reborn*, a new series with a different cast of characters and a new origin for Captain Canuck. The comic provided Comely with the opportunity to return to his original conception of *Captain Canuck*—a national superhero of natural strength and health in a comic with plenty of Canadian references and conspiracy theories.

In the new series, Darren Oak, along with his Native Canadian friend Daniel Blackbird, uncovered an international conspiracy to take over the world, led by none other than Darren's brother, Nathan, and his New World Order conglomerate. As a *Captain Canuck Reborn* commemorative trading card, released in 1993, explained,

> In a desperate attempt to rally a nation against an international conspiracy, Darren Oak becomes Captain Canuck. His big brother, Nathan, is involved in a devious plan to ignite civil war. Canada is to be HQ [Head Quarters] for a New World Order, but first they must gain complete control of Canada's government. Darren, armed only with truth and tremendous courage, must conceal his identity while he exposes the conspiracy. Inspired by a comic book, he becomes Captain Canuck.

Aided by Blackbird and other pro-Canada freedom fighters, Captain Canuck fought the New World Order on Parliament Hill, infiltrated a white-supremacist group in Lucyville, Alberta, and recovered from wounds at his home in Ourtown, Northern Ontario (C.C.R. 0–3).

Comely's skills as an artist, storywriter, and businessman had matured in the two decades since he first released *Captain Canuck*. Unfortunately, Captain Canuck once again fell victim to an enemy he could not defeat: the problems of publishing a comic book in Canada. The new series lasted for only four issues, ending in 1996 and taking with it a *Captain Canuck* newspaper strip that had started to run in various newspapers.

Captain Canuck was not only comic book entertainment, it was part of Canadian consumer culture. From the very first issue, readers were offered a barrage of items, including T-shirts, posters, iron-on crests, pens, pins, and doodle posters. Issue 7 introduced a series of merchandise with "New Captain Canuck paraphernalia to please even the pickiest patron!" There was even a Captain Canuck fan club, including a membership card and special merchandise for members only. The sale of Captain Canuck merchandise eventually made its way from the comic book and into Eaton's department stores in western Canada (Comely 2001). This was a key part of keeping the comic book going. According to Comely, "Captain Canuck merchandising made more than the sale of comic books. Printing costs were too high. The C.C. club, T-shirt licensing deal and other merchandise kept us afloat" (Comely 2001).[11] CKR Productions even went so far as to offer shares in the company to the readers. "This share bonus is not a gimmick!" the advertisement stated. "We've consulted the appropriate representatives of the Government of the Province of Alberta and we've received their cooperation and approval for our proposal to let you, the readers, actually own a part of the company" (14). It may have been a last ditch attempt to keep the company afloat, however, given that the offer was in the last issue of *Captain Canuck* to make it to press. This Canuck commodification was supported by publicity campaigns. Comely drove around Winnipeg in a yellow AMC Pacer with *Captain Canuck* emblazed on the side. As well, a 210-pound, 6'3" karate expert was hired to dress in a Captain Canuck costume and make public appearances at shopping centers and special events. Comely thought the events were quite successful (9, 11).

POST–COMIC BOOK LIFE AND THE TRANSITION FROM NATIONAL DEFENDER TO NATIONAL ICON

Nations need heroes, even fictional ones.[12] Not surprisingly, governments that lay claim to popular heroes, instituting them as representatives and manifestations of national might, validate the national identity and add cultural depth to an institutional hegemonic agent. Embracing popular culture, the Canadian government created a public showing of its comic book superheroes. From February 13 to June 7, 1992, the National Archives of Canada held "Guardians of the North: The National Superhero in Canadian Comic-Book Art," exhibiting Canadian comic books and paraphernalia, and detailing the development of Canadian comic art and superheroes. Canadian superheroes, the exhibition explained, were the "embodiment of our national spirit and identity" (Bell, *Guardians of the North* 50). Captain Canuck's natural strength and abilities, for example, were cited by the exhibition's catalogue as Canadian characteristics:

> … typifying Canadian reticence in so many things, some of these heroes possess no actual superpowers, relying rather on superior physical and intellectual skills to enable them to combat

their enemies. … In a sense, Canuck was the appropriate superhero for a middle power that was somewhat distrustful of heroism and very much aware of the limits of power. (v, 25–26)

The exhibition claimed that comics were much more than adventure stories: they probed Canadian society and reflected the issues within a national context.

> Why superheroes? Why comics? These are not just entertaining fantasy figures. They are important to our history because they are symbols of the Canadian identity. Their creators were probing issues of great concern to the Canadians of the day—World War II, national identity, our relationship with the United States. (v)

There is certainly some truth to this. As Alphons Silbermann has noted, "comics mediate, even as pure entertainment, certain mental values. Since the fact is that entertainment and information do not exclude each other, comics are latently or overtly open to any ideology" (21).

The National Archives exhibition was followed by Canada Post's recognition of five Canadian comic book heroes, institutionalizing them as important cultural icons. On October 2, 1995, Canada Post issued a booklet of ten stamps containing the "Canadian crusaders" Superman, Nelvana of the North, Fleur de Lys (who appeared in the late 1980s comic *Northguard*), Johnny Canuck, and Captain Canuck. Ironically, the government that would not provide funding for Captain Canuck two decades earlier now provided a different form of investment: a symbolic one. The Captain Canuck stamp commoditized his image in a new way, as an official national commodity—forty-five cents of federal currency added to the hats, pins, and pens Comely sold to keep the comic afloat.

Canada Post's inclusion of Superman as a Canadian superhero reflects an interesting part of the Canadian cultural psyche. Striving to establish strong cultural mythologies and heroes, it associates the nation with an internationally recognized, culturally important icon. This has been supported by some cultural nationalists, including Marsha Boulton, who gives him a section and a predominant place on the cover of *Just a Minute: Glimpses of Our Great Canadian Heritage*. Superman co-creator Joe Shuster was born in Toronto, Ontario, in 1914, and that alone was sufficient for Superman to be deemed

Canadian. Shuster left Canada for the United States when he was eight years old, and Superman was not created until a decade later with his friend Jerry Siegal. First a comic strip reflecting American New Deal politics and social consciousness, it was later reconfigured into a comic book action-adventure format. Let's not forget that Superman defended "Truth, Justice, and the American Way," not Canada's motto of "Peace, Order, and Good Government." Heritage Canada reaffirmed the government's claim to Superman through historical tampering, releasing a Superman "Heritage Moment" as part of its series of sixty-second television commercials that dramatize a moment in Canadian history. The spot showed a young Joe Shuster boarding a train, ranting about a new type of superhero he was creating, and passing a drawing of Superman to his friend "Lois" as she laughed about "you Canadian kids!" It was pure fabrication. And, as author Will Ferguson has slyly noted, Captain Canuck is from Canada, Superman is from Krypton (175).[13]

The image of Captain Canuck has become so associated with Canada that the nation itself has been placed in the costume. The April 28, 1997, Canadian edition of *TIME* magazine cast Captain Canuck on its cover, along with a banner declaring that "Canada is the new superhero of global trade (and even Superman is being produced in Winnipeg these days)."[14] Inside the issue, Canada—as Captain Canuck—lifted bar graphs and hurled pie charts detailing Canada's economic strength. In the context of *TIME*, Canada *became* Captain Canuck—Canada *was* strong and powerful. The magazine detached Captain Canuck's image from the comic book and resituated it in a new context and narrative, constructing a new denotative meaning that drew on the established connotation of heroism and strength.[15]

Soon after these developments, Captain Canuck was reconfigured yet again, his status as a national icon attracting the interest of the arts community. Featuring artwork from the *Captain Canuck Reborn* series, "Canada's Own Captain Canuck: Inked Drawings by Richard Comely" was exhibited at the Burlington Art Centre in Burlington, Ontario, during the summer of 1998. By exhibiting the artwork as individual pieces instead of as part of the comic book whole, the segmented, paneled aesthetics separated the artwork from the storylines. *Captain Canuck* was no longer just a comic book; it was now popular art and material for aesthetic critique and display, the images providing content for the exhibition.

Captain Canuck—comic book superhero and national protector, embodiment of Canadian values, forty-five-cent postage stamp, Canada's alter ego, and, finally, popular art—survived not only fictional supervillains, but, perhaps even more heroically, the dangers of the Canadian publishing industry. *Captain Canuck's* history is a story of grassroots cultural production and a distinctly national superhero who became valuable to the government it fictionally protected. The comic's demise, however, may once again be temporary. In 1999, Mark Shainblum (writer and co-creator of popular 1980s Canadian comic book *Northguard*) and Sandy Carruthers, both contributors to the early 1990s *Captain Canuck* newspaper comic strip, attempted to bring back Tom Evans as Captain Canuck in *Captain Canuck: Utopia Moments*. Plans were made for a four-issue miniseries, but these have yet to come to fruition. An issue was compiled and released on a trial promotional run limited to one hundred copies, but has not progressed any further. Comely returned to the comic book scene in 2000 with a plan for yet another Captain Canuck. Establishing media contacts and setting up an Internet Web page, his project is still in the works. Things look hopeful, though. The Canadian publishing industry is not as weak now as it was twenty (even ten) years ago. Captain Canuck may again provide a generation of Canadian comic book fans with a sense of national identity in a cultural arena where New York overwhelms New Brunswick, and one rarely sees a maple leaf.

NOTES

1. Captain Canuck citations will be listed by issue number, not page number.
2. For examples, see J. W. Bengough, *A Caricature History of Canadian Politics*.
3. For a solid overview of the transition from comic strips to comic books, see Ian Gordon, *Comic Strips and Consumer Culture, 1890–1945*.
4. William Kilbourn popularized the term in Canada with the title of his edited collection of nationalist writing, *Canada: A Guide to the Peaceable Kingdom*.
5. Defining just what constituted "Canadian," however, was a more difficult task.

6. In issue 12, Captain Canuck slipped back in time and encountered a group of Micmac Native Canadians. In hopes of ingratiating himself with them, he pulled off his mask, showing them his "Indian blood," and was welcomed by them.

7. The location of issue 3 was identified in issue 4.

8. Interestingly, the Communist leader in issue 1 was drawn so similar to Lenin that a fourteen-year-old reader wrote into the comic about it in the second issue.

9. For an interesting look at comic books and fan mentality, see Matthew J. Pustz's *Comic Book Culture: Fanboys and True Believers.*

10. The 1972 Ontario Royal Commission on Book Publishing's *Canadian Publishers and Canadian Publishing* noted that there may have been "Canadian publishers," but that did not necessarily mean that there was "Canadian publishing" (60). "Commercial realism" and profitability prevented many Canadian publishers, foreign-owned or not, from publishing large quantities of distinctly Canadian content material (63).

11. Comely puts the number of C.C. club members at 1,200–1,500. The phenomenon of comic book commodification first took hold with Detective Comics's trademarking of *Superman* and the extensive merchandising of products during the 1940s, including a toy ray gun and wristwatch. Ian Gordon explains that "In the hands of a corporation, Superman was more important as a business asset than a fictional character" (134). Merchandising hit a high point in the 1990s—with the fusion of comic book characters and global media production—with characters such as Batman commoditized into billion-dollar industries. For more information, see Ian Gordon's *Comic Strips and Consumer Culture*, pp. 133–35 and 152–57.

12. Much can be said about the role of fiction in the stories of nonfictional heroes, of course. History is far from a precise science and, especially in the case of national history, is quite positive and supportive of its heroes. History, after all, is not only written by the victors but also by the heroes.

13. See Will Ferguson, *Why I Hate Canadians*, p. 175.

14. Part of the colorization process for *Superman* was handled in Canada.

15. Swiss linguist Ferdinand de Saussure's semiological work showed how a *signifier* (the communicative) is connected with a *signified* (mental concept, object, and so on) to construct a *sign* (the arbitrary signifying construct). Roland Barthes produced the most influential work on semiology and culture, first outlined in *Mythologies* (1957), *Elements of Semiology* (1964), and *The Fashion System* (1967). Extending Saussure's work on the denotative, Barthes explored the connotative, a subjective meaning produced by the meeting of the sign and the viewer. It is within the connotative that emotions, values, and so on are expressed.

WORKS CITED

Anderson, Benedict. *Imagined Communities*. London: Verso, 1991.

Baudrillard, Jean. *The Consumer Society: Myths and Structures*. London: Sage Publications, 1998.

Bell, John. *Canuck Comics*. Downsview, Ontario: Eden Press, 1986.

Bell, John. "Curator, National Archives of Canada." *Guardians of the North: The National Superhero in Canadian Comic-Book Art*. Ottawa: Minister of Supply and Services Canada, 1992.

Bengough, J. W. *A Caricature History of Canadian Politics*. Toronto: Peter Martin Associates, 1974.

Boulton, Marsha. *Just a Minute: Glimpses of Our Great Canadian Heritage*. Toronto: McArthur & Co., 1998.

Canada Post Corporation. Press release, 26 Sept. 1995.

Captain Canuck. Issues 1–3. Winnipeg, Manitoba: Comely Comix, 1975.

Captain Canuck. Issues 4–14. Calgary, Alberta: CKR Productions Ltd, 1979–1981.

Captain Canuck Reborn. Cambridge, Ontario: Comely Communications, 1993–1996.

Comely, Richard. Correspondence with author, summer 2001.

Ferguson, Will. *Why I Hate Canadians*. Vancouver: Douglas & McIntyre, 1997.

Francis, Daniel. *National Dreams: Myth, Memory, and Canadian History*. Vancouver: Arsenal Pulp Press, 1997.

Gellner, Ernest. *Thought and Change*. London: Weidenfeld and Nicolson, 1964.

Gordon, Ian. *Comic Strips and Consumer Culture, 1890–1945*. Washington, DC: Smithsonian Institution Press, 1998.

Klein, Naomi. *No Logo: Taking Aim at the Brand Bullies*. Toronto: Vintage Canada, 2000.

Land, Jeffrey, and Patrick Trimble. "Whatever Happened to the Man of Tomorrow? An Examination of the

American Monomyth and the Comic Book Super-hero." *Journal of Popular Culture* 2 (1988): 157–73.

Ontario Royal Commission on Book Publishing. *Canadian Publishers and Canadian Publishing*. Toronto: Queen's Printer and Publisher, 1992.

Pustz, Matthew J. *Comic Book Culture: Fanboys and True Believers*. Jackson: UP of Mississippi, 1999.

Silbermann, Alphons. "The Way Toward Visual Culture: Comics and Comic Films." *Comics and Visual Culture*. Ed. A. Silbermann and H. D. Dyroff. New York: K. G. Saur, 1986. 11–27.

TIME. "Canuck to the Rescue." Canadian edition, 9 June 1975: 10.

TIME. "Captain Exporter." Canadian edition, 28 Apr. 1997: Cover.

TIME. "Super Exporter." Canadian edition, 28 Apr. 1997: 34–40.

Yoshino, Kosaku. "Rethinking Theories of Nationalism: Japan's Nationalism in a Marketplace Perspective." *Consuming Ethnicity and Nationalism: Asian Experiences*. Ed. Yoshino Kosaku. Honolulu: U of Hawaii P, 1999.

ARTICLE 2: I AM CANADIAN: NATIONAL IDENTITY IN BEER COMMERCIALS

Robert M. MacGregor

Occasionally a television commercial causes social, political, and business ramifications far beyond anyone's initial expectations. In March 2000, a sixty-second television beer commercial became an overnight phenomenon. For approximately three months thereafter, the advertisement became a national and international focus of debates on Canadian nationalism and identity. Some issues concerning national identity will be discussed.

MOLSON CANADIAN "THE RANT"

Sometimes a single television commercial can have such an impact that it takes on a life of its own. A few examples of such advertisements include:

1. Coca-Cola's 1971 song "I'd Like to Buy the World a Coke" that became "I'd Like to Teach the World to Sing," a one-million-units-sales best seller.
2. LIFE brand cereal—Quaker Oats Company showing Mikey enjoying LIFE brand. "Hey Mikey" entered the lexicon.
3. The greatest commercial ever made—Apple Macintosh's "1984," showing Big Brother (IBM) in an Orwellian nightmare—caused the Macintosh revolution.
4. Clara Peller barked, "Where's the Beef?" for Wendy's and a popular culture phenomenon was born. American presidential candidate Walter Mondale used the phrase in his campaign (Ward Fawcett).

Molson's beer commercial, in a Canadian context, now stands as an example of a single advertisement that now joins the pantheon of selected "best" television presentations.

Montreal-based Molson Company, founded in 1786, is Canada's preeminent brewer and one

hundred percent Canadian owned, with sales in excess of $2 billion. One of its top-selling brands is called CANADIAN. Between 1994 and 1998, Molson had used the tag line, "I am CANADIAN." This line was replaced by "Here's where we get CANADIAN," widely criticized as flat-mouthed. Responsibility for reviving the CANADIAN brand went to Brett Marchand, an Alberta-born marketing executive who had been lured away from Campbell Soup in Philadelphia. Grassroots interviews clearly indicated a growing sense of national pride among the key niche, nineteen- to twenty-five-year-olds. The Toronto agency Bensimon Byrne D'Arcy recommended that Molson revive the "I am CANADIAN" slogan. The "Joe Rant" emerged as a passionate declaration of national pride, a definitive piece of popular culture. As they say, the rest is history.

I AM CANADIAN

Hey
I'm not a lumberjack, or a fur trader.
I don't live in an igloo, eat blubber, or own a dogsled.
I don't know Jimmy, Sally or Suzy from Canada.
Although I'm certain they're very nice.

I have a prime minister, not a president.
I speak English and French, NOT American,
and I pronounce it 'ABOUT', NOT 'A BOOT.'

I can proudly sew my country's flag on my backpack. I believe in peace keeping, NOT policing,
DIVERSITY, NOT assimilation
and that the beaver is a proud and noble animal.

A TOQUE IS A HAT,
A CHESTERFIELD IS A COUCH,
AND IT IS PRONOUNCED 'ZED,' NOT 'ZEE', 'ZED.'

CANADA IS THE SECOND LARGEST LANDMASS,
THE FIRST NATION OF HOCKEY
AND THE BEST PART OF NORTH AMERICA.
MY NAME IS JOE
AND I AM CANADIAN

Thank you.

The copy and visual elements of the advertisement addressed some of the commonly held stereotypes that others perhaps hold of Canadians. Whether it is language pronunciation differences, occupational, eating, and living factors, sports interests, or social

Source: Robert M. MacGregor, "I Am Canadian: National Identity in Beer Commercials," *Journal of Popular Culture*, vol. 37, no. 2, (2003), pp. 276–286. Copyright © 2003 John Wiley and Sons. Reprinted by permission of the publisher.

and political policies, each of these is fleetingly presented. Two major symbolic icons are also invoked in the ad: the beaver and Canada's national flag, the maple leaf. The ad had been in movie theaters since March 17, 2000, and made its national television debut on March 26 during the Academy Awards broadcast.

A possible impetus to the immediate success of "The Rant" may have been Robin Williams's same-night, same-show rendition of the *South Park* film's song "Blame Canada." This song was nominated for an Oscar.

This song satirized Canada as a tool for satirizing Americans. In the song "Blame Canada," all four mums—Sheila, Sharon, Liane, and Ms. McCormick—sing the wows of parenthood. The last ten lines of the song are:

Sheila: With all their hockey hubba baloo
Liane: And that bitch Anne Murray too
Everyone: Blame Canada
       Shame on Canada
       The smut we must stop
       The trash we must smash
       Laughter and fun
       Must be all undone
       We must blame them and cause a fuss
       Before someone thinks of blaming uuuuuus.

Trey Parker and Matt Stone did not create the flip-top headed characters in *South Park* to offend Canadians; they did so to take a jab at Americans' stereotyping of Canadians. They chose to "Blame Canada" before somebody thinks to blame us—Americans—for the sole reason American mentality is that way. Michael Moore wrote *Canadian Bacon* in 1995, a movie about invading Canada that focused on America's need to have an enemy. The song, the movie, and the Oscar presentation appeared to add to the poignancy of "The Rant" commercial and helped to reinforce some prevailing attitudes of Canadians about Americans.

Within days of the initial airing of "The Rant," dozens of Web sites sprung up, numerous parodies of groups and individuals appeared, and Jeff Douglas took on major celebrity status. The many parodies that appeared include: I am a columnist, I am an Albertan, I am a Newfie, I am Chinese, I am Pakistani, I am Indian, I am Italian, I am Irish, I am Jamaican, I am Filipino, I am Torontonian, I am Manitoban, I am British Columbian, I am Not Canadian (parody on Québecers), and I am American. All of the parodies followed the same genre, and the American one read as follows:

I AM AMERICAN

I'm not particularly intelligent, open-minded, or generally well-liked.
I don't live in a clean place.
I don't eat nutritiously very often.
And I abandon my car on the side of the interstate until the tires are stolen.

I don't know Shakespeare, Da Vinci or Gutenberg. Although I'm certain they weren't American.

I drink watery beer.
I don't use utensils when eating.
I believe in guns for settling disputes, not discussions.

And I pronounce it AIN'T, not AREN'T.
I don't say, "you're welcome" in response to "thank you." I say "Uh Huh."
I can proudly sew my country's flag on my backpack … until I go anywhere.

Burger King IS fine dining and Miss America is a virgin.
Ketchup IS a vegetable and WWF wrestling is real.

The UNITED STATES is the ONLY country in the world.

The FIRST nation of ignorance,
And the BEST part of South America!

My name is Johnny Bob Jimmy Joe Ray, I'm married to my sister,
AND I AM AMERICAN!

Joe, the actor, performed at National League Hockey games, appeared on most major television and radio talk shows, did business conferences, and eventually went off to Hollywood. The television commercial won a Bronze Lion at the 2000 Cannes International Advertising Awards, where thirty-two other commercials were on the short list in the alcoholic beverage category. In Canada, it was voted "Best of Show," winning the gold medal for television single over thirty seconds (*Marketing*).

In November 2001, "The Rant" won top honors at the advertising industry's CASSIE awards, picking up the coveted Grand Prix. The CASSIES are awarded based on how successfully the ad moves the client's business. In a release, the award's group said that the Molson Canadian campaign produced "amazing" results for the brand. From March 2000 to March 2001, the Canadian brand grew by 2.5 percent in market share, while archrival Labatt's Blue declined by 2.9 percent (Heinrich).

From a commercial and creative viewpoint, "The Rant" was an extremely successful advertisement. What was unseen initially were the eventual discussions that took place at the political and institutional levels. Ontario Minister of Consumer Affairs Bob Runciman quickly denounced the ad. He was quoted as saying:

> I felt it was saying things that didn't have to be said in terms of saying things of feeling good about our country. You can send out very strong messages about being Canadian—I'm certainly as pro-Canadian as anyone—but I don't think you have to kick anyone else in the shins to do that. I think that this is essentially an anti-American rant which taps into a national lack of self confidence when it comes to dealing with the United States. (Molson Canadian Commercial)

Several well-known Canadian historians, including Michael Bliss of Toronto and Desmond Morton of McGill, voiced their concerns about the negativity of "The Rant." Bliss believed that the advertisement was pathetic, depressing, and an embarrassment to Canada; it was nationalism without content. Morton said that "the mobilization of a sense of Canadianism to peddle beer is a frontal attack on the values Canadians share" (Walker).

Other well-known Canadians took an opposing view and voiced their support of the creative rendition. Bob Rae, former premier of Ontario, said:

> This speaks to every stupid question that Americans always ask Canadians. There is a very strong element of nationalism in Canada that never goes away. The closer we get economically, the more we like thumbing our noses and that's a lot of fun. (Kettle)

Rudyard Griffiths, director of the Dominion Institute in Toronto, saw "The Rant" as an example of tearing a page out of the book of American cultural imperialism—a change in the habits of cultural expression in Canada (a "ra ra-ism").

He believed:

> It's very retro and it's interesting that it's connected with a younger group. Canadian sovereignty has been more of an issue for those who came of age during the late 1960s and early 1970s. That was a time when Canada had a new flag, a hip and glamourous prime minister in Pierre Trudeau, and a world fair. As tensions over the Vietnam war tore at the social fabric of the United States, Canada emerged as a humane alternative society. There was a conscious rebranding of Canada as independent nation ready to take its place on the world stage. (Walker)

Throughout the public debates, two viewpoints were coalescing. The advertisement was seen as an expression of Canadian pride, and critics saw "The Rant" as a declaration of anti-American sentiment. Glen Hunt, who wrote the ad, saw the commercial as pro-Canadian and not anti-American. Brett Marchand, Molson vice president, believed what the ad said "… is what more Canadians wish people would do—scream that they are proud to be Canadian" ("Beer ad").

Marchand also stated that the ad elements—beer, hockey, and the environment, for example—represented "Canada's patriotic DNA." He believed that the young respondents interviewed for their views on Canada were likened to a "dormant volcano." "We definitely didn't expect it to have the impact it's had, beyond its value as a beer ad," Marchand continued. "You couldn't image [sic] the phenomenon it is in Canada. It's been on the front page of newspapers. There are radio talk shows across the country dedicated to the ad. I've been doing interviews almost from first thing in the morning until the end of the day every day. It really has struck a chord with a huge group of consumers." (Bach).

One federal politician who saw the social and political implications of the mass appeal of the ad to many Canadians was the Honourable Sheila Copps, Minister of Canadian Heritage. At the International Press Institute World Congress held in Boston on May 1, 2000, she used "The Rant" beer advertisement to present and discuss the importance of national cultural identity to Canadians. After the video of the ad was shown, she presented the following points to the audience:

> Yes, the ad pokes fun at the U.S., and yes, there is a bit of chest thumping—but it also pokes fun at Canadian efforts at self-validation by posing in contrast to Americans. The ad has spun off a huge raft of subsidiary jokes in which Canadians laugh at our teams, our cities and ourselves. The popularity of the ad raises a serious point, though. Some American business people firmly believe that culture is a good allocated solely by the private sector and free markets. When you are the world's cultural juggernaut, at best, this means serious challenges for other nations.
>
> For Canadians, culture is not just like any other good like pork rinds or brass tack. Culture is not just entertainment. It is the expression of the soul and the identity of the country. (*Speaking notes*)

Ms. Copps continued in the speech to discuss cultural pluralism, cultural diversity, and the disappearance of languages and dialects, encouraging free expression and cultural security. Near the conclusion of her speech, she stated,

> I'll undoubtedly catch flak from some commentors back in Canada for bringing "Joe Canadian" to Boston but I say what better place for a strong call for cultural identity by Joe Sixpack than here where Americans first stated their call for cultural recognition and fair representation. (*Speaking notes*)

The Minister of Canadian Heritage did not have long to wait. The next day, May 2, Mr. John Solomon (Regina-Lumsden-Lake Centre, NDP) rose in the House of Commons in Ottawa and proudly proclaimed "I am Canadian":

I AM CANADIAN

Mr. John Solomon (Regina-Lumsden-Lake Centre, NDP):

Mr. Speaker, I am not a Republican or a Democrat. I do not spend millions to run for office or hire American consultants or go negative. I do not know Stockwell or Tom or Joe but I am sure they are very nice. I have a health card, not an insurance card, I listen to Cross Country Checkup,

not Howard Stern or Rush Limbaugh, I speak for people, not multinational corporations. I believe in inexpensive generic drugs, environmental protection and fair trade deals. I believe that Canada can have an independent foreign policy. Canadian taxpayers are citizens too who value our social programs. And it is pronounced medicare, not Bill 11, okay? Canada is the home of public health care, curling, Codco and the NDP.

My name is John and I am Canadian.

Much of Mr. Solomon's "rant" compares various factors that clearly distinguish America from Canada, and clearly suggests his own political party's electoral platform (Solomon).

Three days later on May 5, Richard Marceau (Charlesbourg, BQ), member of the nationalist/separatist party, openly mocked Ms. Copp's Boston visit. His declaration clearly illustrated some of the tensions that prevail between the English and French populations in Canada. His statements were as follows:

Mr. Richard Marceau (Charlesbourg, BQ):

Mr. Speaker, on May 1, the Minister of Canadian Heritage went to the ridiculous lengths of promoting "Canadian" culture in Boston with a beer ad. How clever.

How can Quebecers define themselves within this selection of Canadiana when the beer in question is not even sold in Quebec? Molson long ago grasped the specific nature of Quebec and serves us in Laurentide.

We in Quebec have a real department of culture, not one for heritage. What we fear is not comparison with the Americans but assimilation with the Canadians.

In Quebec, when we say we are bilingual, that does not mean we just know a few pick-up lines. Our objective is to make Quebec known throughout the world, not to go other countries and put our foot in our mouth every chance we get.

Above all, when we in Quebec want some pro-Quebec advertising, we do not hire an American. (Marceau)

It is not the intent of this article to discuss the individual elements of the ad or to discuss the tensions between the English and French politicians. These will be analyzed in other articles as will the American dimensions—for example, stereotyping of Canadians and whether the ad was anti-American. Some considerations concerning national identity will conclude this article.

NATIONAL IDENTITY

"Who are we?" is a universal and perennial question. It is a particular question of concern to Canadians, most of whom believe that they are distinctive, and that to have a clear identity is to be different from Americans (Hedley). The advertisement highlights some of the perceived value differences: the protection of the state peace, order, good government, and inclusive social policies.

Douglas Kellner believed that today, in modernity, identity is more mobile, multiple, personal, self-reflexive, and subject to change and innovation. Yet in postmodern society, identity remained social- and other-related. Historically, in Canada the dominant ideology of "being a Canadian" was in the process of being defined as speaking English within a British-type institutional system. This British model, a latent unitarian model of identity, was reasonably successful in Canada but was never unchallenged. To varying degrees, tension has existed within the existing cultural diversity of the nation, and especially within the mainly French population of Québec. The symbolic order and cultural capital factors changed dramatically in the 1960s. One of the ways that changes were made to help assuage growing tensions and anxiety between the two founding nations was to change the symbolic character of the Canadian national identity. The Official Languages Act of 1969 made Canada a bilingual country, a Canadian Flag was adopted in 1965, Trans-Canada Airline became Air Canada, the Dominion Bureau of Statistics became Statistics Canada, "O Canada" was proclaimed as the national anthem in 1980, stamps were changed (elimination of the Queen's portrait), money was redesigned with more Canadian symbols, and the constitution was patriated. The point to emphasize here is to concur with Kellner's point that modern national identity more and more has a degree of flexibility to evolve. The state in Canada intervened substantially to reorient the symbolic national identity order. Some groups, not the Québec nationalists, perceived the

changes to be an enrichment of society's symbolic system, and, as a result, their own symbolic identity. Some of these changes are reflected in "The Rant" beer advertisement (Breton).

Consumers, beer drinkers, and advertisement viewers are socially and culturally situated individuals seeking to make sense of their lives, identities, and relationships. Ads such as "The Rant" provided symbolic resources to be used for those purposes (O'Donohue). McCracken suggested that in looking at ads, consumers seek "concepts of what it is to be a man or a woman, concepts of what it is to be middle-aged … (or) a member of a community or a country" (122). Molson's sixty-second television commercial for its brand of beer, CANADIAN, appeared to motivate many people to be proud to stand up and shout, "I am CANADIAN!"

WORKS CITED

Bach, Deborah. "Better Ad Hyping Canada Strikes Chord Across Borders." *Baltimore Sun* 25 Apr. 2000. Available at http:// www.amarillonet.com.

"Beer Ad Gets 19,000 Fans Excited." 15 Apr. 2000. Available at http://www.canoe.ca/2000_NHL_Playoffs_OrrTor.

Breton, Raymond. "The Production and Allocation of Symbolic Resources: an Analysis of the Linguistic and Ethnocultural Fields in Canada." *Canadian Review of Sociology and Anthropology* 21.2 (1984): 123–44.

CASSIES, short for Canadian Advertising Success Stories, created in 1993. For more information see: http:// www.cassies.ca.

Copps, Sheila. *Speaking Notes for the Honourable Sheila Copps. Minister of Canadian Heritage*. International Press Institute World Congress, Boston, 1 May 2000.

Hedley, Alan. "Review Essay, Identity: Sense of Self and Nation." *Canadian Review of Sociology and Anthropology* 31.2(1994): 200–14.

Kellner, Douglas. "Popular Culture and the Construction of Postmodern Identity." *Modernity and Identity*. Ed. Scott Lash and Jonathan Friedman. Oxford, UK: Basil Blackwell Ltd., 41–77.

Kettle, Martin. "Mocked Canada Finds Hope and Glory in a Beer Ad." *Guardian*. 25 May 2000. Available at http://www.guardian.co.uk/Archive/Article.

Marceau, Richard (Charlesbourg, BQ). *House of Commons Debates*. Volume 136, Number 091, 2nd Session, 36th Parliament, Friday, May 5, 2000, 6443.

Marketing. Awards Issue 26 Mar. 2001, 7, 20.

McCracken, Grant. "Advertising: Meaning or Information?" Ed. Melanie Wallendorf and Paul Anderson. Provo UT. *Advances in Consumer Research* 14(1987): 1–2.

"Molson Canadian Commercial." 10 May 2000. Available at http://www.snopes.ca/in_boxer/petition/joerant .htm.

O'Donohue, Stephanie. "Nationality and Negotiation of Advertising Meanings." Ed. Eric J. Arnould and Linda M. Scott, Montreal. *Advances in Consumer Research* 26: 684–89.

Solomon, John (Regina-Lumsden-Lake Centre, NDP). "I AM CANADIAN" *House of Commons Debates*. Volume 136, Number 088, 2nd Session, 36th Parliament, Tuesday, May 2, 2000, 6282.

South Park. Prod. Scott Rudin, Trey Parker, and Matt Stone. Paramount Pictures and Warner Brothers, in association with Comedy Central, 1999.

Walker, Ruth. *Christian Science Monitor*. 4 May 2000 http://www.csmonitor.com.

Ward Fawcett, Adrienne. "The 50 Best." *Advertising Age*. Special Awards Issue spring 1995: 36–39.

QUEERING CANADA

Gay and Lesbian Political and Social Activism, 1969–1982

Matthew Hayday
University of Guelph

● QUEERING CANADA: GAY AND LESBIAN POLITICAL AND SOCIAL ACTIVISM, 1969–1982

● **Introduction by Matthew Hayday**

▲ **Primary Sources**

Document 1: We Demand
  The August 28th Gay Day Committee

Document 2: A Strategy for Gay Liberation
  Brian Waite

Document 3: Defining Lesbian and Gay Liberation
  Tom Warner

Document 4: "Kiss-In" Protest

Document 5: We Need Our Own Banner
  Marie Robertson

Document 6: Gay Men and Lesbians Can Work Together
  Chris Bearchell

Document 7: Police raid *The Body Politic* office

Document 8: Bathhouse Raid

Document 9: Protest Against Police Violence

■ **Secondary Sources**

Article 1: Before the Charter: Lesbian and Gay Rights in Canada
  Miriam Smith

Article 2: Police Repression and Judicial Homophobia
  Tom Warner

Article 3: Coalition Politics: Lesbian Feminists Meet Gay Liberationists
  Becki Ross

● INTRODUCTION

Matthew Hayday

To be gay or lesbian in Canada before 1969 was to be subject to a host of legal, political, social, and cultural sanctions. Under the *Criminal Code*, all forms of gay male sex were classified as criminal acts, covered under the offenses of "buggery," "offences against morality," "indecent assault" and "gross indecency." These laws were used to target any sexual act between two men, even when both individuals were consenting and in a private residence. Police and courts interpreted these offences in a broad manner, and penalties included jail sentences of up to five years and whippings. Under reforms to the *Criminal Code* passed in 1961, individuals who were deemed likely to reoffend could be classified as dangerous sexual offenders.

Beyond the legal arena, psychologists began to label the phenomenon of "gender inversion" among male homosexuals in the early 20th century. During the Second World War, psychologists played a major role in diagnosing homosexuality in male soldiers. The army considered homosexual sex to be grounds for court-martial and discharge for "disgraceful conduct." According to the 1952 version of the *Diagnostic and Statistical Manual of Mental Disorders*, the principal diagnosis tool used by psychiatrists, homosexuality was classified as a sexual deviation under the heading of "Sociopathic Personality Disturbances." Many gay men and lesbians were either forced into or voluntarily underwent terrifying experimental treatments to "cure" their homosexuality, sometimes while incarcerated in psychiatric institutions. Laurier Lapierre, Canada's first openly gay senator, who came out in the 1980s, has publicly discussed the electroshock treatments that he was subjected to in various institutions as part of efforts to eliminate his homosexuality. Lesbian sexuality in this period was less overtly regulated, largely because male authorities had little conception of independent female sexuality. However, lesbians faced all of the same forms of oppression that women faced on account of their gender in this period, with the added burden of discrimination due to their sexual orientation. Despite this repressive climate, networks of gay men and lesbian women did form in major Canadian cities. Bars and bathhouses played particularly important roles as spaces for social interaction. A distinctive lesbian bar culture emerged that centred on a butch/femme dynamic among working-class lesbians. Private social networks also existed, and were particularly prevalent among the professional classes.

The onset of the Cold War in 1940s and 1950s worsened an already hostile climate toward gay male and lesbian sexuality. Fearful of communist subversion, the Canadian and United States governments undertook an active campaign to weed out individuals whom they believed to be vulnerable to foreign influence. Canada's 1952 *Immigration Act* classified homosexuals as subversives, banning them from entry, as well as those with "constitutional psychopathic personalities." Gay men and lesbians were particularly targeted because government authorities believed that their sexuality made them vulnerable to blackmail, which, security officials argued, might lead to their betrayal of Canada. Hundreds of civil servants and members of the armed forces were investigated by the Special Service of the Royal Canadian Mounted Police and many were dismissed for "character weakness." In an effort to scientifically detect homosexuals, the Canadian government experimented with a so-called "fruit machine" in the 1960s, which measured pupil dilation to detect homosexuality. The experiment failed and the project was abandoned. There has yet to be any evidence that any Canadian gay man or lesbian actually passed state secrets to communist agents.

Pressure to change Canadian laws regarding homosexuality came in a variety of forms. A British parliamentary inquiry regarding the regulation of private sexual acts resulted in the Wolfenden report of 1957, which argued that homosexuality should not result in criminal charges unless the acts were in public or involved youth. The report made a distinction between crime and sin, and said that homosexuality should be decriminalized, but regulated by psychiatric and medical agencies. Ten years later, in 1967, the British government decriminalized homosexuality. In the United States, organizations such as the Mattachine Society and the Daughters of Bilitis formed in the 1950s and early 1960s to lobby for gay and lesbian rights—primarily for the right to work and for freedom from persecution. Similar organizations formed in Canada, the first of which was Vancouver's Association for Social Knowledge (ASK), which was founded in April 1964. Canadian legal reform was pushed further by a 1967 Supreme Court decision in the case of Everett George Klippert. The Court upheld the 1966 designation of Klippert as a dangerous sexual offender because he had committed four private sexual acts with men. Reacting to this case, Tommy Douglas, leader of the New Democratic Party, called for a Wolfenden-style committee and the decriminalization of a number of private sexual acts. Liberal Justice Minister Pierre Trudeau replied favourably, ultimately introducing a series of reforms to the *Criminal Code* in 1967 (commonly referred to as the Omnibus bill), which decriminalized consensual sexual activity between two adults in private. Trudeau famously quipped that "the state had no business in the bedrooms of the nation."

The Omnibus bill (Bill C-150) reforms passed into law in 1969, removing some of the legal obstacles facing gay men and lesbians. However, this represented only the first stage for a gay and lesbian social movement that sought to change society's hostile attitudes toward homosexuality. In June 1969, a police raid at the Stonewall Inn, a New York City bar, prompted riots among the bar's patrons, triggering a new wave of gay liberation activism in North America. In Gay Pride marches held the following year on the anniversary of the Stonewall Riots, demonstrators asserted a bold, confident defence of their sexuality, one that went beyond mere antidiscrimination legislation. In Canada, a host of community-based organizations formed in cities across the country, dedicated to working for gay and lesbian rights. The first lesbian and gay rights demonstration on Parliament Hill took place on 28 August 1971. The document "We Demand" outlines the initial demands of the 12 gay and lesbian groups that participated in the rally. Later that year, *The Body Politic*, a Toronto-based newspaper, was founded to be Canada's national gay liberation journal. In 1972, Toronto groups organized the city's first Gay Pride Week.

While many of these early organizations were led by and drew the majority of their members from the gay male population, this was also a period of organization for lesbian feminist groups. While lesbians initially played major roles in the broader women's movement and New Left organizations, many became disillusioned by the marginalization or exclusion of lesbian issues from these groups, and by the sexism of the male-dominated left-wing organizations. Lesbian feminists sought to transform Canadian society to challenge the dual oppression that they lived with both as women and as members of a sexual minority. They observed that many of the gay male leaders were in fact quite privileged on the basis of their gender, and often because of their race and social class. Gay liberation groups were often largely concerned with state repression of their sexuality, and less concerned with systemic societal discrimination against women. Lesbian-specific issues such as child custody or the establishment of rape crisis centres, drop-in centres, and support lines were often marginalized by these groups. Many lesbians also rejected the hierarchical structures of these gay organizations, preferring a consensus-based collective approach to decision making and a greater emphasis on creating safe social spaces and personal empowerment.

The gay liberation movement drew many of its strategies and much of its rhetoric from other civil rights groups and social movements of the late-1960s and early-1970s that sought rights for women, African-Americans, workers and other groups that had largely been excluded from power. However, leaders of gay and lesbian organizations were divided about priorities, tactics, and strategies. As the primary sources from Brian Waite and

Tom Warner indicate, many favoured a direct-action strategy aimed at transforming societal attitudes toward sex and sexuality. Gay liberationists sought full acceptance of their relationships and their sexual activities, and rejected conformity with existing societal norms. The photograph of the July 1976 "Kiss-In" demonstration is an example of protest strategies that sought to increase visibility of gay sexuality, and to challenge laws that criminalized this. However, many activists preferred a human rights or equality-based model to activism, which stressed the pursuit of legal equality and human rights code protections, which could be obtained through legal action or political lobbying. As Miriam Smith demonstrates, the two camps were not entirely opposed to each other, and many liberationists supported the equal-rights strategy as an incremental tactic to gain support for their movement. Others, however, decried what they viewed as a strategy that would mainly benefit middle-class gay men, and not deal with all of the needs of the extremely diverse lesbian and gay community, nor challenge the deeply entrenched antisex attitudes of Canadian society.

Given the wide array of issues facing the gay and lesbian movement, it is not surprising that divisions arose. As the articles by Marie Robertson and Chris Bearchell indicate, lesbians actively debated whether or not they should act in concert with gay men. Many lesbian feminists were less interested in the confrontational direct political action espoused by organizations led by gay men, and more concerned with community-building activities. Moreover, the political priorities of the lesbian feminist groups in the 1970s were often very different from those of gay men, and focussed on issues such as child custody, job protection, and the establishment of women's drop-ins and shelters. Many lesbians were ambivalent about or even opposed to many of the gay men's political priorities such as opposing censorship of pornography and challenging laws about public sex, bawdy houses, and age-of-consent regulations. As Becki Ross explains, there were deep divides within the lesbian community over strategy issues with regards to confronting Anita Bryant's "Save the Children" campaign and the censorship of *The Body Politic*. Indeed, the question of how to define the movement and/or be inclusive has proved to be an ongoing and expanding challenge, as issues related to bisexuality, transgenderism, transexuality, two-spiritedness, intersexuality, and queer and questioning individuals have come to the foreground in recent decades.

As Tom Warner's article demonstrates, the gay and lesbian movement confronted a hostile institutional climate. The cultures of police forces, the courts, and the state were not predisposed to be sympathetic to movement activists. Indeed, the Toronto police responded to the publication of an article challenging laws on youth sexuality by raiding the offices of *The Body Politic* in December 1977 and trying to shut the publication down. As the editorial cartoon from *The Body Politic* wryly illustrates, Canadian police forces were viewed with great suspicion and were certainly not seen as sympathetic. A succession of police raids on gay bathhouses across the country during the late 1970s and early 1980s did little to change these attitudes, and indeed triggered a major demonstration on the streets in downtown Toronto, as shown in the photo from a February 1981 march. Gay and lesbian activists were often working to try to change the attitudes of individuals, including the police and court officials, which posed a different, and often greater, set of challenges from political advocacy.

The gay and lesbian movement won a few of its legal battles in the 1970s, and made major strides in developing more well-established communities and fostering more positive attitudes toward sexuality. However, from a legal and political standpoint, the passage of the *Canadian Charter of Rights and Freedoms* in 1982 would ultimately prove to be the major turning point. Over the course of the 1990s and 2000s, the equality rights contained within section 15 of the *Charter* were broadly interpreted by Canadian courts in favour of gay and lesbian equality, ultimately leading to decisions in favour of equal marriage for same-sex couples. However, as liberation activist Tom Warner reminds us, formal equality for same-sex couples was not the only goal of 1970s liberation activists, who sought, and continue to seek, a much broader transformation of societal attitudes toward relationships and sexuality, objectives that continue to be a major part of the contemporary queer movement.

QUESTIONS

1. What were the top priorities for gay and lesbian activists at the outset of the 1970s? How did they attempt to mobilize support for their cause from the broader Canadian community?

2. Two men kissing in public could be arrested for committing an indecent act, and convicted based on the testimony of a police officer who claimed that they rubbed their groins together. What does this suggest about the social norms regarding sexuality in 1970s Canada?

3. The articles by Miriam Smith and Tom Warner address the divisions within the gay and lesbian community over strategies to follow to obtain political and social change. How did the equal rights and liberationist approaches differ? To what extent were advocates of the two approaches able to work together? How do the photographs and articles from *The Body Politic* illustrate these different strategies? Discuss the advantages and disadvantages of each strategy in the context of 1970s Canada.

4. How did the priorities of gay men and lesbians differ in the 1970s? Why did this lead to tensions within their organizations? To what extent was it possible for the two groups to work together? How do the articles by Marie Robertson and Chris Bearchell inform your opinion on this issue?

5. To what extent was the political and social climate of pre-*Charter* Canada open to the demands of gay and lesbian activists? How did the institutions of the Canadian state (the police, the courts, various levels of government) shape the manner whereby activists tried to change attitudes and secure their rights?

6. Tom Warner was very active in a number of the gay and lesbian organizations that he writes about, including the Coalition for Lesbian and Gay Rights of Ontario (CLGRO). Indeed, many of the most prominent authors and scholars who have written about social activism of various types are themselves either members of, or sympathetic to, the social movements that they write about. How can this be an asset to their writing and research? Does their personal bias necessarily mean that we must reject or be doubtful of their conclusions?

FURTHER READINGS

Stuart Chambers, "Pierre Elliott Trudeau and Bill C-150: A Rational Approach to Homosexual Acts, 1968–69," *Journal of Homosexuality* 57, 2 (2010): 249–266.

Didi Herman, *Rights of Passage: Struggles for Lesbian and Gay Legal Equality* (Toronto: University of Toronto Press, 1994).

Paul Jackson, *One of the Boys: Homosexuality in the Canadian Military During World War II* (Montreal & Kingston: McGill-Queen's University Press, 2004).

Gary Kinsman and Patrizia Gentile, *The Canadian War on Queers: National Security as Sexual Regulation* (Vancouver: UBC Press, 2009).

Becki Ross, *The House that Jill Built: A Lesbian Nation in Formation* (Toronto: University of Toronto Press, 1995).

Miriam Smith, *Lesbian and Gay Rights in Canada: Social Movements and Equality-Seeking, 1971-1995* (Toronto: University of Toronto Press, 1999).

Warner, Tom. *Never Going Back: A History of Queer Activism in Canada*. Toronto: University of Toronto Press, 2002.

▲ DOCUMENT 1: WE DEMAND

The August 28th Gay Day Committee

The following brief was presented to the federal government in August 1971. Written and researched by Toronto Gay Action, the brief was supported by gay organizations across Canada, including: the Community Homophile Association of Toronto, Front de libération homosexuel (Montreal), Gay Alliance Toward Equality (Vancouver), Guelph University Homophile Association, University of Toronto Homophile Association, Vancouver Gay Activist Alliance, Vancouver Gay Liberation Front (GLF), Gay Sisters (Vancouver), Waterloo University's Gay Liberation Movement and York University Homophile Association.

On Saturday, August 28, over two hundred homosexual men and women rallied on Parliament Hill in Ottawa in support of the brief. The action was the first public demonstration of its kind in Canada.

In 1969 the Criminal Code was amended so as to make certain sexual acts between two consenting adults, in private, not illegal. This was widely misunderstood as "legalizing" homosexuality and thus putting homosexuals on an equal basis with other Canadians. In fact, this amendment was merely a recognition of the non-enforceable nature of the Criminal Code as it existed. Consequently, its effects have done but little to alleviate the oppression of homosexual men and women in Canada. In our daily lives we are still confronted with discrimination, police harassment, exploitation and pressures to conform which deny our sexuality. That prejudice against homosexual people pervades society is, in no small way, attributable to practices of the federal government. Therefore we, as homosexual citizens of Canada, present the following brief to our government as a means of redressing our grievances.

We demand:

1. *The removal of the nebulous terms "gross indecency" and "indecent act" from the Criminal Code and their replacement by a specific listing of offences, and the equalization of penalties for all remaining homosexual and heterosexual acts; and defining "in private" in the Criminal Code to mean "a condition of privacy."*

The terms "gross indecency" and "indecent act" in the *Criminal Code* remain largely undefined, thus leaving the degree of offensiveness of many sexual acts open to interpretation by enforcement officials according to their personal prejudices—which, by and large, are anti-homosexual. Therefore a specific listing of public offences is crucial in that only in this way can personal bias be eradicated and the legal intent of the law be preserved.

Sections 147 and 149 of the *Criminal Code* have been used to cover public homosexual acts, an offence which is punishable upon indictable conviction; similar public heterosexual acts have usually been dealt with under Section 158 of the *Criminal Code*, an offence which is punishable on summary conviction.

Moreover, indecent assault upon a female (Section 141) can result in a maximum penalty of five years imprisonment, while a person—in this case, always a male—convicted of indecent assault upon another male (Section 148) is liable to imprisonment for ten years. There is no reason for the continuation of this discrepancy in maximum penalties, since the relevant factor is assault, not the sex of the person assaulted.

"In private" when applied to homosexual acts means strictly in the confines of one's home or apartment. For heterosexual acts this interpretation of "in private" is less stringent,

Source: The August 28th Gay Day Committee, "We Demand", *The Body Politic* 1 (Nov/Dec 1971), reprinted in *Flaunting It*, Vancouver: New Star Press, 1982, pp. 217–220. © Herbert R. Spiers.

as the existence of "lovers' lanes" so well testifies. Persons engaged in sexual acts who have genuinely attempted to create a "condition of privacy" should not be arrested, but—as now happens with most heterosexuals—be told to "move along."

2. *Removal of "gross indecency" and "buggery" as grounds for indictment as a "dangerous sexual offender" and for vagrancy.*

Since persons convicted of homosexual acts are usually charged under Sections 147 and 149 of the *Criminal Code*, they are liable to be labeled as "dangerous sexual offenders" and sentenced to "preventative detention" for an indefinite period under Section 661 of the *Criminal Code*.

Section 164 of the *Criminal Code* labels an individual as vagrant and subject to summary conviction if, *inter alia*, he or she has been convicted of an offence such as "gross indecency." Denying the right of an individual to frequent specified places (school grounds, playgrounds, public parks or bathing areas) on the basis of having been convicted of "gross indecency" is excessive, especially when the specific offence for which the individual was convicted may have been merely an indiscretion and in no way a harmful act.

3. *A uniform age of consent for all female and male homosexual and heterosexual acts.*

Since the federal government of Canada does not recognize legal marriages between homosexual persons, the age of consent for their sexual contact is twenty-one years of age. However, since heterosexual parties can be joined in a legally recognized marriage, their age of consent is dependent only upon the age at which they can legally enter a marriage contract. Further inequities result in that Sections 138, 143, and 144 of the *Criminal Code* specify various ages of consent for heterosexual acts between unmarried persons. We believe that the age of consent (twenty-one) for engaging in sexual acts is unrealistic and should be lowered. A number of provinces have reduced the age of majority. The effect of this is that individuals under the age of twenty-one can enter into contractual agreements, vote and drink alcoholic beverages, but cannot exercise their sexual preferences—no small part of one's life. The principle of maturity should be applied uniformly to all aspects of deciding individual prerogatives.

4. *The* Immigration Act *be amended so as to omit all references to homosexuals and "homosexualism."*

Denying immigration to Canada for any individual merely on the basis of this or her "homosexualism" is inconsistent with the *Criminal Code*. Since "homosexualism" is not, in itself, an illegal practice between consenting adults in private, the *Immigration Act* thus discriminates against a minority group.

5. *The right of equal employment and promotion at all government levels for homosexuals.*

The proposed implementation of Paragraph 100 of the Royal Commission on Security makes one's homosexuality an issue in the promotion and recruitment of civil servants. If an individual freely admits his or her homosexuality and is not afraid of disclosure and engages solely in legal acts, that person is hardly susceptible to blackmail. One cannot profitably threaten to broadcast to others what is already known. The effect of Paragraph 100 is to *force* homosexuals into a furtive situation in which they *might become* susceptible to coercion. Thus, Paragraph 100 becomes self-defeating.

If "homosexuals are special targets for attention from foreign intelligence services," this is evidently due to the threat of dismissal from employment, a situation which could be greatly improved by a more open policy on the part of the government.

6. *The* Divorce Act *be amended so as to omit sodomy and homosexual acts as grounds for divorce; moreover, in divorce cases homosexuality* per se *should not preclude the equal rights of child custody.*

7. *The right of homosexuals to serve in the Armed Forces and, therefore, the removal of provisions for convicting service personnel of conduct and/or acts legal under the* Criminal Code; *further, the rescinding of policy statements reflecting on the homosexual.*

Note (c) of Queen's Regulations and Orders (103.25: "Scandalous Conduct of Officers") and Note (b) of 103.26 ("Cruel or Disgraceful Conduct") both suggest that homosexual acts between consenting adults may be considered punishable offences in the military. This effectively contravenes the *Criminal Code* and, thereby, the principle that military law should be subordinate to civil law.

Paragraph 6 of Canadian Forces Administrative Order 19-20 ("Sexual Deviation— Investigation, Medical Examination, and Disposal") reads: "Service policy does not allow retention of sexual deviates in the Forces" and specifies the manner of discharging persons convicted of homosexual acts while in military service.

8. *To know if it is a policy of the Royal Canadian Mounted Police to identify homosexuals within any area of government service and then question them concerning their sexuality and the sexuality of others; and if this is the policy we demand its immediate cessation and destruction of all records so obtained.*

9. *All legal rights for homosexuals which currently exist for heterosexuals.*

Although numerous instances of the injustices and discrimination embodied by this demand could be cited, the following are indicative of the inequities with which homosexuals must contend:

(1) because homosexuals cannot legally marry, they face economic discrimination in that the benefits of filing joint income tax returns and conferring pension rights are denied to them;

(2) likewise, homosexuals are unable to partake of the benefits of public housing;

(3) they are brought up under an education system which either through commission or omission fosters both a narrow and prejudicial view of homosexuality;

(4) again, owing to the fact that homosexuals cannot enter into legally recognized marriages, they are not permitted to adopt children except under the most unusual circumstances. (Although we recognize that adoption is an area of provincial jurisdiction, we feel that this does not completely remove all responsibility from the federal government);

(5) too often in the private sector, once an individual's homosexuality has become known, he or she is discriminated against in employment, and exploited by unscrupulous landlords;

(6) in known places frequented by homosexuals or in places where they gather, both direct and subtle harassment by police officers is too often commonplace;

(7) since sexuality is not covered under the Canadian Bill of Rights, homosexuals are excluded from protections which are guaranteed to other minority groups such as those of race, religion, or national origin.

As a group, homosexuals are "second class citizens" in a democratic society which purports to recognize only one class of citizenship, based on equality.

10. *All public officials and law enforcement agents to employ the full force of their office to bring about changes in the negative attitudes and* de facto *expressions of discrimination and prejudice against homosexuals.*

The role of public officials must be twofold: (1) to serve as legislators formulating the letter of the law, and (2) to serve as representatives of the spirit of a system founded upon democratic principles. As such, holders of public office must transcend prejudicial attitudes (in this case against homosexuals) in favour of leading society to levels consistent with the principles of human rights.

We call upon government officials, as a show of good faith, to enter immediately into a dialogue with the various Canadian homophile groups regarding all the aforementioned demands and to respond publicly by supporting the purpose of this brief.

▲ DOCUMENT 2: A STRATEGY FOR GAY LIBERATION

Brian Waite

The fight to include the term "sexual orientation" in the *Ontario Human Rights Code* is a fundamental one in the struggle for gay liberation and should be seen as an important priority for all Ontario homophile organizations.

Winning this demand, in itself, will not end our oppression, but in the process of fighting for it many gay men and women will develop a higher level of pride and consciousness. With a victory, thousands more will find it easier to come out and begin the task of educating their fellow workers, neighbours, families and friends about the nature of homosexuality, without fear of losing a job or apartment, being harassed at school, or facing discrimination in innumerable other ways because we have no rights guaranteed by law.

This campaign can give a focus for dealing with many other issues at the local level. Actions to protest police entrapment or conditions in the gay ghetto could also be used to publicize and build the campaign and the organizations that are leading it. Demonstrations don't have to be one-shot affairs aimed at one of a myriad of media establishments which constantly slander us. As well as demanding equal time or space to reply, we can point out the responsibility of the provincial government, which refuses to prosecute such blatant discrimination.

Such a campaign will necessarily be two-pronged, since a prior condition for winning is social recognition of homosexuals as a legitimate oppressed minority. We have a formidable task: to teach the truth about human sexuality to the people of Ontario and to oppose. the powerful resources of the Ontario government's educational and legal systems. If they continue to refuse to recognize our legal rights, be assured that the miseducation mills will continue to grind out ignorant, guilt-ridden and sexually oppressed citizens.

This is an issue which will give us an opportunity to make links with the organized women's liberation movement. They have demonstrated in the past to demand the inclusion of the word "sex" in the *Ontario Human Rights Code*. Victory is due in some part to the demonstrations, but probably more to the general public discussion and awareness that has been generated by the activities of the women's movement on a whole range of issues during the past two years. It was the activist feminists who created a climate in which the Tory government would have found it very difficult to continue to ignore this elementary demand for women's equality.

Although both our demands relate directly to the *Ontario Human Rights Code*, our struggle will have a qualitatively different dynamic. Women have concentrated on the abortion campaign in the recent past because it is an issue which touches the widest layers of

Source: Brian Waite, "A Strategy for Gay Liberation", *The Body Politic* 3 (March/April 1972), reprinted in *Flaunting It*, Vancouver: New Star Press, 1982, pp. 221–223. Reprinted by permission of Brian Waite.

the female population, regardless of their economic position. Repeal of the abortion laws will give impetus to future campaigns by women. Any other possibilities for liberating themselves are inextricably tied to their right to choose whether or not they will bear children. This idea is summed up in one of their slogans—Control of Our Bodies, Control of Our Lives.

Most gays cannot be identified, and we leave ourselves open to economic discrimination only if we declare our homosexuality. This will often leave us feeling psychologically liberated, but jobless or red-circled.

Our "Human Rights" campaign is actually more closely paralleled in the women's abortion fight, rather than their demonstrations demanding inclusion of the word "sex." Winning our demand will give *us* the right to choose whether or not we tell our work-mates or fellow tenants of our sexuality—freely, without fear of reprisals from a bigoted boss or landlord. In the meantime, we must stress to those who support our aims that in our movement they can choose their own level of anonymity, taking into accounts their personal situation. This can range from marching in a demonstration to phoning people to involve them in a meeting or work party, both important activities.

Many feminists are aware of the common source of oppression in the socialization and education which take place in the traditional family structure and its continuation throughout and formal educational system. Those of us who dare to reject such distortions of our real sexuality and human potential face a material barricade of institutionalized discrimination and a lack of facilities which could permit us to gain control over our lives.

The foundations of this barricade are embodied in the governments at Queen's Park and Ottawa. As long as any laws discriminating directly or by omission against gays and women remain on the books, any chauvinist employer, educator, landlord, cop, doctor, psychiatrist or parent can trample on our rights and dignity with the tacit approval of these governments.

The effectiveness of the women's movement to date is partly due to their appreciation of the experiences of other movements for social change. They have learned from their own suffragists and the anti-war movement that along with petition campaigns, local demonstrations and actions, letter-writing and educational meetings, it is extremely important to organize large public demonstrations on as wide a basis as possible, whether provincial, national or bi-national.

Women activists have realized that this is the best way possible to show our common opponents and our supporters the power of our numbers, indicating most visibly that the demands we are putting forward represent the solutions to the problems faced by the overwhelming majority of women and gays. As the movement and the size of the demonstrations increase it will become clear that we are not a tiny, isolated minority, unable to relate to the rest of our brothers and sisters as implied by the media.

It is crucial that we assimilate various lessons of previous social movements:

- Oppression is not in one's head. There are powerful forces in this society which use and perpetuate ignorance, prejudice, hatred, and the divisions and alienation which these produce. If you care to believe this is merely the inertia of the status quo, fine. Nevertheless, this status quo is defended by traditional "natural" mores, social "norms" and laws, backed up by the confessional, psychiatrists' couches and the legal system's police force. This repressive power is generally efficient and well organized.
- Having none of the above apparatus at our disposal individually, we must realize the potential political strength of ourselves and our supporters numerically.
- We have to organize this strength in public actions, relying on the abilities of ourselves and our organizations, not on the goodwill of any individual, be he or she government official, party leader or movement hero.

NEL

- Our movement must devise a programme and strategy which will win full equality. The social activists which are necessary to maintain our morale and alleviate some of our daily stress are extremely important. But the aim of gay liberation is to root out the source of our oppression rather than apply band-aids to a never-ending stream of casualties.
- A conscientious organization recognizes the need for some parliamentary formalities, leadership and an active membership. The election of a leadership body, such as a steering committee, is not "elitist" as long as it reflects the varied composition and experience of the organization, and its power is delegated and controlled by membership meetings.

The vision of a future society free from sexism, which is one I feel we all share, can be turned into a reality sooner or later. Later, if we march haphazardly, ignoring the signposts of past experience; sooner, if we incorporate these experiences into the gay movement's arsenal of strategy and tactics. I am not suggesting that we adopt the programme or demands of other minorities and oppressed groups, for it is only by organizing around issues with which all gays can relate that we will realize our strength. Some individuals, no doubt, will be active in other movements or political parties, thereby raising consciousness about human sexuality in these groups.

I feel strongly that the movement in Ontario will greatly strengthen itself if we organize jointly to demand the inclusion of the term "sexual orientation" in the *Ontario Human Rights Code.*

Winning this demand will give life to the words "gay pride." It will impel and enable thousands more brothers and sisters to join us in future campaigns for the full sexual liberation of humankind—children, adolescents and adults, no matter what their position on the sexual continuum. *Homosexuality is a human right!*

▲ DOCUMENT 3: DEFINING LESBIAN AND GAY LIBERATION

Tom Warner

Tom Warner, author of a number of books and articles on gay and lesbian activism, was and remains actively engaged as an activist in many of the organizations he writes about. How does this perspective as an activist inform and shape his scholarship?

The lesbian and gay movement and the ideology of lesbian and gay liberation are the products of anger and outrage channelled into collective action. Their history is one of resistance and astonishing perseverance, textured with the exuberance of outlaw sexuality. History abounds with testimonies to the power of small bands of committed individuals who succeeded against the most daunting odds. In keeping with this, virtually all progress made over the last three decades for gays, lesbians, and bisexuals has resulted directly from their boldness and militancy. Fed up, they decided to take control of their own destinies despite many obstacles. They dared to confront attitudes and deeds that had led to marginalization and social oppression. Individually and as organized communities, they fought back, coming out of the closet, noisily and defiantly, demanding to be both seen and heard, and revelling in their new visibility. They attacked systemic and institutional prejudice, and combated hatred directed towards them, by demanding that an end be put to centuries of lies, ignorance, prejudice, and fear. By rising up to confront some of Canada's most powerful beliefs and institutions, lesbian, gay, and bisexual activists launched a movement that has changed their world forever. As the movement took root and grew, activists realized they would necessarily need to battle the forces of social conservatism, to prevent these forces from turning back the clock, from erasing even the smallest steps towards change, from returning laws and social conditions to darker, more repressive times. The vast heterosexual majority, in the process, has been forced to deal with lesbians, gays, and bisexuals, even as it has generally resisted their struggle.

What is lesbian and gay liberation? Defining it is, admittedly, daunting. Complex and multifaceted, it is an ideology that resists reduction to a simple sentence or two. Fundamentally, lesbian and gay liberation has been about changing self-image. Like all victimized groups, bisexuals, lesbians, and gays have had to tackle how they see themselves in order, in turn, to change how others see them. They have had to come to terms with their sexual orientation, not only accepting it as healthy and normal, but also celebrating it as special and liberating. Lesbian and gay liberation has militantly rejected notions of gays and lesbians as sick, sinful, criminal, abnormal, deviant, strange, or pathetic. It has condemned the pathologizing of homosexuality and the social oppression of gays and lesbians. Liberationists unapologetically articulate the naturalness of homosexuality as an alternative—but in no way inferior or disordered—sexual orientation and identity. They see gays and lesbians as an oppressed people struggling for sexual and social liberation who, by so doing, advance the liberation of others as well.

Changing a few laws and achieving tolerance are necessary, but insufficient in themselves to achieve fundamental social change. Lesbian and gay liberation means coming to a positive consciousness of oneself and of other gays and lesbians. It requires a personal transformation based on an understanding that gays and lesbians are taught by our society in various ways, both subtle and blatant, to hate and thereby oppress themselves. It means recognizing and fighting against the cultural conventions that reinforce and perpetuate inequities of power. Lesbian and gay liberation requires opposing the repression of sexuality and combating sexual stereotyping, sexism, heterosexual supremacy, violence, hatred, bigotry, and hypocrisy. It is based on an analysis of how and why gays and lesbians, individually and as a group, are oppressed. An important element of this analysis is a realization that sexism and rigid gender-role socialization contribute significantly to that oppression. It further sees the traditional or nuclear family as a key agent of social control, embodying sexism that oppresses women and gays. Other powerful influences contributing to such socialization, and bolstering its effects, have been the state's regulation of sexuality and non-conforming behaviour, the churches' teachings about sin and morality, and the medical models of deviance, abnormality, and perversion. Lesbian and gay liberation means rocking the boat, by confronting harassment, discrimination, and paternalism, so that attitudes, laws, and social institutions are changed. It is predicated on visibility, both in the daily lives of individual gays, lesbians, and bisexuals and in society as a whole; it maintains a public presence on the streets and in the media. Lesbian and gay liberation acknowledges that being impelled to remain invisible by passing as heterosexual is one of the most insidious ways in which gays, lesbians, and bisexuals have been oppressed. Individuals who are unable to pass (e.g., men deemed to be effeminate or women deemed to be masculine), or those who refuse or otherwise fail to do so, face harassment and social censure. As Gary Kinsman, deploying the term *queer,* which gained currency during the last decade, wrote in 1998, 'Queer liberation requires that people achieve control over our bodies, and sexualities and an end to institutionalized heterosexuality.'[1]

Lesbian and gay liberation also means that sex does not have to await a monogamous relationship, that it can be engaged in without guilt or shame, solely as a form of recreation. It can be enjoyed anonymously, with several partners or in groups, and in multiple ways involving acts that are not to be judged by others, provided the participants are capable of giving informed consent and do so. Lesbian and gay liberation acknowledges and celebrates the diversity and complexity of human sexuality. It holds that the body in all of its forms, sizes, and shapes is beautiful and erogenous; that fantasy, voluntary role playing, and dressing up can add excitement and fulfilment to sex acts. Liberationists do not see genitalia as gross and unclean. They reject the notion that sexual acts are inherently dirty, and only appropriately performed in private, with two people behind closed doors. Lesbian and gay liberationists are thus as much in conflict with the tyrannical views of dominant heterosexual society today as they were in the early 1970s. This is because the regimented social order resulting inevitably from heterosexism is maintained by, and benefits, a consortium of powerful interests with vast resources. Belonging to this consortium are the churches, state institutions, conservative organizations and movements, the medical establishment (including psychiatry), the social sciences, the media, the entertainment industries, the educational system, and corporate elites.

NOTE

1. An excellent account of the history of the anti-homosexual religious and criminal laws is found in H. Montgomery Hyde, *The Other Love* (London: Heinemann, 1970).

▲ DOCUMENT 4: "KISS-IN" PROTEST

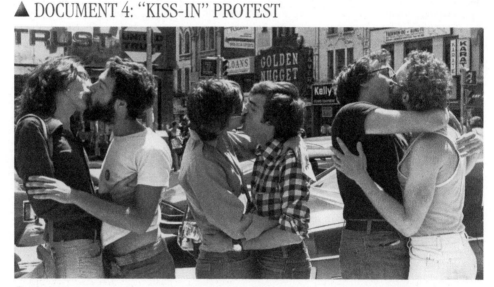

● On February 12, 1976, two gay men, Bill Holloway and Tom Field, were arrested for kissing in public at the corner of Yonge and Bloor streets in Toronto, in front of the Hudson's Bay Company store. The two men were posing for a picture which was to accompany an article on homophobia in the *Alternatives to Alienation* newspaper. Holloway and Field were charged with obstructing the sidewalk by causing a public disturbance, and with committing an indecent act in public. On July 12, they were found guilty of committing an indecent act, and fined $50 each. To protest these convictions the Gay Alliance Towards Equality (GATE) and *The Body Politic* organized a "Kiss-In" in Toronto which was held on July 17. About 20 men participated in the demonstration, parading in couples and triples, kissing as they walked. What does the conviction of Holloway and Field indicate about the culture of the police and judicial community regarding homosexuality? Why do you think the "kiss-in" strategy was used? Do you think this might have been an effective way to challenge societal attitudes?

Source: *The Body Politic*, Sept. 1976, p. 3. Reprinted with permission of Gerald Hannon.

▲ DOCUMENT 5: WE NEED OUR OWN BANNER

Marie Robertson

After four years of asking myself, "Where are all those women?" I've decided to change my focus and question what, if anything, the gay movement has to offer us dykes. Contrary to the belief of many lesbians who are inexperienced in working with gay men, but who nevertheless are amazingly outspoken in their criticism of gay liberation, I have done much more than make coffee and answer telephones. However, of late, I've been looking at the large amount of energy that I expend fighting for equal power in a male-dominated struggle, educating my gay brothers about their sexism and feminism in general, and trying to recruit more women.

Who gains in the amalgamation? It seems to me that men are getting quite a bit for our time. Besides the work we do, having a significant number of active women in an individual group has become a basis for credibility and status in the contest for "Most Together Gay Liberation Group of the Year." But what are lesbians gaining? A growing sense of alienation from our sisters; fatigue as we struggle as a minority to let the public know that the term "gay" also means *female* homosexual. This is not to underplay all the good feelings I've experienced in past years. Spending one's formative years with faggots has definite advantages (I'm a great dancer). Nonetheless, it has begun to strike me as ludicrous when in seminars I expound the virtues of loving women and then upon reflection realize that I've been spending most of my time with gay men.

The problem is obviously much deeper than the superficial male chauvinism in the movement: the meat balls who insist on saying "*man*kind," "him," "he" when referring to both sexes. I perceive a clear conflict of interest. Gay liberation, when we get right down to it, is the struggle for gay men to achieve approval for the only thing that separates them from the "Man"—their sexual preference. All right, all you self-proclaimed "male feminists" who are at this point desiring to bend, spindle and mutilate my poor Polish neck. The point is that if you were not gay you would be part of the powerful prestigious male ruling class that oppresses women, whether you choose to face that reality or not. Your birth as males defines that; you don't. My female birthright places me on the bottom rung, regardless of my sexual orientation and that is where I must fight from. Thanks for letting me take a step up to your rung on the ladder, but no thanks.

Should we dykes then fight alongside our straight feminist sisters? Enter lesbian pride to complicate matters even more. Some lesbians put a lot of energy into the feminist movement, committing themselves to working for the benefit and eventual liberation of *all* women. No one can deny the importance of this since dykes are oppressed first and foremost as women. But it has been my experience, (and I know I'm not alone) that the mere mention of including gay issues in the feminist struggle arouses a complete gamut of negative responses from outright refusal to the more pseudo-liberal (but harder to detect) queasiness of inner parts, characterized by a sudden tightening of the vocal chords and nausea. I refuse to kow-tow to the closetry strongly encouraged by uptight straight women concerned with the "image" of the feminist movement and also, sadly, by those paranoid gay sisters who rationalize their own closetry by viewing their lesbianism as a private personal matter, of little consequence to the liberation of women.

I want a separate dyke movement through which we can fight the women's fight openly and proudly as upfront lesbians. I want gay women finally to get credit for all the work we've been doing and presently are doing under the banners of the gay and women's movements.

Source: Marie Robertson, "We Need Our Own Banner", *The Body Politic* 24 (June/July 1976), reprinted in *Flaunting It*, Vancouver: New Star Press, 1982, pp. 177–178. Reprinted by permission of Marie Robertson.

We need our own banner. We have nothing to lose by separating; we are already losing in movements that do not meet our needs. As feminists we're compromising ourselves in the gay movement, as lesbians we're "hushed up" in the women's movement. If we're going to educate, let us educate our lesbian sisters, not our gay brothers. If we're going to demand equality as women, let us not forget the fact that we are *gay* women, and that as such we must make the dyke issue a prominent one, retrieving it from the closets of feminism.

▲ DOCUMENT 6: GAY MEN AND LESBIANS CAN WORK TOGETHER
Chris Bearchell

In 1968, in a gesture of liberalism, the federal government broadened the grounds for divorce in the *Divorce Act* to include homosexuality. In 1972, in Prince Edward Island, a judge spent twelve pages clarifying that lesbianism constituted homosexuality. Since that time there have been numerous cases, recorded and otherwise, in which the use, or the threatened use of these grounds has separated lesbian mothers from their children. In the eyes of our oppressors, lesbians and homosexuals represent the same perversion—the same threat. "Lesbians and gay men" have many differences and points of disagreement, but we are oppressed by the same legal system, sometimes the same laws, and, more important, we are all oppressed in a hundred and one ways by the same ideology that has given rise to that system and those laws.

Andrew Hodges ... expresses scepticism about the claim that we in fact have these things in common. I always look twice at sweeping generalizations. Especially generalizations that say "men are or want etc, etc; women are or want etc, etc." Especially when the generalization is made by a man, albeit a gay man.

Hodges tells us that the programme of men in the gay movement is "for sexual expansiveness." On the other hand, it seems to me that the Canadian movement, with which I am most familiar, represents the beginnings of a cohesive bi-national movement with a growing lesbian caucus. And it is fortunately based on a strategy of public action and a programme of civil rights. A programme which was developed because it is the most comprehensible to the majority of gay women and men. One which most, if not all of us, could agree on. One which would be able to include and mobilize the largest number of people. One which would allow the handful of us who are gay liberationists to contact, talk to, and—it is hoped—convince many more gay people that civil rights are just a first step toward liberation.

What is missing from Hodges's article is basic gay liberation politics—in fact, politics period. Politics are dismissed and replaced with an unrealistic yearning after a common view of the sexual ideal.

Andrew Hodges has missed the point that it is not just lesbian feminists who think the male bars and baths are objectifying. I have spoken to gay men who think they are too, and who don't like it. I am a lesbian feminist who knows that women's bars can be just as objectifying. Rita Mae Brown, on the other hand, looks forward to the day when there will be "baths" for women with an inspired vision of what they'd be like. I was attacked for walking hand-in-hand with my lover—and yet Hodges says that, as a lesbian, I necessarily stand against "public sexuality." The point is this: not all gay people have reached a consensus about whether or not sexual expression should have a high or low profile. Neither have all gay men. Neither have all lesbians. And a movement that seeks to eventually include all gay people cannot afford to try to reach such a consensus, or to decide how many angels can dance on the head of a pin, either.

Source: Chris Bearchell, "Gay Men and Lesbians Can Work Together", *The Body Politic 32* (April 1, 1977), reprinted in *Flaunting It*, Vancouver: New Star Press, 1982, pp. 184–186. Reprinted with permission, Estate of Chris Bearchell.

I will be the first to admit that, while I see a basis and a need for unity between gay women and men, I don't see the unity. It does not yet exist. Of course, the movement as I hope to see it does not yet exist either; that doesn't mean I'm packing it in and heading back to the hills (though sometimes I'd like to).

Unity will only be forged when those few dykes who are in the gay movement can convince the movement as a whole to give priority to lesbian demands and struggles. Yes, lesbians have been burned by sexism in this movement. No, saying you're sorry won't make it better. Doing something on the other hand just might. Throwing full support behind a child custody fight, for instance, just might. We can't say for sure, because we haven't had the chance to try, yet.

It is also true that lesbians need our own movement—while unity and the needs we share with gay men are political, not *all* lesbians' needs are. Caucuses, or our own organizations, which do not dilute the impact of our common protest, are the only ways to ensure that past mistakes are not repeated. Whether we are in the same organizations or not, we *can* be united. Political unity in action is far more important than formal unity in name. And meantime, autonomous lesbian organizations can work toward mobilizing the lesbian community in a way that the gay movement has never been able to—and can fulfill other, less explicitly political needs. That does not mean that we have to forget the fact that, when the weight of the straight world comes down on queers, they don't care whether we're faggots or dykes.

Sexism is not simply, as Hodges would have us believe, "the institutionalized inequality between the statuses of men and women." It is also, and perhaps more importantly, conceiving of individuals in terms of narrow, stultifying roles determined by gender. Hodges takes many of the ingredients of the traditional stereotype of woman and recombines them to portray lesbians and lesbian sexuality. As if dykes haven't had enough of that very shit. Who is Hodges to tell me what, if anything, I have to overcome to accept the validity of my sexual identity? Who is he to concern himself with lesbian invisibility? We'll do what we can to take care of that ourselves, thank you. What makes him think he can attribute a monopoly on striving for a "sex-positive attitude" to men? We live in a sex-negative society. The psyches of the sexually exploited and the sexually exploiting are equally damaged. Individuals suffering from either *can* do much to overcome them. But no one can do so completely. And, I'd wager that this is one lesbian whose "sensibilities" are probably no more easily offended than Hodges's own.

Hodges's article begins with a reference to words, words, words. Will we ever arrive at universally accepted definitions of all the labels we have ever worn? No. Will we ever cease haggling over them? No. Is it important? Yes, but not enough to lose sleep over. By all means, let's discuss it, but let's not pretend we've concluded the discussion. Yes, "gay" and "homosexual" are male-identified to some gay women and men. The dynamic lesbian culture that Hodges describes includes a whole spectrum of artists who describe themselves variously as: dykes, women who love women, gay and proud, homosexual women, and just plain lesbians. I use gay when I'm tactful and dyke when I'm angry. I think lesbian is a beautiful and overwhelmingly sexual word. My lover, on the other hand, shies away from it as a word that, for her, has always been derogatory. There are probably as many opinions on this subject as there are gay people. But such differences can't be attributed to, nor can they explain, whatever incompatibility exists between lesbians and gay men.

The expressed intention of "Divided we stand" is to provoke a dialogue. Such a dialogue is necessary. But if it is to be a productive one, it must begin by recognizing that we are dealing with a political context. It is doubtful how productive it is for lesbians committed to the gay movement to be both angered and undermined by a supposed attempt at dialogue.

▲ DOCUMENT 7: POLICE RAID *THE BODY POLITIC* OFFICE

"Hi! Mind if we just browse for a while?"

I THINK IT'S ONE OF THOSE "FINE TOOTHED COMBS"

● What does this editorial cartoon, published after the Toronto police raided *The Body Politic's* offices, suggest about how the police force was perceived by gay and lesbian activists?

Source: *The Body Politic*, February 1978. © 1977–2011 Paul Aboud. Used with permission.

Police raid The Body Politic *office: December 30, 1977*

▲ DOCUMENT 8: BATHHOUSE RAID

● In the aftermath of Toronto police raids on gay male bathhouses in 1981, Ontario's provincial attorney-general Roy McMurtry was quoted in *The Body Politic*, claiming that "one police officer took a hammer into the place with him but it was not used. At another establishment, one crowbar was taken and used to open three lockers. This is the total evidence . . . ." What do these two photos, taken in the aftermath of the police raids on a gay male bathhouse in 1981, suggest about how the police acted towards gay men? What does McMurtry's statement suggest about who the provincial government was inclined to believe in allegations of police violence?

Source: *The Body Politic*, March 1981, p. 11. Reprinted with permission of Norman Hatton.

▲ DOCUMENT 9: PROTEST AGAINST POLICE VIOLENCE

● Not all gay men reacted passively to legal and police efforts to control their sexuality. This photograph was taken at a demonstration against police violence in the aftermath of the 1981 bathhouse raids.

Source: *The Body Politic*, April 1981, p. 9. Reprinted with permission of Gerald Hannon.

■ARTICLE 1: BEFORE THE CHARTER: LESBIAN AND GAY RIGHTS IN CANADA

Miriam Smith

GAY LIBERATION DURING THE SEVENTIES

Gay liberation groups were established in the early seventies in Toronto, Ottawa, Vancouver, Montreal, Halifax, Saskatoon, and other Canadian cities. These groups had many of the characteristics typically ascribed to the new social movements, including relatively loose forms of organization, a high level of internal democracy, and a lack of organizational bureaucracy. Indeed, most such groups lived precarious financial and organizational lives. Gay liberation grew out of the counter-culture of the sixties and its meaning frames were transformational, aimed at the elimination of heterosexism, patriarchy and sex and gender roles. As such groups solidified their institutionalized networks over the course of the seventies, they were drawn into the ambit of equality-seeking. Tarrow comments of social movements that 'although [they] almost always conceive of themselves as outside of and opposed to institutions, collective action inserts them into complex policy networks, and, thus, within the reach of the state. If nothing else, movements enunciate demands in terms of frames of meaning that are comprehensive to the wider society.[1] Indeed, the gay liberation movement of the seventies envisioned its demands in this way, concentrating on what its activists termed 'the civil rights agenda.' It worked for the inclusion of sexual orientation as a prohibited ground of discrimination in provincial and federal human rights codes and pursued litigation as a means of drawing attention to the civil rights struggle and building the consciousness, political identity, and organizational base of the movement.

Gay liberation was firmly rooted in the new social movement organizing of the sixties, especially in the challenge to the public/private split and the politicization of sexuality and gender roles that was pioneered by feminism. Its goals were to bring lesbians and gays out of the closet, to build gay community, to gain social acceptance for homosexuality and, generally, to liberate sexuality from the rigid constraints of a patriarchal and heterosexist social system. Like Marxist ideology, which suggests that the state may ultimately whither away, so too gay liberation ideology foresaw the eventual elimination of gender and sex roles. For example, in his manifesto *Homosexual Oppression and Liberation* (1971), Dennis Altman argued that the gay world would eventually die, as the full bisexual potential of all people would be realized and that, as traditional gender roles were eroded, people would be free to choose their sexual preference without rewards and stigmas attaching to particular choices: 'Gay liberation . . . is part of a much wider movement that is challenging the basic cultural norms of our advanced industrial, capitalist, and bureaucratic society . . . It is a movement that is political, not in the traditional way that we have used that word, but because it challenges the very definitions and demarcations that society has created.'[2] Kate Millet's manifesto, reprinted in *The Body Politic,* captured the spirit of sexual liberation, demanding a 'reassessment of the traits categorized into "masculine" and "feminine" with a total reassessment as to their human usefulness and desirability in both sexes'; 'unisex or the end of separatist character-structure, temper and behaviour so that each individual may develop an entire—rather than a partial, limited, and conformist—personality'; 'the end of the ancient oppression of the young under the patriarchal proprietary family'; an end to 'male rule through institutions: patriarchal religion, the proprietary family, marriage, the "home", masculine culture and pervasive doctrine of male superiority'; and 'bisex, or the end of enforced perverse heterosexuality, so that the sex act ceases to be arbitrarily polarized into male and female, to the exclusion of sexual expression between members of the same sex.'[3]

Despite the emphasis on the bisexual potential of the majority, gay liberation required a sharp differentiation of the categories 'straight' and 'gay,' with the aim of building the consciousness and identity that would serve as a base for the movement.[4] Yet these categories were not presented as an unproblematic assertion of an essentialist position. For example, briefs presented to legislatures by gay liberation and homophile groups of the

Source: Miriam Smith, excerpts from Chapter 3: Before the Charter, in *Lesbian and Gay Rights in Canada: Social Movements and Equality-Seeking.* Toronto: University of Toronto Press, 1999. © University of Toronto Press, 1999. Reprinted with permission of the publisher.

seventies are relatively agnostic on the question of the origins of homosexuality, often citing the famous 1948 Kinsey study of sexuality. The importance of this study in the public presentation of the gay liberation movement of the seventies was that it fit with the goals of gay liberation, i.e., liberation from the oppressive gender sex categories of patriarchy. Because Kinsey had discovered evidence of widespread bisexuality as well as finding that homosexuality was more widespread in American society than formerly thought, he was read by the movement as questioning the traditional hetero/homo dichotomy and at least implicitly suggesting that there might for some be an element of choice regarding sexual identity. The tensions for gay politics around the identity/origins of homosexuality are reflected in the 1973 brief to the Ontario Human Rights Commission from the Gay Pride Coalition of Homophile Associations in Ontario (a name that in itself captures a social movement in transition from 'homophile' to 'gay'), which argued that 'Kinsey has challenged the assumption that people are either "heterosexual" or "homosexual". He has shown that for many people sexual feelings are likely to occur for members of the same sex just as for members of the opposite sex. Nevertheless, it is convenient in a brief such as this to speak of "homosexuals" and "heterosexuals". The myth of absolute sexual orientation has such a strong hold on our social custom that those men and women in whom homosexual feelings predominate experience a significantly different position in our society than those who feel themselves to be "heterosexual" do.'[5]

A series of other briefs to government in Manitoba (1974), Saskatchewan (1976), and Alberta (1976) make the same point.[6] This is hardly a medical model of immutable sexuality; in contrast, the presentation expresses the difficulty of forging a stable identity for the purpose of pursuing rights (since society defines sexuality in this manner, it is 'convenient' to do so) while adhering to the view that 'absolute sexual orientation' is a 'myth.' In the short term, then, gay liberation was predicated on the need to construct and assert gay and lesbian identity and to build an institutional and organizational base for the solidification of this identity.[7] The tension between the liberation of sexuality and the need to construct a lesbian and gay identity for political purposes was constant over this period.

The demand for civil rights was central to gay liberation during the seventies, based on the strategic and ideological frame provided by the U.S. civil rights movement, the women's movement, and the institutional opening provided by human rights commissions.[8] The struggle for lesbian and gay civil rights was seen in the mainly male gay liberation movement, in the mainstream gay media, and in gay liberation political organizations of the seventies as inextricably linked to the goal of liberation. While the achievement of rights was significant in itself, it was also a strategy for building a social movement, for creating gay community, for raising gay consciousness, and for bringing gays out of the closet, in short, for the creation of political identity. Tactically, rights claims were not confined to litigation and courts but were the organizing frame used by gay liberation groups across a range of strategies and tactics, including lobbying government, electoralism, picketing, and demonstrations. For example, the first systematic discussion of the ideology of gay liberation, which appeared in the third issue of *The Body Politic* in March 1972, argued that civil rights was the key issue that could unite all gays and would thus serve as a rallying cry and point of unity for the community. Brian Waite, the author of the article, argued that 'Winning this demand, in itself, will not end our oppression, but in the process of fighting for it many gay men and women will develop a higher level of pride and consciousness.'[9] In addition, the substantive achievement of formal equality rights would help build the gay and lesbian movement because, 'With a victory, thousands more will find it easier to come out. . . . without fear of losing a job or apartment, being harassed at school, or facing discrimination in innumerable other ways because we have no rights guaranteed by law.'[10] Similarly, *The Body Politic* collective argued in the spring of 1973 that 'there is no contradiction between the present focus of the struggle, civil rights, and the final object, the full liberation of the human personality, straight and gay alike. Gays are coming to comprehend that the two are intimately interconnected. The present civil rights fight, which is in fact only just beginning, will facilitate the creation and development of a gay liberation consciousness.'[11] As Chris Bearchell recalled, 'how we saw the gay rights strategy was [as] something that would radicalize . . . politicize, and mobilize people . . . The process of being radicalized and politicized and mobilized would mean that the people who were drawn into the process would realize that rights in and of themselves were insufficient... And I think the hope would be that, in making that realization, that they would . . . understand the shortcomings of the way the world was organized.'[12]

In *The Body Politic* in 1975, Ken Popert pointed out that the goal of the civil rights strategy was not to change the law but to raise awareness, especially outside the lesbian and gay communities:

> But why should that struggle be one for 'civil rights'? The history of minority rights reveals that civil rights accomplish little without a corresponding change in public opinion. But the effectiveness of civil rights is much less important than the effectiveness of the public campaign which demands those rights. Of all the questions raised by gay liberation, the issue of civil rights is the one which attracts the greatest support, from gays and straights alike. By a campaign for civil rights, we can penetrate the media and advance the reeducation of the public on the subject of homosexuality . . . It cannot be emphasized too strongly that the campaign for civil rights is a means and not an end.[13]

And, at the Second Annual Gay Rights Conference in 1974, the adoption of a civil rights platform was seen by delegates as 'an important step towards an outward oriented, militant movement.'[14]

Like the U.S. civil rights movement of the fifties and sixties, the rights frames of the main political organizations of gay liberation emphasized formal equality, particularly in the areas of employment and housing. Yet the full implications of equality, including relationship recognition, were demanded from the beginning. For example, the brief presented to the federal Parliament in 1971 demanded equal rights in employment but also 'legal rights for homosexuals which currently exist for heterosexuals including an end to discrimination in adoption, public housing, taxes and pension benefits.'[15] GATE Vancouver's 1971 statement of principles listed its goals as 'full equality for gay people in every area of life and endeavor,' protection from discrimination in housing and employment, and 'the right to homosexual marriage and divorce, recognized by law as the union of two equal partners.'[16] If the goal of gay liberation was societal transformation and if building a lesbian and gay community was key to this goal, then the first step in the process of building a social movement was for people to come out. People would be more likely to do that if they had a meaning frame available that said 'gay is good,' a major slogan of gay liberation in the seventies, and when they no longer feared employment and housing discrimination as a direct consequence of being out. In the context of the gay liberation movement then, the formal equality or civil rights frame was a classic statement of the personal as political.

The main goal of gay liberation groups of this period was to plumb the radical depths of formal equality in order to break the vicious cycle of discrimination and closetry. In both federal and provincial jurisdictions, gay liberation organizations of the seventies advocated formal equality via legislative changes to human rights codes. The impact of the assertion of right claims and litigation in gay liberation organizations can be seen from a select survey of the politics of some of the main organizations of the period: GATE Vancouver,* CGRO, ADGQ, and the NGRC.

During the 1970s, the three regional organizations that are included here, GATE Vancouver, CGRO, and the ADGQ, were all involved (directly or indirectly) in the assertion of rights claims via the courts. These groups were not on the periphery of the gay liberation movement; on the contrary, they formed its organizational, strategic, and ideological core. GATE Vancouver (1971–80), despite its relatively small size, was the main gay liberation organization in Vancouver. Its leader, Maurice Flood, was a leading theoretician of gay liberation and its newspaper, *Gay Tide,* was a major organ for gay liberation organizing and analysis as well as providing the spark for GATE's litigation, the *Gay Tide* case, one of the first lesbian and gay rights cases heard by the Supreme Court of Canada. The ADGQ

---

*There were several organizations at this time in different parts of the country that used the GATE name. They are usually differentiated by appending their locales, e.g., GATE Vancouver and GATE Toronto.

was a Montreal-based civil rights organization, the main gay liberation organization in Quebec at the time and, like GATE Vancouver, had its own periodical, *Le Berdache*. While Quebec's lesbian and gay rights movement has often followed a different path, during the late seventies there were some similarities between Québécois and other Canadian organizations in the pursuit of civil rights claims. However, the ADGQ also provides the exception that proves the rule; the inclusion of sexual orientation as a prohibited ground of discrimination in Quebec's Charte des droits et libertés de la personne in 1977 meant that the principal target of equality seeking in other jurisdictions—the inclusion of sexual orientation in human rights codes—was unavailable as a means of mobilizing the Quebec movement. The third case, the Coalition for Gay Rights in Ontario, founded in 1975, was one of the few provincewide gay rights groups in Canada. Its members included local community groups from smaller urban areas, which were concerned with issues such as the provision of basic social services to their gay and lesbian populations, as well as groups such as GATE Toronto (whose members overlapped with *The Body Politic* collective) and Gays of Ottawa (GO). GATE Toronto and GO, representing urban areas, were strong advocates of gay liberation and the civil rights strategy. Together, these groups and others from across the country formed the pan-Canadian National Gay Election Coalition (NGEC) in 1974, followed, by the National Gay Rights Coalition (NGRC), later renamed [in 1978] the Canadian Lesbian and Gay Rights Coalition (CLGRC), which survived from 1975 to 1980.

The achievement of civil rights for gays and lesbians was the major stated goal of all these groups and their strategies were comprised of an eclectic mix of lobbying, organizing public pickets and demonstrations, electoralism, and litigation. Some cases of discrimination were documented in the pages of the lesbian and gay press during the seventies; many more were brought to gay liberation groups but never received public attention because the people involved did not want to make a public complaint.[17] A small number of lesbians, including Barbara Thornborrow, went public with complaints that they had been dismissed from the Armed Forces for their lesbianism[18] and a lesbian custody case was supported by a fund started by the Saskatchewan gay community.[19] In a case at the University of Saskatchewan, Doug Wilson, a gay activist, brought a discrimination complaint after he was prevented from supervising practice teaching in the public school system. In 1975, four hundred people attended one of the largest gay rights rallies that had been held in Canada up to that time in support of Wilson.[20]

The three cases discussed in more detail here merit particular attention. They were high profile, generated substantial financial and organizational support from within the gay community, and were seen by gay rights activists as legal tests of the state of the law and the attitude of the courts as well as a means of undertaking public education, mobilization, and of drawing attention to the question of discrimination within both the lesbian and gay and straight communities. The cases highlighted one of the central paradoxes of rights claims. Opponents of the inclusion of sexual orientation in human rights codes often claimed that such discrimination did not exist or that there were no documented cases. Gay liberation groups contested this claim, pointing out that the very nature and strength of discrimination meant that lesbians and gays were afraid to come forward for fear that more discrimination would follow. Gay liberation groups called attention to these obstacles, presenting briefs to governments in almost every Canadian jurisdiction during the seventies. Winnipeg's Gays for Equality emphasized the conundrums set up by gay rights opponents: 'there have been no in-depth studies into the area as there have been for other forms of discrimination . . . Furthermore, most cases of discrimination never come to light, as many homosexuals are so frightened of further social censure that they do not seek redress, fully realizing that under the present legal system, it would be impossible to obtain.'[21] Thus, the high-profile cases of the seventies demonstrated that discrimination was widespread. These demonstrations of discrimination resonated deeply within the burgeoning gay and lesbian political communities, which had first-hand knowledge that the few cases brought forward were merely the tip of the iceberg. Moreover, the particular cases profiled below were used in the gay and lesbian communities as levers for political action. They served as a rallying cry and as an assertion of the entitlement to equality.

LITIGATING I: CGRO AND THE DAMIEN CASE

One of the first groups to support an antidiscrimination case in the courts was Ontario's Coalition for Gay Rights in Ontario (CGRO). Although nine groups from five Ontario cities took part in the founding conference of the CGRO in 1975, the main political impetus for its establishment came from the politically active urban gay rights groups, GATE Toronto and Gays of Ottawa (GO), both of which had a strong gay liberation and civil rights orientation. CGRO's main aim was the amendment of the *Ontario Human Rights Code* to include sexual orientation as a prohibited ground of discrimination. However, the code amendment (which was eventually achieved in 1986),[22] was not seen as an end in itself. GATE's original proposal for the coalition pointed out that civil rights issues, especially private discrimination, fell under provincial jurisdiction and that focusing on changing the *Ontario Human Rights Code* was an issue 'of immediate and personal relevance to the vast majority of gays.' The argument continued: 'No one can deny, for example, that one of the principal factors in forcing the vast majority of us to remain in the closet to one extent or another is the fear of job discrimination.' According to the proposal, public attitudes toward homosexuality could not be legislated and, in any case, the Ontario Human Rights Commission was a weak organization in terms of enforcement of the rights of minorities. Nonetheless, 'the importance of winning this demand is that it would force the government to recognize that we are *entitled* to the same rights which are theoretically accorded to other minorities.'[23] The assertion of entitlement, in CGRO's view, would appeal to the majority of gays and lesbians.

While CGRO's main demand centred on amending the human rights code, it was also concerned about other issues, such as education and child custody and adoption.[24] Its tactics included public events like demonstrations and rallies as well as using electoral campaigns for public education.[25] In order to bring gays out of the closet and build gay community, the CGRO, like other gay liberation groups at the time, focused in particular on the public side of political demands. Its early strategy for obtaining the *Ontario Human Rights Code* amendment was typical: securing support from the gay community (mainly providing information about the code); obtaining support from political parties; the preparation of a brief to the government; and public action such as demonstrations.[26]

From the beginning, CGRO was concerned to find test cases that would both document and publicize the problem of antigay discrimination. The organization found exactly such a case in John Damien, a jockey and racing steward who had been fired by the Ontario Racing Commission after a twenty-year career.[27] Prior to his dismissal Damien had not been active in gay politics, according to his own account. However, he subsequently saw an ad for GATE Toronto in a gay bar and contacted the organization. From this phone call came the lesbian and gay movement's twelve-year involvement with his case. Damien first went to the Ontario Human Rights Commission, arguing that sexual orientation was implicitly included in the provincial human rights code. However, the commission declined to accept his complaint. He then undertook a civil suit for wrongful dismissal, which was eventually settled out of court. However, the wrongful dismissal case took years to wind its way through the courts and public attention was difficult to sustain, in part because of the threat of libel action.[28] Following GATE's initial involvement in the case, CGRO founded an independent committee, the Committee to Defend John Damien, to support the Damien defence. The committee worked with Damien and his lawyers to generate support for the case both within the gay community and beyond, linking it to the broader issue of civil rights for gays and to the specific demand for reform of the *Ontario Human Rights Code*. In addition, the committee organized fund-raising for legal costs, called upon the Ontario government to appoint a government inquiry into the actions of the Racing Commission and the ministry responsible for it, the Ministry of Consumer and Commercial Relations, and, in the absence of the specific inclusion of sexual orientation in the code, demanded a broadening of the term 'sex' in the existing code to include sexual orientation. Eleven years after the founding of the Committee to Defend John Damien, the Ontario Human Rights Code was amended to include sexual orientation.[29] Damien himself died six days later.

The Damien case was the *cause célèbre* of the gay political community in the mid- to late seventies and, from the beginning, gay liberation activists saw the potential of the case to mobilize its own constituency. The facts surrounding Damien's dismissal were clear-cut: he had been told he was being fired for being gay.[30] At a time when governments routinely claimed that there were few documented cases of employment discrimination against gays, Damien's case drew attention to the very fact of discrimination. In addition, Damien himself was willing to fight his own case at a tremendous financial, professional, and personal cost. The denial of Damien's complaint by the Ontario Human Rights Commission drew attention to the need to amend the *Human Rights Code.* Most importantly, the Damien case spurred gay and lesbian organizing and community building around the assertion of political identity and the claim for equal treatment. As GO activist Denis LeBlanc recalled: 'I can tell you that, it . . . [took] personal courage . . . for John to go public with his fight and allow us as activists . . . to be his advocate, to run the political strategy around his case, because . . . [it] was a collective effort on his whole case from the very beginning ... He put his trust in us as activists and . . . agreed to the strategy that we proposed, which was very much a political strategy . . . His case was raised over and over and over again, as a symbol of injustice.'[31]

The very length of the case, which facilitated the broader mobilization of which it was a part, laid the groundwork for an ongoing gay and lesbian community that continued to assert rights claims at the provincial and federal level in the seventies and beyond. Thus, during *The Body Politic* trials and the 1978 and 1981 Toronto bath raids, when the gay liberation movement was forced to defend itself in the courts, the state's attempts to repress gay sexuality and gay politics were turned into political claims for the right to privacy with the establishment of the Right to Privacy Committee in 1978.[32] Equality-seeking and the assertion of entitlement had rooted itself successfully in the politically active Toronto lesbian and gay community so that repression was met with rights claims.

LITIGATING II: GATE VANCOUVER AND THE *GAY TIDE* CASE

Another important case and probably the best example of the proactive use of litigation as a deliberate strategy to assert gay civil rights in the seventies was the case of GATE Vancouver against the *Vancouver Sun*. GATE Vancouver was a male gay

liberation group that combined a Marxist analysis of capitalist society with a feminist and gay liberation analysis of heterosexism and patriarchy. Many of GATE's members had belonged to Marxist organizations of the period, such as the Trotskyists; however, the leftist groups of the day were reluctant to recognize gay liberation. Many, but not all, of the members of GATE were from the left, including Maurice Flood, the leader of GATE and an important theoretician of gay liberation in Canada. As former GATE activist Ian McKenzie recalled, 'there was a certain amount of tension around the issue and of course we were baited by other groups who used that . . . as a red herring . . . to avoid the fact that we were doing something publicly and they weren't.'[33] GATE's ideology was thus built on an explicit rejection of multi-issueism and a concentration on gay liberation while maintaining an analysis of the links between gay liberation and other forms of social oppression. This concentration on building the gay movement was a reflection in part of the activists' experiences in leftist groups in which gay liberation, even if recognized or supported, was seen as peripheral or secondary to socialist revolution or socialist transformation.[34] Support for the *Gay Tide* case and for the kind of politics espoused by GATE was not necessarily forthcoming from Vancouver's gay community during that period: '[in] the majority [of] the clubs we got a hostile reaction when we . . . tried to distribute or sell *Gay Tide.* In fact, we were . . . routinely thrown out of clubs, and it wasn't until we had the case before the Supreme Court that . . . we did actually get to make some announcements.'[35] Like other groups included here, GATE's program included civil rights demands as a key element in gay liberation and its tactics emphasized public action, in keeping with the goal of bringing closeted gays and lesbians out and building social and political identity.[36] From its inception, GATE demanded the revision of B.C. human rights legislation to include sexual orientation as a prohibited ground of discrimination. With the election of the NDP government in British Columbia in 1973, GATE presented its position on the need for a legislative change to the government. The minister of labour, responsible for human rights protection in the province, responded to GATE's lobbying effort by telling its members that 'homosexuality should not receive the benefit of legal sanction,' a statement that was publicized by GATE. In fact, GATE publicized its entire correspondence with the government, after which the government agreed to a meeting to discuss the province's human rights legislation. When the new legislation was finally enacted, however, it did not include sexual orientation, although the government claimed that the code's new 'reasonable cause' clause would protect gay rights. GATE immediately held a demonstration to protest the exclusion of gay rights from the code. Like other gay liberation groups of the period, GATE itself had been the object of discrimination. The Vancouver YMCA had refused to rent a room to GATE for a public meeting in 1971 (the ADGQ's court case would also concern discrimination in renting space for meetings). A Vancouver printing shop had refused to print a leaflet for a gay dance. And the *Vancouver Sun* had refused to print a GATE ad in 1973. The ad read: 'Subs. To GAY TIDE, gay lib. Paper. $1.00 for 6 issues. 2146 Yew St. Vancouver.' As one legal scholar has commented, 'Seldom has an advertisement that was refused publication received wider exposure.'[37] According to the *Sun,* the ad was refused because it offended public decency. With the passage of the new human rights legislation and the NDP government's promise that 'reasonable cause' would cover sexual orientation, GATE decided to resubmit its ad to the *Vancouver Sun.* Once again, the *Sun* refused the ad, thus providing the grounds for GATE's deliberate test of the provisions of the new code. The case was referred to the minister of labour, who appointed a board of inquiry. The board held that there had been a violation of the code, that the *Sun* was indeed motivated by bias, and that its decision to refuse the ad was discriminatory. The *Sun* appealed this decision to the Supreme Court of British Columbia, which turned it down; subsequently, the paper appealed to the British Columbia Court of Appeal, which ruled that the newspaper had 'reasonable cause' to refuse to print the ad. GATE then appealed to the Supreme Court of Canada, which ruled that freedom of expression and freedom of the press—in this case, the freedom not to print something—trumped minority civil rights.[38]

The GATE Vancouver case was the fruit of a deliberate strategy by a gay liberation group to provoke discrimination in order to fight it. As GATE later editorialized, 'In part it was the conscious political intention of GATE that the case should strip away any illusions about our status'[39] and 'what was "on trial" was the very social legitimacy of same-sex love and its physical expression and by extension, the right of those of use who define ourselves as lesbians and gay

men, to enjoy full equality before the law.'[40] GATE's audience was in large part the gay and lesbian communities themselves. For closeted lesbians and gay men, GATE wanted to build the consciousness and identity that would aid in constructing a social movement. As GATE activist Don Hann recalled,

> We were conscious, very conscious, [that] it wasn't just a matter of acquiring civil rights. We were building the mass movement, we were building a community identity. The use of civil rights, the demand for those rights was legitimate in itself, but at the same time, we were consciously, deliberately, building a minority identity … trying to encourage people to take on that identity, trying to build a community … and so there wasn't any real contradiction between writing briefs, and street demonstrations. They … went hand in hand with one another and that was very consciously and deliberately framed by us as a strategy that we would use.[41]

In this way, litigation was employed as one strategy among many. As *Gay Tide* argued, 'The legal parameters of our oppression have placed us in the Courts. This has become one form of struggle among many. We seek to utilize this limited forum to our best advantage. However, we are fully conscious that it is only by organizing ourselves into a political force to take what is ours that we will ever be free.[42]

GATE used other tactics in pressing its case, including holding demonstrations and pickets, lobbying, and meeting with the government, as well as using the media (e.g., releasing the minister's homophobic remarks and, in general, refusing to conduct secret meetings with the government), in addition to pursuing its case before the human rights commission. While GATE was a small group, its strategy was by no means unique. Even in Quebec, where gay liberation arrived somewhat later than in the rest of Canada, the civil rights strategy was pursued.

LITIGATING III: THE ADGQ AND THE COMMISSION DES ÉCOLES CATHOLIQUES DE MONTRÉAL

The ADGQ was founded in the fall of 1976, following on the heels of the Coalition Against Repression, a Montreal-based gay liberation group. The coalition had been formed as a result of the bath raids in

1975 and 1976, as well as the antigay police repression ('clean up') of the City of Montreal for the 1976 Olympics. In October 1977, there were more raids as 138 men were arrested at Truxx.[43] The context for the establishment of the ADGQ was different from that of the early Toronto and Vancouver gay liberation groups. While gay liberation ideology was evident in Montreal from the establishment of the short-lived Front de libération homosexuelle in 1971, the linguistic divide, among other factors, impeded lesbian and gay organizing. Sustained organizations were established later in Montreal than in other cities. In Toronto the gay liberation movement was already well established in the pursuit of rights claims prior to the worst attempts at repression, the 1978 and 1981 bath raids and the repeated (and failed) attempts to prosecute *The Body Politic*.

Like other gay liberation groups, the ADGQ espoused a radical gay liberation ideology: 'Notre lutte s'achèvera quand les termes mêmes d'hétérosexualité et d'homosexualité auront disparu du vocabulaire, fondus dans une *véritable* indifferenciation des practiques sexuelles.'[44] At the same time, it defined itself as civil rights organization: 'L'ADGQ est une organisation . . . de libération gaie avec une perspective de lutte publique pour les droits civils des gais et lesbiennes.'[45] One of the first activities of the ADGQ was to present a brief to the Commission des droits de la personne du Québec (CDPQ) demanding the inclusion of sexual orientation in Quebec's Charte des droits. Indeed, the commission recommended this to the newly elected PQ government. The PQ government acted to change the Quebec charter in 1977, making Quebec the first jurisdiction in Canada to include sexual orientation as a prohibited ground of discrimination in human rights legislation.[46] Almost immediately after the passage of the code change, questions arose about the efficacy of the provision. In 1978, the CDPQ ruled against the ADGQ in a case involving the rental of premises for ADGQ meetings by the Commission des écoles catholiques de Montréal (CECM). In November 1977, just after the Truxx raid and before the amendment to the Charte des droits, the ADGQ had requested a room rental from the school board. The CECM had refused. As in the GATE Vancouver case, once the Charte had been changed in December 1977, the ADGQ again requested a room rental from the board in a deliberate test of the new provisions. The board agreed to rent the room but reneged on the decision two months later, citing the 'retombées possibles sur l'éducation des enfants.[47] The ADGQ immediately filed a complaint with the CDPQ; a CDPQ inquiry found that the school board's action was discriminatory but this ruling was rejected by CDPQ commissioners, who allowed the discrimination based on section 20 of the Charter, which permitted discrimination that could be justified by, among other things, the religious and educational goals of a non-profit organization. Following this decision, the ADGQ formed a committee to pursue a legal case against the school board. As part of this strategy, the organization again requested a room from the board and was again refused, at which point it filed a declaratory motion in Quebec Superior Court, marking the first challenge by a gay group to discriminatory action in Quebec and the first case challenging section 20 of the Quebec Charter.[48]

The CECM claimed that its educational and religious objectives justified its refusal to rent space to a group whose behaviour was condemned by the church as permitted under section 20. But the ADGQ was able to show that the CECM had rented space to non-Catholics and to political parties. The group argued that section 20 was a loophole in the law and asked how much human rights protection was worth if 'pour exiger son application un groupe comme le nôtre, aux resources limitées, doit dépenser argent et temps dans un long et très coûteux procès.[49] The ADGQ activists saw the case as concerning not simply rental of space to groups but 'la reconnaissance du plein droit à une orientation sexuelle différente.[50] The court found in favour of the ADGQ, restricting the scope of the application of section 20 in November 1979.[51]

In general, the ADGQ's case did not provide the same drawing card for gay rights organizing in Montreal that the GATE Vancouver and Damien cases had provided in British Columbia and Ontario. The ADGQ had disbanded by the mid-eighties and, unlike the CGRO, did not provide an organizational base for an ongoing provincial gay rights organization. Ironically, the fact that the change to provincial human rights legislation—the key goal in other jurisdictions—was achieved earlier in Quebec than elsewhere and at a time when Quebec gay and lesbian groups had yet to solidify their organizational base, removed one possible rallying point for the lesbian and gay communities. In addition to the linguistic politics that divided the potentially powerful Montreal gay and lesbian community, and the presence of a progressive nationalist movement that attracted activist energies, the early victory for formal equality (however limited) may have undercut gay liberation mobilizng.[52] Hence the short duration of the struggle to assert rights claims denied the Quebec movement a mechanism and a frame for building political identification and community. [...]

RIGHTS CLAIMS AND GAY LIBERATION

The central place of rights demands and rights discourse in the ideology and strategy of gay liberation during the seventies, while not uncontested, has several implications for broader questions about the impact of the *Charter* on social movement organizing and ideology. In the interpretative framework of collective action during this period there was no clear separation between human rights issues and other political demands. Human rights were seen as a means of creating, if only symbolically, one political identity in which all members of the diverse lesbian and gay communities could share, that of a minority group that could challenge Canadian society in terms of its own liberal values. The fact that the lesbian and gay communities were in themselves diverse in many respects was irrelevant to the actual assertion of the political claim. In the view of political activists, human rights served as [a] rallying point for building the movement. Many were gay liberationists and Marxists who were looking for a radical reordering of sex/gender roles in society and the elimination of heterosexism and patriarchy. Such a radical reordering was unlikely to occur through a human rights strategy premised on the inclusion of gays and lesbians as a minority group in human rights codes. Yet such cases were seen as the strategic means of building lesbian and gay community and consciousness. Even if the cases themselves failed, this only served to highlight the battle to be fought and the necessity for political action and political identity. Lesbians and gays who were not directly involved in these struggles and who did not belong to community or political organizations were touched by cases like Damien's, whether by attending a fund-raising dance or demonstration for the Damien defence, reading an article about the case in the gay press, or by hearing Damien on one of his several speaking tours. At the very least, activists hoped that such cases would help create a sense of common identity and community.

Thus, the tendency of left-wing *Charter* critics to separate equality-seeking frames and strategies from broader political or grass-roots mobilization does not reflect the experience of the gay liberation movement of the seventies. Litigation as a tactic and rights as a goal were not seen as antithetical to grass roots mobilization; activists saw these as linked, not as contradictory strategies. Rights struggles were viewed as part of politics, not as separate from the political arena. The potential contradictions of pursuing a rights-based strategy that have been pointed out by *Charter* critics like Mandel were not sufficient to dislodge a rights-claiming politics in the seventies. The stark alternatives that are sometimes posed in the literature between radicalizing strategies that challenge existing categories of oppression and conservatizing strategies imposed by the formal legal rights order, and between the strategies of grass-roots mobilization that empower people 'at the bottom' as opposed to court challenges that empower lawyers and other elites 'at the top' are polarities that were largely absent from the gay liberation movement itself. The contestation that did emerge was diffuse and submerged, in part because the most powerful critiques came from lesbian feminists who were active members of the women's movement. Yet even those women whose politics were centred in the emerging women's communities and in the women's movement did not deny the legitimacy of equal rights. They simply pursued the ideals of equality and liberation in a different political movement or through the creation of community rather than through formal political organizations.

In the pre-*Charter* period, test cases were sought out by local groups and carried forward at an incredibly high financial and organizational cost, despite the fact that legal protections were much weaker than they would become in the subsequent decade. The rights-claiming frame has stronger roots in Canadian politics than some readings of the *Charter's* impact would lead us to believe. The *Charter* did not 'Americanize' the gay liberation movement; in a sense, the gay liberation movement of the seventies was already 'Americanized' in terms of its deployment of a civil rights frame and' strategy. While legal barriers may be stronger or weaker, and the political opportunity structure may be more or less closed to equality-seeking by excluded groups, rights-claiming may still provide the frame and the strategy for social movement politics. Gay liberationists had a very clear understanding of the role of collective action in challenging the dominant codes of society. The activists involved in supporting or pursuing these cases were not wide-eyed innocents in the use of the courts; on the contrary, they had ideologically elaborated and sophisticated justifications for pursuing rights claims. While much debate on the effects of the *Charter* focuses on substantive gains that have been made or could potentially be effected through court decisions, gay liberationists were wielding a symbolic politics that created a new way of thinking about the place of gays and lesbians in Canadian society. By asserting a gay and lesbian right to entitlement and by creating a gay and lesbian 'community' as a mythical unity of rights-bearing citizens (however diverse in reality), they were engaged in building a political movement. That the cases might fail was just further fodder for mobilization. As the case of Quebec suggests, legal and legislative victory—the achievement of substantive policy gains—could actually undermine the potential for mobilization and the creation of political identity. The equality-seeking frame was drawn from the civil rights and counter-cultural movements of the sixties and from the opportunities provided by human rights commissions, before the advent of the *Charter of Rights*. The importance of rights claims to the gay liberation movement was not in the achievement of legal victories or legislative changes but in the role that they played in building the lesbian and gay community and its social and political institutions. However, at the very moment that the government was willing to entertain the views of social groups on the question of civil rights as it considered the constitutional entrenchment of a bill of rights, the gay and lesbian communities lacked the organizational structure to respond to the opening created by the government's constitutional and political agenda. In fact, as other groups were becoming more rights conscious around the Trudeau government's plan for the *Charter*, lesbian and gay politics had already turned away from the civil rights perspective that had animated the early years of gay liberation. Moreover, the federal lesbian and gay rights coalition, fragile as it had been at the best of times, was dissolved and replaced with a lobby group that suffered from

important legitimacy problems from the beginning. To gay liberation activists, it seemed unlikely, to say the least, that any campaign, no matter how well organized or structured, would have had any chance of success, given the failure (with the exception of Quebec) of the campaigns to include sexual orientation in human rights codes at the federal and provincial levels.[53] For the Toronto gay liberation groups, the late seventies and early eighties formed a period of police repression, which galvanized the energies of the communities. Five years later, when the Mulroney government held hearings on the application of section 15 of the *Charter*, the parliamentary committee would be deluged with lesbian and gay groups making submissions on equality rights.

NOTES

1. Sidney Tarrow, *Power in Movement: Social Movements, Collective Action and Politics* (Cambridge: Cambridge University Press 1994), 25–6.

2. Dennis Altman, *Homosexual Oppression and Liberation* (New York and London: New York University Press [1971] 1993), 244.

3. Kate Millet, 'Sexual Politics: A Manifesto for Revolution,' reprinted in *The Body Politic* 3 (March–April 1972), 1.

4. Altman, *Homosexual Oppression and Liberation,* 154.

5. Canadian Lesbian and Gay Archives (CLGA), Community Briefs, *Ontario Homosexuals and the Ontario Human Rights Commission* (A brief presented to the Ontario Human Rights Commission by the Gay Pride Coalition on 24 August 1973), 3.

6. CLGA, Community Briefs, Gay Community Centre (Saskatoon), *The Homosexual Minority in Saskatchewan* (June 1976); GATE Edmonton, *Homosexual: A Minority Without Rights* (1 March 1976); Gays for Equality, *Manitoba Homosexuals: A Minority Without Rights* (1974). See also CLGA, Community Briefs, Coalition for Gay Rights in Ontario, *Discrimination and the Gay Minority* (A brief to members of the Ontario Legislature, March 1978).

7. For other discussions of gay liberation ideology, see Barry Adam, *The Rise of a Gay and Lesbian Movement,* 2nd ed. (Boston: Twayne 1995) and Paul-François Sylvestre, *Les homosexuels s'organisent* (Ottawa: Éditions Homereux 1979). On the relationship between gay liberation and queer theory, see Jeffrey Weeks, *Sexuality and its Discontents: Meanings, Myths and Modern Sexualities* (London

and New York: Routledge 1985); Michael Warner, 'Introduction,' in Michael Warner, ed., *Fear of a Queer Planet* (Minneapolis and London: University of Minnesota Press 1993), vii–xxxi; Altman, *Homosexual Oppression and Liberation*; Steven Seidman, 'Deconstructing Queer theory or the under-theorization of the social and the ethical,' in Linda Nicholson and Steven Seidman, eds., *Social Postmodernism: Beyond Identity Politics* (Cambridge: Cambridge University Press 1995), 116–41 and Steven Seidman, 'Identity and Politics in a "Postmodern" Gay Culture: Some Historical and Conceptual Notes,' in Michael Warner, ed., *Fear of a Queer Planet,* 105–42.

8. On the role that the civil rights movement played as a master frame for other movements, see Doug McAdam, 'Culture and Social Movements,' in Enrique Laraña, Hank Johnston, and Joseph R. Gusfield, eds., *New Social Movements: From Ideology to Identity* (Philadelphia: Temple University Press 1994), 36–57.

9. Brian Waite, 'Strategy for Gay Liberation,' *The Body Politic* (March–April 1972), 4.

10. Ibid.

11. 'Editorial: Never going back,' *The Body Politic* 8 (Spring 1973), 2.

12. Interview, Chris Bearchell, British Columbia, 8–9 February 1996.

13. Ken Popert, 'Gay Rights Now!' *The Body Politic* 19 (July–August 1975), 16.

14. *The Body Politic* 15 (September–October 1974), 5.

15. Brian Waite and Cheri DeNovo, 'We Demand,' *The Body Politic* 1 (November–December 1971), 6–7.

16. Archives Collective, Vancouver, GATE (Vancouver), *Statement of Principles* (adopted 30 May 1971, amended 5 June 1971), 1.

17. Both John Argue and Chris Bearchell recalled cases brought to GATE Toronto and the CGRO that were not pursued. Interview, John Argue, Vancouver, 15 February 1996, Bearchell interview.

18. 'Lesbian goes public,' *The Body Politic* (June 1977), 1.

19. 'Mother fights for children in court,' *The Body Politic* 14 (July–August 1974), 5.

20. 'Saskatoon: 400 rally in defence of teacher,' *The Body Politic* (November 1975).

21. CLGA, *Manitoba Homosexuals,* 10.

22. David Rayside, 'Gay Rights and Family Values: The Passage of Bill 7 in Ontario,' *Studies in Political Economy* 26 (Summer 1988), 109–47.

23. CLGA, Coalition for Gay Rights in Ontario, 82–017/01/13, *Letter to Gays of Ottawa from GATE,* emphasis theirs.

24. CLGA, Coalition for Gay Rights in Ontario, 82–017/01/13, *Memo to groups,* 23 August 1976.

25. CLGA, Coalition for Gay Rights in Ontario, 82–017/01/4, *Working Paper for Provincial Affairs Workshop.*

26. CLGA, Coalition for Gay Rights in Ontario, 82–017/01/13, *CGRO strategy to put sexual orientation in the Ontario Human Rights Code—Phase 2,* 4 September 1977.

27. CLGA, Coalition for Gay Rights in Ontario, 82–017/01 /13, *CGRO: Success or Failure?*

28. Arnold Bruner, 'Sexual Orientation and Equality Rights,' in Anne F. Bayefsky and Mary Eberts, eds., *Equality Rights and the Canadian Charter of Rights and Freedoms* (Toronto: Carswell 1985), 460–1; Didi Herman, *Rights of Passage: Struggles for Lesbian and Gay Legal Equality* (Toronto: University of Toronto Press 1994), 23; and Ken Popert, 'John Damien,' *The Body Politic* 135 (February 1987), 15.

29. Popert, 'John Damien,' 15.

30. Ibid.

31. Interview, Denis LeBlanc, Ottawa, 21 February 1996.

32. On the bath raids and *The Body Politic* trials, see Ed Jackson and Stan Persky, eds., *Flaunting It! A Decade of Journalism from The Body Politic* (Vancouver and Toronto: New Star Books and Pink Triangle Press 1982); Tim McCaskell, 'The Bath Raids and Gay Politics,' in Frank Cunningham et al., eds., *Social Movements/Social Change: The Politics and Practice of Orgnizing* (Toronto: Between the Lines 1988), 169–88; and Gary Kinsman, *The Regulation of Desire: Homo and Hetero Sexualities,* 2nd ed. (Montreal: Black Rose Books 1996), 338ff.

33. Interview, Ian McKenzie, Vancouver, 14 February 1996.

34. McKenzie interview.

35. McKenzie interview.

36. See, for example, GATE Vancouver's constitution. Archives Collective, Gay Alliance Toward Equality (GATE), (1971,1973), *Constitution.*

37. W.W. Black, 'Gay Alliance Toward Equality v. Vancouver Sun,' *Osgoode Hall Law Journal* 17 (1979), 649–75 at 649.

38. *Gay Alliance Toward Equality v. Vancouver Sun* (1979), 97 D.L.R. (3d) 577 (S.C.C). See also Jeff

Richstone and J. Stuart Russell, 'Shutting the Gate: Gay Civil Rights in the Supreme Court of Canada,' *McGill Law Journal* 97, no. 1 (1981), 92–117; Richard A. Goreham, 'Human Rights Code of British Columbia,' *Canadian Bar Review* 59 (1981), 165–79; Harry Kopyto, 'The Gay Alliance Case Reconsidered,' *Osgoode Hall Law Journal* 18 (1980), 639–52.

39. 'Gate vs. Sun: A Chronology of the Case,' *Gay Tide 17* (September 1977), 2–3; 'Supreme Court to hear first gay rights case,' *The Body Politic* (May 1978), 7.

40. 'On to the Supreme Court,' *Gay Tide* 17 (September 1977), 2–3.

41. Interview, Don Hann, Vancouver, 14 February 1996.

42. 'Gate vs. Sun,' 2.

43. Ron Dayman, 'Quebec: Five years of the movement,' *The Body Politic 29* (December–January 1976), 20–3; Ross Higgins, 'Pour une histoire gaie de Montréal,' *Sortie* (mars 1983), 7; 'Du bon boulot . . . et un peu d'essoufflement,' *Le Berdache* 5 (novembre 1979), 3; 'Les gai(e)s du Québec protestant,' *Le Devoir* (24 octobre 1977), 6.

44. *Le Berdache* (juillet–août 1981), 38 (emphasis theirs).

45. Ibid., 46.

46. François Barbeau, 'Les homosexuels réclament une nouvelle formulation des droits civils,' *Le Devoir 27* (octobre 1977), 9; Gilles Garneau, 'Victoire pour les gais,' *Le Berdache* 6 (décembre 1979–janvier 1980), 7; and Suart Russell and Michael Lynch, 'Gay rights: oui!' *The Body Politic* (February 1978), 4–5.

47. Garneau, 'Victoire pour les gais,' 7.

48. Ibid.

49. 'Editorial,' *Le Berdache* 3 (septembre 1979), 1.

50. '1980: une menace, une promesse,' *Le Berdache 7* (février 1980), 3.

51. *L'Association A.D.G.Q. c. La Commission des écoles catholiques de Montréal* (1979), 112 D.L.R. (3d) 230. See also Garneau, 'Victoire pour les gais,' 7–9. See also Nicole Duplé, 'Homosexualité et droits à l'égalité dans les Chartes canadienne et québécoise,' *Les Cahiers de droit* 25 (1984), 836ff.

52. Interview, Claude Beaulieu, Montreal, 2 August 1997. Ross Higgins discusses the reason for a 'distinct' gay politics in Quebec in 'L'impasse linguistique,' *Sortie* 14 (Janvier 1984) 1–2, 7.

53. Interview, Tom Warner, Toronto, 19 September 1995.

■ ARTICLE 2: POLICE REPRESSION AND JUDICIAL HOMOPHOBIA

Tom Warner

Homophobic police, often in collusion with the media, contributed throughout the 1970s and early 1980s to a climate of backlash and bigotry. One notorious incident occurred in Ottawa in 1975, when police announced a 'Homosexual Vice Ring' with great media fanfare. The owner and sixteen clients of the Unique Male Modelling Agency were arrested during an operation police described as 'the most sordid crime we've investigated for some time.' Media coverage, based on police information, used terms such as 'white slavery ring' and claimed that over one hundred boys, some only eleven years old, were involved. In fact, it was later established that all of the escorts charged were between sixteen and twenty-one years of age.[1] To maximize publicity, Ottawa police, over a three-week period, released to the media the names and addresses of all of those who had been charged in the 'ring.' The media reported the names, with devastating consequences. Eight men required psychiatric care and were deluged with hate letters and phone calls. Nine were fired from their jobs, or were suspended or transferred. One was identified in the press by his place of employment and position title. And thirty-four-year-old Warren Zufelt committed suicide after his first court appearance by jumping from the thirteenth floor of his apartment building.[2]

Similar cooperation between police and the media followed a 1978 raid on a Toronto bathhouse called the Barracks. Police disclosed in press releases that items used for sadomasochism, bondage, and other sexual practices had been seized, generating sensational media reports. Following raids on four gay bathhouses in 1981, a Toronto police press release linked those charges with the separate, and unrelated, arrest of a gay man who had been found with 'implements of torture' and 'kiddie porn.' They also alleged links between the bathhouses and organized crime activity, and claimed that drug deals and prostitution were occurring in those businesses.

Yet no evidence of such activities was ever produced and no charges relating to them were ever laid.[3] In a reprehensible and retributive action, a police officer reported the names of three teachers arrested in the raids to school board officials.

Police-initiated publicity, including giving the media the names of men arrested in bathhouses, parks, and public washrooms had, by this time, become a common occurrence. The publicity caused humiliation, social censure for those arrested, and created the impression the police were protecting the public—particularly children—from the evils of homosexuality. Arrests typically followed acts of entrapment—plain-clothes officers enticed other men into making sexual advances or gestures and then charged them with criminal offences. Another tactic involved videotaping public washrooms to record those engaging in sexual acts. In one notorious police operation in a public washroom during 1983, thirty-one men in Orillia, Ontario were charged with sexual offences after having been videotaped by hidden cameras. Assisted by the police, local newspapers reported their names. Extensive media coverage of the first court appearances featured TV camera crews rushing to get pictures of the accused. The men endured insults and catcalls from twenty-five people gathered outside the courthouse in a modern day version of the stocks-and-pillories treatment meted out to offenders in earlier centuries.[4] Three arrested men who were teachers were subsequently fired by their board of education for 'immoral criminal conduct.' One man tried to commit suicide.[5]

Negative police attitudes towards gays and lesbians also were expressed in other ways, through condoning, remaining indifferent towards, or refusing to effectively respond to acts of violence inflicted by homophobic assailants. The most infamous example was a well known tradition in Toronto for many years. Each Halloween, a vicious mob of onlookers gathered on Yonge Street, in front of the St Charles Tavern, within which a Halloween drag show was held. As drag queens or others thought to be gay were spotted on the side streets or entered the bar, they were subjected to jeers, taunts, and a barrage of eggs, tomatoes, and other objects. Some were gay-bashed. This annual spectacle was tolerated by police and civic officials and was prominently reported in the media with photos and commentary as part of the city's Halloween festivities. Few outside the gay and lesbian community saw the event as an outpouring of hate and prejudice; the terror inflicted on that community was rarely reported or was downplayed. In fact, the spectacle was often presented in the news as a kind of good-natured carnival, with no reports of violence.

Toronto activists repeatedly called on the police during the 1970s to either disperse the mob or stop it from forming. Police officials contended there was little they could do, and made only a small number of arrests for throwing eggs, generally charging the perpetrators with breach of the peace. In 1978, Toronto's police chief actually told Toronto GATE that police had no power to stop people from gathering and that, to avoid acts of violence, gays should stay clear of the area surrounding the St Charles.[6] Activists persisted nonetheless, holding pre-Halloween meetings with the police and municipal politicians each year. In 1979, pressure from GATE and the Metropolitan Community Church, aided by the support of progressive politicians, resulted in an increased police presence on Yonge Street. Gay community volunteers also provided their own security network, escorting bar patrons and reporting incidents of violence and harassment to the police. But it was not until 1980, under pressure from activists, gay-owned businesses, Mayor John Sewell, and city councillors that the police finally erected barricades to narrow the sidewalk and did not permit people to stop in front of the St Charles. By 1981, as a result, this particular Halloween tradition was only an ugly memory.[7]

Because of such police actions and attitudes, groups like Gays of Ottawa, GATE in Vancouver and Toronto, and, later, both the Comité homosexuel anti-repression in Montreal and the Right to Privacy Committee in Toronto, focused advocacy efforts on ending police harassment and repression. Activists in larger communities across Canada also attempted to establish police liaison mechanisms in the hope that greater education and awareness would lead to better policing. But their efforts were largely unsuccessful due to distrust of the police, homophobia on the part of the cops themselves, and continued harassment. As *The Body Politic* noted in a 1978 editorial, distrust of the police was widespread, 'so we don't co-operate—even in the solving of murders within our own community.' Sceptical of police attitudes and intentions—'The police are not neutral'—*TBP* acknowledged that 'some kind of co-operation, then, may be necessary. We need to understand what kind it is, and when it should happen.' Still, cooperation did not mean, for *TBP,* 'joining them [police] in the backrooms as quasi-informers, letting them in on where the "troublesome" cans and parks are.' It meant ensuring *'they* co-operate with *us*—calling them into the streets to do their job, for instance, when a gay demonstration has to be protected from straight thugs.'[8]

Vancouver's police liaison efforts were led by SEARCH, the Society for Education, Action, Research and Counselling on Homosexuality, founded in 1974 as a response to 'a crisis in gay bottle clubs' following police raids. Together with other groups, a gay businessman, and a city councillor, SEARCH later formed the Gay-Police Committee to formally communicate with the police and discuss 'approaches to better education on minority issues.'[9] For several years, Vancouver GATE organized strong responses to police harassment, such as a 1977 community forum at which 350 people confronted police over a campaign to 'clean up' the downtown area that featured selective law enforcement. Some at the meeting complained about being harassed by the police for kissing and holding hands on the street.[10] Two years later, three hundred people attended a GATE forum to protest police inaction to increasing violence against gays and lesbians. A few weeks after that, four hundred people rallied in front of the courthouse.[11] In Calgary, the first police liaison initiative started in 1983 to deal with complaints of harassment by people going to gay bars and by men cruising in a city park. The initiative eventually broke down, however, as a result of distrust of the police, and suspicions that information obtained by them at the liaison meetings was being used to increase harassment and arrests of gay men.[12]

POLICE RAIDS AND REPRESSION OF GAY SEXUALITY

From 1975 to 1984, a series of police raids and other actions by the state to repress same-sex sexuality convinced activists that a campaign was underway to recriminalize and demonize gays, and turn public opinion against legislating equality within human rights laws. The police campaign began in March 1975 with the arrests of the clients of the Unique Modelling Agency in Ottawa, and intensified in August 1975 with a raid on Sauna Aquarius, a Montreal gay bathhouse, that resulted in a number of men being charged with bawdy house offences. The raid took place during a period of increased police presence at gay and lesbian bars, and greater entrapment of men in washrooms. These actions were part of a clean-up of Montreal in preparation for the 1976 Olympic games. A police source in a Montreal community paper, *Gay Times,* noted that the campaign was 'designed to frighten gays from frequenting public places where Olympic tourists are likely to be, particularly downtown Montreal.'[13]

Further confirmation of a clean-up campaign occurred when six Montreal gay and lesbian bars were raided in October 1975, with the presence of gun-toting police sending terror through the lesbian and gay communities.[14] Subsequent raids on' the Club Baths and the Neptune Sauna in January and May 1976 resulted in more bawdy house charges.[15] Suspicions that the Olympic clean-up had spread to Ottawa, where some events were to be held, arose following a police raid, and the laying of bawdy house and gross indecency charges, at that city's Club Baths in May 1976, a few days after the Montreal police actions.[16] Angered at the dramatic increase in police repression, Montreal activists formed the Comité homosexual anti-repression/Gay Coalition Against Repression. On 19 June 1976, the Comité held what was to that date the largest gay demonstration in Canada, when some three hundred people protested the raids. Gays of Ottawa (GO) responded with a press conference decrying the Club Baths raid and requesting a meeting with the mayor, which took place a few days later. They also contacted the arrested men, to refer them to sympathetic lawyers, and picketed the Ottawa police headquarters, drawing fifty protesters.

An even more momentous police raid was executed on 22 October 1977 at Truxx, a Montreal gay bar, carried out by fifty officers wearing bulletproof vests and armed with machine guns. One hundred and forty-six men were charged as found-ins and the owner was charged as a keeper of a common bawdy house. Eight charges of gross indecency and two for drug trafficking were also laid. Bar patrons were loaded into police vans, held for eight hours in overcrowded cells without being allowed to call lawyers, and forced to take compulsory venereal disease tests. Some accused the police of verbal and physical abuse.[17] In response, the Comité, now transformed into l'Association pour les droits des gais du Québec (ADGQ), held a demonstration the next night during which two thousand people blocked a downtown intersection. A melee ensued when police attempted to disperse the crowd by riding their motorcycles through it while officers on foot began clubbing them. Protesters fought back, throwing beer bottles and glasses, creating shocking images for a national media coverage that embarrassed the police and the Quebec government. A few days later, three hundred people attended an ADGQ public forum at which a defence committee was set up for the found-ins.[18]

Despite the mass response to the Truxx actions, over the next few years Montreal police continued their raids on bars and bathhouses. They charged twenty-two men at the Dominion Square Tavern with bawdy house offences in October 1978.[19] In April 1980, sixty-one men were arrested as found-ins and six as keepers at the Sauna David; fifteen charges of gross indecency were also laid. Some men claimed they were charged as found-ins while they were outside the sauna walking towards it.[20] And in June 1984, ADGQ once more galvanized community anger with a large demonstration the night after a raid on Bud's, a popular gay bar, during which seventy-five police laid 122 found-in charges, eight keeper charges and thirty-three gross indecency charges. Reprehensibly, police photographs of bar patrons found their way into a weekly crime tabloid.[21] ADGQ demanded a public inquiry, accusing police of arresting the patrons indiscriminately, holding them overnight to sleep on floors and benches, and not informing them of their rights.

Similarly, in Toronto, on 30 December 1977, a police raid on *The Body Politic* sent shock waves through the gay and lesbian community, generating outrage and anger. The pretext for the action was an article by Gerald Harmon, 'Men Loving Boys Loving Men' that a *Toronto Sun* columnist claimed promoted paedophilia. *TBP* held a press conference denouncing the raid as an attack on freedom of the press. The Body Politic Free the Press Fund formed soon afterwards to cover the legal fees of *TBP*'s officers Ed Jackson, Gerald Hannon, and Ken Popert, who were charged under the *Criminal Code* with using the mail to distribute 'immoral, indecent, and scurrilous' material.[22] The raid immediately became a focus of concern for activists nationally. GATE Vancouver held a demonstration protesting it, on 1 January 1978, marking the first of many such events held over the subsequent years. On 14 January, one thousand people marched Toronto's Yonge Street to protest the visit of Anita Bryant—an American evangelical Christian then leading a high-profile campaign against gay rights legislation—and to 'defend the Body Politic.'[23]

In 1978 and 1979, two bathhouse raids by Toronto officers prompted more denunciations of police homophobia and repression. On 9 December 1978, twenty officers descended on the Barracks, which drew a leather and SM clientele, and charged twenty-eight men. Infuriated community activists immediately formed the December 9th Defense Fund to organize legal defences and coordinate community responses. (A few months later, the fund's name was changed to the Right to Privacy Committee.)[24] Following the raid, four hundred people demonstrated in protest and activists held a press conference, at which they accused the police of attacking the entire gay community and attempted to counter the lurid press coverage of SM activities at the Barracks.[25] More protest occurred in October 1979, after police raided the Hot Tubs club and laid forty bawdy house charges. During a separate but related action, the owners of the bathhouse were charged with producing pornographic films.[26]

A particularly outrageous and vindictive police action, also in 1979, transpired when Toronto police charged a gay man, Don Franco, with keeping a bawdy house in his home after a plainclothes officer responded to a classified advertisement Franco placed in *The Body Politic* seeking sexual contacts. The police and the Crown alleged that because Franco publicly advertised for sexual contacts, the sex acts with the men who responded were committed in a public place. They also alleged that the paraphernalia for SM sex found in Franco's residence was offensive to community standards of tolerance. Fortunately, Franco was acquitted two years later. The trial judge actually criticized the use of a plainclothes officer to entice Franco, and ruled that the 1969 consenting adults legislation included the types of acts in question.[27]

But the biggest and most terrifying of all the raids took place on the night of 5 February 1981 during a well-orchestrated, militaristic campaign. Toronto police carried out simultaneous raids on four bathhouses, arresting 304 men as found-ins and twenty others as keepers. The police told the media the raids were the culmination of six months of investigation, and that 'acts of prostitution and indecent acts' were taking place in the bathhouses.[28] The press later revealed that police caused $35,000 in damages to the bathhouses by using hammers, crowbars, and

shears to smash doors, shatter mirrors, rip open mattresses, and wrench doors off lockers. Some officers
kicked huge holes in the walls. In addition, several
of the men arrested were physically and verbally
abused. One man arrested at the Barracks told of
having been 'pushed hard into the wall. My nose was
lacerated and bloodied. The cop kept punching me
in the lower back and pulling my hair and saying,
"You're disgusting, faggot. Look at this dirty place."' A
police officer was quoted saying, 'Too bad the place
doesn't catch fire, we'd have to catch them escaping
custody.' Another was reported as stating, 'Too bad
the showers aren't hooked up to gas.'[29]

Word of the raids reached members of *TBP's*
collective and Jim Monk, the chairperson of the Coalition for Gay Rights in Ontario (CGRO), who went to
the police station at about eleven p.m. to talk to the
people who had been arrested.[30] The next day they
and a network of activists sprang into action, holding
a meeting that organized a demonstration for the
evening of February 6. Initially, three hundred people
gathered at the corner of Yonge and Wellesley Streets,
but their ranks swelled quickly to more than fifteen
hundred. Enraged, they headed to police Division 52,
shouting 'Fuck you 52' as their rallying cry, blocking
traffic and seizing control of Yonge Street.[31] The demonstration grew to over three thousand as it surged
along, becoming more frenzied the closer it came to 52
Division. CGRO activist Christine Donald, who helped
organize the response to the raids, recalls, 'I was
actually quite frightened on that demo. The anger was
enormous, just enormous.'[32] The anger was also fuelled
by clumsy police attempts to curtail the demonstration.
They blockaded the intersection of Yonge and Dundas
with cruise cars, further incensing the demonstrators,
who rocked the cars, smashing windshields and head-
lights. A paddy wagon had its side dented. Two demonstrators urinated on one cop car and a window was
smashed on a streetcar caught in the altercation.[33]

Pressing on along Dundas Street, the crowd faced
more danger as about thirty counter-demonstrators
gathered on the sidewalk, chanting 'Fuck the queers!'[34]
Then, as the protestors arrived at 52 Division, they
encountered a wall of about two hundred police
standing shoulder-to-shoulder, batons held behind
their backs, out of sight. Fearing the police were poised
to start cracking open heads, a small group of activists
huddled to find a way to keep a riot from erupting.
They decided to divert the demonstrators away from

52 Division, so CGRO's Tom Warner exhorted them
to proceed to the nearby provincial legislature to protest the government's refusal to add sexual orientation to the Ontario Human Rights Code.[35] The change
of venue prevented a violent confrontation with the
police at 52 Division but did not defuse the anger.
Demonstration marshals had trouble controlling the
crowd as it approached the legislature. Hordes of protesters charged onto the front lawn, bolting towards
the legislature's main entrance, repeatedly heaving
themselves against the doors and nearly breaking
them down before the police appeared and beat
them back. A violent confrontation between police
and demonstrators broke out, with much punching,
kicking, and shoving. Finally, at the urging of organ-
izers, the crowd dispersed. However, skirmishes
between police and protesters continued for some
time afterwards in the streets nearby.

Relations between the community and Toronto
police worsened dramatically following revelations
published in a community newspaper that, during the
bathhouse raid protests, plainclothes officers acted as
agents provocateurs, inciting demonstrators to acts of
violence and then arresting them.[36] Outraged by the
raids and these events, Brent Hawkes, pastor of the
Metropolitan Community Church, began a hunger
strike on 17 February. He pledged to continue it until
Mayor Arthur Eggleton established an independent
inquiry into relations between the police and the gay
community. On 12 March, supported unanimously by
City Council, Eggleton appointed lawyer and former
journalist Arnold Bruner to prepare a report, at which
point Hawkes ended his strike.[37] Two months after
the raids, however, more fodder was provided for
community fury, as charges of conspiracy—including
conspiracy to obtain proceeds obtained by crime—
were laid against the shareholders and officers of the
Club Baths. Two of those charged, Peter Maloney and
George Hislop, had been vocal police critics, which
fuelled activist suspicions that the charges were a
form of reprisal designed to discredit them. Consequently, thirty-four gay organizations held a press
conference condemning the attempt 'to characterize
our leaders, and by implication the gay community,
as criminal.'[38] But such protestations proved futile, as
police, undeterred, raided two more bathhouses later
in 1981, laying a number of bawdy house charges.[39]
What would turn out to be the last bathhouse raid for
many years occurred on 20 April 1983 when police

laid bawdy house charges against nine customers, the owner, and three employees of the Back Door Gym.[40]

Police action against bathhouses spread westward on 20 May 1981 when forty Edmonton police, six RCMP officers, and two crown attorneys raided the Pisces Spa. Doors to private cubicles were smashed and men found on the premises were videotaped and photographed. In all, sixty men were arrested, four as keepers and fifty-six as found-ins. The membership list of over two thousand names was seized.[41] Within hours, the arrested men were fingerprinted, issued summonses, and loaded into a police paddy wagon. They were then taken to a provincial court where two judges, court clerks, and crown attorneys awaited. The men were questioned about sexual activity they saw or had engaged in at the Pisces. Told that what they said could not be used against them in court, they were not advised that what they said could be used as evidence against others who had been accused, and that what others said could be used against them. They felt intimidated into testifying without benefit of counsel. Later, some said they had asked to speak to a lawyer but had been refused. Michael Phair, one of the men arrested on what he called a 'harrowing' night, recalled, 'I certainly felt extremely powerless because I didn't know anything ... which was very disconcerting to me.'[42]

Phair felt the ordeal was over upon being released, until he later heard a radio newscast featuring the raid as the top story. It was then that he began 'realizing that this wasn't over and it wasn't just going to go away, and it wasn't just a kind of nightmare kind of thing.'[43] Phair immediately called Edmonton GATE, which, along with members of Dignity (the group for gay Catholics) and the Metropolitan Community Church, swung into action. Within twenty-four hours, GATE had a leaflet circulating in the city's gay bars containing information about what had happened and announcing plans for a community response. Counselling and advice was offered to found-ins. A demonstration of one hundred people to protest the raid was held by straight civil libertarians, labour leaders, and supportive churches. A few days later, a public meeting of the gay and lesbian community set up the Privacy Defense Committee to support the found-ins.[44]

Back in Toronto, in April and May 1982, police targeted Glad Day Bookshop, then Toronto's only gay bookstore and, once more, *The Body Politics*. Kevin Orr, manager of Glad Day, was charged with 'possession of obsence material for the purpose of sale' after two morality squad officers visited the store and seized two gay male magazines containing sexually explicit material. Shortly afterwards, nine members of *TBP's* editorial collective and the officers of Pink Triangle Press were charged with publishing obscene material after they ran an article, 'Lust with a Very Proper Stranger' in the paper's April 1982 issue. The Toronto Gay Community Council, an umbrella group of community organizations, responded by holding a press conference to denounce the Glad Day and *TBP* charges, describing them as 'yet another example of selective enforcement of the law designed to discredit harass our community' Spokesperson Harvey Hamburg commented that the charges 'lead us to the conclusion that there is, indeed, a concerted police effort against us.' A few days later, a demonstration of seven hundred people protested the charges. During the demo, Eve Zaremba, a writer and member of the editorial board for *Broadside,* a feminist paper, declared, "This harassment of *The Body Politic,* using obscenity as an excuse, is aimed at destroying one of the few voices open to us."[45]

The community organizing in response to various raids between 1975 and 1984 in Ottawa, Montreal, Toronto, and Edmonton had powerful symbolic significance and an energizing impact on gay and lesbian communities across the country. Indeed, the empowerment achieved from spontaneous, mass uprising in the face of police harassment is the raids' most significant legacy. As sociologist and activist Gary Kinsman stresses, the community response to the 1981 Toronto bathhouse raids closed off certain options for the police and probably prevented some even bigger acts of state repression. The police could no longer conduct mass raids, and the balance of power shifted a little in favour of the gay and lesbian community: 'The mobilization cannot be underestimated. And I think part of that also is that the police actually have been, historically, quite a central regulator of gay men's lives, so I think that the resistance to it had this kind of popular character to it that could really go quite far.'[46] Although the mobilization gradually dissipated, it is clear the lesbian and gay community in Toronto was forever changed by, and became more visible from, the militancy of its response and what that response came to symbolize.

CGRO's Jim Monk, a resident of Windsor, holds similar views, and notes in addition that the massive

Toronto community response was important for gays and lesbians in smaller communities. They feared that if the police in Toronto could get away with brutal acts of repression despite the existence of a well-organized activist community in that city, then more vulnerable and less organized gays and lesbians in smaller places had reason to dread what might happen to them. As Monk saw things, nearly twenty years afterwards, 'We had a victory there over the police that really made a lot of people think things were possible. Always in the '70s, I think we thought we were in this for the long haul and getting the human rights code amended or getting public acceptance of homosexuality was way, way in the future. After the horror of the bath raids had subsided, and people started to fight back, and the determination that they had, I think that what came out of that was a sense of, hey, we can win. We can actually, maybe not right away, we will win.'[47]

As had been the case in Toronto, the period following the bathhouse raid in Edmonton saw increased visibility for the gay and lesbian community there. Phair notes that 'it did unleash probably one of the most active periods for the gay and lesbian community here and a real blossoming of the diversity, and stuff . . . The whole bath raids woke up the community. I mean, I remember people saying to me that they never thought it could happen here, that this [city] was just too quiet and laid back and no one cared and that jarred, took that out from under people's feet, you couldn't argue that, couldn't think that way any more. It really pushed people to have to re-think.'[48] Edmonton's gay pride events, the Gay and Lesbian Alliance, lesbian groups, sports groups, and religious groups began to blossom from 1981 to about 1984. Like Toronto, Edmonton's community was forever changed by the raid.

NOTES

1. Gerald Hannon, 'Anatomy of a Sex Scandal,' *The Body Politic* (TBP), June 1976, 10.
2. Ibid.
3. Arnold Bruner, 'Out of the Closet: Study of Relations between the Homosexual Community and the Police,' *TBP*, 24 Sept. 1981, 120.
4. 'Catcalls Greet 18 Men at Court,' *The Packet*, 20 Sept. 1983, 1.
5. 'Guilty Pleas Smother Real Questions,' *TBP*, July–Aug. 1984, 8.
6. Ken Popert, 'Hallowe'en: Pressure Gets Action,' *TBP*, Dec. 1977–Jan. 1978, 8.
7. Ross Irwin, 'Cops Meet with Gay Community, Say They'll Halt Hallowe'en Mob,' *TBP*, Nov. 1979.
8. Editorial, 'Cops, Co-operation, and Closetry,' *TBP*, Nov. 1978, 7.
9. Geoff Mains, 'A Lot Can Be Gained by Working Together,' *TBP*, Dec. 1979–Jan. 1980, 7.
10. Robert Cook, '350 Demand End to Police Harassment,' *TBP*, May 1977.
11. Ken Popert, 'Pacific Gays and Lesbians Rally to Combat Rising Street Violence,' *TBP*, Sept. 1970.
12. Glenn Wheeler, 'Liaison Committee Cop Goes Spring Cleaning,' *TBP*, May 1984.
13. City Cracks Down,' *TBP*, July–Aug., 1975, 8.
14. Ed Jackson and Stan Persky, eds., *Flaunting It! A Decade of Gay Journalism from* The Body Politic (Vancouver: New Star Books; Toronto: Pink Triangle Press, 1982), 230–1.
15. NGRC, 'The Great Olympic Clean Up: A Chronology of Events,' 30 May 1976.
16. Ibid.
17. 'Thousands Take to the Streets in Protest,' *TBP*, Dec. 1977–Jan. 1978.
18. Jim Bartley, 'Truxx Trial Date Reset,' *TBP*, Dec. 1982.
19. Robin Hardy, 'Montreal Police Storm Tavern in Repeat of Truxx Raid,' *TBP*, Nov. 1978.
20. Stuart Russell, 'Montreal Police Raid on Sauna David Sparks Largest Protest Since Truxx Raid,' *TBP*, June–July 1980.
21. Gary Kinsman, 'Montreal Police- Raid Buds,' *R*, July–Aug., 1984.
22. 'TBP Raided and Charged,' *TBP*, Feb. 1978.
23. 'Support, Loud and Strong,' *TBP*, Feb. 1978.
24. 'Barracks Defence Goes Full Steam Ahead,' *TBP*, March–April 1979.
25. 'Homosexual Leaders Attack "Conspirators",' *Sun*, 13 Dec. 1978.
26. Robert Trow and Bill Lewis, 'Cops Raid Hot Tub Club, Private Homes on Eve of Opening of Ontario Legislature,' *TBP*, Nov. 1979.
27. 'Judge Rules Man's Apartment Is Not a Common Bawdy House,' *TBP*, Dec. 1981.
28. Gerald Hannon, 'Rage! Taking It to the Streets,' *TBP*, March 1981, 11.
29. Ibid.
30. Jim Monk, 2 March 1998.
31. Ibid.
32. Christine Donald, 5 Jan. 1998.

33. Hannon, 'Rage!'
34. Ibid.
35. Jim Monk, 2 March 1998. Gary Kinsman, 27 July 1993.
36 Gerald Hannon, 'Exposing the Big Lie,' *TBP*, May 1981.
37. 'Brent Hawkes: Hungry for Rights,' *TBP*, April 1981.
38. Gerald Hannon, 'Putting On the Pressure,' *TBP*, June 1981, 9.
39. Kevin Orr, 'Fifth Bath Busted in Daytime Police Raid,' *TBP*, July–Aug., 1981.
40. 'Back to the Baths; Back to the Streets,' *TBP*, June 1983. Ed Jackson, 'The Back Door Raid,' *TBP* special supplement, May 1983.
41. Gerald Hannon, 'Edmonton: Bath Raids Move West,' *TBP*, July–Aug., 1981.
42. Michael Phair, 18 June 1997.
43. Ibid.
44. Hannon, 'Edmonton: Bath Raids Move West.' Gerald Hannon, 'Guilty Verdict in Pisces Trial Discouraging Sign for Found-Ins,' *TBP*, Sept. 1981. Gerald Hannon, 'More Guilty in Pisces Trials but Lowers Owners' Fines,' *TBP*, Oct. 1981.
45. Craig Patterson, 'Defending the Right to Read,' *TBP*, June 1982, 8.
46. Gary Kinsman, 27 July 1993.
47. Jim Monk, 2 March 1998.
48. Michael Phair, 18 June 1997.

■ARTICLE 3: COALITION POLITICS: LESBIAN FEMINISTS MEET GAY LIBERATIONISTS

Becki Ross

Our enemies they wish we'd live in silence
They fear us so they often turn to violence
We'll never let them force compliance
Our rights are what we'll have
We will never know our places
We will always be outrageous
We have seen the last of cages
We'll fight until we are free
—Michael Riordan and Heather Ramsay, 1977[1]

Source: Becki L. Ross, "Chapter 7: Coalition Politics: Lesbian Feminists Meet Gay Liberationists", *The House that Jill Built: A Lesbian Nation in Formation*. Toronto: University of Toronto Press, 2002, pp. 99–118. Reprinted by permission of Becki L. Ross.

In January 1977, district councillors in Dade County, Florida, passed an ordinance that prohibited discrimination on the basis of affectional or sexual preference in areas of housing, employment, and services. A landmark victory for gay and lesbian activists, the decision was appealed and overturned in June 1977. Anita Bryant—former Miss America and reigning promoter of Florida orange juice—became the quintessential symbol of rising antigay and antilesbian forces across North America. Bryant's 'Save Our Children' campaign, coordinated and financed by fundamentalist Christian organizations, was intended to exploit the dominant discursive equation of homosexuality and child molestation. Pledging to continue the crusade against homosexuals and their 'perverse, abominable and dangerous' lifestyle, Bryant set out to galvanize anti-homosexual forces in Minneapolis, San Antonio, and San Francisco.

The first major defeat in the struggle for gay and lesbian civil rights in the United States, the Dade County case unfolded in the context of a mobilizing American New Right. Signs of emerging moral conservatism were evinced in reinvigorated organizing and rhetoric that was explicitly anti-abortion, anti-Equal Rights Amendment, anti-affirmative action, antipornography, and pro-family. Consistent with the shift of gender and sexual issues to the political centre in the mid-1970s, the Dade County ruling inaugurated a new wave of violence, state persecution, and legal initiatives directed against minority sexual populations and the commercial sex industry,[2] At the same time, deepening gender/sexual repression was not separable from the larger political and economic climate of escalating inflation, anti-union and pro-Ku Klux Klan organizing, mounting unemployment, and the imminence of economic recession.

As news of the Dade County defeat spread across the U.S./Canada border, organizing efforts in opposition to Bryant's anti-homosexual crusade were launched in most large Canadian cities.[3] For a period of almost one year, mainstream media coverage of the crusade prompted vociferous public debate over homosexuality and homophobia.[4] Former LOOT [Lesbian Organization of Toronto] member and gay liberationist Chris Bearchell commented: 'Anita Bryant did [gays and lesbians] a big favour. She broke the gay story in the mainstream press. If they wanted to cover her, they had to cover us, and she was big news.' The scope and tenor of the stories and letters printed in the *Toronto Sun, Toronto Star, Globe and Mail*, and religious papers like the *Catholic Register* reveal deep-seated antigay and antilesbian hostilities.[5] *Toronto Sun* columnist Claire Hoy described homosexuals as 'morally bankrupt,' 'perverse,' and 'sick,' and then warned his readers of 'the need to protect children from their clawing hands and demented aspirations.' Building directly on the 'Save Our Children' gospel. Hoy exclaimed: '[Homosexuals] want society to condone and institutionalize their disgusting activity so they can then reach out into the schools and twist young minds into thinking they can somehow get fulfillment from this nefarious lifestyle.'[6]

In Toronto, the Ad Hoc Coalition to Stop Anita Bryant was formed in June 1977, coordinated by the Coalition for Gay Rights in Ontario and composed of members from GATE, the John Damien Defense Committee, the Metropolitan Community Church, and CHAT.[7] Representatives from the Revolutionary Marxist Group, the League for Socialist Action and Wages Due Lesbians also attended meetings. A small, loose contingent of LOOT members decided to join the coalition. Convinced of the pressing need to combat Bryant's 'hysterical hate campaign' and its backing by religious and New Right strategists, Chris Bearchell, Fiona Rattray, and several other gay-liberationist members of LOOT plunged themselves into protest work (but not as official LOOT representatives until January 1978).[8] Though keenly aware of the limitations of the cosmetic ideal of gay and lesbian unity, they attended meetings, drafted and distributed leaflets, and helped to plan two summer-time demonstrations. They were also encouraged by the release of the *Life Together* report issued by the Ontario Human Rights Commission in July which, in response to a five-year lobby by largely gay-male activists, recommended the immediate inclusion of sexual orientation in the provincial human-rights code.[9]

As reported in *The Body Politic* and the *Militant*, on 25 June 1977 300 gay men, lesbians, and supporters marched in and out of bars chanting 'Out of the bars, into the streets, gay liberation now,' and on 22 July 700 attended a rally outside city hall.[10] Together, these two public actions signified an unparalleled surge in the history of post-Stonewall gay and lesbian organizing in Toronto. The summer also marked the eruption of national actions across Canada. The National Gay Rights Coalition passed a highly publicized motion calling on the federal government to prevent Anita Bryant's entry into Canada. Splashed across posters, the headline 'Stop Fooling Yourself—Civil Rights Are Your Concern' reminded Toronto gays and lesbians of the need for protection against discrimination in housing, employment, and services. Significantly, it secured legislative reform as *the* key focus of gay-liberationist energy.

Anita Bryant's invitation to Toronto in January 1978 by Reverend Ken Campbell of the People's Church sparked an intensified need for local, organized protest. Campbell's Renaissance International, the Fishers of Men, the Faith Baptist Church, and the Edmund Burke Society began to mobilize in support of Bryant. For lesbians and gay men, the question of derailing the 'Save Our Children' crusade became much more than one of solidarity with American brothers and sisters. *The Body Politic* reported that the Bryant campaign promised 'seed money' to any Canadian group wanting to organize in opposition to gay-rights legislation.[11] Dormant for a year, the LOOT political committee began convening in January and sent representatives to meetings of the Ad Hoc Committee to Stop Anita Bryant.[12]

A mass rally and dance at the St Lawrence Market on 14 January 1978 attracted over 1000 gay men, lesbians, and friends.[13] The following day, five hundred protesters braved arctic conditions to set up a picket line outside of the People's Church in Willowdale while Bryant was inside leading Sunday morning prayers.[14] To Chris Bearchell, 'Anita Bryant was the most visible manifestation of the Right interfering in our community at that time.' As Naomi Brooks recalls, 'It was clear she wanted to get all of us; it was a Hitler kind of crusade.' And as Gay Bell reminisces, 'It's hard to recreate what it felt like. It was very emotional. It was shocking to have someone with that kind of profile in the media making remarks about our core being.'

It was also significant, argues Bearchell, that speakers at the rallies made explicit the connections between 'outrageous homophobia' and the denial of custody rights to lesbian mothers, the deportation of Jamaican domestic workers, and recent government attacks on social spending and job security. Rallying mottoes printed out on chant sheets—'Gays, Women, Children Unite! Same Struggle, Same Fight,' 'Gays, Women, All Workers Unite! Same Enemy, Same Fight,' and 'Lesbian Liberation Now!'—illustrate self-conscious efforts to forge links between oppressions. Among the feminist organizations in attendance were Times Change (women's employment service), Nellie's Hostel, Toronto Women's Hostel, the March 8th Coalition, Women's Credit Union, WCREC, the Women's Educational Press, and WAVAW.

LOOT members tended to disagree on the meaning of the Bryant crusade and on an appropriate set of responses. As Gay Bell recalls, 'At LOOT, there was considerable cold-shouldering and disapproval for being involved in gay male politics. To me, it always felt like walking along a razor blade.' Radical feminists and separatists, in conjunction with members of Wages Due Lesbians, were more concerned to elucidate the differences between lesbians and gay men in defiance of what Pat Murphy saw as 'common-sense efforts to lump us all together.' They maintained that Anita Bryant's campaign was not directly about them—it was largely about gay-male sexual practice, and pedophilia in particular, which was, in their view, *neither* a lesbian nor a feminist issue.

Even though lesbian and straight feminists had argued since the early 1970s that almost all sexual abuse of children is done by heterosexual men, the LOOT membership (with few exceptions) condemned the increasingly public, 'exotic' character of (some) gay men's penchant for man-boy love. [...] In particular, they were disturbed by what they viewed as the exploitative character of adult/child sexual relations, Consequently, as described in [original source], the long-standing disenchantment of LOOT members with highly visible and articulate gay-male sexual culture resurfaced. Some LOOT task-force members maintained that a focus on pedophilia invited the organized wrath of moral conservatives and, in so doing, jeopardized lesbian and gay struggles for legal protection from discrimination and for liberation more broadly defined.

Frustrated and angered by earlier, unhappy confrontations with gay men's sexism, if not overt antifeminism, many radical feminists and separatists were leery of, and in some cases, virulently opposed to, yet another attempt to construct an alliance. Even when political interests appeared to coincide, collaboration was more easily argued in talk than executed in practice. Indeed, from the standpoint of the majority of LOOT-goers, the first signs of organized anti-Bryant protest were hardly reassuring. As Pat Murphy, Susan Cole, and others recall, the 'ugly, blatantly misogynist' tactics deployed by gay-male activists (and borrowed, in part, from the tradition of gay

men's drag and camp) could not be countenanced. Murphy argued, 'It was the same old thing—burn the witch! My heart broke when I'd see [Bryant] with a pie in her face. It hurt me to see her like that.' From the printing of buttons and T-shirts that proclaimed 'Anita Sucks Oranges,' 'Squeeze Anita Out,' and 'Anita Dear, Cram It,' to the delivery of antiwoman speeches and the burning of the Miss Orange Juice Queen in effigy, LOOT members disparaged all initiatives that they felt smacked of woman-hatred.

Many LOOT-goers were influenced by the criticisms made by some American feminists. At a June 1977 rally of women who had separated from the Gay Pride and anti-Bryant demonstration in New York, lesbian poet Adrienne Rich charged that 'Anita was equated with Hitler, or viciously lampooned in terms of her female anatomy by gay men ... The woman-hating tone of large sections of the marches reasserted to us that we could not find real "brotherly" solidarity in the gay movement.'[15] Speaking of gay men who participated in the Toronto anti-Bryant protests, Susan Cole lashed out: '"Cunt," "Bitch," they fumed as they marched down the street. I and others got the sense that Anita Bryant was being used as a convenient target for what was plainly unadulterated woman-hating. For my part, it didn't matter a damn whether it was the fundamentalists who were willing to serve her up as sacrifice or whether it was the boys venting their anger at womankind. It was all the patriarchy to me.'

Aware that Bryant was implicated in discourse and practices that produced gay and lesbian oppression, the majority of LOOT members none the less felt that she was coerced—the puppet of a powerful though mostly invisible male-dominated regime.[16] Thus, they tended not to hold her entirely responsible and blameworthy because she was a women whose *alleged* or *apparent* power to direct and accomplish antigay and antilesbian violence was, Murphy, Cole, and others insisted, illusory.[17] The essentialism of notions of women's natural superiority and universal victimization undergirded and gave shape to feelings of protectiveness harboured by most LOOT members *and* straight radical feminists. Indeed, this was a position that carried serious consequence for the depth and breadth of LOOT's commitment to counterattack.

Importantly, however, not all lesbians agreed with the dominant interpretation advanced by most LOOT-goers. Betty, an older gay women who came out through A Woman's Place but was not a LOOT regular, contended: 'I was so happy when [Anita Bryant] got the pie in the face. I was sorry I didn't do it. I thought it was great. And with the effigy, I would have liked to have been with the boys lighting the first match.' Deb Stinson, a working-class lesbian who had one foot in bar culture and the other in lesbian feminism, explained her position: 'It didn't matter to me that most LOOT women thought that all women were precious. Anita Bryant was fucking me over and that was the bottom line. Being a woman did not excuse her behaviour.' Even within the regular LOOT membership, there was a certain measure of dissent. As Gay Bell asserted: 'The effigy didn't bother me. I also liked the Sisters of Perpetual Indulgence. I don't feel that women are holy and I had no trouble criticizing right-wing women. In fact, it's important to satirize them.' Yet there were few opportunities at LOOT to facilitate a wide-ranging airing of competing analyses.

One meeting of the revived political committee was held at 342 Jarvis Street in early January. Though a number of LOOT members joined coalition committees, instructed gay men on the inappropriateness of 'burn the bitch' tactics, and provided a speaker for the 14 January rally, the organization itself did not assume a position of full, public leadership. This did not mean that lesbian feminists felt distanced from, or uninspired by, the anti-Bryant crusade. Many of the women I interviewed remember the hundreds of angry lesbian feminists present at the January demonstrations and the exuberance engendered by such historically unmatched visibility. However, the lack of leadership, from start to finish, reflected the lack of consensus among LOOT members. Clearly, the ubiquitous desire to devise some semblance of unity among lesbian feminists, however tenuous, was more important than the triumph of one ideological position over another.

Concomitantly, the same fear of conflict that operated internally to thwart the resolution of contentious issues within LOOT, combined with the tentative grasp of new, anti-heterosexist discourse, meant that there was virtually no critical treatment of the anti-Bryant campaign in the LOOT *Newsletter*.[18] Nor was critical commentary carried in other Canadian lesbian or feminist periodicals. Given the potential power of print to educate and mobilize constituencies, this absence was disenabling.

Members of LOOT's task force convened in late January 1978 to evaluate their participation in the coalition and to contemplate their future actions.

The dialogue reproduced in part below (originally taped in February 1978) displays a degree of discord that extended beyond Bryant's crusade to the broader question of LOOT's emphasis and priorities.[19] It reflects the residual reluctance of several LOOT leaders to place anti-Bryant activism atop the organization's agenda:

Chris Bearchell: We have been political but we have not taken responsibility for anything yet. Anita Bryant is coming back to town in April and the feminist and lesbian element really manipulated and, in a sense, led the last action against Bryant. But LOOT didn't initiate that action—we effectively took it over and led it. The next time we should not bother waiting for others to initiate it but do it ourselves.

Judith Bennett: I think that might be laying a guilt trip on us. It's too destructive. We can't get too overly political or we will kill ourselves. We are just not strong. When we took over their organized thing last time, let's face it, we fucked it up . . . and we don't have it together enough to organize one when we fucked it up before.

Chris Bearchell: If we don't have a response to Bryant it will be interpreted that there is more support for her than there is. We tried to make it clear last time to the women in the world that Bryant was not just a homophobic evangelical asshole but also the thin edge of the wedge of the anti-feminist forces from the States. We really didn't get that across. Whatever the media deliberately buries is probably the most important part of it and they buried the feminist response to Bryant. I don't feel like we can let them get away with that.

Brenda Lang: I feel that we dramatize her campaign . . . and feed her with something to hit us with . . . I'd prefer to put that energy into something that's going to get us going rather than hold us back because we're always involved with that and not involved with fulfilling our own needs.

Judith Bennett: Yes, I think that also by ignoring her we can pay attention to other needs in our community, and people will suffer if those aren't paid attention to. It's a matter of priorities.

Chris Bearchell: She puts people back into the closet in droves. It's not an exaggeration when the gay movement says she's responsible for deaths in the States that happened, and I would feel like I was turning my back on that if I didn't do something . . . I think it's possible to sustain the things we need for our community and be able to respond when we feel like we're being offended like that.

Caught up in their own ambivalence towards working with gay men, frustrated by their inability to arrive at consensus, and divided on the objectives of the organization, LOOT members did not mount a unified response to the 'Save Our Children' campaign. Divisions within the membership surfaced along broad radical-feminist and socialist-feminist lines. And with almost no history or experience of mediating different political positions within lesbian activism, compromise proved problematic. At the same time, it became clear that gay-male activists were resistant to, if not threatened by, the prospect of sharing leadership with, or ceding leadership to, lesbian feminists.[20] As Amy Gottlieb recalls, 'Gay men, in their typical way, weren't open to lesbians being represented as much as we needed to be represented. But still, gay men couldn't ignore LOOT members.'

According to Fiona Rattray, 'Mostly LOOT's work consisted of marching in the streets, "gaycotting" orange juice and occasional letter writing.' But overall, the absence of bodies needed to accomplish the work impeded a vigorous, offensive program of action. To quote Natalie LaRoche: 'I don't think the demos or rallies raised the profile of LOOT. They raised the visibility of lesbians, and LOOT was there, LOOT was strongly there, but it was invisible largely because a lot of people were so scared of being out. I repressed the fear, but there were a lot of people who were just terrified.'

From the beginning, lesbian feminists acknowledged the danger of the 'Save Our Children' campaign.[21] However, they were also aware that a civil-rights strategy was insufficient to combat the sexual *and* gender oppression experienced by lesbians, hence their endorsement of legal reform as a politically smart yet insufficient priority.[22] The majority of LOOT members believed that reform offered gay men the right to the same status and privileges accorded straight men.[23] Additionally, they

resisted traditional forms of organizing and decision making adopted by gay-male coalition leaders (for instance, single-issue, mass-action lobbying and an elected executive). Conceptualizing themselves alongside gay men as a 'sexual minority' had definite appeal for LOOT members, particularly as a strategy to garner short-term political gains. Yet for those who were keen to define and defend a lesbian-feminist identity that was distinct from gay maleness, such a strategy was singularly incomplete.

By January 1978, a handful of LOOT representatives did work closely with the coalition and they succeeded in challenging some aspects of gay men's behaviour, such as sexist language and hierarchical process. Radical feminists tended to dispute the utility of converging lesbian and gay-male communities, and yet they could not easily ignore the sequence of developments that placed gay men and lesbians not only under public scrutiny, but also under siege. [...]

AGE OF CONSENT LAWS: THE DILEMMA OF PROTECTION

Though opposed to the criminalization of homosexual sex under the age of twenty-one, the majority of LOOT members were more concerned with how the abolition of age-of-consent laws—a central plank of the National Gay Rights Coalition's platform—would eliminate all judicial measures to prohibit the sexual violation of heterosexual girls and women.[24] A number of LOOT members told me of the pain, humiliation, and fear of unwanted, forced sexual relations with adult heterosexual men. It was often these women, along with the advocates of lesbian mothers, whose angry, impassioned accounts were first and foremost heard and taken seriously at LOOT. Other women added the knowledge that they had gained from work with battered women and children in hostels, rape crisis centres, counselling centres, prisons, and psychiatric hospitals. And refusing to confine discussion of violence to straight men, Pat Murphy and friends retold tales of 'gay men fucking little boys in the basement of the CHAT centre.' Out of these overlapping stories, analysis of women's and children's sexual exploitation by men began to emerge as the dominant feminist discourse at LOOT, WAVAW, the Rape Crisis Centre, and a number of other feminist organizations in the city.[25]

Many LOOT-goers (and straight feminists) were suspicious of claims to consensual sex, whether straight or gay. As stated by Susan Cole, 'Gay men were interested in eliminating age-of-consent laws so that they could find many, many dozen more holes into which they could plug their penises.' Cole and others were not encouraged by the stories that some gay men, as teenagers, delighted in the sexual education they sought and received from older men, or that virtually all boys, as males, are taught to view themselves as sexual subjects. That intergenerational sex among males often entailed a positive and genuinely different experience from intergenerational heterosex was not a tradition with which women, lesbian or straight, identified. In effect, once issues of de facto male sexual power were linked with sexual abuse, there was little room for oppositional narratives.[26]

Working with children as a child-care or day-care worker, a teacher, a youth counsellor, or a girl-guide leader, a lesbian often struggled to hide her sexuality for fear of losing her job. Adult lesbians, most LOOT members contended, were lovers of adult woman-identified women—they were not child molesters, nor did they sexually desire children. As Amy Gottlieb recalls, 'There was a need to say we were really different and, by implication, we wouldn't do *this* with young girls.' Only one narrator mentioned having had sex with an older woman, while two women told me about the sex they had experienced with underage female partners. Perhaps a compulsion to disengage from the messiness of one's past in the service of a politically consistent present prevented others from disclosing similiar acts. Even the lesbian 'crush' popularized by singer/songwriter Meg Christian's 'Ode to a Gym Teacher' (1974) was eulogized in language reminiscent of nineteenth-century ennobling of same-gender romantic friendships. Ultimately, notwithstanding Jane Rule's heretical wish 'to make adults easier to seduce,' breaking the cross-generational taboo was incongruent with 1970s right-on, reciprocal, relational love between adult, women-identified women.'[27] Several years after LOOT's closure, Chris Bearchell remembered the pain of her own sexually active youth (which led her to involvement in youth liberation in Edmonton). In 1983, she wrote: 'There are lesbians doing time in Canada because they've been convicted of gross indecency, because their lovers are under twenty-one. There are lesbians who've opted for suicide rather

than face that prospect. They deserve support, not silence.[28]

Several young lesbians at LOOT called for the abolition of age-of-consent laws (in concert with organized gay liberation), but their call was either ignored or dismissed.[29] LOOT members elected to place a young person's right to protection from exploitation over and above what they perceived as a misguided libertarian emphasis on sexual freedom. There was also conflict among the membership regarding such issues as the calibration of age difference: for instance, What age limits (if any) are appropriate in determining when the impermissible becomes permissible? How do gay and lesbian youth who seek sex from adults make sense of this desire in view of unequal power relations based on age? Given the unpredictable playing out of seduction and the enormous complexity of adult/child sexual relations, can a young person really know what s/he is consenting to?

Consonant with bourgeois norms of propriety, members of LOOT seemed partial to century-old notions of childhood as the age of vulnerability to be guarded at all costs from adult corruption.[30] American theorist Gayle Rubin argues: 'The notion that sex per se is harmful to the young has been chiseled into extensive social and legal structures (i.e., statutory rape laws) designed to insulate minors from sexual knowledge and experience.'[31] In the absence of organized protest, the heterosexist bedrock of the law and the rootedness of age-of-consent rhetoric in the patriarchal definition of children as property remained in place. Cognizant of this tension, most LOOT members felt that securing some sort of legal protection for young girls was a necessary yet unsatisfactory pursuit.

A non-conforming voice at LOOT belonged to Evelyn (Lilith) Finkler. A teenager and one of the six young lesbians who introduced a pro-abolition position on age-of-consent law to the BiNational Lesbian Conference in 1979, she recalls her unpopular stance: 'I remember trying to talk about age of consent and how I found the law really oppressive and how it was important to encourage child sexuality. We don't immediately become sexual at the age of 18 or 21, and if one of the tenets of feminism was control over our own bodies, I thought, "Why can't that be extended to children?" I was sexually abused and I still felt that the age-of-consent laws were wrong. But women at LOOT didn't want to hear what I had to say because it was inconvenient.'

Lesbian feminists in several other organizations across the country established formal policy on age-of-consent laws, but there was no uniformity among them. In 1975, the Lesbian Caucus of the British Columbia Federation of Women (BCFW) stated: 'The present laws provide some protection against the sexual exploitation of young women. Abolition of age of consent laws would worsen the situation.'[32] Contrarily, Toronto's Lesbian Caucus of GATE took a position in favour of the abolition of age-of-consent laws, as did Gay Youth Toronto.[33] A delegate at the NGRC conference in 1975, Chris Bearchell reported: 'Two lesbians, age 16 and 18, felt that people over the age of 21 should base their decision on the recommendation of those under 21—so, youth speaking for themselves . . . No one under the age of 21 spoke in opposition to the abolition of age of consent laws.'[34]

Years later, reflecting on the broad question of sexual self-determination, Lorna Weir laments the lost opportunity to expand feminist discourse to include young women whose sexual agency is subject to both parental and state control: 'Age of consent was bred out of lesbian politics as a potential area of interest and debate and that struck me as manifestly untrue and shortsighted because of delinquency charges. Adolescent women, lesbian and straight, were paying a terrible price for being actively sexual. But then again, this was the era of jackboot lesbian feminism.' The need for a more creative, nuanced approach to the state's regulation of youth sexuality was outlined by Lisa at the LOOT task force meeting in the spring of 1978. Arguing that 'the age-of-consent laws do not articulate the nature of the oppression, and, in fact, are used against lesbian and gay people,' she asserted: 'There must be another way of defining rape or molestation under the law which recognizes the vulnerability of children to assault and violation, but doesn't preclude [their] right across the board to engage in non-coercive sexual involvement with adults.'[35] Had girlhood memories of lust for older women been an admissible subject of dialogue at LOOT, recognition of the disjuncture between practice and ideology may have opened up space for the formation of alternative strategies. Instead, lesbian feminists and supporters tended to apply an analysis of unequal power in adult/child heterosexual relations to adult/youth homosexual relations without considering how same-gender sex might fundamentally alter the dynamic.

DIVIDED LOYALTIES AND THE UNFAMILIARITY OF NEGOTIATION

Though the lines were not impermeable, political differences among LOOT members surfaced and structured debate on *The Body Politic* crisis. Not only did most radical feminists resist working with gay men; they identified the 'Men Loving Boys Loving Men' emergency as a gay men's struggle from which they would benefit little. Despite not being regular readers or contributors to *The Body Politic*, they resented not having been consulted before the decision to publish the controversial article. They were horrified by the raw, brutal OPP/Metro Police incursion; however, their ambivalence towards all forms of male sexuality led to both tacit and openly expressed support (along-side moral conservatives) for state regulation of male homosexual pornography and, by extension, all gay-male sexual expression. In effect, the slide from criticism of sexual practice and representation to support for state sexual censorship was riddled with flaws, not least of all the deflection away from the root causes of sexual and gender inequality in capitalist, racist, and patriarchal culture.

Those women who either felt closely aligned with or were sympathetic to the left tradition of gay-liberationist politics, most of whom also identified as socialists, were the first to critique the oppressive force of state sexual repression. By the late 1970s, Chris Bearchell, Konnie Reich, Sue Golding, Gillian Rodgerson, Anna Marie Smith, and others began to expose the contradictory character of state practices, that is, how the family-court system is set up to protect the adult male who molests his ten-year-old daughter at the same time that it warehouses sexually active, underage 'female delinquents' in reform schools and jails. They questioned the seizures of sexually explicit print materials like *Show Me! The Book of Children's Sexuality* and *The Joy of Lesbian Sex*, which were confiscated in the raid on *The Body Politic*. And they expressed agreement with Gayle Rubin's letter to *The Body Politic* wherein she cautioned against abandoning already vulnerable and stigmatized groups like boy-lovers, sadomasochists, and transsexuals to further attack and isolation.[36]

Unable to reach consensus, LOOT members never hammered out a formal statement and a set of strategies regarding *The Body Politic* crisis. In ways that parallel the Anita Bryant debate, discussion within the membership exposed the complexity of the issue. Stymied by the hardening of divided ideological loyalties and still wedded to the maintenance of organizational unity, LOOT never assumed a full leadership role, though the lesbian and feminist critique of adult men's power over children unsettled the sexual-libertarian posture of some gay men.

That yet another stalemate vexed the LOOT membership is reflective, in part, of an emerging radical versus socialist feminist split. Though lesbians occupied positions on both sides of the radical/socialist divide, most LOOT members, including the majority of the informal leaders, aligned themselves with the vision espoused by radical feminists, both lesbian and straight. In the two instances described above, the discord was characterized by the suspicion of, and unfamiliarity with, modes of compromise; competing estimations of the need to differentiate lesbian feminists from gay men; conflicting analyses of the role of the state; and, hence, divergent takes on the practice of coalition politics.[37]

Convinced that lesbianism was a basis for political activity, members of LOOT demonstrated a degree of political confidence, maturity, and voice unthinkable five years earlier. However, as they wrestled with allegiances to gay liberation and the (straight) women's movement *as lesbian feminists*, the presumed coherence of the category lesbian feminist itself came increasingly under strain.

NOTES

1. This song was composed by Michael Riordan and Heather Ramsay for the anti-Bryant mass rally held at the St. Lawrence Market in January 1978. It was sung, en masse, to the tune of 'The Battle Hymn of the Republic.' On file at the Canadian Lesbian and Gay Archives.

2. On Anita Bryant, see Gayle Rubin, 'Thinking Sex: Notes For a Radical Theory of the Politics of Sexuality,' in Carole Vance, ed., *Pleasure and Danger* (Boston: Routlege and Kegan Paul 1984), 271, and Pat Califia, 'A Personal View of the History of the Lesbian S/M Community and Movement in San Francisco,' in *Coming to Power* (Boston: Alyson 1987), 245–83. Califia states: 'Bryant's hate campaign painted the ugliest, most sensationalistic picture of the gay community, she focused on the fringe and minority elements of the community.

This created a mean-spirited and frightened attitude in the mainstream gay movement. Pedophiles, transsexuals, transvestites, tearoom cruisers, hustlers, young gays and s/mers were disavowed and urged to keep quiet and become invisible' (274).

3. There were similar Stop Anita Bryant coalitions that sprang up in Winnipeg, Saskatoon, Edmonton, and Vancouver.

4. At the end of 1977, *Good Housekeeping* magazine named Anita Bryant 'the most admired woman of the year.'

5. The 'Lunacy' editorial (*Toronto Sun* 28 September 1977) links the rights of gays to adopt children to the 'death-wish that infects Western civilization.' For other pro-Bryant coverage see 'Anita's Day,' editorial, *Toronto Sun*, 15 January 1978, and a column by Mackenzie Porter, ibid. 16 January 1978. One exception to the media attacks led by the likes of Claire Hoy of the *Toronto Sun* is a short article by Betty Lee, 'Bitter Oranges,' *Toronto Star, Canada Magazine*, 23 July 1977.

6. Claire Hoy, 'Stop the Bleeding Hearts,' *Toronto Sun*, 8 September 1977; 'Gay Rights . . . continuing saga,' ibid., 13 November 1977; 'Morality vs. Perversity,' ibid., 21 December 1977; 'Kids, Not Rights, Their Craving,' ibid., 24 December 1977; 'Bryant Speaks Our Mind.' ibid., 15 January 1978.

7. There was some reluctance on the part of *The Body Politic* [*TBP*] collective to take up the Anita Bryant crusade seriously because of the editors' anti-American stance. So, GATE took the organizing lead and called the first meeting at the CHAT office on Church Street. At the first demonstration, a large paper maché effigy of Anita Bryant was burned.

8. The term 'hysterical hate campaign' is coined in the article, 'Anita Must Co!' by Andrea Goth in *The Militant*, 18 July 1977.

9. The *Life Together* report proposed over one hundred changes to the *Human Rights Code*, and in particular identified native people, the physically disabled, youth, and homosexuals as disadvantaged by the current legislation. Released in the summer of 1977, the report strongly recommended the extension of civil rights to homosexuals in the areas of services, employment, and housing.

10. On 26 June 1977, more than a quarter of a million people poured into the streets of San Francisco against the Briggs Initiative—a policy that intended

to prohibit lesbian/gay curriculum in schools and the hiring of lesbian/gay teachers—screaming 'no more Miamis' and 'gay rights now.' For analysis of the defeat of the Briggs Initiative, see Amber Hollibaugh, 'Sexuality and the State: The Defeat of the Briggs Initiative and Beyond,' *Socialist Review,* May/June 1979: 55–71.

11. 'Crisis: In the Midst of Danger, A Chance to Unite,' editorial. *TBP,* February 1978: 1.

12. None of the meetings was held at 342 Jarvis Street because no men were allowed on the premises. It's possible that had mixed-gender meetings been held at LOOT, members might have been able to exert more influence over the structure and content of the community forums.

13. Demands made at the Anita Bryant rally, 14 January 1978, were: stop Anita's crusade: defend *TBP* and freedom of the press; include sexual orientation in the human-rights code along with custody for lesbian mothers; defend Bob and Dave—two gay men who were busted for a week for postering; drop charges against people busted at the WAVAW demo; drop charges against Montreal gays—140 busted at Truxx bar: and ensure full sexual rights for youth, no discrimination against teachers and social-service workers, sexual self-determination for children, and economic independence for women.

14. In January, a bus-load of Toronto gay and lesbian activists travelled to Peterborough to protest Anita Bryant's visit to that community. The rally and demonstration were co-organized by the Ad Hoc Coalition, the Trent Student Union, and the Trent Homophile Association. According to Pat Murphy, 'We weren't sure whether we were going to get out of there alive. Going to Peterborough was a statement that "You will not bury us."'

15. Adrienne Rich 'The Meaning of Our Love for Women Is What We Have Constantly to Expand,' in *On Lies. Secrets and Silence* (New York: W.W. Norton 1980), 223. The essay was first printed as a pamphlet by Brooklyn, New York's Out and Out Books as the first in a series on lesbian feminism.

16. Olivia Records released the album *Lesbian Concentrate: A Lesbianthology of Songs and Poems, 100% Undiluted* (1977) as a protest against Anita Bryant forces in the U.S., with a percentage of profits going to the National Lesbian Mothers Defense Fund. On the album, African American Linda Tillery informs

Bryant, 'You're one of our sisters, and you're going to find that out.'

17. See Susan Cole, 'Sunkist Marriage Goes Sour,' *Broadside*, July/August 1980: 9. In her interview, Susan Cole told me: 'After the crusade died down, Bryant ended up suing for divorce on the basis of mental and physical cruelty and she took back everything she said. She said that her husband forced her to do it, which is something a lot of us had been saying or thinking. *TBP* buried a notice about this in the back of the paper.'

18. See Val Edwards, 'The Invisible Community,' *Broadside*, September 1980, who argues, 'When I took over the LOOT newsletter in 1978, I found that it was virtually impossible to persuade lesbians to contribute meaty political articles' (5). Jeffrey Weeks reports that, not unlike LOOT, *Sappho* in London was founded in 1972 as a grass-roots publication, 'designed more to keep its subscribers in touch with each other's preoccupations than to advance political perspectives.' See Weeks, *Coming Out: Homosexual Politics in Britain, from the Nineteenth Century to the Present* (London: Quartet Books 1977), 214.

19. Anita Bryant debate, taped at LOOT, January 1978; housed at CWMA.

20. Ed Jackson and Stan Persky, the editors of *Flaunting It!* (Toronto and Vancouver: New Star Books and Pink Triangle Press 1982) state: 'A full debate about lesbian political priorities never found its way into the pages of *TBP* . . . the volatile nature of the issue and the fragility of existing alliances apparently inhibited free-wheeling discussion, at least in print. A survey of *TBP* issues spanning the Seventies reveals only fragmentary attempts at dealing with the perceived causes of the problems or at proposing solutions to them' (175).

21. 'Lesbians and the Ontario Human Rights Code' was a printed statement made by members of the Lesbian Organization of Toronto outlining their demand for inclusion of sexual orientation in the *Ontario Human Rights Code*. On file at the Canadian Lesbian and Gay Archives, Toronto.

22. According to Gary Kinsman, members of the revolutionary left, in particular the League for Socialist Action and the Revolutionary Marxist Group, were also critical of the 'human rights' approach for dealing with formal levels of equality rather than substantive social change. But, to quote Gary,

'even though I think our analysis was accurate, we were saying that the alternative was socialist revolution, which was too abstract, not very concrete and not very credible' (personal correspondence with Gary Kinsman). There was a Gay Marxist Study Group at Toronto's Marxist Institute in the mid-1970s, with Tim McCaskell, Richard Fung, Walter Davis, Gary Kinsman, Ken Popert, Brian Mossop, Herb Spiers, Ed Jackson, and Peter Lancastle. This was an early attempt to theorize the connectedness of sexism, homophobia, and class oppression.

23. In her article 'Lesbian Feminism and the Gay Rights Movement: Another View of Male Supremacy, Another Separatism,' in Frye, *The Politics of Reality: Essays in Feminist Theory* (New York: The Crossing Press 1983), Marilyn Frye argues, 'Being gay [male] is not at all inconsistent with being loyal to masculinity and committed to contempt for women' (137).

24. In *TBP*, February 1976, Chris Bearchell reports that at the third annual NGRC conference in the summer of 1975, members voted to include a demand for the abolition of all age-of-consent laws. The alternative was a demand for a uniform age of consent for all, gay and straight. The age of consent varied interprovincially, from 14 to 18 (p. 1).

25. It is hypothesized in the article 'Incest and Other Sexual Taboos: A Dialogue between Men and Women' (*Out/Look*, Fall 1998) that 'the feminist/lesbian movements may be anti-sexual because many of the women involved may have been sexually abused. Whether they remember it or not' (53). I would submit that the connections between women's histories of sexual abuse, feminist politics, and actual sexual practice require much more rigorous investigation.

26. In an article entitled 'Divided We Stand' in *TBP* (February 1977) Andrew Hodges observed: 'Comment on the enormous spectrum of male sexual possibilities has been restricted within the movement, sometimes explicitly for fear of offending lesbian sensibilities' (21).

27. Jane Rule's original article, 'Teaching Sexuality,' appeared in issue no. 53 (June 1979) of *TBP* and has been reprinted in her collection *Outlander: Short Stories and Essays* (Tallahassee, Fla.: Naiad Press 1982), 157–62. Here Rule adds: '[I would want] to make adults easier to seduce, less burdened with fear or guilt, less defended by hypocrisy. If we accepted sexual behaviour between children and adults, we would be far more able to protect our children from abuse and exploitation than we are now' (160–1).

28. Chris Bearchell, 'Why I'm a Gay Liberationist,' *Resources for Feminist Research* 12, 1 (March 1983): 60.

29. At the Bi-National Lesbian Conference in Toronto, May 1979, a workshop of six young lesbians recommended that the conference pass a resolution condemning age-of-consent laws that did not reach the floor of the plenary. See Chris Bearchell's article on lesbian cross-generational relations, 'I Was 15, She Was 43,' *TBP*, December/January 1977–8: 14.

30. See Kate Millett, 'Beyond Politics? Children and Sexuality,' in Vance, ed., *Pleasure and Danger*, 217–24. In 1975, *Show Me! a Picture Book of Sex for Children and Parents* by H. Fleischauer-Hardt, was banned by Customs Canada officials at the border. Though fully heterosexual in content, the book, especially the photographs, attempted to offer a positive portrayal of children as active and curious sexual agents.

31. Gayle Rubin, 'Thinking Sex: Notes for a Radical Theory on the Politics of Sexuality,' in Vance, ed., *Pleasure and Danger*, 268.

32. Reported by Ken Popert in 'Lesbian Group Supports Age of Consent Laws,' *TBP*, April 1976: 1.

33. Robin Hardy reports that the National Gay Youth Coalition, formed in Toronto in May 1978, did not resolve the age-of-consent laws issue. He writes: 'Delegates were divided over whether the demand should be for abolition of age of consent laws or for an equalization which would bring the age for gay youth in line with that for straight youth,' See 'Gay Youth Plan Assault on School System,' *TBP*, June/July 1978: 4.

34. Chris Bearchell, NGRC report, *The Other Woman*, October/November 1975: 4.

35. Lisa, debate, 'Men Loving Boys Loving Men,' at LOOT, January 1978.

36. Gayle Rubin, 'Letter,' *TBP*, February 1978: 2.

37. Judy Springer, in her letter to *TBP* (April 1978), points out 'the lack of feminist viewpoint' in *TBP* on the subject of pedophiles (p. 3). Unfortunately, she herself does not offer a feminist analysis.

Index

A

Abenaki, 23, 48, 89, 96
Aboriginal people, 3-4, 66-71, 73-74, 188-189, 209-217, 227, 229-230, 324, 326-327, 339, 341, 347, 351
Aboriginal population, 210, 229, 343
Aboriginal right, 92, 188, 306
Aboriginal slave, 98, 103-104, 131, 134
Abortion, 404-405, 432
Acadia, 82, 184
Activism, 237, 272-273, 276, 278, 281, 395-396, 398-400, 406, 425, 435-436
Adaptation, 89, 93, 95, 121, 204-205
affirmative action, 432
African American, 440
African slave, 129
Agriculture, 21-22, 91, 108, 110, 116, 125-127, 147, 177-179, 197, 201-202, 204-206, 210-211, 213-214, 321, 338-340, 344, 357
AIDS, 406
AIM, 1, 142, 160, 162, 166, 260, 295, 300, 387, 405-406, 414, 418
Aird Commission, 369
Alberta, 7, 40-41, 80, 90-91, 189-190, 207-208, 213, 215, 222-223, 227, 236, 253, 291, 323, 331, 334, 336, 350-352, 369, 381, 383-385, 387, 389, 415
Alcohol, 53, 65, 71, 73, 77, 212, 226, 235, 267-268
Alert, 358, 360-361, 366
Algonkin, 11
Algonquian, 43, 75, 77, 79-81, 84, 86, 88, 91-96, 99, 103, 115-123
Algonquin, 44, 64, 81, 86, 91-92, 95, 122, 126, 292-294, 296, 306-309
American Civil War, 29, 177
American colony, 130, 133, 142
Amherst, 124
Anglican, 323, 331-332, 342, 344, 347, 350, 352, 355, 357, 359-361, 364-365
Anti-Semitism, 267
Articles of capitulation, 101
Assembly of First Nations, 327
assimilation, 46, 189, 200-202, 205-206, 211, 218, 226, 229, 231, 272, 275, 320, 324-325, 338-341, 347, 357, 389, 392
Assiniboine, 58, 202-203, 206, 214, 358, 365
Autonomy, 25, 45, 142, 209, 272, 303
Aztec, 40

B

Baby, 39, 134, 234, 247, 251-252, 258, 264, 282, 291, 305, 308, 376
Baby boom, 308
Baby Boomer, 376
Bailiff, 110
Bank, 56, 78, 115, 132, 196, 242, 257

Baptist, 184, 354, 363, 433
Battle, 18, 46, 215, 240, 242, 399, 407, 422, 439
Bean, 78
Big Bear, 187, 189, 192, 209, 214, 216
Bilingualism, 383
Bill, 225, 250, 252, 392, 398, 400, 403, 408, 423-424, 431
Birchbark canoe, 61
birth control, 237
Birth rate, 320
Bishop, 47, 87, 92-95, 251, 340, 344, 351, 353, 355, 357, 366
Black Robe, 43, 46
Blackfoot, 58, 90, 131, 194-196, 198, 203-204, 206, 215-225, 230, 323, 331, 337, 339, 362
Borden, Robert, 236
Britain, 46, 101, 141, 157, 160, 195, 201, 210-211, 217-218, 227, 229, 236, 238, 318, 380, 440
British Columbia, 16, 89, 190, 196, 212-213, 217-218, 233, 236-239, 260, 270, 274, 278, 283, 304-306, 309, 311, 326-327, 341-342, 349, 351-352, 359-360, 365, 419-421, 424-425, 438
British North America, 63, 133, 139-141, 153, 209-211
British North America Act, 209, 211
Broadcasting, 369-370, 372, 375-377, 383
Brown, George, 209
Buffalo, 67, 79-80, 90, 187, 189, 193, 200, 203-206, 208-209, 217, 220, 226, 315, 357

C

Cahokia, 22-24, 26, 28
Calgary, 92, 189, 208, 217, 305, 309, 334, 366, 374, 383, 387, 427
Canada Council, 383
Canada East, 142, 211
Canada West, 142-143, 175, 177-178, 184
Canadian Bill of Rights, 403
Canadian Broadcasting Corporation, 370
Canadian expansionist, 207, 218
Canadian Girls in Training, 292, 306, 308
Canadian National Railway, 289
Canadian Radio-television and Telecommunications Commission, 370
Canadian Welfare Council, 321
Capital, 69, 72, 130, 315, 348, 375, 393
Cartier, Jacques, 4-5, 19, 24, 29, 39, 41-42, 49
Catholic, 33, 46-47, 92, 108, 122, 134, 137, 142, 236, 289, 313, 324, 329, 347-348, 351, 353-354, 361-362, 430,

433
Catholic Church, 137, 142, 236, 324, 347-348, 351
CBC, 368, 370-371, 375-378
CCF, 276
Censorship, 358, 399, 438
Champlain, Samuel de, 18
Charitable institution, 244
Charity, 13, 45, 73, 175, 243-244, 289, 292, 298
Charter of Rights and Freedoms, 399, 424
Chesapeake, 24-26, 135
Child, 7, 9, 11-12, 15, 17, 27-28, 35-36, 39-44, 47-48, 52, 63-64, 69, 77, 86, 107-109, 116, 118-121, 123, 129-134, 137, 141, 144, 146, 149, 154, 157, 169, 173, 177, 180-184, 197, 201, 206, 209, 212-213, 219-221, 224-225, 234-235, 237-239, 243-245, 247, 250-251, 256, 258-261, 264-268, 272, 277, 281-283, 285, 289, 291-305, 307-311, 313, 317-321, 324-329, 333-336, 338, 340-350, 352-365, 370, 398-399, 403, 405-406, 410-411, 418, 424, 426, 432-434, 436-441
Child labour, 281, 293, 304
Childhood, 149, 280-283, 291-293, 295-296, 298-300, 303-306, 311-313, 319, 328, 437
Children's Aid Society, 244, 352
Chinese, 33, 236, 266, 272, 274, 276, 390
Chippewa, 71, 73, 75, 77, 80-81, 91, 95
Christianity, 6, 31, 37, 99, 137, 147, 268, 271-272, 338
Church, 32, 39, 47, 100, 110, 134, 136-138, 142, 149, 183, 225, 234, 236, 247, 251, 272-273, 292, 306, 323-326, 329, 333, 336, 339-342, 344-353, 355-356, 358, 361, 363-365, 381, 407-408, 421, 426, 429-430, 433, 439
Church of England, 149, 350, 352
Cinema, 372
City, 15, 19, 24, 110-114, 144, 148, 157-159, 161, 166, 169-170, 173, 175-177, 184, 234, 245, 249, 255, 257-258, 274, 288, 293, 296-297, 308-309, 314, 317, 320, 334, 344, 366, 380, 383, 392, 397-398, 414, 418, 421, 426-427, 429-433, 436
Civil War, 29, 163, 177, 383-384
Clergy, 48, 178, 182
Cod fishery, 130
Code Noir, 98, 100-102, 108, 113, 126-128, 131, 136
Colbert, Jean-Baptiste, 125
Cold War, 299, 397
Commercial development, 188

Commonwealth, 319
Communication, 30, 40, 48, 92-93, 95, 124, 145, 178, 208, 215, 307, 360, 369, 371, 375, 387
Confederation, 1, 24-25, 29, 141, 152, 165, 190, 200, 209, 211, 284, 308, 338, 341
Conscription, 236, 275, 284
Conscription crisis, 284
Conservation, 80-82, 84-89, 91, 93-95, 380
Conservative, 181, 258, 265, 325, 373, 375, 408, 434, 438
Conservative party, 373
Constitutional Act of 1791, 147
Consumerism, 88, 282, 369
COPE, 211, 334
Corn, 288
Council of Public Instruction, 176, 182
Credit union, 434
Cree, 80, 82-89, 91-95, 122, 187, 191-192, 195, 202-206, 208-209, 214-215, 222-223
Creighton, Donald, 200, 226
Crime, 12, 47, 144-145, 148, 162, 181, 250, 255, 259, 266, 269, 289, 311, 314, 319, 322-323, 325-327, 333, 338, 342, 349, 351, 398, 425, 428-429
Criminal Code, 397-398, 401-403, 428
Crown land, 159
CRTC, 370, 378
Cultural diversity, 392-393
Culture, 1, 20-22, 27-29, 31, 40, 43-46, 48-49, 65-67, 70, 72, 76-77, 81, 90, 92-93, 95, 99, 115-116, 118, 120-123, 129, 135, 169-170, 172, 174-175, 200-201, 203-205, 207, 209, 211, 216, 227-231, 266, 268-269, 271, 273, 277-278, 282, 295, 297, 303, 305-307, 313, 316, 319, 324, 338, 341, 358, 367-371, 373, 379, 381, 384-389, 392-393, 397, 399, 408, 411, 414, 424, 434-435, 438
Cypress Hills Massacre, 222

D

Defence, 63, 257, 273, 302, 398, 418, 422, 424, 428, 431
Delegate, 110, 273, 355, 416, 438, 441
Department of Health, 325
Department of Indian Affair, 325, 334, 338, 341, 348, 352, 355, 363-364
Deportation, 433
Depression, 242, 274, 282, 299, 311, 316, 348
Detroit, 78, 135, 315
Dionne quintuplet, 293, 305
Diplomacy, 21-22, 29, 70-71, 116, 208, 212
Disadvantaged, 311, 317, 439
Disallowance, 211
Discrimination, 397-398, 401, 403-405, 407, 414-421, 423, 432-434, 440
Disease, 26, 31, 37-39, 46-47, 79, 83, 85, 120, 160, 162, 172, 206, 226, 247, 254, 298, 314, 323, 325, 334, 342-345, 350, 357, 427
Divorce, 403, 410, 416, 440
Doctor, 12, 144, 160, 162-164, 167, 178, 251, 267, 301, 305, 311-313, 316, 318-319, 321, 343, 345-346, 349, 351,

405
Domestic service, 131, 281
Dominion of Canada, 196, 226
Donnacona, 29-32, 34-39, 41-42
Douglas, Tommy, 398
Doukhobors, 274
Drug, 59, 159, 258, 266, 392, 425, 427
Drunkenness, 164, 270

E

Eaton, 184, 294, 305, 309-310, 384
Economic development, 211, 226, 380
Economy, 20-22, 27, 52, 70, 76, 81, 91, 121, 125-127, 130, 148, 161, 177, 181, 204, 209, 213-214, 227-229, 254, 304, 328, 343, 348, 357, 424
Edict of Nantes, 125
Education, 140, 142-143, 147-148, 151, 169, 172-173, 176-185, 190, 201, 214, 227-228, 234-235, 238-239, 265, 269-270, 273, 280, 292-297, 300-301, 303-311, 317-321, 327-329, 334, 338-342, 345-348, 350, 352, 356-357, 359, 362-365, 403, 405, 417-418, 426-427, 437
Education Act, 176, 178-180, 182
Election, 211-212, 236, 240, 246, 249, 261, 276, 406, 417, 419
Elite, 21-22, 141-142, 174, 229, 292, 408, 422
Emigration, 251
Enemy alien, 275
Enfranchisement, 211
English, 10, 18, 20, 25-26, 29, 31, 41-42, 46, 55, 61, 69, 74-75, 78-79, 84, 87, 89, 92, 94, 96, 110, 121-124, 127-128, 142, 151, 159, 178, 190-191, 194, 208-209, 212, 230, 234, 237, 242, 248-249, 252-253, 260, 264-265, 269-270, 274, 277-278, 280-281, 283, 304, 309, 311, 314, 319, 324, 340, 362, 375, 378, 381, 389, 392-393
English colony, 25-26, 29, 127-128
Environment, 21, 26, 43, 126, 159, 171, 179, 200, 205-206, 208, 220, 228, 230, 268, 292-293, 295, 313, 376, 391
Environmental history, 305
Environmentalism, 379
Epidemic, 25-26, 37, 47, 90, 158, 205-206, 210, 343-344, 346
equality, 13, 45, 64, 86, 210, 217-218, 235-238, 265, 399-401, 403-404, 406, 408, 410, 414-417, 419-420, 422-424, 427, 440
ESP, 26, 29, 123-124
Ethnic group, 228, 270
Eugenic, 266-270, 277, 304, 314
European, 3-7, 10, 12, 14-15, 20-37, 39-45, 47-48, 52-55, 60-61, 63, 65-67, 69-72, 74-75, 77-79, 81-83, 85, 87-88, 90, 92-95, 99, 101, 116, 118, 120, 122, 124, 130, 147, 184, 204, 208-210, 226-230, 256, 265-266, 268, 273-274, 276, 338, 343, 381
Expansionist, 207, 218
Expo, 14-15

F

Factory Act, 245
Family, 11, 22, 39, 45, 52, 56, 58, 64,

68-69, 72-73, 77-78, 81-88, 91-93, 95-96, 100, 117, 119-121, 124, 126, 129-137, 142, 153, 157, 160, 163, 173, 175, 177, 181-183, 196-197, 205, 213, 219, 226, 234-235, 237-239, 243-244, 246, 249-252, 264, 272, 275, 281, 285, 293, 297, 299-300, 302, 304-308, 310-311, 313-317, 320, 324, 328, 336, 354-355, 361, 365, 380, 404-405, 407, 414, 424, 432, 438
Farm, 12, 131, 142, 163, 177, 210-211, 235, 249, 252, 317, 320, 333, 350, 357
Farmer, 142, 166, 169, 177, 210, 236, 252, 321, 340, 350, 357
Fathers of Confederation, 152
feminism, 233, 235, 260, 264, 266, 268-269, 271-273, 276-278, 409-410, 414, 435, 437-438, 440-441
Feminist, 233-237, 257-258, 262-266, 268-269, 271, 273, 275-277, 314, 396, 398-399, 404-405, 409-410, 419, 422, 430, 432-439, 441
Film, 282, 304, 307, 369-372, 388, 390, 428
First Nation, 7, 188, 208-210, 212-213, 215-216, 218-226, 230, 236, 272, 324, 327, 341, 365, 370, 376, 389-390
First Nations people, 218, 220-222, 225
Fishing, 9, 13-14, 21, 31-32, 39, 55, 63, 83, 87, 91, 130-131, 136, 150, 180, 188, 357
Foreign policy, 392
Forest, 8, 13, 17, 44, 61, 80, 85, 91, 93-95, 118, 150, 208, 225, 303, 317
Fox nation, 99
France, 5-6, 8-9, 11-12, 14-15, 24-25, 29-30, 32-35, 37-39, 41-43, 45-46, 48-49, 75, 78, 82, 89-90, 92-93, 98-102, 110, 113, 115, 122-131, 133-138, 159, 227, 236, 266, 269, 355, 366, 381
Franchise, 235-236, 238-239, 246, 248, 250, 261, 270, 274-275, 341
Frederick the Great, 151
Free trade, 127
French, 4-6, 8-15, 18-19, 22-25, 29-39, 41-46, 48-49, 51-52, 55, 60-61, 65-67, 69-70, 74-76, 79-80, 83-84, 94, 98-102, 104, 106, 108, 110, 115-125, 129-131, 133-138, 142, 150, 210-211, 227, 236, 267, 281, 314, 319-320, 324, 362, 381-383, 389, 392-393
French Canada, 101-102, 211
French Canadian, 236, 267, 381-382
French language, 33
Fur trade, 25, 29, 50-54, 58, 60-61, 65-66, 68-77, 79-82, 89-95, 125-126, 200, 204, 206-207, 338

G

Gaols, 145, 159
Garneau, François-Xavier, 99, 102
Gay Pride, 398, 406, 415, 423, 431, 434
Gays and lesbian, 407, 417-419, 422-423, 426-427, 431-433
Gender, 101-102, 116, 131, 152, 169, 236, 264-266, 269, 277-278, 281-282, 313-314, 316, 369, 397-398, 407, 411,

414-415, 422, 432, 436-438, 440
George III, 256
Germany, 169, 266
Government, 1, 31, 66, 68, 99-100, 127, 137, 141-142, 144, 146-149, 158-159, 167-168, 176-179, 181, 183-184, 188-189, 191, 195-197, 200-215, 217, 220, 222-226, 229-230, 235-236, 238-239, 249-252, 257, 267, 270, 272, 275, 292, 309, 312, 324-327, 329, 333, 338-346, 348, 350-352, 354-355, 357-358, 362, 371, 375, 378-379, 381, 383-386, 393, 397-398, 400-405, 410, 412, 415, 417-421, 423, 428-429, 433
Great War, 281, 283-284, 311, 313, 357, 363
Greer, Allan, 102
Groulx, Lionel, 43
Group of Seven, 306
Gun, 13, 25, 52, 65-66, 69, 81-83, 150, 223-225, 338, 387, 390, 427

H

Habitant, 65-66, 75, 78, 149
Habitation, 14
Halifax, 65, 112, 132-133, 136-137, 157-158, 166, 177-178, 184-185, 289, 327, 381, 383, 414
Harper, Stephen, 324, 326
HBC, 79-80, 83-88, 94, 213
health, 37, 127, 145, 153, 156, 161, 163, 165-166, 171, 174, 181, 214, 237, 267, 281, 283, 292, 294, 298-299, 301-302, 307-309, 312-314, 316-319, 321, 325, 327, 333-334, 341-346, 349, 353, 356, 382, 384, 392
Health care, 171, 392
Hell, 8, 252
Histoire du Canada, 99, 128
Hochelaga, 29, 34-37
Hockey, 389-391
Home Children, 317
Horse, 15, 31, 72, 131, 153, 179, 198-199, 208, 219, 223, 225, 243, 350
House of Common, 324, 341, 392-394
Housing, 33, 127, 129, 157, 214, 314, 341, 355, 403, 416, 432-433, 439
Howe, Joseph, 158, 202
Hudson Bay, 53-54, 58, 63, 83-85, 93-94
Hudson's Bay Company, 52-53, 58, 75-76, 79, 89-90, 92-95, 188, 202, 207, 408
Huron, 7, 10-11, 13, 15, 23-25, 27-28, 40, 43, 47-49, 79, 81-82, 90, 99, 107, 188, 190, 248
Huron Confederacy, 23, 47
Huronia, 90

I

Immigrant, 125, 209, 219, 235-236, 264, 267, 270, 275, 313-314, 317, 321, 333
Immigration, 141, 158-159, 171, 181, 213, 234, 264, 269-270, 272, 276, 321, 397, 402
Imperialism, 29, 54, 226-227, 231, 269, 391
Import, 10, 202, 370
Income tax, 403
Indian, 4, 8-9, 16-17, 20-29, 40-45, 49,

51, 53-56, 58, 63-64, 66-67, 69-73, 75-96, 100, 102, 106, 110, 115-120, 123-126, 136-137, 184, 187-191, 195-198, 200-212, 214, 216-218, 223-227, 236, 269, 272, 305, 323-325, 327-329, 331, 333-334, 338-348, 350-357, 359-366, 382, 387, 390
Indian Act, 207, 211-212, 217, 224, 325, 341-342, 362
Indian Territory, 76, 95
Industrial capitalism, 175
Industrialization, 171, 234, 371
Infant mortality, 234
Inflation, 432
Influenza, 37, 353
Innis, Harold, 69
Intendant, 102, 108, 110, 113, 125-128
Internment, 275, 326
Inuit, 324, 341, 380
Invention, 20, 30, 228, 255
Investment, 66, 69, 72, 75, 141, 228, 339, 385
Irish, 75, 390
Iron good, 31
Iroquoian, 5, 23, 25, 31, 35-39, 42-43, 80, 105-106, 123
Iroquois, 6, 18, 23-29, 38, 47, 55, 64, 69, 79-80, 83, 86, 90-91, 98-100, 105-107, 119, 123-125
Iroquois League, 27, 124

J

Japanese Canadian, 273-276, 326
Jesuit, 12, 46, 48-49, 53, 55, 78, 82-83, 89-90, 92-93, 99, 103, 116-117, 119-120, 123-124, 360, 363, 366
Jesuit Relations, 49, 55, 89-90, 92-93, 123-124
Jew, 270, 274, 276-277
Justices of the peace, 159, 162

K

Kingston, 28, 40, 75, 92, 102, 135, 172, 175, 183, 189, 194, 218, 237, 283, 305, 307, 319, 370-372, 400
Kingston Penitentiary, 172

L

Labour, 9, 13, 15, 72, 157-158, 161, 177, 180-181, 184, 205, 227-228, 258, 260, 267, 281-282, 293, 299, 304, 308, 313, 319-320, 340, 419-420, 430
Labourer, 166, 177, 180, 258
Labrador, 30, 80, 190, 383
Land grant, 217
Land ownership, 209
Land tenure, 92, 95
Language, 8, 10, 20-21, 26, 30-36, 38, 44, 65, 67, 74, 76, 80, 84, 91-92, 99, 115-117, 119-124, 144, 150-151, 164, 191, 194-195, 211, 215, 218-219, 223, 227-228, 230-231, 248-249, 276, 294, 300, 306, 324, 341, 365, 370, 373, 375, 379, 389, 392-393, 436-437
L'Anse aux Meadows, 5
Laurier, Wilfrid, 218, 278, 279, 282-283, 285, 291, 304, 318, 367
Law, 4, 6, 10-12, 32, 41, 43, 45, 48-49, 71, 73, 80, 95, 102, 113, 120, 123, 125-127, 131, 135, 137, 144, 154-155,

157, 162-163, 165-166, 170-171, 179, 197-198, 204, 212, 214, 216-218, 220, 223, 226, 233-234, 237-239, 244-245, 250, 252, 256-257, 260, 267-270, 297, 308, 312, 319-320, 364, 375, 397-399, 401, 403-405, 407-408, 410, 415-417, 420-421, 424-425, 427, 430, 436-438, 441
Leacock, Stephen, 233, 235, 237, 254
Legal system, 276, 404-405, 410, 417
Legislative Assembly, 165, 174-176
Leisure, 14, 169, 173-174, 243, 270, 282, 299, 308
Leisure time, 173-174
Liberal, 147, 158, 168, 258, 274, 276, 373, 398, 409, 422
Lieutenant Governor, 202
Literature, 20, 25, 27, 42, 76, 89, 124, 129, 216-218, 265, 277-278, 293-296, 299-303, 422
Longhouse, 27, 29, 48, 124
Louis XIV, 125-126
Louisbourg, 100, 129-130, 132-137
Louisiana, 22, 107, 122, 126, 137, 257
Lower Canada, 112, 210
Loyalist, 136, 210

M

Mackenzie, Alexander, 202
Magazine, 284, 290, 307, 310, 313, 316, 320, 379, 382-383, 386, 430, 439
Maine, 23
Maliseet, 96
Manitoba, 53, 58, 63, 81, 85, 89, 91, 94-95, 101-102, 188-190, 202-203, 207-209, 214, 217, 236, 253, 321, 326-327, 338, 341-342, 348, 350-352, 354-356, 358, 361, 363-364, 381, 387, 415, 423-424
Manufacturing, 22, 88, 338
Maquinna, 366
Marie de l'Incarnation, 49
Maritime, 24, 43, 102, 140, 157, 159-162, 164-166, 184, 190
Maritime colony, 102, 160
Marriage, 21, 77, 81, 108, 125, 127, 130, 132, 134, 212, 234, 239, 241, 246, 250-251, 255-256, 267, 312, 315, 399, 402-403, 414, 416, 440
Mass media, 367-369
Massachusetts, 25, 133, 141, 160, 319
Massey Commission, 369, 372
McClung, Nellie, 233, 236, 253, 271-272, 276-278
McGill University, 74-75, 254, 304, 316, 320-321
Measles, 37, 205
Medicare, 392
Meech Lake Accord, 326
Mercantilism, 89
Merchant, 13, 52, 66-67, 75, 78-79, 99-100, 108, 111-113, 130, 132-134, 159, 257
Methodist, 158, 204, 225, 272-273, 329, 349-350, 356, 359, 361
Miami, 90, 124, 440
Middle class, 173, 175, 177, 228-229, 235, 266
Migrant, 130
Mi'kmaq, 6, 8, 82, 92-93, 132, 327
Military officer, 10, 130

Mining, 196
Minnesota, 29, 65, 74-77, 80-81, 90-91, 94, 122, 277, 305, 340, 424
Minority, 228, 234, 303, 398, 402-406, 409, 416, 418, 420, 422-423, 427, 432, 436, 439
Missionary, 5, 8, 30, 43-49, 55, 78-79, 89, 92, 99-100, 106, 117, 199, 201, 203-204, 207-208, 210-211, 217, 225, 234, 265, 267-270, 325, 328-329, 339-340, 344, 350-352, 354-358, 360-366
Mixed-blood, 66, 328
Mohawk, 25, 86, 326, 340
Mohawk Institute, 340
Montagnais, 51, 53, 55, 61-62, 77-78, 80, 82, 88-89, 91-93, 95
Montreal, 7, 24, 26-27, 40-41, 63, 66-67, 74-76, 89, 99-100, 102, 110-111, 123, 125, 136, 166, 170, 175, 183, 189, 194, 207-208, 218, 237, 277, 283, 305, 316, 319, 321, 351, 365, 371-373, 381-382, 389, 394, 400-401, 414, 417, 420-422, 424-428, 430-431, 440
Moral economy, 228
Morality, 6, 183, 228, 235, 268-269, 290, 380, 397, 407, 430, 439
Mormon, 382
Morton, W.L., 207
Movie, 315-316, 320, 381-382, 390
Métis, 85, 200, 207, 217-218, 272, 324, 341
Music, 161, 282, 370-371
Musket, 56, 106

N

National anthem, 393
National Council of Women of Canada, 267
National Film Board, 304, 369
National flag, 390
National Gallery of Canada, 140, 152
National Policy, 202, 222, 227
Nationalism, 269, 368, 370, 379, 382, 388-389, 391
Nations, 5, 7, 13, 25, 28-29, 41, 49, 52-53, 99-100, 106-107, 123, 150, 181, 188-189, 208-213, 215-216, 218-226, 229-230, 236, 272, 305, 324, 327, 341, 365, 370, 373, 376, 379, 385, 392-393
Native residential school, 326-327, 354
Natural resource, 17, 89-90, 177, 190, 380
Nature, 5-6, 15, 35, 42-43, 53, 64, 66, 73, 77, 81, 91-92, 103, 129, 134, 144, 156, 160-161, 170, 180, 191, 204, 211-212, 214-216, 220-222, 224-225, 229, 234, 237, 247, 258, 265, 269, 277, 283, 292-296, 298-299, 305-306, 309-310, 313-314, 318, 321, 329, 338, 362, 369, 373, 392, 401, 404, 417, 438, 440
Navy, 127, 256, 287
New Brunswick, 92, 101, 132, 137, 142, 157-166, 176, 190, 310, 325, 386
New Democratic Party, 398
New England, 24-28, 60, 79, 89-90, 131-133, 293
New France, 5-6, 11, 24-25, 42-43, 48-49, 78, 82, 89-90, 92-93, 98-102, 110, 115, 122, 124-131, 133-134, 136

New York, 7, 25-29, 40-42, 49, 60, 76-78, 80, 89-92, 94-95, 101-102, 125, 127-128, 133, 135-138, 160, 166, 174, 176, 207, 209, 257, 269-270, 277, 304-307, 315, 318-321, 372-373, 380, 383, 386, 388, 398, 423-424, 434, 440-441
Newfoundland, 5, 129, 132, 136, 325-326, 370
Newspaper, 1, 130, 158, 167-168, 170, 172-174, 227, 241, 244, 273-274, 277, 290, 313, 320, 380, 384, 386, 391, 398, 408, 416, 420, 426, 429
NHL, 393
Niagara Falls, 305-306
Nipissing, 43, 81, 86, 91
Normal school, 178, 180
North, 5-6, 10, 17, 20-30, 32-33, 35, 37, 40-42, 49, 51-54, 61, 63, 65-66, 68, 70, 74-75, 77-82, 84-87, 89-92, 94, 99-103, 107, 110, 115-116, 118, 122-124, 130, 133, 135, 137, 139-141, 153, 166, 174, 188-189, 195-196, 198, 200-204, 206-211, 213, 216-217, 222-223, 226-229, 256, 266, 293, 296-297, 300, 306, 313, 315, 318, 328-329, 340-341, 348, 357, 363-364, 375, 380-382, 385, 387, 389, 398, 432
North America, 5-6, 10, 20-22, 24, 26-30, 32-33, 35, 37, 40-41, 49, 51-54, 63, 66, 70, 78-80, 82, 89, 91-92, 94, 99-103, 107, 110, 116, 122-123, 130, 133, 135, 137, 139-141, 153, 166, 188, 209-211, 228-229, 256, 293, 300, 375, 389, 398, 432
North West Company, 63, 68, 74, 77, 84-87
Northwest, 21, 42, 77, 86, 91, 94, 102, 188, 190-191, 202, 206-207, 217, 226-227, 325, 350, 352
North-West Mounted Police, 189, 195, 216, 222-223
Northwest Territories, 91, 188, 190-191, 202, 325, 350, 352
Notary, 100-101, 110-114, 126
Nova Scotia, 133, 135-136, 140, 142-143, 157-158, 160-166, 176-178, 180, 183-184, 190, 289, 327, 347, 352, 362
Novel, 78, 81-82, 214, 258, 318
Nursing, 85, 244
NWMP, 189, 213, 216, 224-225

O

Official Languages Act, 393
Ojibwa, 51-52, 65-75, 77, 80-81, 85, 87-89, 91-95, 203, 206, 355-357, 365
Ojibwa woman, 365
Olympic Games, 427
Oneida, 91
Onondaga, 28, 48
Ontario, 18, 24, 28, 79-81, 85, 87-95, 101, 140, 142-143, 153, 166, 168-171, 174-176, 188, 190, 237, 260-261, 267, 270, 280, 283, 292-296, 299, 304-306, 308-309, 315, 317, 320-321, 326, 340-341, 345, 352, 355-356, 358, 360, 363, 370, 384-388, 391, 400, 404, 406, 412, 415, 417-419, 421, 423-424, 426, 429, 431, 433, 440
Ontario Human Rights Commission,

415, 418-419, 423, 433
Ordonnances, 113, 128
Ottawa, 42, 67, 75, 77, 81, 91, 93, 95, 99, 117, 120, 128, 152, 184, 207, 209, 273, 306, 327-328, 333-334, 338, 342, 345, 350, 355, 357, 370, 383, 387, 392, 401, 405, 414, 417-418, 423-427, 430

P

Patronage, 159
Penitentiary, 141-142, 144-145, 172
Plant, 17, 39, 43, 78, 197, 247, 274, 338
Planter, 127
Politic, 79, 102, 148, 174, 184, 212, 240, 245-246, 255, 264, 269-270, 277-278, 318-319, 373, 381, 386-387, 396, 398-401, 404, 408-410, 412-419, 421-426, 428, 430-434, 438-441
Political change, 23, 28
Political community, 417-418
Political party, 380, 392, 406, 418, 421
Pontiac, 69
Poor relief, 165
Popular culture, 282, 316, 367-371, 379, 385, 388-389, 393
Population, 21-22, 53, 61, 79-80, 82-85, 87-88, 95, 99, 119-120, 125-126, 129-131, 134, 136, 142, 147-148, 160-161, 163, 177, 179-181, 183, 185, 201, 203, 207, 210-212, 222, 227, 229, 231, 251, 258, 274, 293, 298, 302, 318, 328, 334, 339, 341, 343-344, 351, 392-393, 398, 405, 417, 432
Potlatch, 358, 362
Poverty, 9, 15, 31, 64, 86, 177, 181, 215, 234-235, 242, 244-245, 254-255, 259, 272, 341
Prairie province, 236, 333
Presbyterian, 269-270, 329, 354-356, 358, 361-363
Prince Edward Island, 135, 142, 152, 158, 164, 166, 190, 325, 410
Proclamation of 1763, 188, 202, 210
Progressive movement, 300
Prohibition, 12, 222, 235, 256-257, 267, 270, 314
Prostitution, 425, 428
Protest, 32, 211, 274, 354-356, 358-359, 370, 396, 399, 404, 408, 411, 413, 420, 427-431, 433-434, 437, 440
Protestant, 142, 265-268, 281, 425
Province, 49, 102, 108, 111-112, 114, 128, 140, 145-146, 149, 157-158, 165-166, 168, 175-179, 183-184, 196, 202, 207, 210, 236, 238-239, 244, 250, 256-257, 269, 274, 282, 292-294, 298, 300, 325, 333-334, 348, 351, 385, 402, 419-420
Prudent, 256
Punishment, 10, 106, 108-109, 141-146, 149, 164, 198, 258, 301, 355-356, 363

Q

Quaker, 159, 171, 389
Quebec, 8, 10, 12, 15, 18-19, 24, 48, 53, 77, 80, 82, 92, 101-102, 110-114, 117, 123, 127-128, 134, 142, 175, 190, 210-211, 234, 236, 267, 282, 304, 313, 324, 347, 352, 370, 383, 392, 417,

420-423, 425, 428
Quebec City, 19, 24, 110, 383
Queen Anne's War, 126
Queen's University, 7, 40, 65, 75, 92, 125, 135-136, 166, 175, 183, 189, 194, 218, 237, 277, 283, 305, 307, 371-373, 400

R

Racism, 231, 236-237, 264, 266-269, 271-277
Radio, 285, 292, 368-371, 375-378, 383, 390-391, 430
Radio station, 370
Rae, Bob, 391
Railroad, 80
Railway, 141, 158, 188, 202, 213, 247, 257, 289, 343
Récollet, 79, 92
Rebellion, 25, 119, 144, 192, 218, 272, 315, 361
Reciprocity Treaty, 177
Red River resistance, 188
Reform, 139-142, 149, 158, 160, 170-171, 173, 177, 184, 234-237, 253, 260-261, 265, 267, 269-272, 278, 281, 298, 304, 312, 320, 346, 351, 397-398, 418, 433, 436, 438
Reformation, 145, 162
Reformer, 141, 158-159, 163, 167, 170, 228, 272-273, 275, 281, 313, 320, 338
Regulation, 80, 88, 99, 101, 126-128, 141, 164, 184, 196, 281, 297, 303, 312-313, 316-318, 320, 342, 345-346, 349, 351, 369-370, 383, 397, 399-400, 403, 407, 424, 438
Relief, 38, 157, 165, 225, 249, 316
Religion, 8, 21, 31, 39, 46-49, 94, 108, 134-135, 161, 201, 211, 228, 245, 270, 311, 319, 324, 329, 339, 364, 369, 379, 403, 414
Reserve, 12, 48, 188, 196-197, 201-202, 205-207, 209-214, 224, 323, 331, 333, 335-337, 340, 343-346, 351, 354-358, 361, 363-366
Reserve system, 211
Residential school, 322-327, 334, 336, 338, 340-343, 347, 354-364
Roman Catholic Church, 137
Royal Commission on Aboriginal Peoples, 324, 326-327
Royal Proclamation of 1763, 188, 202, 210
Rupert's Land, 188, 226
Russian, 6, 137
Ryerson, Egerton, 140, 142-143, 147, 178

S

Saint John, 157-159, 164-166, 184
Salmon, 17
Saskatchewan, 85, 95, 187, 189-190, 193, 196, 213, 236, 285, 291, 308, 327, 329, 339, 351-352, 354-356, 363-364, 415, 417, 423
Scandal, 167, 361, 431
Scarlet fever, 205
Schooling, 46, 140-143, 176-178, 181, 183, 185, 293, 304, 308-309, 312-313, 327, 357, 362, 364-365

Schoolteacher, 142
Scot, 75
Secularization, 1
Seigneur, 9, 45
Senator, 397
Senior, 130, 303, 340, 342-343, 345-346, 348, 356
Seven Years' War, 188
Shield, 91, 194, 198-199, 207, 261
Simpson, George, 85-86, 94
slavery, 11, 69, 97-102, 106, 108, 110, 113, 115-121, 123-129, 131, 134-138, 266, 425
Smallpox, 43, 47, 174, 206, 210, 224
Social control, 379, 407
Social Darwinism, 207, 270-271
Social Gospel movement, 281
social history, 165, 217
Social institution, 77, 178, 201, 303, 311, 407
Social life, 228, 258
Social reform, 234, 237, 253, 272
Society of Jesus, 125
sovereignty, 41, 210, 371, 373, 391
Spain, 39
Sport, 39, 55, 92, 173, 257, 300, 305-306, 309, 389, 431
Sport history, 305
Squamish, 4, 6, 16-17, 351
St. John, 93, 136, 151, 165
St. John's, 136
St. Lawrence River, 80
Stability, 171, 180-181, 216, 222, 299-300
Stadacona, 24, 31, 33-39
Standard of living, 33
Status Indian, 212
Strike, 109, 118, 159, 238, 393, 409, 429
Student protest, 370
Subarctic culture area, 92
suffrage, 235-238, 243-246, 248, 252-253, 256, 261-262, 271-274, 276
Sunday observance, 268
Superior Council, 132, 134
Supreme Court of Canada, 215, 416, 420, 425
Susan, 124, 183, 278, 305, 309, 434, 437, 440

T

Tadoussac, 24, 61
Taignoagny, 30, 33-35, 38-39, 42
Talon, Jean, 125
Tamil, 43
Tariff, 87, 141, 258
Tavern, 112, 114, 132, 426, 428, 431
Tax, 141-142, 168, 178, 247, 255, 403, 416
Teacher, 26, 151-152, 177-184, 197, 214, 221, 248, 268, 294, 300-302, 305, 309, 314, 317, 327-330, 333, 359, 364-365, 374, 381, 424, 426, 437, 440
Teaching, 1, 99, 150-152, 178, 180, 201, 220-221, 240, 301-302, 407, 417, 441
Technology, 44, 53, 66, 70, 87, 175, 182, 228, 282, 316, 360, 369, 371, 373, 375-377
Telegraph, 164, 166, 202, 213, 371
Telephone, 365, 371, 409

Television, 283, 285, 360, 370-372, 375-376, 381, 383, 386, 389-390, 393
temperance, 233, 235, 237, 260-261, 267, 272
Texas, 123
Theatre, 274, 282, 302, 370
Tithe, 268
Tobacco, 46-47, 58, 71, 73, 83, 115, 170
Toronto, 7-8, 29, 41, 49, 54, 63, 75-76, 89-92, 94, 102, 106, 136, 140, 143-144, 147, 153-154, 156, 165-176, 183-185, 189, 206-209, 217-218, 237, 240, 254, 260, 264, 269-270, 277-278, 283-284, 289-290, 292-295, 302, 304-309, 314-315, 317-321, 326-327, 341-342, 354-355, 359, 364-365, 369, 371-372, 381, 385, 387-389, 391, 398-401, 406, 408, 412, 414, 416-419, 421, 423-426, 428-434, 438-441
Tourism, 167-169, 171-174, 269, 306
Township, 317
Townspeople, 357
Trade, 5, 21-22, 24-25, 28-29, 31, 33-34, 42, 44, 46, 50-54, 58, 60-61, 65-85, 87-95, 100, 109, 116, 119, 121, 125-127, 129-131, 133, 135, 137, 177, 200, 204, 206-208, 213, 216-217, 219, 222, 226, 266-267, 302, 325, 338-340, 370, 380, 386, 392
Trade school, 340
Transcontinental railway, 202, 213
Treaty, 25, 29, 35, 49, 126, 177, 186-192, 194-198, 200-210, 212-230, 333-334, 338, 341, 357, 364
Treaty Eleven, 188
Treaty of Ryswick, 126
treaty process, 200-201, 203, 206, 214, 222-223, 229
Treaty Seven, 187-188, 194, 202-203, 214-215, 217-218
Treaty Six, 187, 191-192, 200, 202-203, 205, 208-209, 214
Trek, 181
Tribe, 29, 47-48, 64, 72, 75, 79, 83, 87, 93-94, 123-124, 131, 184, 197, 203-204, 208, 210, 218, 220, 222-226, 338, 340
Tuberculosis, 37, 333-335, 342-346, 349-351, 356

U

Unemployment, 432
Union, 102, 233, 235, 237, 260-261, 267-268, 270, 296, 416, 432, 434, 440
United Canada, 211
United Church of Canada, 363, 365
United States, 5, 27-29, 80, 85, 121-122, 141, 144, 147, 157, 159-160, 165, 168, 172, 175, 177, 195, 210, 217, 229, 234, 264-265, 273, 277, 304-305, 311, 315, 318-319, 328, 340, 348, 371, 373, 384-386, 390-391, 397-398, 432
Université Laval, 40, 136
University, 2, 3, 7, 16, 26-27, 29, 39-42, 50, 54, 65, 74-77, 89-95, 97, 101-102, 115, 124-125, 128, 135-138, 139, 143, 160, 165-166, 174-176, 183-184, 186, 189, 194, 209, 217-218, 232, 234, 237, 240-241, 254, 264, 269-271, 277-278, 279, 282-283, 285, 289, 291, 293, 295,

304-311, 314, 316, 318-321, 322, 326-327, 338, 341-342, 354, 363-365, 367, 369, 371-373, 395, 400-401, 406, 414, 417, 423-425, 432
University of Alberta, 7, 40-41, 91
University of Toronto, 29, 41, 54, 75-76, 89, 94, 136, 143, 166, 183-184, 189, 209, 218, 237, 240, 254, 264, 269, 277-278, 283, 289, 293, 295, 304-307, 309, 314, 319-321, 326-327, 341, 354, 369, 371-372, 400-401, 406, 414, 424-425, 432
Upper Canada, 101, 140-142, 144, 147, 178, 190, 210-211, 306-307, 341
Upper class, 161, 177
Urban life, 161, 299
Urbanization, 171, 234, 305

V

Vancouver, 4, 6-7, 16-17, 40, 54, 89, 102, 123, 184, 189-190, 206-207, 217-218, 238, 274, 277, 283, 309, 327, 341-342, 355, 360-361, 365, 387, 398, 400-401, 404, 409-410, 414, 416-417, 419-421, 424-428, 431, 439-440
Vancouver Island, 190, 355, 360-361
Veteran, 356
Victoria, 2, 153, 184-185, 225, 232, 235, 260-261, 274-276, 311
Victoria, Queen, 225
Violence, 15, 23, 28-29, 68, 99, 116, 121, 123, 126, 217, 222, 224-225, 235, 269, 311, 338, 379, 381-382, 396, 407, 412-413, 426-427, 429, 431-432, 434, 436
Virginia, 138
Voting, 184, 212, 246-247, 273-274

W

Wage, 234, 239, 241, 255, 258-259, 281, 433-434
War effort, 236, 275, 299, 380
War Measures Act, 383
War of 1812, 210
Warfare, 21, 23, 28, 31, 44, 79, 120, 224, 338
Wartime Elections Act, 236
Washington, George, 151
West Canada, 142-143, 175, 177-178, 184
West Indies, 43, 125-127, 130-131, 133-134, 137
Wheat, 65, 197
Whiskey trader, 223
White man's burden, 226-227
Winnebago, 119
Winnipeg, 54, 87, 89, 95, 122, 207-208, 273, 277, 288, 316, 321, 326-327, 338, 340, 342, 352, 355, 363, 370, 381, 384-387, 417, 439
Woman, 11-12, 17, 22, 31, 36, 38-39, 43-44, 48, 52, 54, 63-64, 66, 72, 80, 86, 101-102, 106-108, 111, 116, 118-120, 122, 124, 129, 131-132, 135, 153-155, 159, 164, 166, 180, 197, 200, 207, 212-213, 224-225, 232-274, 276-278, 281, 284, 289, 297, 299, 305-306, 309, 314-316, 320-321, 347, 350, 356, 359, 365, 370, 393, 397-399, 401, 404-405, 407, 409-411, 415, 422, 433-441

Women's Christian Temperance Union, 233, 235, 260-261
Women's suffrage, 235, 237, 253, 272-273, 276
Working class, 181, 184
World War I, 235-236, 297
World War II, 299-300, 326, 381, 385, 400

Y

YMCA, 292, 294, 298, 301, 420
Young Women's Christian Association, 234
YWCA, 234, 307-308